D1326454

BILL WYMAN'S TREASURE ISLANDS

BRITAIN'S HISTORY UNCOVERED

BILL WYMAN AND RICHARD HAVERS

SUTTON PUBLISHING

First published in the United Kingdom in 2005 by
Sutton Publishing Limited · Phoenix Mill
Thrupp · Stroud · Gloucestershire · GL5 2BU

Copyright © Bill Wyman & Richard Havers, 2005

All rights reserved. No part of this publication may be
reproduced, stored in a retrieval system, or
transmitted, in any form, or by any means, electronic,
mechanical, photocopying, recording or otherwise,
without the prior permission of the publisher and
copyright holder.

Bill Wyman and Richard Havers have asserted the
moral right to be identified as the authors of this work.

British Library Cataloguing in Publication Data
A catalogue record for this book is available from the
British Library.

ISBN 0 7509 3967 2

Typeset in 8.5/12pt Iowan Old Style
Typesetting and origination by
Sutton Publishing Limited.
Printed and bound in England by
J.H. Haynes & Co. Ltd, Sparkford

Contents

In the Gazetteer sections of this book, the following standard conventions have been used:

[date?]   is used when there is no reliable record of the date of a particular find; (M/D) is used to indicate a find made by a metal detectorist.

Introduction

I bought my first metal detector in 1991 in the aftermath of two years of touring the world, in what had been very difficult personal circumstances. I had spent many long and happy days in the fields around my house in Suffolk during the summer of that year using my new metal detector. I found that I got into a rhythm when methodically searching and for a while detecting became more important to me than my music. Although at that point I did not realise just how interested I was to become in the hobby. To begin with I thought I would find a few bits and pieces, and quickly lose interest – but 'land fishing' grabs you!

I have spent literally thousands of hours searching the fields close to my house and I have been rewarded with hundreds of interesting finds. While I have not been as lucky as many of the people featured in this book I have nevertheless found things that have constantly encouraged me to continue. For me the thrill of finding something a little unusual is further enhanced by what the object can tell me about the past. There is a spot that I go to regularly where I never fail to turn up something interesting with my detector. It's a field close to an old church that I am

pretty sure used to be the site of a lamb fair or market dating from medieval times. I have found many coins, including a gold medieval one, and other artefacts spanning several hundred years. These finds are 'a window on history', helping me to paint a much more detailed, and vivid, picture of the past.

Some men working in the garden of my house dug up a 16thC water jug and I found a small pewter bowl while digging in my rose garden. It was these finds that got me started and I bought a detector to 'search the grounds'. The first thing I found was a coin; at least I thought it was a coin. After

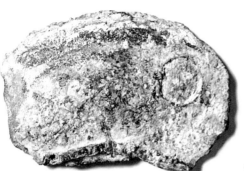

DECORATED
POTTERY SHERD,
ROMAN
(Gedding)

LEATHER
WORKERS
PALM GUARDS
1600–1899

a bit of research I realised it was a Nüremburg jetton (a coin-like object used in the calculation of accounts) dating from between 1580 and 1610. The following year I found my first Roman coins in a local field. In this one field I have since found nearly 300 Roman and medieval silver coins, as well as many Roman brooch fragments and bucketfuls of pottery. In the same area I have found Bronze Age axe blades and fragments as well as two Iron Age coins. The field is ploughed annually and each time it throws up new things. I have surmised that at the top of this field there was a Roman homestead dating from the 3rd and 4th centuries AD, and many of my finds have been in an approximate line running down the slope of the field to where there is a small stream.

My experiences in this one field are similar to many detectorists featured in the book – people who have gone back time and time again to a site, each time finding something new. Back in 1976 a couple decided to try their luck in an area of the New Forest, Hampshire, where several weeks earlier a man had found 33 gold Gallo Belgic staters (coins). Over the course of two weeks the couple found a further 23, and then 27 more staters after the local archaeological society had contacted them and they searched the spot together. The moral of all this is obvious: no matter how many times you search a site there is always something more left to find. Apply that logic to the whole of the UK and Ireland and it's clear that no matter how many finds are made, there is still more lying in wait, ready to be discovered.

SAXON POTTERY
RIM SHERD

GEDDING.

Many interesting things can also be found by 'field walking' without detectors. In a field that I regularly search I found a piece of grey stone measuring 6 inches by 3 inches. I spotted it lying

POTTERY SHERD
IRON AGE
(Flint Gritted)
GEDDING

ROMAN POTTERY
SAMIAN WARE
GEDDING.

on the surface as I was detecting, but at first didn't pick it up. I went back a minute or so later, turned it over and realised that it was handmade. I sent it to my local museum and they told me it was a piece of volcanic rock from Germany and was part of a Roman quern 3 feet in diameter that was used for grinding wheat. People who regularly go field walking discover amazing finds, everything from decorated clay pipes to Stone Age axes and flint tools. A farmer friend of mine found a vertebra from a prehistoric plesiosaur in a muddy ditch on his land.

Just a few days before I started writing this, my wife Suzanne was watching a programme on television that featured an eight-year-old boy with a fascination for archaeology. She told me he said that he loved digging things up all the time because they were 'pieces in the puzzle of history'. No one could put it any better. It can be baffling when you find a piece of metal and you frequently spend longer trying to work out what it is than you spent finding it. I recently found a copper strip with holes in it and realised that it was a medieval purse bar – the material of the purse had long since rotted away. Close by I discovered the original contents, which included Elizabethan silver coins and a seal. Later I found a metal fragment displaying animal shapes and remains of gilding, but I had no idea what it was. I took it

to the British Museum and one of their experts told me it was decoration from an early medieval reliquary box – the question is, what was it doing in a Suffolk field?

When I moved to my house in Suffolk in 1968 I was fascinated by its history. Talking to people from the community, searching through local records and looking at old maps at the library have helped me to piece together its story. The same approach has directed me to some of the places where I go detecting. Getting to know the local farmers has helped me to gain their trust and in turn they have allowed me to detect on their land. Getting permission is one of the first lessons of detecting. At the same time I have built up a good relationship with my local museum in Bury St Edmunds and our County Archaeologist. I regularly send things to them and they are always very helpful with identification, as well as giving

me additional information. I keep a diary of my finds, noting where exactly in a field I've discovered things. This can lead to further discoveries, as well as giving professional archaeologists a pointer to what may be an important site. I also label and scan many of my finds, which helps me to compare new discoveries with what I have already found.

Researching and putting this book together have reminded me what makes finding things fascinating – it's all about our history. We have called this book *Treasure Islands* and I know that some may say many of the finds featured in these pages have little monetary value, so how come they are treasure? The fact is that everything discovered is a part of the treasury that is our past.

Metal detecting has revitalised my childhood interest in history and taught me countless new things.

I hope this book may inspire you to look around your local area, by showing you what has already been found, as well as something of the history that goes along with these discoveries. Make no mistake there are more things lying in wait ready for somebody to discover them. You never know, it might be you – so good luck!

Bill Wyman
Suffolk, 2005

These cards were issued by Churchman's Cigarettes in 1937, the year after Bill was born. The series was not just about archaeological treasures found in Britain but featured finds from around the world including Egypt, Crete, China, Pompeii and Greece.

Foreword

Bill Wyman is best known as a legend of rock rather than as a metal detector user. However, it is clear from reading this book that his real love is for archaeology and history.

Archaeologists and metal-detector users have had their differences, but with the advent eight years ago of the Portable Antiquities Scheme – a voluntary scheme to record archaeological objects found by the public – relations have changed beyond all recognition. In fact many archaeologists now believe that metal-detecting, if practised responsibly by recording finds with the Portable Antiquities Scheme and avoiding sensitive archaeological sites, has great potential to add to our knowledge of the past. Anyone finding an archaeological object should note its location (ideally with a grid reference or an 'x' on a map) and take it to their local Finds Liaison Officer, so that it can be recorded.

Many metal-detector users and other finders of archaeological objects now do exactly this and their information has helped revolutionise our knowledge of artefact types, such as Celtic coins and medieval horse equipment. It has also helped to identify new sites, such as Roman villas, Anglo-Saxon cemeteries and the sites of medieval fairs. Metal-detector users are responsible for discovering 95 per cent of the finds reported under the Treasure Act. All the finds we record are published on our website, www.finds.org.uk, which has become the largest online database of its kind in the world. Of course many objects recorded with the Portable Antiquities Scheme are beautiful works of art or interesting in their own right: so why not explore Bill's gazetteer and learn a little more about some of the amazing objects that shed light on the hidden past of your local area?

Anyone taking up metal detecting needs to be aware that all land in this country has an owner whose permission is needed before you start to use a metal detector, also that it is illegal to use a metal detector on a scheduled ancient monument without permission. We strongly recommend talking to the local Finds Liaison Officer and joining a metal detecting club affiliated to the National Council for Metal Detecting.

Bill has been a great supporter of the Portable Antiquities Scheme since it was established in 1997. He has opened finds identification and recording roadshows in Cambridge and Colchester and his fame helped attract many hundreds of people. But out of public gaze, and unknown to most of his fans, Bill regularly records his discoveries with his local Finds Liaison Officers based at Suffolk County Council's Archaeological Service. Our national network of Finds Liaison Officers provides a comprehensive identification and recording service for all finders of archaeological objects, whether they are metal-detectorists or people out walking or digging in their garden – in fact anyone and everyone. So, what are you waiting for? Record your finds with us and ensure you help write the next chapter of this history of our Treasure Islands!

Roger Bland, Head of Portable Antiquities and Treasure
British Museum

The Bronze Age and the Iron Age

Beginning in around 2500 BC, the early Bronze Age saw a marked improvement in the quality of workmanship on objects made in Britain. But this more skilled society was still a deeply suspicious one ruled by priests. Then, as craftsmanship improved, trade seems to have developed between the south of Britain and the continent and this had an impact on Bronze Age structures of authority and political control. As the power and influence of those who could work metal increased, the power and influence of priests declined, marking a shift in the way that life was led.

A number of Bronze Age hoards have been found in Britain, many of them containing axe heads (or palstaves), pieces of sword, daggers and spearheads. Jewellery has also been discovered – for example, the gold ring dating from 1300–1100 BC that was located by a detectorist in Braishfield, Hampshire, in 1999 (see page 129). Probably the most impressive finds from this period are the wonderful gold torcs discovered in both Britain and Ireland. A visit to the National Museum of Ireland in Dublin will have you marvelling at the richness and the beauty of this jewellery. Gold torcs conferred immense status on the owner; they must have felt wonderful to wear and looked incredible in the sun or the light cast from a fire in a high-status dwelling.

The Celtic 'invasion' of Britain was very different to the arrival of the Romans 400 years later; it did not come in the shape of an army but rather was the result of trade and migration. The Celts were people of a shared a culture as much as a race, bound together by language, religion and, in particular, art. However, they were also accomplished warriors. They were warriors who along with the Druids combined to become a formidable enemy to those they fought, which was as often as not each other. They worshipped in woodland glades and at the site of sacred springs, led by Druids. These 'high-priests' had the right to speak ahead of their kings at council and were at the centre of all forms of cultural expression. The Druids have been described as the glue that held Celtic culture together.

Celtic coins (called staters) are the items most frequently found from the years before the Roman invasion. This period is

> The inland part of Britain is inhabited by tribes who according to their own tradition, are native to the island. Most of the inland peoples do not sow corn; they live on milk and flesh and dress themselves in skins. Notably all Britons dye themselves with woad, which produces a blue colour, and is used to give them a more frightening appearance.
>
> *The Anglo-Saxon Chronicles*

Below, left and right: Gold staters of the Catuvellauni tribe dating from the 1stC BC to 1stC AD were found by a detectorist in a field near Bury St Edmunds, Suffolk, in 1990.

Stone Circles

Stone circles or henges began to appear in Britain from around 3000 to 2500 BC. Today there are around 900 left in Britain and they represent one of the most tangible links with this period of history about which so little is really known. Many other henges may well have been destroyed. The most famous surviving example is the most aptly named: Stonehenge in Wiltshire. Popular myth has it that the Druids built Stonehenge, but they didn't: they came to Britain much later.

called the Iron Age and is considered to have begun in around 600BC. The development of the production of iron changed the nature of domestic life and the art of warfare. Iron made stronger and tougher tools than bronze, which helped in farming; at the same time, weapons made from iron were far more deadly.

Evidence of Bronze Age settlement and activity can be seen throughout the length and breadth of Britain and Ireland. On the site discovered in the 19thC at Skara Brae in Orkney there are eight houses that were occupied from around 3000 BC onwards. Also in Orkney is the tomb site at Maes Howe. In the south of England are the 47-acre Maiden Castle site in Dorset and the remains of the impressive earthworks at Silbury Hill. In the east is the recently opened Flag Fen Bronze Age Centre near Peterborough. From the Iron Age there are Castell Henllys fort in the Pembrokeshire Coast National Park and Old Bewick hill-fort at New Bewick in Northumberland with its tremendous views. A visit to any of these sites, as well as many others from the times before the Roman invasion, always conjures up feelings of being close to Britain's ancient past.

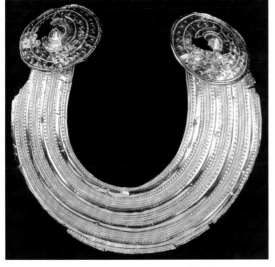

> The inhabitants of Britain who live in the south-west are especially friendly to strangers and from meeting foreign traders have adopted civilized habits. It is these people who produce the tin, cleverly working the land that bears it. They dig out the ore, melt it and purify it. They then hammer the metal into ingots like knuckle-bones and transport them to an island off the coast called Ictis, for the channel dries out at low tide and they can take the tin over in large quantities on their carts. Merchants purchase the tin from the natives there and ship it back to Gaul.

Pytheas, a Greek merchant who explored coastal Britain in around 325 BC

A gold torc, known as the Borrisnoe Collar, dating from 800–700 BC found under a bog at Borrisnoe, County Tipperary in 1836.

A Celtic mirror found among grave goods at Birdlip in Gloucestershire.

Other henges include the Rollright Stones in Oxfordshire, Castlerigg in Cumbria, Arbor Low in Derbyshire and Avebury, also in Wiltshire. Many consider the latter to be the most impressive. Another physical link with this period is provided by the figures carved in chalk hillsides, especially in the south of England. Although many hill figures are of modern origin, some are ancient: the White Horse of Uffington in Oxfordshire, for example, has been dated to 2000 BC.

> The day after the Stones played the Knebworth Festival in August 1976 I drove to Wiltshire with some friends and visited Stonehenge, Avebury and Silbury Hill
> *Bill*

Roman Britain

In 510 BC Rome revolted against the Etruscan king Tarquinius Superbus. Brutus liberated the city and a republic was established, ruled by two annually elected consuls. Over the course of the next 450 years 'Rome' expanded until it stretched from Egypt, along the north coast of Africa, across Syria, almost all the way around the Black Sea and to the northern parts of modern Europe, including France and Spain.

In 23 BC, Augustus (a title granted by the Roman Senate) was awarded a form of authority new to Rome, an 'Imperium'. It is on this date that he is said to have become Rome's first emperor.

THE ROMANS ARRIVE IN BRITAIN

In 55 BC Julius Caesar crossed the Rhine and then invaded Britain for the first time, spurred on by the prospect of securing the islands' natural wealth of iron, silver and tin. Caesar crossed the channel with 10,000 men and landed near Deal after his intended landing place at Dover was blocked by the Celtic tribes. The landing went badly and the day was only saved after Caesar himself led the charge from the boats anchored offshore, shouting, 'Leap forth, soldiers, unless you wish to betray your standard to the enemy. I, at any rate, shall have performed my duty to my country and my general.'

After a short, and what seems to have been an ill-prepared, stay on British soil Caesar retreated with his army largely intact. An invasion in the following year was marginally more successful but in truth did little more than make the Celtic tribes in the south-east of the country aware of Rome's military power. It would be almost one hundred years before Roman legions under Aulus Plautius returned.

In 43 AD four Roman legions landed and this time they were too powerful for the local tribes who had united under Caractacus. The Britons were defeated in a battle close to the River Medway and in 1957 thirty-four

On a ring found at Bowerchalke in Wiltshire in 1997 by a detectorist there are two clasped right hands, a symbol of allegiance or marriage.

Roman Coins

In the 1stC AD the most valuable Roman coin was the gold *aureus*, which weighed 7.85 grams and was 20mm in diameter. An *aureus* was equal of 25 *denarii*. A *denarius*, a silver coin weighing 38 grams and of similar size to the *aureus*, was the equal of 16 asses, the base coinage. Nero (54–68 AD) took the decision to reduce the amount of

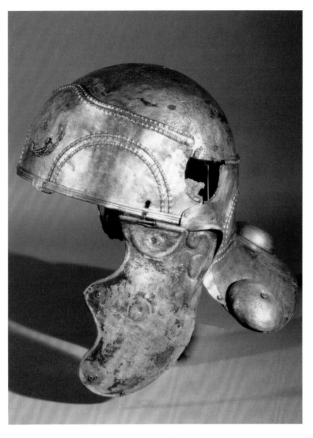

A Roman cavalryman's bronze and iron helmet was found at Witcham Gravel in Cambridgeshire

> The climate is wretched, with frequent rains and mists. . . . The soil will produce good crops, except olives, vines and other plants which usually grow in warmer lands.
>
> *Tacitus (c. 56–120 AD)*

A Romano-British strap fitment found on the borders of Hampshire and Berkshire in the 1990s.

PRINCIPAL ROMAN EMPERORS

Augustus	31 BC–AD 14
Tiberius	14–37
Caligula	37–41
Claudius	41–54
Nero	54–68
Vespasian	69–79
Titus	79–81
Domitian	81–96
Nerva	96–98
Trajan	98–117
Hadrian	117–138
Antoninus Pius	138–161
Marcus Aurelius	161–180
Commodus	180–192
Septimus Severus	193–211
Caracalla	211–217
Macrinus	217–218
Elagabalus	218–222
Severus Alexander	222–235
Maximinus	235–238
Gordian III	238–244
Philip	244–249
Trajan Decius	249–251
Trebonianus Gallus	251–253
Valerian	253–260
Gallienus	253–268
Claudius II	268–270
Aurelian	270–275
Tacitus	275–276
Probus	276–282
Carus	282–283
Carinus	283–285
Diocletian	284–305
Maximian	286–305
Maximinus Daza	305–313
Maxentius	306–312
Constantine I	306–337
Constantine II	337–340
Constans	337–350
Constantius II	337–361
Julian	361–363
Jovian	363–364
Valentinian I	364–375
Valens	364–378
Gratian	367–383
Theodosius I	379–395
Honorius	395–423
Johannes	423–425
Vatentinian III	425–455
Avitus:	455–456
Majorian	457–461
Libius Severus	461–465
Anthemius	467–472
Glycerius	473–474
Julius Nepos	474–475
Romulus	475–476

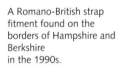

gold coins were found at Bredgar, a little over 10 miles east of the river. Some of these coins, depicting Claudius, were minted in 41 or 42 AD.

By 47 AD Roman legions had penetrated Cornwall and Wales and thirteen years later there was a bridge over the River Thames and the Roman Empire had firmly established itself in much of southern Britain. Queen Boudicca's Iceni attempted to reaffirm Celtic rule in the revolt of 60 AD but they were defeated in 61 AD. There followed over three hundred years of relative peace

THE END OF ROMAN BRITAIN

In 407 AD the Vandals, Suevi and Alans captured much of Gaul and the usurper Constantine was declared emperor by his own troops. He left Britain to attack those who had taken control of Roman Gaul but his departure effectively meant the end of the Roman Empire in Britain. A severely weakened local garrison could not withstand the attacks of the Pictish tribes and in 410 Rome effectively told Britain it was in charge of its own affairs.

gold and silver in coins, as well as the quality of the silver. This was a trend that continued throughout successive reigns until by the time of Caracalla (198–217 AD) a *denarius* contained 60 per cent less silver than when the coin was originally minted. It was in Caracalla's reign that the *antoninianus* was introduced. It weighed 6 grams and was the equivalent of 2 *denarii*. In the late 3rdC the *follis* was introduced (it had just 5 per cent silver content) and the *radiate*, which equated to an *antoninianus*. From Constantine to the fall of the Empire the gold *solidus* was the most valuable coin, worth 24 *siliquae*, a silver coin of 3.4 grams.

The Dark Ages

This is perhaps the most aptly named period in British history, simply because we know less about the 400 years between the Romans leaving and the Viking invasion of Britain than any period during the last two millennia. The term Dark Ages is unpopular with many scholars, but the historian Michael Wood is not one of them. He makes a distinction between the British and the English; he says the former were the people who lived in Britain before, during and after the Roman invasion and the latter were the Anglo-Saxon invaders who poured into the partial vacuum that was created by the fall of the Roman Empire. The 5thC invaders came from Denmark and Saxony, at first to plunder and then to settle the land. During the same period, the Picts and the Scots continued their own marauding activities from north of Hadrian's Wall.

> '*After the Romans went back home, there eagerly emerged from the coracles that had carried them across the sea-valleys the foul hordes of Scots and Picts.*'
>
> *Gildas, c. 540*

THE MAKING OF ENGLAND

The people now known as Anglo-Saxons spoke a language we call Old English, a Germanic tongue that forms much of the basis for modern English. For many years historians attempted to date the colonization of England by the Anglo-Saxons through the study of place names, particularly in eastern England. In more recent times this has proved to be a less scientific process than was at first thought and archaeology is now playing an increasingly important role in establishing patterns of invasion and settlement. In particular the study of cemeteries has added to knowledge of the period and many of the discoveries related to these sites have been aided by metal detectorists.

The decades after the Romans' departure were a period of turmoil and with the country split into seven individual kingdoms – East Anglia, Essex, Kent, Mercia, Northumbria, Sussex and Wessex – it is not difficult to understand why. The *Anglo Saxon Chronicle*, compiled between the 9th and the mid-12th centuries, provides the written outline for much of what we understand of the conquest of England in the 5thC and goes on to record the fighting between the kingdoms. This was also the time when many claim King Arthur lived: the wars between the British and the English continued for many years and Ambrosius Aurelianus, a British 'king', is a possible source for the Arthurian legend. At the end of the 5thC he defeated the Saxons at Mount Badon.

Bede's *Ecclesiastical History of the English People* has provided much of the traditional understanding of the story of the coming of Christianity to Anglo-Saxon England. It

Sceats

By the end of the 7thC silver coins had replaced gold as the main type of monetary currency. These coins were small, about ½in in diameter, and weighed up to 20 grains. The designs on the coins, while clearly Anglo-Saxon, also show

Late 7thC gold jewellery, including a triangular pendant, was found while excavating a barrow grave at Roundway Down, Wiltshire.

tells how Augustine was sent by Pope Gregory I to preach Christianity to the Anglo-Saxons, arriving at the Isle of Thanet in 597. However, Bede portrayed Augustine's influence to suit his own position of support for the Roman Church. It is much more likely that Christianity had hung on in pockets throughout the country after the departure of the Romans. There is strong evidence from Eccles in Norfolk of a continuity of Christian worship stretching back to before Augustine's time and the same can be said of Melrose in the Scottish Borders, Whithorn in Galloway, and Glastonbury. But whatever the precise timing and location of the establishment of the English Church, this was a period of great creativity and much of what detectorists have found from this period has links to the activities of the Church.

Mid to late 9thC Anglo-Saxon silver and niello strap end.

Roman and Merovingian influences. In Northumberland, where silver was in short supply and debased metal was more common, sceats were also called stycas.

The basis for English weights and measures is the grain, and while this unit was originally linked to the weight of a grain of barley, for the purposes of weighing money, wheat was the cereal used (3 grains of barley = 4 grains of wheat). An ounce is 437.5 grains, so a sceat weighed around 0.045oz.

The Vikings and Beyond

Sometime in the middle of his reign (802–839) Ecgberht established the supremacy of Wessex over most of the rest of England. He was the first leader who could justifiably lay claim to the title of King of All England. But it was to be a short-lived supremacy. Some three decades earlier the first Viking raids on England had taken place and in 865, after a period of increasingly frequent attacks, the Danes' 'Great Army' launched a full-scale invasion. While not a conquest like that carried out by the Normans a quarter of a millennium later, it was to have profound and far-reaching effects on the country. East Anglia, Mercia and Northumberland quickly succumbed to Viking rule – Danelaw prevailed in these areas – with only Wessex under King Alfred offering any kind of resistance. The *Anglo-Saxon Chronicle* records that:

> *Alfred ordered warships to be built to meet the Danish ships; they were almost twice as long as the others, some had 60 oars, some more. They were swifter, steadier and with more freeboards. . . . as it seemed to him they could be most serviceable.*

There was almost continual fighting between Alfred the Great and the Vikings with victories on both sides.

For well over a hundred further years the unsettled situation in Britain created fear and uncertainty, a fact that is reflected in the finds that have been made, and in particular those that metal detectorists have unearthed in recent decades. It seems that valuables were hastily buried at locations around the country in an effort to prevent their falling into the hands of an aggressor. There is no better example of this than a hoard of coins from the reign of Edward the Elder, thought to have been deposited around 920 AD soon after the Anglo-Saxon reconquest of East Anglia. They were found at Brantham in Suffolk. The name of the village means burnt hamlet, which alludes to an attack by the Vikings in 911.

While legend has secured Alfred's place in the annals of English history his son Edward the Elder's is, rather unfairly, less prominent. Edward led the reconquest of much of England north of a line that ran approximately from Chester to London (the old frontier of Wessex and the Danelaw) and all the way up to the Humber. Alfred's grandsons, Athelstan, Edmund and Eadred, continued the fight and retook the north of England. When Eadred finally defeated the notorious Norwegian Eric Bloodaxe in 954 the English military victory over the Vikings was complete. As some have said, that was the easy part. Securing and winning the peace by melding the disparate 'kingdoms' and regions into one political society with a central government was the real challenge. Nobles were granted rule over their particular

Coins and Minting

The 10th and 11th centuries saw significant changes in the minting of coinage in England, particularly after the demise of Danelaw and the defeat of the Viking Eric Bloodaxe in 954. The striking of coins became decentralised and mints were established in various economic and administrative centres throughout England.

A Victorian map showing the area ruled by the Vikings, where Danelaw ruled.

regions and in many respects operated independently from the rule of the king. Those 'rulers' whose territory lay on the northern borders of England were vital in preventing raids by the Scots.

When Eadgar died in July 975 this period of peace came to an end and Viking raids recommenced five years later. The Viking campaign culminated in the defeat of the English by the Danes at Maldon in 991.

Aethelred (979–1016) saw gold as his salvation and reportedly paid the Vikings 22,000lb of gold and

> The heathen shall fall in the war. Not so likely shall you come by the treasure; point and edge shall first make atonement, grim warplay, before we pay tribute.

Byrhtnoth, an Essex Alderman to the Danes before the Battle of Maldon

silver, as well as rations, soon after the battle. Three years later in 994 he handed over another 16,000lb of silver and in 1002 a further 22,000lb.

This second Viking period in England culminated with King Cnut gaining the throne in 1017. Later Cnut also acceded to the thrones of Denmark and Norway but chose to have his royal court in England and established a sophisti cated system of devolved government. With his death in 1035 the scene was set for the coming of the Normans. England would never be the same again.

An enamelled and decorated late 10thC gold finger-ring found by a detectorist in Warwick in 2001.

London and Winchester remained the most significant, but York and Lincoln both gained in importance, especially after King Eadgar reformed the coinage in 973.

Eadgar set about establishing a number of mints throughout England which had the effect of boosting the economic importance of the cities in which they were located, as well as ensuring the royal purse was kept topped up. A key feature of Eadgar's reform was that each local mint struck silver pennies to a single design and weight standard.

The Scottish kings included are just the principal monarchs, not a complete list.

1042–66 Reign of Eadward (the Confessor)
1052 Foundations of Westminster Abbey are laid
1066 Harold II defeats the Vikings at Stamford Bridge and is then killed at Hastings by Duke William of Normandy
1066–87 Reign of William I (the Conqueror)
1070 William I defeats Saxons led by Hereward the Wake
1072 William I invades Scotland
1085 Civil war in Ireland
1086 Domesday Book is completed
1087–1100 Reign of William II (known as Rufus – 'The Red')
1094 Welsh revolt against the Normans
1096 The first Crusades begin with attacks on Jewish communities.
1100–35 Reign of Henry I; he held the throne jointly with his wife Matilda until her death in 1118
1113 The Knights of the Hospital of St John, the Hospitallers, are founded to take care of pilgrims to the Holy Land
1135–54 Reign of Stephen
1138 The Scots, under King David I who supported Matilda defeated at the Battle of the Standard
1141 Stephen is captured at the Battle of Lincoln
1147 The start of the second Crusade
1153 The Treaty of Wallingford decrees that Stephen should rule, and Matilda's son should succeed him
1154–89 Reign of Henry II
1165–1214 Reign of William the Lion, King of Scotland
1166 The jury system of trial is founded
1169 The English conquest of Ireland begins
1170 Thomas Becket is murdered
1187 Saladin ravages much of the area held by the Crusaders
1189–99 Reign of Richard I (Coeur de Lion, 'The Lion-Heart')
1199–1216 Reign of John
1209 Cambridge University founded
1214–49 Reign of Alexander II, King of Scotland
1215 King John signs the Magna Carta
1216–72 Reign of Henry III
1230 Around this time jousting becomes popular in England
1249–86 Reign of Alexander III, King of Scotland

The Early Middle Ages – The Normans and Plantagenets

We tend to think of 1066 and the arrival of William the Conqueror as marking 'the coming of the Normans', but links with Normandy were in fact established much earlier. Eadward the Confessor (1042–66), the son of Aethelred II, had been raised in Normandy and there was a strong Norman influence at his court. However, there is no denying that the arrival of the Norman army in 1066 is *the* defining moment of English history, the one date that everyone can remember.

The influence of the conquest on Britain was immense and its consequences are evident to this day. Before the invasion by Duke William, who was himself descended from pagan Vikings who had settled in France in 911, the concept of England as a nation had begun to take shape. But during the twenty years of William's reign it took on a clearer form and was brought into sharp focus by Domesday Book. Commissioned in 1085, the first draft was completed in 1086 and is a great survey ordered by the king to assess who owned what land and resources in England at the time, and the extent of the taxes the crown could raise. Quite simply it defined the country and catalogued the fortunes of most of its two million inhabitants. Historian Michael Wood describes Domesday as a work of 'hypnotic detail', which tells the story of the 90 per cent of the population that lived and worked on the land and records a time when London was a city of just 25,000.

For the next 300 years the history of England, Scotland and Wales was punctuated by periods of massive upheaval, natural and manmade disasters, and milestones in the development of government

Henry II silver penny

> King William rode to all the remote parts of his Kingdom and fortified strategic points against enemy attack. For the fortifications, called castles by the Normans, were scarcely known in the English provinces, and so the English could put up only a weak resistance to their enemies.
>
> Orderic Vitalis (1075–c. 1142), The Ecclesiastical History of England and Normandy.

and society: wars against foreigners, civil conflict, revolts, crusades, plague, famine, the beginnings of an English parliament, and the establishment of universities combined in a rich tapestry that has provided fertile ground for the detectorist and treasure hunter.

The 22 silver Norman *deniers*, dating from around 1030 and found in the Southampton area in 1967, evidence

Left: Found by a detectorist in 1999 in the Buntingford area of Hertfordshire, this late 13th or early 14thC silver-gilt shows either a saint or a prophet.

Right: This 11th or early 12thC silver-alloy cross was found by detectorists near Ipswich in Suffolk.

early trading links with the Normans. A number of coin hoards dating from 1066, some quite substantial, have been found buried in Sussex and indicate the Normans' total victory in that year – a terrified population looked to bury its treasure in the hope of saving it from the hands of the invaders. By the late 12thC, with money in short supply, the practice of clipping, or shaving silver from coins was widespread – this and other measures were employed to help meet the expense of financing the Crusades to the Holy Land.

As the period came to a close French pirates were raiding Kent and Sussex. A very real indication of the impact these attacks had on the people of the area was uncovered in the late 19thC when 700 gold coins were found near Balcombe in West Sussex. The local inhabitants must have been in fear of their lives and livelihoods to have buried this huge amount of money; the fact that it was never recovered when the pirates disappeared almost certainly means that those who owned it were killed in the raids. This and similar finds from the period, often made by detectorists, have led to a far greater understanding of the history of these troubled times.

> In the first place the Lords and the Commons are agreed that, contributions should be made by every lay person in the realm, both in franchises and outside, males and females alike, of whatever estate or condition, who has passed the age of fifteen years, of the sum of three groats, except for true beggars, who shall be charged nothing.

An entry for 1380 from the Parliamentary Rolls (Rotuli Parliamentorum Vol. IV, published in 1771–83), describing the third poll tax issued by Richard III since his accession in 1377. It prompted the Peasants' Revolt in 1381.

Bent Coins

Often coins are found that are bent completely in half. Bill has found quite a number and had assumed that they had either been bent by a plough or damaged in some other way. Some time ago he also read that they could be bent to prove that they were metal. Recently he sent some coins to his local museum to be looked at, including a Harold II penny dating from before the Norman conquest. He was told that this may well have been bent and deliberately put in the ground. Similar to a votive offering, it was placed by someone who wanted to himself or someone close to him to be cured from an illness.

The Late Middle Ages and the Tudors

During the 15thC Parliament began to become something more than just an institution that did the king's bidding. It began to assert its own authority, a trend that was to continue over the course of the next 200 years and beyond.

The wars with France persisted during the later Middle Ages and into the Tudor period, but by the end of the 16thC it was the Spanish who posed the most serious threat to England's sovereignty, a threat that materialised in the form of the Armada in 1588.

Conflict was never far from English shores between 1400 and 1600 and came close to homes all over the country during the Wars of the Roses, which began in the middle of the 15thC. From 1455 to 1487 the rival Houses of Lancaster and York waged an intermittent civil war over who had the rightful claim to the throne of England. Both the Lancastrians and the Yorkists traced their claim to the monarchy through their descent from Edward III (1327–1377). The weakness of the Lancastrian king, Henry VI, allowed first the Yorkists to prevail and in turn the Tudor dynasty. Henry Tudor defeated the Yorkist king Richard III at the Battle of Bosworth in 1485, establishing a royal house that would occupy the throne for the next 118 years, shaping and overseeing a transformation in the life of the country.

THE REFORMATION AND THE DISSOLUTION OF THE MONASTERIES

Pope Clement VII's refusal to annul Henry VIII's marriage to Catherine of Aragon (his brother's widow) in 1529 began a chain of events that ended with Henry's excommunication and, by 1534, a total break between the English and Roman Catholic Churches. Catherine, who was in her forties, had produced no male heir, just a daughter, Mary. Henry was desperate for a son and his desperation triggered the crisis.

The cataclysmic separation from Rome brought about massive change to the religious and social fabric of the country. Prior to Henry VIII's reign there were over 800 religious houses in Britain, home to something over 9,000 monks, nuns and friars. Many thousands of others depended on these institutions in various ways – economic, charitable and educational.

> As for King Richard, he received many mortal wounds, and like a spirited and most courageous prince, fell in battle and not in flight . . . many northerners, in whom, especially, King Richard placed so much trust, fled even before coming to blows with the enemy. . . . Out of this warfare came peace for the whole kingdom . . .
>
> *Crowland Chronicle (Continuations, 1459–86)*

Boy Bishops

The 4thC St Nicholas of Bari, the patron saint of children, was known as the Boy Bishop because he showed remarkable devotion and piety from his earliest years. He was revered during the

Boy Bishop tokens date from between 1480 and 1540. This is one of four found by Bill close to his Suffolk home.

Right: A gilded silver livery badge dating from between 1525 and 1560 that once belonged to the Gainsford family of Crowhurst and was found by a detectorist in 1996 at Chelsham in Surrey.

Below: A coin from Henry VI's reign and a Henry VII groat.

By 1540, 550 monasteries had been closed and their wealth and treasures sequestered. In addition their lands had been sold off, the proceeds helping to double the monarchy's annual income. The ruins of some of these great institutions can still be seen, for example the abbeys in the Border towns of Kelso, Jedburgh and Melrose, and the remains of the great religious house at Fountains in North Yorkshire, which has been named a World Heritage site.

> I am very sorry to know and hear how unreverently that most precious jewel, the word of God, is disputed, rhymed, sung and jangled in every alehouse and tavern, contrary to the true meaning and doctrine of the same.
>
> *Henry VIII's last speech to Parliament, 24 December 1545*

Middle Ages and his saint's day, 6 December, was adopted as a time for special celebrations. In cathedrals and parish churches throughout Britain a choirboy was named 'Boy Bishop', a post he held for three weeks, culminating in the Feast of the Holy Innocents on 28 December when the Boy Bishop and the remainder of the choir performed all church ceremonies except for Mass. The boy was given a coin as an election token and several more that he distributed among the poorest children in the community so they could buy food. The practice was abolished by Elizabeth I, but to this day a 'Boy Bishop' is enthroned at Mendlesham in Suffolk on the Sunday nearest St Nicholas's Day.

1550 English troops are withdrawn from Scotland
1553–1558 Mary Tudor becomes Mary I of England and begins a Counter Reformation
1554 Mary I marries Philip II of Spain
1555 Protestants persecuted and Archbishop Thomas Cranmer is burnt (1556)
1558–1603 Reign of Elizabeth I
1563 Bubonic plague breaks out in London and around a quarter of the capital's population dies
1567 Mary, Queen of Scots is defeated and imprisoned
1567–1603 James VI is King of Scotland
1577 Francis Drake circumnavigates the globe
1587 Mary Stuart, Queen of Scots, is executed
1588 Spanish Armada attempts an invasion of England

THE WARS OF THE ROSES

The House of Lancaster and that of York both claimed the throne through descent from the sons of Edward III. The opening flourish of the war occurred when Richard of York attempted to remove Somerset, a favourite of Henry VI, and his Lancastrian army. The idea of the Wars of the Roses as one long campaign is misleading. It was a series of battles.

The winner of each battle and the estimated number of combatants:

1455 May 22 St Albans (Yorkists) 6,000 men
1459 September 23 Blore Heath (Yorkists) 15,000 men
1459 October 12 Ludford Bridge, near Ludlow (Lancastrians) 12,000? men
1460 July 10 Northampton (Yorkists) 30,000 men
1460 December 30 Wakefield (Lancastrians) 25,000 men
1461 February 2 Mortimers Cross (Yorkists) 20,000 men
1461 February 17 St Albans (Lancastrians) 50,000 men
1461 March 28 Ferrybridge (Yorkists) 10,000? men
1461 March 29 Towton (Yorkists) 75,000 men
1464 April 25 Hedgeley Moor (Yorkists) 10,000 men
1464 May 15 Hexham (Yorkists) 10,000 men
1469 July 26 Edgecote Moor (Lancastrians)
1470 March 12 Losecote Field (Yorkists)
1471 April 14 Barnet (Yorkists)
1471 May 4 Tewkesbury (Yorkists) 12,000 men
1485 August 22 Bosworth (Henry Tudor) 15,000 men
1487 June 16 Stoke (King Henry VII) 30,000 men

Union, Disunion and the Dawning of a Revolution

In 1547 the Scots were defeated by the English at the Battle of Pinkie Cleuch, but 56 years later their king, James VI, ruled all of England, Scotland and Wales. It is somewhat ironical that James VI and I succeeded Elizabeth – he was the son of Henry, Lord Darnley, and Mary, Queen of Scots, whom she had ordered to be executed.

DISUNITY

The difficulties Henry VIII experienced with the Church had been followed by a relatively stable period under Elizabeth I, but the events that rocked 17thC England, Scotland, Wales and Ireland were once again related to religion.

> Oh Lord! Thou knowest how busy I must be this day; if I forget thee, do not forget me.
>
> *Royalist Commander Sir Jacob Astley before the Battle of Edgehill in 1643*

A mid-17thC inscribed silver hawking ring engraved with a shield containing the Royal Stuart arms was found in 1999 by two detectorists at Thwaite in Suffolk.

The English Civil War was precipitated not only because Charles I failed to call a Parliament for eleven years but also because the Scots Covenanters had successfully resisted the reform of the Church. In 1638 they defeated the king's army at Newburn on the River Tyne, which prompted Charles to recall Parliament where he was forced to bow to demands for reform.

When the Civil War broke out in 1642 the extent of the fighting surprised the country: it was felt that a single battle would decide the outcome, but by the time the fighting ceased in 1649 there

Charles I Royal farthing and Charles I gold coin.

Musket Balls

Finds of small pieces of lead shot are extremely common in some parts of the country, particularly in areas that sustained Civil War sieges or major battles. They are also to be found where hunting took place. In either of these locations they may have killed something – or even someone!

In 1782 an English plumber named William Watts worked out that if molten lead could be dropped from a

This early to mid-17thC silver seal matrix was found by a metal detectorist at Plompton in North Yorkshire in 1994.

had been more than fifty battles, sieges and skirmishes. The Battle of Naseby on 14 June 1645 was the defining moment of the Civil War. In three hours the majority of Charles I's Royalist foot soldiers were killed.

In 1648 the violence escalated again in what has become known as the second Civil War. Charles had made an alliance with the Scots which pre-empted a number of uprisings in his favour across the country, but a lack of coord-ination was their downfall. Charles was executed in 1649 after a show trial. When Charles II rallied the Scots in 1650 his disorganised army was routed at Dunbar, a fate that was repeated a year to the day later at Worcester.

> I was moved to write to Oliver Cromwell, and laid before him the suffering of friends in the nation and in Ireland. . . . And he thanked me after I had warned him of many dangers and how he would bring shame and ruin on himself and posterity. And after this I met him riding into Hampton Park and I saw and felt a waft of death go forth against him.
>
> *George Fox, the founder of the Society of Friends (the Quakers), recalls writing to Cromwell when the latter was considering taking the crown*

BEFORE THE DAWN

Following the restoration of the monarchy in 1660 there began a century in which Britain moved from the old to the new. In 1694 the Bank of England was founded, closely followed by the Stock Exchange in 1695. In 1707 the Act of Union brought England, Scotland and Wales together as Great Britain, laying the foundations for the beginning of the modern age. The last execution of an English witch in 1712 was a punctuation mark in history – the end of superstition, the dawn of the age of reason. Eighteen years later agriculture was revolutionised by the introduction of the crop rotation system, a development that would be fundamental to the hobby of metal detecting over two centuries later.

The defeat of the Jacobite pretender, Bonnie Prince Charlie, at Culloden in 1746 was the last battle on British soil: it set the seal on the formation of modern Britain.

sufficient height it would form into spheres, as well as partly solidify. If the lead spheres fell into water, the cooling process would be completed and musket balls produced. To achieve his aim Watts added three further storeys to his already three-storey home and experiments proved his theory correct. Prior to this, shot was made either by casting or by dropping molten lead through a sieve and into a barrel of water, a process that often produced more tear-drop shaped material.

If a cast shot retains its moulding pimple it is likely not to have been fired. However, if the dimple is absent, the find could be a piece of dropped shot. During Civil War sieges some balls had a hole drilled in them and then dung was forced into the cavity in what was an early form of biological warfare.

1692 The MacDonalds massacre the Campbells at Glencoe
1694–1702 William III is sole monarch
1694 The Bank of England is founded
1698 The London Stock Exchange is founded
1702–1714 Reign of Anne
1704 The French are defeated at the Battle of Blenheim by an Austrian and British force under Eugene of Savoy and the Duke of Marlborough
1707 England, Scotland and Wales become Great Britain under the Act of Union
1711 St Paul's Cathedral's rebuilding is completed
1712 Jane Wenham is the last person in England to be convicted of witchcraft
1714–1727 Reign of George I
1718 Banknotes are introduced in England
1721 Robert Walpole becomes Britain's first Prime Minister
1727–1760 Reign of George II
1739 Highwayman Dick Turpin is hanged in London
1745 The French defeat the English at Fontenay
1745 Bonnie Prince Charlie leads the Jacobites to victory over the king's army at Prestonpans
1746 The Jacobites are defeated at Culloden
1753 The British Museum is founded
1756 The Seven Years' War begins

MAJOR BATTLES OF THE ENGLISH CIVIL WAR

The victors are listed in brackets

1642 September: A cavalry skirmish at Powick Bridge, south of Worcester, is the first engagement of the war (Royalist)
1642 October: Edgehill, Warwickshire (stalemate)
1642 December: Tadcaster, Yorkshire (Royalist)
1643 June: Adwalton Moor, Yorkshire (Royalist)
1643 July: Roundway Down (Royalist)
1643 September: Newbury, Berkshire (stalemate)
1644 March: Cheriton, Hampshire (Parliament)
1644 June: Marston Moor, Yorkshire (Parliament)
1644 October: Newbury, Berkshire (stalemate)
1645 June: Naseby, Northamptonshire (Parliament)

THE VALUE OF TREASURE

Establishing the value of objects that have been found is the responsibility of a coroner on behalf of the crown but it is far from an exact science. Items that come up for sale often exceed the estimate of the experts; sometimes they fail to reach the guide price. Historical objects and pieces of treasure are no different from anything sold at auction: it is a question of what the market will pay. This list is of just some of the most valuable items found in Britain during the last 200 years. Prices have been adjusted to take account of inflation where they were sold at auction, or they were valued as treasure trove. In some cases they are purely estimates. Something such as the Bronze Age cape found at Mold in Flintshire is of course priceless, as are some other items on this list.

1811 Cleeve Prior, Worcestershire: Over 3000 Roman gold and silver coins, valued at £500,000
1828 Near Crondall, Hampshire: A

The Modern Era

The history of the world is but the biography of great men.
Thomas Carlyle 1795–1881

Carlyle's words are often quoted and are of course true – but they are only part of the story: history is also the story of ordinary people. History is told through the evidence provided by their tools, their weapons, their jewellery, their money – indeed all of their possessions. This is what helps to make archaeology and metal detecting so fascinating.

Thirty years before Carlyle's birth, and coincident with the dawning of the modern era, a German was working on a book that would encourage the study of archaeology. In 1764 Johann Joachim Winckelmann published his seminal work *Geschichte der Kunst des Altertums – The History of the Art of Antiquity* – which inspired a huge upsurge in the study of the classical age. Born in Germany in 1717 he became the Superintendent of Roman Antiquities in 1763, and soon after was appointed Librarian at the Vatican. Known for his excavations at Pompeii, he is regarded as the father of modern archaeology.

War has frequently been the catalyst for inventions that have later found a peaceful use; one such innovation is the mine detector. In the winter of 1941/2 the British War Office invited designers to submit their ideas for 'a robust and reliable mine detector'. A Polish Army Signals officer, Jozef Stanislaw Kozacki, who had escaped to Britain in 1939 supplied a design that proved to be just the job. Almost immediately 500 were made and shipped to North Africa in time for the advance on El Alamein. This mine detector, which weighed about 30lb, could be operated by one man and saved many lives as well as dramatically increasing the speed of an advance through a minefield; the same design stayed in use for another 50 years. One of the detector's twin coils was connected to an oscillator and the other to an amplifier and a telephone. If it came close to a metal object the balance between the two coils was upset and the telephone received a signal.

Metal detectors for the civilian enthusiast began to appear on the market in the late 1960s and early 1970s. At first they were somewhat primitive, and in truth not too effective. By the late 1970s they had been immeasurably improved but were still unable to discern types of metal like the more sophisticated machines of today. In the early 1980s a standard metal detector cost between £100 and £300 – the equivalent of £280 to £800 in today's money. Today Bill uses a C-Scope CS1220R, which retails for £379.

Grave Goods

When Christianity began to discourage the custom of burying people with their possessions, a window on the past was closed for both detectorists and archaeologists.

Today if a grave is discovered, either by accident or during an organised excavation, and no matter what its antiquity, careful steps are taken to respect the burial. Much of what was originally placed in a grave with the body decays, of course, particularly drapes or clothing. In recent years over 2,000 coffins from

An 18th–19thC Georgian gold fob seal found by a detectorist in Oxfordshire.

While the last 250 years have seen the greatest advances in our understanding of the past, in part through opportunity and education but also because of technology, the objects made and buried or lost in this period are generally the least interesting finds. Coins, and mainly gold ones, have been the most valuable and informative discoveries, but the need to bury coins, for legitimate reasons, has largely been consigned to history by the rise of the banking system. High-value coins have been replaced by banknotes and the character of money has changed forever. When most people wanted to hide their money during the last hundred years or more they usually put it under the bed!

In the 1970s, during the early days of the detecting hobby, there were rumblings about laws being introduced in Britain to restrict metal detectorists. There was talk of making it difficult to obtain a licence to operate a detector. None of this actually happened, and while the Treasure Act was revamped, the hobby has remained unregulated. While there are some who question the value of detecting, in part because of the activities of rogue detectorists who rob sites and those who fail to report important finds, the vast majority of people act responsibly. In particular the introduction of the Portable Antiquities Scheme has helped the hobby to mature and develop. Throughout the modern era the number of finds has rapidly accelerated, and in the past decade advances in electronics have meant that detectors have become even more sophisticated, which has resulted in a massive upsurge in both discoveries, and their quality.

‘ History is more or less bunk, ’ As Henry Ford famously said. For many who go metal detecting history can often be junk! But it can also be treasure and that's what makes it so fascinating.

vaults in London were exhumed and just two of the occupants were dressed in 'normal' clothing – one in full military uniform, the other in fashionable clothing. There were also a good number of wedding rings found.

In recent times one of the most interesting examples of 'grave goods' is associated with the burial of singer Frank Sinatra. In his coffin is a bottle of Jack Daniel's, a ring put there by his third wife Mia Farrow, some sweets, a cigarette lighter and a roll of dimes.

hoard of 7thC gold coins and jewellery, valued at £750,000

1834 Long Framlington, Northumberland: 300 gold coins from the 14th and 15thC, valued at £350–400,000

1907 Benhall Green, Suffolk: The bronze head of Emperor Claudius, valued at £750,000

1939 Sutton Hoo, Suffolk: A 7thC hoard of gold and silver coins and objects, valued at more than £20M

1940 Mildenhall, Suffolk: A hoard of Roman silver, valued at more than £20M

1966 Fishpool, Nottinghamshire: 14th and 15thC gold coins and jewellery, valued at more than £3M

1968 Belstead, Suffolk: 5 gold torcs dating from the 1st C BC, valued at £450,000

1969 Colchester: 14,065 silver mostly long-cross pennies of Henry III, valued at £900,000

1971 Rattlesden, Suffolk: A 12thC gilt bronze statuette of St John, valued at £250,000

1972 Prestwich, Bury: A hoard of 12thC silver coins, valued at £400,000

1977 Pentney, Norfolk: 6 9thC Anglo-Saxon silver brooches, valued at £475,000

1978 Mildenhall, Wiltshire: Over 50,000 Roman coins, valued at more than £1M

1979 Thetford, Norfolk: Roman gold and silver objects, valued at more than £3M

1980 Coed-y-Wenallt Cardiff: 86 silver coins from the 12thC, valued at £270,000

1982 York: An 8thC Anglo-Saxon helmet, valued at £500,000

1985 Middleham, North Yorkshire: A gold and sapphire pendant, valued at £4M

1989 Near Norwich, Norfolk: A hoard of 12thC coins, valued at £1M

1991 Whitwell, Rutland: A hoard of Roman coins, valued at £240,000

1992 Hoxne, Suffolk: A hoard of Roman gold and silver coins, gold and silverware, valued at £2.3M

1992 Near Kelso, Scottish Borders: over 1200 coins from the 16th and 17thC, valued at £500,000

2000 Near Milton Keynes: Gold torques and bracelets from 1150–750 BC, valued at £290,000

2000 Winchester Area, Hampshire: Iron Age gold jewellery from 80 BC and 30 BC, valued at £500,000

2001 River Ivel, Bedfordshire: A 9thC gold coin, valued at £230,000

2001 Ringlemere, Kent: An early Bronze Age gold cup from c.1700–1500 BC, valued at £270,000

The Treasure Act 1996

The Treasure Act 1996 replaced the common law of treasure trove in England, Wales and Northern Ireland. Under the law of treasure trove there was a requirement that finds of gold or silver objects be reported to the coroner. Before an object could be declared treasure trove and so crown property it had to pass three tests: it had to be made substantially of gold or silver, to have been deliberately hidden with the intention of recovery, and its owner or his heirs unknown. In practice, national and local museums had the opportunity to acquire treasure trove finds. If a museum chose to do so, the lawful finder normally received the full market value (assessed by the Treasure Trove Reviewing Committee); if not, the object was returned, normally to the finder. The new act removes the need to establish that objects were hidden with the intention of being recovered, except in a very few cases; it sets out the precious metal content required for a find to qualify as treasure; and it extends the definition of treasure to include other objects found in archaeological association with finds of treasure. The act further confirms that treasure vests in the crown or the franchisee if there is one, subject to prior interests and rights. It simplifies the task of coroners in determining whether or not a find is treasure and it includes a new offence of non-declaration of treasure. Lastly, it states that occupiers and landowners will have the right to be informed of finds of treasure from their land and that they will be eligible for rewards.

DEFINITION OF TREASURE

(i) *Objects other than coins*

Any object other than a coin provided that at least 10 per cent by weight of metal is precious metal (that is, gold or silver) and that it is at least 300 years old when found. This means that objects plated in gold or silver will not normally be treasure (unless they are found in association with objects that are treasure).

(ii) *Coins*

All coins that contain at least 10 per cent of gold or silver by weight of metal and that come from the same find, provided a find consists of at least two coins with a gold or silver content of at least 10 per cent. The coins must be at least 300 years old at the time of discovery. In the case of finds consisting of coins that contain less than 10 per cent of gold or silver there must be at least ten such coins; they will also need to be at least 300 years old. This definition only includes coins and tokens made after the introduction of the first coinage into this country during the Iron Age period and excludes objects made earlier such as iron currency bars. Jettons or reckoning counters are also excluded from this definition.

(iii) *Objects found in association with objects that are treasure*

Any object, of whatever composition, that is found in the same place as, or that had previously been together with, another object that is treasure. The object may have been found at the same time as, or later than, the item of treasure.

Roman gold lamella plaque (1ˢᵗ–2ⁿᵈC AD), a sheet of gold with a magical inscription scratched on to it invoking the protection of the eastern god Abrasax.

(iv) Objects that would have been treasure trove

Any object that would previously have been treasure trove but does not fall within the specific categories given above. (Only objects that are less than 300 years old, that are made substantially of gold or silver, that have been deliberately hidden with the intention of recovery and whose owners or heirs are unknown will come into this category. In practice such finds are rare and the only such discoveries that have been made within recent years have been hoards of gold and silver coins of the eighteenth, nineteenth or twentieth centuries.)

If you are in any doubt, it will probably be safest to report your find.

REPORTING A FIND

You must report all finds of treasure to the coroner for the district in which they are found either within 14 days of the day on which you made the find or within 14 days after the day on which you realised that the find might be treasure (for example, as a result of having it identified). The obligation to report finds applies to everyone, including archaeologists. You may report your find to the coroner in person, by letter, telephone or fax. The coroner or his officer will send you an acknowledgement and tell you where you should deliver your find.

You will normally be asked to take your find to a local museum or archaeological body. Local agreements have been drawn up for each coroner's district in England and Wales to provide the coroner with a list of such museums and archaeological organisations. The Department is publishing a series of leaflets, roughly one for each county of England and one for Wales, listing the relevant coroners, museums and archaeological services in each area. The body which receives the find on behalf of the coroner will give you a receipt. Although they will need to know where you made the find, they will keep this information confidential if you or the landowner wish – and you should do so too. The body receiving the find will notify the Sites and Monuments Record as soon as possible (if that has not already happened), so that the site where the find was made can be investigated by archaeologists if necessary.

If you fail to report a find that you believe or have reasonable grounds for believing to be treasure without a reasonable excuse you may be imprisoned for up to three months or receive a fine of up to level 5 on the standard scale (currently £5,000) or both. You will not be breaking the law if you do not report a find because you do not initially recognise that it may be treasure, but you should report it once you do realise this.

REWARDS

There is an obligation under the act to pay rewards for the discovery of what is deemed to be treasure, providing certain criteria are met. In broad terms these are:

where the finder has permission to be on the land, rewards should continue to be paid in full to him or her. (The burden of proof as to whether he or she has permission will rest on the finder.) If the finder makes an agreement with the occupier/landowner to share a reward, the Secretary of State will normally follow it:

- if the finder does not remove the whole of a find from the ground but allows archaeologists to excavate the remainder of the find, the original will normally be eligible for a reward for the whole find;

- rewards will not normally be payable when the find is made by an archaeologist;

- where the finder has committed an offence in relation to a find, or has trespassed, or has not followed best practice as set out in the Code of Practice, he or she may expect no reward at all or a reduced reward. Landowners and occupiers will be eligible for rewards in such cases.

The Code of Practice states that you should receive a reward within one year of you having delivered your find, although this may take longer in the case of very large finds or those that present special difficulties. If no museum wants to acquire the find it should be disclaimed within six months or within three months if it is a single object.

If you are in any doubt of any aspect of the act check the full text at:

http://www.hmso.gov.uk/acts/acts1996/1996024.htm

or

The Stationery Office Ltd
PO Box 29
Norwich, NR3 1GN
Telephone orders and general enquiries: 0870 600 5522
Text telephone for the hard of hearing: 0870 240 3701

There are minor variations in the act as they apply to Northern Ireland; these can be checked at the above website or are included in the printed copies of the act.

East Anglia offers everyone interested in the past, from the professional archaeologist to the detectorist, a landscape rich in Britain's history and the potential for fascinating finds. Despite the enormous number of finds that have occurred, there seems to be an unlimited supply still waiting to be discovered.

Some of Britain's greatest treasures have been uncovered in the region. There are the amazing hoards from Snettisham, Mildenhall and Thetford – the first dating from the hundred years before the Roman invasion, the latter from 400 to 500 years later. The richness of some of the Roman finds from around Colchester is illustrated by the temple site at Gosbecks and there have been many other Roman discoveries, such as the gladiator's helmet found at Hawkedon and numerous Roman coins in caches both large and small.

In the centuries after the Romans left these shores East Anglia saw more than its fair share of upheaval and this resulted in many interesting finds. Among the finest are a 7thC seal ring found near Norwich that may have belonged to Queen Balthilda and Anglo-Saxon silver brooches from Pentney in Norfolk. The grave of the Anglo-Saxon monarch found at Prittlewell, Essex, in 2003 confirms the region's potential for yet more fantastic discoveries.

Subsequent periods have perhaps yielded fewer important finds, probably because of the changing nature of the rural economy, but there have been, and continue to be, numerous discoveries associated with Tudor times, the Civil War and later.

EAST ANGLIA

Saxtead Green Windmill

NORFOLK

Hunstanton
Cromer
Snettisham
Kings Lynn
Pentney
Beachamwell
Norwich
Great Yarmouth
Wisbech
Swaffham
Fincham
Oxborough
YARE
Caistor St.Edmund
Lowestoft
Peterborough
NENE
Stonea
WISSEY
OUSE
Water Newton
Brandon
Thetford
WAVENEY
CAMBRIDGESHIRE
Ely
Lakenheath
Hoxne
Wingfield
Huntingdon
Mildenhall
CAM
Bury St. Edmunds
Saxmundham
Cambridge
Newmarket
Stowmarket
SUFFOLK
Sutton Hoo
Ipswich
Great Chesterford
ESSEX
COLNE
STOUR
Felixstowe
Harwich
Colchester
Clacton-on-sea
CHELMER
Ely Cathedral
Chelmsford
MALDON 991
Epping
Basildon
Southend
Prittlewell

N
W E
S

· Km ·
0 10 20 30 40 50
0   10   20   30
· Miles ·

ACTON, SUFFOLK

1973 81 silver coins of Edward VI, Philip and Mary, Elizabeth I, James I, and Charles I and II, spanning the years 1551–1679.

AKENHAM, SUFFOLK

1981–2 59 Roman *denarii* and a small fragment of a gold bar possibly dating from the 1stC BC to the 3rdC AD. A detectorist first found 43 of the coins in a pot, and then the remainder with a fragment of pottery.

ALDEBURGH, SUFFOLK

1743 Great quantities of Roman copper coins from the 4th and 5thC AD on the seashore between Aldeburgh and Orford.

ASHBOCKING, SUFFOLK

1849 3 16thC silver coins, thought to have been concealed in 1595.

ASHDON, ESSEX

1984 12 silver coins, 7 fragmented coins and over 100 other fragments, dating from the 9thC, found in a field by Bob Spall (M/D) over the course of several months. Many were Danish Viking imitations of Alfred the Great pennies; the hoard was thought to have been buried AD 890–5 and declared treasure trove.

1984 1 gold and between 1,100 and 1,120 silver coins, dated 1552–1649, found in a bag in a field by Richard Fisher and his wife Cherry. While they were out walking their dog one Sunday morning, they spotted a coin glinting in the sun among some loose earth scraped from a barrow by some rabbits. This led to the discovery of the hoard, estimated to be worth £20,000 (possibly double that today). A week later another 79 coins came to light near the burrow. The vast majority were Tudor issues but there were a few Charles I coins. It seems likely that the coins were buried by a Royalist living in an area of Parliamentary sympathies.

ASHWELLTHORPE, NORFOLK

1998 Medieval silver cross-shaped pendant: J. Worton (M/D).

2000 13thC silver finger-ring: finder A. Womack (M/D); later returned to the finder.

c. **2003** Copper-alloy coin of British Emperor Carausius (AD 286–93). The obverse shows both the emperor and Sol the sun god in profile.

ATTLEBOROUGH AREA, NORFOLK

1866 7 Henry VI gold angels, thought to have been hidden *c.* 1483.

AYLSHAM AREA, NORFOLK

1999 Mid-7thC Anglo-Saxon gold pendant, with a garnet setting: finder Jim Blackburn (M/D).

THE ANGEL

The coin was introduced in 1465 by Edward IV and these remain extremely rare; angels of Henry VI are relatively common. It was introduced after the gold noble was revalued to 8s 4d. The standard fee for all sorts of professional services was 6s 8d and so it was felt necessary to have a coin of the same value as the old noble. Throughout the 200-year life of the angel its value fluctuated and it was so called because on the reverse side it depicted the archangel St Michael spearing a dragon, a metaphor for Satan. The half-angel and quarter-angel were also introduced before the angel eventually disappeared in 1643, when the final issues were minted during Charles I's reign.

BACONSTHORPE, NORFOLK

1878 9,000–17,000 Roman copper coins dating from the 3rdC AD found in a large pot during ploughing on Barningham Hall estate, about half a mile east of the ruins of Baconsthorpe Castle. Contemporary reports spoke of 'over a hundred-weight of brass and billon coins', many of which 'took wings in all directions'. Around 5,000 coins were recovered, almost all *antoniniani*.

Norwich Castle Museum

BACTON, NORFOLK

>1991 Early 7thC Anglo-Saxon pendant with a gold coin (585–602) in a cloisonné and garnet setting.

1999 13thC gold finger-ring, set with a green stone, was found by Tim English and Tim Pestell (M/D) while they were engaged upon an archaeological survey.

BALE, NORFOLK

1943 42 silver and 1,063 bronze Roman *antoniniani* from AD 249 to 296 found in a jar in a field 500 yd west of Bale Hall.

Norwich Castle Museum

BARKING, SUFFOLK

>1813 Bronze statuette, almost 2ft high, of a Roman emperor, probably Nero (AD 54–68) found at Barking Hall. Although the left arm is missing, inlaid silver and niello patterning is clearly visible in the armour and clothes. The statue was presented to the British Museum by Lord Ashburnham in 1813.

British Museum

BARNEY, NORFOLK

1815 Large Viking gold shield and gold torque were discovered during ploughing near Barney Hills Convent. Seven years later several brass coins were dug up close to the original find site.

BARWAY, CAMBRIDGESHIRE

1979–81 24 Roman *denarii* from the 1st and 2ndC AD found scattered in a field.

BARWAY AREA, CAMBRIDGESHIRE

>1960 4 Roman *aurei*, 364 *denarii* and 1 *drachm* from the 1st and 2ndC AD found scattered in a field with pottery between Old and New Forday Farms. They were thought to have been deposited *c.* AD 192.

1977 21 Roman *denarii* found scattered over a large area in a field; they were thought to have been deposited *c.* AD 192.

BEACHAMWELL, NORFOLK

5th–6thC earthwork in the area known as Bichamditch, used to control movements along the Roman road, which today is part of a field boundary. The thatched Norman church in the village has a round tower that may pre-date the church itself.

1846 About 50 Roman *denarii* from the 1st and 2ndC AD found in an urn, which was inside another urn 2ft deep, by a boy digging in a sandpit on Wellmere Heath.

1989 1stC BC silver coin of the Iceni tribe found at Toot Hill by a detectorist.

1998 14thC silver-gilt brooch: finder K. Matthews (M/D); returned to the finder.

1998 Back-plate of a 7thC AD gold pendant: finder M. Carlile.

1999 13thC silver cross pendant: finder Steven Brown (M/D).

2001 Part of an early 6thC Anglo-Saxon silver-gilt buckle loop fragment: finder Steven Brown (M/D).

BEALINGS, SUFFOLK

1943 90 tiny Roman gold coins found in a sandpit by an 11-year-old boy. Sandmartins tunnelling near the lip of the pit had broken into a Roman coin hoard; the main hoard was never found. The pit has been filled in and forms part of the garden of a modern house.

BECK ROW, SUFFOLK

1979 258 Roman *denarii* dating from the 1stC BC to the 1stC AD found at Wilde Street Farm, just to the north of Mildenhall airfield: finder David Tilbrook and John King. Discovered during the course of a week, the coins lay scattered in a cornfield belonging to Percy Webb. They were centred on what had been a small mound bulldozed flat some years before, about 200 yards from the site of a Roman settlement. They were thought to have been deposited in AD 80 and were declared treasure trove. A year later 19 more coins of a similar date were found in the field.

Fitzwilliam Museum, Cambridge

BELSTEAD, NEAR IPSWICH, SUFFOLK

1968 5 gold torcs dating from the 1stC BC unearthed by a mechanical digger driver. At first the driver thought they were brass coffin handles or perhaps horse-brasses, and only when he noticed that they were not tarnished did he realise that they were gold. The torcs have a 90 per cent gold and 10 per cent silver content, indicating that they were probably made shortly after 75 BC – between 150 BC and that time there was a tendency to have more gold and less silver. Each torc is about 7in in circumference and is made of twisted wire with the terminals cast on to each end of the wire, using a technique known as lost wax. They were declared treasure trove, and the finder awarded £45,000 (the equivalent of £450,000 today). Around a year later, when the new homeowners moved into the houses on the same site, they had topsoil dumped at the bottom of their gardens. One lucky owner found another, the sixth, torc and was awarded £9,000 when it too was declared treasure trove.

British Museum

BENACRE, SUFFOLK

1786 About 920 Roman *denarii*, in a good state of preservation, dating from the 1st and 2ndC AD, found by a workman making a new road when his pickaxe struck a stone bottle that contained the coins.

1876 Roman coins found in a group of trees beside the road; the site is known as Money Tree Clump.

BENFLEET, ESSEX

1700s About 1,500 Roman coins found in an urn by men ditching in a field.

1996 Bronze coin from the Byzantine Empire dated AD 850–950 found by Paul Elmy while digging the footings for a new shed in his back garden at Hall Farm Road. It was only eight years later when he took the coin to Southend Museum that he found out its significance. It dates from the period of the Battle of Benfleet, when King Alfred defeated and drove out the Danes from their stronghold. There were also some pieces of 4thC AD pottery.

BENHALL GREEN, SUFFOLK

1907 Bronze head of Emperor Claudius found by a small boy in the River Alde where it passes through the grounds of Benhall Lodge. It has been suggested that the statue originally stood in Colchester and that the head was removed as a trophy by Boudicca's victorious Iceni warriors when the town was sacked in AD 61. It was bought from Sotheby's by the British Museum for £15,500 (the equivalent of over £750,000 today).

BIRDBROOK, ESSEX

1790 Small number of silver and copper 17thC coins, including some of James I found by a group of workmen near the gravel pit at Bathorne End.

1977 99 gold sovereigns of 1825–45 found in what remained of a metal cash box at Yew Tree Cottage. When Michael Wrintmore was preparing to put in a damp course and dug up the old stone floor, his pickaxe struck a container with coins of George IV and Victoria. Thought to have been deposited soon after the last sovereigns were minted, they were estimated to be worth £10,000 – £1,000 more than Mr and Mrs Wrintmore had paid for the cottage.

BLAKENEY, NORFOLK

1998 Late 13th or early 14thC silver-gilt finger-ring set with a purple stone (possibly an amethyst): finder Jim Tamosaitis (M/D); returned to the finder.

2001   18thC or later gold finger-ring: finder J. Blackburn (M/D); returned to the finder.

2001   Late 15th or early 16thC highly decorated silver-gilt dress fitting: finder Jim Renfrew (M/D).

BLYFORD, SUFFOLK

>1978   Roman bronze statuette of Venus found near Blyford Bridge.

BOCKING, ESSEX

>1754   Vast quantity of 3rdC AD Roman coins found by 'a countryman', who disposed of them.

1834   1stC AD Roman coins found in an urn in the grounds of High Garrett House. A large number of coins were preserved, but many were lost or sold on by the workmen. At the time of the find former army lieutenant Joseph Jagger lived with his wife and two sons in a nearby house on Bocking's Church Street!

BOOTON, NORFOLK

1998   13th or 14thC highly decorated silver brooch: finder A. Woods (M/D); returned to the finder.

BOYTON AREA, SUFFOLK

1835   Early Bronze Age gold flanged torc 5in in diameter and dating from c. 600 BC found by a villager 10ft deep in a loam pit near the rectory. Attached to the torc were two small gold rings, but these were removed the torc snapped in two.

British Museum

BRADWELL, ESSEX

1998   Late 12th or early 13thC broken gold finger-ring, with its gem missing, found by D. Crawford at a metal detector rally; returned to the finder.

2001   Damaged 13thC gold finger-ring: finder M. Weale (M/D); returned to the finder.

BRAINTREE, ESSEX

1828   About 300 (although some reports say 3,000) Roman silver and copper coins from the 3rd and 4thC AD found in a pot by a gardener close to the road that divides Bocking and Braintree; the finder gave them away or sold them.

2000   Roman gold phallic amulet dating from the 1st or 2ndC AD: finder G.R. Lee (M/D).

Braintree District Museum, Essex

BRANCASTER, NORFOLK

>1985   28 Roman *denarii* and a brass coin dating from the 1st to the 3rdC AD found to the south-east of the site of the Roman fort of Branoduno; an altar stone was also discovered there.

BRANCASTER AREA, NORFOLK

1942–5   300–350 Roman coins from the 3rdC AD found in a pot to the north-west of Choseley Farm. Many of the coins were dispersed by the finders but 171 were retrieved. Three years later about 600 Roman coins from the same period were discovered in a pot in the same field but this time 306 coins were retrieved. Choseley had been a village but it was deserted during the Middle Ages.

BRANDON, SUFFOLK

>1889   Roman coins found at Fenhouse Farm and a Roman curse plaque dredged from the Little Ouse says 'To the person slave or free, who stole my pot, may they be cursed in the name of the God Neptune.'

Moyse's Hall Museum, Bury St Edmunds

>1913   About 3,000 Roman silver coins, possibly dating from the 3rdC AD found in a large urn at Wangford Heath. The urn can be seen at Moyse's Hall Museum.

Moyse's Hall Museum, Bury St Edmunds

1978   9thC Anglo-Saxon gold plaque. Finder Tony Langwith was fishing on the bank of the Little Ouse with his nephew when, scouring the river bank, he got a good signal. Digging just 2in he unearthed a flat gold block. On one side was a carved representation of a saint with the head of an eagle, as well as some exquisitely carved script. Tony contacted the curator of Norwich Museum, who confirmed it was Anglo-Saxon and the engraving represented St John the Evangelist. Sotheby's valued it at £14,400 (the equivalent of over £50,000 today); it was bought by the British Museum.

British Museum

>1980–8 Selection of early to middle Anglo-Saxon finds in Staunch Meadow: finder Suffolk Archaeology Unit. The best of the finds is a gold plaque depicting St John described in the previous entry. Since that find the excavation has also uncovered 3 styli, 3 runic inscriptions, as well as decorative silver and bronze objects that all date from the 7th to 9thC. The finds are thought to indicate that this site was either of royal or monastic status.

BRANTHAM, SUFFOLK

2002–3 90 Anglo-Saxon coins of Edward the Elder, thought to have been deposited c. AD 920. This hoard is of considerable importance as it dates from soon after the Anglo-Saxon conquest of East Anglia. Members of the East Coast Searchers Club found the coins over a four-day period at Brantham Hall Farm. Brantham means burnt hamlet, which alludes to an attack by the Vikings in 911.

BRENTWOOD, ESSEX

1948 Late 4thC Romano-British Christian gold signet ring found in a garden where tomatoes were being grown. It was later sold at Christie's for £5,606 (the equivalent of over £120,000 today).

1957 5 billon coins from the 16th and 17thC, thought to have been concealed in 1672.

2003 Silver penny of Edward I found in a school playground by 12-year-old George Hughes. It was minted in London and was probably struck between AD 1272 and 1307.

BRISTON, NORFOLK

2001 15th or early 16thC silver-gilt pilgrim's badge, depicting St George slaying the dragon: finder Paul Dawson (M/D); declared treasure trove.

BUMPSTEAD, ESSEX

[date?] 19thC hoard found during deep ploughing at Ford Meadow.

BUNGAY AREA, SUFFOLK

1997–8 103 Roman radiates found by D.J. Riches over a period of about 6 months. 7 Roman base-silver coins followed, probably deposited c. AD 269; returned to the finder.

1999 15thC gold finger-ring, decorated with lines; finder C. Hammond (M/D); returned to the finder.

BURES, ESSEX

2001 19thC decorated gold finger-ring: finder M.J. Matthews (M/D); returned to the finder.

BURGATE, SUFFOLK

1998–9 5 Roman silver coins, ranging in date from AD 337 to 395, and a silver spoon fragment: finder I. Charity (M/D). These items had been added to a previous hoard found sometime before 1997; the total number of coins from this hoard stands at 1 gold solidus, 174 siliquae, 1 silver half-siliqua, 3 silver finger-rings, 1 complete silver spoon and 4 spoon fragments.

BURGH CASTLE, NORFOLK

1958–61 A total of 1,180 Roman copper coins from AD 330–48 found during excavation of the Roman fort of Gariannonum in 16 small hoards.

BURNHAM-ON-CROUCH, ESSEX

1984 2 Celtic Gallo-Belgic gold staters from the Ambiani tribe dated 57–45 BC found by Michael Day while clearing an overgrown garden.

BURNHAM MARKET AREA, NORFOLK

1998? 200 late Iron Age silver coins from the 1stC AD, thought to have been deposited c. AD 47, found by a detectorist; they were declared treasure trove.

BURY ST EDMUNDS, SUFFOLK

1812 380 silver coins of Henry VII (1500–9), concealed in 1544 or earlier.

1851 Quantity of William I coins, concealed in the late 11thC, found in Mill Lane.

1852 6 copper tokens/jettons from the 16th and 17thC, thought to have been concealed in 1669.

1957 18 silver coins from the 16th and 17thC , probably concealed in 1645.

1977 13thC silver-gilt brooch found by a bricklayer in Abbey Gardens.

1978 Silver stater dating from 15 BC to AD 45, probably minted by an unknown Bury tribe, found in a field 5in below the surface by Dorothy Bailey (M/D). At the time of the discovery only one other coin with similar markings was known to exist.

BURY ST EDMUNDS AREA, SUFFOLK

1990 31 gold staters of the Catuvellauni tribe from the 1stC BC to 1stC AD found in a local field by Dorothy Bailey (M/D). They were sent to the British Museum to be recorded.

[date?] 60 Roman denarii from the 1st and 2ndC AD.

2000 Early 7thC Anglo-Saxon gold pyramid mount from a scabbard: finder Lady Kemball (M/D). The mount has a well-cut square garnet and is similar to the better-known ones found in the ship burial at Sutton Hoo.

6

CAISTER-ON-SEA, NORFOLK

1946 847 Roman silver coins from the 1st and 3rdC AD. Although found by three separate people the coins appear to belong to the same hoard. 628 coins were found in a pot during work to dig a trench for a water main of a new housing estate at Belstead Avenue, an additional 200 coins were later produced by another finder, and a further 19 found later. Altogether there were 664 *denarii* and 183 *antoniniani*. During the 18thC Roman coins were regularly found on the beach after storms, and coins and other relics still turn up after severe weather.

CAISTOR ST EDMUND, NORFOLK

This was once an extremely important town, known as Venta Icenorum. Capital of the Iceni tribe, it was also a large market town and a centre of entertainment. The impressive Roman walls still stand 20ft high on the north side of town. Much of the town is built from stone taken from Romano-British buildings.

1895 20 Roman *denarii* from the 1st and 2ndC AD found in an urn on the Caistor Hall estate.

1989–91 Anglo-Saxon brooch of AD 610–50 and other jewellery found at a grave site at Harford Farm during the building of the southern bypass around Norwich. The brooch is made of gold and silver, inlaid with cloisonné garnets and filigree interlace decorative work. Pieces such as this have hardly ever been found outside Kent and it would certainly have belonged to an extremely wealthy Anglo-Saxon woman. On the back of the brooch are 16 runes that have caused speculation among scholars. 'Luda made me' and 'Luda repaired this brooch' have both been put forward as possible meanings but perhaps the most interesting is, 'May Luda make amends by means of the brooch'. Friends of the Norwich Museums raised £91,600 to purchase the Harford Farm treasure.

Norwich Castle Museum

c. **2003** Roman gilt plate brooch from the 3rdC AD, unusually set with a late 1stC carnelian intaglio that depicts Victory crowning Providence; normally this type of brooch has a glass setting.

CAMBRIDGE, CAMBRIDGESHIRE

>1854 Silver coins and 3 gold rings from the 13thC found in a purse close to Trinity College. The coins were dated 1247–78.

1875 41 gold coins from the 16th and 17thC found close to Pembroke College; they were thought to have been concealed in 1640.

1889 About 2,500 Roman *antoniniani* found in two jars by men digging a post-hole. 2,308 were sold to a collector, the rest disposed of by the finders.

1897 207 Roman silver coins from the 2nd and 3rdC AD found in a fused lump. Some were broken as they were prised apart but 155 *denarii* and 52 others remained.

1954 37 gold coins possibly dating from the 19th and 20thC. They were possibly concealed in 1912.

1964? A quantity of 16th or 17thC copper tokens/jettons.

2001 Silver finger-ring, dating from after 1700, found on the surface of drained millpond; it was returned to the finder.

[date?] Bronze Age side-piece, part of a horse bridle.

[date?] Bronze Age bronze razor dating from *c.* 500 BC.

CAMBRIDGE AREA

1980s 6thC Anglo-Saxon spear, dagger and shield-boss found in a grave about 15in below the surface by Chris Montague. On being informed of the discovery the Cambridge Museum of Archaeology and Anthropology organised a thorough archaeological excavation of the site.

[date?] Bronze bracelet, thought to date from 50 BC.

1987 30 Roman *denarii* from the 1st and 2ndC AD and the remains of an upside-down pot found on a development site by Bill Parkinson and Derek Glover (M/D).

1990–1 6 Ambiani gold staters from 50–40 BC, found over a period of time in a field by Chris Montague (M/D).

CAMPSEA ASH, SUFFOLK

1832 About 600 coins, mainly of Edward the Confessor and Harold II found in two thin lead cases. Surprisingly, given Harold's short reign (January–14 October 1066) he issued three types of silver pennies.

CANVEY ISLAND, ESSEX

2000 Hoard of around 100 silver Iron Age coins and another of stone coins of *c.* 500 BC found by Clive Smith (M/D) on what is believed to be the site of a Celtic harbour dating from 350 BC. After a number of weeks of searching a total of 700 coins were found, leading Clive to suggest that many were thrown overboard by sailors departing on ships as an offering to the Gods. As well as coins there were several ivory bracelets.

CARLETON ST PETER, NORFOLK

1807 Roman gold and silver coins from the 4th and 5thC AD found in a vase, of which just 3 gold *solidi* and 11 *siliquae* were not dispersed.

CARLTON COLVILLE, SUFFOLK

1998   Anglo-Saxon part-gilded silver pendant figure from the first half of the 7thC: finder Adrian Charlton (M/D).

CASTON, NORFOLK

1816   Roman gold coin and a quantity of silver coins from the 4th and 5thC AD found in an urn.

1820   About 300 mostly Roman silver and brass coins, as well as a silver ring from the 1st and 2ndC AD found about 5ft deep in the course of making a clay pit.

CASTOR, CITY OF PETERBOROUGH

1924   2 silver coins of Henry VIII (1509–44) were found, thought to have been concealed in 1544 or earlier.

CAWSTON, NORFOLK

1999   Roman openwork gold finger-ring from the 4thC AD: finder J. Blocksidge (M/D).

CHATTERIS, CAMBRIDGESHIRE

According to *Kelly's Directory of Cambridgeshire* (1900), 'Various other relics of the Romans have been met with at several times hereabout, as well as Celts and a double-edged sword, the hilt of which was embossed with figures of men fighting; this, when found, was in a perfect state of preservation.'

1824   About 1,000 Roman copper coins, mostly of Constantius (AD 305) and Constantine (AD 306) found in an earthenware pot during ploughing about 2 miles from the town.

1983   1 gold and 8 silver British coins along with 1 gold, 30 silver, and 215 bronze Roman coins found by a metal detectorist at Langwood Hill. The British coins date from the 1stC BC and the Roman from the 4thC AD, and were identified as two separate hoards.

CHATTERIS AREA, CAMBRIDGESHIRE

1960   34 Roman billon *antoniniani* from the 3rdC AD, thought to have been concealed *c.* AD 273, were found at Westmoor.
Wisbech and Fenland Museum

CHELMSFORD AREA, ESSEX

1982   Bronze perpendicular Omega design brooch from the 1stC BC found by Jack Basham (M/D), just a few inches down in a ploughed field.

[date?]   6 Roman gold coins from the 4th and 5thC BC found by a detectorist. They were valued at just under £1,000 and declared treasure trove.

2000–1   23 Iron Age gold staters from the 1stC AD: finder G. Newitt (M/D).
Chelmsford and Essex Museum

CHIPPENHAM, CAMBRIDGESHIRE

1981   2 separate hoards comprising 41 Roman gold and silver coins from the Republic to Claudius I and 5 Iron Age gold staters of Cunobelin and artefacts dating from the 1stC BC to the 1stC AD found in King's Fen field at Manor Farm.

1997   Early 9thC Anglo-Saxon highly decorated silver hook tag found by R. Allison (M/D); it was valued at £500.

CHIPPING ONGAR, ESSEX

1999   2 gold Merovingian tremisses from the early to mid-7thC were found by C. Kutler (M/D). They were valued at £1,500.
British Museum

MEROVINGIAN TREMISSES
The Merovingians were Frankish kings who ruled parts of present-day France and Germany from the 5th to the 8thC AD. They struck gold tremisses, whose design evolved from earlier Roman coins, which in turn went on to influence the design of later British coins. Tremisses found their way to Britain through trade, and are found mostly in southern England.

CLARE, SUFFOLK

1865   Gold crucifix, studded with pearls and attached to a 2ft-long gold chain found by Walter Lorking, a 'poor village lad' employed in digging the castle bailey. It is believed to have belonged to Edward III. On hearing of its discovery Queen Victoria claimed it and rewarded Walter with three gold sovereigns.
British Museum

COCKFIELD, SUFFOLKNHAM, SUFFOLK

Early 1900s?   A number of coins, tiles and a bronze bust. Roman earthworks known as the Warbanks are located near the village.
British Museum

[date?]   Bronze mirror and cover decorated with a bust of Nero and a sacrificial scene dating from the 1stC AD.

British Museum

COLCHESTER, ESSEX

Colchester, the Roman Camulodunum, lies on the River Colne. There are numerous Roman remains in the area, and the 11thC castle has the largest Norman keep in England.

1849 800 Roman copper coins from the 3rd and 4thC AD with fragments of two small lead-lined boxes found at Union House.

c. **1866** 36 Roman brass coins, 12 of Agrippa and 24 of Claudius, plus 37 Roman objects from the 1stC BC to the 1stC AD found at the Roman cemetery near Beverley Road and Lexden Road. Among the finds were fragments of cups, an elaborate and highly ornamented casket and a sphynx-like piece.

c. **1890** 32 Roman *denarii* and 1 *antoniniani*, possibly dating from the 1st and 3rd C AD, found during excavations on farmland.

1897 Large hoard of Roman *denarii* from the 1st to the 3rdC AD found in a jug on the Maldon Road.

1901 Silver and billon coins, thought to have been concealed between 1820 and 1837, but possibly belonging to the period 1727–60.

1902 10,926 silver coins, mainly English Henry III short-cross silver pennies, with several hundred Scottish and Irish coins, dating from the 13thC, found in a lead bucket 2ft beneath the surface by workmen on land belonging to the Church. Somewhat ironically, the workmen were building the London and County Bank in Colchester's High Street. The coins were probably buried in 1256 by the town's Jewish money-lenders, who lent a great deal of money to Roger de Quincy, Earl of Winchester in 1244. De Quincey's father was one of the surety signatures on the Magna Carta and inherited through marriage large portions of Galloway. Later he was one of the barons who revolted against Henry III.

1926 28 Roman brass coins found in a pot during building work to extend the telephone exchange behind St Martin's House. Although the workman destroyed the pot and burnt the coins, the coins were recognisable as mostly being from the reigns of Agrippa and Claudius.
Colchester Castle Museum

1958 192 Roman copper coins from the 3rdC AD found during excavations in the debris of a hypocaust.

1965 4 Roman bronze *asses* of Claudius, AD 50–60 found in Balkerne Gardens after demolition of a house in an area known for Roman finds.
Colchester Castle Museum

1969 14,065 silver coins mostly long-cross pennies of Henry III dated 1216–72, along with about 20 laminated forgeries, dug up in a lead bucket by a workman cutting a trench on the site of an old chemist shop in Culver Street. The condition of the coins was such that when the workman broke open the box with his pickaxe he thought they were modern sixpences. They were estimated 12 years later to be worth almost £500,000 (perhaps over £1 million now). The find was only about 30ft from the similar hoard found in 1902. The first hoard was deposited in 1256, the second *c.* 1268–78; both are thought to relate to the Jewish community in the town which was forcibly ejected from Colchester *c.* 1290. The community was not allowed to return until 1656.

1977 128 Roman bronze coins from AD 294 to 317 were dug up over three to four days on a building site in Balkerne Gardens. The coins were examined and found to contain 3 per cent silver.

1979 About 140 Roman coins found by Nigel Richards and Mike Scilleto while exploring an area due to be covered in concrete for a new road. Some thick black clay taken from the River Colne had been dumped there and among it they found some very fine Roman *sistertii* and *denarii* of the Emperors Claudius, Tiberius and Vespian, as well as some Constantine *folles*.
Colchester Castle Museum

1979–80 11 silver coins and 1 gold stater, minted in Colchester between AD 10 and 40: finder Nigel Richards. The coins were declared not treasure trove.

1980 8 Roman gold coins found on the banks of River Colne: finder Nigel Richards (M/D).

1995–8 A total of 6 Anglo-Saxon silver sceattas found by Christopher Behn (M/D) on separate occasions; they were thought to have been deposited *c.* AD 710.
Colchester Castle Museum

1996 Celtic gold torc terminal from *c.* 100–50 BC found 1ft below the surface by Ken Kirtley (M/D). The walnut-sized lump of pure gold was unearthed in a field on a farm on the eastern outskirts of the town.

2000 A 1stC AD Roman silver buckle and a 2nd or 3rdC AD finger-ring found during excavations by the Colchester Archaeological Trust.

COLCHESTER AREA, ESSEX

1927 298 Roman copper *antoniniani* from the 3rdC AD found in a pot by men digging a drainage trench a few miles from the town.

[date?] 14th or 15thC bronze cauldron found by Keith Hampton (M/D) 3ft below the surface at the base of a tree in the woods on a farm.

1988 Almost 1,000 Roman silver and bronze coins from the 1stC AD. Sharon Dyden found the coins while visiting the rebuilt Norman castle; she noticed a chicken scratch the dirt by a rabbit warren, revealing the coins.

2001 5thC AD post-Roman gold finger-ring, with 2 small cabochon stones: finder C. Behn (M/D).

Colchester Castle Museum

COLKIRK, NORFOLK

1999 2 Roman silver coins from the 4thC: finder N. Abram (M/D). Thought to have been deposited *c.* AD 395; returned to the finder.

2001 15thC highly decorated silver mount fragment found by N. Abram (M/D); returned to the finder.

2002 Some decorated harness mounts from the late 1stC AD, with fine metalwork and highlighted with red enamel, were found by a detectorist.

CONGHAM, NORFOLK

1997 Early 7thC AD Anglo-Saxon silver sword pommel found by John Wells; it was valued at £900.

1999 6thC Anglo-Saxon silver square-headed brooch fragment was found by John Wells; returned to the finder.

CORRINGHAM, THURROCK

[date?] Hoard of 2,300 Iron Age coins cast in Potin (a form of bronze with a high tin content). It was one of the largest of this type of coin ever found.

NEAR COTTENHAM, CAMBRIDGESHIRE

1986 5,084 Roman bronze coins from the 3rdC AD. A detectorist made the initial find, but the entire hoard was excavated later.

CROMER, NORFOLK

1979 9thC Late Bronze Age smith's hoard found in an urn on the edge of playing fields at Beeston Hall School by schoolboy Jimmy Ellis. The hoard comprised 18 Bronze Age axe heads (three of which were broken), a spearhead, half of a mould, and a big piece of bronze that Jimmy left in the ground, for fear of breaking it; the next day it was dug up by Andrew Lawson of the Norwich Castle Museum. Although it broke it was later put back together by conservators.

DENTON, NORFOLK

1973 5 sixpences of Elizabeth I (1578–1602 and 1603), and a James I shilling (1605–6) found at Pear Tree Farm, thought to have been concealed after 1606.

DERSINGHAM, NORFOLK

1979 3rdC Roman ring found on a footpath near Peddars Way.

1984 About 129 silver coins and a silver goblet hallmarked 1607–8 found by digger driver Terry Graver after he spotted a metallic object shining through the sandy soil while digging a trench on the Old Hall site.

DISS, NORFOLK

1871 325 gold and silver coins from the 13th to the 15thC found in an earthen vessel in a house in Mount Street. Believed to have been deposited *c.* 1465, the coins included gold nobles as well as silver pennies of Edward I, II, III and IV, and Henry V and VI. They were probably someone's life savings, accumulated over a long period.

> **THE NOBLE**
>
> The noble was the first English gold coin produced in real quantity. It was valued at 6s 8d and is found with many different inscriptions, mintmarks, as well as designs. It was introduced during King Edward III's reign *c.* 1344–6. Edward's early nobles were inscribed 'Edwar Dgra Rex Angl Z Franc Dns Hyb' (Edward by the grace of God King of England and France Lord of Ireland). Later in his reign, when he renounced his claim to the French throne, the word Franc was replaced by ACQ (Aquitaine). From 1369 Edward reasserted his claim to the French throne and so Franc once again appeared on the coins. Nobles were struck during Henry VI's first reign, from 1422 to 1461 but, owing to a gold shortage, there were fewer made. Initially coins were struck in both London and Calais but later on just in London.

DITCHINGHAM, NORFOLK

1812 More than 1,000 Roman copper coins from the 4th and 5thC AD found in a pot during ploughing on Bath Hills to the west of Outney Common.

DOCKING AREA, NORFOLK

1990 153 silver coins of the Iceni tribe from the 1stC AD found in a field along with fragments of a pottery vessel and some small pieces of cloth probably from a purse. They were thought to have been buried *c.* AD 60.

DOWNHAM, ESSEX

1999 8 silver pennies of Edward I and II and a continental imitation, dating from the 13th and 14thC, found by members of the Essex Detector Society. They were thought to have been deposited *c.* 1330–40 and were valued at £145.

Chelmsford Museums Service

DUNWICH, SUFFOLK

>1908 352 silver coins from the 13thC found on a beach. There were 46 silver pennies, 143 cut halfpennies and 163 cut farthings of Henry I, II and III, Edward I, William the Lion and Alexander III of Scotland. They were thought to have been concealed *c.* 1279 or later.

Dunwich Museum

EARITH, CAMBRIDGESHIRE

1956 10 silver coins from the 16th and 17thC, thought to have been concealed in 1645.

EARSHAM, NORFOLK

[date?]   Roman and Saxon artefacts found near Camp Hill; the village name derives from 'the station of the army'.

EAST RAYNHAM, NORFOLK

1910   67 gold nobles of Edward III (1327–77) and 133 other coins from the 14thC found by workmen digging a drain. They are thought to have been concealed *c*. 1377. The gold nobles alone would now be worth around £80,000. Many of the coins from this hoard were in excellent condition and are in the collection of the Royal Mint.

EAST RUDHAM, NORFOLK

1719   Roman coins found in a small pot in the ruins of Coxford Priory.

2000   4thC AD Roman silver crossbow brooch: finder Barry Mears; later returned to the finder.

EAST SOMERTON, NORFOLK

2000   15thC gold finger-ring set with a sapphire: finder E. Bagguley; returned to the finder.

EASTON BAVENTS, SUFFOLK

1956   Edward III gold half-noble found on the beach.

ELM, CAMBRIDGESHIRE

c. **1713**   Roman copper coins from the 3rd and 4thC AD found in an urn near a tumulus.

1785   21 Roman billon coins, thought to have been concealed *c*. AD 400, found in an earthen pot.

ELMHAM, NORFOLK

c. **2000**   Gold quarter-stater of the Iceni from *c*. 50–40 BC found by a metal detector (M/D) during archaeological excavations at Flixton Park Quarry.

ELMSTEAD, ESSEX

1930   Gold coins found in a ploughed field west of the church near the manor house.

ELSENHAM, ESSEX

[date?]   2ndC AD bronze box, possibly an inkwell, found in a grave. Decorated with intricate and well-preserved enamel.
British Museum

ELVEDEN, SUFFOLK

1953   965 Roman *denarii* and 181 *antoniniani* from the 2nd and 3rdC AD were found in a pot, in woodland, on the estate of Lord Iveagh by a man digging out rabbit warrens. The hoard was declared treasure trove, but most of the coins were returned to Mr Trett, the finder.

ELY, CAMBRIDGESHIRE

2000   Late 15th or early 16thC plain gold finger-ring found during an archaeological excavation.
   The superb cathedral that dominates the surrounding Fenland is Norman. The Norman earthworks date from William I's defeat of Hereward the Wake in 1071.

ELY AREA, CAMBRIDGESHIRE

[date?]   11thC spearheads found near the Norman earthworks, located at Braham Farm, a mile south of the town.

EMNETH, NORFOLK

1938   About 2,000 Roman copper coins from the 3rdC AD found in a pot between Emneth and Smeeth Road Stations. The finder concealed the hoard before disposing of around 500 coins; later, 1,594 coins and the remains of the pot were recovered.

1941   More than 650 Roman silver coins, all *antoniniani* except for 5 *denarii*, from the 3rdC AD found in a pot between Emneth Station and Long Lot Crossing during ploughing.

EPPING FOREST, ESSEX

1977   53 Roman billon *antoniniani* of AD 220–70 found in the bed of a stream near Baldwin's Hill. Thought to have been deposited in AD 275, they were declared treasure trove.

EPPING UPLAND, ESSEX

1971–2   Of the 12 Celtic gold coins, 4 were of the Tasciovanus and 8 of the Cunobelin, and they dated from AD 20. They were declared treasure trove and the finder received their full market value.
British Museum

ERISWELL, SUFFOLK

1972   327 Iron Age and Roman silver coins, thought to have been concealed *c*. AD 60–1, were found on a building site in Lord's

Walk. There were 255 British silver coins of the Iceni and 72 silver Roman coins from the Republic (45), the reigns of Augustus (11), Tiberius (13), Caligula (1), Claudius (1), and Nero (1). They were declared treasure trove and the finder awarded the full market value.

British Museum

ESSEX

1993   114 Anglo-Saxon silver sceattas were found in two small batches beside a road by two detectorists. Half the coins were continental types, and the find was later declared treasure trove.

1994   6 Bronze Age axe heads found by R. Fry (M/D) about 2ft beneath a pile of bronze scrap in a field; in all there were 36 pieces of bronze.

1994   9 Bronze Age axe heads along with 52 other pieces of bronze were found in a field by Mike Sinclair (M/D).

EYE, SUFFOLK

1781   500–600 Roman gold coins from the 4th and 5thC AD found in a case covered with lead 2ft below the surface by two men digging in a sandpit. In pristine condition, the find included coins of Valentinian I, Honorius and Constantine III. The case was probably a military chest.

[date?]   Mid-9thC bronze seal-die of Bishop Aethelwald of Dunwich (AD 818–28).

British Museum

EYE AREA, SUFFOLK

1999   4 Roman *siliquae* of AD 360–93: finder J. Scopes (M/D). Thought to have been deposited *c.* AD 402, they were returned to the finder.

2000   Early 7thC Anglo-Saxon gold conical fitting, inlaid with garnets: finder John French (M/D); later declared treasure trove.

2001   4 Roman silver coins, thought to have been deposited *c.* AD 402: finder J. French (M/D) returned to the finder.

FAKENHAM, NORFOLK

>1837   About 1,600 Roman copper coins from the 3rd and 4thC AD.

FELIXSTOWE, SUFFOLK

1977   9 billon coins from the 2ndC AD, thought to have been concealed in AD 187 or later.

1978   More than 25 copper coins from the 3rdC AD, thought to have been deposited *c.* AD 240 or later.

FELMINGHAM, NORFOLK

1844   Hoard of Roman votive bronze statuettes and a pottery jar found at Felmingham Hall. The hoard, which also included a bronze wheel, a head of Jupiter, another of Minerva and a pair of ravens, may have come from a shrine or temple. Some of the pieces indicated a Celtic connection, while others were obviously Roman.

British Museum

FELTWELL, NORFOLK

>1880   300 Roman *denarii* from the 1st to the 3rdC AD found during ploughing.

2001   3rdC AD Roman silver finger-ring found by D.G. Woollestone (M/D); returned to the finder.

FIELD BAULK, NEAR MARCH, CAMBRIDGESHIRE

1982   860 silver coins from the Iceni tribe found in a pot by farmer Samuel Hills, who was digging his orchard to plant apple trees. The coins were thought to have been buried in about AD 60, the period when Queen Boudicca was staging her rebellion against the Romans. The coins were declared treasure trove and were estimated at £100,000.

FINCHAM, NORFOLK

The last Roman legions left the town in 410; the area had long been very vulnerable to German raids. Ten years later it was occupied by the Angles.

1801   7 Roman coins of AD 360–95 found in a silver *ampulla* (a small two-handled bottle) during ploughing. They date from the reigns of Emperors Valentinian (AD 360), Arcadius and Honorius (AD 395); the latter two had divided the Roman Empire between them.

1860   Gold coin of Julius Caesar, probably minted in France, found in the roots of a large elm tree after it was blown over in a severe gale.

1860s   Gold coin of the Iceni tribe, probably from after 10 BC, found in the rectory gardens.

1990s   Silver penny of Edward the Confessor (1042–66) was found by Carol Little (M/D).

2000   A 2nd or 3rdC Roman silver finger-ring, with a nicolo paste intaglio of a male figure, found by S.E. Sproule (M/D).

FLAG FEN, NEAR PETERBOROUGH

1982   This important site first came to light when a digger driver, working on improving the drainage ditches, pulled out some very old-looking timbers. Archaeologists, led by Dr Francis Pryor, dated them to 1000 BC and work began on piecing together the history of this crannog settlement. The site has yielded tools and a bronze ring. In August 2004 the first human remains, a part of a skull, were found by a student on work experience at the site.

FLAGGRASS, NEAR MARCH, CAMBRIDGESHIRE

There is speculation that this may have been the site of the Roman fort of Durovigora ('fortification at the Vigora', or fort at the windy river).

1949   1 silver and 14 Roman billon coins from the 3rdC AD were found along with the base of a coloured beaker; they were thought to have been concealed *c.* AD 260–73.

1949–51   9 Roman *sesterii* from the 3rdC AD, thought to have been concealed *c.* AD 273.

1949–50   2 Roman *denarii* and 28 *antoniniani* from the 3rdC AD found in a beaker during ploughing.

FLETTON, CITY OF PETERBOROUGH

1904   15 Roman coins from the 2nd and 3rdC AD found in a pot.

FORDHAM, CAMBRIDGESHIRE

2001   A 13thC silver decorated annular brooch found by S. Smalley (M/D).

FORNCETT END, NORFOLK

1997   328 Iron Age Icenian silver coins, 41 Roman *denarii* and pot sherds from the 1stC BC to the 1stC AD: finder Paul Thrower. Later declared treasure trove.

FORNHAM PARISH, SUFFOLK

1900–52   20–30 'Tealby' silver pennies of Henry II (1154–89). In October 1173, Robert of Leicester's army of Flemish mercenaries was destroyed at Fornham St Geneviève, by knights from Bury and local peasants armed with pitchforks and flails.

FORNHAM ST MARTIN, SUFFOLK

1978   A Roman filigree gold band with a garnet stone of *c.* AD 300: finders Dorothy Bailey and Josephine Fuller (M/D). The band was declared not treasure trove and returned to the finders.

FRECKENHAM, SUFFOLK

1948   595 Roman copper coins from the 4thC AD found in a pot during ploughing.

1980   Roman silver coins dated AD 360–423 found in a ploughed field by Thornton Vale. The hoard was declared treasure trove.

British Museum

FRING, NORFOLK

1998   8 Iron Age silver coins, thought to have been deposited about AD 50: finder John Bocking (M/D); returned to the finder.

2001   1st or 2ndC AD Roman silver finger-ring, with a missing setting: finder John Bocking (M/D); returned to the finder.

FULBOURN, CAMBRIDGESHIRE

2001   3rdC AD Roman silver finger-ring; set with an oval cornelian with an engraved hare: finder Mr Williams (M/D).

Cambridge University Museum of Archaeology and Anthropology

GIMINGHAM, NORFOLK

1999   9thC AD Anglo-Saxon silver pinhead decorated and engraved with crosses and triangles: finder S. Burgess and A. Kedge; returned to the finders.

GODMANCHESTER, CAMBRIDGESHIRE

1956   Roman coins and jewellery from the 3rdC AD found scattered in a rubbish pit during excavations. The find included 60 coins, a bronze

brooch, a gold pendant and chain, three intaglio gems, a string of glass beads, four bronze finger-rings and one silver, and was judged to be the contents of a woman's jewellery box.

Cambridge University Museum of Archaeology and Anthropology

GOOD EASTER, ESSEX

1992–36   Roman gold *solidi* from the 4th and 5thC were found by M.J. Cuddeford (M/D).

1998   6 Roman gold *solidi* of Arcadius, Honorius and Constantine III, covering the period AD 395–411: finder M.J. Cuddeford (M/D). The coins were valued at £1,700.

2002   2 Roman gold *solidi*, thought to have been deposited *c.* AD 408, found by M.J. Cuddeford (M/D). Weeks later another gold coin was found, bringing the total from this site to 15.

Chelmsford Museum Service

GOODERSTONE, NORFOLK

2001   16thC highly decorated silver-gilt dress-hook: finder Barry Hamilton (M/D); returned to the finder.

GOREFIELD, CAMBRIDGESHIRE

1998   1,084 13th–14thC silver coins, mostly silver pennies, halfpennies and farthings of Edward I and II, were found by T. Stamp and J. Fisher, while laying a patio. They were thought to have been deposited *c.* 1310–14. 141 of the rarest coins were valued at £5,270.

GOSBECKS, ESSEX

About 3 miles south of Colchester a square Roman temple was built *c.* AD 150 and remained in use until *c.* AD 390. It is unclear who the temple was built for but it was probably, as was often the case, dedicated to both a Celtic deity and a corresponding Roman god. In May 1983 the farmer at Oliver's Orchard Farm discovered, while ploughing, a pot containing 1,559 Roman coins. Calling in local archaeologists, two more pots were quickly discovered within 4 yd of the first one. The second pot contained 4,071 coins, and the third 494 coins. The coins dated AD 80–270 and were thought to have been buried by a single family or individual within five years of each other. The first hoard seems to have been buried in AD 269, the second in AD 270 and the fourth in AD 274. The hoard was declared partial treasure trove because only 1,600 coins had a high enough silver content to qualify.

GREAT BARTON, SUFFOLK

c. **1850**   About 50 silver pennies from the 10th and possibly 11thC were found in the garden of a house. They were thought to have been buried *c.* AD 1004, when the Vikings were attacking East Anglia.

1953   Roman coins on Red Castle Farm.

GREAT BIRCHAM, NORFOLK

1978   Gold Tudor ring from 1552.

GREAT BURSTEAD, ESSEX

c. **1820**   About 1,100 Roman coins found by a man ditching at Tiled Hall Farm; they were sold in London.

GREAT CHESTERFORD, ESSEX

The Roman site, which is strategically well sited slightly to the north-west of the village on the banks of the River Cam, is one of the earliest to have been occupied by Aulus Plautius in AD 43. The fort itself is thought to date from the winter of AD 60/1, the time of Boudicca's revolt.

1873   200 well-preserved Roman *denarii* from the 1st and 2ndC AD found by a boy digging a ditch in Chesterford Park.

1923   Bronze trumpet mouthpiece, the first piece of evidence to suggest Roman military occupation.

>1934   89 Roman silver *antoniniani* from the 3rdC AD.
Saffron Walden Museum

1949   About 326 Roman silver and 1 copper coin dating from the 1st to the 3rdC AD were found by the driver of a mechanical digger. The hoard comprised 171 *denarii*, 155 *antoniniani*, and 1 copper coin, but it is possible that some gold coins were undisclosed.

1978   5 Roman silver items dating from the 2ndC found on the site of a Roman temple by an amateur archaeologist.

GREAT CHISHILL, CAMBRIDGESHIRE

1954   Roman copper coins from the 4th and 5thC AD found in an urn during excavation of a burrow near Chishill Grange.

GREAT CORNARD AREA, SUFFOLK

2002–3   5thC AD penannular brooch.

GREAT EASTON, ESSEX

>1779   Large quantity of Roman bronze *antoniniani* from the 3rdC AD found on Lord Maynard's estate.

GREAT FINBOROUGH, SUFFOLK

2001   Late 13th or early 14thC decorated silver brooch: finder J. Wilding (M/D).

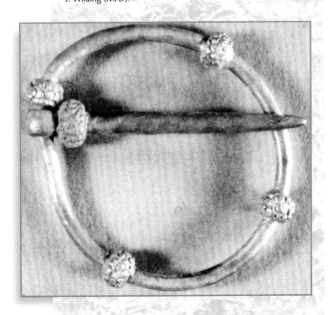

GREAT GLEMHAM, SUFFOLK

1999   2 16thC silver-gilt dress-hooks: finder P. Berry; returned to the finder.

GREAT LEIGHS, ESSEX

1997–8   27 Iron Age Gallo-Belgic gold staters, thought to have been deposited *c.* 50 BC, found by Greg Newitt and R. Pearce (M/D). They were sold for £40,000 to Chelmsford and Essex Museum. Two years later Greg Newitt returned to the same farm and, using a mechanical digger to strip away a layer of subsoil, found 11 more Gallo-Belgic gold staters lying on top of the clay; these were valued at £8,000.

Chelmsford and Essex Museum

GREAT MELTON, NORFOLK

1887   Roman *denarii* from the 1st and 2ndC AD found in a pot at Melton Hall.

1994–8   268 Roman *denarii* from the 1stC BC to the 2ndC AD found over the course of a 4-year period at Algarsthorpe Farm on the Great Melton estate.

GREAT SHELFORD, CAMBRIDGESHIRE

>1933   44 Roman copper *antoniniani* from the 3rdC AD found in a pot.

GREAT WALTHAM, ESSEX

1998   10 Iron Age gold staters from *c.* 50 BC: finder G. Newitt and B. Smith (M/D); valued at £4,500.

GREAT WITCHINGHAM, NORFOLK

2003   Silver late-Saxon pendant of Thor's hammer with gold filigree inlay on its head.

GREAT YARMOUTH, NORFOLK

1860   70 silver coins from the 16thC, thought to have been concealed 1544–61.

GREAT YARMOUTH AREA, NORFOLK

1827–8   A quantity of silver coins, thought to have been concealed *c.* AD 835.

HADDISCOE, NORFOLK

2003   250 Civil War era sixpences, shillings and half-crowns uncovered during excavations by Norfolk Archaeological Unit.

HADLEIGH, SUFFOLK

The *House of Commons Journal* of December 1642 stated that 'The Town of Hadleigh in the County of Suffolk shall be allowed the Sum of One hundred and Fifty Pounds, out of the Contribution Monies in the said Town; to be employed in providing of Arms, and making some Fortifications for the Defence of the said Town.'

1841 Some 16th and 17thC silver coins, thought to have been concealed 1625–49.

1936 97 gold coins from the 16th and 17thC, thought to have been concealed in 1649.

HADLEIGH AREA, SUFFOLK

1998 13thC silver-gilt finger-ring, set with an amethyst: finder T. Davis (M/D); returned to the finder.

HALESWORTH AREA, SUFFOLK

1999 Roman gold ring, with an openwork bezel-panel: finder G. Barker; returned to the finder.

1999 Roman silver finger-ring fragment: finder R. Allen; returned to the finder.

HAPPISBURGH, NORFOLK

Many gold, silver and copper coins, believed to originate from offshore wrecks. This is one of the best treasure-hunting beaches in the area.

HARKSTEAD, SUFFOLK

1999 Late 15thC gold finger-ring, set with a stone: finder A.R. Dunnett (M/D); returned to the finder.

HARTFORD, CAMBRIDGESHIRE

1964 1,108 silver coins from the 14th to the 16thC found in an urn during the bypass construction. There were coins of many denominations and eight different reigns, as well as foreign coins. The hoard is believed to have been buried *c.* 1509.

British Museum

HARWICH AREA, ESSEX

1878 Small cache of early 13thC French coins of Louis VII, Philippe II and Augustus discovered in the remains of a wooden box.

HASLINGFIELD, CAMBRIDGESHIRE

1865–75 Iron sword blade, a spearhead and the point of another spear found with a skeleton near Cantelupe Farm. There were also 2ndC Romano-British and 5th and 6thC Anglo-Saxon grave goods from graves that were found here, associated with the coprolite diggings. The find included brooches, wrist clasps, beads and bracelets.

British Museum, London, and Ashmolean Museum

[date?] A mid-5thC gilded bronze 'equal-armed' brooch.

Cambridge University Museum of Archaeology and Anthropology

HAUXTON, CAMBRIDGESHIRE

c. **1875–90** Anglo-Saxon swords, daggers, amulets, combs, tools and shield bosses, along with human and animal bones, found during digging

for coprolite near Hauxton Mill. On the west side of Hauxton Road, approaching the mill, a Roman cemetery containing 33 bodies was found. They were 5–8ft deep and apart from pottery there were coins of Postumus, Salonia, and Constantine II. Between 1914 and 1918 when digging resumed near the chalk quarry, a Bronze Age palstave was discovered.

HAVERHILL, SUFFOLK

1788 About 50 Roman gold coins from the 4th and 5thC AD found and then sold by the finders.

HAWKEDON, SUFFOLK

1965 Roman gladiator's bronze helmet from the 1stC AD discovered during ploughing. With its wide neck guard it weighed twice as much as a legionnaire's helmet and would originally have had a tinned surface, giving it a shiny silver appearance, and eye guards. Similar to helmets found elsewhere in the Roman Empire, this one is thought to have originated from Colchester, where gladiatorial contests are known to have taken place.

HEACHAM, NORFOLK

c. **1974** Tony Framlingham, a fisherman, caught some cod and then cut one open to use as bait; in the fish's gut was a Roman coin. It is probable that the coin came from a site that had been eroded by the sea, or perhaps from an ancient shipwreck.

HEMINGFORD ABBOTS, CAMBRIDGESHIRE

c. **1870** Roman gold coins from *c.* AD 50 found in a beaker inside a stone coffin at Hemingford Park. The coffin and beaker are now in Hemingford Abbots church.

HEMINGSTONE, SUFFOLK

1999 Late 17thC inscribed gold memorial ring: finder Gary Finbow (M/D); returned to the finder.

HEMSBY, NORFOLK

1980 Silver coins from before 1942 found inside a flower pot by Mike Olley and George Page during building work. The silver value amounted to £3,000.

HEVINGHAM, NORFOLK

2000 Early 16thC silver lid to a cruet set: finder B. Mathewson (M/D); returned to the finder.

c. 2000 Late Bronze Age hoard dated 900–650 BC found in a field. The 32 items included 12 axes, a knife/dagger, spearhead, and many fragments. The hoard also contained the second known example of an axe mould with asymmetrical decoration on the valves, which led the British Museum to recognise this new form of socketed axe, decorated only on one side.

Norwich Castle Museum

HEYBRIDGE, ESSEX

>1913 Many hundreds of Roman silver and bronze coins, and bronze and iron ornaments found in a vessel. The coins dated from 65 BC to AD 117.

HILLBOROUGH, NORFOLK

1999 4thC AD Roman silver finger-ring: finder K. Matthews (M/D); later returned to the finder.

HILLINGTON, NORFOLK

2000 Late 12th or early 13thC gold finger-ring set with a garnet: finder C. Merchant (M/D); later returned to the finder and sold at auction for £1,495.

2000 5th or 6thC Anglo-Saxon silver brooch: finder C.K. Merchant (M/D); later returned to the finder.

HOCKLEY, ESSEX

[date?] 3 silver coins – an Elizabeth I half-groat, a sixpence dated to 1573 and a shilling minted in 1602 – found in Hockley Wood.

HOCKWOLD-CUM-WILTON, NORFOLK

1861 About 500 silver coins, Henry II and III short-cross silver pennies, found in woodland.

1999 811 Roman copper-alloy coins from the 3rd and 4thC AD found by Derek Woollestone (M/D); they were thought to have been deposited *c.* AD 350.

HOCKWOLD AREA, NORFOLK

1962 7 Roman silver cups from the 1st and 2ndC AD, thought to have been buried *c* AD 60–1 during Boudicca's rebellion, found in a wood by Frank Curtis. Although badly damaged, having been crushed and broken up before burial, they were restored by conservators at the British Museum.

British Museum

2001 3rd or 4thC Roman decorated silver plaque: finder Derek Woollestone (M/D).

2001 Roman silver bracelet of 1st–4thC AD: finder Derek Woollestone (M/D).

2001 2ndC Roman silver finger-ring, with a missing setting: finder Derek Woollestone; returned to the finder.

HOLBROOK, SUFFOLK

1841 Large quantity of Roman copper coins from the 3rd and 4thC AD found by a boy tending sheep on the banks of the River Stour.

HOLBROOK AREA, SUFFOLK

1959 3,118 Roman copper coins dated AD 324–48 found in a large pot, with a small pot on top, by Russell Thompson during ploughing on Potash Farm, just to the north of the village.

Ipswich Museum

HOLME HALE, NEAR SWAFFHAM, NORFOLK

1943 42 Roman silver *antoniniani* from the 3rdC AD found ¾ mile south of Holme Hale Lodge.

HONEDON, SUFFOLK

1687 200–300 silver coins, thought to have been buried *c.* AD 953, found in a grave.

HORSEHEATH, CAMBRIDGESHIRE

c. 1840 More than 200 Roman *denarii* and copper coins from the 1st to the 3rdC AD found when a wagon's wheels sank into a deep rut and crushed a pot to reveal the coins. The wagon driver sold them in Cambridge.

HOUGHTON, CAMBRIDGESHIRE

1876 25 gold and 288 silver coins from the 16thC, thought to have been concealed in 1580.

HOWE, NORFOLK

1979–87 15 gold, 125 silver and some bronze Roman coins from the 1stC BC to the 1stC AD. In 1979 Christopher Pears (M/D) found a bronze

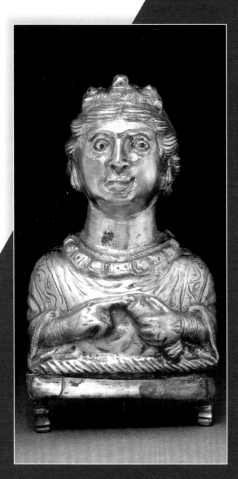

Roman coin in a field near Sheep Lane, Howe. Two years later he found 2 gold and 14 silver Roman coins in the same field; a few days later still he discovered 7 more gold and silver coins widely scattered over a large area thanks to ploughing. Members of the Norfolk Archaeology Unit moved on to the site and uncovered evidence of at least 7 tile and flint structures, which pottery suggests were in use mid-2nd–4thC AD. They also found more coins, although no container ever came to light. The hoard was thought to have been deposited *c.* AD 87, when evidence suggests no one else was living in the area. The find was later declared treasure trove.

British Museum

1998 140 Roman coins: finder Christopher Pears (M/D); later declared treasure trove.

2000 Late Bronze Age hoard of axes and metal fragments: finders Ian Roberts and James Woodrow (M/D).

HOXNE, SUFFOLK

1992 One of the greatest and luckiest treasure finds in recent years was found by metal detectorist Eric Lewes on Peter Watling's farm. Eric had been given a detector as a birthday present. As well as finding some interesting, yet uninspiring pieces, he had made himself useful by finding things that others had lost, which is why he was at the farm. Peter Watling had lost some tools in a field and as Eric was searching for them he found a Roman silver coin. Shortly afterwards he found a gold coin and soon was getting signals from all over the area of the ploughed field in which he was searching. He told reporters afterwards: 'By that time I was really excited. The signals were becoming even louder, so I probed down to the bottom of the ploughed soil and uncovered hundreds more Roman coins. There were so many I had to run to the farmhouse and ask the farmer to help me to gather them all up.' He did not remove all the objects from the ground and immediately informed the Sussex Archaeological Unit, who were able to supervise a controlled excavation. The Hoxne Hoard, as it has become known, was made up of 565 gold *solidi*, 14,191 *siliquae* and *miliarenses*, and 24 bronze coins, along with a whole range of items. There were 29 pieces of gold jewellery: six chain necklaces, one elaborate chain, three finger-rings, 19 bracelets (one of which was inscribed 'Vtere Felix Domina Ivuana' – Good luck to Mistress Juliana – and a body chain. Silver items included a solid silver statuette of a prancing tigress, 4 pepper pots, 2 small decorated pots/vases, a set of 4 small plain bowls, a shallow plain dish, 20 round-bowled ladles, 78 spoons, 3 small handled strainers, a handled strainer-funnel, toothpicks and ear-picks, 2 silver locks, a quantity of right-angled brackets and decorated studs. The hoard was stored in what remained of a wooden chest. The items were carefully buried, some time after AD 407–8, which indicates that their owner was intending to retrieve them at a later date. This was of course a time when Roman rule was breaking down and there may have been local troubles that necessitated the burial. It was, according to the British Museum, 'the most valuable find of Roman coins ever to have been recovered in Britain'. The hoard was later declared treasure trove and valued at £1.75 million.

2000–1 4 Roman coins were found by Christopher Pears (M/D); later declared treasure trove.

HUNDON, SUFFOLK

1687 200–300 silver pennies from the reigns of Ethelstone, Edmund and Eadred, thought to have been concealed *c.* AD 953, were found by the sexton digging a grave in the village churchyard. The hoard was sold to two local antiquarians.

HUNTINGDON, CAMBRIDGESHIRE

1963? 64 lead tokens from the 16th and 17thC were found.

1999 Anglo-Saxon silver hooked tags of late 9th–early 10thC found during excavations by Cambridgeshire County Council Archaeological Field Unit.

HUNTINGDONSHIRE

1990 5 gold coins of Henry IV, in pristine condition, were found on farmland by T. Johnson (M/D).

ICKLINGHAM, SUFFOLK

This settlement village was at the centre of the Iceni tribe's land before the Romans arrived. Known as Camboritum, it was an important junction on the Icknield Way.

1874 About 350 Roman silver coins from the 4th and 5thC AD found during ploughing.

1885 230 Roman *siliquae* from the 4th and 5thC AD found in a pot.

1902 70 silver, 22 *antoniniani*, and 972 copper coins, a silver spoon, some rings, and beads and other items from the 4th and 5thC AD found in an earthen bowl.

INGATESTONE, ESSEX

1896 5 Anglo-Saxon silver pennies from the time of the Danish raids.

1999 Late 16th or early 17thC decorated and engraved gold *memento mori* ring was found by David Scheinmann (M/D). *Memento mori* is a Latin phrase meaning 'remember that you must die'.

INGOLDISTHORPE, NORFOLK

1989 1stC BC Celtic gold quarter-stater, a unique Norfolk Wolf type, found during a Norfolk Archaeological Unit excavation.

IPSWICH, SUFFOLK

1863 About 500 10thC silver pennies, in a remarkably good state of preservation, were found in the Buttermarket. The hoard was thought to have been buried *c.* AD 983, about the time that Ipswich was twice raided by Viking looters.

IPSWICH AREA, SUFFOLK

1990s 11th or early 12thC silver-alloy cross found by Mickey Seager and Andy Slinn of the Ipswich and District Metal Detecting Club. It is the front plate from a reliquary or eneolpium that depicts the figure of Christ with the hand of God above.

2000 15thC gold finger-ring, engraved with the virgin and child: finders Mark and James Armes (M/D); returned to the finders.

2001 17thC, highly decorated, silver dress-hook was found by David Cummings (M/D); it was returned to the finder.

2001 Highly decorated late 16th or early 17thC gold ring in two pieces was found by David Cummings (M/D); it was returned to the finder.

2001 3 *denarii* and 1 plated *denarius*, thought to have been deposited about AD 75: finder David Cummings (M/D); returned to the finder.

2002–3 Bronze Age hoard of 29 items found, including 10 socketed axes, 3 spearheads, 2 double-edged knives, and a sickle.

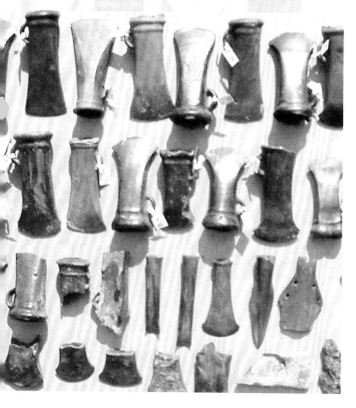

ITTERINGHAM, NORFOLK

2000 62 *denarii* and 42 copper-alloy coins, 3 silver rings, a bronze key, and 2 copper-alloy cosmetic sets from the 2ndC AD: finders Mr and Mrs A. Dawes, and C. Hawes (M/D).

British Museum

IXWORTH, SUFFOLK

[date?]   An Anglo-Saxon gold pectoral cross set with garnets.

Ashmolean Museum

KELVEDON, ESSEX

2000 Late 12th or early 13thC silver-gilt finger-ring, set with a garnet: finder R. Gold (M/D).

Braintree District Museum

KESWICK, NORFOLK

c. **1995** Anglo-Saxon small 'brassy' metal disc inscribed with runes found in the River Yare and taken to Norwich Castle Museum. It was taken away by the finder and has since been sold. The find site was only about a mile from Harford Farm where the beautifully inscribed brooch was found.

KING'S LYNN, NORFOLK

1972 41 silver pennies, mostly of Edward I, an Irish coin of Edward I, and Scottish coins of Alexander III, found during archaeological excavations; they were thought to have been deposited in 1290 or earlier.

1979 441 19thC silver coins found in a box, partially buried in the river bank, by five boys while fishing. Some coins dated back to 1853 and the entire hoard was valued at £700.

KING'S LYNN AREA, NORFOLK

1991–2 153 silver coins of the Iceni tribe found by a detectorist. They were declared treasure trove and it was reported that this was the normal size for Iceni hoards. It may be another hoard linked to the time of Boudicca's revolt against the Romans *c.* AD 60–1.

KIRTLING, CAMBRIDGESHIRE

1842 5 gold and a quantity of silver coins of Henry VIII, thought to have been concealed in 1544 or earlier. The brick gate-tower of the moated mid-16thC Kirtling Tower, where Queen Elizabeth I was entertained, can still be seen.

KNAPWELL, CAMBRIDGESHIRE

1840 78 Roman *denarii* from the 1st and 2ndC AD found 18in below the surface by workmen digging a drain.

KNETTISHALL, SUFFOLK

1998 12thC silver finger-ring, with an elongated bezel and decorated with three square panels: finder I. Charity (M/D); valued at £250.
Moyse's Hall Museum, Bury St Edmunds

LACKFORD, SUFFOLK

1979 251 Roman copper coins and 20 fragments from AD 330–40, thought to have been buried *c.* AD 360, found along with small pieces of wool during ploughing.

LAKENHEATH, SUFFOLK

1959 3 gold and 411 silver Iron Age coins and 67 Roman silver coins from the 1stC BC to the 1stC AD found in a pot in a field known as Roman field. William Mackender was ploughing deeper than usual, at about 9in, and turned up the base of a pot. He picked up the pot and out poured a whole mass of coins. He contacted Lady Grace Briscoe, his employer, and together they collected over 400 coins. Over the course of the next few months over 30 more coins were found more than 3ft from the depression where the original pot was found. Yet more coins were found in an area that had been unploughed. The pot, a little over 8in high, was typical of the kind that is found in the Colchester area and is generally regarded as dating from before the invasion. 481 coins are held in the Fitzwilliam Museum, Cambridge.

Fitzwilliam Museum, Cambridge

1960–1   Roman and Iceni coins found in April 1960 after deeper ploughing on Joist Fen, a mile to the west of Lakenheath. The coins were found on a string of small sand islands surrounded by black peat. It turned out that coins had been found for some years and the finders were selling or giving them away. Eventually 55 coins were traced, 32 Iceni and 23 Roman, including Republican coins. The next year a mine-detector was used to track down more in an area where a ploughman had found several coins. They found another Iceni and 12 Roman coins. Previously a skeleton of a 25-year-old man had been found in the black peat and it could have been that the coins had belonged to him when he drowned in the bog.

1982   202 Roman *siliquae* from the 4th and 5thC AD found in an undamaged clay pot 1ft below the surface during the ploughing of an area that had previously been unfarmed heathland to the east of the B1112. The hoard was declared treasure trove.

1997   Anglo-Saxon bridal fittings with appliqué silver mount from the mid-6thC AD found by Suffolk County Archaeological Service during their excavations at RAF Lakenheath. It was a horse and rider grave, surrounded by graves of children; the find was valued at £15,000.

1999   5 late 6th or early 7thC AD Anglo-Saxon silver pendants and 4 silver finger-rings found by Suffolk County Archaeological Service during their excavations of grave burials at RAF Lakenheath.

LAMARSH, ESSEX

c. **1543**   Gold coins of Henry VI found in a secret wall cavity after a house had burnt down.

LANGHAM, SUFFOLK

1856   1,000 silver coins, thought to have been concealed between 1649 and 1660.

LANGLEY WITH HARDLEY, NORFOLK

1997–8   1,890 (possibly 1,941) Roman silver coins from the 3rdC AD: finder Mr Canham (M/D).

1999   47 Roman base-silver radiates from the 3rdC AD found in a pot: finders T. Phillips and K. Usler (M/D); thought to have been deposited *c.* AD 278 and were returned to the finder.

2001   22 Roman base-silver radiates from the 3rdC AD: finder Mr Canham (M/D); thought to have been deposited *c.* AD 278; returned to the finder.

LAVENHAM, SUFFOLK

1874   197 Roman *denarii* from the 1st and 2ndC AD found in an earthenware pot, about 12in deep, during the ploughing of a field near Lavenham Lodge.

LAWFORD, ESSEX

1930   Scattered hoard of Roman coins found in a field south-east of Lower Barn Farm.

LEIGH-ON-SEA, ESSEX

1769   Roman coins found after a cliff fall.

LESSINGHAM, NORFOLK

>1998   Late 15thC gold finger-ring, engraved with zigzags, flowers and lettering: finder S. Jefferson (M/D).

LEVINGTON, SUFFOLK

1801   About 100 Roman coins from the 2nd and the 3rdC AD found in an urn during the digging of gravel above Levington Creek.

LEXDEN, ESSEX

1924   Iron Age gold chainmail tunic, a silver coin of Augustus struck in 17 BC, and mounted as a portrait medallion, statuettes, 7 wine jars and a bronze table found when a burial mound was excavated. Local legend claimed that a king was buried in the round barrow wearing a suit of golden armour, along with weapons and a gold table. The barrow did indeed contain a skeleton with a mail tunic made of gold cloth and a bronze table, and it may be the last resting place of Cunobelin or one of his family, or possibly Addedomaros of the Trinovantes.

LINDSELL, ESSEX

1998   25 Roman *siliquae* dating from AD 361 to 393: finder J. Stolworthy and G. Bailey (M/D). The coins were probably deposited *c.* AD 402 and were valued at £200.

Saffron Walden Museum

LITTLE GLEMHAM, SUFFOLK

1998   17thC gold inscribed finger-ring decorated with enamel: finder P.S. Bradley (M/D); the ring was returned to the finder.

LITTLE MASSINGHAM, NORFOLK

2000   Early 16thC silver-gilt pendant: finder Chris Merchant.

British Museum

LITTLE SNORING, NORFOLK

1997   Late 9th or 10thC Viking silver pendant: finder G. Parsons (M/D); valued at £5,000.

British Museum

LITTLE THETFORD, CAMBRIDGESHIRE

1978 6 silver coins of Mary and Elizabeth I found on a path, close to a ford; thought to have been deposited after 1565.

LITTLE WALTHAM, ESSEX

1901 180 Roman small bronze coins from the late 3rdC AD found 3ft below the surface by two workmen at a gravel pit on Sheepcotes Farm.

LITTLE WILBRAHAM, CAMBRIDGESHIRE

[date?] A square-headed brooch, 2 cruciform brooches, and 2 sleeve-clasps from the mid-6thC.

Cambridge University Museum of Archaeology and Anthropology

LITTLE WITCHINGHAM, NORFOLK

2001 14th or 15thC silver brooch: finder Debbie Jones (M/D). The brooch was crushed and was returned to the finder.

LONG STRATTON, NORFOLK

2001 Roman silver finger-ring broken into four pieces from the 4th or 5thC AD: finder Les Laing (M/D). The bezel has the inscription VTI FELIX (Good luck).

British Museum

2001 13thC silver-gilt brooch: finder M. Harmer (M/D).

LORDS BRIDGE, CAMBRIDGESHIRE

[date?] Iron Age chain with collars found at Heyhill, Bourne Brook.

Fitzwilliam Museum, Cambridgeshire

LOWESTOFT, SUFFOLK

1877 More than 38 Roman *denarii* and a fibula brooch dating from the 1st or 2ndC AD found in a pot.

1905 Silver pennies of Henry I (1100–35) found on the beach following a cliff fall.

1979 2 lead ampullae, each just 2in high, and dating from between the 12th and 16thC, found by Ronald Littell in his back garden.

MALDON AREA, ESSEX

1996–7 10 Celtic Gallo-Belgic gold staters found by R. Pearce and another detectorist a few inches below the surface in a field on farmland; they were later declared treasure trove.

1997 19 Celtic gold staters found by R. Pearce and another detectorist a few inches below the surface in a field. There were 14 Gallo-Belgic staters, two quarter and three full Apollo staters.

MARCH, CAMBRIDGESHIRE

1730 About 400 Roman *denarii* from the 1st and 2ndC AD, and some burnt bones, found in three urns 'in a place called Robin Good-fellow's lane' during the building of a new roadway from March to Wisbech.

>1844 Roman copper coins found in a large pot.

1934 816 Roman silver *antoniniani* from the 3rdC AD found in a small pot during ploughing at Linwood Farm.

Cambridge University Museum of Archaeology and Anthropology

1961 42 silver coins from the 16thC found at Norwood Farm; probably concealed in 1580.

MARCH AREA, CAMBRIDGESHIRE

1979 9 silver coins of the Iceni from the 1stC AD, thought to have been concealed *c*. AD 40–50, found closely scattered, in a field on West Fen.

MARGARETTING, ESSEX

1930 Roman coins found near Whites Place.

MATTISHALL, NORFOLK

1968 1,095 Roman silver coins and 15 fragments from the 2nd and 3rdC AD found in a jar by two workmen building a driveway to garages on the Walnut Tree site near the centre of the village. The 763 *denarii* and 321 *antoniniani*, which were fused together in a solid mass, were declared treasure trove.

Norwich Castle Museum

MERSEA ISLAND, ESSEX

1980 333 Roman silvered bronze coins from AD 268 were found by Peter and Margaret Oakley, and John and Moira Russell (M/D) on farmland. The coins, collected over a number of visits, scattered by ploughing over an area of 300 sq. yd.

MALDON, ESSEX

1999 3 Iron Age gold staters of Dunovellauno of the Trinovantes dating from 20 BC to AD 10 found by David Mann (M/D) on three separate occasions; valued at £2,100. The Trinovantes were the first Britons to sign a non-aggression treaty with the Roman settlers.

Colchester Castle Museum

1980–1   657 Roman silver *antoniniani* from the 3rdC AD found by a detectorist in a ploughed field in the north-east part of the island.

early 1990s   5 Roman *denarii* from *c.* AD 50: finder J. Marley (M/D).

Colchester Castle Museum

MESSING, ESSEX

1975   2,223 silver coins spanning five reigns from Edward VI to Charles I of England, as well as 3 Scottish coins, found in an earthenware pot. They were concealed *c.* 1648 when Colchester was besieged. John Milton the 'Puritan Poet' wrote a short poem entitled 'On the Lord Gen. Fairfax at the siege of Colchester' to congratulate the Parliamentarians' general-in-chief on his success.

> Fairfax, whose name in armes through Europe rings
> Filling each mouth with envy, or with praise,
> And all her jealous monarchs with amaze,
> And rumors loud, that daunt remotest kings . . .

MICKFIELD, SUFFOLK

1999   2ndC AD Roman silver snake finger-ring fragment: finder G. Stribling (M/D); returned to the finder.

MIDDLE HARLING, NORFOLK

1980–1   37 Saxon silver coins from the 8thC found by Tony Frost, scattered by the plough over an area of approx 20 sq. m. The coins are of the East Anglian King Beonna, and date to *c.* AD 758. They were described as 'extremely valuable' by the British Museum and later declared treasure trove.

MIDDLETON, NORFOLK

2001   1st or 2ndC Roman silver finger-ring, set with a bezel of a male head facing to the right: finder Kevin Boldero (M/D); returned to the finder.

MILDENHALL, SUFFOLK

c. 1832   Roman coins from the 3rdC AD found in three pots by labourers in a field near Holywell Row. Most were disposed of by the finders but one pot containing 1,286 coins survived; they were all *antoniniani*, except for one *denarius*.

1897   Roman coins found in a container by a woman searching for mushrooms; they were described as 'weighing about 5 pounds'.

>1942   Roman silver coins from the 4th and 5thC AD. Only 13 *siliquae* survived.

MILDENHALL AREA, SUFFOLK ▷ ▷ ▷ ▷ ▷ ▷

1940   34 pieces of Roman silver tableware dating from the 3rdC AD found in a field, at Thistly Green, West Row; this has become known as 'The Mildenhall Treasure'. Tractor driver Gordon Butcher was deep-ploughing a 4-acre field on Thistly Green, a large area of common land. He was ploughing more deeply than usual as sugar beet was to be planted. He was also keeping his eye out for any coins that might be turned up as this field often produced them, being just 30 yd from the site of a Roman villa. When the plough struck something solid, Gordon got down off his tractor and found a metal dish more than 2ft in diameter, which he took to show Arthur Ford, the landowner. They both went back to the field and together dug up many more objects, including dishes and spoons. Ford took them all home and did nothing with them for six years, thinking they were made of too badly tarnished lead or pewter to be worth anything. In 1946, however, he showed them to an archaeologist friend, who insisted that the hoard should be reported to the British Museum. The museum revealed that it was far from worthless and was Romano-British silver, probably deposited in the 4thC AD, and worth more than £1 million (perhaps as much as £20 million today). In total there were 34 highly decorated pieces, weighing over 55lb, including the 2ft 'great dish', two convex platters, a circular niello dish, a covered bowl, six flanged bowls, a fluted bowl and swing handles, five ladles, a pair of goblets, and a number of spoons. Much of the decoration relates to Bacchus, god of wine, a common motif on silver tableware throughout the Roman period. The large dish showed a central figure of the sea god Neptune at its centre, surrounded by mythical sea creatures, who were in turn surrounded by Bacchus, Pan and female companions. An inquest awarded Butcher and Ford just £1,000 as their find had been concealed for six years. This is the most beautiful (and probably the richest) treasure ever found in England.

British Museum

1980   212 Roman silver *siliqae* from the 4th and 5thC AD found in a field outside the village by a detectorist at West Row.

MORLEY ST BOTOLPH, NORFOLK

1958   883 Saxon coins thought to have been buried *c.* 925 found in what are now the grounds of Wymondham College, a little to the south of the village. Two workmen were laying pipes for some staff houses at the college one Friday in January. When they returned to work on Monday the snow had melted, exposing some coins and a wheel-made Thetfordware pot. The college called in Norwich Castle Museum and archaeologists undertook a full excavation. The coins fall into three distinct groups. In the first group are 107 coins foom the reign of Ceolwulf II of Mercia (*c.* 875), some East Anglian rulers, including Athelstan II, and some commemorated St Edmund (martyred in 869); but most were coins of Alfred, struck in the last decade of his reign. The second group was of 16 Northumbrian coins struck at York between *c.* 900 and *c.* 915. The remaining coins were of Edward the Elder, struck late in his reign, with the exception of a single coin, a penny of Athelstan, whose first coins were minted in 924. From a historical perspective, what makes this hoard so interesting is the fact that most of the coins were struck after 917, which shows that Edward the Elder was very much in control of this part of the country when he retook East Anglia from the Danes in that year. The find was declared treasure trove and the finders shared £2,700 – enough to allow one of them to swap his caravan for a new house.

1999   Medieval silver annular brooch: finder W. Brooker (M/D).

1999   20 silver short-cross pennies and halfpennies from the 13thC: finder W. Brooker (M/D). Thought to have been deposited *c.* 1270–80; returned to the finder.

MUCKING, THURROCK, ESSEX

1961   Early 5thC Saxon belt-fittings, made of cast bronze with silver inlay, and other military bronzes found during excavation of a grave. They probably would have belonged to Germanic mercenaries who settled there.

NARBOROUGH, NORFOLK

2001   13thC gold finger-ring, with its stone missing: finder A.J. Oliver (M/D); returned to the finder.

NARFORD, NORFOLK

2000   2nd or 3rdC AD Roman silver finger-rings, a spoon and a bracelet were found by Mr and Mrs J. Wells (M/D); later returned to the finders.

NETTLESTEAD, NEAR BLAKENHAM, SUFFOLK

1999–2003   Silver coin dating from *c.* 50 BC, probably the Iceni tribe: finder James Armes (M/D). Embossed with a wild-haired head on one side and a Celtic horse on the other, it was declared treasure trove. James found 5 coins of this type since 1999, all held in the British Museum. He was paid £80 for them.

British Museum

1999   16thC silver-gilt dress-hook found by James Armes (M/D); it was valued at £600.

NEWMARKET, SUFFOLK

1980   94 gold sovereigns and 12 half-sovereigns, dated 1817–25, found in an earthenware pot underneath floorboards by Frank and Barbara Bendon while carrying out home improvements in their cottage. The hoard was thought to be worth at least £6,000 (over £140,000 today).

NEWMARKET HEATH, SUFFOLK

>1789   Roman coins found in a large pot during the digging through of the Devil's ditch.

NORFOLK

1988   Roman enamelled brooch in the form of a leaping hare: finder Paul Searle (M/D).

1996   Early 17thC gold signet ring found in a field by a detectorist. This highly decorated ring had a swivelling bezel and was thought to have belonged to Thomas Anguishe (Mayor of Norwich in 1611) or his son Edmund; later declared not treasure trove and sold at auction for £20,700.

2000–1   Bronze Age hoard, comprising 23 socketed axes, all but one complete. They display casting errors and are unfinished, probably buried by the smith.

2000–1   2 gold coins, one dated AD 461–5, the other AD 474–5, found on the site of an early Anglo-Saxon cemetery.

2003   Celtic gold torc of 21–50 BC, found by a farmer in his fields.

CENTRAL NORFOLK

1999–2000   An elaborate medieval copper-alloy openwork buckle plate, a high-quality dress accessory: finder Bill Dodgson (M/D).

EAST NORFOLK

2001   8thC Anglo-Saxon highly decorated silver-gilt mount fragment: finder J.M. Scanlon (M/D).

British Museum

MID-NORFOLK

1998   12 silver pennies and cut halfpennies, thought to have been deposited about 1230–50, found by members of the Anglian Historical Searchers (M/D); returned to the finders.

1999   19 silver short-cross and 5 silver long-cross pennies: finder Monique Slaven (M/D). Probably deposited *c.* 1240–50 and 1260–70; returned to the finder.

1999   13thC decorated silver-gilt brooch: finder Monique Slaven (M/D); returned to the finder.

NORTH NORFOLK

2000   Anglo-Saxon silver-gilt square-headed brooch fragment from the early 6thC: finder Gary Owen (M/D).

NORTH-WEST NORFOLK

2001   Celtic gold stater of 30–20 BC: finder Mark Ashton (M/D). It was the first of this type to have been found. This was christened the 'Norfolk cross type'. It had two crescent moons back to back on a cross wreath pattern with a horse galloping to the left and a wheel on the reverse.

SOUTH NORFOLK

1994   184 Roman high-quality *denarii* dated AD 30–169 found in a pot in a field by a metal detectorist. They were discovered over a number of days with the help of the farmer, who scraped the topsoil from an area of 15 sq. m.

SOUTH-WEST NORFOLK

1990s   Anglo-Saxon square-headed brooch: finder Steve Brown. The brooch had lost its foot in antiquity, and its head plate was smashed when a plough raised it into the topsoil from a grave.

1995 7thC AD gold and cloisonné garnet mount, probably from a sword scabbard: finder Kevin Wright (M/D).

1997–9 Almost 300 coins found over a lengthy period of time by metal detectorist C.E. Sproule. The finds included many Bronze Age silver coins of the Iceni, Roman gold, silver and bronze coins from the 1st to the 3rdC AD as well as some medieval silver pennies. Some of the coins were very rare and were acquired by the British Museum. Others were acquired by Norwich Castle Museum.

British Museum and Norwich Castle Museum

2003 Iron Age gold torc of 250–200 BC found by farmer Owen Carter. The finding of the electrum twisted gold and silver wire torc measuring 8in in diameter was extremely lucky. 'I tripped over it! I was loading some hay up that had been cultivated, and I felt it under my boot. I had a look at it and thought it was an old bit of wire. Then I realised it was one of those necklaces.' It was later declared treasure trove.

WEST NORFOLK

>1908 635 Roman copper coins from the 4th and 5thC AD.

Norwich Castle Museum

1984 Gold and silver necklet dating from around the 1stC BC found by digger driver Gary Gotobed in a quarry. Apparently the necklet went through the mineral crusher but came out undamaged.

NORFOLK AREA

1982 5 middle Bronze Age axes were found on a Roman site: finder Peter Day (M/D).

1985–6 Saxon strap-end cast in gold, possibly 9thC, found on ploughed land: finder Tony Langwith (M/D). Measuring 2¼in × 1in was in two parts, depicting an ox on one half and what looks like a horse and rider on the other.

NORTH CREAKE, NORFOLK

1799 About 2,000 Roman copper coins well preserved from the 3rd and 4thC AD found in a pasture by a shepherd. A bullock had been treading ground near the edge of a ditch and exposed two pots containing the coins.

[date?] Gold torc terminal similar to those found at Snettisham and Sedgeford, suggesting it may have been made by the same smith.

NORTH ELMHAM, NORFOLK

c. **1750** Roman *denarii* from the 1st and 2ndC AD found by a man sowing carrots south of the town. Contemporary reports spoke of 'a pint and a half of coins'.

NORTH TUDDENHAM, NORFOLK

2001 Bronze Age founder's hoard, 900–800 BC, found by a detectorist. In all there were 82 pieces, including 9 socketed gouges, 8 socketed spearheads, 2 socketed axes, 2 sword chapes, and numerous fragments of axe, spear, sword, knife and rapier, part of a button and other metalworking debris.

NORTON SUBCOURSE, NORFOLK

1982–91 113 Roman silver coins, 3 Celtic silver coins and a Romano-British brooch (from the mid-1stC AD) found in a field at Low Road. This was the total number of coins spread over nine years. The first group of finds was made up of 97 Roman *denarii* and 3 Celtic coins (although these may have been buried or lost separately). Recovered on various occasions between 1982 and 1986, they were declared treasure trove. The first find was a single *denarius* found by Ken Woodhose in a ploughed field in November 1982. The remainder of this first group of finds were made with the help of the Norfolk Archaeological Unit. 16 further coins were discovered in 1989 and 1991 from the same site.

British Museum

NORWICH, NORFOLK

1743 Large quantity of silver coins from the 16th and 17thC found in the Catton Grove area; thought to have been concealed after 1603.

1927 1 Roman *denarius* and 15 *antoniniani* from the 2nd and 3rdC AD found just outside the town.

1972 9 silver pennies of William I and 4 fragments, thought to have been deposited *c.* 1069, found during an excavation of Saxon kiln debris on the former site of Garland's store.

Norwich Castle Museum

1970s Massive hoard of late 19thC coins was found in the Norman well at Norwich Castle Museum. Almost 2 tons of coins were brought to the surface, and finders were still knee-deep in coinage at 116ft. It is believed the coins, estimated to be worth several thousand pounds, were thrown down the well by visitors to the castle.

NORWICH AREA, NORFOLK

1970 Celtic bronze terret ring, probably dating from the mid-1stC BC, found by a farmer's son on the surface while he was hoeing beet. The finder put it in a trinket box until the early 1980s, when he took it to be examined. The open ring was used to contain the reins for guiding the horses.

1984 190 Roman *denarii* from 30 BC to AD 195–7 found by Derek Woolestone (M/D) at Algarsthorpe Farm on the Great Melton estate. They were declared treasure trove and estimated to be worth £3,000–£5,000.

Norwich Castle Museum

1987 50 Roman *denarii* from 52 BC to AD 192 found by two detectorists; thought to have been buried *c.* AD 195.

1989 482 silver pennies and halfpennies dated 1110–68 and mainly from the reigns of Henry I (17 coins), Henry II (over 100 coins) and Stephen (270 pennies) found by Mervyn Bone and Russell Chamberlin

(M/D), scattered in a medieval ditch on farmland belonging to Alan Goodings. There were also coins of David I of Scotland and the Empress Matilda. Reports suggested they were worth around £1 million.

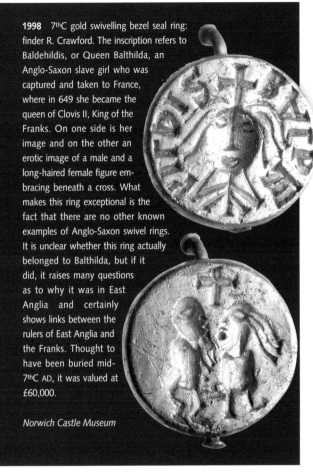

1998 7thC gold swivelling bezel seal ring: finder R. Crawford. The inscription refers to Baldehildis, or Queen Balthilda, an Anglo-Saxon slave girl who was captured and taken to France, where in 649 she became the queen of Clovis II, King of the Franks. On one side is her image and on the other an erotic image of a male and a long-haired female figure embracing beneath a cross. What makes this ring exceptional is the fact that there are no other known examples of Anglo-Saxon swivel rings. It is unclear whether this ring actually belonged to Balthilda, but if it did, it raises many questions as to why it was in East Anglia and certainly shows links between the rulers of East Anglia and the Franks. Thought to have been buried mid-7thC AD, it was valued at £60,000.

Norwich Castle Museum

2001 Celtic gold quarter-stater from 65 to 55 BC found by an American, Michael J. Martin (M/D) during a detecting trip organised by Discovery Tours. This was only the second Norfolk Wolf-type stater found. Mr Martin donated the coin to the Norfolk Museums and Archaeology Service.

ORFORD, SUFFOLK

2001 Late 15th or early 16thC decorated silver-gilt finger-ring: finder A.G. Calver (M/D); returned to the finder.

ORFORD NESS, SUFFOLK

>1936 About 3,000 Roman copper coins from the 4thC AD found in what was described as a 'casket' on or near the beach. Many of the coins were dispersed by the finders.

ORWELL RIVER, SUFFOLK

1985–6 5th or 6thC gold Saxon pendant with an unblemished garnet at its centre, found by Russell Wright (M/D), buried 4in deep beneath black mud on the riverbank.

OVER, CAMBRIDGESHIRE

1883 Great quantity of Roman copper coins from the 3rd and 4thC AD found in the remains of a metal box.

1974 11 gold sovereigns and 65 half-sovereigns from 1825 to 1878 found by Gerald Smith in an old teacup under the floor of a cottage at 5 Randalls Lane during renovations.

OXBOROUGH, NORFOLK

1990 6thC Saxon cemetery was excavated following pre-Saxon finds in the area.

1998 2 14th or 15thC silver-gilt decorated and inscribed appliqués, probably coming from a casket: finder Adam Oliver (M/D); returned to the finder.

1998 7thC Anglo-Saxon gold fragment of one end of an axe-shaped mount, or pendant with a stylised bird and garnet: finder S. Brown (M/D); returned to the finder.

1999 11 Iron Age silver, and 1 bronze coin thought to have been deposited about AD 50: finder M. Carlile (M/D); returned to the finder.

1999 Mid-5th–mid-6thC AD Anglo-Saxon silver finger-ring: finder M. Carlile (M/D); returned to the finder.

1999 13th or 14thC inscribed silver brooch fragment: finder Adam Oliver; returned to the finder.

2001 Silver-gilt decorated angular finial, probably dated to the first half of the 7thC: finder Adam Oliver (M/D). These triangular buckles became popular on the continent in the last part of the 6thC and the fashion spread to England.

OXBOROUGH AREA, NORFOLK

2000–1 5thC AD gold Roman *solidus* of Libius Severus (AD 461–5) with suspension loop, probably originating from an Anglo-Saxon cemetery site.

OXNEAD, NORFOLK

c. 1650 Roman *denarii* from the 1stC BC to the 3rdC AD found in an urn.

PEBMARSH, ESSEX

1841 269 silver coins from the 16th and 17thC, thought to have been concealed 1685–9.

PENTNEY, NORFOLK

1977 6 Anglo-Saxon silver brooches from the 9thC found by part-time gravedigger William King while preparing a new grave. King gave them to the vicar, who locked them in the vestry. Three years later the new rector, the Revd John Wilson, sent them to the British Museum for examination which announced that they were 'among the most intricate and finely-wrought pieces of late-Saxon metalwork, and of national importance'. The finder was awarded £135,000 (£475,000 today).

Norwich Castle Museum

2001 2 Iron Age gold staters of the Iceni, thought to have been deposited early in the 1stC AD: finder D. Coggles (M/D); returned to the finder.

PETERBOROUGH

>1889 2 silver pennies of Stephen, possibly part of a small hoard, thought to have been deposited *c*. 1150.

c. **1904** Large quantity of Roman copper coins from the 3rdC AD found in a vase 8ft below the surface in a brickfield. Most were disposed of by the finders, with just 15 copper coins being retrieved.

1978–9 3 George II gold crowns, together with shillings, florins, and half-crowns, 720 coins in all, from the 18th to the 20thC found in a plastic bag by divers searching the River Nene. Police believed the coins to be part of a stolen numismatic collection.

1980 Silver penny in mint condition from the reign of Offa, Anglo-Saxon King of Mercia, dated 780–770 BC found by Ernest Parkes (M/D) 1in below the surface on a corporation development site. Believed to be worth £4,000–£5,000, it was declared not treasure trove and returned to the finder, who presented the coin to a local museum.

1984 7 Iron Age swords found by a workman on a construction site.

PLESHEY, ESSEX

1998 16thC decorated gold finger-ring: finder R. Stuteley (M/D); returned to the finder.

PORINGLAND, NORFOLK

1969 46 silver and 1 copper coin from the 19thC, thought to have been concealed in 1851.

Late 1990s Roman gold ring set with a rare gold coin of the Emperor Postumus (AD 259–68). The British Museum paid the finder £20,000 for the ring.

British Museum

POSTWICK, NORFOLK

1986–91 80 Roman *denarii* and some bronze coins from the 1st and 2ndC AD: finder Roy Crawford and Terry Gallagher (M/D). They were later declared treasure trove and three of the coins were acquired by the British Museum; the remainder returned to the finders. In 1988 45 Roman *denarii* of a similar vintage were found and over the next three years 63 more were discovered.

1999 7 Roman *denarii*, thought to have been deposited *c*. AD 192, found by Roy Crawford (M/D); returned to the finder.

2001 3 Roman silver coins, thought to have been deposited *c*. AD 192, found by Roy Crawford; returned to the finder.

2002 3 Roman *denarii* from the 2ndC AD found by a detectorist. There have evidently been other finds on the site with a total of 285 coins recovered to date.

PRICKWILLOW, CAMBRIDGESHIRE

1930s? 2ndC AD Roman bronze saucepan or skillet with a highly decorated inlaid handle bearing the maker's name 'Buduogenus'. The find may date from the time of archaeological digs at Plantation Farm and Peacocks Farm, to the east of the village, in the 1930s, which identified the remains of Roman and earlier human habitation.

PRITTLEWELL, SOUTHEND-ON-SEA

2003 The grave of a Saxon monarch (*c*. AD 630) found by archaeologists. The local council asked the Museum of London Archaeology Service to evaluate the site before a potential road-widening scheme. Archaeologists found a wood-lined chamber beneath Priory Crescent, close to the railway line, that contained treasures and grave goods, including gold coins, gold buckles, a ceremonial cross, a lyre, a copper box, bronze cauldrons and flagons, a sword and shield, and drinking vessels. There was also a silver spoon which experts believe to be one of the earliest christening spoons found in Britain. The fact that tiny foil crosses lay around the body indicates that this was a Christian grave. It has been suggested that the deceased was either King Saeberht, the first Christian King of Essex, or King Sigebert II, who ruled Essex shortly afterwards; or perhaps some unknown ruler or member of the royal family.

Museum of London

QUIDENHAM, NORFOLK

c. **2003**   10thC convex disc brooch, in a fine state of preservation, and decorated with Scandinavian-style beasts, found on a site occupied between the 8th and 11thC. When Boudicca was defeated by the Roman army she escaped with her daughters and, to avoid humiliation of capture, they took poison. It has been rumoured that they were buried at Quidenham.

RAMSDEN CRAYS, ESSEX

1800s   1,100 coins found in a field.

RAMSEY, CAMBRIDGESHIRE

c. **1890**   Roman copper coins from the 4thC AD found in a pot during ploughing at Worlick.

RATTLESDEN, SUFFOLK

1971   A gilt bronze statuette of St John the Evangelist from *c.* 1180 found by Arthur Davey, farm labourer, while hoeing sugar beet in a field at Cansell Green Farm. He gave the statuette to his son (aged 7), who tried to swap it with a schoolfriend for a toy car. Sometime afterwards a friend saw the statuette on Arthur's mantelpiece and said he ought to have it looked at by experts. On 5 December 1972 it was sold at Christie's for 35,000 guineas (£36,750), over £250,000 today.

RAYDON, SUFFOLK

1999   Early 16thC highly decorated silver-gilt livery badge: finder R. Ratford (M/D); valued at £1,800.

British Museum

RAYLEIGH, ESSEX

1849   More than 230 Roman *denarii* from the 2nd and 3rdC AD found in a pot during the ploughing of a field called Fish Ponds; the finder sold the coins.

REDENHALL, NORFOLK

>1895   144 Roman copper coins from 4th and 5thC AD found in an urn.
Norwich Castle Museum

REEDHAM, NORFOLK

1831   Roman coins and a bronze lion's head from the 2nd and 3rdC AD found in a pot 1ft below the surface near Low Street.

c. **2002**   Almost 300 post-medieval coins along with fragments of a salt-glazed vessel.

REEPHAM, NORFOLK

2000   15thC gold finger-ring with missing stone: finder M. Cornwell (M/D); returned to the finder.

RENDHAM, SUFFOLK

2001   12thC highly decorated silver terminal: finder R. Lilley (M/D); returned to the finder.

RENDLESHAM, SUFFOLK

1687   Anglo-Saxon silver crown, melted down purely for the value of its metal. It was said to be the crown of Redwald (AD 599–625), King of the East Angles, partly because Rendlesham was the capital of the Anglo-Saxon kingdom of East Anglia. It was home to the Wuffingas, the Saxon royal family, the most prominent among them being Redwald.

RIDGEWELL, ESSEX

1980   175 silver coins, including 74 shillings and 79 sixpences, dated 1461–1625, and from the reigns of Edward V, Elizabeth I, James I, and Charles I and II, found at Little Meadow End Cottage, Tilbury Green. Robert Hall put his foot through the floorboards of the loft of his 15thC cottage and found the coins in a black leather pouch. Probably concealed in 1660 or later, they were subsequently declared treasure trove.

ROCHFORD, ESSEX

1936   More than 100 silver coins, possibly from the 18th and 19thC, thought to have been concealed between 1820 and 1837.

ROUGHAM, SUFFOLK

1843–4   There were reports of 'Roman Antiquities being found here'. Roman burial urns from AD 80 to 150 have been found near St Mary's church. There is a Roman villa site close by.

SAFFRON WALDEN, ESSEX

1876   Late 9thC Viking necklace discovered in a woman's grave, in what was once a Roman cemetery. The necklace had ornamented silver-gilt pendants, a plain silver pendant, beads of silver, cornelian, crystal and glass.

Saffron Walden Museum

SAHAM TONEY, NORFOLK

2000   2nd or 3rdC AD Roman silver finger-ring and two ring fragments found by Chris Aldridge (M/D); they were later returned to the finder.

SANDRINGHAM, NORFOLK

1987   43 Celtic gold coins found on the Queen's estate by a detectorist; they were later declared treasure trove.

SANTON DOWNHAM, SUFFOLK

1869   107 silver coins of the Iceni and 2 Roman copper coins of Claudius found by men digging gravel near the Little Ouse.

SAXMUNDHAM AREA, SUFFOLK ▶ ▶ ▶ ▶ ▶ ▶ ▶ ▶ ▶

1988–2000   Fragments of 2 Anglo-Saxon brooches were found by a detectorist in 1988. It was thought that they may be associated with a cemetery, although subsequent investigation yielded nothing more to confirm this hypothesis. Then, in autumn 2000, a detecting rally was organised by Ken Willcox of East Coast Searchers in the field, which led to the discovery of ten brooches, including an almost complete cruciform brooch. In addition, belt mounts and buckles were also found, some melted by cremation pyres. The finds date from the late 5thC to 6thC.

SCOLE, NORFOLK

>1883 'Many Roman coins have been found in this parish,' according to William White's *History, Gazetteer and Directory of Norfolk*, 1883.

1982–3 202 Icenian and 87 Roman silver coins found on a building site at Scole House. Initially a hoard of 142 Roman silver and bronze coins was found by digger driver Brian Read while cutting a trench. He spotted some corroded coins in the trench shortly before a stream of coins poured out from the side of the trench. The remaining coins were discovered in nearby spoil heaps after Norwich Museum were called in to assist in the search. The coins were probably mixed together when they were buried. The hoard was declared treasure trove.

SEDGEFORD, NORFOLK

1965 and **2004** 1stC AD gold and silver necklace, with a missing terminal, found in a field by a farm worker using a harrow machine; valued at £3,500 (the equivalent of over £40,000 today). It has been suggested that the necklace may have belonged to Queen Boudicca. In 2004 a gold and silver necklace terminal was found by Steve Hammond (M/D) 4in below the surface only 400yd from the spot where the original discovery was made.

British Museum

1999 4 Iron Age Gallo-Belgic gold staters from the 1stC BC: finder R. Ludford for the Sedgeford Archaeological Project. Initially 3 were

found, and then another at a later date. They were declared not treasure trove and returned to the finder.

c. 2003 18 Gallo-Belgic gold staters of 60–50 BC were found inside a cow bone on the site of an Anglo-Saxon cemetery. The bone was X-rayed at Sandringham Hospital after being taken there by the Sedgeford Archaeological Project. Reports are confusing but there may have been two additional hoards of 8 and 11 coins.

SHELTON, NORFOLK

1998 2ndC AD Roman silver finger-ring: finder Paul Thrower (M/D); returned to the finder.

SHIMPLING, SUFFOLK

2001 Highly decorated silver-gilt brooch from the second half of the 13thC: finder Linda White (M/D).

SHIPDHAM, NORFOLK

2001 18thC gold posy ring found while extracting a mole from a lawn; returned to the finder.

SHOTLEY, SUFFOLK

1998 3 Iron Age gold staters of Cunobelin from the 1stC AD: finders V.H. Thomas and J. French. Thought to have been deposited about AD 25. 6 coins had previously been found on this site.

SNETTISHAM, NORFOLK

1948–90 Farmhand deep-ploughing in a field known as Ken Hill in 1948 found what he thought to be three pieces of scrap metal, possibly part of a brass bedstead – he threw them away. Then several days later some coins and more pieces of metal were found near the same spot. After cleaning, the pieces of metal were identified as Celtic gold torcs, and the original discarded torcs retrieved. After examination of the whole field by experts from the British Museum, nothing more significant was found. Then, in 1950, after another round of deep ploughing, more torcs came to light. Not all were gold; some were silver while others were electrum, an alloy made of gold and silver with some bronze added to make for ease of working. In total 61 torcs, bronze jewellery, gold coins and over 80 tin coins, believed to have been buried *c.* 70 BC, were discovered. After the first two finds, enquiries confirmed that this was treasure trove and both times the farmer was given a reward. Over the next twenty years or so more torcs were discovered along with gold ingots, rings and silver coins dated 87–85 BC. But this was not the end: in August 1990 fragments of 50 more torcs, 70 gold ingots and rings were found in the same field by metal detectorist C.A. Hodder. The British Museum then decided that the area should be searched yet again and found at least another five separate locations where there was gold and silver. In one 'pit' they discovered, in the upper part, 7 silver and bronze torcs, and an opening into a larger pit which had the richest treasure of all. 2 bronze bracelets at the top, 2 silver torcs and finally 10 gold torcs (shown on the front cover). The grand total of finds made at Snettisham by farmers, the detectorists and the archaeologists came to 180 torcs and torc fragments, 100 ingots and rings, and 234 gold and silver coins (mostly Gallo-Belgic staters). In an interview with *Coin Monthly* in 1973 Sir Stephen Green, the owner of Ken Hill, gave an interesting insight into the ongoing search. 'I did have one good try a few years ago. I got all my men together and used every plough we could get onto the field. We gave the soil a good, deep going over while the rest of the farmhands followed behind, checking all the time. What did we find? Precisely nothing! It was the same when the BBC turned up and set up a search for the *Chronicle* programme. All they discovered were a few rusty nails and pieces of old ploughs. A week later one of my men was dressing the field with fertiliser when he saw an empty plastic bag lying in a furrow. Being a tidy chap, he went to pick it up, and lying on the soil underneath the bag was another gold torc! It happened again quite recently when one of the boys working a seeding machine spotted something fouling one of the drills. He went to remove the object and – yes, you've guessed it – it was yet another torc. It's simply a mystery the way they keep turning up.' In 1948 it was assumed that the hoards were buried by refugees fleeing from Julius Caesar in *c.* 55 BC. The Gallo-Belgic staters, though, indicate the more likely date of 70 BC. The mystery remains as to why they were here, who exactly owned them and what caused them to be buried. In 2003 a further 37 Iceni silver units and Trinovantian coins were discovered in the area.

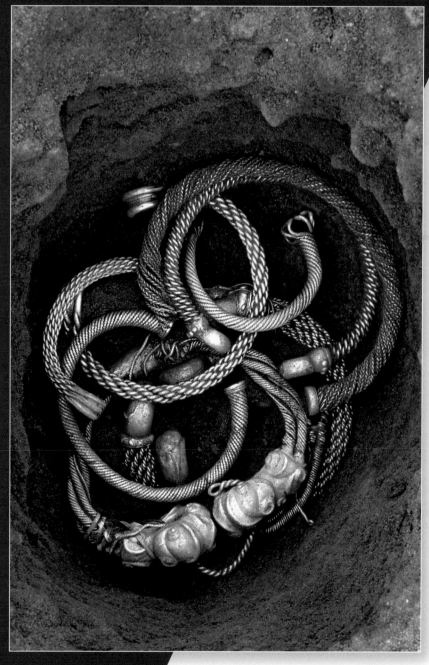

1985   83 Roman silver and 27 brass coins, and a mass of jewellery from the 1stC BC to the 2ndC AD were found in a greyware vessel by George Onslow on a building site while digging a trench with a mechanical excavator. George took the pot home and found the hoard inside, which he took to his employer, and from there it was eventually forwarded to the British Museum for a complete analysis. It is thought to be a jewellery worker's hoard; among the finds were 117 engraved red cornelians, many silver rings, bracelets, necklaces, pendants and silver bars. Many of the silver coins are of the Emperor Domitian (AD 81–96), and it is thought they would have been melted down to be made into jewellery. The latest coins are posthumous issues of the deified Empress Faustina I (AD 154–5), which is why the hoard is thought to have been buried *c.* AD 155. The silver was declared treasure trove and George Onslow received £39,000 from the British Museum. The hoard has absolutely nothing to do with the Iron Age torc finds, although it may indicate a tradition of metalworking in the area.

British Museum

1991   Hoard of over 8,000 Iron Age coins found in a bronze, or possibly silver, bowl, illegally removed from the find site, unreported and then smuggled out of the country to be sold. This has been named the 'Bowl Hoard' and we are unlikely ever to know the truth of what might have been a spectacular find.

1999   15thC gold finger-ring, engraved with figures of saints: finder Maurice Gibbons (M/D); returned to the finder.

2001   2ndC AD Roman silver snake finger-ring fragment found by Glen Tucker during work on a building site; returned to the finder.

SOMERLEYTON, SUFFOLK

1926   Bronze Age implements found in the rectory garden.

SOUTH ELMHAM, SUFFOLK

1998–9   19 silver pennies of Edward I and II and Alexander III of Scotland: finder D. Witham. Thought to have been deposited *c.* 1314–15; returned to the finder.

SOUTH WALSHAM, NORFOLK

2001   3 silver Venetian coins: finder D. Soanes/ (M/D). Thought to have been deposited *c.* 1400–15; returned to the finder.

SOUTHEND-ON-SEA

1985   33 Celtic gold coins from *c.* 55 BC: finder William Rowntree (M/D). Found 6in below the surface, in just 30 minutes on a building site. Valued at £10,000; later declared treasure trove.

2002   3 Anglo-Saxon silver coins from the 8thC, found by Edward Storozynski (M/D) on a golf course off Eastern Avenue; declared treasure trove.

Southend Museum

SOUTHWOLD AREA, SUFFOLK

c. **1745**   Small number of coins, possibly from the 14thC but possibly earlier, found on the site of Bedingfields Hall.

SPIXWORTH, NORFOLK

1998   12 silver pennies and cut halfpennies from the 13thC AD: finders members of the Anglian Historical Searchers (M/D); deposited about 1230–50; returned to the finders.

1999   13th to 15thC silver decorated annular brooch: finder A. Womack (M/D); returned to the finder.

STANNINGFIELD, SUFFOLK

2001   15thC silver-gilt pilgrim badge of St Nicholas: finder S. Atkinson (M/D).

STANSTEAD, SUFFOLK

2001   Silver-gilt mount engraved with the image of a winged dragon from *c.* 1300–50: finder J. McLeish (M/D); returned to the finder.

STETCHWORTH, CAMBRIDGESHIRE

1980   106 gold sovereigns and half-sovereigns of George II and IV, dated 1817–25, found in a cottage at 6 Mill Lane.

STIFFKEY, NORFOLK

>1931   18 Roman *antoniniani* from the 3rdC AD.

STODY, NORFOLK

2001   A 13thC silver brooch: finder J. Hull (M/D).

STONEA, CAMBRIDGESHIRE

The hill fort to the west of the village may have been the site of the battle in AD 47 between the Iceni and the Romans under the second governor of Britain, Publius Ostorius Scapula.

>1827   Roman silver coins from the 3rdC AD found by men digging a post hole. Contemporary reports spoke of 'nearly half a peck of base silver'.

1848   At least 2,000 Roman copper coins from the 3rdC AD found in a vase during ploughing at Stonea Grange Farm.

1979   Roman gold plaque: finder Michael Carlisle. Between 1980 and 1988 Roman coins have been found on the site of the camp as well as a gold votive leaf dedicated to Minerva and a bust of the goddess, which suggests that there may also have been a shrine of some significance to the Iceni.

[date?]   25 Roman billon coins from the 3rdC AD found at Stonea Camp, thought to have been concealed *c.* AD 273.

STONHAM ASPAL, SUFFOLK

1915   Roman *denarii* were reported as having been found here.

1980   270 silver threepences, sixpences and shillings of Edward VI, Elizabeth I and James I buried beside a dilapidated cottage; they were thought to have been concealed in 1613 or later.

STOWBRIDGE, NORFOLK

1825   11 silver and 9 billon coins from the 16th and 17thC found on a skeleton by the River Ouse; they were thought to have been concealed between 1603 and 1625.

STOWLANGTOFT, SUFFOLK

1764   About 7,000 Roman bronze *antoniniani* from the 3rdC AD found buried in a pot by two men who then sold them to a man in Bury St Edmunds for 1s per lb.

STOWMARKET AREA, SUFFOLK

2001   13thC highly decorated silver-gilt brooch: finder R. Watcham (M/D).

STRETHAM, CAMBRIDGESHIRE

1939   865 Roman copper coins from the 4th and 5thC AD found in a pot while a drain was being dug at Tiled House Farm.

SUDBOURNE, SUFFOLK

1879   2,800 silver pennies, mainly English, with some Scottish and Irish coins, from the 12th and 13thC found buried on church land.

SUDBURY, SUFFOLK

1963   17th and 18thC gold and silver coins, thought to have been concealed in 1715.

SUFFOLK

1845   About 960 silver coins, thought to have been concealed between 1625 and 1649.

(POSSIBLY BURY ST EDMUNDS AREA)

>1972   83 Roman *antoniniani* from the 2nd and 3rdC AD.

Ipswich Museum

1980   Rare Beonna coin *c*. AD 758, found in a field by Terry Marsh (M/D) which proved, according to the British Museum, that Beonna ruled Suffolk around this time and was trading with the French. It was valued at £5,000, over £13,000 today.

2002–3   Fine Roman cameo ring featuring a woman in profile.

CENTRAL SUFFOLK

1999–2000   Base silver cross from the late 11thC to the early 12thC: finders Mickey Seager and Andy Slinn of the Ipswich and District Metal Detecting Club. The cross formed the front plate of an *encolpium* (reliquary), would have belonged to a senior ecclesiastical figure. In the form of a cross the reliquary's hinged back is missing, but the niello inlay and traces of gilding remain.

NORTH SUFFOLK

1995   110 Roman silver-plated *denarii* from the 1stC AD found by a detectorist; they were all forgeries.

NORTH-WEST SUFFOLK

2002–3   Quote-headed pin and a spearhead from the middle Bronze Age.

SURLINGHAM, NORFOLK

2001   Fragments of a 4thC AD decorated Roman silver bracelet: finder J. Scanlon (M/D); returned to the finder.

SUTTON, NEAR WOODBRIDGE, SUFFOLK

c. **1870**   Roman copper coins from the 4thC AD found in a vessel during digging for coprolite.

1987   204 Roman *denarii* from the Republic to Galus (AD 37) found in a greyware jar in a field near Sutton Hall. There also seem to have been some stray coins of Claudius (AD 41–54) not associated with the main hoard.

SUTTON HOO, SUFFOLK ▷

1939   The 7thC Sutton Hoo hoard was considered to be the most important treasure in the British Museum in a recent BBC poll. The 86ft long ship burial included a helmet, sword, shield, ornaments, mostly gold inlaid with garnets, cloisonné shoulder clasps, Byzantine silverware and kitchen equipment, 37 Merovingian gold tremisses (AD 575–620), three gold blanks and two gold ingots. The 40 coins were to pay the oarsman while the ingots were the stearsman's wages. The hoard was discovered by a self-taught archaeologist named Basil Brown, just a few days after the outbreak of the Second World War during excavation of the 18 burial mounds at the site; many of which had been robbed. Given the status of the burial, the body is thought to be that of one of 4 East Anglian kings – Raedwald, Eorpwald or the co-regents Sigebert and Ecric. Some scholars suggest

it belongs to Raedwald , who died about 624–5. In his *History of the English Church and People* Bede says Raedwald was the first East Anglian Christian king, although he also hedged his bets by keeping pagan shrines as well. There are two spoons among the hoard, one inscribed Saul and the other Paul; these are christening spoons. The site is now owned by the National Trust and the Sutton Hoo Centre was opened by the poet, Seamus Heaney, who translated the epic poem *Beowulf*. 'The hoard is laid bare – I have been inside and seen everything amassed in the vault. Let us go again swiftly and feast our eyes on this amazing fortune heaped under the wall, I will show the way and bring you close to those coffers packed with bars of gold . . .'

British Museum

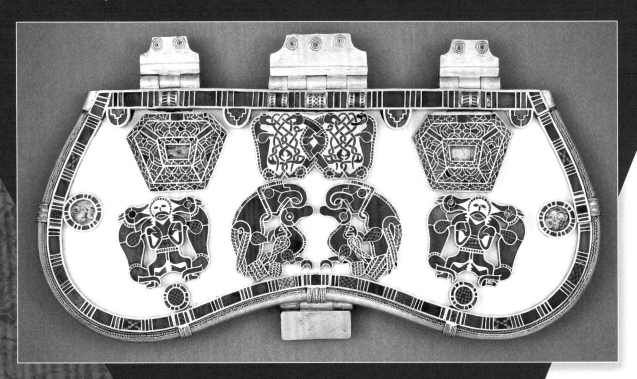

SUTTON, CAMBRIDGESHIRE

1695   100 silver pennies of William I, 5 gold rings and an Anglo-Saxon silver disc brooch, believed to be a military deposit associated with Hereward's revolt, and thought to have been deposited *c.* 1071. The 'Sutton Brooch' is decorated in the 'Ringerike' style (an ornate style of decoration found on ornamented stone slabs in Norway). The reverse shows a potent curse engraved in Anglo-Saxon.

SWAFFHAM, NORFOLK

1699   One of the most enduring legends of treasure relates to Swaffham. According to Francis White's *History, Gazetteer and Directory of Norfolk* (1854), 'John Chapman, *a tinker*, who dreamt that if he went to London bridge he would hear news greatly to his advantage, and having gone thither he was, after walking about for some hours, accosted by a man, who asked him what he wanted, to which he replied that he had come there on the vain errand of a dream, and the man answered, "Alas, good friend, if I had heeded dreams I might have proved myself as very a fool as thou hast; for 'tis not long since I dreamt that at a place called Swaffham, in Norfolk, dwells John Chapman, a pedler, who hath a tree at the back of his house, under which is buried a pot of money." On hearing this the tinker hastened home, dug under the tree, found a large brass pot full of money, and inscribed "under me doth lie another much richer than I"; but being in Latin it was some time before the tinker discovered the meaning, after which he dug deeper, and

found a much larger pot filled with old coin.' The story is enhanced by the fact that a wealthy parishioner, named John Chapman, was churchwarden in 1462 and funded the building of the north aisle of the church.

SWEFFLING, SUFFOLK

c. **1909**   'Roman finds' were reported here in contemporary papers.

TENDRING AREA, ESSEX

1999   3rdC Roman gold earring: finder S. Keeble (M/D); it was valued at £125.

Colchester Castle Museum

TERLING, ESSEX

1824   About 30 Roman *aurei*, between 300 and 400 *siliquae*, and 2 gold rings from the 4th and 5thC AD found in two pots by men building a new road. After some very heavy rain the wagons moving the earth had formed deep ruts in the mud and one of the drivers saw what he thought were buttons in one of the impressions; they were in fact around 300 coins. Several days later the owner of the land visited the site and found an almost perfectly preserved small vase containing the rings and the gold coins.

1979   77 gold and silver Roman objects from the late 4thC AD were found on a building site at Gallows Hill to the north of the town by Arthur and Greta Brooks. The Thetford Treasure, as it is known, comprised a rectangular gold plate, 22 gold rings, 4 gold bracelets, a gold brooch, 5 gold necklaces, clasps, silver wine strainers, and 33 silver spoons, many of which were decorated with gold and bear inscriptions to the woodland fertility god Faunus. There was also a 2in gold belt buckle with a dancing satyr, which was possibly intended for a Roman army officer. Most of the gold was in mint condition, and the jewellery had never been worn, some pieces were even unfinished. The finds were dated *c.* AD 390–400 and were possibly buried *c.* AD 410, when the Roman legions left Britain. It is also possible that they were buried before the end of the 4thC AD as some kind of ritual deposit. Unfortunately, the find was not reported for six months, because Arthur Brooks was taken seriously ill. The British Museum said this was particularly unfortunate, since a warehouse was erected on the site in the interim and any chance of evaluating and excavating the site had been lost. Experts estimated that the items would have fetched at least £1 million on the open market. Mrs Brooks shared the reward with Breckland District Council, and it is thought she received something in the region of £125,000 (worth well over £300,000 today).

British Museum

TERRINGTON ST CLEMENT, NORFOLK

1940 189 silver coins, mainly of Edward I silver pennies (1272–1307), found in a small earthenware pot, believed to have been concealed c. 1425.

King's Lynn Museum

1979 17thC gold ring, dated 1619, found in a back garden.

2000 13thC silver decorated annular brooch: finder Gorden Hunter (M/D); returned to the finder.

THETFORD, NORFOLK

The town's name comes from the old English *Theod-ford*, 'people's ford'. There was an Iron Age fort here, which remained an important centre throughout Roman times. The Danes occupied the fort in 869, marching out to defeat and kill one of the last of the Wuffing kings of East Anglia, St Edmund, on 20 November 869. Thetford was attacked and burnt by the Danes in 1004 but once again became one of East Anglia's major towns and the seat of the region's bishops from 1075 until Norwich Cathedral was built in the 1090s. The 81ft high Norman motte on Castle Hill is one of the largest manmade mounds in England and was built soon after 1066; it remained a stronghold until it was confiscated by King Henry II in 1157.

1975 168 billon Thetford Industrial Co-operative Society Limited tokens from the 19thC.

1978–82 47 Roman *siliquae* from the reigns of Constantius II to Magnus Maximus, thought to have been deposited in AD 385, found packed together in a clod of earth by D. Perkins (M/D) on Gallows Hill. Four years later he found another 74 coins from the 4thC AD in a fused mass at the same site; they were later declared treasure trove.

Norwich Castle Museum

THEYDON MOUNT, ESSEX

1977 365 silver coins from the 17thC found in a pot by William Ferris and his son Mark (M/D); the hoard is thought to have been buried by a highwayman after 1656.

THORPENESS, SUFFOLK

1911 Silver coins from many different time periods were washed out of old wells in the cliff during gales.

THWAITE, SUFFOLK

1998 11thC highly engraved gold pendant: finder M. Seager; valued at £1,500.

British Museum

1998 22 short-cross and long-cross silver pennies and halfpennies along with 3 lead seal matrices dating from the 13thC: finder A.C. Slinn and M.D. Seager (M/D). Thought to have been deposited c. 1260–70, they were valued at £450 (£300 for the coins and £150 for the seal matrices).

1999 Mid-17thC inscribed silver hawking ring, engraved with a shield containing the Royal Stuart arms: finder A.C. Slinn and M.D. Seager (M/D); valued at £1,000.

British Museum

TIBENHAM, NORFOLK

2003 9thC Anglo-Saxon ring: finder Peter Day (M/D); later declared treasure trove.

TUDDENHAM ST MARTIN, SUFFOLK

1938–9 114 Roman *siliquae* and a gold ring, inset with a blue stone, from the 4th and 5thC AD, found in a pot in a sandpit.

UPWELL FEN, NORFOLK

1837 3rdC AD Roman coins in an excellent state of preservation found in two pots by men digging on the site of an old Roman road.

WALTHAM ABBEY, ESSEX

1955 8 gold coins and 52 old banknotes were found inside an old sideboard in a house in William Street by a man removing some shelves.

WALTON-ON-THE-NAZE, ESSEX

1885 180 gold coins, possibly from the 17th and 18thC, thought to have been concealed between 1760 and 1816.

1970s Gold stater of Cunobelin, struck in Colchester, of c. AD 10–40, found on the beach beneath the Naze Cliffs.

Colchester Castle Museum

WASHBROOK, SUFFOLK

1979 Gold coin of James I, 298 silver coins from Edward VI to Charles I (1547–1649) and a small bronze ring. John Faulds, the farmer at Coles Green Farm, was ploughing when he found a silver coin; searching around he found about 30 more coins lying on the surface. Once the crops were harvested, he searched the area with a metal detector and uncovered the remaining coins. It is almost certain they were buried during the Civil War, after 1646. They were deemed treasure trove, and the finder received full market value for the pieces.

WATER NEWTON, CAMBRIDGESHIRE

Around this small village are the remains of the Roman town of Durobivae, built where Ermine Street crossed the River Nene. It was initially a minor settlement located next to the fort, and by the 2ndC AD had grown into an important regional capital with massive walls.

1974 30 gold Roman *solidi* dating from Constantine I to Constantine II in the 4thC AD found by Peter Chamberlain in the remains of a leather purse which was in a bronze bowl, in a pottery bowl with lid, together with two pieces of folded silver plate. The hoard was valued at £6,000 (close to £40,000 today).

British Museum

1975 Hoard of Roman silverware from the 3rd and 4thC found almost a year to the day from the first find. Alan Holmes was walking along a furrow in a ploughed field when he spotted a grey object protruding from the soil. The object turned out to be silver, and, along with 26 other pieces, made up a complete set of the oldest Christian church silver ever found. Although damaged by ploughing the hoard included a wine strainer, a tray, wine carafe, cups, chalice, and dishes. A mixing bowl carries the inscription O LORD, I, PUBLIANUS, RELYING ON YOU, HONOUR YOUR HOLY SANCTUARY. Some of the other pieces have the names of three females, Amcilla, Innocentia and Viventia, who are assumed to have been part of the congregation. There were also 18 silver plaques, 9 of which carry the *chi-rho* symbol, an anagram of the first two letters of Christ in Greek, the *Chi* (the English CH) and *Rho* (English R). Together they stood for Christianity in the late Roman and early medieval period.

WELLS-NEXT-TO-THE-SEA AREA, NORFOLK

>1849 Large quantity of Roman copper coins from the 3rd and 4thC AD found in the sand on the seashore.

WEST ACRE, NORFOLK

1985, **1988** and **1998** 81 Roman *antoniniani* from the 3rdC AD and some brooches from the 1stC AD: finder S. Brown (M/D). The 1998 find had an additional 18 base silver radiates that would appear to have been concealed after AD 274.

WEST ROW, SUFFOLK

See 'The Mildenhall Treasure', this section.

WEST RUDHAM, NORFOLK

1998 14thC silver-gilt cross pendant: finder A. Mears (M/D); returned to the finder.

WEST WALTON, NORFOLK

1998 Anglo-Saxon silver hooked tag: finder M. Carlile (M/D).

WESTHORPE, SUFFOLK

2000 4th or 5thC AD Roman silver finger-ring: finder Brian Welsh (M/D); returned to the finder.

WESTON LONGVILLE, NORFOLK

1852 About 300 silver coins found in an urn by men digging a ditch. It appears that the majority were of the Iceni tribe but there were at least two Roman coins of Antoninus.

WETHERINGSETT, SUFFOLK

2000 13thC gold finger-ring: finder Keith John Lewis. The ring, probably a man's ring: was engraved with the legend IASPAR : MELCHIOR : BALTAZAR, the names of the three wise men or Magi. In medieval times the names of the Magi were seen as a talisman against illness, and in particular the prevention of fever.

WEYBOURNE, NORFOLK

1999 Late 1st or 2ndC AD Roman silver finger-ring, with oval intaglio setting: finder J. Morrison (M/D).

1999 13thC gold finger-ring: finder J. Morrison; returned to the finder.

WHERSTEAD, SUFFOLK

1803 About 2,000 Roman coins from the 1st to the 3rdC AD found in a pot during ploughing.

1810 Roman coins found on farmland on a hillside overlooking Downham Reach, where a Roman causeway crossed the River Orwell.

WICKHAM MARKET, SUFFOLK

1981 Gold stater of the Trinovantes found by a metal detectorist.

1983   1,588 Roman bronze *antoniniani* from the 1st to the 3rdC AD found in a pot during the building of some industrial units. A mechanical digger exposed a pot 2½ft below the surface.

2001   1st or 2ndC fragmented and distorted Roman silver finger-ring: finder Ian Humphrey (M/D); returned to the finder.

WICKHAM MARKET AREA, SUFFOLK

2002   9thC AD Viking silver pendant depicting a male warrior wearing a long dress-like tunic holding a shield and sword. It is probably an Anglo-Scandinavian product, from the time of the main Danish settlement in East Anglia in *c.* AD 879; declared treasure trove.

Ipswich Museum

WICKHAM SKEITH, SUFFOLK

1999   16thC silver-gilt dress-hook: finder J. Stringer (M/D); returned to the finder.

2000   Roman silver finger-ring: finder Dennis Payne (M/D). The bezel has the inscription VTI FELIX (Good luck); later returned to the finder.

WICKHAMBROOK, SUFFOLK

[date?]   Roman fibula brooch in Four Acre Honeycomb Field.

WICKLEWOOD, NORFOLK

1999   17thC inscribed gold finger-ring: finder W. Brooker (M/D); returned to the finder.

WICKMERE, NORFOLK

1999   Early 17thC silver counter: finder Edward Lamb (M/D). One side a portrait of James I with the inscription 'Give Thy Judgements O God Unto The King'; the other with his son Henry, Prince of Wales, with the inscription 'And Thy Righteousnesse Unto The Kings Sonne'. It was part of a set of Passe counters depicting English monarchs, so named after Willem de Passe who developed this technique of casting from engraved originals.

2001   11th or 12thC distorted silver finger-ring: finder John Love (M/D); returned to the finder.

WIDDINGTON, ESSEX

1827   Large number of Roman *denarii* from the 1st to the 3rdC AD.

WIGGENHALL ST MARY MAGDALEN, NORFOLK

c. **1860**   28 silver Roman coins from the 3rdC AD.

Ashmolean Museum

WILBURTON, CAMBRIDGESHIRE

1844   Heavy gold torc and three palstaves.

1882   163 bronze objects including 115 spearheads, leaf-shaped swords and socketed axes. This Bronze Age find has become known as the

Wilburton Hoard and lent its name to a particular form of craftsmanship found in other parts of the country.

WILLINGHAM, CAMBRIDGESHIRE

1881   About 500 Roman copper coins from the 3rdC AD found in a fused mass along with a pot during the ploughing of a field called Middle Fen.

WILTON, NORFOLK

>1981   7thC Anglo-Saxon Wilton Cross containing a gold coin of the Byzantine Emperor Heraclius (610–41 or 615–32) in a cloisonné garnet setting. It closely resembles the garnet work at Sutton Hoo.

WINGFIELD, SUFFOLK

>1836   Large quantity of Roman silver coins found in the most extra-ordinary circumstances. A woman had a dream in which she saw a well-dressed woman walking near her home, who suddenly disappeared when she got near the pigsty. Once aware the woman told her husband he should dig in the pigsty as there was buried treasure there. He did so and found a hoard of silver coins and some silver objects. Unfortunately the couple gave the silverware to two men who promised to sell it for them; the silver was never seen again. Fortunately the couple had kept the coins, which they sold for enough money to buy some land and build their own house. There is a Goulder's Farm on the northern edge of the village – a possible connection?

WISBECH, CAMBRIDGESHIRE

1785   Many Roman copper coins from the 4th and 5thC AD found in a pot during digging at Waldersea.

1852   8 Roman billon coins from the 3rd and 4thC AD found in a pot; they were thought to have been concealed *c.* AD 400.

1874   9 Roman billon coins from the 4thC AD found at North Brink; they were thought to have been concealed *c.* AD 400.

1948   9 billon coins from the 3rdC AD, thought to have been deposited *c.* AD 293.

WITCHAM, CAMBRIDGESHIRE

[date?]   Roman cavalryman's bronze and iron helmet found at Witcham Gravel; coins are also reported to have been found there.

WITHAM, ESSEX

1936   170 copper tokens from the 17thC, thought to have been concealed in 1669.

WIVETON, NORFOLK

2000   10thC Anglo-Saxon silver brooch: finder J. Blackburn (M/D); returned to the finder.

2000   A 13thC gold finger-ring, set with a sapphire: finder J. Love (M/D); returned to the finder.

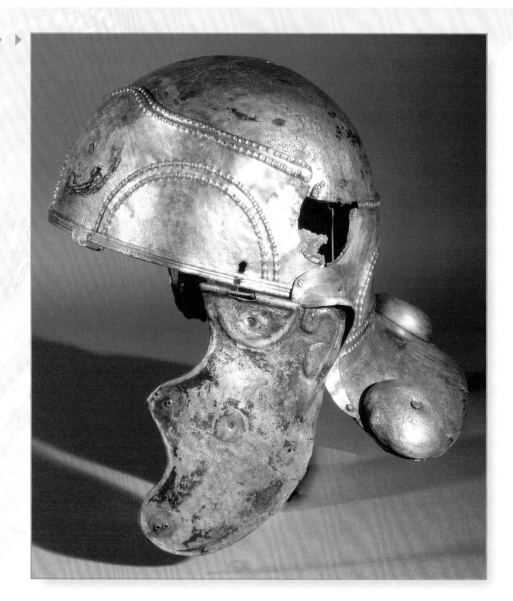

2001 14th or 15thC silver belt mount, in the shape of a flower, was found by E. Middleton (M/D); it was returned to the finder.

WIXOE, ESSEX

2000 Roman gold necklace element from the 1st to the mid-3rdC AD: finder A. Allen (M/D); returned to the finder.

WOOD NORTON, NORFOLK

2001 2 Roman gold coins from the 4thC: finder A. Pearson (M/D). Thought to have been deposited after AD 392, returned to the finder.

WOODBRIDGE, SUFFOLK

1934 More than 536 Roman copper coins from the 4th and 5thC AD.

WOODBRIDGE AREA, SUFFOLK

1996 3 silver pennies of Cnut: finder B. Warren and R. Damant (M/D). The coins were all fragmentary and valued at £40; they were thought to have been deposited c. 1035.

1996–8 18 gold staters from c. 50 BC found by B. Warren and R. Damant (M/D) over a two-year period on the same site as a 1stC AD Roman brooch fragment that they found in 1998. The two finds were not linked in antiquity.

1998 37 Roman *denarii* and one Iron Age gold stater of Cunobelin: finder Stephen Andrews (M/D). The Roman coins covered the Republic, Mark Antony, Augustus, Tiberius and Claudius; they were probably buried shortly after AD 47. Given that Claudius invaded Britain it seems likely that the hoard belonged to a member(s) of the invading army. The stater is thought to have been lost separately.

2001   Gold penannular ring from 1150 to 750 BC: finder B. Warren.
Ipswich Museum

WOODHAM MORTIMER, ESSEX

1991   190 silver coins from the 2ndC AD found by John Davey and Arthur Greenway (M/D) between July and November 1991 in a ploughed field about half a mile north of the village. The coins were scattered by the plough over a large area, and the finders also submitted a *denarius* of Antoninus Pius (AD 138–61) found in the same area as the rest of the hoard but which cannot have belonged to the hoard. In the November 3 Iron Age gold torcs from 1200 to 1000 BC were found in the same field. Both hoards were declared treasure trove and valued at £20,000.
Colchester Castle Museum

WOODWALTON, CAMBRIDGESHIRE

c. **1886**   Hoard of Roman bronze coins from the 3rdC AD found in two pots by men making a post hole at Hill Top Farm, about half a mile south of the village.

WORLINGTON, SUFFOLK

2001   7 Roman silver coins from the 4th and 5thC found by S. Foster (M/D); they were thought to have been deposited *c.* AD 402.
Mildenhall Museum

2002–3   Roman enamelled copper alloy brooch dating from AD 150 to 300. Probably continental, the 'Knee Bow' brooch is extremely unusual for a British find.

WORLINGWORTH, SUFFOLK

2000   13thC silver finger-ring, known as a 'stirrup ring', was found by M. Seager (M/D); returned to the finder.

WORMEGAY, NORFOLK

1998   2 Gallo-Belgic gold staters from the 1stC BC: finder J. Coggles (M/D). They were thought to have been deposited about 50 BC and brought the total finds there to four. They were returned to the finder.

WORTHAM, SUFFOLK

1995   172 Roman *denarii* from 2 BC to AD 51 found by Nick Davies and his mother, Eve Davies (M/D), in a field on farmland near the church. Elsewhere it was reported that there were 160 coins of Claudius and two of Tiberius, but it appears that they were all contemporary forgeries. They were later declared not treasure trove and the British Museum later bought 90 of the coins for £18,000.
British Museum

WORTHING, NORFOLK

1947   Pieces of 2 Roman copper cavalry parade helmets, possibly from the 3rdC, dredged from the River Wensum. There is evidence of a Roman fort near Billingford.
Norwich Castle Museum

WYMONDHAM, NORFOLK

1895–1900   About 250 silver coins from the 15thC found by a workman who gave away 2 groats of Edward IV and Richard III, the latter dated 1483, and left town the day after discovering the coins and was never seen again.

he counties of the East Midlands are as rich in history as any in England. The region was frequently traversed by armies and fighting forces from earliest times.

Finds from this part of the country are not just diverse; they are also some of Britain's most significant. The hoard of over 1,200 coins buried during the Wars of the Roses at Fishpool in Nottingham and found in 1966 remains one of the largest hauls of gold coins ever found. The discovery of a hoard of 3,000 Iron Age coins almost 35 years later is another indication of the richness of the region's history. An Iron Age find in north Nottinghamshire shows another side of life 2,000 years ago: two gold coins were found by a detectorist and her husband – one of the pieces turned out to be a forgery. The activities of the Vikings are also evidenced by the discoveries of coins throughout the area, many minted at Lincoln.

The Civil War troubled this region too and there have been many finds associated with the siege at Newark. In 1987 3,000 coins were found at Rhyall in Leicestershire; the British Museum identified them as having been buried during this period of upheaval. The number and variety of coin hoards show how in times of trouble, and without the facility of a local bank, burying your wealth was the only safe option. If you were killed or captured in the upheaval that prompted the burial, your treasure probably remained hidden.

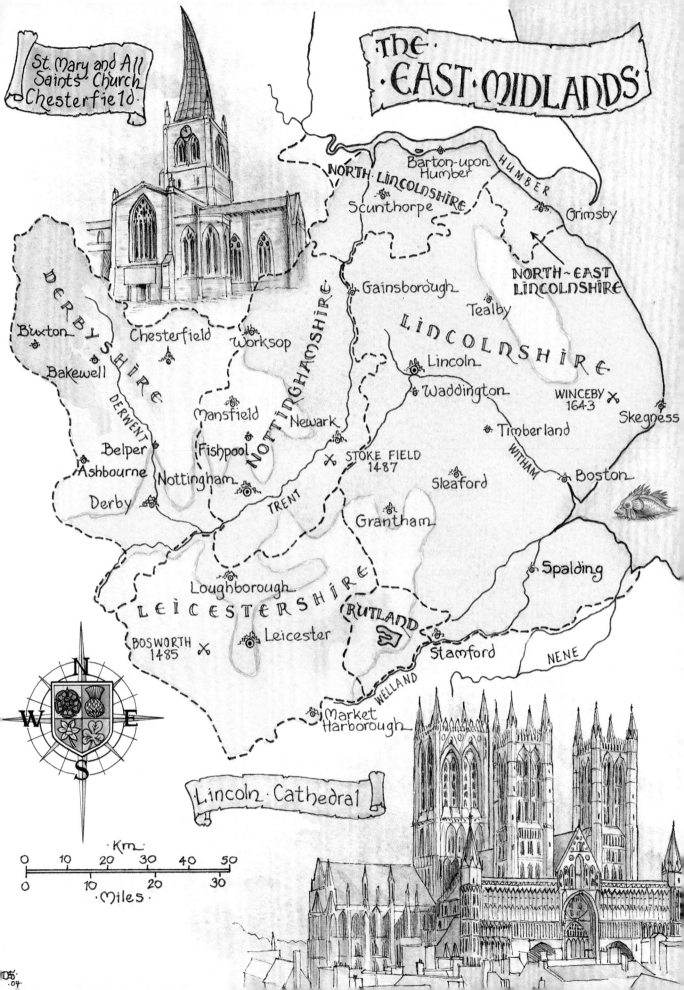

The East Midlands

St. Mary and All Saints' Church Chesterfield

NORTH LINCOLNSHIRE

Barton-upon Humber

HUMBER

Scunthorpe

Grimsby

NORTH-EAST LINCOLNSHIRE

Gainsborough

Tealby

LINCOLNSHIRE

Buxton

DERBYSHIRE

Chesterfield

Worksop

Lincoln

Bakewell

Waddington

WINCEBY 1643

Skegness

DERWENT

Mansfield

NOTTINGHAMSHIRE

Newark

Timberland

WITHAM

Belper

Fishpool

STOKE FIELD 1487

Sleaford

Boston

Ashbourne

Nottingham

Derby

TRENT

Grantham

Loughborough

Spalding

LEICESTERSHIRE

RUTLAND

BOSWORTH 1485

Leicester

Stamford

NENE

WELLAND

Market Harborough

Lincoln Cathedral

Km

0   10   20   30   40   50

Miles

0   10   20   30

N W E S

D.S. .04.

ALFORD, LINCOLNSHIRE

1918 170 gold coins from the 19thC found at the Elms, thought to have been concealed in 1828.

ALFRETON, DERBYSHIRE

1748 1,500–3,000 Roman *denarii* from the 1st to the 3rdC AD found 3in below the surface in a boggy piece of ground on New Grounds Farm, near Greenhill Lane. When news of the discovery spread, local people took around 500 coins from the site. The tenant farmer sold many of the remaining coins.

AMBER HILL, LINCOLNSHIRE

1964 22 gold coins from the 19thC, thought to have been concealed in 1869.

ANCASTER, LINCOLNSHIRE

1841 2,159 Roman coins from the 3rdC AD found during the digging of a post hole in front of a house, close to the edge of Ermine Street. Contemporary reports talked of the coins as 'a mass weighing 28 lbs'.

APPLEBY, NORTH LINCOLNSHIRE

>1872 Large quantity of Roman coins found in a vase in a rabbit warren. Appleby lies on the Roman road from Lincoln to Winteringham.

ASHBY DE LA ZOUCH, LEICESTERSHIRE

1856 Roman copper coins from the 3rdC AD found in two brass urns during ploughing on a high point on Lawn Hills; the field is now called Money Hill.

ASHBY DE LA ZOUCH AREA, LEICESTERSHIRE

1788 450 silver pennies of Henry I, Stephen and Henry II, dated 1100–89, found on Ashby Wolds, a large area of heath. They were thought to have been buried in the latter half of the 12thC, when Henry II was curbing the powers of the barons.

ASHOVER, DERBYSHIRE

1922 42 Roman coins, one Ancient British coin, and a silver ring dating from the 1stC BC to the 3rdC AD found by three boys in a recess or shallow cave in the cliff above East Wood. The local policeman, claimed the coins as treasure trove, then climbed up to the site and found the ring.

1934 27 16th–17thC silver coins found, thought to have been concealed between 1500 and 1634.

ASKHAM, NOTTINGHAMSHIRE

1850 Roman silver and bronze coins from the 1stC AD found in an urn, in a cutting of the Great Northern Railway. There were at least 14 silver coins and some bones. They were thought to have been deposited *c.* AD 81–96.

BABWORTH AREA, NOTTINGHAMSHIRE

1802 29 silver and 62 copper Roman coins from the 1st and 2ndC AD found in an urn about 200yd to the south of Morton Hall, East Retford.

BAKEWELL, DERBYSHIRE

>1778 Roman copper coins from the 4thC AD found by an old woman caving for lead ore between Winster and Bakewell. Contemporary reports spoke of 'about a quart full'.

BARDNEY, LINCOLNSHIRE

1787 2 Iron Age swords and scabbards found in the River Witham near Bardney Abbey. They were owned by the antiquarian and naturalist Sir Joseph Banks, who destroyed one of the swords while carrying out experiments in metallurgy.

City and County Museum, Lincoln

BARKSTON, LINCOLNSHIRE

2001 Late 16th early 17thC decorated gold posy ring found by D.T. Baker.

City and County Museum, Lincoln

BARROW-UPON-SOAR, LEICESTERSHIRE

1861 57 silver coins thought to have been concealed in 1613.

BARROWBY AREA, LINCOLNSHIRE

1871 Some 11thC coins found, including two coins of Aethelred II and 12 of King Cnut, dated 1016. Most of the coins were in superb condition, probably because they were found inside the shinbone of an ox with its ends stopped with clay. Most of the coins were disposed of by the finder, but an antiquarian secured 14 coins and the bone.

BARTON IN FABIS, NOTTINGHAMSHIRE

1858 Roman coins found when the villa was discovered near Glebe Farm. The Romans called the place Barton in the Beans.

BARTON-UPON-HUMBER, NORTH LINCOLNSHIRE

1979 1 Roman gold *solidus* and 260 *siliquae*, dated AD 350–90, found in a pot by farmer Charles Lawe in a 5-acre field of barley at Deepdale, to the south of the town. He found 6 silver coins on the surface and after marking the spot, he returned next day, and with the help of his son found the remains of a Roman urn containing the rest of the coins about 1ft deep. The coins were all in fairly good condition and were later declared treasure trove.

1983 56 Roman *denarii*, 23 *antoniniani* and 2 billon coins from the 2nd and 3rdC AD found by Barry Kirk (M/D) in a ploughed field on Burwell Farm, situated between Horkstow Road and Waterslacks Lane. They were declared treasure trove.

BELPER, DERBYSHIRE

1998 Late 16th or 17thC engraved and decorated gold signet ring: finder D. Cashmore (M/D); returned to the finder.

BELVOIR, LEICESTERSHIRE

c. **1787** Several 2ndC AD Roman coins found in a field.

BESTHORPE, NOTTINGHAMSHIRE

1964 1,347 Roman copper coins from the 4thC AD found during the extraction of gravel from pits between the River Trent and the Fosse Way. The hoard was thought to have been deposited in AD 354. A site at Ferry Lane is undergoing excavation; the site where the coins were found is 4 miles north-north-west of the Roman site of Crococalana, at Brough.

BINBROOK AREA, LINCOLNSHIRE

2003 15thC gold ring found in a field: finder David Holland (M/D). It was inscribed 'Ne Vieil Autre' (Not Wanting Another) and was declared treasure trove.

BOLSOVER, DERBYSHIRE

1954 £900 in 20thC money found in a metal box attached to the roof joists of a house.

BOSTON, LINCOLNSHIRE

1885–6 291 silver shillings and half-crowns from the 16th and 17thC found at Brand End, thought to have been concealed in 1643 around the time that Oliver Cromwell's Parliamentarians established a field HQ in the area. The find was in an earthenware jar which was smashed during ploughing.

BOURNE, LINCOLNSHIRE

2000 Late 15th–early 16thC silver finger-ring: finder Anthony Burton (M/D); returned to the finder.

BRACEBRIDGE HEATH, LINCOLNSHIRE

1977 16 Roman *denarii* from the 1st and 2ndC AD found scattered over a large area; they were declared treasure trove.

BRANSTON, LINCOLNSHIRE

1928 18 gold coins, probably from the 18thC, thought to have been concealed in 1802.

BRASSINGTON, DERBYSHIRE

1907 4 bronze coins and a bronze fibula found during some excavations carried out by an amateur archaeologist.

[date?] Mid-7thC gold necklace with garnets.

BROUGH, NOTTINGHAMSHIRE

Many Roman coins – so many that they are known locally as 'Brough Pennies'. It was the site of the Roman station called Crococalana.

BROUGHTON ASTLEY, LEICESTERSHIRE

1882 More than 14 silver and 2 copper coins from the 16th and 17thC found, thought to have been concealed in 1697.

BURTON-LE-COGGLES, LINCOLNSHIRE

2000 9thC Anglo-Saxon silver strap-end: finder F. Cholmeley (M/D); returned to the finder.

BURTON ON THE WOLDS, LEICESTERSHIRE

1802 Large quantity of Roman copper coins from the 3rd and 4thC AD found in a field about a mile from Cotes Hall. 214 of the coins, in very fine condition, were preserved.

BURTON OVERY, LEICESTERSHIRE

1994 Hoard of Charles II silver coins found by an electrician working in the loft of a house.

BUXTON, DERBYSHIRE

1984 Bronze Age knife of *c.* 1000 BC found by schoolboy Jan Collier (aged 13) while out climbing with friends. The knife was sticking out of the mud on the river bank, in almost perfect condition, believed to have been washed out of a burial site.

Buxton Museum

CALVERTON, NOTTINGHAMSHIRE

Site of a Roman marching camp. There are coins from the area exhibited in Calverton Village Museum.

Calverton Village Museum

1959 1,460 Roman copper coins from the 3rdC AD found in a pot during work on the foundations of Manor Park Infants' School in Collier Road.

1960 About 1,500 Roman copper coins from the 3rdC AD found during the building of a house in Crookdole Lane. Apparently the workmen threw many of the coins away, thinking them to be worthless.

CALVERTON AREA, NOTTINGHAMSHIRE

>1797 Nearly 200 Roman silver coins from the 2ndC AD found in a pot.

CARLBY, LINCOLNSHIRE

1837 100 Roman copper coins, in a fine state of preservation, from the 3rd and 4thC AD found in a small urn in an enclosure called Holmes Paddock. An elevated ridge had recently been cut away, disclosing the coins.

CASTLETON, DERBYSHIRE

1814 Some 9thC Anglo-Saxon stycas, presumed to have been deposited in the early 9thC.

CAUNTON, NOTTINGHAMSHIRE

2001 Highly decorated 9thC Anglo-Saxon silver strap-end: finder J. Inslipp (M/D).

Brewhouse Yard Museum

CHESTERFIELD, DERBYSHIRE

1934 40 silver coins from the 16th and 17thC found in Vicar Lane, thought to have been concealed in 1643.

1939 18 silver coins from the 16th and 17thC were found, thought to have been concealed in 1644.

1939 About 28 Roman coins from the 1st to the 3rdC AD found about 2ft below the surface in clay by men excavating a trench for telephone cables in Malvern Road in the Brockwell district of the town. Some coins were dispersed but later 19 were recovered; all but one coin were *denarii*.

CHESTERFIELD AREA

2000–1 Almost 1,400 Roman coins from the 4thC AD on farmland: finder Slenn Shaw(M/D); thought to be worth around £5,000.

CHURCH LANEHAM, NOTTINGHAMSHIRE

2001 Late 16th or early 17thC inscribed gold posy ring found by Mark Stephen (M/D).

Bassetlaw Museum, Retford

CLAXBY, LINCOLNSHIRE

1983 28 silver pennies from *c.* 1200 found 9in below the surface by Anthony Marshall and his son David, while laying footpaths to two bungalows. They were handed to the police, subsequently declared not treasure trove and returned to the finders.

CLAXBY AREA, LINCOLNSHIRE

2003 16thC silver oval pendant found by Paul Braithwaite (M/D) in a field in the Binbrook area. Less than an inch in size it was engraved with Christ on the cross and the initials INRI (Jesus, King of the Jews); it was declared treasure trove.

CLAYBROOKE MAGNA, LEICESTERSHIRE

The village is about a mile from where the Fosse Way and Watling Street cross; many Roman coins have been found in the area.

CLEETHORPES BEACH, NORTH-EAST LINCOLNSHIRE

1979 More than 700 coins, consisting mainly of worn pennies, halfpennies and threepenny pieces, dated 1870–1950: finder Mark Wagerman (M/D).

CLEETHORPES AREA, NORTH-EAST LINCOLNSHIRE

1993 Large hoard of Roman bronze coins from the 3rd and 4thC AD found in a field, on the side of hill, by Adrian Caley and another metal detectorist.

COLEBY, LINCOLNSHIRE

1975 About 8,500 Roman silver coins from the 3rdC were found by Brian Kilshaw (M/D) on land belonging to G.E. Overton. He sold them without declaring them to the authorities, which came to the notice of the police, who recovered 7,800 coins dated AD 260–80. Some reports have talked of 10,000–20,000 coins and while they were originally declared treasure trove this decision was reversed. The coins, all *antoniniani* except for 67 *denarii*, were initially estimated to be worth £15,000–£20,000 (the equivalent of £75,000–£100,000), but they were found to be very low in silver content.

COLSTERWORTH, LINCOLNSHIRE

1875 18thC gold coins, thought to have been concealed between 1760 and 1816.

CORRINGHAM, LINCOLNSHIRE

1994 100 silver pennies of Edward the Confessor, Harold II and William I, dated 1065–1071, found by John Matthews and five other detectorists in very good condition. The coins were found in topsoil dug out to make foundations for a new cowshed on a farm; they were later declared treasure trove.

COWLOW, DERBYSHIRE

[date?] Mid-7thC gold chain and pins.

Sheffield City Museum

CRICH, DERBYSHIRE

1761 Some Roman copper coins of Domitian, Hadrian and Diocletian found in the foundations of a small building on Crich Cliff.

1788 About 700 Roman copper *denarii* of Hadrian, Diocletian and Constantine found by two labourers removing a heap of stones in Culland Park. They found a large flat stone lying on two others, under which was an urn; they sold the coins locally. The Romans were engaged in exploiting the lead ore to be found in the area.

DEEPING ST JAMES, LINCOLNSHIRE

1807 782 Roman coins from the 1stC BC to the 3rdC AD found in a pot 16in below the surface, along with a skeleton, by workmen digging on Deeping Common.

1967 515 billon *antoniniani* from the 3rdC AD found in a pot at Priory Farm, thought to have been buried in AD 274.

1980 2,000–3,000 Roman coins from the 3rdC AD found in two pots about a foot below the surface in a paddock at Frognall.

DERBY, CITY OF

1879 30 silver coins from the 16th and 17thC, thought to have been concealed in 1641.

1886 Small quantity of silver coins from the 16th and 17thC, thought to have been concealed in 1642.

1937 634 silver pennies, the majority of Edward I, believed to have been concealed at the time of the Black Death in 1348.

1957 50 gold coins probably from the 19thC but possibly earlier, thought to have been concealed in 1893.

DERBY AREA, DERBYSHIRE

1987 14thC bronze bell was found under a tree about 300yd from a moated manor house: finder Tim Corser (M/D). The bell was six-sided, each side decorated with coats of arms and inscribed with the names of Belgian towns. The British Museum dated it and identified it as a priest's bell valued at about £100; it was returned to the finder.

DERBYSHIRE

1989 14thC solid silver seal matrix found by Kevin Darby (M/D) at a depth of about 8in. Authenticated by the British Museum it was sold by Sotheby's to Leicester Museum for £4,000.

New Walk Museum, Leicester

SOUTH DERBYSHIRE

1987 61 hammered silver coins of Edward I, II and III found by Molly Chamberlain (M/D) at a depth of about 18in. Included in this total are 13 coins which she found when she returned to the site a few days later.

DRIBY AREA, LINCOLNSHIRE

1978? Late 2nd or early 3rdC AD Roman silver ring found at Ulceby Cross.

DUFFIELD, DERBYSHIRE

1945 61 gold coins from the 19th and possibly 20thC, thought to have been concealed in 1905.

EASTON, LINCOLNSHIRE

1807 151 silver coins from the 16th and 17thC, thought to have been concealed 1625–49.

EDLINGTON, LINCOLNSHIRE

1957 824 Roman copper coins and two silver rings from the 3rdC AD found in a vase while ploughing on Barr's Farm, a few yards from the River Bain. A Romano-British building lies 100yd to the north of the find site.

EDWINSTOWE, NOTTINGHAMSHIRE

This is where legend has it that Robin Hood married Maid Marion.

1910 367 Roman *denarii* from the 1st and 2ndC AD found in a small clay pot during the ploughing of a field at King's Stand Farm to the east of the village.

1988 50 Roman *denarii* from the 1st and 2ndC AD found in the same field as the 1910 hoard by members of the Chesterfield Metal Detector Club.

EGMANTON, NOTTINGHAMSHIRE

c. **1990s** 22 Roman silver coins from the 2ndC AD: finders A. Henshaw, R. Pincott and C. Pincott-Allen (M/D). Several years later a *denarius* was found in the same area by the same people; it was thought to have been deposited about AD 160.

ENDERBY, LEICESTERSHIRE

1866 88 silver coins from the 16th and 17thC, thought to have been concealed in 1644.

EPPERSTONE, NOTTINGHAMSHIRE

1776 About 1,000 Roman copper coins from the 3rdC AD. Some were disposed of by the finders but 784 were saved.

EVERTON, NOTTINGHAMSHIRE

1881 600 Roman copper coins from the 3rdC AD found in a jar during ploughing on land between Bawtry in Yorkshire and Everton.

EYAM, DERBYSHIRE

1814 About 100 Roman copper coins from the 3rdC AD found by workmen removing soil from limestone rock, near where the road branches out of Middleton Dale to Eyam.

FISHPOOL, NOTTINGHAMSHIRE ▷ ▷ ▷ ▷ ▷ ▷ ▷ ▷ ▷ ▷

1966 1,237 gold coins, 4 rings, 4 pieces of jewellery and 2 lengths of chain from the 14th and 15thC found on a building site by a mechanical digger driver and five other workers. It is the biggest hoard of gold coins so far found. Among the jewellery was a brooch decorated in blue and white enamels – the colours of the House of Lancaster. Thought to have been buried in 1464 at the time of the Battle of Hexam, it consisted of gold nobles, half-nobles and quarter-nobles of Edward III, Richard II, Henry IV, V and VI, and

Edward IV, as well 223 foreign coins of James II of Scotland (1436–60), Charles VII of France (1422–61) and Philip the Good, Duke of Burgundy (1419–67), who dominated the Netherlands. The face value of the hoard in the 15thC was about £400, the equivalent of around £290,000 today. The assumption is that they were hidden by a supporter of the House of Lancaster after defeat at the battle by the House of York in May 1464. In all likelihood, it was done in great haste and given its hiding place deep in Sherwood Forest where it was probably deemed unlikely to be found by opponents. Of course, we have no way of knowing why it was not retrieved at the time.

Maybe whoever buried it was killed, maybe captured or maybe his hiding place was too good even for him to find again. At the coroner's inquest the hoard was valued at £250,000 but they also found that four workmen, who between them had found nine-tenths of the hoard, did not immediately inform the police. Because they wilfully concealed their finds, it was recommended that no award should be made, and that their finds should be forfeited. Only after an appeal were they awarded a token sum.

British Museum

FISKERTON AREA, LINCOLNSHIRE

[date?]   3 late 8thC Anglo-Saxon silver-gilt bronze pins with circular heads, engraved with ornate stylised animals with blue glass eyes and linked together with engraved plates, found in the River Witham; they are known as the Witham Pins.

British Museum

FLAWBOROUGH, NOTTINGHAM

1877   327 silver coins from the 16th and 17thC , thought to have been concealed in 1643.

FLEET, LINCOLNSHIRE

c. **1698–1701**   Large quantity of Roman coins from the 3rdC AD found in a pot about 3ft below the surface by a man

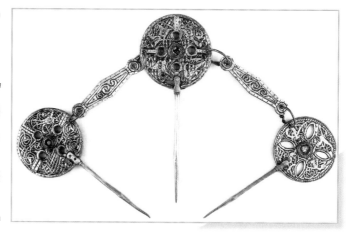

digging to fence in a haystack near Ravensclough. The finder disposed of the coins locally, contemporarily described as 'no less than 36lbs weight'.

FLIXBOROUGH, NORTH LINCOLNSHIRE

1997   16thC silver-gilt dress pin: finder M. Keightley (M/D); valued at £900.

North Lincolnshire Museum

FRISKNEY, LINCOLNSHIRE

1833   16th and 17thC silver coins, thought to have been concealed 1603–25.

FROGNALL AREA, LINCOLNSHIRE

1981   Almost 3,000 Roman silver and bronze coins from the early 3rdC, covering a span of 65 years and 12 emperors, found in two broken pots by Ian Parker (M/D), near a fenland dyke.

GAINSBOROUGH, LINCOLNSHIRE

1987–8   Roman gold ring, valued at Sotheby's at £800, found in a field: finder D. Jones (M/D).

GEDNEY, LINCOLNSHIRE

2000   15thC gold finger-ring: finder Joanna Birdseye (M/D). On one side of the hoop are two hands ending in a lover's knot and on the other a rather worn inscription.

British Museum

GLENFIELD, LEICESTERSHIRE

2001   Engraved 15thC gold finger-ring found by B. Biddles (M/D); it was damaged and distorted.

GOADBY MARWOOD, LEICESTERSHIRE

c. **1953–5**   1,917 Roman billon *antoniniani* from the Emperors Valerian to Probus found in a pot by an excavator driver, clearing topsoil between the road from Waltham-on-the-Wolds to Harby. They are thought to have been deposited in AD 280.

GRANTHAM, LINCOLNSHIRE

There is thought to have been an Anglo-Saxon mint in the town.

1726   Some silver coins found in a pot during the digging of a garden.

1735   According to the minutes of the Peterborough Gentlemen's Society of 11 June 1735, 'Rev. Mr Mason, Rector of Cotesworth, near Grantham presents a "Peter's peny" found with several others of the same sort in digging a grave in his churchyard. It is a coin of Wm. the Conqueror.'

1865   180 silver coins from the 16th and 17thC, thought to have been concealed 1625–49.

GRANTHAM AREA, LINCOLNSHIRE

c. **late 1990s**   13thC gold finger-ring, set with a green stone (possibly an emerald): finder Alan Crofts (M/D). Somehow the ring was lost while in the possession of the Brewhouse Museum in Nottingham and so the finder was paid compensation.

[date?]   8thC BC Bronze Age hoard found by Robin Green and members of the Grantham and District Search Club (M/D). 60 items were found in a field that included nearly complete socketed axes. They were assumed to have belonged to a bronze smith who had buried them for safe keeping.

GRASSMOOR, DERBYSHIRE

2001   1,421 Roman silver coins from the 4thC AD: finder G. Shaw (M/D). Thought to have been deposited *c.* AD 340 they were base-silver nummi and one base-silver radiate.

GREAT CASTERTON, RUTLAND

1950   327 Roman copper minims from the 4thC AD found during excavations of a Roman villa.

1955   Small quantity of 9thC Anglo-Saxon coins found beside the river between Great and Little Casterton. The hoard can be associated with the intense Viking penetration of Mercia.

GRIMSBY, NORTH-EAST LINCOLNSHIRE

1979   Gold stater dating from 30 BC to AD 10 found by Frank Barber while planting a rose bush; it was valued at up to £750.

GRIMSBY AREA, NORTH-EAST LINCOLNSHIRE

1808   3,400 gold guineas and hundreds of farthings found in a cottage that belonged to Elizabeth Fridlington, a woman renowned as a skinflint. The police who investigated her death found small parcels of coins concealed all over her cottage.

HAMBLETON, RUTLAND

1975   6 silver long-cross pennies and cut halfpennies of Henry III found while excavating at the foot of a wall in the deserted medieval village of Nether or Lower Hambleton; they were believed to have been concealed *c.* 1256. The village was flooded to make Rutland Water in 1976 and the excavations were carried out shortly before.

Rutland County Museum

HARLAXTON, LINCOLNSHIRE

1968   1 gold and 141 silver coins from the 16th and 17thC, thought to have been concealed in 1642.

HARWORTH, NOTTINGHAMSHIRE

1999   17thC silver finger-ring: finder D. Kent (M/D); returned to the finder.

HATTON, DERBYSHIRE

1954   405 gold and 8 silver coins, possibly from the 18th and 19thC, thought to have been concealed in 1869.

HAUGHTON, NOTTINGHAMSHIRE

1998   Gold ring of 1300–1100 BC: finder Robert Johnson (M/D). Declared to be not treasure trove, it was returned to the finder.

HEANOR, DERBYSHIRE

1800s   More than 800 Roman coins found in a vase by men working on building the railway.

HICKLING, NOTTINGHAMSHIRE

1771   About 200 Roman *denarii* from the 1st and 2ndC AD found in an urn during ploughing.

HIGHAM-ON-THE-HILL, LEICESTERSHIRE

1773   43 gold and some silver coins consisting of an Edward VI gold crown, an Elizabeth I gold crown, and 2 Ormonde crowns, thought to have been concealed in 1676.

HIGHAM-ON-THE-HILL AREA, LEICESTERSHIRE

1607   Hoard of coins, rings and artefacts found when a man removed a large square stone located where Watling Street crossed a road leading to Coventry. Beneath the stone, which may have been part of a Roman altar, there were a few Roman silver coins, about 250 silver coins of Henry III, a gold ring with a ruby, a gold ring with an agate, a silver ring with a flat stone, pieces of silver, and links of a gold chain. The hoard was thought to have been deposited *c.* 1210.

HINCKLEY, LEICESTERSHIRE

1871   About 200 or 300 Roman silver coins, in a good state of preservation, and from the 1st and 2ndC AD, found in a dirty white pot by workmen building the Ashby and Nuneaton railway. A pickaxe broke through the pot, which lay about 18in below the surface, near the Harrow Inn. The Inn was located on Watling Street between the Roman stations of Manduessedum (Witherley) and Vennones (High Cross).

HOLWELL, LEICESTERSHIRE

1864   About 900 English or Scottish silver coins from the 15thC, of many different types and denominations and from different reigns, believed to have been concealed *c.* 1450.

HONINGTON, LINCOLNSHIRE

1691   Hoard of 1stC AD bronze weapons, including spears, bridles and sword fragments as well as coins, found in two urns during ploughing. They are believed to have been found on the site of an Iron Age hill fort that was also occupied by the Romans. More coins were found in the area during 1999 but the details are unknown.

HORNCASTLE, LINCOLNSHIRE

1734   Roman coins and rings found in an urn by a girl digging sand by the roadside.

2001   13thC gold finger-ring set with a blue stone (possibly a sapphire): finder K. Pritchett (M/D); returned to the finder.

HORNCASTLE AREA, LINCOLNSHIRE

2000   2nd or 3rdC Roman silver finger-ring, inscribed with the letters TOT: finder Neil Wooton (M/D).

2000   Early to mid-7thC Anglo-Saxon gold and garnet pendant: finder Neil Wooton (M/D).

HOVERINGHAM, NOTTINGHAMSHIRE

1949   289 3rdC Roman *antoniniani* found in a pot during gravel working. The workmen discarded many coins 'as useless', but 289 were recovered.

Nottingham Castle Museum

HOWELL, LINCOLNSHIRE

1999   Mid-17thC inscribed gold finger-ring: finder D. Woodthorpe (M/D); returned to the finder.

HUCKNALL, NOTTINGHAM

1967   9 gold coins, probably 19thC, thought to have been concealed 1837–1901.

HUNGERTON, LINCOLNSHIRE

[date?]   Coin of Constantine I (AD 306–37) found near this village, where it is known the Romans smelted iron.

ILKESTON, DERBYSHIRE

1948   21 gold and 42 silver coins, probably from the 19th and 20thC, found, thought to have been concealed in 1912.

KELSTERN, LINCOLNSHIRE

2001   2ndC AD Roman silver finger-ring, with the stone missing: finder Stephen Wilkinson (M/D); returned to the finder.

KETTON, RUTLAND

2002–4   Roman coins found by the Northamptonshire Archaeology Group at a site at Garley's Field.

KINGERBY, LINCOLNSHIRE ▶ ▶ ▶ ▶ ▶ ▶ ▶ ▶ ▶ ▶

1998   16thC silver-gilt and cameo dress-hook, valued at £2,000: finder H. Hibberd and A. Thomas (M/D).

KIRKBY, LINCOLNSHIRE

1999   3rdC AD Roman gold finger-ring: finder D. Lambert (M/D). The ring, which contained a gemstone, was distorted but still valued at £350.

KIRKBY IN ASHFIELD, NOTTINGHAMSHIRE

1986 304 Roman copper *antoniniani* from the 3rdC AD found in a pot in the back garden of a house in Greenholm Close.

Nottingham Castle Museum

1990 29 silver Roman coins from the 1st and 2ndC AD found in a vase by a detectorist at Grives Farm, in the Portland Park area of the town. They were declared treasure trove.

Brewhouse Yard Museum

KIRMINGTON, NORTH LINCOLNSHIRE

1960 About 10,000 Roman copper *antoniniani* from the 3rdC AD found in a pot during ploughing.

KIRTON-IN-LINDSEY, NORTH LINCOLNSHIRE

1999 875 Roman base-silver radiates from the 3rdC AD: finders Stephen and Lorraine Reynolds and Alan Smithies (M/D). They were thought to have been deposited *c*. AD 274. They were returned to the finders, who presented the British Museum with six coins.

2001 111 Roman base-silver radiates from the 3rdC AD: finder M. Gennard (M/D). Thought to have been deposited *c*. AD 276; they were returned to the finder.

LANGTOFT, LINCOLNSHIRE

c. **1820** About 1,000 Roman copper coins from the 4th and 5thC AD found in an urn about half a mile from the Car Dyke and Langtoft. Car

Dyke is possibly an Imperial Roman Estate boundary; whatever it is, everyone agrees that it dates to the Roman period.

LEICESTER, CITY OF

1718 Large quantity of 4th–5thC AD Roman copper coins found in a jug 6ft below the surface while digging out a cellar for a new house at the entrance into the White Friars, near the north gate. Contemporary reports talked of 'about 3 pints or 2 quarts of Roman coins'.

c. **1721** Some 12thC silver pennies.

1735 About 600 Roman copper coins from the 3rd and 4thC AD found in an urn after a heavy rainstorm had washed away earth from a farm gateway. The farmer drove his wagon through the gate and broke the urn to reveal the coins.

1805 Roman coins from the 1stC AD found in earthenware pot by workmen building a cellar at the corner of St Peter's Lane, High Cross Street.

1937 79 silver coins from the 16th and 17thC, thought to have been concealed in 1645.

1983 14thC bronze seal matrix, inscribed in Latin with 'Glory to God in the Highest and Peace on Earth', showing an angel holding a scroll: finder Anthony Jackson (M/D).

Newarke Houses Museum, Leicester

LINCOLN, LINCOLNSHIRE

1800 1,142 silver coins, both British and foreign, thought to have been deposited *c*. 1308.

1957 11 Roman bronze coins from the 1stC AD were found in a trench outside the National Provincial Bank, Castle Hill; on the west side of the main north–south street in the Roman city (Ermine Street). The theory is that they were the contents of a dropped purse, having all been found together.

City and County Museum, Lincoln

1971–2 More than 744 silver pennies and cut halfpennies of Henry I found along with fragments of a linen container. Council workmen were repairing the road when silver coins started pouring from the wall of a trench. One theory is that they were buried by a merchant fleeing the Battle of Lincoln in 1141; another is that they were deposited in 1230–5. 274 coins are held in the British Museum and 470 in the Lincoln Museum. Known as the Malandry Hoard, it is named after the hospital of the Holy Innocents or the Malandry that was founded *c*. 1100 for lepers; it stood outside the town walls.

British Museum and City and County Museum, Lincoln

1977   404 sixpences, shillings, florins and half-crowns of Victoria and George V and VI found in a tin, in a wall, during restoration of Ellis's Windmill, Mill Road. They were deposited on 3 September 1951.

c. **early 1980s**   5 silver pennies of Henry I, deposited in *c.* 1135. These are possibly strays from the Malandry Hoard.

1985–6   About 48,000 Roman bronze coins of 7 different emperors and dated AD 260–80 found in a field on the northern outskirts of the city. They were found by a detectorist under a few feet of soil in a pot 2½ft tall; a large stone was placed on top of the pot to act as a lid.

1986–7   152 Roman bronze coins from AD 330–61 found in a field on the outskirts of the city.

[date?]   20 Roman billon coins from the 4thC AD found in a pottery money box; they were thought to have been deposited in AD 330.

LINCOLNSHIRE

1985   9 Saxon silver pennies from the 9thC found by a detectorist. They were stacked one on top of the other and almost completely encrusted in iron. There were 6 of Alfred (King of Wessex), 2 of Burgred (King of Mercia) and 1 of Aethelred I. This was the first hoard of Saxon coins to be found with a metal detector in Lincolnshire and was also the earliest dated hoard of pennies found in the county, pre-dating the Tetney Hoard by 25 years.

1988   13th or 14thC inscribed gold ring with an uncut sapphire of Gothic French origin: finder Eric Taylor (M/D).

1989   109 silver coins (65 shillings, 43 sixpences and 1 groat) of Elizabeth I, James I and Charles I were found on a hilltop: finder John Derry (M/D).

[date?]   15 gold staters from the 1stC BC found scattered in a field near a village: finder Andrew Riddle (M/D); declared treasure trove.

SOUTH LINCOLNSHIRE

2000   20 Celtic coins of the Corieltauni from the 1stC BC found by a father and son on a number of different occasions scattered in a field on farmland.

LINDSEY, LINCOLNSHIRE

1990s   2 Anglo-Saxon solid gold pendants with intricate filigree decoration from the 6thC were found by Craig Allison. They were valued at about £10,000 each.

LISSINGTON, LINCOLNSHIRE

2001   Anglo-Saxon silver sword ring showing some signs of decoration, of AD 550–600: finder Keith Kelway (M/D). This was an important find as they had previously only seemed to be associated with Kent.

City and County Museum, Lincoln

LITTLE CARLTON

1999   Late Iron Age bow brooch of the Birdlip type, made from copper alloy, found by a detectorist.

LITTLE CHESTER, CITY OF DERBY

c. **1887**   More than 80 Roman silver and brass coins from the 1stC AD found in a vase during the building of a road through the lower part of Strutt's Park.

LITTLE GRIMSBY, LINCOLNSHIRE

2000   Roman silver finger-ring, a bronze finger-ring, and 11 *denarii* from 8 different rulers from the late 1st or 2ndC AD: finders Malcolm Hammond and Russell Taylor (M/D); returned to the finders.

LONDONTHORPE, LINCOLNSHIRE

1976   420 Roman Nero–Hadrian *denarii* from the 2ndC AD found in a pot near Alma Wood by workmen building a new road; they were thought to have been deposited in AD 154.

British Museum and City and County Museum, Lincoln

LONG BENNINGTON, LINCOLNSHIRE

1944?   980 silver coins from the 16th and17thC, thought to have been concealed in 1641.

LOUGHBOROUGH, LEICESTERSHIRE

1840   Over 1,000 Roman copper coins from the 3rdC AD found in a pot, about 1ft below the surface, during ploughing on Charnwood Forest at Mount St Bernard, near Loughborough.

LOWESBY, LEICESTERSHIRE

1997   16thC silver-gilt dress-hook: finder C. Dawson (M/D); returned to the finder.

LUDDINGTON, NORTH LINCOLNSHIRE

1901   Several hundred gold guineas, all dated 1774, found when two girls playing ball lost their ball in the garden of an unoccupied house and found a coin in a flower bed. They took it home and, with the help of their mother, found 40 more. As news spread, many people from the village came and hundreds were found before the local policeman came to break up the crowd. The coins were thought to have been concealed in 1775.

LUTTERWORTH, LEICESTERSHIRE

1725   Vast quantity of Roman coins from the 1st and 2ndC AD found near Bensford Bridge in a hole in fields between Loughburrow and Watling Street.

1869   254 Roman silver *antoniniani* from the 3rdC AD were found.

LYDDINGTON, RUTLAND

c. **1862**   150 gold coins and some silver coins were found in two small jars by men working in a gravel pit; they were claimed by the Crown.

1992   17thC inscribed gold posy ring: finder A. Brown (M/D); returned to the finder.

M1 MOTORWAY, LEICESTERSHIRE

[date?]   435 Roman radiates and *denarii* from the 2nd and 3rdC AD found by a digger-operator, while working on the Leicestershire stretch of the M1; he died before divulging the find spot.

MALTBY, LINCOLNSHIRE

1999   5 silver pennies of William I (1066–87) found by C.P. Hodson and D.K. Lascelles (M/D), thought to have been deposited *c.* AD 1075–80; they were valued at £1,500. The find site of Maltby Springs was next to the site of a medieval village.

MANSFIELD, NOTTINGHAMSHIRE

1849   300–400 Roman *denarii* from the 1st to the 3rdC AD found in a pot 2ft below the surface in a field near Kings Mill by workmen making alterations for the Mansfield and Pinxton railway. The Duke of Portland claimed them as treasure trove.

MANSFIELD AREA, NOTTINGHAMSHIRE

2002   7 gold and 35 silver coins from the 14thC: finders John Kirk, Dave Perkins and Kevin Smith (M/D). The hoard included 7 gold nobles of Edward III and Richard II, and about 24 silver groats, some half-groats and a few silver pennies, most of which were in very good condition. They were sold at auction and fetched just over £7,000.

MANSFIELD WOODHOUSE, NOTTINGHAMSHIRE

1787   Roman *denarii* from the 1st and 2ndC AD found in an urn, near a stream, on a hill half a mile from the Mansfield Woodhouse Roman villa.

MANSFIELD WOODHOUSE AREA, NOTTINGHAMSHIRE

1990–1   59 silver coins and 22 fragments from the early 12thC found on farmland at Oxpasture Wood, 3–12in below the surface: finders John Wood and Stephen Pegg (M/D); later declared treasure trove.

MARKET HARBOROUGH, LEICESTERSHIRE

2001   13thC silver buckle: finder John Holland (M/D).

MARKET HARBOROUGH AREA, LEICESTERSHIRE

2000–3   More than 3,000 Iron Age gold and silver coins of *c.* AD 1–40 found by Ken Wallace (M/D) while field-walking with a local community archaeology group on a hilltop site. Besides the hoard was a unique Roman iron and gilded silver auxiliary parade helmet. The fragile helmet had to be lifted while still inside a block of earth for further examination at the British Museum. It has led experts to suggest that whoever buried the coins probably travelled to continental Europe prior to the Roman invasion. It could have meant that the man may have served in the cavalry. After initially finding the site when with the Leicestershire Museums Archaeological Fieldwork Group, Mr Wallace returned with a metal detector and discovered the coins. Subsequent excavations, funded by English Heritage, the British Museum and the BBC, have identified it as an important open-air religious site, dating back some 2000 years. The coins were mostly made by the local Iron Age tribe, the Corieltauvi, and evidence at the site suggests that the coins were offerings, possibly associated with the Druids. In the end over 15 separate hoards of coins were found in the position that they were originally buried. The hoard was declared treasure trove. Speaking after the hearing, Mr Wallace said it had been difficult keeping the discovery under wraps for the past two and a half years. 'It's been very enjoyable. It's been almost a perfect piece of community archaeology.'

MARKET RASEN AREA, LINCOLNSHIRE

2001   8 silver coins, thought to have been deposited *c.* 1420–50, found fused together in a pile: finder D. Toobie (M/D); returned to the finder.

MARKET STAINTON, LINCOLNSHIRE

1915–16   305 Roman bronze coins, in mint condition, dated AD 296–305, found in a pot by a ploughman in a pasture called Hillside Field, alongside the Caistor Road.

1938–9   About 400 Roman bronze coins, dated AD 296–305, found in a pot during deep ploughing in the Third West Field near the Caistor Road. It is thought that it was a part of the same hoard as the one discovered 20 years earlier.

MEDBOURNE, LEICESTERSHIRE

>1797   Silver coins, composed mainly of Edward I halfpennies, dated 1272–1307, were regularly found during ploughing. According to the farmer, 'Every time the field between the Mill and Slauston Field is ploughed the men stop work to collect the hundreds of coins that are turned up. They're a damned nuisance.'

c. **1799**   230 Roman silver coins, in the highest state of preservation, were found in an urn at Holt Wood by a boy who slipped and fell into a ditch.

MORTON, DERBYSHIRE

1986–7   80 Roman *denarii* from the 1st C BC to the 3rd C AD found on ploughed farmland by a detectorist. At first 20 coins were found and later another 60; they were declared treasure trove.

MOULTON, LINCOLNSHIRE

1811   22 silver coins from the 16th and 17th C, thought to have been concealed 1625–49.

NETHER HADDON, DERBYSHIRE

1824   Roman copper coins from the 4th C AD and 2 skeletons were found in an urn by labourers in search of stone, while opening a 60ft diameter tumulus in Haddon Field, near the River Lathkiln.

NEWARK, NOTTINGHAMSHIRE

During the Civil War, Newark withstood 3 sieges before finally surrendering in 1646.

>1724   Roman coins found in a pot at Charlton-Scrope, near the Fosse Way.

1957   17 gold and 466 silver coins from the 16th and 17th C, thought to have been concealed in 1641.

1961   97 gold coins from 1639 or earlier found at Balderton Gate, thought to have been concealed during the siege.

1963   64 gold coins from the 16th and 17th C, thought to have been concealed during the siege.

1999   Early 7th C Anglo-Saxon sword pyramid found ¾in below the surface in a field during a metal detector club rally: finder Malcolm Ellis (M/D). This is known as the Collingham Jewel and was declared treasure trove. One theory is that it belonged to a nobleman who was killed at the Battle of the Trent in AD 679.

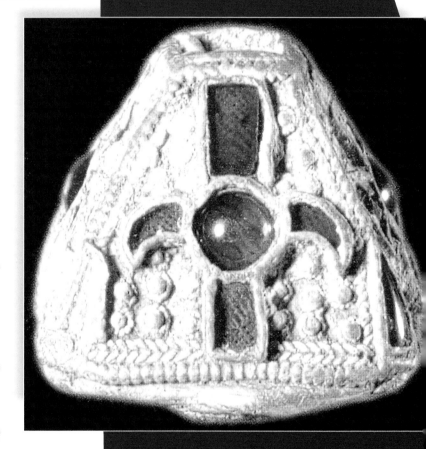

NEWARK AREA, NOTTINGHAMSHIRE

1988   1,000 silver coins from the 17th C found on a footpath in Muskham Wood by metal-detecting club members. Thought to have been buried *c.* 1644, they were declared treasure trove and valued at £25,000.

NEWBALL, LINCOLNSHIRE

1998   Early 13th C inscribed silver seal matrix, decorated with fleur-de-lis: finder Peter Marshall (M/D); valued at £1,200.

City and County Museum, Lincoln

1985 Around 47,900 Roman silver and billon coins dated AD 253–87 found in a large jar about 1ft below the surface of a ploughed field: finder Tom Cook (M/D). The find site was half a mile east of Ermine Street and the top of the jar was covered by a large stone. They were silver and billon *denarii* and *antoniniani*, with about 18,000 being washed silver. The hoard was declared not to be treasure trove and they were auctioned by London dealers C.J. Martin, and sold for an average of about £1 per coin; a large portion was sold on the American market.

NORMANTON, LINCOLNSHIRE

1998 2 Anglo-Saxon scutiform pendants were found by a detectorist.

NORTH ORMSBY, LINCOLNSHIRE

2001 Decorated cube-shaped 12thC silver, gold and niello finial: finder G. Taylor (M/D); returned to the finder.

NOTTINGHAM, CITY OF

c. **1789** 16th and 17thC silver coins, thought to have been concealed in 1638.

1880 More than 300 silver pennies, many from erased dies, found at Bridesmith (or Bridlesmith) Gate; many of the coins were blackened by fire, bent and buckled. Nottingham was burnt in 1141 so it is more than likely that that is when they were deposited.

c. **1910** 19 Roman silver and 46 bronze coins from the 1st and 2ndC AD found in an earthenware pot, which was inside a larger pot, about 3ft deep by workmen laying a gas main at the junction of Leslie Road and Berridge Road.

Nottingham Castle Museum

1952 3 billon coins were found at St Barnabas Cathedral, thought to have been concealed in 1806.

NOTTINGHAM AREA

1980s 152 Roman bronze coins from the 4thC found by members of Nottingham Co-op Club.

1986 Roman coin: finder Grenville Shuttleworth (M/D). Sent to the British Museum for examination, it was valued at £1,000–£10,000 and was declared treasure trove.

NORTH NOTTINGHAMSHIRE

1992 Celtic bronze bracelet, in two bits, found in a sugar beet field by Mick Sims of the Mansfield and District Detector Club.

1992 2 gold staters from 80 BC, 1 of which was a contemporary forgery, found in a field by a member of the Mansfield and District Detector Club. Having found one, she and her husband then found another. The British Museum identified them as coming from the Coritani tribe. They were declared not treasure trove.

OAKHAM, RUTLAND

1749 About 900 Anglo-Saxon silver pennies, cut halves and quarters, a silver chain-ring, and many pieces of 'brass or gold wires' from the 10thC, found on a pathway leading to a mill. Thought to have been buried *c.* AD 980.

OLD DALBY, LEICESTERSHIRE

1978 11 silver coins of Elizabeth I, dated 1553–85, found by three members of the Melton and Belvoir Search Society. They were thought to have been concealed *c.* 1585 and were valued at £200.

ORSTON, NOTTINGHAM

1952 2 gold and 1,413 silver coins from the 16th and 17thC found during ploughing, thought to have been concealed in 1641. The report says Orston Spa, but there is no such place; there is a Spa Lane that runs north-west from the village.

OSBOURNBY, LINCOLNSHIRE

c. **1980** 311 Roman *siliquae* and 1 miliarens in a fine state of preservation, found at a depth of around 10ft, in a small beaker after a trench for a water pipe was cut. Dating from the 4th and 5thC; they were declared treasure trove.

1980 270 Roman silver coins, dated AD 356–95, found on farmland on the Whichcote estate by Timothy Camm, aged 11, of Osbournby. He discovered a silver coin and rushed home to show it to his parents. Next day Timothy and his father, along with the couple who own the land, dug deeper and found a broken earthenware pot 18in down, which contained the coins.

OSGODBY, LINCOLNSHIRE

1999   44 Roman *denarii*, a finger-ring, a bronze brooch, and the pottery container from the 1st and 2ndC AD found while digging a drain on farmland: finder R. Heath; thought to have been deposited about AD 163, they were valued at £1,600.

British Museum

OWMBY, LINCOLNSHIRE

c. **1953**   Roman *denarii* from the 1st and 2ndC AD.

OWSTON FERRY, NORTH LINCOLNSHIRE

1952   4 Roman *denarii* and 116 bronze coins from the 1st and 2ndC AD found in a pot during ploughing.

OXCOMBE, LINCOLNSHIRE

1818   46 silver coins from the 16th and 17thC, thought to have been concealed 1561–1634.

OXTON, NOTTINGHAMSHIRE

1765   Roman coins found in a vessel at Robin Hood's Hill on the road to Rufford.

PARTNEY, LINCOLNSHIRE

1932   Large quantity of silver coins from the 16th and 17thC, thought to have been concealed 1561–1634, but possibly later.

PARWICH, DERBYSHIRE

c. **1769**   About 80 Roman *denarii* and a military weapon from the 1st and 2ndC AD were found in an urn about 2½ft below the surface by a man digging for lead.

PECKLETON, LEICESTERSHIRE

2001   Roman gold earring from the 1st to the 4thC AD: finder Kenny Dorman (M/D).

PINCHBECK, LINCOLNSHIRE

1742   Roman coin of Commodus (AD 180–92) found in the manor house gardens.

PLEASLEY, DERBYSHIRE

c. **1770**   Large quantity of Roman silver coins from the 1st to the 3rdC AD found by a man at Stuffine Wood; he was apparently poor and sold them to a person in Mansfield for £5.

POTTERHANWORTH, LINCOLNSHIRE

1928   18 gold Spanish peseta pieces, thought to have been concealed 1837–1901, found by a farmer while ploughing.

REEPHAM, LINCOLNSHIRE

1999   15thC gold finger-ring, engraved with figures of the Virgin and Child, St Barbara and St Katharine: finder N. Broadbent (M/D).

RHYALL AREA, LEICESTERSHIRE

1987   More than 3,300 silver coins found by a detectorist. The British Museum said they were probably lost during the Civil War; they were valued at more than £100,000.

RIBY, LINCOLNSHIRE

1953   15,000–20,000 well-preserved Roman copper *antoniniani* from the 3rdC AD found in a large urn during deep ploughing at Riby Wold Farm, 4–5 miles north-east of Caistor.

RIBY AREA, LINCOLNSHIRE

c. **1953**   More than 495 Roman billon coins from the 3rdC AD, thought to have been buried in AD 276.

RIDDINGS, DERBYSHIRE

c. **1850**   800 Roman coins found, that were never catalogued, nor is their fate known.

RISEHOLME AREA, LINCOLNSHIRE

1979–80   Hoard of silver bracelets, necklaces and bangles found buried under a clump of trees: finder Michael Foster (M/D). He immediately handed it over to the police, who thought it was stolen jewellery, but the owner was never traced, and the hoard was later returned to the finder.

ROPSLEY, LINCOLNSHIRE

1820   125 silver coins from the 16th and 17thC, thought to have been concealed between 1603 and 1625, although they may be Civil War-related.

ROTHERBY, LEICESTERSHIRE

2001 Highly decorated gold finger-ring of continental origin from the 10th or 11thC: finder J. Palmer (M/D).

ROTHLEY, LEICESTERSHIRE

c. **late 1800s** Roman brass coins, which, according to the Leicestershire Archaeological Society report of 1904–5, were exhibited 'by Mr. H. Hartopp (for Captain Burns-Hartopp). A Roman coin of Julius Caesar (1st brass) bearing the inscription IVLIOS DIVOS CAESAR, found with others at Rothley some years ago.'

ROXBY, NORTH LINCOLNSHIRE

[date?] Copper coins found by the handful on numerous occasions on the top of Risby Warren.

SANTON, NORTH LINCOLNSHIRE

>1882 Roman coins found according to *White's Directory of Lincolnshire* for 1882: 'among the sands of Santon was a Roman Pottery, of which remains of the furnace and numerous fragments of urns and pots, together with several coins, and a large brass were found some years ago.'

SCARCLIFFE, DERBYSHIRE

1876 About 2,000 Roman *antoniniani* found 2ft below the surface while a drain was being cut, about a quarter of a mile from the village; 1,647 held at the British Museum.

British Museum

SCARTHO AREA, NORTH-EAST LINCOLNSHIRE

1851–6 7 staters , probably Iron Age, found during the digging of a trench at Scartho Hill.

SCOTTON, LINCOLNSHIRE

1998 15thC gold finger-ring, engraved with the figures of St John the Baptist and St Katharine: finder Christopher Kilner (M/D); valued at £2,500.

North Lincolnshire Museum

2001 Fragment of a 2ndC AD Roman silver snake finger ring: finder Grenville Shuttleworth (M/D); returned to the finder.

SCUNTHORPE, NORTH LINCOLNSHIRE

1985 3,000-year-old solid gold belt found by Ralph Pointer on his farmland. Thought to be worth more than £10,000, it was declared treasure trove.

SCUNTHORPE AREA, NORTH LINCOLNSHIRE

1997 Bronze Age gold bracelet from 1200 BC found 10in below the surface of a field: finder Jason and Wayne Coleman (M/D); declared treasure trove.

SELSTON, NOTTINGHAMSHIRE

c. **1830** Roman silver coins from the 1st and 2ndC AD, in an excellent state of preservation, found in a pot about 18in deep during ploughing.

SHELDON, DERBYSHIRE

1867 95 silver coins and 7 cut halves from the 12thC found in a lead container on the Duke of Devonshire's land. There were 3 coins of Henry I, 2 of David I of Scotland, and 84 of Stephen among the hoard and it was believed they were concealed in 1140.

SHELFORD, NOTTINGHAMSHIRE

1989 9thC Saxon gilded bronze mount found in a field on crown lands: finder D. Ford (M/D).

SHIPLEY, DERBYSHIRE

1890 More than 1,000 Roman copper coins from the 3rdC AD found in a jar 1ft below the surface by a workman during railway excavations; he quickly disposed of them.

SLEAFORD, LINCOLNSHIRE

>1724 Large quantity of Roman copper coins from the 4thC AD found near the castle.

1882 Excavations revealed an Iron Age enclosure and a Roman mint, one of the largest to be found in Britain. A large number of moulds in 3 different sizes, denoting gold, silver and bronze coins.

[date?] 24 Roman silver dupondii of Vespasian to Pius, and 18 asses, thought to have been deposited in AD 160.

SLEAFORD AREA, LINCOLNSHIRE

2002 Gold iconographic ring with 5 cartouches engraved with scenes from the life of Christ: finder Alan Croker.

SOUTH FERRIBY, NORTH LINCOLNSHIRE

1909 4 Roman silver miliarenses and 224 *siliquae* and a silver ring from the 4th and 5thC AD found in a vase by a man walking on the north Humber shore.

Hull and East Riding Museum

1930s Thousands of Roman coins found when the house of a local beachcomber was searched after his death. In 1903 Celtic coins started appearing on the beach, and more recently medieval coins have also been found.

SOUTH KYME, LINCOLNSHIRE

1998 15 silver coins from Henry III to Elizabeth I: finder M. Bell (M/D); returned to the finder.

1999 12th or 13thC gold finger band set with a garnet: finder D.J. Duffy (M/D); valued at £1,500.

City and County Museum, Lincoln

SOUTH KYME AREA, LINCOLNSHIRE

>1922   324 Norman silver pennies from 1141.

SPROXTON, LEICESTERSHIRE

1811   About 100 Roman *siliquae* from the 4th and 5thC AD found in a pot 9in below the surface by a man lessening the slope of the hill on the road to Saltby a quarter of a mile from Sproxton church.

STAINTON BY LANGWORTH, LINCOLNSHIRE

1962   660 silver coins from the 16th and 17thC, thought to have been concealed in 1656.

STAMFORD, LINCOLNSHIRE

The town was one of the 5 boroughs of Danelaw in the 9th and 10thC and built its economy on wool, becoming one of the ten largest towns in England by the 13thC. As the wool trade went into decline through the 15thC so did the town. In the 16thC William Cecil became Elizabeth I's secretary of state and built the beautiful Tudor mansion Burghley House just outside the town, which was besieged by Cromwell in 1646. Through the remaining centuries the town saw very little of the industrial revolution and because of its somewhat feudal relationship with the Cecils the town has become one of the jewels of British provincial architecture.

1847   33 gold coins dating from the 16th and 17thC, thought to have been concealed between 1603 and 1635.

1866   More than 3,000 English and Scottish silver groats from the 15thC found in a broken coarse brown clay pot at the east end of St George's church. They were thought to have been buried *c.* 1465 during the Wars of the Roses.

1902   28 Anglo-Saxon, Danish and foreign silver coins buried in AD 901, of which 15 were later traced. The finder failed to inform the police and when he was asked what had happened to the remainder, he said that he lost them on his way from London to Stamford.

1969   14th or15thC silver coin clippings found in a plaster floor during an archaeological excavation, thought to have been deposited after 1465.

STAMFORD AREA, LINCOLNSHIRE

c. **1750**   More than 17 silver coins, probably from the 10thC, thought to have been deposited *c.* AD 979.

1980   2,868 Roman coins from the early 3rdC, spanning approx 65 years, found in two earthenware urns in a paddock by George Lovett and Ian Parker (M/D). The coins had very little silver content and were deemed to be not treasure trove.

1999   2,649 Roman bronze coins from the 3rdC AD found in a pot in a field by Peter Hartmann and another detectorist. The Roman fort of Great Casterton is just north of this site.

STANFORD ON SOAR, NOTTINGHAMSHIRE

1896   Roman copper coins from the 3rdC AD, in a corroded mass, found in a pot in a field to the north of the village, during the building of the main railway line to London.

STOCKERSTON, LEICESTERSHIRE

1799   230 Roman silver coins from the 4thC AD found by a boy collecting nuts in Holyoaks Wood. His foot slipped into a ditch and struck a glass urn containing the coins. There is another story that dates to 1814 when 600 Roman silver coins from the 4thC AD were found in an earthen vessel by a woman and her son while gathering nuts in a small wood called Holyoak Spenney, about 4 miles from Uppingham. The boy saw part of the vessel emerging from the bed of a small stream. This may be the same find or two separate ones. Uppingham is about 3 miles from Stockerston.

1964   62 gold coins from the 16th and 17thC , thought to have been concealed in 1698.

STOW, LINCOLNSHIRE

2001   Broken 3rd or 4thC Roman silver mount in the form of an eagle: finder Michael Wilson (M/D).

City and County Museum, Lincoln

SUDBROOK, LINCOLNSHIRE

1996   Late Bronze Age gold torc from *c.* 750 BC found by a farmer in his fields. The torc is one of only seven of this particular style, the only one to be found in Britain.

SURFLEET, LINCOLNSHIRE

1986   93 gold coins of Edward III and Richard II, in remarkably good condition, found by a farmer while working his land.

SUTTON BONINGTON, NOTTINGHAMSHIRE

c. **1895**   About 180 Roman silver and copper *denarii* and *antoniniani* from the 3rdC AD found in a pot 2½ft below the surface in a railway cutting now called Rushcliffe Halt.

SUTTON ST EDMUND, LINCOLNSHIRE

1741   Roman coins found in an urn beneath a large square stone.

SWABY, LINCOLNSHIRE

1934   Roman *denarii* from the 1st and 2ndC AD found in a jug by a man rolling a field after ploughing. 162 coins are held at the City and County Museum, Lincoln.

City and County Museum, Lincoln

SWANWICK, DERBYSHIRE

1977   Rare Henry VIII silver groat dated 1524 found by Oliver Canfield, licensee of the Boot and Slipper, Swanwick.

TATTERSHALL THORPE, LINCOLNSHIRE

1982 5,074 Roman copper *antoniniani* from the 3rdC AD found by P. Bourne, a dragline operator, at a gravel pit.

TEALBY, LINCOLNSHIRE

1807 More than 6,000 silver pennies of Henry II, dated 1154–80, some in an excellent state of preservation, found in a coarse glazed earthen pot during ploughing. The Tealby Hoard, as it was known, did not survive intact as the Royal Mint melted down over 5,000 of the coins for their silver content.

TETNEY AREA, LINCOLNSHIRE

1945 394 Anglo-Saxon and Danish silver pennies, concealed in AD 970 during the Viking raids on England's east coast. Following a treasure trove inquest, some of these coins were retained by the British Museum.

THIMBLEBY, LINCOLNSHIRE

2001 16thC highly decorated silver-gilt dress-hook: finder C. Hodson (M/D).

British Museum

THIMBLEBY AREA, HORNCASTLE, LINCOLNSHIRE

2003 6th or 7thC Anglo-Saxon gold pendant, decorated with garnets, was found in a field: finder Michael Shaw (M/D); declared treasure trove and then bought by the British Museum.

British Museum

THISTLETON AREA, RUTLAND

Coins and brooches from the late Iron Age (pre-Roman) to the late 4th and early 5thC found in the area, providing evidence that this was a Romano-British settlement. It was possibly a small market settlement on the border between the Catuvellauni and the Coritani tribes.

THORNTON ABBEY, NORTH LINCOLNSHIRE

1952 23 silver coins from the 16thC, thought to have been concealed in 1578 or 1590.

THRUSSINGTON, LEICESTERSHIRE

>1950 Roman copper coins from the 4thC AD found in a pot.

1992–7 9 Viking silver coins from the 10thC were found by Brian Kimberley (M/D) over a period of 5 years and in 1999 he found 3 more coins from AD 921–7. Valued at £3,000, they were thought to have been deposited c. AD 930. These coins were struck by Sihtric (921–7), one of the Norse kings of York. These were probably struck in Sihtric's territory in the East Midlands, perhaps at Lincoln.

Fitzwilliam Museum

THURGARTON, NOTTINGHAMSHIRE

>1801 Roman copper coins from the 4th and 5thC AD found while removing part of Thurgarton Priory. Contemporary reports talked of 'more than would fill a peck basket'.

TIMBERLAND, LINCOLNSHIRE

1808 1,400–1,500 Roman copper coins found in a pot in a field that was being ploughed. The *Coventry Mercury* of 14 November 1808 said: 'A few days since a considerable quantity of Roman copper coins . . . were contained in an Etruscan earthen ware pot which was broken by the plough. The coins are of Augustus, Tiberius and the First Claudius. Many of them are in fair preservation.'

c. **2004** 12th to 14thC ancient silver cross pendant found in a field by David Duffy. The cross measures roughly 1¼in across and was inscribed with the letters EMW. The initials could have been those of a prosperous yeoman, a trader or a member of their family.

TINTWISTLE, DERBYSHIRE

1968 11 gold sovereigns and 32 half-sovereigns, all struck before 1870 and in mint condition, found under the floorboards of a house: finder 14-year-old John Crossland. Following an argument with his parents, he locked himself in his bedroom and levered up the floorboards, where he found the coins. They were thought to have been concealed in 1878.

DANELAW COINS

The Danes, who settled in the north and east of Britain late in the 9thC, ruled an area where Danish customs prevailed; it was known as Danelaw. These Vikings were not used to using coins and this was one area where local customs prevailed. They based their wealth on the weight and the purity of precious metal, with silver the most used. Pieces of silver that were cut from larger pieces were known as 'hacksilver'. The Vikings quickly adapted to the idea of using coins. The rulers of York struck their own coins both to show their authority and as a source of revenue. But it was also necessary for trading with people who were already accustomed to using coinage. It would be wrong to think that even silver pennies were in wide circulation; most poor people never saw or even handled such wealth. In the same way as the Danes copied the idea of using coins, they also copied the designs of existing British coins; some even carried Alfred's name. What is also interesting is the fact that the coins of Danelaw also carry Christian symbols. Some bear the words 'Ominus Deus Rex' (Lord God and King), while others carry images of saints alongside pagan gods.

TINWELL, RUTLAND

1999 2,830 Roman base-silver radiates found by P.K. Hartman (M/D), thought to have been deposited *c.* AD 275; they were valued at £5,850.

UFFINGTON, LINCOLNSHIRE

1969 1 gold and 48 silver coins from the 18th and 19thC, thought to have been concealed in 1820.

UPPINGHAM, RUTLAND

1764 About 200 silver coins found in the house of Cornelius Nutt. It was said that they were revealed to his daughter in a dream.

1888 16th and 17thC silver coins, thought to have been concealed 1625–49.

UPTON, NOTTINGHAMSHIRE

>1709 About 20 Roman silver coins and other artefacts from the 1stC BC to the 1stC AD found in a pot in a furrow during ploughing, after sudden rains had washed away earth.

WADDINGTON, LINCOLNSHIRE

1976 2,958 Roman silver-dipped bronze coins of Constantine the Great, dated AD 309–17, found in a greyware pot 1ft below the surface by Arthur Greensmith and Dorothy Harrison at Grange Farm, on the outskirts of the city. They first found 11 scattered coins before finding the main hoard. Thought to have been deposited in AD 318, they were tentatively valued at £25,000.

1976 5 silver and 2 billon Roman coins of Vespasian–Pius, Trajan and Hadrian in the 2ndC AD; they were probably the contents of a lost purse.

1977 16 silver coins from the 2ndC AD found at Bracebridge Heath, having probably been concealed in AD 161.

WAINFLEET ALL SAINTS, LINCOLNSHIRE

1875 Silver coins of Edward I, II and III found in Rumbolds Lane, close to Wainfleet Hall. They were thought to have been deposited after 1351.

WALTHAM ON THE WOLDS, LEICESTERSHIRE

2001 13thC decorated gold triangular finger-ring: finder K. Pritchett (M/D).

WARSOP VALE, NOTTINGHAMSHIRE

1973 341 Roman copper coins, dated AD 315–30, in an unusually good state of preservation, found in a pot during the excavation of a trench on a building site on the Glebe estate, Bury Lane. They were declared treasure trove and are held in the British Museum (122 coins), and the Nottingham Castle Museum (219 coins).

British Museum and Nottingham Castle Museum

WELBOURN, LINCOLNSHIRE

1998 57 Roman base-silver coins from the 4thC AD found in a pot: finder David Philips (M/D). A further 379 were found 6 months later. They were thought to have been deposited *c.* AD 354. The British Museum acquired 8 coins, valued at £400, and the rest were returned to the finder.

WELL, LINCOLNSHIRE

1725 600–700 Roman coins, of which four were said to be gold, from the 3rdC AD found in two pots about 1ft below the surface during the digging of a ditch on the heath at Well Walk, near Allford. The coins in the second pot were thought to have been silver, but they crumbled to dust when touched.

WEST LINDSEY, LINCOLNSHIRE

1999 13thC gold finger-ring, set with a sapphire: finder Keith Smallwood (M/D); valued at £1,250.

City and County Museum, Lincoln

WHAPLODE, LINCOLNSHIRE

1890 29 silver coins from the 16thC found at Fosdyke Bridge; it is thought that they were concealed in 1569.

WHITTON, NORTH LINCOLNSHIRE

[date?] Roman coins of Claudius Gothicus (AD 268–70) and Constantine I (AD 309–37) found on the cliff.

2000 Late 10th or 11thC silver-gilt Viking brooch: finder Mr Rhodes (M/D).

WHITWELL, RUTLAND

1991 2 gold solidi and nearly 800 Roman *siliquae* and a gold finger-ring from AD 337 to 400 found by a detectorist in a field. Most of the silver coins had been clipped and the hoard was thought to have been buried no later than AD 410. The majority of the hoard was declared treasure trove and was valued as high as £240,000.

WIGSTON MAGNA, LEICESTERSHIRE

1927 16th and 17thC gold and silver coins, thought to have been concealed 1625–49.

WILLOUGHBY ON THE WOLDS, NOTTINGHAMSHIRE

1999 6thC Anglo-Saxon gold finger-ring, inlaid with two garnet discs above and a square garnet below: finder J.E. Smith (M/D).

WINSTER, DERBYSHIRE

[date?] Mid-7thC gold cross with garnet found at Winstermoor to the south of the village.

WINTERINGHAM, NORTH LINCOLNSHIRE

1989 A 15thC gold pendant cross found by Barry Williams (M/D) 4in below the surface on farmland. Found in 2 pieces it has been dated to *c.* 1450–1500 and is an English-made Tau that has become known as the 'Winteringham Cross'. Having been declared not treasure trove, it sold at Sotheby's for £60,500.

WIRKSWORTH AREA, DERBYSHIRE

1735 83 silver Roman coins from the 1stC BC to the 2ndC AD.

WORKSOP, NOTTINGHAMSHIRE

1835 940 Roman copper coins from the 4thC AD found in a pot during the digging of a trench before planting a belt of trees on the north side of the Retford and Worksop road.

1958? More than 17 silver coins from the 16thC found on Lindrick Common, thought to have been concealed in 1547.

WRAGBY, LINCOLNSHIRE

A Roman *denarius*, minted in North Africa *c.* 47–46 BC: finder Adge Winstanley (M/D); returned to the finder.

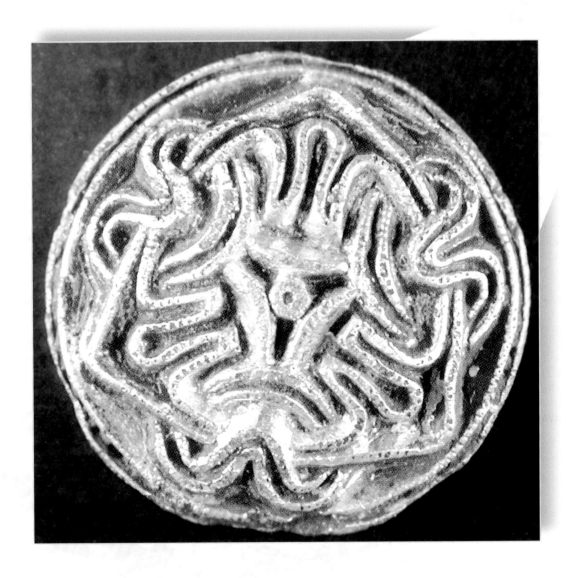

The landlocked counties of Buckingham-shire, Hertfordshire, Northamptonshire, Oxfordshire and Bedfordshire, with their proximity to London, offer a deep and varied slice of history. Many of the country's main arterial routes linking the capital with the rest of Britain run through this region.

In 2003 over 5,000 Roman coins were found at Chalgrove in Oxfordshire. The hoard, which spanned five emperors and about a quarter of a century, included a single coin from the reign of the Emperor Domitianus. He probably ruled Britain for just a matter of days but his mints still found the time to produce coins bearing his head. The only other coin of this emperor ever found was discovered in the Loire in 1900 and until the Chalgrove one turned up the French find was thought to have been a fake. This single Oxfordshire coin discovery proves the value of the responsible detectorist.

Coins known as Whaddon Chase staters are found throughout the region. They date from the period before the Roman invasion; they are named after an area of Buckinghamshire and a find of golden staters dating from 1849, over a century before the advent of the metal detector.

Around 800 years after the Roman invasion of Britain, Alfred the Great established the royal borough of Wallingford. He constructed ramparts and a castle, traces of which can still be seen. Around 200 years later William the Conqueror received the submission of the Archbishop of Canterbury in the town. Both these events influenced what has been found in the surrounding area.

The Heart of England

St. Albans Abbey

WELLAND

× NASEBY 1645

● Desborough
▲ Kettering

NORTHAMPTONSHIRE

1460

NENE

Northampton ×

EDGCOTE 1469

Towcester

OUSE

BEDFORDSHIRE

Bedford

CROPREDY BRIDGE 1644

Banbury

CHERWELL

Buckingham

BUCKINGHAMSHIRE

Milton Keynes

Shillington

Ashwell

OXFORDSHIRE

EVENLODE

Minster Lovell

THAME

Aylesbury

Dunstable

Luton

Stevenage

HERTFORDSHIRE

Hertford

1455, 1461

St. Albans

LEA

Oxford

Abingdon

THAMES

CHALGROVE 1643 ×

Hemel Hempstead

BARNET 1471

Chorleywood

Watford

High Wycombe

THAMES

N E S W

Magdalen College, Oxford

·Km·

0   10   20   30   40   50

0   10   20   30

·Miles·

ABINGDON, OXFORDSHIRE

One of the wealthiest and most important monasteries in Anglo-Saxon England was established here in 675. It met with destruction at the hands of the Vikings during the reign of King Alfred but was re-established by Aethelwold in 955. Many royal charters were granted to the abbey and these documents form one of the most important archives for the study of the period. The last abbot was Thomas Pentecost, who signed the surrender of his monastery in 1538 at which time the abbey's revenues were valued at £1,876 10s 9d (close to £900,000 today).

1828 Large quantity of 19thC gold coins found in a tea canister in a fishpond. It was believed to have been part of the £800 stolen 15 years earlier from the previous owner of the land.

1870 Large quantity of 16th–17thC silver coins, thought to have been concealed in 1641.

[date?] Anglo-Saxon sword pommel with silver plates, adorned with animals, human figures and plants.

Ashmolean Museum

2002 7thC Anglo Saxon gold finger-ring found about 3ft below the surface by Nigel Himpson while digging a friend's patio. Thought perhaps to be worth 'thousands of pounds', it was later declared treasure trove.

[date?] A 6thC AD Anglo-Saxon disc brooch.

ALDBURY, HERTFORDSHIRE

1870 10 Roman silver and 96 bronze/brass coins, and other metal articles and some pottery from the 1st to the 3rdC AD, found by workmen making a road a few hundred yards to the south of Moneybury Hill. The site is close to the Icknield Way.

1977 30 Roman silver coins from the 3rdC AD found 1ft below the surface by a detectorist illegally searching a Scheduled Ancient Monument at Moneybury Hill. The coins, which were all *antoniniani* except 1, were confiscated. These may be connected to the hoard discovered in 1870.

ALDENHAM, HERTFORDSHIRE

1882 16 gold and 264 silver coins from the 16th and 17thC found on Letchmore Heath; thought to have been concealed between 1660 and 1685.

AMERSHAM AREA, BUCKINGHAMSHIRE

c. **1751** 3rdC AD Roman copper coins found during the making of an artificial lake.

1999 Highly decorated Anglo-Saxon silver buckle from the mid-9thC AD: finder T. Jenner (M/D).

AMPTHILL, BEDFORDSHIRE

1836 146 silver coins from the 12thC found inside a hollow in sandstone. The coins were mainly Henry II Teaby silver pennies, and

were buried *c.* 1168–79. The find site is not far from the site of a former castle.

APPLEFORD, OXFORDSHIRE

1954 5,752 Roman copper coins from the 3rd to 4thC AD found in 2 pots a little below the surface during ploughing between Sutton Courtenay and Appleford, 50yd south of the road. They were thought to have been buried *c.* AD 350.

ASHWELL, HERTFORDSHIRE

1876 More than 500 Roman *denarii* from the 1st and 2ndC found by men working at the coprolite works at Ashwell End, close to the River Rhie. This is very near the Roman camp of Marborow or Arbury Banks.

1914 3rd and 4thC Roman bronze coins, in almost mint condition, found by a ploughman, who smashed the pot that contained them and carried them home. When told they were of little value, he gave them to someone who in turn presented them to Ashwell Village Museum.

Ashwell Village Museum

1998 Roman silver finger-ring with a missing stone, from the 4thC AD: finder B. Tattingham (M/D); valued at £75.

Ashwell Village Museum

1988 Roman silver leaf-shaped object: finder H. Cross (M/D); returned to the finder.

1999 Late 13th or early 14thC highly decorative silver-gilt brooch, broken into three pieces: finder H. Cross (M/D).

2000 Roman silver finger-ring, with missing gem, from the 1st or 2ndC AD: finder A. Phillips (M/D); returned to the finder.

ASTON ROWANT, OXFORDSHIRE

1971–4 324 silver coins from the 8thC AD found in a badger's earth in Grove Wood beside the A40. In 1971 Barrie Thomson (M/D) unearthed 175 Anglo-Saxon sceattas, scattered over several square yards, and the remainder of the coins were found by Barrie Thomson and John Reeves over many visits to the site. At this point it was the largest hoard of Anglo-Saxon silver coins (sceattas) ever discovered in England; they were dated AD 715 or earlier. They were declared treasure trove and valued at approx £8,000 (the equivalent of £50,000 today). 188 of the coins are in the British Museum.

British Museum

AYLESBURY, BUCKINGHAMSHIRE

c. **1938** Large quantity of 4thC AD Roman copper coins found by a farm boy in a field. Contemporary reports talk of 'more than half a bucket full'. When the boy showed them to the farmer he was told they were no good, and was advised to throw them away.

AYLESBURY AREA, BUCKINGHAMSHIRE

1835 2,436 silver coins from the 16th and 17thC found in the grounds of Hartwell House, thought to have been concealed in 1641. Between

1809 and 1814 this was the home of Louis XVIII of France and the coins were found by Dr Lee, the owner of the house, and first President of the Royal Numismatic Society.

1997　38 Iron Age gold staters from about 50 BC: finder P. Hampton, D. Shelly and G. Groucher (M/D). Thought to have been deposited in the late 1stC BC; they were valued at £13,100. Two years later 2 more were found and in 2001 another came to light

Buckinghamshire County Museum

AYOT ST LAWRENCE, HERTFORDSHIRE

1851　About 230 Roman silver coins, mostly *denarii*, found by workmen widening a ride in Prior's Wood, close to the village. They came upon an urn of dark-coloured earthenware about 6in below the surface, which contained the coins. Lionel Ames claimed them for the lord of the manor.

BALDOCK, HERTFORDSHIRE

[date?]　Many Romano-British urns, lamps, beakers, jugs and other items from the 2nd to the 4thC AD found in Wall's field. It was an extensive burial ground close to the settlement site where the Icknield Way crosses the Roman Stane Street. Most of the finds are now in Letchworth Museum. In 1150 the area was given to the Knight's Templars by King Stephen; they called it Baldock, Baudoc being the Norman French for Baghdad.

Letchworth Museum

BAMPTON, OXFORDSHIRE

1851　456 silver coins from the 16th to 17thC, thought to have been concealed in 1673.

BARKWAY AREA, HERTFORDSHIRE

1743　A number of silver votive leaves, including a large one inscribed with a dedication to Mars Toutatis, a native deity linked to the Roman god, found in a copse on what was the site of a temple. Mars, the Roman god of war, is on many of the other leaves, as is Vulcan, the god of fire.

British Museum

BEACONSFIELD, BUCKINGHAMSHIRE

1797　65 silver Roman coins, many in a state of fine preservation, from the 1st to the 2ndC AD, found in a pot by workmen removing the roots of a tree.

BEDFORD AREA, BEDFORDSHIRE

1980　Roman openwork gold ring and 2 Roman silver coins from the 1stC AD were found on the edge of public footpath at Queen's Park by a detectorist. The ring was declared treasure trove and is now in the British Museum.

British Museum

BEDFORDSHIRE

1997–8　446 Roman silver coins of AD 360–92 and 3 silver spoons, 2 gold rings and silver rings from the 4thC AD: finders Paul Summers,

Alistair Lee and Andy Horwood (M/D); the hoard was later declared treasure trove.

BENINGTON, HERTFORDSHIRE

1999　A 9thC Anglo-Saxon silver hooked tag: finder A. Cracknell (M/D).

BERKHAMSTED, HERTFORDSHIRE

1999　2 Iron Age gold staters from the 1stC AD, thought to have been deposited about AD 25, found during an archaeological survey. 8 coins had been found earlier, making 10 in all.

BICESTER, OXFORDSHIRE

1979　440 Roman billon coins, thought to have been deposited in AD 348.

2001　A 16thC silver strap-end, decorated with a man sitting astride a lion: finder A.J. Rogers.

BICESTER AREA, OXFORDSHIRE

1979　440 Roman copper coins and fragments from the 4thC AD found by workmen removing a tree stump on a farm. The coins were scattered, but retrieved by the use of a metal detector.

1995　14thC gilt brooch: finder Len Rees.

Ashmolean Museum

BIGGLESWADE, BEDFORDSHIRE

1770　About 300 gold coins from Edward III to Henry VI found in a pot during ploughing near Stratton House; thought to have been deposited after 1422.

1978–9　More than 40 pieces of jewellery from the 19th and 20thC found in a plastic bag on the common by 13-year-olds Kevin Smith and Darren Huckle. The bag was just an inch below the surface and contained rings, brooches, a wristwatch, and 2 ladies' evening bags. Inside the bags were two rings dated '12.8.30' and '23.5.1873'.

BLEDLOW, BUCKINGHAMSHIRE

1998　2 silver pennies of Stephen (1135–54): finder R. Piercy (M/D); thought to have been deposited c. AD 1145–50 and valued at £750.

Buckinghamshire County Museum

BLETCHLEY, MILTON KEYNES

1943　418 gold and a large quantity of silver coins probably from the 18th to 19thC, thought to have been concealed in 1881.

BLETCHLEY AREA, MILTON KEYNES

1991?　A forger's hoard in 3 pots: finder Andy Smith (M/D). The discovery was made during the building of a bypass in the vicinity of the old Roman town of Magivinium. The Roman pots were filled with blank bronze coin flans, and 2 iron dies.

1991　A 13thC silver coin found by Andy Smith (M/D). Although worn and bent, it turned out to be a unique Henry III halfpenny, and was later sold for £2,500.

BLETSOE, BEDFORDSHIRE

1936   2nd and 3rdC AD Roman coins found during the building of the new rectory, now the Grange. Also found, along with several skeletons, was a silver spoon with a curved handle.

BODINGTON, NORTHAMPTONSHIRE

1873   About 360 Roman copper coins from the 3rdC AD found in a pot in White-Leys, a field to the north-west of the village. The coins were dispersed, but 150 were recovered.

BOTLEY, BUCKINGHAMSHIRE

1888   200 16th–17thC gold coins, thought to have been concealed in 1633.

BOURNE END, HERTFORDSHIRE

1976   5 silver *antoniniani* and 35 bronze Roman coins from the 1st to the 3rdC AD, thought to have been deposited in AD 270, found in a river near Bourne End.

Verulamium Museum

BOXMOOR, HERTFORDSHIRE

[date?]   A 9thC cast bronze brooch, apparently modelled on a Frankish gold *solidus*.

Ashmolean Museum

BRAUGHING, HERTFORDSHIRE

[date?]   Enamelled Roman bronze cup from the 1stC AD.

BRAUGHING AREA, HERTFORDSHIRE

1956   61 Roman *denarii* from the 1st and 2ndC AD found in a pot on the bank of the River Rib: finder F.R. Bower.

BRICKENDON, HERTFORDSHIRE

1895   387 Roman *denarii* and 45 *antoniniani*, probably from the 2nd and 3rdC AD, found in a recess in clay by workmen during draining work.

BRIGHTWELL BALDWIN, OXFORDSHIRE

1759   Almost 1,500 Roman coins in an urn found while ploughing the common field.

BRIGSTOCK, NORTHAMPTONSHIRE

1966   278 Roman coins from the 1st to the 4thC and a number of bronze items (the head of a female, a model axe, votive leaves, and 3 pairs of equestrian statues) found during excavations of this temple complex.

BRIXWORTH, NORTHAMPTONSHIRE

1892   25 Roman *denarii* from the 1st and 2ndC AD.

BUCKINGHAM, BUCKINGHAMSHIRE

1997   38 Iron Age gold staters of *c.* 100–10 BC found in a field near Buckingham and declared treasure trove. 15 of the staters were of the 'Whaddon Chase' type.

Buckinghamshire County Museum

2001   A gold ring decorated with a fox and inscribed with lettering of the late 16th–17thC: finder G.R. Sarvis (M/D).

Buckinghamshire County Museum

BUCKINGHAMSHIRE

1993   An Iron Age Celtic gold bracelet found in tree roots: finder Derek Critoph. He took it to the British Museum, where it was valued at £8,000; later declared treasure trove.

1999   736 Roman bronze folles, mostly Constantine, from the 3rd and 4thC AD found in a pot in a field by Dougie Valverde (M/D) at a metal-detecting rally. The area was roped off to allow the coins to be retrieved and while this was in progress a second, smaller hoard of 2nd and 3rdC AD *denarii* was found in an adjacent field by Kevin Kelly (M/D).

NORTH BUCKINGHAMSHIRE

1981–2   9thC bevelled gold ring found by a tree stump in a field, just 4in below the surface: finder Roy Foster. The ring was declared not treasure trove and returned to the finder.

BULWICK, NORTHAMPTONSHIRE

1878   1stC AD silver Roman coins found in a pot. About 100 coins, in far from good condition, were given to the police.

BUNTINGFORD AREA, HERTFORDSHIRE

1999 Late 13th or early 14thC silver-gilt figure: finder D. Lambert. The figure, either a saint or a prophet, was valued at £50,000.

British Museum

BURTON LATIMER, NORTHAMPTONSHIRE

1954 124–40 Roman *antoniniani*, in a fine state of preservation, from the 3rdC AD: finder W.D. Evans; thought to have been concealed *c.* AD 295.

BUSHEY, HERTFORDSHIRE

1965 4 copper and 4 lead tokens from the 17thC found beneath floorboards of an upper room at 6 High Street. They were thought to have been concealed sometime after 1669.

1970? 5 copper tokens/jettons from the 16th or 17thC, thought to have been concealed in 1669.

1984? Rare Edward III silver hammered half-groat, which was over-stamped with a design from the time of Edward V, found by Colin Wiles and Steve Hammond (M/D), among tree roots, in a garden. Declared not treasure trove, it was returned to the finders and valued at around £7,000.

CADDINGTON, BEDFORDSHIRE

1974 17 gold sovereigns and 35 half-sovereigns of George IV, William IV, and Victoria, thought to have been concealed in 1861. They were valued at over £3,000.

CASTLETHORPE, MILTON KEYNES

c. **1826** About 20 Roman silver and 35 brass coins, 2 silver armillae, and a ring from the 1st to the 2ndC AD found in a pot south of the village in a field called Burtles Hill by a farmer while ploughing. The 2 silver armlets (penannular snake bracelets) and ring (with a cornelian intaglio bearing a nude figure) are held at the British Museum.

British Museum

CHALFONT ST GILES, BUCKINGHAMSHIRE

1934 40 Roman silver and 12 copper coins from the 1st to 2ndC AD found in an urn by workmen digging for a new road on land north of Narcot Lane.

CHALFONT ST PETER, BUCKINGHAMSHIRE

1989 6,682 Roman copper coins from the 3rdC AD found in 4 pots in a field near Welder's Lane: finder Christopher Conway (M/D). Three of the pots were buried together, with the 4th about 4 yards away. The majority of the coins were *antoniniani*, with the exception of 333 *denarii*. They were later declared treasure trove.

CHALFONT ST PETER/CHALFONT ST GILES AREA, BUCKINGHAMSHIRE

1840 200 Elizabeth I gold coins found by a small boy, who had started breaking up an old discarded window frame for firewood. The coins, of varying denominations, were beautifully preserved and had been hidden inside the wooden frame.

CHALGROVE, OXFORDSHIRE

1989 4,145 Roman copper coins from the 3rdC AD found scattered and in 2 pots less than 2ft below the surface by Brian and Ian Malin (M/D) and their father at Chalgrove Farm.

2003 Over 5,000 Roman coins of AD 250–mid-270, at a time of great upheaval for the Roman Empire, spanning 5 emperors, found in a field 10 miles south-east of Oxford: finder Brian Malin (M/D). The hoard was given to the British Museum for examination, and Richard Abdy, the Roman coin curator said: 'The Roman empire was beginning to fray. Domitianus ruled in 271AD; he was the penultimate emperor and there was only one coin with his image. There have been references to Domitianus in two ancient texts but they described him as an officer who had been punished for treason. Domitianus probably ruled Britain for only days which would explain why only two coins bearing his image exist.' The only other bronze coin of Domitianus was found in the Loire, France, in 1900, and until this second coin turned up it was thought it could have been a fake. The coin is estimated to be worth over £10,000.

British Museum

CHESHUNT, HERTFORDSHIRE

c. **1904**   About 280 Roman copper coins from the 3rd and 4thC AD found in an urn.

CHILDREY, OXFORDSHIRE

1937   44 gold coins from the 16th and 17thC found at Childrey Manor; thought to have been concealed in 1639.

CHIPPERFIELD AREA, HERTFORDSHIRE

1972   67 Roman billon folles of AD 294–307, thought to have been deposited *c.* AD 307.

British Museum

CHORLEYWOOD, NEAR AMERSHAM, HERTFORDSHIRE

1970s   Small hoard of Roman coins found while excavating for a new reservoir. The coins were spotted when the earth-removing machine scraped off several feet of topsoil.

1977   4,358 4thC AD Roman bronze and copper coins found in a pot by workmen during the construction of a new reservoir at Stag Lane. They were believed to have been concealed *c.* AD 348.

CLAY COTON, NORTHAMPTONSHIRE

1865   433 Henry VII silver coins, concealed in 1544 or earlier.

COMBE, OXFORDSHIRE

c. **1692**   4thC AD Roman copper coins found in an urn under the roots of an oak tree, in the parish of Combe by Woodstock.

1823   16th and 17thC silver coins, thought to have been concealed between 1561 and 1634.

1970?   9 copper tokens/jettons from the 16th and 17thC. These lead seals or bale marks were possibly used as tokens.

COPLE, BEDFORDSHIRE

1969   35 silver coins from the 16th and 17thC, thought to have been concealed in 1680.

COSGROVE, NORTHAMPTONSHIRE

1801   60 Roman *denarii* from the 4thC AD 18in below the surface by workmen during the construction of the Grand Junction Canal.

CRANFIELD, BEDFORDSHIRE

1946   1,700 Roman copper coins from the 3rd and 4thC AD found in a pot 3ft below the surface after draining operations in a field at Wharley Farm.

Bedford Museum

DESBOROUGH, NORTHAMPTONSHIRE

1976   Pendant gold cross on a gold beaded necklace of AD 650–700 found in a woman's grave, 1 of 60, by workmen digging for ironstone. They handed over the necklace only after being offered a reward, and

[date?]   Engraved bronze mirror of 50 BC–AD 50, measuring 10½in across, one of the finest surviving Celtic mirrors. Richly decorated on the back, the front would have been highly polished. The circumstances of its discovery remain a mystery.

British Museum

it is still possible that there were other items that were never recovered, as the men had apparently split the necklace between themselves. This necklace is one of the earliest Christian crosses ever found in Britain and the 37 separate pieces were put back together by experts at the British Museum.

British Museum

DIDCOT AREA, OXFORDSHIRE

1995   126 Roman gold coins from the 1st to the 2ndC AD found in a pot by William Darley (M/D) on his first solo detecting outing. The coins were *aurei* from AD 54–160 and were all excellently preserved, having, it's thought, been buried prior to AD 169. This hoard would have equated to over 10 years' pay for a Roman legionary and whether this was an offering or buried for safe keeping, with the owner dying before he could recover it, is open to conjecture. The coins were declared treasure trove and the finder was given a reward of £141,850; the coins were acquired by the British Museum for the same amount.

DORCHESTER, OXFORDSHIRE

[date?]   13 copper tokens/jettons from the 16th to the 17thC.

DRAYTON, OXFORDSHIRE

1800   Large quantity of 4thC AD Roman copper coins found in perfect preservation in the sandy soil.

DRAYTON BEAUCHAMP, BUCKINGHAMSHIRE

1998   Decorated gold finger-ring with a pointed stone from the late 16th to early 17thC: finder Paul Johnson (M/D); returned to the finder.

DUNSTABLE, BEDFORDSHIRE

The town stands at the intersection of the Icknield Way and Watling Street. The divorce proceedings of King Henry VII from Queen Catherine of Aragon took place here.

1770   A great quantity of Roman copper coins, as well as many small ornaments of bridles and armour from the 3rd and 4thC AD found in an urn while digging for gravel on a down near the Shepherd's Bush.

1835   Coins, mainly of French origin from Louis XII and Charles VIII; thought to have been concealed *c.* 1500.

1850–1   A quantity of silver pennies, possibly Anglo-Saxon, found near where Watling Street crosses the Icknield Way.

DUSTON, NORTHAMPTONSHIRE

1910   4thC AD Roman copper coins, of which only 120 were later retrieved.

ECTON, NORTHAMPTONSHIRE

1762   A small quantity of 10thC silver pennies found at a Saxon cemetery.

EDWORTH, BEDFORDSHIRE

2001   Late 16th or early 17thC highly decorated gold armorial signet ring: finder Russell Fergie (M/D); returned to the finder.

ELLESBOROUGH AREA, BUCKINGHAMSHIRE

1777   12thC silver coins, the majority of which were Henry II silver pennies; believed to have been buried in 1180.

EVENLEY, NORTHAMPTONSHIRE

1826   Several hundred Roman coins found during the irrigation of Addington's Meadow, near the River Ouse in the direction of Brackley.

1854   3,153 Roman copper coins from the 3rd and 4thC AD were found in a vessel while ploughing a field south-east of the village. The horse's hooves broke the vessel to reveal coins in an excellent state of preservation.

1965   1.5in-high livery badge, known as the Swan Jewel, made of opaque white enamel feathers over gold, with a gold chain and coronet attached. Probably made by a London goldsmith *c.* 1400, it was found during excavations in Friary field, the site of a Dominican priory from 1259 and 1538. The House of Lancaster adopted the swan emblem in 1380 when Henry (later Henry IV) married Mary de Bohun. It may well have links to the House of Lancaster or some other supporting family.

EWELME, OXFORDSHIRE

1722   Large quantity of 3rdC AD Roman copper coins found in an urn about 65 yd from the Icknield Way.

1953   202 Roman silver and bronze coins from the 3rdC AD found in a pot during the planting of fruit trees, 300 yd south of Ewelme House. The haul comprised 20 silver quinarii and 182 *antoniniani*.

Ashmolean Museum

FENNY STRATFORD, MILTON KEYNES

1962   About 650 Roman copper coins from the 4thC AD found 4ft below the surface during excavation by the Bletchley Archaeological and Historical Society: finder R.W. Griffiths. 251 coins were loose and about 400 were fused together in a mass. They were found together with a barbed arrowhead made of iron, south of Watling Street, close to Magiovinium.

Buckinghamshire County Museum

FLAMSTEAD, HERTFORDSHIRE

1886   100 gold and 195 silver coins from 1745 or earlier.

FLITWICK, BEDFORDSHIRE

1880   177 Roman brass coins from the 3rdC AD found 2½ft below the surface during the cutting of a drain on Priestley Farm. The coins fused together in a round lump and many broke into pieces.

FOREST HILL, OXFORDSHIRE

1842   More than 560 Roman copper coins from the 3rdC AD found in a pot when a wagon was passing alongside a small copse. The wheel broke the vessel revealing the coins, many of which were in a good state of preservation.

FOSCOTT, BUCKINGHAMSHIRE

1955   199 16th–17thC silver coins, thought to have been concealed in 1641.

FOTHERINGHAY, NORTHAMPTONSHIRE

1988   45 Roman *denarii* from the 1st and 2ndC AD found at Fotheringhay Lodge Farm; they were later declared treasure trove.

FYFIELD, OXFORDSHIRE

1944   2,105 Roman coins (all folles except for 1 *antoniniani*) from the 3rd to 4thC AD found by a man using a mechanical excavator about 1¼ miles south-west of the village, on land owned by the St John Baptist College.

Ashmolean Museum

GAYTON, NORTHAMPTONSHIRE

1998   147 silver pennies of Henry II (1154–89) found by K.W. Jones and F.G.H. Bason (M/D), having been deposited *c.* AD 1170–80. They were valued at £10,500.

Ashmolean Museum

1999   161 silver pennies of Henry II (1154–89) and 7 fragments found by K.W. Jones and F.G.H. Bason (M/D), thought to have been deposited *c.* AD 1170–80. They were valued at £4,050.

Ashmolean Museum

GLYMPTON, OXFORD

1948   44 silver coins from the 16th and 17thC, thought to have been concealed in 1643.

GREAT OFFLEY, HERTFORDSHIRE

1998   A Roman silver finger-ring, missing its stone and crushed, from the 1st or 2ndC AD: finder K. Skelton (M/D); returned to the finder.

GREAT TEW, OXFORDSHIRE

1817   Roman copper and brass coins found in several large ornamental red jars during the construction of a road on the north-east side of the village.

GREAT WYMONDLEY, HERTFORDSHIRE

1940   62 Roman bronze coins from the late 3rdC AD found on the site of the Roman villa.

Letchworth Museum and Art Gallery

GRENDON AREA, NORTHAMPTONSHIRE

2004   Inscribed 13thC crucifix found in a field by Steve Kane at Grendon House Farm, owned by Jim Brodie. It was just 2in below the surface and is just 1.5in long, and has IESVS (Jesus) inscribed on it. Steve Kane had previously found some 18thC coins in the same field on what is thought to be the site of a medieval market. It was declared treasure trove and is probably worth £500–£1,000.

GRETTON, NORTHAMPTONSHIRE

1972   More than 48 Celtic iron currency bars found during excavations at Park Lodge Quarry. The area was used for iron-making during Roman times.

HACKLETON AREA, NORTHAMPTONSHIRE

2000   15thC gold brooch and early 14thC silver brooch: finder Steve Marchant (M/D). The silver one was returned to the finder and the gold one is held by the British Museum; the gold brooch was possibly worn by King Edward IV and was declared treasure trove. 4 months later Steve Marchant found a 15thC silver-gilt finger-ring; it was returned to him.

HADDENHAM, BUCKINGHAMSHIRE

1999   2 silver and 29 bronze Roman coins from between the 1stC BC and 4thC AD: finder W. Jackman (M/D); returned to the finder.

HAMBLEDON VALLEY, BUCKINGHAMSHIRE

1912   294 Roman copper coins from the 3rd to the 4thC AD found in a small pot buried below the floor during excavation of a Romano-British homestead.

Buckinghamshire County Museum

HANDBOROUGH, OXFORDSHIRE (1930)

1930   4 silver coins from the 16th and 17thC, thought to have been concealed in 1645.

HANWELL, OXFORDSHIRE

1828   70 silver Roman coins from the 1st to 2ndC AD found in an urn by workmen in a field, a little to the south-west of the Roman villa.

HARDINGSTONE, NORTHAMPTONSHIRE

>1712   Roman coins found beside a riverbank. The *History of the Antiquities of Northamptonshire* (1712) stated, 'Upon the northern bank of the river a little above Northampton nigh Queen's Cross have been plow'd up Roman coins and particularly a Nero in silver.'

1882   Celtic swords, scabbards and other items found during quarrying at Hunsbury Hill.

HARPOLE, NORTHAMPTONSHIRE

1955   16 silver coins from the 19th and 20thC, thought to have been concealed in 1918.

HATFIELD, HERTFORDSHIRE

1910   Silver coins, probably from the 16thC or possibly from the 17thC; thought to have been concealed between 1603 and 1625.

1912   Silver and copper coins, possibly from the 17th and 18thC; thought to have been concealed 1727–60. It is possible that these may have been single finds rather than a hoard.

[date?]   Gold and sapphire ring found in Hatfield Forest.

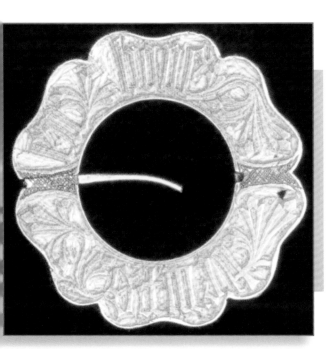

HEADINGTON, OXFORD

1937   65 silver coins from the 16th to the 17thC, thought to have been concealed in 1644.

HEMEL HEMPSTEAD, HERTFORDSHIRE

>1852   19 Roman *denarii* from the 1stC BC to the 1stC AD found in a field to the north-west of town.

1968   173 Roman copper coins from the 4thC AD found during excavation of the Gladebridge Park villa. Along with the coins were fragments of 15 bronze bracelets, 11 bronze rings, fragments of 4 penannular brooches, 2 tweezers, a fragment of a bronze mirror, a bronze spoon, fragments of worked bronze and pieces of iron knives.

1972   62 Roman silver washed coins found in Scatterdells Wood; they were declared treasure trove.

1981   11thC bronze Viking clasp found while digging the foundations for a garden shed: finder David Evans. The clasp was a few inches below the surface, and has the design of a serpent intertwined with a beast.

Verulamium Museum

HERTFORD, HERTFORDSHIRE

1964   1,108 silver groats, half-groats, pennies and halfpennies dated 1450–1503, some in mint condition, found in 2 pots by a mechanical digger driver. One pot was standing on the other and it is supposed that the coins were buried *c.* 1500 and were the proceeds of a robbery.

HERTFORDSHIRE

1993–4   A hoard of late Iron Age gold coins, jewellery, ingots and artefacts found by 4 detectorists after searching the site for 2 weeks; their find was declared treasure trove.

2001   A Celtic gold stater of AD 10–42 found in a field: finder Dave Chennells; the very rare coin was later sold for £3,000.

2002   A hoard of Roman silver and gold objects found by a detectorist. The site is now a coordinated dig with archaeologists.

HIGH WYCOMBE AREA, BUCKINGHAMSHIRE

1983   Pair of Celtic enamelled bronze harness mounts: finder Derek Robinson (M/D). There have only been 7 of these found in Britain and these were the first in Buckinghamshire. At auction they sold for £54,000 (the equivalent of £112,000 today).

HINXWORTH, HERTFORDSHIRE

[date?]   Roman statuette of Venus . Roman coins have also been found in large numbers.

HITCHIN, HERTFORDSHIRE

1895   7 9thC Anglo-Saxon silver pennies, thought to have been buried *c.* AD 870–5. The theory is that they are a part of an as yet undiscovered hoard.

1977 Late 2nd C AD gold Roman ring found by Colin Kane (M/D) in a friend's garden. An engraving on the gem depicts Mars standing with a spear and shield. The engraving is very like that on a gem found at Corbridge, Northumberland.

HOUGHTON REGIS, BEDFORDSHIRE

1938 A quantity of Anglo-Saxon silver pennies.

1973 A quantity of Anglo-Saxon silver pennies.

IRCHESTER, NORTHAMPTONSHIRE

1963 42,000 3rd C Roman copper *antoniniani*, in an excellent state of preservation, found in a huge storage jar 3ft below the surface by workmen with a bulldozer in an ancient yard by the Midland Railway Bridge, during road widening work between Irchester and Higham Ferrers.

Northampton Museum

IVEL RIVER, BEDFORDSHIRE

2001 King Coenwulf of Mercia (796–821) gold penny found by a man walking along the riverbank. This is the oldest gold penny ever found and was struck in the Wick of Lun dene (London). It sold in London in October 2004 to an American collector for £230,000, having been expected to fetch in the region of £150,000.

KEMPSTON, BEDFORDSHIRE

1976 53 Roman *siliquae* from the 4th C AD found grouped together by workmen digging a trench on a building site at Hillgrounds; they were thought to have been concealed in AD 388, and were declared treasure trove.

1978 13 Roman silver coins from the 4th C AD found in a field near All Saints' Church: finder Barry Walker (M/D): 'I got a very strong signal, which I thought was an old can. Then I discovered a Roman coin about the size of a 10p piece. The remaining coins were all just a few inches down.' There were 11 large miliarenses and 2 smaller *siliquae*, in an exceptional state of preservation. The coins, struck in Rome, Lyon and Trier, were thought to have been concealed c. AD 390. They were declared treasure trove, 2 coins being retained by the British Museum. Most of the rest were sold to Stanley Gibbons for around £10,000 (around £35,000 today).

KETTERING, NORTHAMPTONSHIRE

1928 63 silver coins from the 16th and 17th C, thought to have been concealed in 1645. In 1527 a man was prosecuted for demanding money to show where treasure could be found. He said: 'Ther was thousands of pounds of gold an sylver in a bank beside the crosse nygh hand to Kettering.'

KIDDINGTON, OXFORDSHIRE

>1783 4th and 5th C AD Roman silver and copper coins found opposite a lane going to Ditchey; the finders disposed of most of the coins.

c. 1870 More than 80 Roman silver coins, a brooch, and a strip of silver found in a vessel on the surface of a field on the Assarts Farm, adjoining Hill Wood, after ploughing.

1921 Large hoard of Roman silver and copper coins from the 4th and 5th C AD found in Not Oak Field on Wood Farm. The finder disposed of a large number of coins but 16 silver and 87 copper coins were retrieved.
>1935 1,176 Roman copper coins from the 4th and 5th C AD found in a broken pot just north of the hedge between Box Wood and Out Wood. The coins, which were in a solid mass, were 600–700yd north-north-east of the Roman villa in Watts Wells Field South.

Ashmolean Museum

KIDLINGTON, OXFORD

1940 More than 13 silver coins from the 16th and 17th C, thought to have been concealed in 1641.

LANGFORD, BEDFORDSHIRE

1977 25 Roman billon coins from the 2nd C AD, thought to have been concealed in AD 155.

LAXTON, NORTHAMPTONSHIRE

1936 339 Roman copper coins from the 4th and 5th C AD found 18in below the surface, under a stone, during levelling operations on the cricket field at Blackfriars School.

LEAGRAVE, BEDFORDSHIRE

[date?] 12 Roman bronze coins from the 2nd C AD found at Waulud's Bank; thought to have been deposited c. AD 190.

LETCHWORTH AREA, HERTFORDSHIRE

1990 13th C silver pendant seal matrix inset with a gemstone cut in Roman times of a lion with a bull's head, found by Paul Hing (M/D) in a field close to a Norman church.

LETCOMBE REGIS, OXFORDSHIRE

c. 1750 Roman gold and silver coins in 3 or 4 pots found in a field at harvest time.

LIDLINGTON, BEDFORDSHIRE

2001 A late 16th or early 17th C highly decorated gold ornamental ring: finder Robert Barton (M/D).

Bedford Museum

LITTLE BRICKHILL, MILTON KEYNES

1967 296 Roman *denarii* from the 1st and 2nd C AD found by amateur archaeologists Adrian Knight and Hedley Pengelly, while examining a ditch dug for a gas pipeline, in a field next to the Roman Watling Street. They were declared treasure trove.

1987 627 Roman *denarii* from the 1st and 2nd C AD found on the edge of the Roman town of Magiovinium, at the same site as the 1967 hoard. They were declared treasure trove.

LITTLE HADHAM, HERTFORDSHIRE

1999   13thC silver-gilt finger-ring, with a missing setting, found by N.J. Bickel while gardening; it was returned to the finder.

LITTLE WYMONDLEY, HERTFORDSHIRE

1973   652 silver coins of Henry VI, VII and VIII and Edward IV and V found by building worker Michael Lawrence beneath a floor when renovating a medieval cottage. They were believed to have been concealed in 1547.

LONG BUCKBY, NORTHAMPTONSHIRE

2000   Late 8thC Anglo-Saxon silver-gilt strap-end fragment, engraved with serif runes: finder Mark Scholler (M/D). At first the finder was unaware of the age of his find or that it was silver.

LONG CRENDON, BUCKINGHAMSHIRE

1831   1stC AD Roman coins found in a pot close to the Roman cemetery, where earlier discoveries had been made. Some of the coins, most of which were corroded, were of Claudius.

1885   210 gold and 846 silver coins from the 16th and 17thC, thought to have been concealed between 1649 and 1660.

LONG HANBOROUGH, OXFORDSHIRE

1930   12 silver coins, possibly from the 18th and 19thC, thought to have been concealed between 1820 and 1837.

LONG WITTENHAM, OXFORDSHIRE

1936   102 Roman coins from the 3rdC AD. The coins were all *antoniniani* except for 1 *denarius*.

Ashmolean Museum

1977   3,000-year-old circular bronze shield found by Oxford Sub-Aqua Club member David O'Halloran, while diving in the Thames at Long Wittenham. In fields close to the village hundreds of skeletons and weapons have been found. They are thought to be of the Saxons who were ambushed on their way to attack the hill-fort of Wittenham Clump.

Ashmolean Museum

LUTON, BEDFORDSHIRE

1862   800–1,000 Roman coins from the 3rdC AD found in a vase by workmen on the estate of Luton Hoo; many were dispersed by the finders.

LUTTON, NORTHAMPTONSHIRE

1961   183 silver coins from the 16th and 17thC, thought to have been concealed in 1641.

MAIDFORD, NORTHAMPTONSHIRE

1910   About 40 silver coins, possibly from the 16th and 17thC, found near the farmhouse on Manor Farm, thought to have been deposited *c.* 1642.

1979   24 silver coins of Elizabeth I, James I and Charles I found about 20 yd from the farmhouse on Manor Farm. A few months later another 17 silver coins of the same vintage were found. The coins were found in 2 distinct groups, 30 yd apart, and were thought to have been deposited after 1642–3.

MAPLEDURHAM, OXFORDSHIRE

1910   Roman coins, 'a pint in volume', from the 1st to the 2ndC AD, dredged from the River Thames immediately below Mapledurham lock.

MARCHAM, OXFORDSHIRE

1900   About 68 clippings, thought to have been concealed in 1662.

CLIPPINGS

During the late 12thC it had become common practice for people to cut coins, clipping them to take the silver for their own use. The shaving off of the edges of silver coins obviously decreased their silver content and also allowed for forging. It appears that King Richard's Crusades and King John's wars in Normandy had taken so much money out of circulation in taxes that the supply of silver was drastically reduced. This encouraged large-scale clipping. In 1205 King John ordered all these clipped pennies to be withdrawn and replaced by new coins, in order to help restore the value of the currency. Clipping of course went right back to the Byzantine era and continued until means were devised for marking the edges of coins, so preventing the widespread practice.

MILTON KEYNES

1978 76 Roman billon folles from the 4thC AD found during excavations at the Bancroft Roman villa. They were thought to have been concealed *c*. AD 330–41.

1985–6 Gold coin of AD 325–30: finder George Allan (M/D). This solid gold *solidus* of Constantine I was minted at Heraclea, in modern Turkey. It was declared not treasure trove, and deemed the property of the Milton Keynes Development Corporation, the finder being given a reward of £250. The British Museum had wanted the coin, and had valued it at £2,500 (the equivalent of £4,500 today).

1990–1 124 Roman bronze coins from the 3rdC AD found scattered across a field over a period of a week: finder Richard Colliass (M/D).

1991 Dress ring set with a rectangular-cut diamond from *c*. 1580 found near a 12thC church: finder Jonathan Gray.

1991 13thC silver-gilt amulet seal found by Jonathan Gray (M/D) on land being prepared for building houses. Inscribed in French it was a rare intaglio amulet seal, set with a carnelian semi-precious stone of Roman origin (27 BC–AD 14).

MILTON KEYNES AREA

1980–1 Gold stater of Cunobelin of AD 10–40 found by Arthur Eisher in fields; thought to be worth £400.

2000 2 gold torcs and 3 gold bracelets of 1150–750 BC were found in a fineware bowl: finders Gordon Heritage and Michael Rutland (M/D). Known as the Milton Keynes Treasure, their find was valued at £290,000.

MINSTER LOVELL, OXFORDSHIRE

1860 The Anglo-Saxon Minster Lovell Jewel is similar to the Alfred Jewel found at Athelney, Somerset. This one is round rather than pear-shaped and not as large or as elaborate. It features a cloisonné round-armed cross and is assumed to have an ecclesiastical connection. In King Alfred's *Cura Pastoralis* he says he sent each of his bishops an æstel (a pointing device), which is what these jewels are assumed to be.

Ashmolean Museum

1881 24 1stC AD Roman copper *sestertii* of Claudius I, in fine condition, found close to the Priory and the Windrush.

MOULSFORD, OXFORDSHIRE

1960 Bronze Age gold torc from 1200 BC found while ploughing. Known as the Moulsford Torc it was declared not treasure trove on the basis that it was probably a casual loss, which allowed the museum to acquire it at a reasonable price.

Museum of Reading

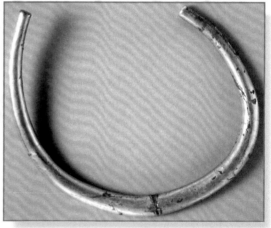

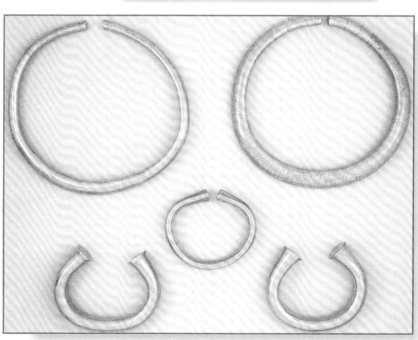

c. **1924** 4thC AD Roman copper coins found; of which 57 were recovered.

NASSINGTON, NORTHAMPTONSHIRE

20thC Saxon bracelets, filigree brooches and strings of beads have been found in a quarry near the village, where an Anglo-Saxon cemetery was discovered prior to 1944. The 13thC prebendal manor house in the centre of the village, opposite the church, was featured on Channel 4's *Time Team*, and it has been suggested that this may have been part of King Cnut's estates. Large post holes were found beneath the floor of the manor house, which indicated that it had been part of an early Saxon hall. Pottery from the early 11th and 13thC was found, including a small piece of high-status 11thC Rhineland pottery.

NOBOTTLE, NORTHAMPTONSHIRE

1928 814 Roman copper coins from the 4th and 5thC AD found in a cloth bag during excavation of a Romano-British building in Sharaoh Field, on the east side of Nobottle.

NORTHAMPTON, NORTHAMPTONSHIRE

1976 45 Roman billon coins from the 3rdC AD, thought to have been deposited *c.* AD 273.

NORTHAMPTON AREA

1873 194 silver coins of Edward I, mostly silver pennies, thought to have been buried in 1290.

1979–80 22 silver shillings and sixpences of Elizabeth I, James I and Charles I (1558–1649) found 13in deep and under a thin slab of stone: finder Ray Brice, assisted by Gordon Atkinson and John Brignall; the coins were handed to the police.

1989 A 16thC gold ring: finder Jim Possinger. It was declared not treasure trove and bought by the Guildhall Museum, Northampton for £2,700.

Northampton Museum

2001 Gold torc of 1150–750 BC found by Colin Hennell (M/D) in a wheatfield close to the 1960 find. It is one of only 5 found in the UK and weighed more than 2½lb. It was Colin's sixth visit to the field and proves the value of persistence.

Museum of Reading

MUCH HADHAM, HERTFORDSHIRE

1990 129 Roman *denarii* and 36 brass sistertii from the 1st and 3rdC AD found in a pot in a field: finder Kim Sandwell (M/D); the silver coins were declared treasure trove.

Hertford Museum

NASEBY, NORTHAMPTONSHIRE

1974–5 38 Roman *denarii* from the 1st and 2ndC AD found in a vase during drainage operations.

NORTHAMPTONSHIRE

1974 27 Roman billon coins from Gallienus to Tetricus (AD 253–74), thought to have been deposited in AD 276.

1982 12thC bronze dish found in a river; later fetched £11,000 (the equivalent of £24,000 today) at Sotheby's.

1988 45 Roman *denarii* from the 1st and 2ndC AD found on farmland: finder James Green (M/D).

1996 7th or 8thC Anglo-Saxon grave found at a Pioneer Agregates (UK) Ltd sand and gravel workings by a detectorist. The grave was thought to be that of a Saxon prince, and besides the skeleton there were a shattered bronze hanging bowl, an iron sword, and the remains of a Pioneer Helmet.

NORTHCHURCH, HERTFORDSHIRE

1813   Roman bronze helmet from the mid-1stC AD, around the time of the invasion, found during the digging of the Grand Junction Canal. The dome and neck-guard of the helmet would have been made from a single piece of bronze, but when found both the cheek pieces were missing.

OLD AMERSHAM, BUCKINGHAMSHIRE

1976   More than 26 Chinese billon coins from the 18th and 19thC AD were dug up in a garden, thought to have been concealed *c.* 1851.

OXFORD, OXFORDSHIRE

1790   3 gold coins from the 16th and 17thC, thought to have been concealed in 1638.

1868   213 silver pennies from the 14thC, thought to have been concealed *c.* 1351.

1896   Small quantity of Anglo-Saxon silver pennies from the 10thC was found on the site of Carfax Church; believed to have been buried *c.* AD 930.

Ashmolean Museum, Oxford

1903   12 gold coins, possibly from the 17th and 18thC, found at Merton College; thought to have been concealed in 1723.

1931   36 Portuguese coppers coins of 1509–44 found in the Carfax area of the city.

1932   4 copper and 10 lead tokens/jettons from the 16th and 17thC found in Holywell Street.

1938   3 copper and 3 lead tokens/jettons from the 16th and 17thC found in Holywell Manor.

1940   184 silver coins from the 16th and 17thC, thought to have been concealed in 1645.

1942?   16th and 17thC silver coins found at All Souls College, thought to have been concealed in 1697.

1969   4 billon coins found at St Ebbe's thought to have been concealed in 1806.

OXFORDSHIRE

1990s?   18th–19thC Georgian gold fob seal: finder Brian Linzey (M/D). The grey agate or amethyst has a crest but no one has been able to identify it.

1993   An 8thC Anglo-Saxon silver sword pommel with unusual openwork design found by W. Stowell (M/D) 5in deep on farmland. Taken to the British Museum, it was valued at £50,000–£60,000 and was later declared not treasure trove and returned to the finder.

SOUTH OXFORDSHIRE

1982   5 bronze axes (palstaves) from 1000 BC were found in a field: finder Michael Hodges.

Ashmolean Museum

OXHEY, NEAR WATFORD, HERTFORDSHIRE

1818   1,127 12thC silver coins, thought to have been buried *c.* 1140, found in an earthen vessel in a field close to the site of the manor house. The hoard comprised 1,094 silver pennies and 33 cut halves and gave its name to the 'Watford'-type coin of Stephen, as 632 coins of this type were found here. Also present were a coin of Matilda and 3 of uncertain baronial origin. Soon afterwards, another 100 12thC silver pennies were found with fragments of an earthenware vessel, close to the original hoard.

PIDDINGTON AREA, BUCKINGHAMSHIRE

1978   18 gold coins, including Elizabeth I half-pounds, Henry VIII angels, and Henry VII half-sovereigns, discovered by Paul Willis (aged 17) and Andrew Stonham (aged 16) from Piddington. The coins were handed over to the police, who sent them to the British Museum, where they were estimated to be worth £5,000 (the equivalent of over £17,000 today).

PITSTONE, BUCKINGHAMSHIRE

1977   30 Roman billon coins from the 3rdC AD. The coins were thought to have been concealed *c.* AD 270–80 and were from the reigns of 6 emperors.

PITSTONE GREEN, BUCKINGHAMSHIRE

>1870   1stC AD coins, including a coin of King Cunobelin and some Roman coins.

1890   2 Elizabeth I silver coins and 8 square-type farthings found on a body at the site of an irregular interment in a churchyard; thought to have been buried before 1603.

POTTERS BAR, HERTFORDSHIRE

>1860   19thC copper coins and tokens found at the foot of an elm tree, during the building of a car park at Wyllyotts Manor. They were thought to have been deposited before 1860.

PRESTWOOD, BUCKINGHAMSHIRE

1999   110 Roman silver coins and 1 base-silver coin from the 1st to the 3rdC AD found by D. Bird, K. Gee, C. Griffiths, K. Kelly, N. Payne and M. Weselby (M/D), during a metal-detecting rally, thought to have been deposited *c.* AD 220, they were valued at £1,923.

Buckinghamshire County Museum

1999   735 Roman base-silver coins from the 3rd and 4thC AD found in a pot by V. Valverde and E. Duffield (M/D) during a metal-detectors' rally. Thought to have been deposited *c.* AD 317, they were valued at £6,500.

Buckinghamshire County Museum

RADLETT, HERTFORDSHIRE

1999   A Roman silver finger-ring of the 1st–2ndC AD: finder P. Glenister.

RADLEY, OXFORDSHIRE

2000   Late 15thC silver-gilt finger-ring: finder Keith Liddiard (M/D).

RADNAGE, BUCKINGHAMSHIRE

[date?]   A glass flagon and marbled bowl found in a 1stC grave.

ROYSTON, HERTFORDSHIRE

1721   12thC silver pennies.

ROYSTON AREA, HERTFORDSHIRE

c. **1833**   Several 1st–2ndC AD Roman coins, along with the remains of an urn and some bones, found by workmen digging for stone at Limbury Hill.

ST ALBANS, HERTFORDSHIRE

The Roman city of Verulamium, the third largest in Britain, was sacked in AD 68 by Queen Boudicca's Iceni. In 793 the abbey was founded by King Offa of Mercia and later it was rebuilt by the Normans, beginning in 1077. In 1455 the first Battle of St Albans began the War of the Roses; 6 years later the second battle brought victory for the House of Lancaster.

1749   345 Roman copper coins from the 3rdC AD found in a vase.

1872   29 gold coins, possibly from the 15th and 16thC; thought to have been concealed in 1561.

1886   221 Henry VIII gold coins, thought to have been concealed in 1520, found in Park Street.

1932   About 100 Roman *denarii* from the 1stC BC to the 2ndC AD, thought to have been deposited *c.* AD 130, found by workmen 14ft below the surface during sewerage operations in Beech Bottom Dyke, west of Harpenden Road. They were dispersed by the workmen, but 41 were recovered.

1932   52 Roman silver *antoniniani* from the 3rdC AD found while excavating the foundations of the west wall of the eastern tower of the Roman city.

c. **1933**   About 1,000 Roman copper coins from the 3rdC AD found 9in below the surface during excavations.

1956   249 Roman copper coins and some small items from the 4th and 5thC AD found on the river bank in silt. The hoard included fibulae, a silver spoon, two pewter plates, and small chalice of tin or lead.

1958   50 Roman *denarii* from the 1st and 2ndC AD found in the clay floor of a wooden building (late 1stC AD), which lay beneath a later stone-built building.

1975   46 Roman silver coins from the 3rdC, thought to have been deposited *c.* AD 220.

1984   4 Roman coins and other items from the 1stC AD found during excavations in the grounds of Sheldon and Halsmead, in King Harry Lane, about 600 yd south of the London Gate. There were remains from 31 cremations and 29 burials and the principal grave was that of a child. The latter contained a wooden casket containing 4 glass vessels, 3 flagons, a beaker, and 4 Roman coins that had originally been in a purse.

2001   Silver finger-ring with an escutcheon dating from after 1700 found by a detectorist; it was returned to the finder.

SANDFORD ST MARTIN, OXFORDSHIRE

1768   Large quantities of gold and silver coins of Elizabeth I, James I and Charles I from the 16th and 17thC found behind loose bricks during alterations to a house. They were thought to have been concealed between 1625 and 1649.

SANDY AREA, BEDFORDSHIRE

1981   4thC Roman pewter bowl found by 14-year-old Susan Clark (M/D) 5in below the surface of pasture land. Subsequently other important artefacts, including coins, tools, weapons, jewellery, human remains and clothing fragments have been found on this site.

SCALDWELL, NORTHAMPTONSHIRE

1914–18   250 Anglo-Saxon and Norman silver pennies of 1066–87 found by the churchyard. There is speculation that the hoard could be related to the 'Norwich Bride Ale' revolt that was mentioned in the *Anglo-Saxon Chronicle*. This revolt was hatched at Earl Ralf's bridal ale (wedding feast), and involved Earl Waltheof, whose estate was 10 miles from Scaldwell.

c. **1920**   11 silver pennies of William I, thought to have been concealed *c.* 1080.

SHEFFORD, BEDFORDSHIRE

1949   5 Elizabethan coins, all in excellent condition, found during the restoration of a 15thC house.

SHILLINGTON, BEDFORDSHIRE

1871   More than 250 silver coins from the 11th and 12thC were found in a small pot by workmen. Most were English silver pennies of William II (Rufus), but there were also some of William I and Henry I, and it is thought that they were concealed *c.* 1110–20. Other Roman jars were subsequently found in the same field and it is thought that some coins were kept by the workmen.

1998–9   123 Roman gold coins from the 1stC AD found in 1998, followed a year later by 4 more. Both finds were by Shane Pyper and Simon Leete (M/D) and the *aurei* were dated about AD 79. They were valued at £200,000.

Wardown Park Museum

1998–9   7 Roman *aurei* of 100 BC–AD 79 found in October 1998 and almost a year later another 11 Roman *aurei* of *c.* AD 128 found by Shane Pyper and Simon Leete. The latter hoard was valued at £4,500.

Wardown Park Museum

2000   1st C BC silver brooch and bronze mirror found along with some pottery in a disturbed grave: finders Shane Pyper and Simon Leete (M/D). The British Museum thought the mirror, which was of 75–2 BC, one of the finest they had ever seen, and in exceptional condition. Declared treasure trove, it is thought that the mirror could be worth £30,000.

1983   Saxon weapons found by mechanical operator Stuart de Bank, who at first thought they were just sheep bones. There was a sword, spearhead, and cauldron of the Saxon period. The bones turned out to be those of a Saxon warrior, as well as those of a child.

SIBBERTOFT, NORTHAMPTONSHIRE

1866   16th and 17thC gold coins, thought to have been concealed between 1625 and 1649. Nearby are extensive earthworks and Moot Hill, the site of the Battle of Naseby, one of the most important battles of the Civil War in 1645, which effectively marked the end of Royalist hopes of winning the war.

SHIRBURN, OXFORDSHIRE

>1724   Roman coins found in a pot.

SHRIVENHAM, OXFORDSHIRE

1825   38 gold coins of Charles I and II, and 1 of Mary, found by labourers at a depth of 4ft while road-making. Viscount Barrington, the lord of the manor, claimed the coins.

SNELSHALL, BUCKINGHAMSHIRE

1857   About 140 Roman brass coins from the 3rdC AD found in a pot by drainers near the site of the old Priory of Snelshall.

SONNING COMMON, OXFORDSHIRE

1965   About 100 Roman silver coins from the 1st and 2ndC AD found and immediately dispersed by the finders.

STANFORD, NORTHAMPTONSHIRE

1753   Roman coins found in an urn in Sowthorpe Pits.

STANFORD-IN-THE-VALE, OXFORDSHIRE

1944   96 gold coins possibly from the 18th and 19thC, thought to have been concealed in 1857.

STANTON ST JOHN, OXFORDSHIRE

1647   Roman coins found in an urn by a butcher in Stow Wood, near the village; he sold them to a scholar.

STEEPLE CLAYDON, BUCKINGHAMSHIRE

1620   3rdC AD Roman copper coins found in a pot under the roots of a tree, by a pond.

STEPPINGLEY, BEDFORDSHIRE

1912   518 silver short-cross pennies, dated 1268, found in the church.

STEVENAGE, HERTFORDSHIRE

1987   2,579 Roman silver coins (387 *denarii* and 2,192 *antoniniani*) from Septimus Severus (AD 193) to Postumus (AD 260) found on a large Roman site on a housing development near Chells Manor after aerial photographs had revealed crop marks and archae-ologists had been called in to excavate. The British Museum kept the rarest coins; the remainder were returned to the landowners, who gave them to local museums.
British Museum and Stevenage Museum

1998   16thC silver-gilt dress-hook: finder K. Stazaker (M/D); valued at £150.
Stevenage Museum

STOKENCHURCH, BUCKINGHAMSHIRE

1982   24 gold sovereigns of 1872–1900 found beneath a hedge in a field at Horsleys Green by retired machinist Frederick Craft. There were no remnants of a container and the coins were stacked one on top of the other; they were declared treasure trove.

STONESFIELD, OXFORDSHIRE

1959   4 billon coins, thought to have been concealed in 1794.

STUCHBURY, NORTHAMPTONSHIRE

2001   9thC Anglo-Saxon silver strap-end: finder S. Barker (M/D); returned to the finder.

SWALCLIFFE, OXFORDSHIRE

1630   Coins found in a pot in a field, later known as Money Acre, at the bottom of the hill on which Tadmarston Castle stands.

TAPLOW, BUCKINGHAMSHIRE

[date?]   Gold belt buckle, inlaid with garnets, from *c*. AD 600, found in a grave.

THAME, OXFORDSHIRE

1889   About 500 silver coins from the 13th and 14thC from various reigns, including foreign rulers, thought to have been deposited after 1313.

THRAPSTON AREA, NORTHAMPTONSHIRE

1778   360 silver coins, mainly pennies of Edward I and II.

TINGRITH, BEDFORDSHIRE

1961   About 4,000 Roman copper coins, 'about 30lbs weight of bronze coins', from the 3rd and 4thC AD found in a pot while a mechanical digger was being used high on the sand cliffs. They were dispersed by the finders but 2,050 coins, all in mint condition, were later retrieved.

TITCHMARSH, NORTHAMPTONSHIRE

1979–82   9 silver pennies of Harold I (1037–40) found by James Green (M/D) on the south bank, in mud dredged from the River Nene. Thought to have been deposited *c*. 1040, they were reported to the coroner before being returned to the finder.

TOTTERNHOE, BEDFORDSHIRE

1998   Highly decorated Anglo-Saxon silver strap-end from *c*. 875: finder Peter W. Barbour; valued at £550.
Wardown Park Museum

UPPER DEAN, BEDFORDSHIRE

1875   11 gold, 5 silver and 34 copper coins, possibly from the 17th and 18thC; thought to have been concealed in 1734.

UPPERTON, OXFORDSHIRE

2001   13thC decorated silver brooch: finder A. Irvine (M/D).

UPTON, OXFORDSHIRE

1960   7 silver coins from the 16th and 17thC, thought to have been concealed in 1638.

WALGRAVE, NORTHAMPTONSHIRE

1997   Highly decorated 9thC Anglo-Saxon silver strap distributor: finders P. Flett and C. Brooks; valued at £500.

WALLINGFORD, OXFORDSHIRE

Established by Alfred the Great in the 9thC, Wallingford has preserved sections of earth ramparts and traces of the castle, demolished in 1644. After the Battle of Hastings, William made for the town and received the submission of the Archbishop of Canterbury.

1726   3rdC AD Roman coins.

1889   50 silver coins of Henry VII, thought to have been concealed in 1544 or earlier.

1949   Bronze Age socketed axe, a bronze chisel, and spearhead fragments found on the banks of the River Thames.

1999   Late 13thC silver seal matrix: finder M.J. Absolom (M/D). The ring was set with a Roman glass intaglio from the 1st or 2ndC and carried a legend.

WALSWORTH, HERTFORDSHIRE

1930s   2 17thC farthing tokens and a French Louis XIII double Tournois, deposited some time after 1662, found in Purwell field.
Hitchin Museum

WANTAGE, OXFORDSHIRE

1968   264 gold coins from the 19th and 20thC, thought to have been concealed in 1915.

WATCHFIELD AREA, OXFORDSHIRE

1903   16 Roman *antoniniani* from the 3rdC AD found during excavations of a Romano-British homestead west of Little Wellington Wood, near Watchfield.
Museum of Reading

WATFORD AREA, HERTFORDSHIRE

1980   6 Saxon silver pennies of AD 915–30: finders Tony Gill and Dennis Williams; valued at £900. 2 coins, of Edward the Elder and Athelstan, are in the British Museum and the other 4 are in the Watford Museum.
British Museum and Watford Museum

WELWYN, HERTFORDSHIRE

1961   149 Roman coins, mostly silver and silver-washed *antoniniani*, from the 3rdC AD found in a pot at 22 Glebe Road, Welwyn.
Verulamium Museum

NEAR WENDOVER, BUCKINGHAMSHIRE

1978   Bronze Age jewellery of 850–700 BC found by Kenneth Beasley while searching a wooded hill site. The jewellery fragments were about 4–6in below the surface. According to the British Museum, 'The fragments are severely damaged, but have been determined as a matching pair of gold tress rings'.

WEST WYCOMBE, BUCKINGHAMSHIRE

1978   18 gold coins of Henry VIII, Edward VI and Elizabeth I found, thought to have been concealed *c.* 1590 or later.

WESTON, HERTFORDSHIRE

2001   Late 16th or early 17thC inscribed gold mourning ring: finder Julian Evan-Hart (M/D).

WESTON UNDERWOOD, MILTON KEYNES

1858   More than 166 Roman *denarii* from the 1st and 2ndC AD found in a pot by labourers in White's Close. Sir Robert Throckmorton, as lord of the manor, claimed the coins for treasure trove; most were in a good state of preservation.

WHADDON CHASE, BUCKINGHAMSHIRE

Coins that have become known as Whaddon Chase staters carried a stylised laurel wreath with a realistic horse, and have been found widely in Buckinghamshire, Bedfordshire, Essex and Hertfordshire.

1849 Gold staters were found beneath tree stumps by a farmer while he was clearing an old woodland; they were immediately claimed by the lord of the manor.

1858 3 gold coins, thought to have been concealed 1660–85.

1997 38 Iron Age gold staters from *c.* 50 BC found by a metal detectorist.

2001 An Iron Age gold stater from the 1stC BC: finder D. Shelley (M/D).

Buckinghamshire County Museum

WHEATHAMPSTEAD, HERTFORDSHIRE

1974 8 gold coins of James I and Charles I, and 24 silver coins from Edward VI, Philip and Mary, Elizabeth I, James I and Charles I found on Normansland Common. They were believed to have been concealed after 1641–2, during the Civil War.

Verulamium Museum

[date?] 153 Roman artefacts found in 2 burial pits: finder Dave Phillips (M/D). The find included 13 bronze vessels, 14 Samian vessels, 9 glass vessels, 3 iron blades, 2 silver brooches with connecting chain, and a bronze lamp-holder.

WHITCHURCH, BUCKINGHAMSHIRE

1897 16th and 17thC silver coins, thought to have been concealed between 1625 and 1649.

2003 56 silver pennies and halfpennies of Henry III found in a field at Creslow Manor: finders John Hughes, Arthur Reynolds, Bill French and Val Crutcher (M/D).

WHITTLEBURY, NORTHAMPTONSHIRE

1999 2 Iron Age gold staters of the Corieltauvi from the 1stC BC: finder L.J. Owen (M/D). Thought to have been deposited about 50 BC, they were returned to the finder.

WOBURN, BEDFORDSHIRE

1829 About 1,000 gold coins, mainly guineas, of James II, Queen Anne and George II, found in a canvas purse by thatchers at a cottage near Northern Woods. They ran off with most of the coins, which were never recovered.

WOLVERCOTE, OXFORDSHIRE

1937 9 silver coins from the 16th and 17thC, thought to have been deposited between 1625 and 1649.

WOOBURN, BUCKINGHAMSHIRE

1770 About 100 gold coins from the 16th and 17thC, thought to have been concealed between 1625 and 1649.

WOODCOTE, OXFORDSHIRE

1939 78 Roman silver coins, 1 *denarius* and 77 *antoniniani*, from the 2nd and 3rdC AD, found in a jar 2ft below the surface during the digging of foundations for a bungalow at Woodcote, to the north-west of Newbarn Farm.

Museum of Reading

WOODEATON, OXFORDSHIRE

1717 1,551 Roman copper coins from the 4thC AD found during ploughing on the Romano-British site, together with many small bronze objects.

>1930 1,565 Roman billon coins from AD 341 or earlier, of which 94 were imitations. On a hill by the manor house a silver coin of Cunobelin (AD 10–40) was also found, and the eagle head of a Roman standard and a small statue of Venus were also found nearby.

WOOTTON, NORTHAMPTONSHIRE

1844 3rdC AD Roman copper coins found in an urn in the side of an earth bank. Many were dispersed by the finders, but 616 were saved.

WORMLEY, HERTFORDSHIRE

1948 A large quantity of silver coins and 1 copper coin, thought to have been concealed in 1946.

WRAYSBURY, WINDSOR AND SLOUGH

1979 Bronze sword from 750 BC found by workmen 6ft down at Hall's (gravel) Pit.

WROXTON, OXFORDSHIRE

1950 136 Roman silver and copper coins (all *folles* except for 3 *antoniniani*) from the 3rd and 4thC AD found after heavy rain. Mechanical diggers had earlier removed topsoil to expose ironstone near Rignall House.

WYCOMBE MARSH, BUCKINGHAMSHIRE

1902 16thC silver coins, thought to have been concealed in 1576.

WYMINGTON, BEDFORDSHIRE

1971 131 gold sovereigns and 242 silver coins from the reigns of Victoria, Edward VII and George V, 1838–1914, found in roof thatch of derelict cottages at 2–4 Church Lane. The thatch had caught fire and the firemen found a metal box crammed with the coins. They were thought to have been deposited in 1914 and were later returned to the finders.

Northumberland and what we used to call Yorkshire are huge areas of Britain with vast areas of open countryside, moorland and a long coastline. They also contain cities and areas of urban development that built up during the industrial revolution. This diverse topography has offered up some fascinating glimpses of history.

One find very nearly remained lost forever, even after it had been uncovered. In the 1970s a farmer found a cross. He put it in a drawer where it lay discarded until 1998 when his daughter took it to Hull Museum and asked experts to help in its identification. The 7thC gold cross was identified as being of an extremely rare type, only three others having been discovered; it sold at auction for almost £70,000. Perhaps the most spectacular find in the region was a gold and silver amulet dating from the time of Richard III and found at Middleham in Yorkshire. It was bought by the Yorkshire Museum for £2.5 million.

Since times before the arrival of the Romans, marauding Scots travelling south had to come through this region and many finds are associated with their raids on England. Similarly English armies heading north often went this way and their activities also resulted in objects being scattered across the landscape.

The eastern half of Hadrian's Wall runs through Northumberland and over the centuries many discoveries have been made that are associated with it. The combined importance of this frontier of the Roman Empire and the area's significance as the location for plundering and eventual settlement by the Vikings have made the region a rich and rewarding tapestry of discovery.

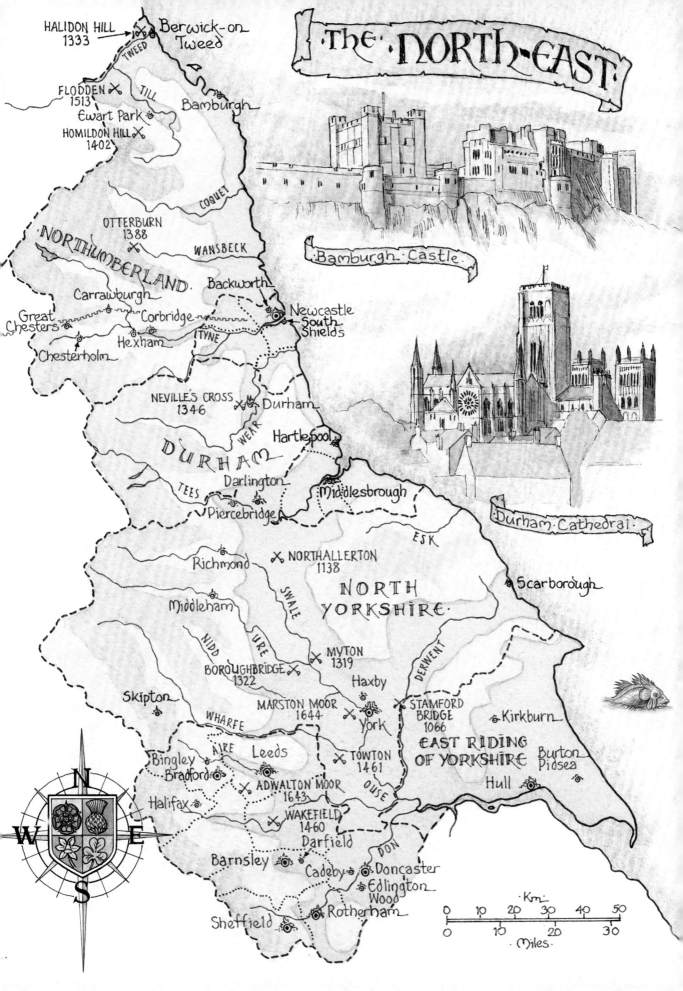

THE NORTH-EAST

HALIDON HILL
1333

Berwick-on
Tweed

TWEED

FLODDEN
1513

TILL

Bamburgh

Ewart Park

HOMILDON HILL
1402

COQUET

NORTHUMBERLAND

OTTERBURN
1388

WANSBECK

Backworth

Carrawburgh

Great
Chesters

Corbridge

Newcastle
South
Shields

Hexham

TYNE

Chesterholm

NEVILLE'S CROSS
1346

Durham

WEAR

Hartlepool

DURHAM

Darlington

Middlesbrough

TEES

Piercebridge

ESK

Richmond

NORTHALLERTON
1138

Scarborough

SWALE

NORTH
YORKSHIRE

Middleham

NIDD

URE

MYTON
1319

DERWENT

BOROUGHBRIDGE
1322

Haxby

Skipton

MARSTON MOOR
1644

STAMFORD
BRIDGE
1066

Kirkburn

WHARFE

York

EAST RIDING
OF YORKSHIRE

Burton
Pidsea

Bingley
Bradford

AIRE

Leeds

TOWTON
1461

Halifax

ADWALTON MOOR
1643

OUSE

Hull

WAKEFIELD
1460

Darfield

DON

Barnsley

Cadeby

Doncaster

Edlington
Wood

Rotherham

Sheffield

Bamburgh Castle

Durham Cathedral

N
W E
S

Km
0 10 20 30 40 50

0 10 20 30
Miles

ABERFORD, LEEDS

1870 A 9thC gold ring decorated with niello found during ploughing. It may have belonged to Aethelswith, Queen of Mercia, as her name was scratched on the back of it. She was the daughter of Aethelwulf, King of Wessex, and the sister of King Alfred. It is also thought that they did not themselves wear the rings, but they may have been gifts, or possibly some kind of mark of office. There is an A and a D on the ring representing the Agnus Dei. ('Agnus Dei, qui tollis peccata mundi, miserere nobis' – Lamb of God, Who takest away the sins of the world, have mercy on us.)

British Museum

ACKLAM, NORTH YORKSHIRE

late 1800s Early 7thC Anglo-Saxon decorated disc pendant found in a chalk pit. Decorated with filigree and garnet inlay, it is similar to many other such pendants found in the country and was an early indication of a trend in fashionable design.

ADDERSTONE, NORTHUMBERLAND

c. **1850** 22 Roman copper coins, a horse harness, and an apothecary's brass scale and beam from AD 117–267, found in a small oak box when a peat bog was drained. The coins dated from Hadrian to Postumus, and several of the latter were in very good condition.

ADEL, LEEDS

1742 About 500 Roman bronze coins from the 3rdC AD, in a pot during digging on the site of the Roman fort of Burgodunum.

ALDBROUGH, EAST RIDING OF YORKSHIRE

1997 Anglo-Saxon gold sword pommel from the early 7thC AD found by Nigel Wilding and John Sutton (M/D) in a lump of compacted soil that had been eroded from the cliff top. It was later declared treasure trove and acquired by the Sewerby Hall Museum, near Bridlington, for £50,000.

Sewerby Hall and Gardens

ALLERTON BYWATER, LEEDS

1922 299 Roman *denarii* from the 1st and 2ndC AD found 5–6in below the surface by the sexton of Bywater church.

ALMONDBURY, KIRKLEES

1828 About 290 silver and copper Roman coins found, reported in the *Gentleman's Magazine* of 1828 as follows: 'As a labourer was removing the soil from a stone-quarry in the neighbourhood of Huddersfield, on the supposed site of the ancient Cambodunum, he discovered upwards of 290 silver and copper Roman coins, which appear to be of the era of the latter part of the Dictatorship and the reigns of Julius and Augustus Caesar, as many of them bear effigies and inscriptions of these emperors, as well as those of many of the generals and other great men of and previous to that time. They seem to have been coined in various provinces of the empire, as some of them have Egyptian, others Grecian characters on them, mixed with the common Roman letters. Out of the whole, there are scarcely two alike.'

ALNE, NORTH YORKSHIRE

2001 14thC silver-gilt brooch found by M. Phelps (M/D); returned to the finder.

ALNWICK, NORTHUMBERLAND

1982 A 12in piece of a Viking sword with an engraved brass hilt was found by Shaun Cairns and Kenneth Middlemas (both aged 12) in a neighbour's vegetable garden. Ten years earlier some Viking coins had been found in a nearby field.

AUBURN, EAST RIDING OF YORKSHIRE

1570 1st and 2ndC AD Roman silver coins found by villagers when the foundations of a house were washed away by the sea. The villagers sold the majority of the finds. Auburn has since been entirely washed away.

AUSTERFIELD, DONCASTER

1963–4 42 silver Roman coins from the 2nd and 3rdC AD found in a pot. Initially 34 coins were unearthed by workmen with a bulldozer during preliminary excavations for a gravel pit in a field in Thorne Road. This find comprised 9 *denarii* and 25 *antoniniani*; the following year 8 more *antoniniani* were found.

Doncaster Museum

BACKWORTH AREA, NORTH TYNESIDE

1811–12 300 Roman coins, and gold and silver items from the 2ndC AD unearthed by workmen. The find included 2 gold chains, some small silver spoons, several gold finger-rings, a harp-shaped brooch and a silver trulla. It is supposed that the hoard was stolen during the Roman advance from the Tyne to the Forth in AD 143, as it appears to have been concealed when it was almost new. The finders secretly sold their treasures to a Newcastle goldsmith, from whom they were bought by a local collector, who willed everything to the British Museum.

BAINBRIDGE, NORTH YORKSHIRE

1998 9 silver coins and 64 clippings from Edward VI to Charles found by A. Lambert, T. Peacock and J. Hodgson while rebuilding a farm wall. They were thought to have been deposited in the early 1660s and were valued at £500.

Dales Countryside Museum, Hawes, North Yorkshire

BAINTON NORTH, EAST RIDING OF YORKSHIRE

1982 133 silver pennies and halfpennies, from 1182 to 1204, on land belonging to farmer Richard Welburn: finder Keith Bayles (M/D). They were thought to be worth £2,000–£3,000.

[date?] 12 silver short-cross pennies from the 12th and 13thC found in a field: finder J. Sutton (M/D). Thought to have been deposited *c.* AD 1200, they were valued at £440.

Hull and East Riding Museum

BAMBURGH AREA, NORTHUMBERLAND

1844 12thC Scottish coins found but not reported at the time. 7 coins, all of Scottish origin dated before 1124, have since been identified as coming from this hoard. They were probably concealed at the time of the Battle of the Standard in 1138, fought near Northallerton, in which the Scots under King David were defeated by a Norman English force of barons and civil militia.

1999   253 base metal coins, including silver sceattas, from the kingdom of Northumbria, dated AD 830–55, found by members of the Ashington and Bedlington Metal Detecting Club; thought to have been deposited *c.* AD 875–900. They were scattered across a ploughed field but were probably originally hidden under a hedgerow or some other marker. There were coins of several Northumbrian kings, including Eanrad (810–40), Aethelred II (840–4) and Redwulf (*c.* 855). 223 coins were found in January, and 30 more in June. Many had combinations of images which had not been seen before on Northumbrian coins. The find has suggested to experts that there was still a Romano-British or Celtic population living in the area, despite occupation by the Angles. Most of the coins were of low denomination, indicating that they belonged to a trader or possibly a mercenary. Valued at £10,000–£15,000, half the money went to the detecting club with the rest going to the landowner, Francis Armstrong.

Museum of Antiquities, Newcastle

BAWTRY, DONCASTER

1999   A decorated Roman gold marriage ring, possibly from the 3rdC AD: finder D. Rodgers (M/D). The ring was broken at the shoulder and flattened; it was valued at £850.

Doncaster Museum

BAWTRY AREA, DONCASTER

1980s   10thC Viking sword found in the River Idle by Leslie Topham (M/D).

BEDALE, NORTH YORKSHIRE

1991–7   13 10thC Anglo-Saxon silver pennies of the period of Offa: finder B. Court (M/D); returned to the finder.

BENTLEY, DONCASTER

1865   1st and 2ndC AD Roman *denarii* found in a pot by men working on the new railway from Doncaster to Thorne. The coins were dispersed among the workmen.

BEVERLEY, EAST RIDING OF YORKSHIRE

1981   23 bronze/copper coins from the 9thC AD found during archaeological excavation at an early collegiate site beside Beverley Minster. The coins were thought to have been deposited *c.* AD 850.

BEVERLEY AREA, EAST RIDING OF YORKSHIRE

1999   46 Iron Age staters of the Corieltauvi from about 50 BC: finders Alec Thompson and Jack Cooper; valued at £3,000.

Hull and East Riding Museum

2001   A further 21 Iron Age staters of the Corieltauvi from about 50 BC: finders Alec Thompson and Jack Cooper.

Hull and East Riding Museum

BINGLEY, BRADFORD

1850   91 gold coins, possibly from the 17th and 18thC, found at Gawthorpe Hall; thought to have been concealed in 1745.

1948   320 silver coins from the 16th and 17thC found in an earthenware pot in Gawthorpe Hall Wood, to the west of the town; thought to have been concealed in 1641. The find comprised a shilling and a sixpence of Edward VI; 5 shillings of Philip and Mary; 42 shillings and 109 sixpences of Elizabeth I, 46 shillings and 15 sixpences of James I, 13 half-crowns, 77 shillings and 11 sixpences of Charles I.

BINGLEY AREA, BRADFORD

1775   Many hundred Roman *denarii* and a 6in silver image from the 1st and 3rdC AD in a brass or copper chest by a farmer at Morton Banks while making a field drain. The chest was 20in below the surface and contained almost a hundredweight of the silver coins and the silver image. The coins were in a perfect state of preservation and came from 15 different periods, including Julius Caesar. The container may have been a Roman military chest, or possibly associated with a Roman temple. Elam is on the Roman road that passes over Harden Moor, Riddlesden, Norton Banks, and Rombald's Moor to the Roman camp at Ilkley.

BINNINGTON, NORTH YORKSHIRE

c. **1875**   12 Roman silver coins and a bronze bell from the 1stC AD found during ploughing near the village.

BIRDFORTH, NORTH YORKSHIRE

>1821   A considerable quantity of silver coins, found during the widening of Bickforth Beck, near a Roman road. The coins were dispersed by the finders.

BIRSTWITH, NORTH YORKSHIRE

1853   A large number of forged 17thC farthings, thought to have been concealed between 1625 and 1649.

BISHOP AUCKLAND AREA, DURHAM

1980   3rdC Roman ring found on the banks of the River Wear, not far from the Roman camp at Binchester: finder Paul Atkinson (M/D); it was ruled not treasure trove and was returned to the finder.

BOLAM, NORTHUMBERLAND

1804   Large quantity of gold coins from the 16th and 17thC found at Gallow Hill; thought to have been concealed between 1625 and 1649.

BOLTON, EAST RIDING OF YORKSHIRE

2001   Late 9th or early 10thC decorated Viking silver finger-ring: finder P.S. Birkett (M/D).

British Museum

BOLTON PERCY, NORTH YORKSHIRE

1846   A quantity of copper coins from the 9thC found in a field on the banks of the River Wharfe. These were probably strays from the hoard found in 1967.

1967   More than 1,775 copper coins from the 9thC found in a pot on the banks of the River Wharfe. Two brothers, John and Malcolm Miles, were walking across the newly ploughed field and found some coins, which they took to show their teacher. A few weeks later a careful search of the field was made by the Keeper of the Yorkshire Museum, with the help of two men from the Royal Commission on Historical Monuments. Their search revealed more coins, some of German origin, buried in an earthenware pot, and others which had been buried
in a wooden box that had long since rotted. Besides the coins there were some barely recognisable fragments and stycas of four Northumbrian kings.

BOSSALL, NORTH YORKSHIRE

1807   About 300 Anglo-Saxon coins and jewellery from the 10thC found in a leaden box on a farm. The hoard was thought to have been buried in *c.* AD 927, when the Vikings were ravaging and plundering the area.

BOSTON SPA, LEEDS

1848   About 200 Roman silver coins from the 1stC BC to the 2ndC AD found in a pot by workmen about a mile from the old Roman road between Aldborough and Castleford. Some were disposed of by the finders, but 172 were recovered, of which all were *denarii*.

Yorkshire Museum

BOWES AREA, DURHAM

1983   21 Viking silver ingots from the 10thC found by Brian Wilson, on the farm of Joe Brown. In AD 954 Eric Bloodaxe, the Viking King of York, met his death at Stainmore. The hoard was later declared not treasure trove and returned to the finder, who decided to sell it to the museum. In the same month (July) Brian Wilson also found a late Bronze Age sword from *c.* 800 BC. He sold the sword to the museum as it needed expert attention to treat the bronze disease.

Bowes Museum

BRADFORD

1982   716 silver coins, mainly English with some Scottish, Irish and continental, along with 20 fragments from the 16th and 17thC, found in a pot beside a footpath in Low Wood by Roy Mackenzie. He at first found 12 coins and then, when he had dug down to around a foot, he found pieces of the pot and many more silver coins. Returning to the site for three more visits he found an additional small number of coins. They were declared treasure trove and he received £7,000 (the equivalent of £15,000 today). Several weeks later Roy returned to the site and, upon removing a boulder, he found a second pot just a few inches below the surface. It was almost intact and contained 325 silver coins. The two hoards dated from the Civil War.

◀ BRAITHWAITE, DONCASTER

2001   Early Bronze Age gold crescent dated *c.* 2500–2000 BC: finders P.B. Williams and R.I. Smith (M/D). The strip of flimsy gold was folded and was 5in below the surface. It tapered towards its ends and had terminals at each end, although one had been broken off in antiquity.

British Museum

BRAMHAM MOOR, LEEDS

>1756   12thC silver coins, thought to have been deposited *c.* 1168–70.

BRAMLEY, LEEDS

1909   2,997 Roman copper *antoniniani* from the 3rdC AD found in an iron pot by a labourer, who broke up the pot and threw the pieces away. He hid 200 coins in a plant pot and buried them; some of these were later recovered. A further 200 coins seem to have been discovered by some boys, who disposed of them.

BRIDLINGTON, EAST RIDING OF YORKSHIRE

1921   61 gold and 61 silver coins from the 18thC or earlier, thought to have been concealed in 1796.

BROMPTON, NORTH YORKSHIRE

1999 5 silver coins, silver shillings and sixpences of Elizabeth I (1558–1603) found by R. Horseman and C. Crooks (M/D), thought to have been deposited *c.* 1600. They were returned to the finders.

BURGHWALLIS, DONCASTER

1999 A highly decorated Anglo-Saxon silver-gilt wrist-clasp fragment from the early to mid-6thC AD: finder D. Pearce (M/D).

BURTON PIDSEA, EAST RIDING OF YORKSHIRE

***c.* 1970s** 7thC gold cross with garnet inlay found on the peninsula on which Burton Pidsea stands, giving rise to the name, the Holderness Cross. It was found by Ronald Wray, a farmer, on the surface of a muddy field in which he kept his pigs, but it was not recognised for what it was until 1998. (He took it home, washed it, and put it in his kitchen. It was his daughter who took it to Hull Museum.) The cross, which may have been made in East Anglia, has rectangular arms with cloisonné cell-work. This is filled with shaped garnets and at the centre of the cross is a boss formed by a large garnet, whose face is incised with a deep circle, probably originally inlaid with gold. It was acquired by the museum for £69,548 and it is one of only four known crosses of this type. One found at Stanton in Suffolk has been in the Ashmolean Museum's possession for a number of years. Another is in the British Museum and the fourth, found in the coffin of St Cuthbert (d. AD 687), is in Durham Cathedral.

Ashmolean Museum

CADEBY, DONCASTER

1912 28 Roman *denarii* from the 1st and 3rdC AD found during construction of the mineral railway from Denby colliery. They may well be the first find from the hoard found in 1978.

1978 1,653 Roman billon *antoniniani* from Valerian to Tetricus dated AD 274 or earlier, found in a pot beside a rock outcrop on the north-east side of the former Dearne railway cutting by John Ball. He described his find as follows: 'I was standing up above Cadeby Valley. A large outcrop of rocks caught my eye. I hurried down, switched on my detector, and started searching. Within seconds I was unearthing a coin, quickly followed by 5 more, then nothing. I decided the main hoard must be buried right under the rocks. I dug for nearly an hour and a half before I was again rewarded with a very faint signal. I pushed my hand into the hole and brought out a pot sherd. Thrusting past that into the softened earth beyond, I brought out handful after handful of small, dull coins. The pot itself was wedged between some tree roots and the rock and I couldn't get it out without damaging it, so I left it for the archaeologists to extract. I tidied the site to avoid attracting too much attention and set off home in the dark.' 13 coins are held in the British Museum, and the rest in Doncaster Museum.

British Museum, and Doncaster Museum and Art Gallery

1981 110 Roman *denarii* and 4 silver bracelets, 2 of which were inlaid with gems, possibly from the 2nd and 3rdC AD, found by Brendan Kennedy (a face worker at Yorkshire Main Colliery, Doncaster) in a wood at Cadeby, near Mexborough.

CAMPSALL, DONCASTER

1841 More than 300 Roman coins found on the Campsmount estate, West of Campsall.

CANTLEY, DONCASTER

1999 A Roman silver ring key from between the 1st and the 3rdC AD: finder Peter Jones (M/D).

2001 Gold torc, bronze spearhead fragment and bronze instrument of 1500–1100 BC: finders Peter Jones and Malcolm Hibberd; returned to the finders. They were discovered within 22 yd of one another and while they were first thought to have belonged together, later study indicated that they were not all contemporary.

CAPHEATON, NORTHUMBERLAND

1747 Roman coins and silver plate, found by labourers who sold all the coins and some of the silver plate. Some pieces were given to Sir John Swinburne, the lord of the manor, and he managed to recover a few more pieces from a silversmith in Newcastle. The collection includes a sacrificial vessel called a 'trulla' or 'skillet'. On the handles of four other ornaments were figures of heathen gods. The find site is called Silver Lane. The nine silver fragments are held at the British Museum.

British Museum

CARRAWBURGH, NORTHUMBERLAND

Carrawburgh was a fort on Hadrian's Wall, located on the moors in the Tynedale area, close to the most northerly point of the wall. The fort was excavated by John Clayton, who discovered a military bath-house in 1873; and three years later he took charge of the excavations at Coventina's Well. In 1949 a temple to Mithras was found and ten years later another shrine to water nymphs.

1872   87 Roman bronze coins from the 3rd and 4thC AD.

Grosvenor Museum, Chester

1875   66 Roman *denarii* from the 1st to the 3rdC AD found in a pot, under a large boulder, by a man digging in the centre of the Roman camp of Procolitia.

Museum of Antiquities, Newcastle

1876   15,000–20,000 (one report very definitely says 13,487) gold, silver and bronze coins, as well as jewellery, discovered by a party of lead miners at a spring, which was the source of a local brook, about a quarter of a mile from the fort. Underneath about a foot of loose debris they found what appeared to be a solid mass of greenish metal, which turned out to be the coins. John Clayton and other antiquarians took charge of the excavations and identified gold coins of Emperors Nero, Sabina, Antoninus Pius, and Julia Domna, and silver coins of 30 emperors. The thousands of bronze coins covered a span of nearly 300 years. There were also rings, brooches, buttons, fibulae, bronze busts, bronze animals and a life-size bronze hand – as well as a large number of stone altars, earthenware jars and glass bottles. There was even a human skull, full of coins. The reason for the vast number of coins and offerings was that the Romans had built a temple over the spring, which was dedicated to Coventina, a Celtic water goddess.

CASTLE EDEN, DURHAM

1776   Saxon drinking vessel found by workmen uprooting a hedge at the upper end of the wooded Dene, about 100yd from the castle lodge. The vessel was in wonderful condition and was discovered alongside a skeleton.

British Museum

CASTLEFORD, WAKEFIELD

1955   12 Roman *denarii* from the 1st and 2ndC AD found in the Airdale area.

CATTAL, NORTH YORKSHIRE

1684   12thC coins from the time when Stephen and Matilda disputed the crown; the hoard was deposited after 1142. There were an unknown number of coins of Stephen, including irregular issues of York district, Eustace Fitzjohn and Robert de Stuteville. The latter two are extremely rare baronial issues.

1998   11 Roman *siliquae*, thought to have been deposited *c*. AD 402: finder M. Killeen (M/D); valued at £300.

Yorkshire Museum

CATTERTON, NORTH YORKSHIRE

2000   Roman silver finger-ring, with a missing gemstone, from the 1st or 2ndC AD: finder Peter Ireland (M/D); returned to the finder.

CHERRY BURTON, EAST RIDING OF YORKSHIRE

1999   Roman silver finger-ring, engraved with a swastika motif, and possibly from the 3rdC AD: finder P. Fullard; returned to the finder.

CHESTERHOLM, NORTHUMBERLAND

The Roman fort of Vindolanda and the surrounding civilian settlement are some 2 miles south of Hadrian's Wall. Much of what we know about life for the soldiers at Hadrian's Wall has been gleaned from what have become known as the Vindolanda tablets. Many are letters or official documents written on wooden blocks, although some are on wax tablets. The first ones were found in 1973 and they continue to turn up during archaeological excavations at the fort. Of the 2,000 that have been found, among the best were the 200 that came out of a Roman midden in 1993. The letters all date from the period AD 92–125 and give us a fascinating account of life on the frontier: 'The Britons are unprotected by armour. They are very many cavalry. The cavalry do not use swords, nor do the wretched Britons take up fixed positions in order to throw javelins.' In another, more domestic matters are addressed: 'Please send me 20 chickens, 100 apples (if you can find nice ones), 100 or 200 eggs (if they are for sale at a fair price).' The tablets are generally 6–8in long, 0.2in thick, and made of sapwood from local birch or alder wood. The smooth surface would be scored with a metal-tipped wooden pen dipped in ink made from carbon, water and an emulsifying agent. Remarkably the tablets have survived very well after having been buried for nearly 2,000 years, showing only some discoloration. (They had often been partially burnt before being dumped.) One of the most famous of the tablets was written in AD 100 from Sulpicia Lepidena, the wife of the commander of a nearby fort, to Claudia Severa, wife of the commandant of Vindolanda, inviting her to a birthday party.

1833   300 Roman copper coins from the 4thC AD found in stones of a wall.

1837   3 gold and 60 silver Roman coins from the 1stC BC to the 2ndC AD found in a bronze boat-shaped arm purse in an old quarry. There are two versions of the find location: near Long Stone, Thorngrafton Common, or Borcum Hill, Thorngrafton, Haltwhistle. They were found by workmen quarrying for stone for the Newcastle and Carlisle railway. Among the coins were some from Hadrian's time. After the finder had disposed of them he was caught and sent to prison for a year.

Chesters Museum

1976   112 Roman bronze billon *antoniniani* from Volusian to Claudius II found during excavations; thought to have been deposited in AD 270.

[date?]   A Roman betrothal medallion carved from Whitby jet, probably in York, found at the fort.

CLEASBY, NORTH YORKSHIRE

1958   15 silver coins from the 16th and 17thC, thought to have been concealed in 1699.

CLECKHEATON, KIRKLEES

c. **1695** Several hundred Roman coins from the 2nd and 3rdC AD found in an urn in a field called Hedleshaw.

CLIFTON, DONCASTER

1705 3rdC AD Roman bronze coins found in two pots by workmen at the east entrance of Clifton, after cart tracks had worn the earth off the top of an urn. Most were disposed of by the finders, but about 150 were preserved.

CONSETT AREA, DURHAM

1983 A hoard of 54 rings, possibly from the 18th and 19thC, in Fellside Field: finder Paul Rennoldson (M/D). They are all 15ct gold and are thought to be of German origin, probably stolen and dumped.

COOKRIDGE, LEEDS

1708 About 20 Roman *denarii* and 1 brass coin from the 1st and 2ndC AD found during ploughing. There may have been more but this was all that was 'declared' by the finders.

CORBRIDGE, NORTHUMBERLAND

1735 4thC AD Roman silver rectangular dish with an engraved 'picture' measuring 19in by 15in found on the banks of the River Tyne by a 9-year-old girl. It shows deities associated with the Aegean Island of Delos and may have been made to commemorate the Emperor Julian's visit to Apollo's Shrine in AD 363. It was sold to a local goldsmith, possibly with some other pieces that were melted down. The dish was rescued by the 7th Duke of Somerset.

British Museum

1907   Almost 700 Roman copper coins from the 4thC AD found just over 2½ft below the surface, during excavations close to the outer face of a north wall. The coins were fused together and may have originally been contained in a wooden box.

1908   400 Roman copper coins from the 4thC AD found on the opposite side of the street to the 1907 find.

1908   48 Roman gold coins and a gold ring from the 4thC AD found wrapped in lead sheeting 14in below the field surface during excavations.

British Museum

1911   160 Roman *aurei* and 2 bronze coins found at the site of the Roman town of Corstopitum. They date from the Emperor Nero (AD 64–8) to Marcus Aurelius (*c.* AD 157) and were found in a bronze jug whose neck was 'stopped' with the two bronze coins. Found under the remains of a floor during excavations, the hoard may have been dropped during flight from invaders from the north.

British Museum

1911   1 gold and 7 silver Roman coins from the 1st and 2ndC AD.

1914   32 Roman *denarii* and 12 copper coins from the 1stC BC to the 2ndC AD found as a corroded and fused mass on the eastern area of the excavations.

1965   6 Roman *denarii* from the 1st and 2ndC AD were found during excavations.

1969   12 Roman *denarii* from the 1st and 2ndC AD found during excavations.

COTHERSTONE, DURHAM

1782   A large quantity of coins from the 13thC, believed to have been concealed during the Barons' Revolt in 1214–16. All that remains of this hoard is a Henry II silver penny.

COWLAM, EAST RIDING OF YORKSHIRE

1958   About 14,000 Roman copper coins from the 4thC AD found in a large vessel by labourers ploughing and sowing. They were quickly dispersed by the finders and contemporary reports spoke of '6 stones or 84 lbs' in quantity.

CRAWCROOK AREA, GATESHEAD

1982   Hoard of silver coins and jewellery found in a walnut chest in a ditch beside a road by 10-year-old schoolboys Ian Thompson, Steven Hurst and Mark Dixon. The lock was broken and inside were dozens of rings, bracelets, pendants and silver coins. It was later discovered that the hoard was stolen from a house in Hexham, Northumberland.

CRIDLING STUBBS AREA, NORTH YORKSHIRE

1967   About 3,247 Roman copper coins from the 4thC AD found in a pot by W. Frost.

CRIGGLESTON, WAKEFIELD

1928   170 silver coins from the 16th and 17thC, thought to have been concealed in 1641.

CUDWORTH, BARNSLEY

1983   12thC Scottish silver penny found by a man digging a trench; it was estimated to be worth £700.

DARFIELD, BARNSLEY

1680   Roman gold and other coins found in a large pot during ploughing. The finder sold them to a goldsmith for a pound.

1691   481 Roman gold coins found in a field.

1947   481 Roman silver coins from the 1st to the 3rdC AD found in a pot 14in below the surface by a man digging a trench on the North Street housing estate. All but 1 were *denarii* and 30 of them are held in the Darfield School Museum, 33 at the British Museum, and 417, together with the pot, at the Sheffield Museum Services.

British Museum

1948   500 Roman *denarii* from the 1st to the 3rdC AD found in a pot 2ft below the surface by a man laying a water main on a new housing site, known as Clarney Place. The site was only 200yd from the 1947 find. 14 coins are held at the British Museum, and the other 486 coins and the pot at the Sheffield City Museum.

British Museum

1950   541 Roman copper coins from the 3rdC AD found in a pot by a workman digging a trench for a gas main in Clarney Avenue.

1950   500 Roman silver coins found by builders digging the foundations of a house in Fensome Way.

DARLINGTON

>1854   A vast quantity of Roman copper coins from the 4thC AD found in the Cockerbeck, between Mowden Bridge and Darlington, and in Baydalebeck near the same bridge.

1912   Silver coins, a collection of forger's blanks, thought to have been concealed between 1760 and 1816.

[date?]   203 Roman billon coins from the 3rdC, the reigns of Valerian to Tetricus; thought to have been deposited in AD 274.

DARLINGTON AREA

1790   1st to 3rdC AD Roman silver coins, in 'almost mint' condition, found on the bed of the River Tees; they were dispersed by the finders.

1980   Silver tankards and other silver items found by boys swimming in the River Wear. The find was identified as coming from a burglary in Darlington and when police frogmen searched the river they found more stolen property from house burglaries in Darlington's West End.

RIVER DEARNE, DONCASTER

1983–4 740 coins from 1862 to 1967, thought to have been stolen, found on the riverbank.

1985–6 Bronze Age axe from 600 BC found in the riverbank.

DENBY, KIRKLEES

1887 51 silver coins from the 16th and 17thC; thought to have been concealed in 1641.

1888 36 silver coins from the 16th and 17thC; thought to have been concealed between 1603 and 1625.

DEWSBURY, KIRKLEES

1863 1stC AD Roman gold and silver coins found with the remains of two Roman querns on Dewsbury Moor; they were sold to the jeweller in Dewsbury.

1925 26 Roman *denarii* from the 2ndC AD found beneath a large stone in Crow Nest Park by workmen planting trees. They were 3ft below the surface and there were traces of a leather bag.

1924 24 Roman *denarii* from the 1st and 2ndC AD found in the angle of High Street and Scot Lane.

DONCASTER

1945 1,220 Roman copper *antoniniani* from the 3rdC AD found in a pot 1ft below the surface during ploughing in Sheepcote Meadow, on Folds Farm, near Sandbeck Hall. The coins, which registered a tiny silver content, were declared treasure trove.

1977 15 Roman bronze coins from the 1st and 2ndC AD found in a pit in the High Street during an excavation. The hoard included 4 intaglios (2 set in silver rings, 1 in an iron ring, 1 in a copper-alloy brooch), 5 brooches, and a bronze scalpel handle.

DONCASTER AREA

1841 Nearly 300 Roman bronze coins from the 3rdC AD found at Campsmount, about 7 miles from the town.

1861 More than 472 silver short-cross pennies of King John and Henry III.

DOWNHAM, NORTHUMBERLAND

c. **1830** Roman silver coins, buried in a vase.

DRIFFIELD AREA, EAST RIDING OF YORKSHIRE

2001 5 14thC silver groats of Edward III: finder I.K. Bayles. They were thought to have been deposited *c.* 1360–70 and were returned to the finder.

>2002 More than 50 gold staters of the Corieltauvian tribe from the late 1stC AD: finder David Scott (M/D).

Hull and East Riding Museum

DUNNINGTON, YORK

1998 17thC silver-gilt Royalist badge of Charles I; deposited in the second half of 17thC: finder M. Dandy (M/D); valued at £700.

Yorkshire Museum

DUNSFORTH, NORTH YORKSHIRE

1924 75 coins , possibly two hoards close to each other, as their dates span a 200-year period, AD 875–1075.

DURHAM

1756 About 170 silver coins from the 14thC found in a pot on Elvet Moor; thought to have been concealed *c.* 1390.

1930 572 silver coins, mainly English silver pennies of Edward I, from the 14thC, found in a light redware pot on Beach Crest. They were thought to have been buried *c.* 1360.

British Museum

1930 150 silver pennies, all in excellent condition, of Edward I and II, and David and Robert the Bruce of Scotland, found in an earthenware pot in the house of Mr Lee of the Durham County Council.

1998 13thC silver-gilt brooch: finders Mr Bolam and Mr P. Rennoldson (M/D); valued at £1,000.

DURHAM AREA

1995 14th or 15thC gold seal ring, decorated with a rampant lion, found by Mick Batey, 7in below the surface of a field which was once part of a royal hunting park, near the site of the Battle of Neville's Cross (1346). It was declared not treasure trove.

EASBY, NORTH YORKSHIRE

1981 14 coins from 1643 found on the site of the abbey by a detectorist who had been granted permission to search there.

EAST LUTTON, NORTH YORKSHIRE

2001 A 3rdC AD Roman silver finger-ring, set with a red cornelian engraved with a wolf: finder K. Umpleby (M/D).

Yorkshire Museum

ECCLESHILL, BRADFORD

1953 Hoard of gold and silver coins found in bags in an old cottage at Bank Farm, which had been empty since 1925, when its occupants had died. Just prior to its demolition, 30 schoolboys decided to spend their lunch-hour playing in the derelict old cottage, which was near their school. Pulling up the floorboards they found 12 small bags of gold and silver coins: 230 sovereigns, 200 half-sovereigns, and around £20 face value of silver. Today this would be worth around £15,000.

EDLINGTON WOOD, DONCASTER

1935   80 Roman *denarii* and 1 *antoninianus* from the 2nd and 3rdC AD found in a pot by Colin Cameron and his family. Shortly afterwards they found another hoard of 356 Roman *denarii* and 172 *antoniniani* from the 2nd and 3rdC AD in another pot. This was followed by a third hoard of 59 Roman copper *antoniniani* from the 3rdC AD, found by Mr Cameron and his son among rocks known as the Crags, fairly close to the two earlier hoard finds. This latter hoard was thought to have been deposited *c.* AD 269.

Doncaster Museum

1975   8 silver coins (Philip I to Victorianus Antoniniani) from the 3rdC AD, thought to have been deposited *c.* AD 269. This may have been connected with the 1935 hoards.

1978   84 Roman silver coins of AD 250–70 found by 16-year-old Scott Fletcher (M/D) on a path close to his home in Edlington.

1978   23 Roman *denarii* from the 3rdC AD found by Terence Cottle at the base of a large upright limestone block at the foot of the Crags. 20 coins were located first and then 3 more a few weeks later. They were thought to have been deposited in AD 226.

Doncaster Museum

EGTON, NORTH YORKSHIRE

1928   23 silver coins from the 16th and 17thC, thought to have been concealed in 1640.

ELLAND, CALDERDALE

1932   1,807 silver coins dated 1520–1602 or possibly 1605 found in a jar by a man digging in his garden's cabbage in Elizabeth Street. They were thought to have been concealed *c.* 1641.

[date?]   856 silver coins from the 16th and 17thC, thought to have been concealed in 1641.

ELLOUGHTON, EAST RIDING OF YORKSHIRE

[date?]   Bronze Age flat axe from *c.* 2000 BC: finder David Haldenby.

Hull and East Riding Museum

ESTON, REDCAR AND CLEVELAND

Roman copper coins have been reported, from the Emperors Nero, Vespasian, Trajan, Maximian and Constantine.

EWART PARK, NORTHUMBERLAND

1811   A Bronze Age hoard was found from *c.* 900 BC, comprising axe heads, a socketed gouge, a socketed spearhead, fragments of axe heads, swords, bronze rings of various types, and several casting moulds. In all about 61 items were found and it gave rise to the naming of a style of Bronze Age items as the 'Ewart Park' type. The three swords have two or three holes in the hilt, and were buried standing vertically in the ground.

FENWICK AREA, NORTHUMBERLAND

[date?]   More than 224 gold Edward III nobles (1327–77) found by farm labourers. Several hundred coins are said to have been carried off by the finders before the find was reported. Today the nobles would be worth in excess of £250,000.

FIELDHOUSE, DURHAM

1806   60–70 silver coins of Elizabeth I found at the base of a hedge on the estate of John Barras (one of the founders of Scottish and Newcastle Brewery). They were thought to have been deposited after 1558.

FLAMBOROUGH HEAD, EAST RIDING OF YORKSHIRE

Gold coins have regularly been found on the beach beneath the cliffs and are believed to come from an unidentified wreck lying close to the shore to the north of the point.

FOUNTAINS ABBEY, NORTH YORKSHIRE

1800s   350 Charles I silver coins found near the fishponds.

2001   2 silver shillings of James I: finders A. Grange and S. Baxter (M/D). Thought to have been deposited in the early to mid-17thC, they are held by the National Trust.

2001   Late 19th or early 20thC silver spoon: finders A. Grange and S. Baxter (M/D); held by the National Trust.

FOXHOLES, EAST RIDING OF YORKSHIRE

1995   14thC silver-gilt brooch found by Charles Pelham (M/D).

GAINFORD, DURHAM

1864   9thC AD Anglo-Saxon silver pennies, concealed *c.* AD 875, the time of the Viking raids. A considerable number of the coins were discreetly disposed of by the finders.

GATESHEAD

1790   A large number of Roman coins, possibly from the 1st and 2ndC AD, found in an urn by workmen, who are thought to have disposed of many of them.

GAWBER, BARNSLEY

1991   112 gold sovereigns from the 19thC found by teenagers digging a hole. They were returned to the finders and were bought by the British Museum.

GIGGLESWICK, NORTH YORKSHIRE

1794   Large quantity of Roman coins from the 3rd and 4thC AD found in a crevice between two rocks by workmen digging for stones in a quarry by the roadside at Craven Bank, above Giggleswick. A bronze ring was also found nearby.

GILLING WEST, NORTH YORKSHIRE

1976   9thC Anglo-Saxon chieftain's sword, with a hilt decorated with silver, found by 9-year-old Garry Fridd while out fishing for tadpoles in the stream. The sword blade was made of iron and had been saved from complete corrosion by being buried in the peat. It was acquired by Yorkshire Museum for £10,000 (the equivalent of £44,000 today).

Yorkshire Museum

GOLDSBOROUGH, NORTH YORKSHIRE

1858   39 Anglo-Saxon and oriental coins, silver ingots and ornaments from the 10thC found by workmen digging a trench for rebuilding the

church wall. The coins were in a broken earthenware pot and are thought to be a Viking raider's plunder, concealed *c.* AD 925–30.

1999   17thC decorated and inscribed gold posy ring: finder Helen E. Smith (M/D).

GREAT CHESTERS, NORTHUMBERLAND

The Roman fort overlooks the Caw Burn and was called Aesica by the Romans. It was one of the last forts to be built on Hadrian's Wall and was finished AD 128–38. The banks and ditches around the fort can still be seen today.

1894   A 1stC AD gilded bronze brooch decoration in a Celtic style was discovered during excavation of the west guard chamber of the south gate of the Roman fort. It was in a hoard of jewellery which included 3rdC pieces. Known as the Aesica brooch, it was cast in two parts which slot together. The brooch is decorated all over by swirling designs of trumpet scrolls, and is thought to have been made in a Celtic workshop, possibly in Yorkshire, *c.* AD 70–80.

1895   About 20 Roman *denarii* from the 2ndC AD found behind a water trough during excavations of the fort.

1897   120 Roman copper-alloy coins, including a few base-silver coins from the 3rdC AD, found during excavations of the Roman fort.

GREAT LUMLEY, DURHAM

1950   678 silver coins from the 16th and 17thC found at Black Row Farm, thought to have been concealed in 1641.

GRINTON, NORTH YORKSHIRE

1924   53 Roman *denarii* and 9 fragments from the 1st and 2ndC AD found scattered in a field adjacent to Scarr House in Grinton. They were declared treasure trove.

Yorkshire Museum

GUISBOROUGH, REDCAR AND CLEVELAND

[date?]   Roman bronze helmet, found with both embossing and engraved decorative work depicting Mars, the god of war, and Victory. Experts are unsure whether this was a combat helmet, or one used in sports or on parade; possibly it may have been both.

GUISBOROUGH AREA, REDCAR AND CLEVELAND

1848   195 silver coins, mainly English and Irish silver groats, half-groats, and pennies; thought to have been buried before 1471, during the Wars of the Roses.

HALIFAX, CALDERDALE

1774   A hoard of jewellery was found inside an old sideboard after a sale of household goods at the town's vicarage. The man who bought the sideboard for a half-crown found secret drawers containing 2 pendants set with diamonds, valued at £2,000 (worth maybe £150,000 today). There were also 9 gold rings, 9 wedges of gold, some of which were very large, a ladies equipage, a great number of antique pieces of silver, coins and medals, 3 gold girdles and a large purse exquisitely wrought in gold and silver with 3 buckles suited to them set with brilliants, the largest of solid gold, with several others of the same metal, a tortoiseshell snuffbox, gold bezelled, and a casket of jewels of 'immense value'.

c. **1828**   Gold Iron Age coins and Roman silver coins from the 1stC BC to the 1stC AD found in a field, opposite Lightcliffe Chapel. According to a fairly contemporary report, there were silver consular and imperial coins found within a few yards of the present road, in a Roman vessel. There were at least 4 British gold coins in a beautiful state of preservation, 'two of the gold coins are Boudicca's, twenty-six consular coins and five Imperial Coins'.

1915   1,075 Roman copper coins from the 4thC AD found near a footpath by schoolchildren playing at 'the Rocks'.

HALSHAM, E1AST RIDING OF YORKSHIRE

>1841   Roman copper coins, together with a considerable number of skeletons, found in several urns by workmen opening a tumulus. The finders took many of the coins.

HAMPSTHWAITE, NORTH YORKSHIRE

c. **1845**   9 Roman *denarii* from the 1st and 2ndC AD.

HAREWOOD, LEEDS

1895   11thC coins, thought to be loot from the harrying of Northamptonshire in 1065.

HARTLEPOOL

2002   Hoard of Bronze Age artefacts found 18in below the surface by Charlie Pounder (M/D) in a large earthen pot on a building site above Hartlepool Bay. It included a spearhead, rings, beads, and horse attachments. It was found just before the land was bulldozed 24 hours later.

HATFIELD, DONCASTER

1996?   15thC gold ring, set with a sapphire and believed to date from about 1450, found a few inches below the surface by Allen Kendell. The supposition is that it was lost by a female member of the nobility while out riding, as the area was a royal palace and deer park.

HAXBY, YORK

1993–4   838 Roman bronze coins from the 4thC AD found in two pots; the latest coins were from AD 358. One of the pots was broken, the other intact. The coins were split up and shared between the finder, his companion, and the farmer, who sold coins to tourists.

1993–4   21 Roman bronze coins from the 4thC AD found in a field by Derek Myers (M/D). The coins, later declared treasure trove, are part of the Haxby Hoard found earlier. Between 1996 and 1998 Derek found 44 more billon coins from emperors ranging from AD 307 to 361. Some of the coins found after the Treasure Act came into force in late 1996

were declared treasure trove and acquired by Yorkshire Museum. The remainder were returned to the finder.

Yorkshire Museum

HEADINGLEY, LEEDS

1846   1st and 2ndC AD Roman coins found in an earthenware vessel by workmen building a house on the ridge of the hill above Battyewood. The workmen broke the pot and disposed of most of the coins; only 7 copper-alloy coins were recovered.

HEDDON-ON-THE-WALL, NORTHUMBERLAND

1752   About 3,000 Roman copper coins, well preserved and from the 4thC AD, found in decayed wooden boxes by road builders in the ruins of Hadrian's Wall.

HENSHAW, NORTHUMBERLAND

[date?]   Highly decorated Roman dragonesque brooch with the green and red enamelling from the 2ndC AD found at the site of a Romano-British settlement at Milking Gap. The brooch, 2in in diameter, was used to keep clothing fastened.

British Museum

HESLEYSIDE AREA, NORTHUMBERLAND

1854   257 silver pennies from the 14thC found in a bronze vessel on Shaw Moss, having, it is thought, been hidden in the troubled times between 1300 and 1320.

HESLINGTON, YORK

1966   2 billon and 2,798 bronze coins, including 1,640 copies, from the 4thC AD, found in a pot 3ft below ground level while digging the footings for a new building at York University, on the south-facing slope of Heslington Hill.

HEWORTH, GATESHEAD

1813   8th and 9thC Northumbrian stycas of Ecgfrith found in a small bi-conical pot at Chapel Yard.

HEXHAM, NORTHUMBERLAND

1832   About 10,000 gold and silver coins from the 6th to the 9thC AD found in the remains of a stone coffin by the sexton and his assistant while digging a grave in Hexham's Camp-Hill churchyard. The coffin was at a depth of 8ft and inside was a 10in-high brass bucket-shaped vessel containing the coins. Some coins were of Ethelred and other Saxon kings, and some dated to as early as AD 510. It is thought that as many as 2,000 coins disappeared before the authorities were informed of the find. Also in the coffin was an ancient helmet covering a skull. According to the *Newcastle Chronicle* of 21 October 1832, 'the helmet [was] more as a sort of crown with curious devices on it'. There are reports of another hoard of coins being found close by the church in 1841 but there are no specific details.

1800s   Anglo Saxon silver plaque from the 7th or 8thC AD. This may be a part of a reliquary or could have been for use in some other form of worship. The sheet has been etched with an image of a figure with a halo, and who appears to be holding a book with a cross on it.

British Museum

HICKLETON, DONCASTER

1946 15 silver coins, mainly Henry III short-cross silver pennies from 1230, found in the churchyard.

Doncaster Museum and Art Gallery

2001 350 Roman silver and 36 copper-alloy coins from the 1stC BC to the 2ndC AD, thought to have been deposited c. AD 180: finder M. Perry (M/D).

Doncaster Museum and Art Gallery

HIGH GREEN, KIRKLEES

2001 738 Roman base-silver radiates from the 3rdC AD, thought to have been deposited c. AD 274: finder M. Gennard (M/D).

HIGH HUNSLEY, EAST RIDING OF YORKSHIRE

1967 Late Bronze Age gold bracelet found by a farmer while ploughing.

HOLY ISLAND, NORTHUMBERLAND

1962 50 silver coins, thought to have been concealed in 1562.

HONLEY, KIRKLEES

1893 5 British silver coins of the Coritani, 13 silver and 5 copper Roman coins, and other small objects from the 1stC AD, found inside a hollowed-out ox bone, in a rock cavity by workmen breaking away the rock. Besides the coins there was a small bronze seal-box, a bronze bow fibula brooch with ring for attachment to a chain, and 2 small bronze rings. The 5 Coritani coins are held at the British Museum, the rest at the Tolson Museum, Huddersfield.

British Museum and Tolson Museum

HORNSEA, EAST RIDING OF YORKSHIRE

>1907 250 Roman copper coins from the 4thC AD found in the remains of a bag on the cliffs.

HOVINGHAM, NORTH YORKSHIRE

1980 44 Roman *siliquae* of AD 360–420. Initially 18 coins found by four boys throwing stones into a stream. Later local archaeologist Anthony Pacitto found a further 26 coins; they were all declared treasure trove. According to the *National Gazetteer* of 1868: 'There are three mineral springs, yielding respectively sulphurous, chalybeate, and clear water, near which a Roman bath, tesselated pavement, hypocaust, and coins of Antonine, &c., were found in 1745.'

HOW STEAN BECK, NORTH YORKSHIRE

1868 25 Roman *denarii* and 4 brass coins from the 1st and 2ndC AD found by two youths playing in the cavern known as Tom Taylor's Chamber, in How Stean Gorge.

HOWDEN AREA, EAST RIDING OF YORKSHIRE

1770 Roman coins found in several urns about 3 miles north-east of the village.

HUDDERSFIELD, KIRKLEES

1770 Roman coins found in several urns during digging for gravel.

HUSTHWAITE, NORTH YORKSHIRE

c. **1902** About 400 Roman copper coins from the 4thC AD found underneath a thick slab of stone, resting on another stone, by workmen digging a trench for water pipes. They appeared to have been buried in what was probably a leather bag and both it and the coins were in a poor state of preservation.

JARROW, SOUTH TYNESIDE

1980–1 Hoard of silver jewellery found by Terry Weightman, while digging a trench for leeks in his back garden. The hoard included a commemorative medal, a locket, a pocket watch, wrist watches, bangles and a ring, and appeared to have been delivered in some topsoil.

KILHAM, EAST RIDING OF YORKSHIRE

1998–9 Late 6th or early 7thC Anglo-Saxon highly decorated silver-gilt pyramidal strap-mount: finder Ian Bayles (M/D); returned to the finder.

KINGSTON UPON HULL

1909 9 silver coins from the 16th and 17thC, thought to have been concealed between 1625 and 1649.

1946 £600 in banknotes found in biscuit tin up a chimney by a lady when spring cleaning a bedroom of a house in Princes Avenue.

KINGSTON UPON HULL AREA

1979? Roman statuette found in a market garden.

KIRBY WISKE, NORTH YORKSHIRE

1985 30 gold and more than 1,500 silver coins from the 17thC found in an earthenware jug at Castle Farm, south of the village. Along with the coins were receipts for requisitioned provisions signed by the Deputy Provider General of the Royalist army at York. This hoard may well have been buried shortly after or during the siege of York in 1644.

KIRK DEIGHTON, NORTH YORKSHIRE

1998   14thC silver seal matrix, decorated with heraldic design: finder K. Jackson (M/D); valued at £625.

Royal Pump Room Museum

KIRK HAMMERTON AREA, NORTH YORKSHIRE

1984   105 silver coins found at a depth of about 6in on the edge of a pasture at Launde Farm. They are thought to be 12thC York short-cross silver pennies: finders Mr Roebuck and Mr West.

KIRKBURN, EAST RIDING OF YORKSHIRE

[date?]   A Celtic sword and scabbard from the 3rdC BC found in a grave during excavation. The sword is magnificently decorated and consists of 37 pieces of iron, bronze and horn, decorated with red glass. The scabbard is of polished bronze and is engraved and decorated with a scrollwork pattern as well as glass studs and insets. The scabbard showed signs of repairs made sometime before it was placed in the grave with the man who was its final (?) owner. The ritually buried man was aged around 30, and had three spears thrust into him after he was already dead. There was also a chariot found nearby that was buried with a man; two lynchpins from the chariot are also in the British Museum.

British Museum

KIRKLEATHAM, REDCAR AND CLEVELAND

1954   1,197 silver coins from the 16th and 17thC found in a pot, under a hedge in a field at Yearby Farm by the farm manager Charles Auty. He was ploughing when he spotted some silver coins in a furrow. Stopping his tractor he collected the hoard on what was close to the site of Turner's Hospital, founded in 1676. The coins were thought to have been concealed in 1697. This find is known as the Yearby Hoard.

Dorman Museum

LANCHESTER AREA, DURHAM

1891   Anglo-Saxon Sword, 4 scythes, and 8 axe heads found by a farmer fishing in Stanhope Burn near Hurbuck Farm. The site was just 2 miles north-west of the location of a Roman fort.

LANGDON BECK AREA, DURHAM

1944   13 Roman coins of Constantine from the 4thC AD found in a field by a ploughman.

Bowes Museum

LANGTOFT, EAST RIDING OF YORKSHIRE

2000   975 Roman coins (2 *denarii*, 575 radiates, and 398 folles) from the 3rd and 4thC AD found in a pot 1ft below the surface on farmland by Stephen Best, Jimmy Haley and Paul Rennoldson (M/D). They were

thought to have been deposited *c.* AD 305. Soon afterwards they found a second hoard about 15ft away from the first, containing 926 Roman folles of the family of Constantine the Great, struck in the early AD 320s, thought to have been deposited *c.* AD 325. Both hoards were later declared treasure trove. Yorkshire Museum kept 54 of the coins and the rest were sold at auction for £16,503.

Yorkshire Museum

LANGWITH, NORTH YORKSHIRE

1891   More than 6,000 Roman copper coins from the 4thC AD found in a large pot during ploughing.

LAYERTHORPE, YORK

1829   10th and 11thC Anglo-Saxon silver pennies.

LECONFIELD, EAST RIDING OF YORKSHIRE

1998   A fragment of a silver Thor's hammer pendant from the 10th or 11thC: finder S.K. Sansom; valued at £500.

British Museum

1999   Mid-17thC decorated and inscribed gold ring: finder S.K. Sansom (M/D); valued at £850.

LEEDS

1899   350 Roman copper coins from the 4th and 5thC AD found during the demolition of an old house.

1923   About 40 Roman copper coins from the 1stC AD found at 37 Thorpe Road, on the Middleton housing estate. A man digging in his garden found them, of which only one was legible, a copper *denarius* of Nero.

LONG FRAMLINGTON, NORTHUMBERLAND

1834   300 gold rose nobles of Edward III, Richard II and Henry IV (1327–1413) found in a medieval bronze pot, under a large hollow stone in a burnt-out wooden building, 50 yd south-west of the church. Today they could be worth £350,000–£400,000.

LONGHORSLEY, NORTHUMBERLAND

2003   Roman coins found by a detectorist.

MALTBY, ROTHERHAM

1978   3,496 (although some reports suggest 3,053) Roman copper and silver-dipped coins from the 3rdC AD found in a pot 1ft down by Peter O'Nion (a false name!) (M/D), 220yd from St Bartholomew's church. The coins, which were badly corroded, were found inside a brown earthenware pot. He took the hoard, undisturbed, to the local museum, where some of the coins were identified as Roman *antoniniani* from AD 250, thought to have been deposited in AD 282. The British Museum has acquired 33 coins, and the remainder are being bought by the local Clifton Park Museum.

British Museum and Clifton Park Museum

MALTBY AREA, ROTHERHAM

1979   56 Roman coins, possibly from the 3rd and 4thC AD, unearthed in some woods by James Rickett. Thought to have been deposited in AD 332, it is possible that these are part of a larger hoard in some kind of container that has yet to be found. The coins were declared treasure trove.

Clifton Park Museum

MALTON, NORTH YORKSHIRE

1863   12th and 13thC silver coins found in a Baluster jug. The coins were dispersed, but the jug, which dated the coins, was later advertised for sale.

MARR, DONCASTER

1949–52   79 Roman bronze *antoniniani* and 2 rings of silver or an alloy from the 3rdC AD found in a jar in woodland on Marr Thick.

Doncaster Museum

MARSKE, NORTH YORKSHIRE

1844   16th and 17thC silver coins, thought to have been concealed between 1561 and 1634.

MASHAM, NORTH YORKSHIRE

1951   19 gold coins from the 19thC, thought to have been concealed in 1869.

MIDDLEHAM, NORTH YORKSHIRE ▶ ▶ ▶ ▶ ▶ ▶ ▶ ▶ ▶

1985   A gold and sapphire pendant amulet dating from the reign of Richard III (1483–5), known as the Middleham Jewel, was found by Ted Seaton and two other detectorists on a bridle path 15in deep, and a few hundred yards from the castle. It was at first valued at £10,000–£15,000 but later sold to a private buyer for £1.43 million. He in turn sold it to the Yorkshire Museum for £2.5 million. The jewel is almost certainly a reliquary that may have once contained a fragment of wood reputed to come from the Cross, or some other artefact associated with Christ. The pendant was probably made between 1450 and 1475 and the use of the sapphire, a symbol of the splendour of heaven, is indicative of its religious status, which is endorsed by the inscription 'ecce agnus dei qui tollis peccata mundi miserere nobis tetragramaton ananizapta' (Behold, the Lamb of God, you who take away the sins of the world, have mercy on us! Tetragramaton Ananizapta), combining the words John the Baptist used when he baptised Jesus in the River Jordan with a medieval charm against epilepsy. It has been described as the finest piece of work by a 15thC English goldsmith. What makes the find even more remarkable is the luck of it all. Ted Seaton and his friends had effectively finished detecting for the day and were walking back to their cars, but Ted had not switched off his metal detector. He got a strong signal and on turning over the top of some grass roots he found the amulet.

1990 Late 14th or early 15thC inscribed silver ring found in a field at Park Farm, near Middleham Castle, during a metal-detecting rally: finders Bob Angus and Brian Snowden. The ring is believed to have belonged to a supporter of the Lancastrian kings, somewhere between the reigns of Henry IV and Henry VI. Initial estimates valued it in six figures, possibly inspired by the Middleham Jewel, but it eventually sold for £41,800, having been declared not treasure trove.

MIDDLESBROUGH

1935 27 silver coins from the 16thC, thought to have been concealed in 1569.

1954 Silver coins of Henry VIII, thought to have been concealed in 1544 or earlier.

MIDDRIDGE, DURHAM

1974 3,072 silver pennies and halfpennies of Edward I and II, and Irish, Scottish and continental coins from the 14thC found in a pot. It is thought they were concealed around the time of the Battle of Bannockburn in 1314 (between 1310 and 1315). 200 coins were retained by the Dorman Museum and the British Museum. The remainder were returned to the finder.

Dorman Museum and the British Museum

MILLINGTON, EAST RIDING OF YORKSHIRE

1845 Roman coins found about half a mile north-east of the town, together with Roman pavements, tiles, and other relics.

MINDRUM, NORTHUMBERLAND

1826 600 Roman *denarii*, in an excellent state of preservation, and from the 1st and 2ndC AD, found in a brass urn by a farmer.

MINSKIP, NORTH YORKSHIRE

c. **1886** Roman bronze coins found in an earthenware vessel by a farm worker during drainage operations. He took them away but they were later recovered.

MORPETH AREA, NORTHUMBERLAND

1862 Silver ingot found by drain-layers at Bothal Castle. Today the ingot would be worth around £20,000.

MYTHOLMROYD, CALDERDALE

1952 597 Roman silver or silver alloy *antoniniani* and fragments from the 3rdC AD found in a pot at Scout Rocks, Scout Wood, Mytholmroyd.

NETHERTON, KIRKLEES

1892 80 silver coins from the 16th and 17thC, thought to have been concealed in 1645.

NEVILLE'S CROSS AREA, DURHAM

1889 219 silver coins from the 14thC found in a small yellow glazed earthenware jug in woodland. A ruined cross commemorates a battle fought here in 1346 between the Scots under King David and the English in which the English archers inflicted heavy damage on the Scots and David was taken prisoner. The finder disposed of the coins to a silversmith in Durham and two private collectors; but when this was discovered, steps were taken to recover the hoard which were entirely successful. The coins were probably deposited *c.* 1377–80, and so are unlikely to be linked to the battle.

NEWCASTLE UPON TYNE

1771 1st and 2ndC AD Roman coins found close to where the Swing Bridge crosses the Tyne, which is near to the old Roman bridge.

1832 Coins of Edward III and Henry IV found in a tunnel during demolition of Anderson Place, which was built in 1580, on the site of a former nunnery.

1844 4 copper Scottish and French jettons from the 16th and 17thC.

1937 More than 300 gold coins from the 19th and 20thC, thought to have been concealed between 1901 and 1936.

NEWMINSTER, NORTHUMBERLAND

1925 472 silver coins, the majority of which were silver pennies of Edward I, from the 13th and 14thC; thought to have been concealed *c.* 1307.

NORHAM, NORTHUMBERLAND

1950 23 silver coins of Henry VII, thought to have been concealed in 1544 or earlier.

NORTHALLERTON, NORTH YORKSHIRE

1788 4th and 5thC AD Roman copper coins found in a large urn by a man digging a field close to the hills. The coins were in a good state of preservation and were so numerous that they got into circulation as farthings. They were known as 'Lawrie's farthings' after the man who discovered them.

NORTON, DONCASTER

1963   39 Roman *denarii* from the 1st and 2ndC AD found in a pot by workmen in soil that was being dumped from building excavations.

2000   13thC gold finger-ring set with a sapphire, known as a stirrup ring: finder J. Halliday (M/D).

Malton Museum

NUNBURNHOLME, EAST RIDING OF YORKSHIRE

1855   3,236 Roman copper *antoniniani* from the 3rdC AD found in a vessel by a farmer ploughing a field called Mead Hills (or Methill), about 3 miles from Pocklington. He gave them to Lord Muncaster, the owner of the land.

ORMESBY, REDCAR AND CLEVELAND

1838   Large quantities of gold and silver coins from the 16th and 17thC. This may have been two hoards, one of which may have been located in the grounds of the vicarage. The first hoard was from the reign of Henry VIII, thought to have been concealed between 1509 and 1544. The second hoard is thought to have been concealed between 1603 and 1625.

1999   A Bronze Age gold penannular ring found during archaeological excavation.

OTLEY, LEEDS

1999   16thC inscribed gold posy ring: finder Paul Mortimer (M/D); returned to the finder.

OULTON, LEEDS

1906   260 silver coins from the 16th and 17thC, thought to have been concealed between 1625 and 1649.

OUTCHESTER, NORTHUMBERLAND

1817   Over 1,000 silver pennies from the 12thC found on land belonging to Greenwich Hospital. It is thought that this hoard was concealed in 1170, at the time of the Barons' Revolt.

PIERCEBRIDGE, DARLINGTON

There are visible remains of the East Gate and the defences, courtyard building and part of an internal road of this Roman fort. It guarded the bridge, of which there are also some remains, and stands where Dere Street crossed the River Tees.

1974   130 Roman silver coins, *denarii* and *antoniniani*, possibly from 3rdC AD, thought to have been deposited *c.* AD 260–8, found in Kilngarth Field in the top of the flood bank at Piercebridge Beck. They were found during archaeological excavation, secreted behind a stone in the wall of the Roman civil settlement, in the vicinity of clay pits and quarries.

1979   6 Roman *denarii*, probably lost between AD 155 and 165 on the south bank of the River Tees, 30ft west of the modern bridge: finder Alan Clough (M/D); returned to the finder.

1981–2   Roman gold ring found in the bed of the river: finder Arnold Atkinson (M/D).

[date?]   Roman bronze statuette of a ploughman with a team of oxen about 3in in length.

PIERCEBRIDGE AREA, DARLINGTON

1921   About 250 Roman brass coins dated AD 254–379 found in an urn during ploughing on a farm 5 miles north of Piercebridge, about 18in below the surface.

PLOMPTON, NORTH YORKSHIRE

1994   Early to mid-17thC decorated silver seal matrix found by a metal detectorist; returned to the finder.

POCKLINGTON, EAST RIDING OF YORKSHIRE

c. **1880**   4thC AD Roman silver coins, in mint condition, found in a field. The farmer is said to have given them to his many sons.

2000   9thC Anglo-Saxon silver strap-end: finder B. Freeman (M/D).

Hull and East Riding Museum

POCKLINGTON AREA, EAST RIDING OF YORKSHIRE

1991   15thC iconographic ring, inscribed with the figure of a saint, found in a field by Les Hill (M/D); declared not treasure trove.

1991   Late 16thC posy ring found in a field by Les Walker (M/D). The inscribed gold band broke into three pieces while being repaired; declared not treasure trove.

PORTINGTON AREA, EAST RIDING OF YORKSHIRE

1814   About 100 well-preserved Roman coins from the 1st and 2ndC AD found in an urn in a lane near Portington.

PUDSEY, LEEDS

1775   About 100 Roman silver coins found hidden in a horse's thigh bone on Pudsey Common. A man clearing rubbish from a place called King Alfred's Camp, adjoining an old cave, found the bone, in the cavity of which were the coins, many of which pre-dated Julius Caesar.

RAMSHAW FELL, NORTHUMBERLAND

1762   A large quantity of silver pennies, possibly from the 14thC found among rocks.

RICHMOND, NORTH YORKSHIRE

1720   About 600 Roman silver coins and a silver instrument from the 4th and 5thC AD found while digging on the steep slope between the castle and the River Swale. The silver object was thought to be a ladle or an instrument of sacrifice.

c. **1867**   14 Roman coins from the 1stC AD found at Gillingwood Hall.

RIEVAULX ABBEY, NORTH YORKSHIRE

1920s   A gold crucifix and two caskets, probably for saints' relics, found during renovations at the Cistercian establishment beneath some tumbled-down masonry. Close by, some lead ingots were found carrying the impressed stamp of Henry VIII.

RIPON, NORTH YORKSHIRE

2000   Gold penannular ring of 1150–750 BC found by Norman Smith (M/D), 2in below the surface in a field on farmland. It was a Celtic money ring that was used as currency before the introduction of struck coinage. It was declared not treasure trove and returned to the finder, who donated it to Ripon Cathedral.

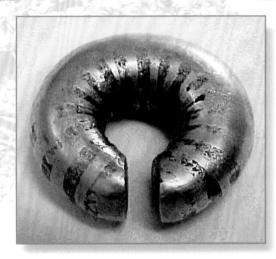

RIPON AREA, NORTH YORKSHIRE

1992   200 coins, mainly silver sixpences, shillings and half-crowns, of Elizabeth I, James I and Charles I, found by workmen while renovating a cottage in a village near Ripon.

ROTHERHAM AREA

1939   43 Anglo-Saxon and Norman coins from the 11thC, thought to have been buried in 1069. The finders attempted to keep their discovery from the authorities, but police recovered 32 of the coins, 20 of which went to Rotherham Museum, and the remainder to the British Museum.
Clifton Park Museum and British Museum

1984   Gold torc from the 1stC AD found on a public footpath in a small wood by James Rickett (M/D).

1985   183 Roman coins and a silver stater.

RUDCHESTER, NORTHUMBERLAND

1776   More than 16 gold and 500 silver Roman coins from the 1st and 2ndC AD found in a small urn near Rudchester Burn by two labourers digging up the foundations of an old fence. They sold some of the coins in Newcastle before the landowner heard about it and claimed them; he recovered 16 gold and 500 silver coins. He in turn was forced to surrender them to the Duke of Northumberland after the duke initiated legal proceedings.

SCARBOROUGH, NORTH YORKSHIRE

1907   About 320 forged copper farthings from the 17thC found in the castle, having probably been concealed between 1625 and 1649.

1967–8   Bronze Age gold ring from 1000 BC found by a lady digging her garden. She kept it and forgot all about it until in 1981 she decided to take it to a jeweller, who advised her to take it to the Yorkshire Museum. Having had it identified, she gave it on permanent loan to the Rotunda Museum
Rotunda Museum

SCOTTON, NORTH YORKSHIRE

1924   310 silver coins, mainly silver pennies of Edward I (1272–1307), thought to have been buried after 1324; returned to the finder.

SEATON CAREW, HARTLEPOOL

1867   Spanish gold coins dated 1720–1804 found on the beach after a bad storm cleared much of the sand from the shore. Two labourers saw what looked like a mass of black washers, which turned out to be Spanish gold dollars and gold dubloons. Over the next two days thousands of coins and a gold ingot were recovered. 110 years later, after another storm, dozens of gold coins were again found on the beach.

SETTLE, NORTH YORKSHIRE

1958   4 gold coins from the 19thC, thought to have been concealed in 1879.

SEWINGSHIELDS CRAGS, NORTHUMBERLAND

[date?]   Bronze wheel brooch from the 2ndC AD, decorated around the outside edge with pale blue and red enamelled squares, found among the rubbish in a turret on Hadrian's Wall between Housesteads fort and Sewingshields Crags. A little over 1¼in in diameter, it was used to fasten clothing.

SHEFFIELD

1854   48 Roman silver coins from the 1st and 2ndC AD found by labourers digging for clay on a brickfield at Hall Carr or Holme Carr, on the north bank of the River Don.

1860   Between 100 and 1,000 Roman brass coins from the 1st and 2ndC AD found in a jar by a workman just below the surface in a brickfield between Cricket Road Park and the railway line. The coins were distributed by the finders.

1891   19 Roman coins and an inlaid brooch from the 1st and 2ndC AD found by workmen under a flat stone in the 'Roman Rig' linear earthworks (in the centre of the bank of the dyke) while building the railway. The finders dispersed the coins.

1906   About 40 Roman silver coins from the 1st and 2ndC AD found 2½ft below the surface by men working on the Duke of Norfolk's land off Scotts Road, Pitsmoor. Some were sold, or given away, or exchanged for beer; 35 *denarii* were recovered.

1913   3 gold and 100 silver coins from the 16th and 17thC, thought to have been concealed between 1603 and 1625.

100

1949   16 copper tokens/jettons from the 16th and 17thC.

1980   10 Victoria gold sovereigns and half-sovereigns, from 1843 to 1872, found by four workmen on a building site in Freedom Street. They were later returned to the men, by permission of the British Museum, as a reward for their honesty.

SHIPLEY, YORKSHIRE

1899   Several hundred Roman silver coins found in a quarry near Catstones Wood.

SILSDEN, BRADFORD

1998   27 Iron Age gold staters, mostly of Cunobelin, and a Roman iron finger-ring with an intaglio of a standing figure from the 1stC BC to the 1stC AD: finder J. Walbank. They were thought to have been deposited about AD 40, were declared treasure trove, and valued at £10,000.
Cliffe Castle Museum, Keighley

SKIPSEA, EAST RIDING OF YORKSHIRE

Early 1970s   A Roman silver trumpet brooch from the 2ndC AD, on the beach: finder P. Alcock (M/D); returned to the finder.

2001   A 14thC gold brooch, in the shape of a heart: finder Jack Cooper (M/D).

SKIPTON AREA, NORTH YORKSHIRE

1949   373 silver coins, mainly pennies of Edward I from the 14thC, found in a tall, slender, earthenware water jug; they were thought to have been concealed after 1399. 203 of the coins were selected by museums: 20 went to Ripon Museum and others to York Museum and the British Museum; the remainder were returned to the finder.

SNAPE, NORTH YORKSHIRE

1999   A 15thC gold finger-ring: finder Darren Thompson (M/D). It was engraved with the figures of saints and valued at £800.

SOUTH SHIELDS, SOUTH TYNESIDE

The Romans built a major fort (called Arbeia) on a hill overlooking the river mouth.

1778   Large quantity of gold and silver coins from the 16th and 17thC found in ballast brought from the River Thames. They were thought to have been concealed between 1561 and 1603.

1874–84   12 Roman billon folles, thought to have been concealed c. AD 300. 59 Roman billon coins, Constantinian folles, thought to have been concealed c. AD 329. 19 Roman billon coins, thought to have been concealed c. AD 353. These were all found during archaeological excavations.

1878   10 Roman gold coins and 200–300 silver coins from the 1st and 2ndC AD found by a labourer excavating in Fisher Street, near the site of a Roman station.

1878   12 *aurei* from Nero to Antoninus Pius and more than 120 *denarii* from Nero to Commodus (2ndC AD) found during archaeological excavation. They were thought to have been concealed c. AD 185 or later.

1954   20 gold coins from the 20thC, thought to have been concealed in 1913.

1976   More than 1 gold coin from the 4thC AD found during building work; they were thought to have been concealed c. AD 388.

1977   44 Roman billon coins from the 3rdC AD found during excavation. 13 were *antoniniani* from Gallienus to Tetricus. The other 31 were radiate copies; they were thought to have been concealed c. AD 273.

[date?]   A Roman helmet cheek piece made from copper-alloy with a figure of Dioscurus with horse.
Museum of Antiquities, Newcastle

SPITTAL, NORTHUMBERLAND

1886   More than 100 silver coins, possibly from the 17th and 18thC, thought to have been concealed in 1797.

SPOFFORTH, NORTH YORKSHIRE

1998   9thC Anglo-Saxon highly decorated silver hooked clasp and pinhead fragment: finder G.P. Stebbins (M/D).
Royal Pump Rooms Museum

SPROTBOROUGH, DONCASTER

1980 638 Roman copper coins from the 3rdC AD found in a pot by a metal detectorist in woodland known as Sprotborough Plantation, about 3 miles south-west of Doncaster.

STANHOPE AREA, DURHAM

1843–72 Large hoard of Bronze Age artefacts, including 8 bronze rings, 6 bronze cylinders, spearheads, knives, axes, bracelets, brooches, necklaces, a bronze cauldron, a gold ring and many other items of 1150–800 BC, found at Heathery Burn cave during quarrying operations. They are preserved as the Heathery Burn Collection in the British Museum.

British Museum

STANLEY, DURHAM

1956 14 silver coins of Henry VII, thought to have been concealed in 1544 or earlier.

STANLEY, WAKEFIELD

1905 7,198 Roman copper coins from the 4thC AD found in a vase by a farmer walking behind his horse-drawn plough at Smalley Bight Farm. He spotted the top of an urn in the bottom of a furrow less than 2ft below the surface.

STANWICK, NORTH YORKSHIRE

[date?] Bronze Age horse mask made from bronze from the late 1stC BC to the 1stC AD found during excavation of Iron Age earthworks. Possibly a fitting from a chariot.

British Museum

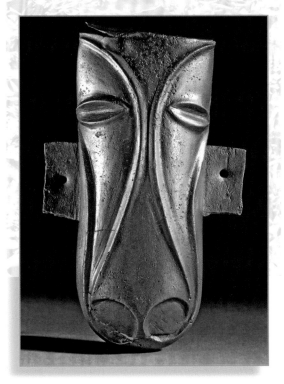

STOCKTON-ON-TEES

1792 More than 840 16th and 17thC silver coins, which could have been concealed between 1685 and 1689, or possibly deposited in 1644.

SUNDERLAND

1979 Bronze Age burial urn found near a pond.

SUNDERLAND AREA

1982–3 50 gold sovereigns dated 1844–94 found by handyman George Fairley in a cloth bag, behind a false ceiling in a cottage. They were declared treasure trove.

British Museum

SUTTON-ON-THE-FOREST, NORTH YORKSHIRE

1999 17thC inscribed gold posy ring: finder Robin Sykes (M/D); returned to the finder.

2000 Mid- to late 9thC Anglo-Saxon gold fitting, possibly a strap-end: finder Robin Sykes (M/D). The fitting is in the form of an animal head, with protruding eyes of cut glass and blue glass studs. It is decorated with filigree wirework and, while its use remains a mystery, it does have similarities to the Alfred Jewel. It was declared treasure trove.

Yorkshire Museum

SUTTON UPON DERWENT, EAST RIDING OF YORKSHIRE

1998 A late 2nd or 3rdC AD Roman gold earring was found by archaeologists working on the Humber Wetlands project.

Hull and East Riding Museum

SWINE, EAST RIDING OF YORKSHIRE

1826 14,000–15,000 well-preserved 4thC AD Roman copper coins found in an urn by boys playing in a newly ploughed field near the earthworks. Many coins were dispersed by the finders.

1940 28 Roman *denarii* and 24 brass coins from the 1st and 2ndC AD found in a field.

1964 3,000 Roman copper coins of AD 320–35 found in a pot on the farm of F.H. Johnson.

Hull and East Riding Museum

SWINTON, ROTHERHAM

1853 300–400 Roman *denarii* from the 1st to the 3rdC AD found while excavating for a cellar of a new house. The site is where the Roman road passed from Templeborough to Castleford.

TADCASTER, NORTH YORKSHIRE

1982 A 14thC silver spoon found in a field.

TEMPLE NEWSAM, LEEDS

1959   216 silver coins from the 16th and 17thC, thought to have been concealed in 1641.

TEMPLEBOROUGH, SHEFFIELD

1828   1,600 Roman copper coins from the 4th and 5thC AD found in a jar on Guilthwaite Common.

1916–17   19 silver Roman coins from the 1st and 2ndC AD found a foot below the surface during excavation of the Roman fort.

Clifton Park Museum

THORNHILL, KIRKLEES

1938   27 Roman silver coins from the 1st and 2ndC AD found under a large rough stone at Overthorpe.

THORPE-ON-THE-HILL, LEEDS

1902   11 Roman *denarii* and 8 brass coins from the 1st and 2ndC AD found by workmen 18in below the surface, while preparing to move some rock with a crane. Some were disposed of, but 19 were secured.

THORPE WILLOUGHBY, NORTH YORKSHIRE

1939   1 gold and 2,678 silver coins from the 16th and 17thC found at Thorpe Hall; thought to have been concealed in 1641.

THROAPHAM, ROTHERHAM

1864   1,500–2,000 Roman copper coins from the 3rdC AD found in two vases during the ploughing of a field called the Leys, adjoining the road from St John's to Dinnington. About half of the coins were dispersed by the finders; those that remained were *antoniniani*, with a few *denarii*.

THROCKLEY, NEWCASTLE UPON TYNE

1879   A hoard of over 5,000 Roman silvered *antoniniani* of AD 260–70 found in a pot, 4ft deep, during the laying of water pipes at Throckley Bank Top, near Hadrian's Wall. The site is midway between the Roman station of Condercum (Benwell) and Vindobala (Rudchester). A few coins were dispersed by the finder, but 5,024 were recovered.

THURSTONLAND, KIRKLEES

1838   600–800 Roman copper and a few silver coins from the 3rdC AD found by a man digging in a field at Winstance, not far from Thurstonland. They were dispersed throughout the neighbourhood but 64 *antoniniani* and 1 *denarius* were later retrieved.

ULLESKELF, YORKSHIRE

1846   Several thousand 9thC stycas of the Northumbrian kings found by a labourer in a field, together with fragments of leather, dated AD 865.

> ### STYCAS
> By the end of the 7thC, small silver coins known as sceats were the principal means of exchange. In Northumbria these coins were known as stycas and were more often as not struck in a debased metal because of a lack of silver in the region. By the end of the 8thC, sceats and stycas were replaced by silver pennies.

UPTON, EAST RIDING OF YORKSHIRE

1927   303 Roman *antoniniani* coins from the 3rdC AD found in a pot by a man digging in a field at Walton Wood Farm.

WAKEFIELD

1812   5,000–6,000 Roman copper coins from the 4thC AD found in a vessel in a field about 100yd to the left of the road from Wakefield to York. It was said that there were upwards of 40lb of coins and they were sold to local people. About 2lb of coins were melted down by one of the purchasers. The find was about a mile from Lingwood Gate, the site of a Roman station.

1980   A quantity of various coins and other objects, found in an old tin can in a garage. The finder gave the 5 Roman coins, an Elizabeth I silver half-crown (1635), an eighth of a farthing, a penny-weight, and some temperance society medals to a coin collector friend.

WALLSEND, NORTH TYNESIDE

1895   14 Roman *denarii* of Vespasian, Domitian and Trajan, thought to have been concealed *c*. AD 100, found during excavations of the Roman fort (Segedunum).

WARMSWORTH, DONCASTER

1999   122 silver coins of Elizabeth I, James I and Charles I found in pots while excavating the foundations of a new house. They were thought to have been deposited *c*. 1635.

WASHINGTON, SUNDERLAND

1939   4thC AD Roman copper coins found in a pot by a man digging a hole to build an air-raid shelter. 59 cententionales, in a good state of preservation, were eventually recovered; they were thought to have been deposited *c*. AD 335.

WEIGHTON LOCK AREA, EAST RIDING OF YORKSHIRE

1963   Small hoard of Roman jewellery found on the banks of the River Humber.

WENSLEYDALE, NORTH YORKSHIRE

1832   1,100 Roman bronze coins from the 3rdC AD found in an urn by a girl digging in a potato patch; they were well preserved.

1909   236 silver coins from the 16th and 17thC found at Constable Burton; thought to have been concealed in 1641.

WEST WHELPINGTON, NORTHUMBERLAND

1976   5 silver pennies of Edward I dated 1272–1307 found in the wall of a barn. It is thought they were concealed *c.* 1310 or possibly later. By 1720 West Whelpington was a deserted medieval village that had been destroyed by quarrying.

WESTGATE IN WEARDALE, DURHAM

1870   15 Roman silver coins from the 1st and 2ndC AD found in a pot, near the castle. Other coins were found close by, as well as a ring with a stone symbolising Cleopatra and the asp.

1983   9 Roman *denarii* from the 1st and 2ndC AD found; declared treasure trove.

Bowes Museum, Barnard Castle

WHITBURN, SOUTH TYNESIDE

>1704   3rd and 4thC AD Roman copper coins found in sand by boys throwing stones. Reports spoke of 'a peckful', and said that they were 'as fresh as if they were new coins'.

1777   A large quantity of silver coins from the 16th and 17thC found, thought to have been concealed between 1625 and 1649.

WHITLEY BAY, NORTH TYNESIDE

1981   18 half-crowns, 244 halfpennies, and foreign coins from the 19th and 20thC found on the beach near St Mary's Lighthouse by Denzil Webb (M/D). The hoard was located at the extreme north end of the beach near a flight of steps leading to Curry's Point. Most of the foreign coins were from Commonwealth countries, while the earliest British half-crowns were dated 1947.

WHITTINGHAM, NORTHUMBERLAND

1880   2 Bronze Age swords and 3 leaf-shaped spearheads from *c.* 500 BC found by men draining a boggy patch of land at Thrunton Farm. All 5 pieces were bronze and in near-perfect condition.

WHITTONSTALL, NORTHUMBERLAND

1958   About 1,200 silver coins from the 13th and 14thC found by a man clearing the site for a police office beside the Corbridge to Ebchester Road. His spade hit a corroded metal container and as he picked it up it fell to pieces to reveal 5 or 6 rows of neatly stacked coins. The hoard was made up of almost 1,150 silver pennies of Edward I and II, 13 coins minted in Dublin or Waterford for Edward I, 42 Scottish coins of Alexander III and John Balliol, and 5 continental coins. They were believed to have been buried *c.* 1333, at the time of the Battle of Halidon Hill. The coins were declared treasure trove.

WHORLTON, NORTH YORKSHIRE

1810   Many thousands of Roman *siliquae* from the 4th and 5thC AD found in a vase with 3 silver rings, silver bars, a fragment of sheet silver, and 2 copper-alloy rings by a man ploughing on Whorle Hill. Only 38 coins have survived from the hoard, thought to have been concealed *c.* AD 415.

WILBERFOSS, EAST RIDING OF YORKSHIRE

2001   A 16th or early 17thC decorated gold posy ring: finder Michael Dobson (M/D).

British Museum

2002   9th or 10thC Viking silver ring found on farmland, about 1ft below the surface: finder Peter Birkett; later declared treasure trove.

WILTON, NORTH YORKSHIRE

1856   About 80 Roman silver coins from the 4th and 5thC AD found in a silver vessel during ploughing near the ice-house at the castle.

WISTOW, NORTH YORKSHIRE

1943   119 silver coins from the 16th and 17thC, thought to have been concealed in 1611.

WOMERSLEY, NORTH YORKSHIRE

[date?]   A mid-7thC gold pendant, inset with stylised boar's head and garnets.

WORTLEY, LEEDS

1992   76 Roman silver coins from *c.* AD 148 found in a field by Roy Oates (M/D).

2001   288 Roman bronze coins from the 3rdC AD found in a field by Michael Gennard (M/D); later declared treasure trove.

2002   449 Roman bronze coins from the 3rdC AD found in a field by Michael Gennard (M/D); later declared treasure trove.

WYKE AREA, BRADFORD

1700s   Hoard of gold coins of Elizabeth I, Mary, James I and Charles I found in a large earthenware jar by a man ploughing at Woodside Farm, north of Wyke. He reported the fact to the landowner Edward Rookes Leedes, who was so impressed with the man's honesty that he gave him land and built him a house. It is thought the coins were buried during the Civil War by a Royalist called Rookes, an ancestor of Leedes, when things went against the king.

1836   About 2,000 silver coins from the 14thC found, believed to have been concealed shortly after 1321, when Robert the Bruce's Scots army was harrying Northumberland and North Yorkshire.

1982   700 coins from the Civil War period found in a pot in woodland near the village. A few weeks later the same man found another 1,000 coins and another pot.

1985   26 silver shillings and sixpences of Elizabeth I, James I and Charles I found in woodland by Colin Garner and Paul Drake (M/D).

YEARBY, REDCAR AND CLEVELAND

1962   More than 250 Georgian bronze coins from the 17thC, thought to have been concealed in 1694. They may be related to the Kirkleatham find, which is also known as the Yearby Hoard.

YORK

George VI said, 'The history of York is the history of England.' After the Roman invasion, York became a garrison town, covering 50 acres, with 6,000 soldiers based there; and soon Eboracum, a civilian town, grew up alongside the military base. When the Romans withdrew in about AD 400, York became Eoforwic, the centre of the kingdom of Northumbria. In 866 Eoforwic was overrun by the Vikings and became Jorvik. The town then settled into a more peaceful existence until King Eadred of Wessex drove out the last Viking ruler of York, Eric Bloodaxe, in 954. William the Conqueror went to York in 1069 to suppress the northern rebellion and over the next three centuries York grew and became the country's second city and capital of northern England. Later it suffered with the decline of the wool industry, the Wars of the Roses and the dissolution of the monasteries, before seeing a revival under Elizabeth I. When Charles I set up court in York (he left in 1642), things were flourishing. After the outbreak of the Civil War, York came under siege in 1844 and saw many of its buildings destroyed. From 1688 onwards York grew into the modern-day city aided in no small measure by the arrival of the railway in 1839.

1704   250 Norman silver pennies from the 11thC found in a small oak box in High Ousegate. They are believed to be dated about 1069–70, probably linked to William's harrying of the North.

1840   About 244 Roman silver coins from the 1stC BC to the 3rdC AD found in a pot on the site of a house erected for the Secretary of the North Eastern Railway.

1842   10,000 Celtic stycas from *c.* AD 865 found at St Leonard's Place.

1845   600 Anglo-Saxon and Norman silver pennies found with no apparent container at the Jubbergate. They were thought to have been concealed *c.* 1069–70, when William I was harrying the North.

1849   1 silver and an unknown quantity of billon coins from the 16th and 17thC found at Lamel Hill. They were thought to have been concealed between 1625 and 1649.

1856   More than 105 Danish silver coins from the 10thC found at Walmgate.

c. **1868**   About 200 Roman *denarii* from the 1st to the 3rdC AD found near Foss Island; all dispersed by the finders.

1882   More than 25 Anglo-Saxon and Norman silver pennies from the late 11thC found in a pottery crucible in the Bishophill area of the city. They were thought to have been loot from the harrying of Northampton in 1065.

1896   163 silver pennies from the 15thC, concealed after 1480, found in the Bootham Stray area of the city.

1898   Almost 200 Roman silver coins from the 1st and 2ndC AD found in a jar in Railway Street.

1930   30 Roman silver coins from the 2ndC AD, thought to have been concealed in AD 155, found by men working on the new Parcels Office near the station. They divided the finds among themselves but some were retrieved and are now in the museum.

Yorkshire Museum

1953   903 silver pennies, buried *c.* 1320, found in a bronze vessel in the Bootham Stray area of the city.

1954   110 copper coins from the 18th and 19thC found at Wath upon Dearn, thought to have been concealed between 1760 and 1816.

1975   34 *denarii* of Vespasian in the 1stC AD discovered during archaeological excavations. They were found in the Praetentura of the legionary fortress, in Blake Street.

1982   8thC Anglo-Saxon helmet found on a building site for a shopping centre. Andrew Shaw was using a mechanical digger to remove clay when he came upon the helmet which was made of iron and bronze. It was valued by the British Museum at £500,000, which prompted the finder to seek a bigger award than the £50 he had been given. He failed after incurring legal costs of £200.

1983   Anglo-Saxon sword pommel, decorated with silver, found by Edward Ross while planting marrows in his back garden. The sword would have been owned by a warrior of noble rank. It was declared not treasure trove and returned to the finder.

[date?]   Norman silver pennies concealed *c.* 1070 found near York Minster.

YORK AREA

>1692 More than 100 Roman copper coins from the 3rd and 4thC AD.

1992 812 silver pennies, groats and half-groats, and seven Belgian pattards from the 15thC, found in a pot 2ft down in a leek field by Stephen Pickles (M/D).

1998 A suite of mid to late 9thC Anglo-Saxon highly decorated silver and niello strap-ends: finders M.F. White, T. Garaghan, M. Brookes and J. Fieldson, during a metal-detecting rally; valued at £18,000.

Yorkshire Museum

1999 8th or 9thC Anglo-Saxon silver dress pin found by P.R. Ireland (M/D); returned to the finder.

1999 9thC Anglo-Saxon silver strap-end found by a detectorist; valued at £1,500.

Yorkshire Museum

2000 9thC Anglo-Saxon silver brooch pendant fragment found by a detectorist.

Yorkshire Museum

YORKSHIRE

1800s 226 silver half-crowns of James I and Charles I dated 1625–45 found during the demolition of a house. They were thought to have been concealed after 1645.

1850 161 silver coins from the 16th and 17thC, thought to have been concealed in 1643.

1977 Gold stater of the Coritani tribe found in a market garden by Victoria Cumberland after a storm had disturbed the soil. It was sold at Christie's in London for £1,100 (£4,200 today).

1996 39 Saxon silver pennies comprising a coin of Eadmund, of Eadred, 8 of Eadwig, and 28 of Eadgar, spanning the years AD 939–75, were found by Ennis Brain and another detectorist in a field on farmland.

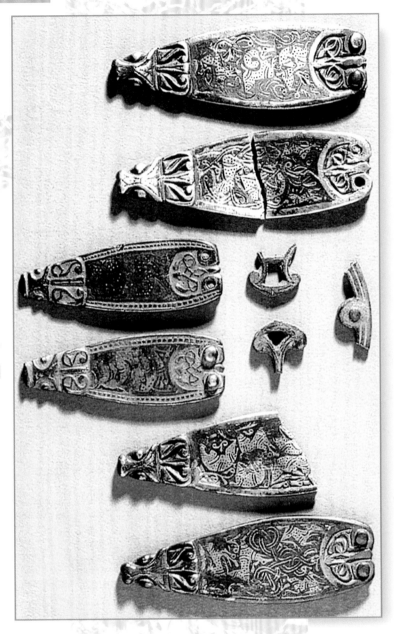

EAST RIDING OF YORKSHIRE

1990s 22–3 Iron Age gold staters of the Corieltauvi: finders Messrs Thompson and Cooper (M/D). Found at a depth of 3–4in over an area in excess of half an acre.

NORTH YORKSHIRE (NORTH)

1980–1 Tudor gold George noble identified by Sotheby's after a man took a box of coins to the auction house for identification. The coins had been given to the man when he was a schoolboy; the noble was sold for £13,000 (the equivalent of over £30,000 today).

he region is similar to the North-East of England with large areas of urban development dating from the industrial revolution as well as spectacular open country-side that includes the mountains and fells of the Lake District. Like Northumberland, Cumbria has yielded many discoveries associated with border wars and armies raiding back and forth between England and Scotland.

Further south, a series of finds made at Congleton, Cheshire, in 1992 illustrates one of the basic principles of metal detecting – never assume you have found everything at the first attempt. A detectorist discovered 1,144 silver coins dating from the 16th and 17th centuries; a week later in the same field he found another 791 coins and after a month a further 1,474. At Cuerdale, near Preston, in 1840 a hoard of over 7,000 silver coins associated with the Viking raids was unearthed. It included Anglo-Saxon and Danelaw issues, Frankish coins, some from Scandinavia, Islamic dirhams and a single Byzantine coin. There are frequent finds of coins minted in Scotland before the union of the crowns, which provide evidence of cross-border raids as well as trade. Coins tell you much more than just the wealth of a former owner.

At Rushton in Cheshire a 400-year-old gold finger-ring with an enamelled skull was found bearing the inscription *Hodie mihi cras tibi* – 'Today it is me but tomorrow it will be you'. It could easily be the motto for the modern detectorist with 'mine' and 'yours' substituted for 'me' and 'you'.

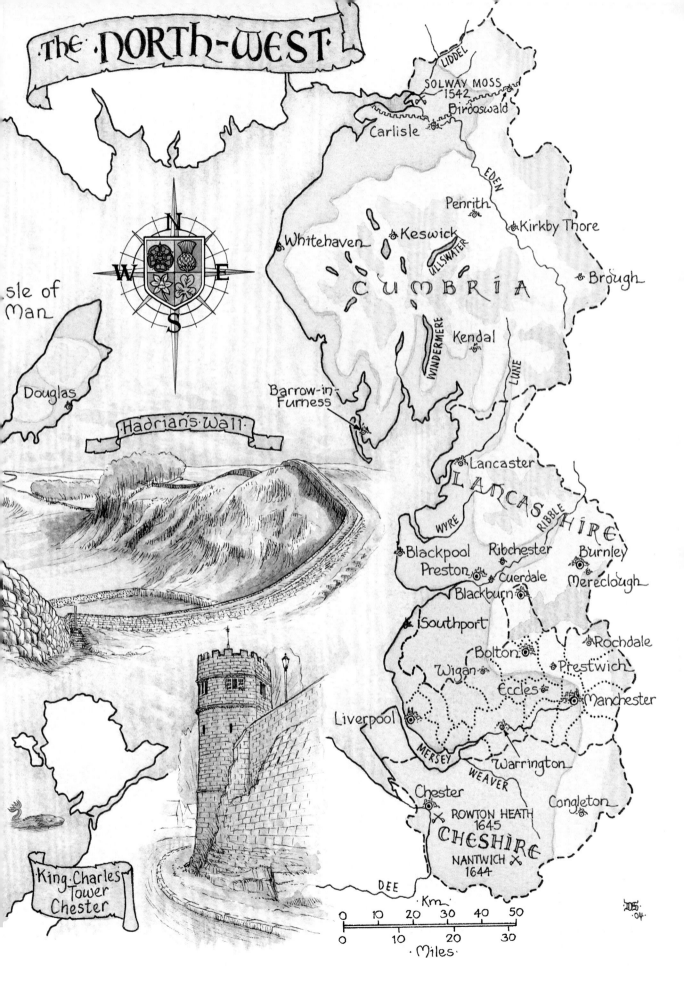

The NORTH-WEST

Isle of Man

Douglas

Hadrian's Wall

King Charles' Tower Chester

LIDDEL

SOLWAY MOSS 1542

Birdoswald

Carlisle

EDEN

Penrith

Keswick

Kirkby Thore

Whitehaven

ULLSWATER

Brough

CUMBRIA

WINDERMERE

Kendal

LUNE

Barrow-in-Furness

Lancaster

LANCASHIRE

WYRE

RIBBLE

Blackpool

Ribchester

Burnley

Preston

Cuerdale

Mereclough

Blackburn

Southport

Rochdale

Bolton

Prestwich

Wigan

Eccles

Manchester

Liverpool

Warrington

MERSEY

WEAVER

Chester

Congleton

ROWTON HEATH 1645

CHESHIRE

NANTWICH 1644

DEE

Km

0   10   20   30   40   50

0   10   20   30

Miles

JDS 04

ACTON, CHESHIRE

1939 More than 2,000 Henry II silver pennies dated 1154–89 found by men digging a drainage trench at a factory. They first thought they were old pig tags used by farmers, and threw them back; experts identified them from the few the workmen kept.

1984 Extremely rare 8thC BC Bronze Age gold bangle found by David Stubbs (M/D) at a depth of 6in on farmland. The 22-carat bangle was dated 750 BC. Later declared not treasure trove and returned to the finder.

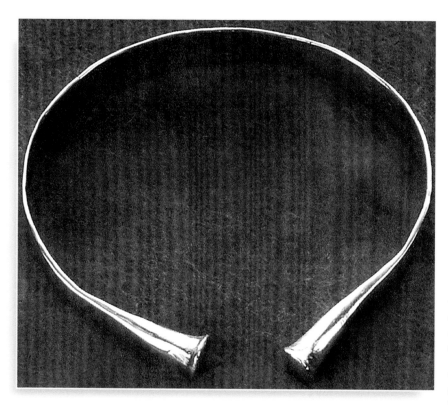

ADLINGTON, CHESHIRE

1925 20 Roman silver coins from the 1st and 2ndC AD, in a decomposed leather bag, dug up in a garden.

AGDEN, WARRINGTON

1957 Almost 2,500 Roman bronze coins dated AD 253–74 found on farmland.

Grosvenor Museum

Early 1980s 52 Roman bronze coins from the 3rdC AD found, stragglers from the 1957 find.

AINSWORTH AREA, BURY

1822 14th and 15thC gold coins and 60 silver coins, thought to have been deposited after 1413, found inside a cow's horn on Cockey Moor, which is east of the village and adjacent to Watling Street.

ALDERLEY EDGE, CHESHIRE

1980s–90s Bronze Age palstave found by John Laverack, a man involved in the Alderley Edge Archeological Project. A 19thC mining hammer and 4thC AD Roman coins were also found at Pot Shaft.

AMBLESIDE, CUMBRIA

[date?] 2nd and 3rdC AD Roman silver coins found in a pot at a quarry under Gilbert Scar.

ARNSIDE, CUMBRIA

2000–1 An 8thC bronze bowl mount in the form of a human face, made in Ireland. The bowl is decorated with traces of inlaid yellow enamel on a red background. It was originally one of a set which would have included a second inverted head. Similar examples have been found at some Viking ship burial sites.

BARTON UPON IRWELL, SALFORD

1880 109 silver coins from the 16th and 17thC found at Barton Old Hall; thought to have been concealed in 1645.

BEAUMONT, CUMBRIA

1855 1,100 Roman bronze coins from the 4thC found in an earthenware vase south of Hainings Farm. Thought to have been deposited c. AD 323.

1884 About 2,090 silver coins, including silver groats, half-groats and foreign coins; believed to have been buried in 1360.

1976 4thC AD Roman coins, thought to have been deposited c. AD 323.

1977 223 Roman billon coins from the 4thC AD found south of Hainings Farm.

BEETHAM, CUMBRIA

1834 About 100 coins from the reigns of Edward the Confessor, William I and William II found at the base of a pillar in the Church of St Michael and All Saints during reconstruction work.

BIRDOSWALD, HADRIAN'S WALL, CUMBRIA

This fort was known to the Romans as Banna and it guarded the bridge over the River Irthing. Covering 5 acres, the garrison would have housed around 500 men, possibly including 300 cavalry. Birdoswald was, according to legend, the site of King Arthur's last battle.

BLACKBURN AREA, BLACKBURN WITH DARWEN

1804   Gold and silver coins dated 1660–1702 found in a large purse hidden between the thatch and wall of a cottage, between Whalley and Hibchester. The purse contained 5 smaller purses containing gold sovereigns, crowns and half-crown pieces of Charles II, James II, William and Mary and Queen Anne. They were thought to have been hidden in 1715, the year of the 'Preston Fight', when rebel supporters of James Stuart were surrounded by a smaller cavalry force of the king's men and tamely surrendered.

2001   15thC silver-gilt finger-ring: finder S. Smith (M/D); the bezel was formed of two joined hands.

BOOTHSTOWN, SALFORD

1947   540 Roman *antoniniani*, a few fragments, and a few beads from the 3rdC AD, found in 2 pots in the grounds of the Garden Canneries in Boothstown.

BOWNESS-ON-SOLWAY, CUMBRIA

1580–86   More than 15 Roman coins from the 2ndC AD found under an inscribed flagstone by a rector while digging his garden. During 20thC excavations at the Roman fort, the second largest on Hadrian's Wall, a number of coins have been found, including some of Hadrian, Crispina, Domitian, Trajan, Postumus and Gratian.

BOWNESS-ON-SOLWAY AREA, CUMBRIA

1884   22 silver English and Scottish pennies of Edward I and Alexander III, all dated prior to 1280, found on the roadside between Bowness and Wigton. It was thought they had dropped from a cart laden with soil taken from the foreshore.

BRAYSTONES, CUMBRIA

Late 1800s   1st and 2ndC AD Roman coins found when a well was being sunk.

BROUGH, CUMBRIA

1783   1stC AD Roman coins found in a pot near Maiden Castle; most were sold off and not recorded.

c. **1850**   Roman silver coins found while digging in the peat-moss, not far from Maiden Castle.

BROUGHAM, CUMBRIA

c. **1914**   23 Roman billon *antoniniani* dating from the 3rdC found while digging a grave in St Ninian's churchyard; thought to have been deposited *c.* AD 280. This small hoard is often referred to as having been found at Ninekirks, the local name for St Ninian's, which is close to Brougham Castle, where the Roman station of Brovacu once stood.

1930   30 Roman *denarii* from the 1stC BC to the 2ndC AD, in a pot-base pushed into the floor, found during excavations of a barrack block in the fort.

1949   Bronze wrist purse containing 28 *denarii* dated 125 BC–AD 119 found by staff from the old Ministry of Works, who were consolidating the east wall of the fort, north of the main gateway. The coins were later declared not treasure trove.

BLACKBURN, BLACKBURN WITH DARWEN

1986   4,000-year-old Bronze Age axe head found on farmland.

BURNLEY, LANCASHIRE

1905 24 silver coins, possibly from the 17th and 18thC; thought to have been concealed in 1723.

CALDER BRIDGE, CUMBRIA

1905 6 Edward III gold nobles, buried some time after 1369, found near Calder Abbey; would be worth the equivalent of £10,000 today.

CARLISLE, CUMBRIA

1782 Large quantity of Roman *denarii*, in a high state of preservation, from the 1st and 2ndC AD found 'a few feet below the surface' by a labourer excavating in Fisher Street.

1860 200–300 silver Roman coins from the 1st and 2ndC AD found in the line of the wall on the south side of the North British Railway Engine Sheds. Most were dispersed and just 62 survived.

1977 120 Roman bronze coins found in a field by Bob Tweddle.

1979 30 Roman bronze coins and 1 silver were found by Bob Tweddle, close to the first hoard. The money raised from the sale of these coins was given by Bob to Save the Children Fund.

[date?] 1st or 2ndC AD Roman bronze jug.

1887 200–300 Roman silver coins from the 1st and 3rdC AD found during excavations to erect the new market. Sold to a Liverpool dealer.

CARTMEL, CUMBRIA

1806 574 *denarii*, well preserved, from the 2nd and 3rdC AD, found in an unglazed earthenware pot by two men gathering stones on an estate belonging to Lord Cavendish.

CASTLESTEADS, BRAMPTON, CUMBRIA

1825 About 5,000 Roman copper coins, all *antoniniani*, except for 1 *denarius*, from the 3rdC AD, found in a pot by the son of the farmer during ploughing at Foot Farm. A pond had been drained and the hoard was referred to as 'about a stone weight [14lb] of copper coins'.

CHATBURN AREA, LANCASHIRE

1778 900–1,200 Roman *denarii* and a small bronze lamp from the 1st and 2ndC AD found in an earthenware pot by labourers during roadwork between Chatburn and Worston. The coins weighed about 8lb and were seized by Josias Robinson, the lord of the manor.

CHESHIRE

1980 13thC gold ring, set with a garnet, found in a field by Douglas McAll (M/D).

1990s Elaborate medieval key: finder Andy Harper (M/D).

1990s Romano-British strap fitment: finder M.D. Callow (M/D).

1990s Late 8th or early 9thC copper-alloy cross with gold plaques on the arms: finder John Gibbons (M/D).

2000 29 silver shillings and 3 groats from the late 16thC found by Colin Bailey (M/D) in a field; they were thought to have been deposited c. 1603–4 and were later eclared treasure trove.

CHESTER, CHESHIRE

The Roman city of Deva on the River Dee was first settled in AD 79. Ancient walls, 2 miles long, are wonderfully preserved, studded with towers and gates, and the Roman amphitheatre built in AD 100 is still visible. The Chester Rows, the timber buildings that the town is famous for, were established in the 13th and 14thC, but most of what is visible now is of 19thC origin.

1724 1st and 2ndC AD Roman *denarii*.

1855 43 Roman *denarii* from the 1st and 2ndC AD found at Heron Bridge.

1857 70–80 silver pennies, probably deposited in AD 960, found in Eastgate Street.

1858 More than 64 Roman billon coins found in a pot.

1862 40 Anglo-Saxon and Danish coins, deposited in AD 925, found during rebuilding work at St John's church.

1883 Large quantity of bronze Roman coins from the 1st and 2ndC AD was found along with an altar, sunk in rock with cut steps, 30ft from the front of Mr Harvey's ironmonger shop in Northgate Street.

1884 About 118 Roman copper coins from the 3rdC AD found in a jar at Bollands Court. Initially about 50 coins were found in a fused mass before two other groups of coins were located, together with pottery and other items.

1901 25 silver Edward III groats, thought to have been deposited c. 1360 or later, found in a pot in Northgate Street.
Grosvenor Museum

1914 122 Anglo-Saxon silver pennies, deposited c. AD 980–5, found at Pemberton's Parlour. They were buried at a time when the Vikings were harrying Cheshire.

1922–3 12 Roman *denarii*, 37 bronze coins, and a bronze ring from the 1st to the 3rdC AD found in two small hoards during excavations at Deanery Field.

1936 6 silver and 3 billon Roman coins and bronze finger-ring, from the reigns of Constantius I and II, Valentinian and Valens, thought to have been deposited after AD 364, found while excavating for a water main.

1946 101 silver pennies, deposited before 1350, found in Pepper Street.

1950 More than 540 Anglo-Saxon silver pennies and a small number of cut halfpennies of AD 871–973 and over 50 silver ingots found under old paving slabs during cable-laying at Castle Esplanade. The discovery was not reported and some of the workmen took coins and a few ingots home, or gave them to friends. Eventually the news of the discovery reached the Curator of the Grosvenor Museum, Chester, who succeeded in collecting some 525 coins and 40 ingots, which were taken to the British Museum. The majority of the coins were from the reigns of Athelstan, Edmund, Edred, Edwig, and Edgar and the hoard was dated c. AD 970. In 1976, an additional 15 coins and 5 ingots were handed over to the Grosvenor Museum.

1985–6 42 silver coins and a gold ring from the 15thC or earlier found in a field on land belonging to Chester Cathedral, where the old abbey of St Werburgh had stood. Found by Dave Dickinson and George McKean (M/D) over a few days, there was no sign of a container, and the latest coin was dated 1420–34. The hoard was later declared treasure trove.

CHESTER AREA, CHESHIRE

1980–1 17thC sword with a rusted 29in blade, like those used by Cromwell's troops, found by a gardener on his allotment. It was bought by a Civil War collector in Chester.

CHORLEY, LANCASHIRE

c. **1830** 2ndC AD Roman coins and a silver chain with two enamelled silver brooches.
British Museum

CHORLTON, CHESHIRE

1818 2nd and 3rdC AD Roman coins found in a pot by workmen about 3ft below the surface of a field.

CHORLTON-CUM-HARDY, MANCHESTER

1860 2,000 silver coins from the 18th and 19thC.

CLIFTON, LANCASHIRE

1947 61 silver pennies found at a sandpit.

CONGLETON, CHESHIRE

1956 18 gold coins from the 16th and 17thC, thought to have been concealed in 1640.

1992   1,144 silver coins of 1554–1649 found by Keith Pay (M/D), in a black-glazed earthenware jar with a lid and single strap handle on the shoulder of a field on 18 April 1992. (The jar shattered when removed from the ground.) A week later on 25 and 26 April he returned to the field and found a further 791 silver coins in a brown bottle with its neck broken, about 40yd from the first hoard. The coins were sixpences and shillings of Elizabeth I, James I, and Charles I and II, with many half-crowns from the later reigns. Just about a month later on 18 May 1992 Keith Pay and Philip Bordley, another detectorist, found another 833 silver coins in a black-glazed earthenw jar about 4yd from the first hoard site. The latest coin of this haul wa dated 1670. Later that day they found 641 silver coins in an earthen bottle with the latest coins dated 1660–2. In all, the 4 hoards totalled 3,409 coins and was one of the largest deposits of such coins ever recorded in Britain. The composition of the hoards is considered typic the period 1640–70.

CONGLETON AREA, CHESHIRE

2002   10thC silver penny of Eadger (AD 959–75) found in a field by Keith Pay (M/D).

CREWE AREA, CHESHIRE

1982   12 Roman silver coins and 2 bronze brooches from the 1stC AD found in a field by John Morris (M/D).

1984   3 bronze flat axes and a bronze dagger dating from 2000 BC found by Cyril Montague (M/D) 8in below the surface on farmland.

1985   7 silver coins from the 13th and 14thC found in a field.

CROSTHWAITE, CUMBRIA

1841   12thC silver and other coins found during the restoration of the 11thC church. The hoard included a leaden coin of Stephen (1135–54).

CROSTON, LANCASHIRE

1884   200–300 Roman coins found in a shallow dish 2–3ft below th surface by men digging for clay at the Littlewood Tile and Brick Work The coins were distributed among the workers, but 65 were later recovered.

CUERDALE, PRESTON AREA, LANCASHIRE

1840   Over 7,000 silver coins and 1,000oz silver ingots dating from the 9th and 10thC found in a decayed, lead-lined, wooden box on the banks of the River Ribble, near a dangerous ford, anc close to Cuerdale Hall. A group of workmen were walking abou 400yd from the riverbank when they came upon a large waterlogged mass of soil that had slipped down towards the riv and where it had slipped were the exposed remnants of the wooden chest. The hoard was believed to have been buried dur the flight of the Viking army from Edward the Elder c. AD 911. *Anglo-Saxon Chronicle* says: 'a Viking army harried the north o

England at will until King Edward sent his own army and also summoned his allies from Mercia. And they came up with the rear of the enemy as he was on his way homeward, and there fought with him and put him to flight, and slew many thousands of his men.'

The hoard's make-up clearly shows the geographical scale of Viking activity. Although most of the coins were English, including about 1,000 official Anglo-Saxon issues (919 silver pennies of Alfred the Great, and 51 of Edward the Elder) and around 4,800 Danelaw issues (both Northumbrian and Danish coins minted in York), there are many from elsewhere. There are about 1,000 Frankish coins, some early

Scandinavian, about 50 Islamic Kufic dirhams, and a single Byzantine silver hexagram of Heraclius and Heraclius Constantine, minted AD 615–30. While some of the coins came from Viking raids on the Netherlands, western France and as far away as Italy, some came through Scandinavia's geographical links to Russia. Careful study of the English coins has suggested to experts that many were acquired as a result of trading rather than raiding. This hoard, more than any other, has helped in the dating of Danelaw coins. Some of the hoard went missing with the finders before the Bailiff of Cuerdale Hall arrived to take charge of the recovery operation.

CUMWHITTON, CUMBRIA

2004   A Viking hoard comprising swords, spears, jewellery, fir-making materials, and riding equipment: finder Peter Adams.

DEE, RIVER, CHESHIRE

1981   Extremely rare Roman silver intaglio ring from the early 2ndC found on common land on the banks of the river by Kenneth Jones (M/D). The ring, which featured a blue onyx stone with a dark jet background depicting a satyr walking and holding a bunch of grapes and a staff, probably belonged to a high-ranking officer.

DISLEY, CHESHIRE

1962   £1,700 in old banknotes, made up of 1,500 pound notes and 400 ten-shilling notes, found in an old biscuit tin, in the rafters of a detached house by builders carrying out renovations.

DISTINGTON, CUMBRIA

1811   16th and 17thC silver coins, thought to have been concealed between 1625 and 1649.

DOCKER MOOR, LANCASHIRE

1975–80   123 Roman billon coins from the 3rdC AD found in the bank of the River Keer on a number of separate occasions; thought to have been concealed c. AD 275.

ECCLES AREA, SALFORD

1864   More than 6,000 short-cross silver pennies from the 12th and 13thC found in an earthenware jug. A local mill worker noticed the glint of a coin on a footpath where soil had been disturbed by road builders. He found 20 coins, which he showed to the mill owner, who advised him to take them to the landowner, John Harland, a fellow of the Royal Society and a noted local historian. On Harland's advice, he looked more carefully, and found a solid mass of silver coins inside the remains of an earthenware pot. Both he and John Harland returned the following day and found the remainder of the hoard. During the 13thC the land belonged to Stanlaw Abbey, and later to the Cistercian abbey of Whalley, near Blackburn. It was believed that the coins were concealed in 1230.

Monks Hall Museum, Eccles and Salford Museum

FLEETWOOD, LANCASHIRE

1840   About 400 Roman *denarii* from the 1st to the 3rdC AD found by brick makers between Rossall Point and Fenny.

FORMBY, SEFTON

1869   More than 19 silver coins from the 16th and 17thC, thought to have been concealed in 1669.

FRODSHAM, CHESHIRE

1658   £500 in gold and silver found behind some oak panelling at Halton Castle. Colonel Henry Brooke purchased the castle and renovated parts that had been damaged when Royalist Captain Walter Primrose held it in 1642–3. Today that £500 would be the equivalent of £48,000.

GREAT ORMSIDE, CUMBRIA

The village name relates to Orm the Viking.

> **1823**   The silver and gilt bronze cup now called the Ormside Bowl found in St James's churchyard by gravediggers. It is one of the great artistic items of the Dark Ages and was probably made c. AD 800–50.
>
> *York Museum*

1899   A quantity of 9thC Viking weapons found in a warrior's grave.

Tuille House Museum

HALSALL, LANCASHIRE

1920   20 Henry V and VI gold nobles, believed to have been buried not later than 1428. Today these would have the purchasing power of £20,000.

HALTON, NEAR RUNCORN, CHESHIRE

1658   16th and 17thC gold coins found near the ruins of the 11thC Halton Castle; thought to have been concealed between 1625 and 1649.

HALTON MOOR, LANCASHIRE

1815   860 Anglo-Saxon and Danish silver pennies, 2 gold pendants, a beautifully decorated silver-gilt cup and a large silver torc. The cup is decorated with four large animals and foliage and was made in the late 8th or 9thC somewhere on the continent. All the silver coins date from King Cnut, with the latest coin minted in 1027.

British Museum

HARGRAVE, CHESHIRE

1997   6 silver pennies of Edgar (959–75) found by Denis Price (M/D), thought to have been deposited c. AD 970–5; returned to the finder.

HASLINGDEN, LANCASHIRE

1892   132 copper coins, including three pattern farthings, thought to have been concealed in 1714.

HEAPEY, LANCASHIRE

1835   A large quantity of Roman coins, mainly brass with some silver, in an excellent state of preservation.

HOLME CULTRAM ABBEY, NEAR ABBEY TOWN, CUMBRIA

>1896   81 silver pennies of Edward I and II dated 1272–1316 found during the digging of a grave on the site of Holme Cultram Abbey. The abbey was founded in 1150 by Cistercian monks from Melrose Abbey in the Scottish Borders. During the 13th and early 14thC the abbey was raided by the Scots, who took manuscripts, vestments and altar silver. Both in 1300 and 1307 the abbey provided shelter to Edward I's retinue. In 1319 Robert the Bruce sacked the abbey, and after another raid in 1332 the abbey was left destitute. It continued to function but finally

c. **1820**   Roman silver coins found in an urn near the River Lune at Killington Hall.

KIRKANDREWS-ON-EDEN AREA, CUMBRIA

1855   About 1,100 Roman copper coins from the 3rd and 4thC AD found in a vase in a field at Hainings Farm, west of Kirksteads, a mile and a half south of Kirkandrews.

1977   About 300 Roman bronze and silver coins dating from the 3rd and 4thC AD found by Bob Tweddle (M/D) in the field on Hainings Farm. He gave half to the farmer, and sold his half for £300, and gave the money to the Save the Children's Fund and Cancer Research. Later he found 36 more bronze coins in the same field.

KIRKBY, KNOWSLEY

1953   41 gold and 25 silver coins from the 19th and possibly the 20thC, thought to have been concealed in 1905.

closed when the abbot joined the Pilgrimage of Grace against Henry VIII's seizure of church properties in 1536. It has been suggested that the coins were concealed *c.* 1313–16, in anticipation of a Scottish invasion, but it may well have happened closer to the 1319 sacking by Robert the Bruce.

HOOLEY BRIDGE, ROCHDALE

1856   About 1,000 Roman copper coins from the 3rdC AD found by workmen erecting a house close to Hooley Wood, near the village. They found a pot, which they broke to reveal a mass of fused coins, which they shared among themselves.

HOOTON, CHESHIRE

c. **1889**   Large number of Roman copper coins, all in an excellent state of preservation, from the 4thC AD, found in an urn by workmen excavating the Manchester Ship Canal.

HULME, MANCHESTER

[date?]   19 Roman billon and 7 copper coins, dating from the 3rdC AD, thought to have been deposited *c.* AD 275 on the site of a Roman military station and Mithraeum.

KENDAL, CUMBRIA (*See also* Stainton, this section)

1981   355 coins from Henry VIII to Charles II, all in virtually mint condition, although some showing signs of clipping, found by two children playing in a garden, within an area of a square foot and only a few inches down.

KENDAL AREA, CUMBRIA

1893   106 Roman copper coins from the 4thC AD, thought to have been buried *c.* AD 333.

KIRKBY THORE, CUMBRIA

The name 'Kirkby' means 'village by a church'. Thore is a Viking name, Thor being the god of thunder. A Roman cavalry camp, Bravoniacum, was found here. It guarded the Stainmore gap and was on the Roman road that led to Carvoran (Magna), just south of Hadrian's Wall.

1838   Large hoard of Roman silver and brass coins, jewellery and artefacts dating from the 1st to the 3rdC AD found by workmen within the channel of a stream called the Troutbeck, while removing the foundations of an old structure, before building a new bridge. The hoard included a vast quantity of coins, fibulae, the cusp of a spear, bronze greyhounds, idols, gold bracelets, pins, intaglios, and an immense number of small implements in brass and iron. 13 inscribed Roman stones, thought to be altar stones, were found as well as 3 Roman tombstones. Some items were carried off by the workmen.

1863   167 or 234 *denarii* from the 2ndC AD found at Newbiggin Hall. Thought to have been concealed in AD 180, they included coins from Nero to Crispina.

KIRKHAM, LANCASHIRE

1923   35 Roman *denarii* from the 1st and 3rdC AD found in a Samian-ware jar.

Harris Museum, Preston

KIRKOSWALD, CUMBRIA

1808   542 stycas from the 9thC found after an old tree blew down. Hidden in its roots was an earthenware vessel containing the coins, thought to have been concealed in AD 865.

KNOTT END-ON-SEA, LANCASHIRE

1927 400–500 3rdC AD Roman billon *antoniniani* from Valerian to Tetricus were in a leather container at Hackensall Hall, half a mile south of the village; thought to have been deposited in AD 274.

KNUTSFORD, CHESHIRE

1918 81 gold coins possibly from the 18th and 19thC, thought to have been concealed in 1836.

LAKE GRASMERE, CUMBRIA

1978 63 silver groats, half-groats, pennies and halfpennies of Henry V, VI and VII, Edward IV, and Richard III found near Pennyrock Falls, on the shores at the southern end of the lake. Leonard Price first discovered 20 coins, which he handed to the archive office at Kendall. A week later he returned to the spot and uncovered another 43 coins. Thought to have been concealed *c*. 1500, they were later declared treasure trove.

LANCASHIRE

1790 About 20 Roman *denarii* from the 1st and 2ndC AD found during the ploughing of a field which had until shortly before been woodland.

1980–1 Small quantity of coins and jewellery found in a back garden by 13-year-old Paul Aspden, who was demonstrating his metal detector to his cousin. The hoard was handed to the police, who believed it was connected with a robbery. Unable to trace the items' owners the police returned them to the finder.

1990s Late Bronze Age socketed spearhead found by Matt Hepworth (M/D).

1990s Late Bronze Age sword was found by Matt Hepworth (M/D). It was broken in a way that indicated it had been offered to the gods.

1990s Roman strap fitting found by Daniel Daly (M/D).

LANCASTER, LANCASHIRE

c. **1775** 1stC AD Roman coins found during the digging of a cellar in a house on Church Street. The coins were found under several large hewn stones and some steps, which were thought to be the corner of a temple.

1856 100 Roman silver coins of 81 BC–AD 118 found in a pot at Bridge Lane. They were uncovered by a workman cutting away the embankment at the foot of the 'Wery Wall', before building two cottages. The coins were quickly dispersed, but 38 were later retrieved.

1975 15 billon coins of 6 emperors from the 3rdC AD found in Mitre Yard; they were thought to have been deposited *c*. AD 286 or later.

1975, 1979–80 123 Roman silver *antoniniani* from the 3rdC AD were found in the bank of the River Keer, on Docker Moor.

LATHOM, LANCASHIRE

1999 13 Roman *denarii* and 1 copper-alloy coin from the 1st and 2ndC AD found by Liverpool Museum Field Archaeology Unit. They were thought to have been deposited about AD 138.

National Museums and Galleries,
Merseyside

LEYLAND AREA, LANCASHIRE

1850 126 Roman copper *antoniniani* from the 3rdC AD found 18in below the surface in Worden Park to the south of Leyland.

LINDAL IN FURNESS AREA, CUMBRIA

1778 Late 14th or 15thC gold fede-ring brooch found to the north of the village in Whinfield Park during ploughing. In the 14th and 15thC Whinfield was a deer park. A fede-ring has two hands clasped together to indicate faith; they were popular as far back as Roman times, usually as finger-rings, but also in the form of a brooch.

LITTLE BOLLINGTON AREA, CHESHIRE

1957 Almost 2,500 Roman copper *antoniniani* from the 3rdC AD found in a jar while ploughing the edge of a field bordering Agden Brook, at Woolstencroft Farm.

LITTLE CROSBY AREA, SEFTON

1611 300 Anglo-Saxon and Danish coins, together with some silver bullion believed to be dated AD 900–15, found by a cowherd on William Blundell's estate. The coins were sent to Wales for safe keeping during the Civil War but were lost. The bullion was used to make religious plate for St Mary's church, Little Crosby.

LIVERPOOL

1955 28 gold coins from the 19th and 20thC found in the area of Anfield; thought to have been concealed in 1915.

LONGTON AREA, LANCASHIRE

1819 11 Roman silver and 17 copper coins from the 1st and 2ndC AD found in a small wooden box by a man cutting turf in an area called Longton Moss.

LONGTOWN, CUMBRIA

1949 25 gold coins from the 17th and 18thC, thought to have been concealed in 1794.

LYTHAM ST ANNE'S, LANCASHIRE

1961 7 gold and 376 silver coins from the 16th and 17thC, thought to have been concealed in 1641.

MALLERSTANG EDGE, CUMBRIA

1926 138 Roman *denarii* from the 2ndC AD concealed in a hole in the ground, covered by a flat stone at Steddale Mouth.

MANCHESTER

1828–9 89 1st and 2ndC AD Roman coins were found while moving soil on the Castlefield estate; it was thought that they were originally deposited in a wooden box.

1840 10 gold coins and around 190 mostly silver and copper-alloy coins from the 1stC AD found at the Crown Inn, Trafford Street, on the road to Slack.

1840–50 Roman silver coins from the 1st to the 3rdC AD found in a pot, probably in the Castlefield area.

c. 1852 1,664 Roman copper coins from the 4thC AD found during the digging of the foundations for the Knott Mill Railway Station, Castlefield.

1895–6 192 Roman bronze coins from the 3rdC AD.

MANCHESTER AREA

1993 A Saxon gold clasp of AD 600–25 found by Bob Foster (M/D) on farmland. Inset with five red stones, it was thought to have been part of a buckle, or clasp, from the cover of a religious book. Declared not treasure trove, it was returned to the finder.

MARYPORT, CUMBRIA

>1915 About 125 Roman silver coins, including 17 forged *denarii*, from the 1st and 2ndC AD, found at Netherhall with numerous other items. The Senhouse Roman Museum in Maryport is home to the oldest collection of Roman artefacts in Britain. The collection was started by John Senhouse of Netherhall about 1570. It was passed down through successive generations until a charitable trust was set up in 1970 to display the many items.

MEOLS, WIRRAL

A silver tetra*drachm* of Tigranes II of Armenia, minted in Syria *c*. 1stC BC and bronze coins of Augustus (31–14 BC). Many Roman brooches have also been found and in the late 1990s 6th and 7thC Byzantine coins were discovered.

MERECLOUGH, LANCASHIRE

There has been much debate about where the Battle of Brunanburh (AD 937) was fought. One possible site is between Mereclough and Worsthorne, which lies to the north-west of the village. The battle was a victory for the West Saxon army led by King Athelstan over the forces of Olaf III, Guthfrithson (the Viking King of Dublin) and Constantine, King of Scotland. Both sides suffered heavy losses, which we know from the *Anglo-Saxon Chronicle*.

> In this year King Aethelstan, Lord of warriors,
> ring-giver to men, and his brother also,
> Prince Eadmund, won eternal glory
> in battle with sword edges
> around Brunanbur . . .
>
> . . . Never was there more slaughter
> on this island, never yet as many
> people killed before this
> with sword's edge.

The importance of this battle is that it signified the coming together of the Anglo-Saxon kingdoms into a unified kingdom; it was the beginning of what we understand as England.

1695 22 Roman silver coins from the 1stC AD, thought to have been concealed in AD 98, found by workmen close to a considerable heap of stones that showed evidence of the ruins of a Roman fort (there are earthworks to the north-west of the village). Only 12 *denarii* were recovered from the workmen.

1761 About 200 Roman copper folles from the 3rd and 4thC AD found in a glass vessel while clearing away a heap of rubbish in a field called Law House Wood, half a mile south of the village.

MERSEYSIDE

1983 3,463 half-crowns, 4,884 florins, 1,812 shillings and 1,629 sixpences from the Victorian era found by workmen erecting a garden fence. The coins were in tallow inside 5 lead-lined barrels buried in the ground. They were declared not treasure trove and returned to the finder, who sold them to a dealer for many thousands of pounds.

MICKLE TRAFFORD, CHESHIRE

1895 38 silver shillings and sixpences of Elizabeth I found in a pot, thought to have been concealed in 1594.

Grosvenor Museum

MIDDLEWICH AREA, CHESHIRE

1820 About 1,000 Roman coins from the 3rdC AD found by a mole-catcher on farmland near Kinderton Lodge. They were fused together in a decayed wooden box, and many were broken or corroded.

MILLOM, CUMBRIA

1759 Roman silver coins found in two large urns during digging at Millum Castle, on the River Duddon. The coins were sent to London, where they were sold by pound weight.

NELSON, LANCASHIRE

1977 44 gold sovereigns dated 1838–53 found in a leather bag in a stable wall at Pinfold Farm.

OLDHAM, LANCASHIRE

1887 About 200 Roman copper coins from the 3rd and 4thC AD found in what remained of a wooden box by workmen excavating for cellars for a new mill midway between Chamber Road and Manchester Road, in the Werneth district of Oldham.

ORMSKIRK AREA, LANCASHIRE

1949 119 *denarii* from the 1st and 2ndC AD found by children playing on Ottershead Farm. They were in the bed of a stream and were thought to have been concealed *c*. AD 120.

PARKGATE, CHESHIRE

1897? 16th and 17thC silver and billon coins, along with a collection of bronze horse paraphernalia of distinctive design found with a skeleton; thought to have been buried between 1685 and 1689.

PENRITH AREA, CUMBRIA

1785, 1830 and **1989** In 1785 a very large silver penannular brooch of the Viking period was discovered on Flusco Pike, 3 miles to the west of Penrith. In 1830 it was reported that somewhere 'near Penrith' a slightly more elaborate brooch was found; also probably from Flusco Pike. In 1989 2 thistle brooches and 3 bossed penannular brooches were found by Gerald Carter to the east of Flusco Pike in an area called Silver Field. Experts assess that fewer than 50 pennanular brooches have been found in Britain and no more than 40 of the ball-type penannulars, including those of the thistle type.

British Museum

PREESALL, LANCASHIRE

1926 About 325 Roman bronze coins from the 3rdC AD found in a semi-fused mass in the remains of leather pouch while removing sand from a pit.

1934 3rdC AD Roman billon coins, thought to have been deposited in AD 274, found during the digging of a sandpit; a considerable number were dispersed by the finders.

PRESTON, LANCASHIRE

1975–6 About 185 Roman copper coins from the 4thC AD found in Frenchwood.

PRESTWICH, BURY

1972 1,065 silver coins and cut coins dated 1142–5 found when a bulldozer driver and a young gardener were levelling ground at Prestwich Jewish School in preparation for a new playing field. They noticed a metal disc in the earth they had shifted, and soon after saw several more. The gardener showed these to the school caretaker, who thought they might be old seals, so they went back to the site and began digging, whereupon the ground caved in and they found many coins. The caretaker's stepson recognised them as silver coins and instinctively knew they were old and probably valuable, so the men decided they should hand over the 600 they had so far found to the police. A team of local archaeologists then investigated the site with metal detectors but found only a few coins and soon abandoned the search. The caretaker and his son remained convinced that there were more coins and so carried on digging, in places as deep as 6ft. Their diligence produced a further 216 pennies and 11 halfpennies, which they also handed to the police. A few weeks later they had another go and found 71 more coins. The hoard turned out to be both rich and diverse. There were 42 coins that bore the legend 'Pereric'. It is thought that the moneyers who made these coins during Stephen's reign did so to imitate coins of Henry's reign that carried the word Henricus. It was their way of disassociating themselves from the war between Stephen and the Empress Matilda. There were also Scottish coins of David I, Northumberland coins of David's son Henry, and Angevin issues of the Empress Matilda and Henry of Anjou, and others which could only be classed as 'uncertain'. There were also coins from erased dies of Stephen. A conservative estimate of their value was £50,000 (over £400,000 today) and 294 coins were retained by various museums; the remainder were returned to the finders.

RIBCHESTER, LANCASHIRE

The place was named Bremetenacum Veteranorum by the Romans, which translates as 'The Hilltop Settlement of the Veterans'. Established in the late 1stC AD, it was garrisoned by cavalrymen from Spain and Hungary. When the men retired from the army they were allowed to farm the fertile land of the nearby Fylde country. By the time of the Domesday Book the village was known by its modern name, which simply means 'Roman Fort on the River Ribble'. The village then spent many years with nothing of significance to report. According to the Pictorial History of the County of Lancaster in 1844, 'the chief employment is weaving, which is carried on in connection with farming operations. But we heard heavy complaints of rack rents and miserably low wages, with uncertain work; and in truth, the place had every appearance of poverty, and offers a painful contrast with the historical recollections which it bears.'

>1746 More than 600 Roman *denarii* from the 1st to the 3rdC AD found in a copper urn between Overborough and Ribchester. Some sources mention just 200 coins.

1796 Roman bronze ceremonial helmet of an élite trooper dating from *c.* 100 AD found after the River Ribble changed its course following severe floods. This event brought to light much other Roman military paraphernalia, mainly cavalry sports equipment. The helmet was briefly used as a football by the son of a clog maker playing truant from school. It is decorated with a battle scene showing both infantry and cavalry, and would have been even more pectacular when worn on special occasions, as streamers, or manes, would have been attached to its top.

British Museum

1920 5 well-preserved Roman *denarii* from the 1stC AD found on the edge of the old Roman road about 40yd north of the north gate of the (Roman) fort.

1978 9 Roman silver coins from the 1st and 2ndC AD found by Mary Davies, a Lancashire University archaeological student, during excavations of the Roman fort site. The coins appeared to have been wrapped in a piece of cloth and were thought to have been lost when the fort was occupied by Roman cavalry.

RICKERBY, CUMBRIA

1986–7 1,732 pennies, 488 halfpennies, and 58 farthings, and some broken coins and pottery shards, all from the reigns of Edward I, II and III, and a penny of King John (1205), found by Neil Marshall and Ken Jones in a field. They were declared treasure trove.

ROCHDALE

>1870 1stC AD Roman brass coins found in the Castlemere area. A report from near the time described 'A discovery made several years since consisting of several coins of the middle brass and of the Higher Empire, one if I am not mistaken (for I am compelled to write from recollection) as early as Claudius'.

RUSHTON, CHESHIRE

[date?]   A late 16th or early 17thC gold finger-ring found with an enamelled skull, and inscription *Hodie mihi cras tibi* (Today it is me but tomorrow it will be you).

ST HELENS

1983   3,674 half-crowns, 4,825 florins, 1,941 shillings, 1,638 sixpences, 6 silver threepenny bits, 5 brass threepenny bits, and a halfpenny from the 19th and 20thC, found in the back garden of a house in Atherton Street. Fred Hartley came across three metal canisters, each 2ft long, while digging his garden and at first thought they were wartime bombs. They were removed by the refuse department and when they opened them, out poured more than 12,000 coins. They were thought to have been buried *c.* 1940, when this hoard would have represented around eight years' wages for an agricultural worker.

SALFORD

1928 31 silver coins from the 16th and 17thC, thought to have been concealed in 1645.

SAMLESBURY, LANCASHIRE

1900 More than 37 silver coins from the 16th and 17thC found in a leather bag inside a chimney in Higher Barn Cottage; thought to have been deposited after 1645.

SANDSFIELD, NEAR CARLISLE, CUMBRIA

1845 Silver coins thought to have been buried in 1344 sold by the finders to a Carlisle silversmith, who melted most of them down. Others he gilded and sold as cufflinks and charms. 40 years later just 9 coins remained and these were presented by the silversmith's son to the museum at Carlisle.

SCARISBRICK, LANCASHIRE

1655 1stC AD Roman silver and bronze coins.

SCOTBY, NEAR CARLISLE, CUMBRIA

1855 About 100 silver coins from the 10thC, thought to have been buried *c.* AD 935–40 ; not reported by the finders. Later the authorities retrieved 19 coins, which were Anglo-Saxon silver pennies of Edward the Elder and Athelstan.

SHAP AREA, CUMBRIA

c. **1830** 19 gold and 580 silver Roman coins from the 1stC AD were found under some blocks of granite that were being removed by labourers repairing the road north of Shap on the way to Kendal, a little to the north of Brinns Farm.

SKELTON, CUMBRIA

1999 13th or 14thC bronze cauldron found by Ken Philips (M/D) during a detectorist rally organised by the West Lancashire Metal Detecting Club. This is a comparatively rare find in that it is complete; normally just the legs or rim are found.

SPURSTOW, CHESHIRE

2000 Late 14th or early 15thC silver-gilt pendant crucifix: finder Andrew Harper (M/D).

SPURSTOW AREA, CHESHIRE

1982–3 Bronze Age axe of 1800–1500 BC found by Stephen Murphy (M/D) in a field used for grazing.

STAINTON, CUMBRIA

1981 391 silver and 1 copper coin, in virtually mint condition, from Henry VIII through to Charles II, dated 1509–1671. Eric Clare found a silver coin while working on his land, close to a river. The following day, his small son Louis dug up a handful of silver coins. Eric then bought a metal detector and he and his family searched the area. They got a

sounding from behind a large boulder, and as they moved the rock coins came pouring out from among some tree roots. His farmhouse had been built over an earlier mill alongside Stainton beck and it is thought that a 17thC mill owner had hidden the coins.

STANDISH, WIGAN

>1700 About 200 Roman coins, mostly *denarii* with some brass, and 2 gold rings from the 1st to the 3rdC AD, found in a copper container by a man ploughing a field.

1926 131 Roman silver coins from Nero to Severus Alexander (2nd and 3rdC AD), thought to have been deposited in AD 222 or later.

STATHAM LYMM, CHESHIRE

c. **1778** Between 300 and 1,200 Roman copper coins from the 3rdC AD found in a large pot by a man and his son while working at the side of a field near a piece of wall. Contemporary reports told of 'about 2 quarts of copper coins'; they were quickly disposed of by the finders.

STOCKPORT AREA

1988 An 18thC Georgian silver-gilt vinaigrette: finder Eric Taylor (M/D).

TARBOCK GREEN, KNOWSLEY

1838 33 Roman silver and 47 copper coins from the 1st and 2ndC AD found on farmland on the estate of the Earl of Sefton.

WADDINGTON, LANCASHIRE

1989 30 Roman *denarii* from the 1st and 2ndC AD found at Waddow Hall; declared treasure trove.

WALKDEN, SALFORD

1896 500 gold coins, possibly from the 19thC, thought to have been concealed between 1837 and 1901.

WALMERSLEY, BURY

1864 500–700 Roman silver and bronze coins, as well as other silver items from the 3rdC AD found in an urn. The hoard was covered by a flagstone not far from a farmhouse on moorland at Throstle Hill, close to a Roman road, about 4 miles north-east of Bury. The silver items included 2 broad bracelets, 1 silver bracelet, 2 silver armlets, broken pieces of other bracelets and armlets, a bronze spoon, 2 silver rings, and a large amber bead or bulla. Most of the items were sold by the finders.

WARTON, LANCASHIRE

1997 3 Viking silver coins and 6 pieces of strap silver dating from the 9th and 10thC: finders M. Hepworth and D. Kierzak (M/D). The coins were Islamic silver dirhems dated AD 898–913 and were valued at £300.

Lancaster City Museum

WATERLOO, BLACKBURN WITH DARWEN

1974 18 Victorian gold sovereigns and half-sovereigns, and 75 Victorian silver coins, dated 1839–96. This scattered hoard was thought to have been deposited after 1896.

Liverpool Museum

TOCKHOLES, BLACKBURN WITH DARWEN

1973 59 short-cross silver pennies and cut halfpennies of Henry II and III, believed to have been buried *c.* 1218–19.

Blackburn Museum

TUNSHILL, ROCHDALE

1793 Silver arm from a Roman statue found by workmen at a quarry. The 9½in arm had a loose armilla around the wrist and a silver chain bearing a silver plate which read: VITORIAE LEG. VL. VIC. VAL. RUFUS. V.S.L.M (To victory of the Sixth Legion the Victorious Valerius Rufus performs his vow willingly to a deserving object).

UPHOLLAND, LANCASHIRE

1921 18th and 19thC gold coins, thought to have been concealed in 1853.

WEAVERHAM AREA, CHESHIRE

1984 Bronze socketed axe from 2000 BC found in a field.

WESTON, CHESHIRE

1982 12 Roman *denarii* from the 2ndC AD found at Green Farm, Weston.

WHALLEY, LANCASHIRE

1966 9th or 8thC BC Bronze Age hoard found by men working for Manchester Corporation, digging a ditch in a meadow at Portfield Farm. They found a gold armlet, a gold tress ring (hair ornament), a carpenter's gauge, and a number of bronze axe heads and other tools.

WIGAN AREA

1926 More than 137 Roman *denarii* from the 1st to the 3rdC AD found about 10in below the surface by a man digging a trench at Boar's Head in the parish of Standish. He distributed them among his workmates but later 137 were recovered and were found to be in a fine state of preservation.

WINSFORD, CHESHIRE

1970   246 silver coins from various reigns, dated 1552–1643, found in a pot during construction work.

WINSFORD AREA, CHESHIRE

1978   4 gold coins from the 17th and 18thC found by Dave Kitchen (M/D) in a small field behind Bill Whittaker's farmhouse. There were 2 coins of Charles II (1678 and 1684), a William III (1698), and a George I (1718), all in beautiful condition. The coins were thought to be worth as much as £7,500 (the equivalent of £26,000 today).

WYNBUNBURY, CHESHIRE

1969   Antique silverware found by the Revd Stanley Jones and his son while spring-cleaning the 15thC tower of the parish church. They opened a chest that had lain undisturbed for years, and inside they found silverware that was valued at more than £26,000 (worth over £260,000 today). The most valuable item was a lidded Charles II silver tankard, dating from 1677, thought to be worth £10,000.

Isle of Man

BALLAMODHA

1840   Coins of Edward I and II, Alexander III of Scotland, and Robert the Bruce, thought to have been deposited in the 14thC, found in a jar in a field.

BALLAQUAYLE, NEAR DOUGLAS

1894   More than 400 silver coins from the 10thC, believed to have been concealed in the late AD 970s. The coins included 133 silver pennies and 5 cut halfpennies, spanning the reigns of 6 British kings and 2 Viking rulers during the 10thC.

Manx Museum

1800s   Large quantity of coins and jewellery from the 11thC found inside a stone box during the digging of foundations for a house.

BALLAQUEENY, CRONK

1874   41 silver pennies and 2 cut halfpennies, spanning the reigns of more than 9 rulers during the 10thC, found while excavating gravel. They were believed to have been concealed just after AD 960.

Manx Museum

BALLAQUEENY AREA, CRONK

1873   10thC coins, believed to have been concealed from Norse pirates.

Manx Museum

BALLASLIG, BRADDAN

1978   Over 200 silver coins of Edward I and II, with Irish, Scottish and continental coins from between 1279 and 1327: finders Robert Farrer and Kevin Robinson (M/D). They were thought to have been concealed when the Isle of Man suffered raids from Irish and Scottish marauders.

BALLATOES AREA

1826   20 English silver short-cross silver pennies of Richard I.

BALLAYELSE, ARBORY

1977   5 silver coins, thought to have been deposited after 1302.

BRADDA HEAD

1848   Several hundred 11thC Anglo-Saxon silver pennies found. The majority were sold to a watchmaker who probably melted them down.

BRADEN

1982   565 high-quality silver pennies dated 1279–1307 and 22 fragments found by Lillian Moore and Frederick Blacknall in the entrance of a field at Kilkenny Farm. They were thought to have been deposited in 1313 and were later declared treasure trove; the finders were paid the full value of the coins.

CASTLETOWN

1691   17thC gold and silver Spanish dollars and moidores, thought to have been concealed between 1625 and 1649.

1814   15 gold coins from the late 17th and early 18thC found in the wall of a house.

1869   2 silver coins, thought to have been concealed in 1570.

DALBY

1835   A large quantity of silver coins from the 16th and 17thC, thought to have been concealed between 1625 and 1649.

DOUGLAS

1849   A large quantity of gold coins of Henry VII, thought to have been concealed in 1505.

1880   4 gold and 55 silver coins from the 16th and 17thC, thought to have been concealed between 1625 and 1649.

1894 Several hundred Anglo-Saxon and Danish silver coins, jewellery pieces and ornaments dating from the 10thC, believed to have been deposited *c.* AD 970s, found by John Stephen. It is thought that he gave away many coins, and broke a large number attempting to clean them. 95 coins and 11 pieces of jewellery were declared treasure trove, but it is said that Stephen failed to declare a further 93 coins and 9 pieces of jewellery.

1956 8 silver coins of George III and IV, dated 1818–44, found while sewer laying at North Quay. Thought to have been concealed *c.* 1850–75.

Manx Museum

ISLE OF MAN

1982–3 Viking gold finger-ring made of interlacing gold wire and dating from the 10th or 11thC found on farmland by Colin Gough just a few inches below the surface. Part of the field in which it was found once contained an ancient chapel and burial ground. It was declared to be treasure trove.

[date?] 12 gold coins of Edward IV, Henry VI, and Richard III.

KIRK ANDREAS

1866 About 100 silver coins from the 10thC, found buried in the ground. 13 coins were of Eadred, Eadwig, and Eadgar and it is thought the hoard was concealed *c.* 970 or later. 8 years later more 10thC coins were found in the same area.

Manx Museum

KIRK MICHAEL

1795 More than 50 silver Hiberno-Norse coins from the 11thC found during demolition of the medieval church. These were thought to have been deposited *c.* AD 1075.

1834 12 gold and 208 silver coins from the 19thC found wrapped in some material in a wall cavity during the demolition of the old church. These were Hiberno-Norse, early coins of Dolley *c.* 1075; 46 of these are held in the British Museum.

British Museum

1972 and **1975** 79 silver pennies, 3 silver ornaments and 2 fragments from the 11thC found in the remains of a cloth bag during the digging of a grave in 1972 and again when it was reopened in 1975. The coins were largely from the reigns of 6 British rulers and 2 others and were thought to have been concealed *c.* AD 1060.

Manx Museum

LAXEY

1786 237 silver coins.

PARK LLEWELLYN, KIRK MAUGHOLD

1835 Silver Anglo-Saxon and Hiberno-Danish coins found in a cow or ram's horn, thought to have been deposited *c.* 1031. The find was concealed from the authorities and many coins were dispersed. 7 are at the new Manx Museum.

Manx Museum

PEEL CASTLE, WEST SIDE

1982 41 Viking Hiberno-Norse silver pennies from the 11thC found during an archaeological dig; declared treasure trove.

RAMSEY

1940 About 12 billon penny and halfpenny tokens from the 18thC, thought to have been buried in 1773 or later.

1945 2 gold sovereigns, 10 half-sovereigns, and 208 silver coins (78 half-crowns, 5 florins and 125 shillings) of George III and IV, William IV and Victoria found by workmen, wrapped in material in the cavity of a wall during demolition work. They were thought to have been hidden *c.* 1853.

SCARLETT

1974 8 billon Manx, Irish and British coins from the 18th and 19thC.

SILVERDALE

1938 3 silver, 44 billon, and 3 other Manx, Irish and British coins from the 18th and 19thC found in St Jacob's Well, deposited before 1950.

Manx Museum

STRANDHALL

1921 2 silver Scottish coins of David II and Robert II found on a beach; they were thought to have been deposited *c.* 1370–90.

WEST NAPPIN

1885 11thC silver coins and a silver armlet found in a mound. They were thought to have been deposited *c.* 1041.

Today the South-East of England is the gateway to Britain, especially for those arriving via the Channel Tunnel. Two thousand years ago it was the gateway for the Romans when they landed in Kent; they immediately began to leave behind evidence of their arrival and settlement. The activities of the Roman invaders and the people who followed them have made the region the most representative template for the history of Britain.

The fantastic finds made in the South-East include a Bronze Age cup found at Ringlemere, Kent, in 2001 by a detectorist; a hoard of silver pennies thought to have been buried at the time of the Norman invasion and found at Sedlescombe, East Sussex, in 1876; and a 19thC gold and diamond encrusted scabbard found in a Surrey river – it is believed to have been presented to Lord Nelson after the Battle of the Nile in 1803.

Sadly, as an increasing number of buildings spring up on farmland in the South-East, much of the region's history is being covered over forever. The one saving grace is that developers sometimes accidentally stumble across important evidence of the past.

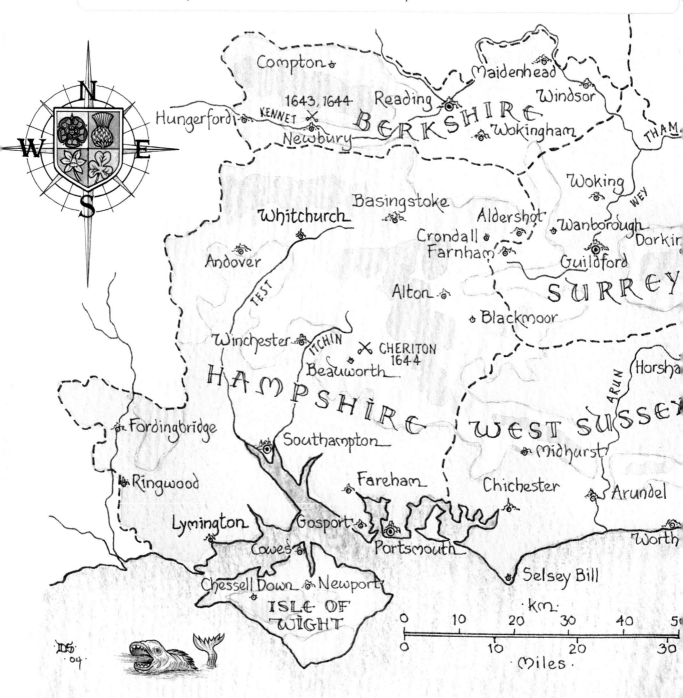

·THE·
SOUTH·EAST·

Windsor Castle

LONDON
AREA

Dartford

See
separate
map

Springhead

Margate

Rochester

Ramsgate

Monkton

Chatham
Tunstall

Faversham

Canterbury

STOUR

Bredgar

Richborough

Sevenoaks

Wrotham

Hollingbourne

Ringlemere

Godstone

Maidstone

Kingston

Deal

Reigate

K E N T

Dover

Ashford

Lyminge

Royal Tunbridge
Wells

Folkestone

Crawley

Tenterden

Haywards
Heath

EAST SUSSEX

ROTHER

Lydd

Rye

OUSE

MEDWAY

1264
Lewes

1066
Hastings

Hailsham

Newhaven

Brighton
and
Hove

Eastbourne

H.M.S. Victory

ABBOT'S BARTON, HAMPSHIRE

1999 Roman silver ring bezel, probably from the 3rdC AD: finder J. de Montfalcon (M/D). Within the bezel was a niello paste engraved with a figure of Bonus Eventus.

ALCISTON, EAST SUSSEX

1925 12 16thC silver coins, thought to have been concealed in 1586.

ALDINGBOURNE, WEST SUSSEX

[date?] 13thC gold brooch found by R.D. Frost (M/D).

Chichester Museum

ALDWORTH, WEST BERKSHIRE

1984 75 Roman *denarii* and 2 bronze coins from the 1st to the 2ndC AD found in a pot by a metal detectorist, thought to have been deposited *c.* AD 176–7. The coins were declared treasure trove.

West Berkshire Museum

ALTON, HAMPSHIRE

1999 Gold pendant featuring a male portrait and a triangular red gem: finder Peter Beasley (M/D).

2001 Highly engraved 15thC silver finger-ring: finder B. Ham (M/D).

ALTON AREA, HAMPSHIRE

1995 206 Celtic gold staters, a Roman ring and bracelet from the 1stC BC to the 1stC AD found 1ft below the surface on farmland: finders Peter Murphy and Peter Beasley (M/D). Shortly afterwards they found a second hoard a few feet away from the first, made up of 50 Celtic gold staters. Both hoards were declared treasure trove and valued at £102,074.

British Museum

2000 Solid gold jewel, possibly from the 1stC AD, found on farmland: finders Peter Murphy and Peter Beasley (M/D). It was 3in high, weighed almost 8oz and was in remarkably good condition. It was found about 25yd from their 2 earlier hoards of Celtic gold coins. The British Museum identified it as not Roman, and undatable.

ANDOVER AREA, HAMPSHIRE

1985 3,055 Roman bronze and silver washed coins found by Stephen Cole (M/D) in a pot, in a hazel coppice. The hoard pot, 10in tall and 6in across the top, was 8in below the surface beneath a young tree and collapsed as he attempted to remove it. Many of the coins were fused together.

APPLEDORE, TENTERDEN AREA, KENT

1997 450 Saxon silver coins and 30 cut halves dating from the 11thC AD found in a field by Philip Collins and Herbert Douch (M/D) along with 26 pieces of a clay pot. The coins were exceptionally well preserved and came from 30 different mints from the reigns from Cnut to Edward the Confessor. Thought to have been deposited *c.* 1050–3, each coin was worth £100–£2,000; it was the largest Saxon hoard found this century.

British Museum

1998 12 silver coins from the 11thC AD found in a field: finders Philip Collins and Herbert Douch (M/D). The silver pennies of Edward the Confessor (1042–66) were thought to have been deposited *c.* AD 1051–2 and were valued at £1,400.

British Museum

APPLESHAW, HAMPSHIRE

1985 3,502 Roman copper *antoniniani* from the 3rdC AD found by a metal detectorist in a pot in a field near Appleshaw, about 4 miles north-west of Andover. They were thought to have been deposited *c.* AD 282.

ARRETON DOWN, ISLE OF WIGHT

1998 10 silver groats and 8 half-groats of Edward II to Henry VI: finder D.I. Cole (M/D); they were thought to have been deposited in the late 1420s and were valued at £600.

Isle of Wight Museums Service

ARUNDEL AREA, WEST SUSSEX

1744 4thC AD Roman copper coins found in a small pot on the estate of Sir John Shelley.

ASH AND NORMANDY, SURREY

1904 115 Roman copper coins dated 3rd–4thC AD found in a pot by a child in a stream which runs through the garden of Manor Nurseries, near Guildford.

Guildford Museum

ASHFORD, KENT

1999–2000 9thC Anglo-Saxon silver strap-end: finder V.A. Butcher (M/D); later returned to the finder.

ASHAMPSTEAD GREEN, WEST BERKSHIRE

1935 62 silver coins from the 16th to the 17thC, thought to have been concealed in 1640.

ASHURST, HAMPSHIRE

1987   19 gold coins from the 1stC BC: finders Mike Sleeman and Pat Mulholland (M/D). The Chute-type Celtic gold staters, of 85–55 BC, were found at a depth of 2–5in and were valued at £4,000. They were later declared treasure trove.

Andover Museum

AWBRIDGE AREA, HAMPSHIRE

1902–3   About 180 silver pennies of Stephen (1135–54) and Henry II (1154–89) were found 2½ft below the ground on farmland. 50 coins were disposed of by the finder before the discovery was reported.

BALCOMBE, WEST SUSSEX

1897   More than 700 gold, and possibly silver, coins from the 14thC found in an iron container that resembled a modern-day coffee pot. The coins found on a piece of ground called Stockcroft opposite the rectory and were probably buried *c.* 1380, to avoid detection by French pirates, who were raiding the West Sussex coast at that time.

BARHAM, KENT

>1841   About 30 well-worn Roman *denarii* from the 2ndC AD found in a grave by labourers when removing a heap of stones on the road crossing Barham Downs.

BARHAM AREA, KENT

1998   Highly decorated Anglo-Saxon silver hooked tag from *c.* AD 880: finder Ian Lee (M/D).

1998   5 Anglo-Saxon silver-gilt sword rings from the late 6thC AD found two months after the silver hooked tag: finder P. Castle (M/D).

BARTON WOOD, ISLE OF WIGHT

1853   Large hoard of coins.

BASINGSTOKE, HAMPSHIRE

1967?   27 19thC gold coins, thought to have been concealed between 1837 and 1901.

[date?]   17thC coins found by workman digging the Basingstoke Canal. This Civil War hoard was valued at £120,000.

BEACHY HEAD, NEAR EASTBOURNE, EAST SUSSEX

1899   2,073 poorly preserved Roman copper *antoniniani* from the 3rdC AD found on Frost Hill close to the site of a Roman farmstead.

1914   550 Roman copper *antoniniani* from the 3rdC AD found by a labourer in one of the 'coombes' of the Eastbourne Downs, near Bullock Down. The badly preserved coins had been unearthed by rabbits and were lying loose on the ground.

1961–73   5,294 Roman copper *antoniniani*, dated AD 254–75, found in a broken pot by farmer Edgar Williams and his son while ploughing at Bullock Down Farm in 1961. Initially they found about 100 copper coins scattered on the surface and over the next few days collected the remainder of the hoard. In 1964 another 3,173 Roman coins were found in a pot on the same farm. The hoard comprised 27 *denarii* and 3,146 *antoniniani* and were found by R.P. Williams. In 1973, 5,445 Roman coins found in a bronze bucket by Derek Aldred (M/D) on Edgar Williams's land, the *antoniniani* dating from AD 273 or earlier, thought to have been concealed close to that date. Each hoard was buried separately. The bucket is held at the British Museum.

BEAUWORTH, WINCHESTER AREA, HAMPSHIRE

1833   More than 12,000 silver coins dating from the 11thC were found in a large leaden chest under a track close to the local manor house. Four boys were playing marbles when one of them noticed a piece of lead protruding from a hole in a wagon rut. When they went to look at the hole one of the boys pulled out a handful of silver coins. Soon most of the village were digging up the chest and dividing the coins between them. Many of the coins were silver pennies of William I and II, dating from before 1087. 6,282 of the coins were saved and were recorded by Edward Hawkins. It was Hawkins, the Keeper of the Coin Collection at the British Museum who advised the trustees of the British Museum to aim for completeness of their collection. It is a principle that is still followed today. The chest is held at the Winchester Museum.

City Museum, Winchester

BENENDEN, KENT

1964   98 gold and 35 silver coins from the 20thC found, thought to have been concealed in 1912.

BENTLEY, FARNHAM AREA, SURREY

1955   Roman coins found in the garden of Ash Cottage, close to the Pilgrim's Way.

BENTWORTH, HAMPSHIRE

1879   87 Celtic gold coins (82 Verica and five Epaticcus staters) from the 1stC AD, thought to have been deposited *c.* AD 25.

BERKSHIRE

1985   30 gold and 1,551 silver coins of Elizabeth I, Charles I and James I found by Chris Greensit, while levelling an area for concreting. The tractor bucket cracked open a pot lying 9in below the surface. The hoard was estimated to be worth over £50,000.

1987   About 150 Roman bronze coins dated AD 256–73 found in a pot in a ploughed field: finder Denny Hurst (M/D).

BERKSHIRE/HAMPSHIRE

1990s   2 Roman gold coins from the reigns of Theodosius I (AD 379–95) and Valentinian II (AD 375–92): finders A. and M. Parker (M/D).

BILSINGTON AREA, KENT

1999 15thC silver finger-ring, engraved with a female saint: finder P.J. Castle (M/D); returned to the finder.

BINSTEAD, WEST SUSSEX

1998 2 Bronze Age gold rings of 1500–1300 BC: finder C. Longridge (M/D). The rings were linked together and slightly crushed; they were valued at £800.

Littlehampton Museum

BISHAM, WINDSOR AND MAIDENHEAD

1878 318 gold coins from the 16thC found near Bisham Abbey, thought to have been concealed in 1565.

BISHOP'S WALTHAM, HAMPSHIRE

2001 17thC silver thimble, decorated and inscribed with lettering, found by a metal detectorist.

City Museum, Winchester

BITTERNE, CITY OF SOUTHAMPTON

>1798 3rdC AD Roman silver coins in a number of earthen vases found in fields and ditches adjoining the manor house at Bittern. Besides the coins were ash and pieces of bone.

*c.***1908** 1stC AD Roman coins. A contemporary report stated, 'Mr H Guillaume exhibited four similar coins recently found on the site of the Roman city Clausentum (Bitterne) near Southampton, together with bronze coins of the Roman Emperors Claudius I and Nero.'

1916 700 silver coins, thought to have been concealed in 1808.

BLACKMOOR, HAMPSHIRE

1741 Several hundred Roman coins and medallions found by children after an exceptional drought when Woolmer Pond dried out. The coins and medallions were lying closely grouped, as if they had been in a container that had rotted away.

1860s Bronze Age hoard found near Blackmoor House.

1867 About 100 Roman coins of Gallienus, Tetrici and Victorinus (AD 253–73) found near Blackmoor House.

c. **1870** 100 Roman bronze coins from the 3rdC AD found in a pot in a cottage garden west of the road from Eveley corner to Hogmore.

1873 More than 29,802 Roman billon *antoniniani* from the 3rdC AD found in 2 earthenware jars in Blackmoor Park, about a quarter of a mile north-west of Woolmer Pond. They were found during trench work on the Earl of Selbourne's Hampshire estate and were offered to guests over the years as souvenirs. Thought to have been deposited *c.* AD 296 or later, the *antoniniani* were of Gordianus III (AD 238–44) to Allectus (AD 294–7), and were thought to have been buried *c.* AD 294–6. This was such a large hoard that it could have been a military pay chest, or in some way connected to the government.

1875 46 Roman bronze coins from the 3rdC AD found in a pot.

BLENDWORTH, HAMPSHIRE

1860 240 silver coins from the 16th to the 17thC found, thought to have been concealed in 1644. The latest coin was a 1644 Exeter shilling.

BOGNOR REGIS, WEST SUSSEX

[date?] Small gold bar found on the beach. It was probably swept ashore from a wreck of Spanish origin.

BOSSINGHAM, KENT

2000 13thC gold finger-ring: finder Alan John Punyar (M/D). The original setting had been lost and it was returned to the finder.

BRABOURNE LEES AREA, KENT

1999 16thC silver-gilt dress-hook: finder J. Sinclair; valued at £350.
British Museum

BRACKNELL, BRACKNELL FOREST

1956 More than 9 silver coins from the 16th to the 17th C, thought to have been concealed in 1640.

1998 2 Henry IV gold half-nobles from the 15thC found by N. White (M/D), possibly deposited *c.*1420–30; they were returned to the finder.

BRAISHFIELD, HAMPSHIRE

1999 Middle Bronze Age gold ring (1300–1100 BC): finder D. Palmer (M/D). It had become distorted in the ground but was valued at £450.

BREDGAR, KENT

1940 120 14thC gold coins in an earthenware jug found under ivy roots, near an old flint wall, in the garden of Chantry cottages. It was the former site of the old Chantry Hall (built in 1398). The hoard comprised 93 gold nobles, 24 half-nobles, and 3 quarter-nobles, of Edward III and Richard II. The latest coin was dated 1388. The finder thought that they were of no value when he first discovered them, but it was estimated in 1980 that they would be worth a minimum of £40,000, maybe c. £100,000 today.

1957 34 Roman gold coins from between the 1stC BC and the 1stC AD found during the digging of foundations for a bungalow in Gore Road. 33 *aurei* were found together and further search produced another coin, but no trace of a container. Some of the coins were still stacked together and lying on their edges, so it is probable that they were packed in rolls and wrapped in cloth that had rotted in the ground. The *aurei*, dated from Julius Caesar and Claudius, and the four of Claudius were in mint condition. 2 years later 3 more *aurei* were found, bringing the total to 37. They were thought to have been buried in AD 43 and valued at £40,000–£80,000 in 1980, £100,000–£200,000 today.
British Museum

BRENZETT, KENT

c. **2000** 13thC gold finger-ring, set with a garnet, ruby or amethyst: finder M. Longman (M/D); later returned to the finder.

BRIGHTON AND HOVE

>1761 About 1,000 Roman *denarii* from the 2nd to the 3rdC AD found in an urn.

1840? 9 silver coins and 1 billon of William IV and Victoria, thought to have been deposited in 1840, found during the digging of foundations for the church hall of the Countess of Huntingdon church. They were later returned to the finder.

1888–9 2ndC AD Roman coins found by labourers digging for flints on the downs. The coins were in poor condition and were found in several urns about 3ft below the surface.

1904 928 Roman billon *antoniniani*, thought to have been deposited *c.* AD 275, found in a lead container during building work.

1939 About 455 Roman copper coins from the 3rdC AD found in a pot by workmen digging a trench for a water main on the building estate at Woodlands Avenue in Hove.

1984 Very fine silver penny of Edward the Confessor (1042–66): finder J. Hancocks (M/D). It was struck at the Nottingham mint by the moneyer Wolnoth and is the only hammered cross type known to have been produced by him.

1984 A silver quarter-stater from AD 10–40: finder J. Hancocks (M/D); only two other specimens are known.

BUCKLEBURY, WEST BERKSHIRE

1981 19thC silver communion plate found in a wood by Robert Lawes (M/D), who was able to read the inscription. He took it to the vicar, who was delighted, but said there was a chalice with it. Robert went back to the spot and came across the chalice nearby. These items had been presented to Frilsham church in 1864 and were stolen in 1962.

BUCKLER'S HARD, HAMPSHIRE

1970? 4 billon coins, thought to have been concealed in 1806.

BURGESS HILL AREA, WEST SUSSEX

1980 A rare Roman bronze fibula-type brooch from the 2ndC: finder Peter Bish (M/D).

BURGHCLERE, HAMPSHIRE

1971 167 silver coins of Edward IV to Charles II found in a pot, in a cottage wall, thought to have been deposited after 1660.

BURLEY, NEW FOREST, HAMPSHIRE

1979 4 gold staters from 50 BC found in a wooded area, between Picket Post and Burley.

BURMARSH, KENT

1999 Anglo-Saxon silver hooked tag (an all-purpose fastening used to secure clothing) from the mid-9thC: finder I. Lee (M/D).

CADNAM, HAMPSHIRE

>1853 About 1,700 Roman bronze coins from the 3rdC AD found in a pot.

1983 More than 610 Roman copper coins from the 4thC AD found in a pot during work to dig footing trenches for an extension for a house named Oakley in Southampton Road. The workman who found them removed the coins, but later surrendered the greater majority of them, together with the shards of the pot.

CAMBERLEY/BAGSHOT AREA, SURREY

1998 15th–16thC gold posy ring found by Adam Parker (M/D) in perfect condition; it was inscribed in Gothic-style lettering. The ring was later declared treasure trove.

CANTERBURY, KENT

The Romans under Julius Caesar arrived in Canterbury c. 55 BC and following the AD 43 invasion the importance of the town was recognised, as it became an important settlement. During the reign of King Ethelbert St Augustine arrived in England and converted many to Christianity. Ethelbert's son began building a monastery in AD 602, which became the present-day cathedral, the centre of Britain's Christianity. The stone castle and city walls were built early in the 12thC. A great part of the archaeological history of Canterbury has become known following the Second World War, when much of the city was damaged, which allowed for excavations in areas which could have remained hidden for ever.

[date?] 117 Roman copper coins from the 3rdC AD discovered when they fell from some roof timbers.

1901 358 silver coins from the 12thC discovered during work on the Archbishop's Palace. They were thought to have been buried c. 1130–5 and taken to Bournemouth, where experts believed they originated.

1947 49 silver coins, thought to have been concealed in 1643.

1956 1 silver and 3 billon coins from the 16th to the 17thC, thought to have been concealed between 1561 and 1603.

1961 50 Roman silver *antoniniani* from the 3rdC AD found hidden in the area west of the hypocaust stokehole in the Roman building in Butcher's Lane.

1962 A hoard of Roman gold and silver items from the 4th to 5thC AD found during the digging of the foundations of a new bridge for the A2 bypass, on the right bank of the western branch of the River Stour, a few yards south-west of the city wall in Westgate Gardens. The hoard comprised a gold ring and bezel, a gold clasp in two pieces, 4 silver ingots, 12 silver spoons, a silver spoon with a prong at the other end, a silver pin, and a few silver and copper coins. It was declared treasure trove.

[date?] Late 6thC gold items recovered from a grave in St Martin's church. There was a brooch, a Roman intaglio, 5 imperial (or pseudo-imperial) and Merovingian gold coins, and a 'medalet' mounted as a pendant.

Liverpool Museum

CARISBROOKE, ISLE OF WIGHT

1998 A 15thC gold finger-ring, engraved with a representation of St Christopher: finder Keith Stuart (M/D); returned to the finder.

CHADDLEWORTH, WEST BERKSHIRE

1850 About 100 Roman silver coins from the 4thC AD found in a vase 2 miles north of the Upper Baydon Road.

CHALTON, HAMPSHIRE

1850 Roman coins found in a crock and they were disposed of in Portsmouth by the finder.

1999 17th–18thC gold finger-ring, decorated and inscribed with lettering, and dated about 1670–1720: finder P.D. Beasley (M/D); returned to the finder.

CHARTHAM, KENT

1999–2000   7 Iron Age gold coins from the 1stC BC: finders C.A. Smith and D. Villanueva (M/D). These Gallo-Belgic gold staters were thought to have been deposited about 50 BC. The 6 found together were valued at £1,157.

CHELSHAM, SURREY

1996   Gilded silver livery badge of 1525–60, which had belonged to the Gainsford family of Crowhurst, found in a field: finder Martin Hay (M/D).

British Museum

1999   16thC silver-gilt dress-hook: finder M. Hay; valued at £420.

British Museum

CHERTSEY, SURREY

[date?]   14thC pewter cruet found near the abbey river which was close to the remains of the abbey at Chertsey.

CHESHAM, SURREY

1999   Roman gold bulla probably dating from the 1stC AD: finder M. Hay; valued at £350.

Guildford Museum

CHESSEL DOWN, ISLE OF WIGHT

1855   Anglo-Saxon silver-gilt and niello brooch, probably made *c.* AD 515, found by George Hillier in the grave of a woman during the excavation of a cemetery. There were also two stamped pendants, a pair of tweezers, an iron knife and a waist buckle. It has become known as the great square-headed gold brooch.

British Museum

CHESSINGTON, SURREY

1998   4 Iron Age gold coins from the 1stC BC found by PC Gary Roy and PC Andrew Dunn (it was Andrew's second time out with a metal detector.) The Gallo-Belgic gold staters were thought to have been deposited about 50 BC. A year later they found two more at the same site which was on farmland with no evidence of an Iron Age settlement.

Kingston Museum

CHICHESTER, WEST SUSSEX

1774   1st and 2ndC coins of all the emperors from Claudius to Commodus (AD 43–192) found in a pot at Woolmer Lake Pond.

1819   About 700 silver Roman coins from the 1st to 2ndC AD found in an urn by workmen digging out soil from Palace Field. There was also a skeleton, the head of a Roman spear, pottery, glass and many other artefacts.

1998   Inscribed mid-17thC silver huntsman's whistle: finder S. Burch (M/D); valued at £2,000.

Chichester District Museum

CHIDDINGLY, EAST SUSSEX

1999   Late 15thC silver badge found by a metal detectorist. The badge is in the form of a boar, a symbol of allegiance to Richard III.

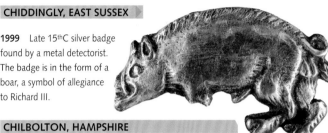

CHILBOLTON, HAMPSHIRE

1941   About 900 Roman copper coins from the 4thC AD in two vessels found by Royal Artillery gunners digging a trench on Hill Farm on Chilbolton Downs. The coins, which were in very fine condition, were dispersed among the finders but 820 were later recovered and are held at City Museum, Winchester.

City Museum, Winchester

CHILHAM, KENT

1999   13th or 14thC decorated and inscribed silver-gilt brooch: finder D. Villanueva (M/D); returned to the finder.

CHOBHAM, SURREY

1772   About 200 Roman silver and copper coins from the 4th to 5thC AD found in a pot during ploughing.

CLAYTON, BRIGHTON AREA, WEST SUSSEX

1979–80   Bronze Age axe head, 2 ingots and pottery were found near to Clayton Windmills: finder Gerald Gaston (M/D).

CLIMPING, WEST SUSSEX

2000   18 Celtic gold coins found on farmland during a metal-detecting rally; they were of a type never seen before. At the same rally 89 Roman silver coins dated AD 81–140 were found 15in below the surface: finder Anthony Hunt (M/D); both hoards were later declared treasure trove.

COBHAM, KENT

1883   836 Roman copper coins from the 4thC AD found in a pot by labourers while grubbing the roots of a tree in Cobham Park.

COBHAM AREA, KENT

1984   A gold terminal of a torc dating from 1400 to 900 BC found in a field: finder Lawrence Mulcrow (M/D).

2000–1   Late 8thC silver penny of Cynethrith, wife of Offa, King of Mercia: finder Ray Barker (M/D). *(Illustration shows obverse and reverse.)*

COMPTON, WEST BERKSHIRE

1852   500 Roman silvered coins from the 3rdC AD found in an urn in a wood below Compton Cowdown.

[date?]   Roman gold, silver and copper coins found in a jar on Lowbury Hill. The coins ranged from the Emperors Claudius to the Constantines.

1981   281 Roman *siliquae* from the 4th to 5thC AD found by Alan Clark (M/D) over a section of the Ridgeway on Compton Downs to the north-west of the village. They were declared treasure trove.

West Berkshire Museum

COMPTON DOWN, HAMPSHIRE

1758   More than 300 silver coins from the 12thC found buried with a skeleton. They were silver pennies and cut pennies, dated 1154–89.

CORHAMPTON, HAMPSHIRE

1850–5   291 Roman copper coins (all folles except for 1 *antoniniani*) from the 3rd to 4thC AD found in a pot at the Mill Barrow, at the north-west corner of Preshaw Park, near the Fox and Hounds Inn, Beauworth.

CRAWLEY, HAMPSHIRE

2001   Highly decorated 9thC Anglo-Saxon silver strap-end: finder T. Austin (M/D).

City Museum, Winchester

CRONDALL, HAMPSHIRE

1869   About 300 Roman coins from the 3rdC AD found at Barley Pound, Crondall.

CRONDALL AREA, HAMPSHIRE

1828   101 Anglo-Saxon gold coins and jewellery from the 7thC found on Bagshot Heath. Two young brothers named Lefroy went shooting snipe and partridge, accompanied by their gamekeeper. On a stretch of flat ground, about a mile from the old earthwork known as Caesar's Camp, one of the brothers noticed that a turf-cutter had been at work. A piece of turf had been lifted and in the centre of the bare soil there was a small heap of what seemed to be brass waistcoat buttons. On examination they were found to be gold coins of unusual design; along with the coins were 2 jewelled ornaments and 2 gold chains. The Crondall Hoard, as it has become known, now consists of 97 coins, the others having been lost. There are 18 French, 19 Saxon copies, 52 native Saxon design, 7 of dubious origin and a forgery. Two unusual pieces of jewellery were also found, but these have since been lost. They turned out to be Merovingian gold tremisses (or thrymsa) of French origin, which were copied by the Anglo-Saxons. They were in circulation for a very short time in the 7thC and were thought to have been buried AD 645–75. This was one of the most valuable hoards ever discovered, estimated to be worth *c.* £250,000 in 1979, making it worth *c.* £750,000 today.

Ashmolean Museum

CRUNDALE, KENT

1861   An Anglo-Saxon silver-gilt 'fish' buckle, dating from the mid-7thC AD. It is believed to have belonged to a Christian; the fish was an early symbol of Christianity, and may have housed a relic within the hollow buckle plate. Artistically, it fully reflects the pagan culture of early Anglo-Saxon life. It was found in a man's grave along with a copper-alloy buckle with garnet inlays and a sword with a decorated pommel.

British Museum

CURRIDGE, WEST BERKSHIRE

1998–9   425 Roman bronze coins from the 1st to 3rdC AD found in a jar with a Samianware dish: finders B. Aldridge and H. Haddrell. The coins were worn sistertii, except for 6 dupondii, thought to have been deposited *c.* AD 209; they were valued at £3,000.

West Berkshire Museum

DAMERHAM, HAMPSHIRE

>2002   16 silver coins from the 14th and 15thC found over several years up to 2002, thought to have been deposited *c.* 1480–1500: finder A. Truepenny (M/D); returned to the finder.

DARTFORD, KENT

1825   60 silver coins dated 1100–35, believed to have been buried *c.* 1160, when the country was in turmoil. Among the silver pennies there were coins of Henry I, Stephen (including irregular issues), Empress Matilda and David I of Scotland.

[date?]   Decorated Saxon glass bowl dating from *c.* AD 450, found in a 5thC grave in the grounds of the old Darenth Park Hospital. Known as the Darenth Bowl, it is a Christian artefact and is one of the most spectacular bowls found in Britain. It is dedicated to St Rufinus of Soissons and is in the Frankish tradition.

Dartford Borough Museum

DEAL, KENT

1765   Silver coins in an urn found in a field.

1832   About 2,000 Roman coins from the 3rdC AD found in a pot.

DENGE MARSH, BETWEEN DUNGENESS AND LYDD, KENT

1739   200–500 coins and cut coins from the 11thC found during the digging of a hole for a fence post. They were silver pennies, cut half-pennies and quarter-pennies of Harold II and William I, thought to have been buried *c.* 1068, possibly connected with the Kent rising of 1067.

DETLING AREA, KENT

1999   Early 13thC silver cross pendant: finder B. Petit (M/D); valued at £1,050 and returned to the finder.

DORKING, SURREY

1817   12 silver and 962 Anglo-Saxon coins and foreign coins from the 9thC found in a wooden box, which fell to pieces as it was discovered. It included silver pennies of Coenwulf of Mercia, Ethelwulf of Wessex and Archbishop Ceolnoth of Canterbury and was thought to have been buried in AD 861, when the Vikings unsuccessfully attempted to storm Winchester. 174 coins were retained by the British Museum.

British Museum

1911 Roman coins discovered in a pot.

1999 Gold penannular ring dating from 1150 to 750 BC: finder Jason Thurbin (M/D); valued at £350.

2003 2 bronze axe heads and the end of a sword scabbard chape, also made of bronze, dating to the late Bronze Age (1150–900 BC) was unearthed in Norbury Park at Mickleham, near Dorking, by Martin Hay (M/D) on land belonging to Surrey County Council. The finds were discovered 450yd from the west bank of the River Mole. They were declared treasure trove.

[date?] An Iron Age urn.

DOVER, KENT

1765 About 300 pennies of Henry II and III, dated 1154–1272, found in a lead case during ploughing. It was possibly buried during the French raid of 1295.

1817 Gold, copper and other coins, a belt and a breastplate in 2 metal vessels found on a hill. Thomas Page had apparently dreamed of a large sum of money buried on a hill near Dover. He memorised the exact spot, obtained permission to search, took a party to the spot, and found the hoard.

1955 686 silver coins from the 13thC found in a lead box during work to install a new gas main in Market Street. A workman's pickaxe struck what seemed to be a lead pipe at about 2ft deep and it rolled to the bottom of the trench. The lid of what was in fact a box came partially off and some silver coins were exposed. The foreman collected them and took them to the local museum, where the curator recognised their importance. The latest datable coin was 1295, the year that 10,000 Frenchmen landed at Dover and plundered and burnt houses on 2 August. Later the British Museum took possession of 92 coins.

British Museum

1991 Macedonian gold stater from the 2ndC BC near to Dover: finder Roger Reid (M/D). It features the head of Philip II of Macedonia and is an imitation of a 4thC BC coin.

1995 17thC gold memento mori ring: finder George Watman (M/D). The ring was set with a white skull and inscribed with lettering; it was returned to the finder.

DUMMER, HAMPSHIRE

1919 More than 123 silver coins from the 16th to the 17thC, thought to have been concealed in 1643.

DUNDRIDGE, HAMPSHIRE

1999 Anglo-Saxon silver and nielloed strap-end from c. 870–900: finder M. Gillham (M/D).

Hampshire Service

EARNLEY, WEST SUSSEX

1824 About 840 Roman *denarii* from the 2nd to the 3rdC AD found in an urn during ploughing near Almondington Common.

EAST GARSTON, WEST BERKSHIRE

1998 2 silver pennies of Edward I and III from the 13th to 14thC found by A.J. Gray while searching at a detectorist rally. They were thought to have been deposited c. 1375 and were returned to the finder.

EAST GRINSTEAD, WEST SUSSEX

1977 150 bronze/copper pennies dating from the 1890s to 1917 found near the railway bridge over Station Road.

EAST MEON, HAMPSHIRE

1998 17 silver coins from the 16thC: finder C. Longridge and L. West (M/D). The coins were of Philip and Mary and Elizabeth I, thought to have been deposited c. 1570. They were valued at £550.

EAST WITTERING, WEST SUSSEX

[date?] Roman coins and gold pieces found along this 6-mile stretch of beach.

EASTBOURNE, EAST SUSSEX

1956 10 gold coins from the 19thC, thought to have been concealed in 1870.

1878–9 About 682 Roman copper *antoniniani* from the 3rdC AD found in a pot 2ft below the surface by men digging for flints between Beachy Head and Birling Gap.

1980 62 silver coins, all Victorian save for one George III crown and dated 1819–1900. They belonged to two elderly residents and were thought to have been concealed c. 1910.

1981 3 gold staters found on the beach: finder local farmer Eddie Williams. 1 was in the mud under the pier, while the other 2 were found along the low-tide line.

EASTCHURCH, KENT

1977 1stC BC Belgic quarter-stater found sticking out of the cliff face by Victor Cato when he was fossil-hunting. Dated 356–336 BC, it was made in France and is worth about £500.

ECCLES, KENT

[date?]   Fish-type buckle, similar to the one found at Cundle in Kent, found in a man's grave.

EXTON, HAMPSHIRE

2001   Gold penannular ring of 1300–1100 BC: finder Keith Hutchings (M/D).

City Museum, Winchester

FAREHAM, HAMPSHIRE

1959   254 silver coins from the 19th and 20thC, thought to have been concealed in 1920.

FAREHAM AREA, HAMPSHIRE

1979   Middle Bronze Age transitional palstave and a spearhead of 1400–1000 BC.

FREEFOLK, HAMPSHIRE

1940   642 gold coins from the 19thC found by workmen repairing an old cottage on the farm estate of Lord Portal. They found an earthenware jug containing 358 gold sovereigns and within the hour a second jug was found containing a further 254 gold half-sovereigns. The latest coin was dated 1876, around the time they were thought to have been concealed.

FARNBOROUGH, KENT

1980–1   Silver coin of AD 780, struck during the reign of King Offa of Mercia: finder John Harlin (M/D). When sold at Sotheby's it fetched £1,400, which equates to around £3,000 today.

FARNHAM, SURREY

1968   Part of a 19thC gold scabbard studded with 663 diamonds found in the River Wey: finder Fred Besch; 2 large stones had been removed, but 633 small diamonds remained, set in enamel and gold. The scabbard was believed to have been one of the many that were presented to Lord Nelson following his victory at the Battle of the Nile in 1803.

1976   68 silver coin clippings and a small piece of silver dating from the 15th to 17thC found near the edge of Farnham Castle moat in Farnham Park, thought to have been deposited in 1660 or later; they were declared treasure trove.

1993   Tudor gold cloak pin found by Ian Fletcher (M/D) under an oak tree, in Farnham Park. Made from enamelled gold and set with a sapphire it was valued at £35,000. It was declared treasure trove, and returned to the finder.

FAVERSHAM, KENT

According to the Anglo-Saxon Chronicle, 'In this year [1154] died the King Stephen; and he was buried where his wife and his son were buried, at Faversham; which monastery they founded.' Faversham was a centre of jewellery manufacture in the Anglo-Saxon period.

[date?]   2 highly decorated and enamelled Roman dragonesque brooches.

[date?]   Anglo-Saxon gold and garnet pendant.

[date?]   Anglo-Saxon necklace, with amethysts, dating from the late 6th to early 7thC.

[date?]   2 Anglo-Saxon disc brooches.

c.**2000**   Excavations at Syndale Park, an estate near Faversham, revealed a small ribbon development alongside a cobbled section of Watling Street. There were numerous Roman finds.

FAWKHAM, KENT

2000   13th or 14thC gold finger-ring found during archaeological excavation at Fawkham manor house.

FINGLESHAM, KENT

1964   7thC Anglo-Saxon gilt bronze buckle, showing the figure of a naked man wearing a 2-horned headdress and holding 2 spears. It was indicative of the cult of Woden. The site at Finglesham was an Anglo-Saxon cemetery extensively excavated by Sonia Hawkes. The Finglesham Man, as he has become known, features on the village sign.

Ashmolean Museum

FIVE ASHES, EAST SUSSEX

1044   5 silver coins from the 16thC, thought to have been concealed in 1551.

FOLKESTONE, KENT

1870   3 gold Gallo-Belgic quarter-staters from the 1stC BC found in a cliff.

1999   Gold ingot, which could be anything from Iron Age to Roman: finder Mr Coyne (M/D); returned to the finder.

[date?]   Elizabeth I florins found on Sandgate beach and other beaches. They were thought to come from a hoard buried on the cliff top that had fallen onto the beach as erosion took place.

FORDINGBRIDGE, HAMPSHIRE

c. **1845**   16 Roman silver coins from the 4thC AD found in a small crock by a labourer while grubbing an earth bank at Amberwood, on the borders of the New Forest.

1893   4,020 Roman copper coins from the 3rdC AD found in a pot by ploughmen in a field at Brookheath to the north-west of the village; all were in a remarkably good state of preservation.

1910   30 gold coins from the 18th to 19thC, thought to have been concealed between 1760 and 1816 on the Breamore estate.

1998   1,782 Roman base-silver radiates found on the Breamore estate, with the latest coins from the reign of Probus (AD 276–82). Later 398

136

Roman base-silver coins from the 3rdC AD found in a pot by Mr Gifford (M/D) about 100yd from the first hoard. It is thought that these make up just a part of a much larger hoard.

FRENSHAM, SURREY

1999 390 Roman and Iron Age silver and bronze coins from the 1st and 2ndC AD found by members of the Surrey Archaeological Society (M/D). There were 2 Iron Age silver and 2 bronze coins, and 6 Roman silver and 380 bronze coins; they were thought to have been deposited c. AD 160.

2000–1 1 Iron Age silver coin, 2 Roman *denarii* and 73 copper-alloy coins from the 1st to the 2ndC AD found by members of the Surrey Archaeological Society (M/D). They were thought to have been deposited c. AD 160.

FRESHWATER, ISLE OF WIGHT

1863 250 Roman bronze coins from the 3rdC AD found in an urn by a labourer.

FRIMLEY, SURREY

c. **1708** Roman coins and intaglia found in an urn.

FULLERTON, HAMPSHIRE

2001 15thC silver finger-ring with a heart-shaped engraved bezel: finder M. Crate (M/D); returned to the finder.

FUNTLEY, HAMPSHIRE

1978 1stC BC gold stater: finder Michael Chapman (M/D).

GILLINGHAM, MEDWAY

1909 722 4th–5thC AD Roman copper coins in a small vase found by a workman grubbing up a tree on the outskirts of the village. The coins were in an advanced state of oxidation.

Guildhall Museum, Rochester

GODSTONE, SURREY

1999 15thC silver-gilt finger-ring fragment: finder D. Hunt (M/D). The fragment of the ring consisting of the bezel and part of the hoop was decorated with figures of saints; it was valued at £300.

2000 Roman silver finger-ring from the 1st to 2ndC AD found during archaeological excavation: finder David Hunt (M/D); returned to the finder.

c. **2001** 13thC copper-alloy seal found by a detectorist belonging to a sheriff of Kent in the 1260s. The seal has 2 boars' heads face to face and fleurs-de-lis above and below along with the inscription, S FULCONIS PEYFORER (The seal of Fulk Peyforer). They were an old Kent family dating back to the Domesday Book.

GOODNESTONE, KENT

1994–8 29 Roman silver coins from the 4thC AD found by Les Hetherington (M/D) over a four-year period. There were 28 base-silver nummi and a half-nummus, thought to have been deposited AD 316–28.

GORING, WEST SUSSEX

1907 About 435 Roman copper coins from the 3rdC AD found in a pot by a brickmaker digging in the Courtlands brickfield.

GRAFFHAM, WEST SUSSEX

1982–3 10 gold sovereigns, 2 silver coins, and 50 copper farthings dating from the early 19thC found by Derek Powell (M/D) quite close together on farmland on Graffham Downs. They were thought to have been dropped by a trader and may have been in a leather pouch; they were declared not treasure trove.

GRAVESEND, KENT

1838 540 gold and silver coins and a gold cross, thought to have been concealed in AD 875, at the time Alfred the Great was fighting the Danish invaders. There were Anglo-Saxon silver pennies and foreign gold coins. The gold cross was looped and inset with a roundel of coloured glass.

GREAT SHEFFORD, WEST BERKSHIRE

1889 16th and 17thC silver coins, thought to have been concealed between 1625 and 1649.

GREENHITHE, KENT

1894–5 1stC AD Roman coins found by a gardener in a lead receptacle, in grounds of Eagle Cliff. In a letter in 1954 from the Revd H.E.E. Hayes, St Stephen's Vicarage, Mernda, Victoria, Australia, he said, 'The find was not disclosed but some odd coins crept out for sale! I was a small boy at the time and acquired a Denarius of Tiberius Caesar and another of Claudius Caesar in EF condition.'

GUILDFORD, SURREY

1983 173 silver coins dating to the 1550s put through the letterbox of the Guildford Museum by an anonymous person. The hoard was declared treasure trove.

GUILDFORD AREA, SURREY

1979 33 gold half-sovereigns and other coins from the 18th and 19thC found in scrub woodland, on land once part of the Lovelace estate: finder Eric Hill. In 1936 it was sold to the Surrey County Council; the site was in a triangle formed by an old footpath and the A3. The find was valued at c. £1,500.

1984 12 Celtic British/Roman silver coins found in the area known as the Hog's Back: finders Rick Goodale and Malcolm Bridger (M/D). They were mostly Celtic British, dating from the late Iron Age, and were later declared treasure trove.

1984 10 gold and 125 silver and bronze coins of 20 BC–AD 35 found in the next field to where the earlier finds (above) had been located: finders Tom Chuter, Stuart Hazelwood and Cliff Kill (M/D). They were declared treasure trove and valued at £10,000, roughly worth double that today.

HAILSHAM, EAST SUSSEX

1950 22 gold and 7 silver coins from the 19thC found by a 14-year-old schoolboy raking earth at the bottom of a ditch near his home. He found 14 gold sovereigns, 8 gold half-sovereigns, 6 half-crowns, and a Victorian shilling, which were thought to have been concealed in 1871.

HAMBLE, HAMPSHIRE

1964 2,494 Romano-British billon coins from the 4thC found on the recreation ground in Hamble, believed to have been buried in AD 349. A number of these coins were not represented in the national collection, and the British Museum retained 200.

British Museum

1968 2,466 Roman copper coins from the 3rd to 4thC AD found during work for the extension of a playing field at College Copse.

HAMPSHIRE

1970s An *aureus* from c. AD 290, struck for the Emperor Carausius, who was ruling in Britain, found in crazy paving by teacher Clive Bell while weeding in his grandmother's garden. It was valued at £60 by the local museum, but he sold it to Seaby's for £8,000, which would equate to around 3 times that amount today.

1987 142 Bronze Age gold coins from the 1stC BC: finders Ron Holmes and the Andover Metal Detecting Club (M/D). The coins were from two separate hoards of 34 Gallo-Belgic coins and 108 British coins; later declared treasure trove.

2000–1 68 late Bronze Age socketed axe heads were found in an area a yard in diameter: finder Jason Rogers.

NORTH HAMPSHIRE

1991 Mid-7thC gold pendant found on an old pathway on farmland: finder Bernard Pye. It was 9in down beneath a Georgian penny of 1806. The British Museum identified it as Pagan-Saxon with a garnet setting.

HARTING BEACON, NEAR PETERSFIELD, WEST SUSSEX

1892 5 silver pennies from the 10th to the 11thC found by men digging for flints on the south side of Harting Beacon.

HARTLEY, HAMPSHIRE

1773 700 gold coins dating from the 17thC found in a pot in a field. During the Civil War, Sir Nicholas Stuart had buried 1,550 broad pieces,

his entire fortune. In 1773 his grandson, Sir Simon Stuart, found a note in his grandfather's handwriting giving directions to the hoard. Upon discovery it was found to contain just 700 coins, having been disturbed by ploughing.

HASLEMERE, SURREY

1972 Hoard of early 20thC jewellery in a rusty tin: finder Douglas Oram. It comprised a diamond necklace, and 20 gold, diamond, ruby, and sapphire rings, identified by the police as having been stolen from a local house 50 years earlier.

HASTINGS, EAST SUSSEX

>1862 50 to 60 Roman coins from the 1st to the 2ndC AD found with 5 or 6 broken vases while digging the foundations of a house on the west side of Warrior Square.

1901 150 gold coins from the 18th and19thC, thought to have been concealed between 1816 and 1820.

1989 59 Roman silver and 92 bronze coins dated 32 BC–AD 125 were found on a building site at Wilphinstone Road: finder L. Drake and Bert Douch (M/D). The coins were in two groups: the first consisted of 92 bronze coins and the remains of a pot; the second, buried 40–50ft away, had 59 *denarii*.

HAWKSHILL, KENT

1989 Victorian gold button brooch: finder Roy Pilkington.

HAWKSHILL AREA, KENT

1989 2 Saxon gilded brooches from the 5th to 6thC AD found in a field within 20ft of each other: finder David Barwell (M/D).

HAYLING ISLAND, HAMPSHIRE

1964? 2 gold and 30 silver coins dating from the 16th or 17thC were found, thought to have been concealed in 1623.

1966 16thC silver coins found in a brass box on the foreshore by Terence Davey, who was fishing with his brothers. Two months later, after apparently arguing with his brothers, and after a claim by the Customs and Excise on behalf of the Receiver of Wrecks over the ownership and reward sharing, he threw the box and the coins back into the sea.

HOLLINGBOURNE, KENT

1959 5,470 Roman copper coins from the 3rdC AD found in a pot 2ft below the surface by William Reddick while ploughing a field on Old Mill Farm. The coins, which were all *antoniniani* apart from two *denarii*, were declared treasure trove.

1998 8 silver coins, of Mary I and Elizabeth I, thought to have been deposited around mid- to late 1570s: finder B.E. Petit (M/D); returned to the finder.

2003 Bronze Age hoard dating from *c.* 800 BC found 18in below the surface: finder David Button (M/D). He reported the find to Kent County Council's Heritage Conservation Team and a thorough excavation was organised. In all there were 12 axe heads, 6 blades, 2 spearheads, and 2 sword/dagger handles; it was later declared treasure trove.

HOLYBOURNE, HAMPSHIRE

1976 117 Roman billon coins from the 4thC AD found during an excavation. They were thought to have been deposited *c.* AD 378.

HORSTED KEYNES, WEST SUSSEX

1929 64 gold nobles of Edward II found in an area newly cultivated 50yd north of the manor house at Horsted Keynes.

HOUGHAM WITHOUT, NEAR DOVER, KENT

1780 About 300 7thC silver coins, believed to have been concealed.

HURSTBOURNE TARRANT, HAMPSHIRE

[date?] A 17thC pewter beaker found in a well, thought to date *c.* 1610–12.

ICKHAM, KENT

1974 29 billon coins from the 4thC AD found during archaeological excavations. The coins were dated 364–83, from the reigns of Valentinian I, Valens and Gratian.

INKPEN, WEST BERKSHIRE

1950 9 gold coins from the 17th to 18thC , thought to have been concealed in 1719.

IPING, WEST SUSSEX

>1909 Roman coins in an urn found while digging at the fortified camp on a hill over Milland Place, north-north-west of Iping.

ISLE OF SHEPPEY, KENT

1968 415 silver coins from Edward VI to Charles I, thought to have been concealed in 1648, found in an old pot during the building of a new school at Clarke's Farm. A digger driver struck an earthenware pot containing the coins; he was allowed to keep the coins, worth several thousand pounds. In 1648 the area was owned by Sir Edward Hales, a secret Royalist sympathiser. The money was perhaps to pay Royalist soldiers.

ISLE OF WIGHT

c. **1890** 9 billon coins dated AD 188–9 were found in a cave.

2000 A gold ribbon bracelet of 1150–750 BC was found at West Wight: finder Ben Griffiths (M/D).

ITCHEN ABBAS, HAMPSHIRE

1914 234 silver coins from the 16th and 17thC found at Manor Farm, thought to have been concealed in 1644 as Royalist troops fled through Hampshire.

ITCHEN NAVIGATION CANAL, NEAR WINCHESTER, HAMPSHIRE

1977? A 19thC silver communion set of three pieces found on the towpath: finder Malcolm Hill (M/D). About a foot down he discovered a solid silver wafer tray, a chalice and a wine bottle. Each piece was engraved HIS and hallmarked 'London 1885 by JNM'. It was a 'sick communion set' used by priests to bring the Sacrament to the sick or infirm in their homes.

KENT

1912 14 gold coins from the 2ndC BC found in a hollow stone.

1957? 62 silver coins from the 16th and 17thC, thought to have been concealed in 1645 (Mr Binney's Hoard).

1962 4thC silver objects found by Graham Dixon; the find only came to light 20 years later when his parents died. He had taken them home and failed to declare them, which resulted in him only being awarded £853, 10 per cent of their value.

1970s 6thC Anglo-Saxon silver-gilt brooch with garnet settings and a black niello border: finder a Mr Holbrook. In between the garnets are stylised bird motifs; similar brooches have been found in the Kent area, but they are extremely rare.

1970–80s 14thC Edward III gold noble found by schoolteacher Mr Bennet in the lawn of his back garden.

1970–80s 3 gold coins, an Edward IV hammer gold angel (based on the design of the Edward III noble), a Henry VII gold angel, and a James I gold half-crown: finder Dennis Butcher (M/D).

>1980 18 gold sovereigns and 42 half-sovereigns dated 1891–4 found in an old cocoa tin behind an old copper-brick surround in the scullery of a house.

>1984 11 gold coins found close to the verge of a road: finder Phil Connoly (M/D); estimated to be worth over £12,000, around £24,000 now.

>1998 Rare silver penny of Wulfred (Archbishop of Canterbury 805–23) was found by Josh Davies (M/D) on an old pathway where a gate used to be near a wood. It was thought to be worth around £2,000.

2000–1 Mid-5th–early 6thC copper-alloy insular 'radiate-headed' bow brooch: finder Doug Arms.

>2001 Anglo-Saxon Kentish jewelled disc brooch: finder Neil Wynn (M/D).

2004 An early 5thC Roman *solidus* of Jovinus (AD 411–13): finder Richard Malin (M/D). It was expected to fetch £5,000–7,000 at auction.

KINGSTON, KENT ▶

1771 Anglo-Saxon gold inlaid brooch and other pieces from the early 7thC were found in a burial mound by the Revd Faussett at Barham Downs. The Kingston Brooch, as it is known, is cloisonné, inlaid with garnet, glass, white shell, and gold filigree panels and is the finest of its kind. There were 2 gold pendants and 2 silver-gilt crosses from a necklet consisting of beads that include 12 amethysts.

Liverpool Museum

KINTBURY, WEST BERKSHIRE

1762 47 Anglo-Saxon silver pennies from the 10thC found under a skull in the churchyard. They were thought to have been buried c. AD 957–60.

LAMBOURN, WEST BERKSHIRE

1931 9 billon coins from the 18thC, thought to have been concealed in 1797.

[date?] 660 gold coins dating from the 16th and 17thC found at Lyle Farm, thought to have been deposited c. 1640.

2004 2 gold torcs and 3 bracelets from c. 1500 BC found in a field by Shaun Raynsford and his wife Ann.

LANCING, WEST SUSSEX

1982 Small hoard of 3rdC Roman bronze coins by 16-year-old Stephen Whittle (M/D) in the hills behind his home.

LAUGHTON, EAST SUSSEX

1959 524 silver coins dating from the 16th and 17thC, thought to have been concealed in 1653.

LENHAM HEATH, KENT

1954   60 gold and 33 silver coins from the 19thC, thought to have been concealed in 1894.

LEWIS, EAST SUSSEX

1855   49 gold coins of Charles II, James II and William III, dated 1664–83, found in a crevice of a timber from a demolished house in the St Ann's area. They were deposited after 1695.

1934 and **1959**   Tudor coins found in a field at Loughton, on the outskirts of Lewes, by a farm labourer. Twenty-five years later a schoolboy spotted some pieces of broken urn in the same field. Knowing the story of the earlier find he looked closer and found 600 half-crowns of the late Tudor and early Stuart period.

1995   13thC gold brooch, engraved on both sides and with amethysts: finder John Isted (M/D). Thought to have been lost at the Battle of Lewes in 1264; it was declared treasure trove.

LEWES AREA, EAST SUSSEX

1849   Bronze Age hoard found with the remains of a skeleton at Hanley Cross Barrow, between Lewis and Brighton. It comprised a quote pin, a massive pin with a disc head and stem perforation, protected by a decorated diamond-shaped plate, and a pair of 'East Sussex loop pins'.

LEYSDOWN-ON-SEA AREA, KENT

1968–9   492 Roman copper sestertii dated c. AD 260 found by J.V. Brett while digging for worm bait on the mudflats in Warden Bay.

Maidstone Museum

LINCHMERE, WEST SUSSEX

1924   812 Roman copper coins in very fine condition from the 3rdC AD found in a vase in a field north of the road leading from Haslemere and Shotter Mill to Liphook.

LINTON, KENT

1883   About 180 silver coins and cut coins from the 12thC found in earthenware jar buried about 15in below the surface, believed to have been deposited c. 1140–2. The hoard comprised Norman silver pennies and cut coins of Henry I and Stephen, some of which were irregular Pereric issues, about which little is known.

LITTLEBOURNE, KENT

1998   Silver-gilt buckle with triangular plate, broken into two pieces, and dating from AD 600 to 650: finder R.H. Riley (M/D); valued at £3,500.

LITTLEHAMPTON AREA, WEST SUSSEX

1978   Rare Saxon seal dating from the 7th to the 9thC found in a picnic area.

LOWER HALSTOW, KENT

1977   Belgic quarter-stater dated 356–336 BC found on farmland: finder Anthony Judges. The coin was made in France and is worth about £500.

LUDDESDOWN, KENT

1850   Coins, possibly Roman, found in an urn in a field called Old Lands, close to Little Buckland.

LYMINGE, KENT

1953–4   18 Anglo-Saxon brooches of at least 9 styles were found dating from the 6thC. The earliest are penannular and annular brooches decorated in a Romano-provincial style. Workers erecting a prefabricated mushroom shed had struck bones and metal that included what turned out to be an Iron Age spearhead. The wife of one of the workers had contacted the Maidstone Museum and an extensive dig involving the Kent Archaeological Society was organised on what turned out to be a Jutish cemetery of 44 graves. The Lyminge cloisonné jewellery is among the earliest of this type of work found in England. The field in which the cemetery was located adjoins the back garden of Riversdale in Canterbury Road.

2000   A 14thC gold finger-ring decorated with a triangular motif: finder P.J. Castle (M/D); returned to the finder.

c. **2001**   9thC boldly decorated silver hooked tag: finder M. Jennings (M/D).

LYMINGTON, HAMPSHIRE

1744   4th and 5thC AD Roman copper coins found in 2 urns in a field half a mile from Rimbury in the New Forest. Contemporary reports talk of 'about 176 pound weight' of coins.

LYMPNE, KENT

1999   6thC Anglo-Saxon keystone garnet disc brooch: finder Peter Welsh (M/D); returned to the finder.

MAIDENHEAD, WINDSOR AND MAIDENHEAD

1837 Up to 800 Roman silver coins from the 1st and 2ndC AD found in an earthen jar by workmen digging on a railway line a mile east of the Maidenhead bridge. They were about 2ft below the surface and most of the coins were sold for very little (75 for 5s).

1979 £3,000 worth of modern jewellery found on a rubbish tip by two boys; it had been stolen from a nearby hotel.

MAIDSTONE, KENT

1952 About 500 gold and silver coins from the 15th and 16thC found during the clearing of a building site in Lower Street. Many of the coins were grabbed by various people but the museum curator managed to recover some, which turned out to be from the reigns of Henry V to Henry VIII, dated 1413–1509.

1970 16th and 17thC copper tokens/jettons.

1979 39 Roman bronze/silver-dipped folles from Gallianus to Tetricus in the 3rdC AD by Steve Martin and Alex Page on a slope of a hill below a footpath in the Vinters Park area over a period of 6 months. It is thought that they may be part of a far larger hoard.

1979 58 Roman silver *antoniniani* from the 3rdC AD found in Vintner's Park.

MAIDSTONE AREA, KENT

1979 A 12thC silver penny found in tree roots on a footpath (the former 'Travellers Way' to the north of Maidstone) by Leslie Clayton. This unique King Stephen silver penny of 1135–54, was just a few inches below the surface and was so small that he almost threw it away. In near perfect condition, he was offered £10,000 (which equates to £24,000 today) by an American coin auctioneer shortly after the find. Leslie Clayton said: 'It frightens me when I think I nearly threw it away.'

1983 68 Roman coins found by Ray Cox on the edge of a footpath beneath some stones; they were in mint condition.

1987 7 silver coins from the 16th to 17thC were found by a detectorist on an old footpath. The 3 Elizabeth I sixpences, an Elizabeth I shilling, 2 James I sixpences, and James I shilling were slightly scattered, with no sign of a container.

MARGATE, KENT

1997 7thC Anglo-Saxon gold composite disc pendant: finder J. Laing (M/D); declared treasure trove and returned to the finder.

MARTYR WORTHY, HAMPSHIRE

1998 16thC silver-gilt dress-hook valued at £1,500: finder J.E. Cousins (M/D).

British Museum

MEDWAY RIVER, KENT

1984 8 gold bars were found in the river by Mr Bullock (M/D), who was initially arrested under suspicion of theft.

MEONSTOKE, HAMPSHIRE

2001 Medieval silver-gilt coin brooch dating from *c.* 1300: finder Ken Ross (M/D). It was made from a Louis IX of France coin, minted 1266–70; it was returned to the finder.

MEOPHAM, KENT

1973 2 gold nobles and 1 gold half-noble of Edward III from the 14thC, thought to have been concealed in 1369 or later, found beneath a tree stump in a garden.

1976 11 14thC gold coins found on steeply sloping ground below the garden where the 3 coins had been found 3 years earlier. This hoard was found by Philip Connolly and included 6 Edward III gold nobles, and an extremely rare Richard II quarter-noble of 1354–99. They were valued at almost £10,000 (which equates to over £38,000 today).

MICHELDEVER WOOD, HAMPSHIRE

1843–4 More than 1,400 Roman copper coins from the 4th to 5thC AD found during excavations by the Revd W.H. Gunner on the remains of a Roman villa.

MICKLEHAM, SURREY

1716 Roman coins, said to measure 'near a peck', found in an earthen vessel in a ploughed field at Bagden.

MICKLEHAM AREA, SURREY

1971 24 4thC Roman billon coins found, thought to have been deposited *c.* AD 324.

Guildford Museum

MILTON REGIS, KENT

1916 6 Anglo-Saxon silver sceattas and 3 gold pendants from the late 7thC. The 3 gold pendants were purchased by the British Museum.

British Museum

MINNIS BAY, KENT

1938 Bronze Age items including axes, ornaments, and bronze ware.

MINSTER, ISLE OF SHEPPEY, KENT

1986 3,235 3rdC AD Roman copper *antoniniani*, in a poor state of preservation, found in a large pot by builders digging foundation trenches for a development of new houses next to the junction of Scrapsgate Road and Kent Avenue at Minster. The hoard was declared treasure trove.

MINSTER IN THANET, KENT

1630 Roman silver *antoniniani* and *denarii*, probably from the 3rdC AD, found in a pot by farm workers. Apparently they had been made to work on a holiday and so tried to break the plough by ploughing at a greater depth than normal when they broke the pot.

MONKTON, KENT

1971–2 Saxon coins, gold and jewellery, probably from the 7thC, found during drainage work alongside a 7thC cemetery in which 12 graves were discovered. The coins were found in 1971; in 1972 the jewellery was found, which included a square-headed gilt-bronze brooch set with garnets, an ornate bronze belt buckle, a bronze chatelaine, and a gold bracteate. 'The Monkton Brooch' has a framework of bronze cells enclosing bosses of shell with garnet eyes, and panels of gold filigree and garnets on gold foil backing with blue glass insertions. All are mounted together on a silver back plate and bound with a gold rim. The Ashmolean Museum bought the brooch in 1972 for £4,000 (the equivalent of £32,000 today).

Ashmolean Museum

1998 41 silver coins and fragments dating from the 14th to 16thC found by members of the Thanet and Wantsum Relic Association (M/D). They were silver pennies and half-groats from various reigns, many broken or in poor condition, thought to have been deposited *c.* 1510 or 1540–50. They were returned to the finders.

MOUNTFIELD, EAST SUSSEX

1863 Gold torc and gold ornaments about 2,000 years old were discovered by a farmworker while ploughing. He thought they were brass, and sold them for 5s 6d. The Hastings man who bought the items knew they were gold and sold them for over £500 (the equivalent to over £27,000 today); the buyer melted the things down. Both men were prosecuted.

NEATHAM, HAMPSHIRE

1976 196 Roman copper coins dated AD 364–78 found during excavations of a Roman site.

NETLEY, HAMPSHIRE

1867 Almost 2,000 Roman *antoniniani* from the 3rdC AD found in two urns, 2ft below the surface, during the digging of the foundations for a lunatic asylum in the rear of Netley Hospital.

NEW FOREST, HAMPSHIRE

1747 Roman coins from the 2nd and 3rdC AD were found in 2 urns.

1970 or 1981? 45 gold coins, 43 staters of the Barocaser tribe from Normandy, 1 Gallo-Belgic quarter-stater, and 1 Westerham-type dating from around 2,000 years ago were found by A. White near his home. The British Museum paid the finder just under £4,000 for the coins.

British Museum

NEW ROMNEY, KENT

1999 16thC silver-gilt dress-hook: finder J. Mead (M/D).

NEWBURY, WEST BERKSHIRE

1997 75 17thC silver coins dating from the 17thC found on and just below the surface in a field by Brian Jenner and Andy Stewart (M/D)

during the Newbury Metal Detecting Rally. The coins were mostly from the reign of Charles I.

NEWBURY AREA, WEST BERKSHIRE

1999 More than 400 Roman coins, dated AD 68–211, found in a pottery jar by Harry Haddrell and Bernard Aldridge (M/D). The hoard included 416 bronze sestertii and was declared treasure trove.

1756 3,499 silver coins (English, Scottish and continental, mainly silver pennies) from the 14thC or earlier, believed to have been buried in 1307.

[date?] 65 gold coins inside a round flint stone. A young boy threw the flint stone, which broke in two, revealing the coins. This was not an unusual method of concealing coins. Two of these coins are now in the West Berkshire Museum.

West Berkshire Museum

1981 240 Roman coins from the middle of the 4thC to the beginning of the 5thC found on Berkshire Downs: finder Alan Clarke (M/D); they were declared not treasure trove.

1985 24 gold and silver coins dated 1673–1715 were found in a small lead tube on a footpath by Keith Butcher (M/D) about 6in below the surface. There were 16 gold guineas and 8 silver crowns in very good condition, thought to be worth £7,000. The theory is that they were a highwayman's hoard; they were declared treasure trove. West Berkshire Museum bought the silver crowns and 1 guinea of each monarch. The rest of the coins were returned to the finder.

West Berkshire Museum

NEWHAVEN, EAST SUSSEX

1806 Gold bracelets found after a landslide.

1920 A large hoard of Roman bronze coins from the 3rdC AD found in a pot by workmen refilling a trench near the fort at Newhaven. The coins were dispersed by the finders with only 73 being recovered.

NEWPORT, ISLE OF WIGHT

1833 Roman brass coins from the 1st and 2ndC AD found at Barton Wood. Contemporary reports talk of 'nearly a gallon measures' of coins. Most had fused together and corroded and were unable to be easily separated.

NEWPORT AREA, ISLE OF WIGHT

1849 2,392 silver pennies from the 14thC found in a container, thought to have been buried *c.* 1340. A few of these coins are in the Carisbrooke Castle Museum.

Carisbrooke Castle Museum

NORTH FORELAND, KENT

1999 63 Iron Age British coins from the 1stC BC found during archaeological excavation by the Canterbury Archaeological Trust.

NORTH WARNBOROUGH, HAMPSHIRE

1998 15thC inscribed gold finger-ring: finder Adam Parker (M/D); valued at £3,500.

NUTFIELD, SURREY

1755 Around 900 Roman copper coins from the 4th and 5thC AD found in a vessel during ploughing.

OLD ARLESFORD, HAMPSHIRE

1871 17 silver coins from the 16th and 17thC found in Godsfield Row, having been been concealed in 1640.

OTTERBOURNE, HAMPSHIRE

1978 543 Roman silver coins (seven miliarenses and 536 *siliquae*) from the 4thC AD found in a pot on a footpath on the south side of Poles Lane by Terence Carroll. 'About a foot down I found some coins. I scooped up more soil and saw the top of a pot containing more coins. I dug very carefully around the pot and tried to lift it out intact, but it disintegrated.' He took the coins, which were in excellent condition, and pottery fragments to the police. They were found to be 90 per cent silver and were declared treasure trove.

1980 155 Roman *siliquae* from the 4th and 5thC AD found by members of the Hampshire Detectors' Club (M/D) near the Incinerator Plant at Poles Lane; it was close to the find two years earlier. Later still, 5 more coins were found.

OWSLEBURY, HAMPSHIRE

2001 5 Roman silver coins in a worn state from the 2ndC BC to the 1stC AD found by a detectorist.

PATCHING, WEST SUSSEX

1997 23 Roman gold solidi and 26 silver coins (3 silver miliarenses and 23 *siliquae*), 2 gold rings, 50 small pieces of silver and some small iron or bronze objects of AD 340–461 were found on farmland: finder Terry Bromley and Terry Silver (M/D). The hoard was scattered by ploughing and thought to have been buried after AD 46; it was declared treasure trove.

POLEGATE, EAST SUSSEX

[date?] 17 billon Roman coins dating from the 3rdC and the reigns of Gallianus to Tetricus, thought to have been deposited in AD 273.

PORTCHESTER, HAMPSHIRE

>1758 3rd and 4thC AD Roman copper coins found in an urn by a man digging under an apple tree in a garden at Portchester Castle.

1979 Early 6thC gilt Anglo-Saxon brooch found near the site of the Roman fort. The brooch, of circular design and studded with red glass with a central green glass stone, is one of the earliest Anglo-Saxon items found in Britain.

PORTS DOWN, CITY OF PORTSMOUTH

1976 10 billon Roman coins found from the 3rdC AD from the reigns of Valerian, Gallienus and Postumus; they were declared treasure trove.

Portsmouth Museum

1994 22 silver pennies and fragments of King Stephen (1135–54) scattered in a field on farmland: finder David Lodder and Julia Steele (M/D); declared treasure trove.

PORTSMOUTH AREA

1830 About 100 Celtic silver staters and quarter-staters, thought to have been deposited during the 1stC BC.

PRESTON, KENT

1999 Medieval gold finger-ring, set with a blue stone (probably a sapphire), dating from the first half of the 13thC: finder P.D.F. Thomas (M/D); returned to the finder.

PRESTON CANDOVER, HAMPSHIRE

1914 14 silver coins from the 16th and 17thC, thought to have been concealed between 1625 and 1649.

1917 1 gold and 117 silver coins from the 16th and 17thC, thought to have been concealed between 1625 and 1649.

PULBOROUGH, WEST SUSSEX

1880 Large quantity of 16th–17thC copper tokens, thought to have been concealed in 1669.

PURBROOK HEATH, HAMPSHIRE

1981 More than 200 Roman silver and bronze coins dated AD 249–70 were found in a pot, beside a footpath, thought to have been buried *c.* AD 272. Schoolboys Peter Warren and Kevan Thompson (M/D) at first found scattered coins and then discovered the main hoard and the remains of a pot. The coins were in a very clean condition. They took them to the local police station; later declared not treasure trove.

PYREFORD, SURREY

1957 82 Roman *denarii* from the 1st and 2ndC AD in a greyware pot found by a mechanical excavator driver in a field adjoining Bolton's Lane. As the pot was being cleaned, pieces broke off to reveal the coins. 8 are held in the British Museum, and the rest in Guildford Museum.

British Museum and Guildford Museum

RAINHAM, MEDWAY

1849 200 gold nobles of Edward III uncovered by a ploughman.

c. **1864**   16 Roman bronze coins, a silver armilla, and 2 silver finger-rings with intaglios of red carnelian, from the 1st and 2ndC AD, found in an urn on the Slayhills Marsh to the west of the Greenborough Marshes. The silver armlet and two silver rings are held at the British Museum.

British Museum

1952   37 bronze Roman coins from the 1st and 2ndC AD found in a small urn on the Slayhills Marsh, on Upchurch Marsh; the majority were very worn.

RAMSGATE, KENT

At Abbey Farm, Minster near Ramsgate there is a large Romano-British site that has been extensively excavated by the Kent Archaeological Trust in recent years.

1962   731 gold coins from the 18th and 19thC, thought to have been concealed in 1850.

1969   27 Roman copper coins from the 2nd and 3rdC AD found scattered in the ground by workmen laying gas pipes near Pysons Road.

[date?]   34 Roman sestertii were found 3ft down in trench during the laying of a pipe.

READING

There are the remains of the Norman abbey in Reading, where King Henry I was buried in AD 1135.

1885   26 copper tokens/jettons from the 16th and 17thC, thought to have been concealed in 1666.

1890   Silver pennies, thought to have been concealed *c.* 1150.

1895   About 50 Roman silver coins from the 4thC AD found in a vessel by boys playing at an unused gravel pit at Bobs Mount. There had been a severe frost and the coins were lying on the ice. Some of the coins were taken by the finders, but 9 *siliquae* were recovered.

1926   5 Roman sestertii from the 2ndC AD found during reconstruction work on the Berkshire side of Caversham Bridge.

Reading Museum

1934   17 gold coins from the 16th and 17thC found at Yield Hill, thought to have been concealed in 1641.

1970s   Beautifully decorated casket containing a sacred relic found among the rubble of the ruins of Reading Abbey.

READING AREA

1998   Hoard of Celtic gold staters from the 1stC BC found by Gerald Futcher (M/D), scattered in a field. They were declared treasure trove.

RECULVER, KENT

1980   Silver ingot, possibly Roman, found to the west of Reculver by Leonard Charingbould (M/D). It was 95 per cent silver and stamped 'Exoffi Istatis' (from the workshop of Istatis). It had probably fallen off the cliff, which had been eroding for many years. 7 other ingots of this type have been found in Kent, at Canterbury, Wingham and Richborough.

REDFORD, WEST SUSSEX

1855   1,800 Roman copper coins from the 3rd and 4thC AD found in the bank, near the surface, when the reservoir of the spring was being cleared. The coins were thought to have been buried in a wooden box which had rotted.

REIGATE, SURREY

1972   2 gold nobles and a gold quarter-noble of Henry VI and 984 silver coins from the 15thC found in a pot at Wray Lane, near Gatten Park. The silver coins were mainly of Edward III, Richard II, Henry V, Henry VI, and Robert II of Scotland and were believed to have been concealed *c.* 1450–55, possibly during the Peasants' Revolt in 1450 or during the Wars of the Roses, which began in 1455. 43 of these coins are in the British Museum, and 4 are in Guildford Museum. The rest were returned to the finder.

British Museum and Guildford Museum

1979 2 extremely rare pots, one dated 1350 and the other from the late 16thC found in the garden of an old vicarage.

1990 135 gold nobles, half-nobles and quarters and 6,566 silver groats, dated 1272–1455: finder Roger Mintey. Found in 2 pots buried together, they were thought to have been deposited in 1450–60. The site was 50yd from a medieval track, and close to the 1972 hoard. Roger had almost given up for the day as it was getting dark, and at first thought the loud signal on his detector was a fault and ignored it. When he got the signal again he decided to dig as it was getting too dark to detect properly. As he dug he came upon bits of the pot and inside were the coins, stacked vertically in concentric circles. Having unearthed about 2,500 that night he and a local archaeologist went back the next day to finish the task. At over 6,700 coins it is the largest post-1350 hoard ever to have been discovered and a Henry VI leaf trefoil half-noble had never been found before. There were also a few French and Scottish coins among the total. They were declared treasure trove before being auctioned, when they were expected to raise £150,000.

RICHBOROUGH, KENT

Situated a mile and a half north of Sandwich, the Roman fort, or Richborough Castle as it is known today, dates back to AD 43 and the Roman invasion. The original defences were 2 double ditches and around AD 83 the Romans built an 80ft high triumphal arch; 200 years later the fort had 25ft high flint walls, still visible today. The Roman

Watling Street starts at the east gate and proceeds to Canterbury and then London.

[date?] More than 8,000 Roman coins and artefacts, including axes, ingots and pottery, found at the fort.

>1904 4,000–5,000 Roman copper coins from the 4th and 5thC AD found by Canon Routledge, who died in 1904.

1924 16 Roman sestertii, beads and counters from the 1stC AD found in the remains of a small brass-bound box during excavations at the fort. Although badly corroded, the coins were otherwise in mint condition.

1926 1,202 Roman copper coins from the 4th and 5thC AD found 3ft below the surface during excavations at the fort.

1928 430 Roman copper coins from the 4th and 5thC AD found during excavations at the fort.

1930 85 Roman copper coins from the 4th and 5thC AD found during excavations at the fort.

1931 875 Roman copper coins from the 4th and 5thC AD found during excavations at the fort. The coins were found in a mass, and were possibly buried in a wooden box.
British Museum

1931–8 96 Roman copper coins from the 4th and 5thC AD found during excavations at the fort.

1931–8 124 Roman copper coins from the 4th and 5thC AD found during excavations at the fort.

1932 91 Roman copper coins from the 4th and 5thC AD found during excavations at the fort.

1937 76 Roman copper coins from the 4th and 5thC AD found during excavations at the fort.

RINGLEMERE, KENT

2001 Partly crushed early Bronze Age gold cup of c. 1700–1500 BC found 18in below the surface in a ploughed field: finder Cliff Bradshaw. Named the Ringlemere Cup it was declared treasure trove and valued at £270,000. Since its discovery archaeologists have excavated the area surrounding where it was found and revealed a previously unknown grave and funeral complex.
British Museum

RINGLES CROSS, EAST SUSSEX

1893 749 copper coins from the 17th and 18thC, thought to have been concealed in 1776.

RINGWOOD AREA, HAMPSHIRE

1976 23 gold Gallo-Belgic (Chute) staters of 75–55 BC found on a footpath in a wooded glade by John Sibley, who immediately handed them over to the local police.

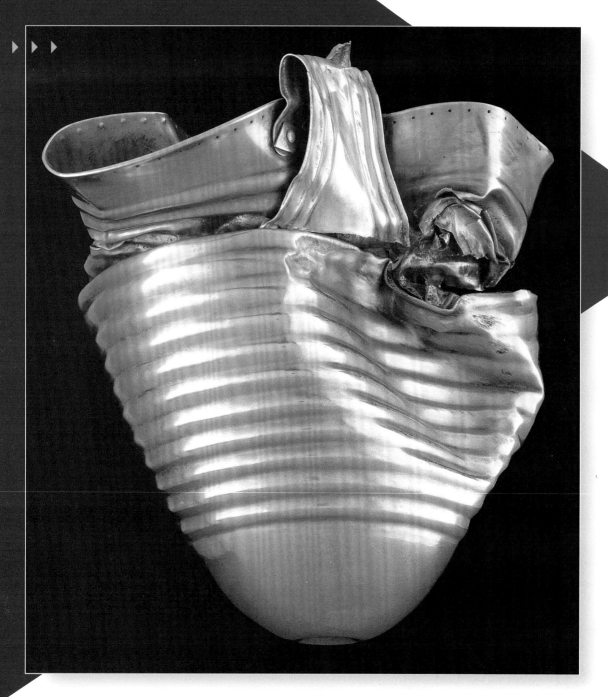

1976 23 gold Gallo-Belgic (Chute) staters were found, dated 75–55 BC. 2 months after the first hoard was discovered a Mr and Mrs Freeman decided to try their luck along the same footpath where the first hoard was found, using a metal detector. After rising up a slight incline they found a Gallo-Belgic gold stater. A search of the immediate area produced a further 6 staters. The following day they found 9 more staters, and over the next 2 weeks, 7 more.

1976 27 gold Gallo-Belgic (Chute) staters dated 75–55 BC. The local archaeological society contacted the Freemans and the couple agreed to take them and representatives from Hampshire County Council Museum Department to the site. Further meticulous excavations resulted in the discovery of a further 27 staters. Over the course of the next year more came to light, bringing the total to 119.

1979 4 gold staters of 50 BC were found in a wooded area between Picket Post and Burley. The staters were thought to have originated in Normandy.

RISELEY, KENT

1937 Set of 4 Anglo-Saxon gold pendants, a silver pendant with a decorative glass centre and 4 amethyst beads, which would have been strung together to form a necklace, were found in the cemetery at Horton Kirby. The gold pendants were decorated with pagan and Christian motifs; 2 with crosses, and 1 with a man wrestling 2 snakes. The site was in use from the 5th to the 7thC AD and its discovery was made by workers preparing for the building of council housing at the appropriately, and subsequently, named Saxon Place.

Dartford Borough Museum

ROCHESTER, KENT

1838 158 silver coins from the 16th and 17thC, thought to have been concealed between 1625 and 1649.

ROCKBOURNE, HAMPSHIRE

1967 7,717 Roman coins of AD 250–90 were found in a storage jar 1ft below the surface during excavations near an outside wall of the West Park Roman villa. The bronze and silvered bronze coins included three *denarii* and were mostly in mint condition.

1986 and **1988–9** 20 Roman gold coins from the 4thC AD found at Toyd Corner, about 2 miles from the well-known late Roman villa.

ROMNEY MARSH, KENT

1999 A silver penny and two halfpennies of Richard II found by P. Beving, while walking on a public footpath. They were thought to have been deposited in the late 14th or early 15thC and were returned to the finder.

ROTTINGDEAN, EAST SUSSEX

1798 Large hoard of 3rdC AD Roman bronze coins, in an extraordinarily good state of preservation, was found in a pot during ploughing near the town.

RUSCOMBE, WOKINGHAM

1965 150 gold coins, from 1854 or earlier, thought to have been concealed in 1854.

RYE, EAST SUSSEX

1936 1 silver and 5 billon coins from the 16th and 17thC, thought to have been concealed between 1625 and 1649.

ST NICHOLAS AT WADE, KENT

Late 1970s 10th or 11thC late Saxon or Viking gold finger-ring found by C.E. Bradshaw (M/D), while searching soil supplied for a garden. It was returned to the finder.

2001 Anglo-Saxon gold disc pendant or bracteate dating from the second half of the 6thC: finder A.P. Wainwight (M/D); returned to the finder.

SARRE, KENT

1860–8 Saxon jewellery and glass objects from the 5th and early 6thC found over an 8-year period. The site of this Anglo-Saxon cemetery first came to light during work on the Sarre windmill in 1860 when gold coins and a bronze bowl, among other things, were found. Some of these items were purchased by the British Museum. Work on the site began in earnest in 1862 when members of the Kent Archaeological Society began their excavations. They found iron spearheads, silvered shield studs, gold bracelets, silver rings, iron keys, gold pendants and numerous other items of jewellery among the graves. Of particular interest was a 'quoit'-style brooch from the mid-5thC.

Maidstone Museum and British Museum

SEAFORD AREA, EAST SUSSEX

1991 Gilded silver religious pendant dating from the second half of the 15thC found by Geoff Wicks (M/D) about 5in down in a paddock, 50yd from a medieval church. On the front of the pendant is the head of Christ, and on the back the Lamb of God. It was declared not treasure trove and returned to the finder, who was offered £2,000 by Sotheby's but he declined.

SEDLESCOMBE, EAST SUSSEX

1876 2,000–3,000 silver pennies and a silver bar dating from the 11thC in a rotted leather bag inside a corroded iron pot unearthed by a farm worker laying drainage pipes. At least half of the coins were sold or given away to local people. Among the hoard were various types of Edward the Confessor silver pennies, which were believed to have been buried at the time of the Norman invasion in 1066. The coins possibly belonged to the moneyer Duninc, who minted at Hastings, as his name was on many of the coins.

SELLINDGE, KENT

1974–5 16 silver coins of Mary I, Philip and Mary, Elizabeth I, James I and Charles I, thought to have been deposited in the late 17thC.

SELSEY, WEST SUSSEX

>1926 Several Roman copper coins and a gold ring from the 3rd to the 4thC AD found on the beach.

>1932 975 Roman silver coins (all *antoniniani*, except for 9 *denarii*) dated AD 258–70 found in an urn by two gardeners in a garden at Halton, near the corner where Fish Lane joins Albion Road, about a quarter of a mile from the seashore. They found the urn over 2ft down beneath the potato crop.

SELSEY BILL, WEST SUSSEX

***c.* 1873** About 300 gold coins and gold nuggets and ingots from 20 BC to AD 40 found by a man walking on the beach. He first found a gold coin among the pebbles and then some others. Over the next few years around 300 British gold coins, including 20 that had never come to light before, were discovered in the same area. There were also small nuggets and ingots of gold and fragments of broken jewellery, all of which were probably part of a single hoard.

1924–5   A gold torc found on West Beach.

British Museum

1936–7   A gold torc found on West Beach.

British Museum

SEVENOAKS AREA, KENT

1973   104 gold sovereigns and 86 half-sovereigns dated 1860–1910 found in jar on Ide Hill.

SHANKLIN, ISLE OF WIGHT

1833   6 silver Roman coins and 600 copper coins from the 4th and 5th C AD found in a vessel during ploughing at Cliff, near Shanklin.

SHEERNESS, KENT

1952   3 gold coins from the 18th C found with a skeleton, thought to have been concealed in 1785.

SHEERNESS AREA, KENT

1968   415 silver coins dated 1550–1650 .

SHELDWICH, KENT

1848   About 60 silver coins were found, thought to have been concealed 1544–61.

SHOREHAM AREA, WEST SUSSEX

1999   4,105 Roman silver and base-silver coins of *c.* AD 221–74 found in a pot by J. Howe (M/D) on the downs several miles north of the town. Thought to have been deposited after AD 274, they included *denarii* and radiates and were valued at £12,500. They were returned to the finder.

SILCHESTER, HAMPSHIRE

c. **1894**   253 Roman *denarii* from the 1st to the 3rd C AD found 3–4ft below the surface, in the earth on the side of a pit, during the excavation of the Roman city.

SITTINGBOURNE, KENT

1977   Rare 11th C Saxon seal matrix found by Stuart Bryant, hunting through his garden shed for a screw. He at first thought it was an old ivory disc. It bore the name 'Wulfric' and would have been worn around the neck and used to make a mark in wax to seal documents and letters. It sold at auction for £4,800.

SOBERTON, HAMPSHIRE

1851   259 (could be 300) Anglo-Saxon and Norman coins and 2 gold rings from the 11th C found in a pot, in a field, near Wickham Lodge. The hoard comprised silver pennies of Edward and Harold, and Norman silver pennies of William I, and two gold rings.

SOUTH STONEHAM, HAMPSHIRE

1869   1 Roman gold *solidus* and 53 *siliquae* from the 4th to the 5th C AD found in a pot by a labourer sinking a ditch on farmland at Allington.

SOUTH WONSTON, HAMPSHIRE

1999   46 Roman bronze coins from the 1st and 2nd C AD, thought to have been deposited *c.* AD 192: finder T. Hinds (M/D).

CITY OF SOUTHAMPTON

c. **1966–9**   9 halfpenny coins of George II and III, dated 1729–75, found during archaeological excavations of a cesspit.

1967   22 silver coins, Norman French deniers, from the 11th C AD, found during archaeological excavations of a rubbish pit; they were thought to have been deposited *c.* AD 1030.

2000   Anglo-Saxon gold and silver finds from the 7th and 8th C AD discovered during archaeological excavations at St Mary's Football Stadium. The items came from different graves in a Saxon cemetery and included a 7th C gold pendant, a gold pendant and silver coins (late 7th or 8th C), and a skein of gold thread/wire.

SOUTHAMPTON AREA

1981   Roman silver coins of the Emperor Valentinian (AD 375–92) found in a bulbous pot on farmland by teenager Sue Staples (M/D). The top of the pot had been broken by ploughing and a few coins had been scattered. The hoard was estimated to be worth £15,000 (the equivalent of around £35,000 today).

1985   Roman bronze coins found in a pot in a ploughed field on the edge of a hazel coppice by Stephen Cole (M/D). Some of the coins were fused together and the pot broke as he attempted to move it.

SOUTHSEA, HAMPSHIRE

1897   About 1,000 Roman silver coins from the 1st and 4thC AD found in a jar by workmen in a field near Lumps Lane.

1929   Large quantities of 19th and 20thC gold and silver coins found, thought to have been concealed 1901–36.

SOUTHWICK, HAMPSHIRE

1982   207 Roman silver *antoniniani* from the 3rdC AD found at Purbrook Heath.

SPRINGHEAD, KENT

The site is believed to be the Roman town of Vagniacae.

c. **1887**   120 Roman silver *antoniniani* from the 3rdC AD.

1925   168 Roman copper coins from the 4th to the 5thC AD found during the making of New Watling Street.

1964   3 gold and 444 silver Roman coins from the 4thC AD found on spoil heaps by workmen during roadworks on the A2 at Springhead. Some of the coins were disposed of by the finders, but later, members of the Gravesend Historical Society found more coins. The coins that were retained were 3 gold solidi, 12 silver miliarenses, and 432 *siliquae*; they were declared treasure trove.

1976   4 *aureii* of Nero and 1 of Titus, dated AD 58–75, found by John D. Shepherd, an archaeology student, during excavations by the Springhead Excavation Group and the Council of Kentish Archaeology. The coins were retained by the British Museum and later sold to the Ashmolean. The finder received a sum believed to be in the region of £5,000 (around £22,000 at today's values).

Ashmolean Museum

STAPLE, KENT

1942   138 silver coins from the 16th and 17thC, thought to have been concealed in 1673.

STEDHAM, WEST SUSSEX

1926   414 silver coins from the 16th and 17thC, thought to have been concealed in 1662.

STOWTING, KENT

1777   300–400 Roman brass coins from the 1st to the 3rdC found in a wooden box, which crumbled to dust, during ploughing.

STREATLEY, WEST BERKSHIRE

2002   1 Roman silver and 48 base-silver and copper-alloy coins dating from the 3rd and 4thC found by A. Tegg, on the surface while walking past a collapsed bank. They were returned to the finder.

SULLINGTON, WEST SUSSEX

1866   Nearly 3,000 Anglo-Saxon silver pennies of Edward the Confessor and Harold II dated 1042–66 found in a crock at Sullington Manor Farm. A stretch of land at the farm was being cleared of trees before sowing crops when the farm workers found the hoard beneath the roots of a big tree. The exact number is not known because many of the coins were sold by the finders to local people, before 1,720 were taken to the British Museum. The coins were all in very fine or near mint condition and were thought to have been buried in 1066.

SURREY

1821   Roman bronze coins found in a pot in a wood.

c. **1970**   9 Roman coins dating from the 3rdC, thought to have been deposited *c.* AD 293.

1978   44 Roman coins were found.

1985   2nd or 3rdC AD gold and onyx ring found by John Young (M/D) 8in below the surface. The 22ct gold ring with black and white banded onyx, with an intaglio design depicting a man and child, was declared not treasure trove and returned to the finder.

SWALLOWFIELD, WOKINGHAM

1890   30 Roman silver *antoniniani* dating from the 3rdC AD.

Ashmolean Museum

TADLEY, HAMPSHIRE

1963   21 gold guineas and half-guineas of George III were found in a tin in a garden in Winston Avenue. 4-year-old Christopher Forrest was playing in his garden and kicked a half-buried rusty tin beneath a pear tree. Thought to have been concealed in 1801, it was declared treasure trove; he received the full market value of the coins.

TESTON, KENT

1845   36 silver pennies dated 1154–1272.

THURNHAM, KENT

2003   204 bronze coins and 158 coin fragments from *c.* 85 to 60 BC were found on farmland: finders Peter and Christine Johnson (M/D).

[date?]   Anglo-Saxon gold cross dug up in a garden and valued at £5,000.

TIMSBURY, HAMPSHIRE

1907 18 ancient British and 43 Roman copper-alloy coins dating from the 1stC BC to the 1stC AD found in an earthenware vessel.

TONBRIDGE, KENT

1748 500 gold coins found hidden in an old desk, thought to have been concealed *c.* 1600–62.

[date?] Late 14thC pewter flagon found in the River Medway not far from the castle.

TUNBRIDGE WELLS, KENT

1936 3 silver coins from the 16th to the 17thC found in a load of peat from Glastonbury. They were thought to have been concealed in 1606.

TUNBRIDGE WELLS AREA, KENT

1986 Mid-14thC gold cross with Scottish garnets found by Simon Wicks (M/D) behind 14thC buildings by an drawbridge.

TUNSTALL, KENT

1737 More than 614 gold coins from the 16th to 17thC , thought to have been concealed *c.* 1648. A boy playing in wood on land owned by Sir Edward Hales, a Royalist sympathiser during the Civil War, found the hoard.

1873 3 gold coins from the 1stC BC to the 1stC AD found near the eastern boundary of the parish of Borden, near the farmhouse called Hart's Delight, during the digging of ground for a garden. Contemporary reports said: 'Mr. Prentis' men discovered three gold coins. At first 2 were found together, 1 being Roman, and bearing the profile of Claudius Caesar, the other being a British coin of Cunobelin . . . The second discovery brought to light only 1 coin; another Cunobelin, but of a type

which has never before been engraved.' It is possible that this may have been a scattered hoard, as reports talk of some other coins being found and dispersed.

TWYFORD, HAMPSHIRE

1977 12 guineas, 83 sovereigns and 2 half-sovereigns, dated 1773–1822, found in a copse by Jeremy de Montfalcon, aged 15, and his friend Harry King while searching with a metal detector. There was a heavy downpour of rain, and they took shelter in a small copse. Here they found the gold coins, heaped together 8in below the surface. They were thought to have been deposited 1822–3 and were estimated to be worth in the region of £12,000 (the equivalent of over £40,000 today). The hoard was declared treasure trove.

UPPER FROYLE, HAMPSHIRE

1999 17thC silver-gilt bell: finder R. Perry (M/D); valued at £175.

VENTNOR, ISLE OF WIGHT

1860 Roman copper coins and a bronze ring from the 4th and 5thC AD found in an urn while excavating the south end of the Ventnor tunnel.
1928 About 260 late 3rdC AD Roman bronze coins found during ground-levelling for a house in Castle Road, Ventnor. The coins were among debris from a Romano-British midden on the cliff above.

WALTHAM ST LAWRENCE AREA, WINDSOR AND MAIDENHEAD

1977 58 gold and 143 silver Celtic coins from about 50 BC found along with pieces of a black pot and flints by songwriter and producer Bill Parkinson, of Waltham Abbey, Essex, He was on holiday when he came across what was one of the most important finds of Roman and Celtic coins this century, using his metal detector. At the farm, near the site of a Roman temple, he dug up the coin hoard along with a small silver snake head, which was probably part of a bracelet. The coins, thought to have been deposited in AD 43, included some that were unique.

British Museum

WANBOROUGH, SURREY

The Romano-Celtic temple at Wanborough has been one of the most important finds of the last three decades. In 1999 the excavations revealed a circular temple, which pre-dated the square Romano-British temple found in 1985. Wanborough became big news in the mid-1980s when looting of the site led to changes in modern treasure laws; the Surrey Archaeological Society was instrumental in the changes to the law. It has been estimated that as many as 20,000 mainly coins were looted from the site; apparently one enterprising looter drove away with a lorry-load of soil. Interestingly, and fortunately, the looters were so concerned with the coins that they missed some of the more valuable temple arte-facts which included temple priests' head-dresses. The coin market was hit with a huge upsurge in coins, to the extent that existing values dropped rapidly.

1984 More than 80 Celtic and Roman coins found by Stuart Hazelwood, Cliff Kill and John Castle (M/D) over a two-week period near the site of the temple. 11 of the coins were unknown at this point in time.

1985   More than 1,000 gold and silver Celtic and Roman coins from the 1stC AD found during the excavation of the temple. The 1,000 coins or so that were recovered, many by the police, consisted mainly of Atrebatic silver and gold, but there were some Republican and early issues. Thought to have been deposited c. AD 60, the coins that were recovered are in the British Museum.

British Museum

1999   44 Iron Age and 42 Roman coins from the 1stC AD found by the Surrey Archaeological Society. The finds included 5 gold, 28 silver and 11 bronze Iron Age coins, and 8 silver and 34 copper-alloy Roman coins; they were thought to have been deposited about AD 50.

1999   5 silver short-cross pennies from the 12th and 13thC, thought to have been deposited c. AD 1205–20, found by the Surrey Archaeological Society.

WATERINGBURY, KENT

1872   More than 10 billon *antoniniani* coins of Gallienus and Postumus from the 3rdC AD, thought to have been concealed c. AD 265.

WATERSFIELD, WEST SUSSEX

1815   About 1,700 Roman copper coins found in a pot by a labourer who disposed of the coins.

WELFORD, WEST BERKSHIRE

1825   Almost 800 Roman coins from the 4thC AD found 18in below the surface by men repairing an earthen bank in Hangmanstone Lane, near the ruins of Poughley Priory.

WEST MALLING, KENT

1998   12th or 13thC gold finger-ring, set with a sapphire: finder N.J. Betts (M/D). 3 months later he found an early 13thC gold finger-ring, set with a ruby. Both rings were returned to the finder.

WEST MALLING AREA, KENT

1999   16thC silver-gilt dress-hook: finder N. Betts; valued at £400.

Maidstone Museum

WEST MEON AREA, HAMPSHIRE

1992   3 silver pennies of Stephen (1135–54), and 30 silver pennies and 1 cut halfpenny of Henry II (1154–89) found by Adrian Boswell (M/D) among the roots of trees in a small coppice, at crossroads, beside a stone circle; it was declared treasure trove.

WEST SUSSEX

1985   8 silver coins, including a Henry VIII groat, 3 medieval silver pennies, 2 James I silver shillings, a soldino of Venice (1501–21), and a double patera (1467–77) found in woodland close to an old coaching road: finder Mick Hall (M/D). The coins were valued at around £500, were declared not treasure trove, and returned to the finder.

1980   2 gold coins dating from the 20thC found in a puddle by 3 schoolboys while on their way to school. Initially they thought it was chocolate money covered in gold paper. They gave them to the police and received a reward of £173 each (almost £500 today!).

WEST WICKHAM, KENT

c. **2003**   2ndC AD Roman finger-ring: finder John Hughes (M/D); valued at £180 and declared treasure trove.

Bromley Museum

WEST WITTERING, WEST SUSSEX

1847   12 Roman gold solidi from the 4thC AD found during the levelling of an old earth bank in a field called the Green Duer at Cakeham, West Wittering.

WESTMESTON, EAST SUSSEX

1984   61 Roman silver *antoniniani* from the late 3rdC AD found on the northern scarp of the South Downs: finder L. Gaston (M/D). The following year another 9 Roman *denarii* from the 2ndC AD found in the same area: finder L. Gaston (M/D); both hoards were declared treasure trove.

WESTERHAM, KENT

2000–3   25 Celtic gold coins from the 1stC BC: finder Nicholas Moon (M/D). During the autumn of 2000 he found a single coin; a year later a search of a 100 sq ft area revealed a further 14 gold coins. 2 years later another search unearthed a further 11 coins. At the coroners' inquest it was reported that the British Museum had examined them and believed that they were local Iron Age coins made by tribes living south of the Thames. They were declared treasure trove.

WESTGATE, KENT

1845–6   About 200 Roman copper coins from the 3rd and 4thC AD found on the beach together with a large quantity of broken fibulae, rings, buckles, and bracelets in bronze.

WEYBRIDGE, SURREY

1907   Roman coins from the 3rd and 4thC AD found in a jar 2ft 6in below the surface during the building of the Brooklands motor racing circuit. There was a scramble for the contents and many were dispersed although 137 folles were recovered.

WHITCHURCH, HAMPSHIRE

1989   48 silver coins from the 4th and 5thC AD found by members of the Andover Metal Detecting Club (M/D). They were declared treasure trove, and returned to the finders.

WIGGONHOLT, WEST SUSSEX

1977   Georgian silver plate from the 18th and 19thC found on Wiggin Holt Common: finder Peter Clements (M/D). He received a fairly weak signal and later said, 'I started digging, when the soil suddenly caved in. I put my hand down the hole and pulled out a couple of spoons. At first I thought it was just picnic junk, but when I rubbed the back, to my delight, I saw a crest.' The hoard, including a cigarette box, ashtray and cutlery, some dating to George III, was valued at £400. The cutlery was thought to have either been stolen and then promptly hidden, or buried by the owner during the Second World War.

WILLINGDON, EAST SUSSEX

1980   144 Roman coins from the 3rdC AD found scattered on the northern slopes of Combe Hill: finder Roy Lock (M/D). The coins were all *antoniniani*, except for 4 sestertii.

WINCHESTER, HAMPSHIRE

1996   15thC silver-gilt finger-ring engraved with 2 saints: finder M. McGovern (M/D); returned to the finder.

2000   10thC Anglo-Saxon silver-gilt dress-tag found by D. Palmer (M/D).

2000   13thC silver pendant, set with an amethyst: finder Alan Steele (M/D).

British Museum

[date?]   Late 10thC Anglo-Saxon strap-end.

Winchester City Museum

WINCHESTER AREA, HAMPSHIRE

1991   10th or 11thC gold pendant found by Terence Hinde (M/D) on an old trackway used by pilgrims to Winchester and Salisbury.

1996   Imitation gold *solidus* of the Byzantine Emperor Anastasius (AD 491–518), which had been made into a gold pendant dating from about AD 600: finder M. McGovern (M/D).

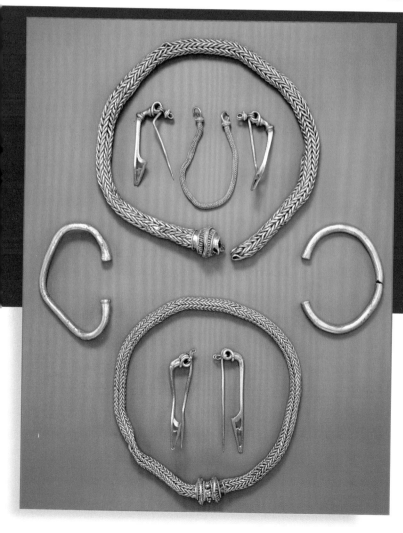

2000   Iron Age gold jewellery of 80–30 BC found in a field on farmland: finder Kevin Halls. Kevin had been metal-detecting for 25 years when he stumbled on the greatest find of his life. The hoard of 2 necklaces (torcs), 2 pairs of brooches, and a pair of bracelets were of almost pure gold and weighed 2¼lb. The hoard is one of the most significant discoveries ever made in Britain, and certainly the most important since the discovery of the Snettisham Great Torc in 1950. The objects are unique, and no other gold necklaces like these have been found anywhere in Europe. One of the torcs is bigger than the other, leading historians to the view that they may have been made for a king and queen, who lived when Julius Caesar was conquering France. They did not come from a settlement, a grave or temple, but were buried on top of a small hill, which means they were either buried for safe keeping or perhaps as a religious offering. They were declared treasure trove, and valued at £500,000.

British Museum

2000   11thC Anglo-Saxon silver coin brooch: finder J. Bennett. The brooch was made with a silver penny of Edward the Confessor and had been gilded on the rear.

City Museum, Winchester

2001   5 Roman *denarii* from the 1stC AD: finder K. Halls (M/D); thought to have been deposited after AD 37.

British Museum

2001   Gold ring dating from 1300 to 1100 BC found in a field: finder Keith Hutchings; later declared treasure trove.

WINDSOR AND MAIDENHEAD

1859   150 silver coins from the 16th and 17thC found at Shaw's Farm estate in Windsor Great Park, thought to have been concealed between 1625 and 1649.

1968   19thC diamond-studded gold scabbard locket found by Fred Besch while diving in the Thames. This item formed part of the scabbard of a sword reputed to have been presented to Lord Nelson by the Sultan of Turkey after the Battle of the Nile in 1798. It was auctioned at Christie's and fetched £7,500, the equivalent of around £75,000 today.

1982   19thC diamond-studded gold scabbard locket found by Ken Crosby while diving in the Thames. This item formed part of the scabbard of a sword reputed to have been presented to Lord Nelson by the Sultan of Turkey, after the Battle of the Nile (1798).

WOKINGHAM

1817   About 1,000 well-preserved Roman copper coins, from the 4thC AD, found in a jar during ploughing.

1877   Gold ryals of Edward IV, concealed in the beams of an old house.

1970   1,800 Roman copper coins from the 4thC AD found in a pot at Matthews Green, on the north-western outskirts of the town.

WOODLAND ST MARY, WEST BERKSHIRE

1949   60 gold coins dated 1603–49 found in the bank of hedgerow at Lye Farm.

WOODNESBOROUGH, KENT

2001   A 9thC highly decorated Anglo-Saxon silver strap-end: finder C.E. Bradshaw (M/D).
British Museum

WORTHING, WEST SUSSEX

1948   About 2,100 Roman copper coins from the 3rdC AD found in a pot during the digging of a sewer trench in Mill Road.

1979   A rare 17thC gold seal ring, found on the beach. The 15–18ct gold ring, inset with a red cornelian stone and an oared galley intaglio, was worth in the region of £450.

[date?]   A Bronze Age hoard, including tools, an axe, a knife and a gouge.

WOTTON, SURREY

1837   30 gold coins from the 16th and 17thC found on Leith Hill; thought to have been concealed 1561–1634.

WROTHAM, KENT

1849   15 silver coins from the 16th and 17thC, thought to have been concealed 1660–85.

1999   A silver-gilt Frankish hinged arm-ring fragment from the late 5th to early 6thC: finder John Darvill (M/D). The terminal was cast in the form of a lion's or horse's head inlaid with garnets.

1999   A 13thC gold finger-ring, set with a blue stone: finder Keith Smallwood (M/D); returned to the finder.

2001   A Roman silver finger-ring from the 2ndC AD: finder Nigel Betts (M/D). The engraved cornelian gem, which had become detached, shows the figure of a dolphin. The ring was returned to the finder.

WROXHALL, ISLE OF WIGHT

1863   About 5,000 Roman copper coins from the 4th and 5thC AD found in an earthen jar 5ft below the surface in a cutting of the Ryde and Ventnor railway. A large proportion of the coins were disposed of by the finders, and so only a few hundred were retrieved.

WYTHAM, BERKSHIRE

1963   7 silver coins, thought to have been concealed between 1760 and 1816. The coins were very worn and may have been forgeries.

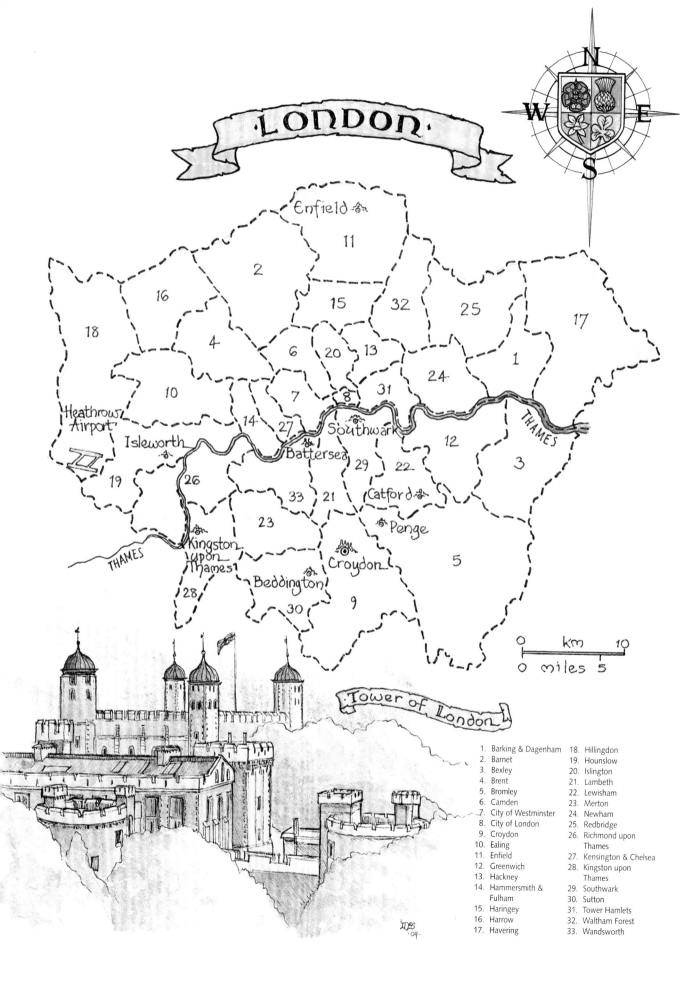

LONDON

N
W E
S

Enfield

11

2

16

15   32   25

17

18

4

6   20   13

1

10

24

7   31

8

THAMES

Heathrow
Airport

14   27   Southwark

12

Isleworth   Battersea

3

19   26

29   22

33   21   Catford

23   Penge

THAMES

Kingston
upon   Croydon

5

Thames

Beddington   9

28   30

0   km   10

0   miles   5

Tower of London

1. Barking & Dagenham   18. Hillingdon
2. Barnet   19. Hounslow
3. Bexley   20. Islington
4. Brent   21. Lambeth
5. Bromley   22. Lewisham
6. Camden   23. Merton
7. City of Westminster   24. Newham
8. City of London   25. Redbridge
9. Croydon   26. Richmond upon
10. Ealing   Thames
11. Enfield   27. Kensington & Chelsea
12. Greenwich   28. Kingston upon
13. Hackney   Thames
14. Hammersmith &   29. Southwark
    Fulham   30. Sutton
15. Haringey   31. Tower Hamlets
16. Harrow   32. Waltham Forest
17. Havering   33. Wandsworth

ACTON, EALING

1899 7 Roman *denarii* and a small lamp from the 1st to 2ndC AD found on the Springfield estate.

ADDINGTON, CROYDON

c. **1977** 177 *antoniniani* of various rulers from the 3rdC AD found at Addington Palace, thought to have been concealed in AD 270.

British Museum

ALBERT BRIDGE AREA, ROYAL BOROUGH OF KENSINGTON AND CHELSEA

1973 A 19thC diamond-encrusted sword chape was extracted from the mud near the bridge by Roger Coyle. It was believed to have been one of the many sword scabbards presented to Nelson following his naval victories, and was valued at £36,000, perhaps two to three times that amount today. Some reports suggest the sword was found at Old Windsor.

BATTERSEA, WANDSWORTH

1851 A bronze shield, probably made in Britain, dating from *c*. 350 BC, decorated with red glass studs, was extracted from the mud on the Thames foreshore. The shield was not made for warfare, being too short, but probably for ceremonial use. Like many other items found in the Thames, it had probably been deposited as some kind of votive offering.

British Museum

1900s A hoard of 20thC jewellery and objects found by a house painter and his son (aged 11) who were walking along the Thames mudflats at low tide. The father saw something glinting in the mud and pulled up a ruby-studded bracelet, a silver cup, candlesticks, an assortment of clocks, a tray and several snuffboxes.

1965 83 gold and 13 silver coins from the 19thC, thought to have been concealed in 1893.

BEDDINGTON, SUTTON

1978 4 silver coins from the 11thC were in Beddington Park close to Carew Manor, where Queen Elizabeth I was entertained for three days in 1599. The hoard, found by J. Dabkowski, consisted of silver pennies and a cut halfpenny of William I. Dated 1075–8 they came from Canterbury mints, Thetford and London and were buried in what was once part of the bank of the River Wandle. They were later declared treasure trove.

Central Library, Sutton

BERMONDSEY, SOUTHWARK

1820   12 silver pennies of William II and Henry I (1087–1135), thought to have been buried in 1101.

1927   46 20thC gold coins were found, thought to have been concealed 1901–36.

BEXLEY

1969   4 cast lead tokens, thought to have been concealed 1760–1816.

BEXLEYHEATH, BEXLEY

1860   19 silver coins.

BLACKFRIARS, SOUTHWARK

[date?]   A 15thC sword, found on the foreshore.

[date?]   A 16thC pewter baluster, found on the Thames foreshore near Three Cranes Wharf.

BLACKFRIARS BRIDGE, SOUTHWARK

1840   16thC gold coins and 200 silver coins found at a house near the old Blackfriars Bridge; thought to have been concealed in 1564.

BLACKHEATH, LEWISHAM

1807   253 silver coins found, thought to have been concealed 1561–1634.

BRENTFORD, HOUNSLOW

1970   67 bronze Roman coins, dated AD 322–30.

BROMLEY, KENT

1955   300 Roman copper folles from the 3rd to 4thC AD found in a pot by boys at Hayesford Raglan Secondary School, while digging a long jump pit in the sports field.

1966   299 silver coins from the 20thC, thought to have been concealed in 1941.

CATFORD, LEWISHAM

1937   110 gold coins of Charles I (1625–49), found by workmen digging a shallow trench in Oldstead Road on the Hall Park estate. They first found just 1 gold coin and when they dug into the walls of the trench they found over 100 more. They were thought to have been concealed in 1644 or, like the Lewisham hoard, could date from the 1648 Kent Royalist uprising.

CATFORD AREA, LEWISHAM

1979   A Georgian silver hoard from the 18thC: finders Dennis Deadman and Brenda Hitchman (M/D), in a recreation area. The hoard included a silver dish, 8 tumbler holders, a mustard pot, 2 spoons, a serviette ring, and a set of 6 tablespoons, all highly decorated. It was declared treasure trove but was later returned to the finders.

CHISLEHURST, BROMLEY

1974   307 silver half-crowns, and florins of Victoria, Edward VII and George V dated 1872–1917 found on Chislehurst Common.

CRANHAM, HAVERING

1998   A 15thC inscribed silver-gilt finger-ring: finders Nick Rowntree and B.A. Smyth (M/D); valued at £850.

Colchester Castle Museum

CRAYFORD, BEXLEY

1906   8 gold Celtic bracelets; a year later 9 more were discovered on Crayford Heath.

British Museum

CROYDON

1860   Roman silver coins from the 4th and 5thC AD found in gravel pit in Park Street.

1862   About 250 Anglo-Saxon foreign and oriental silver pennies from the 9thC AD found in a canvas bag by workmen. The bag fell to pieces when it was picked it up, having been buried *c.* AD 875. Most of the coins were acquired by the editor of the *Croydon Journal*.

1893   121 Roman copper *antoniniani* from the 3rdC AD.

1903   About 3,600 Roman copper coins from the 4thC AD found 2ft deep in 2 pots during the digging of a drain-trench opposite 56 Wandle Road.

1905   More than 281 Roman copper-alloy coins from between the 1stC BC and the 2ndC AD found in a greyware pot by workmen digging a drain for new buildings in South End, Croydon. The coins, which were corroded, were shared out among the men.

1998   3 silver pennies of Edward I, II and III found by the Museum of London Archaeology Service.

[date?]   About 7 Anglo-Saxon silver pennies from the 9thC AD found on the site of the old archbishop's palace.

DEPTFORD, LEWISHAM

1908   A 16thC pewter flagon, found in the Thames.

ELTHAM, GREENWICH

1919   18th and 19thC silver coins, thought to have been concealed in 1807.

ENFIELD

1820   About 70 Roman silver and brass coins from the 1st to the 2ndC AD found in a pot during ploughing near Catcherhatch Lane.

1863   13thC silver coins found in an earthenware vessel: Henry I and II silver short-cross pennies, concealed during the 13thC, probably at the time of the Barons' Revolt in 1264.

1976   326 Roman billon coins from the 4thC AD found during an excavation by the Inner London Archaeological Unit; thought to have been deposited *c*. AD 335.

FINCHLEY, BARNET

1755   About 20 gold coins from the 14thC found on Finchley Common.

1820   Silver George II coins and 2 pistols from the 18thC found in 2 large chests under tree roots at Cold Fall Wood, Near Finchley Common. As workmen were cutting timber, they pulled the roots of a large tree, unearthing the chests. This may have been part of the loot of a gang of highwaymen who were hanged for their crimes in the mid-18thC.

FULHAM, HAMMERSMITH AND FULHAM

1804   700 gold George I guineas dated 1714–27 and many rings and valuable trinkets in a silver cup, found in the roof tiles of Captain Duncan's House.

GROVE PARK, HOUNSLOW

1915   A large quantity of 18thC billon coins, thought to have been concealed between 1727 and 1760.

HAMMERSMITH, HAMMERSMITH AND FULHAM

>1929   A large quantity of 3rdC AD Roman copper coins and 1 silver coin, found on the south side of the Thames.

HEATHROW AIRPORT, HILLINGDON

During the building work on the 250-acre site for the airport's Terminal 5, 80 archaeologists unearthed 80,000 items, the oldest from 6000 BC. Along with some 40,000 flints were 18,000 pieces of pottery and the only wooden bowl ever to be found from the Middle Bronze Age (1500–1100 BC).

HIGHGATE, CAMDEN

c. **1830–50**   Roman copper coins in a vase and a bronze sword handle from the 3rdC AD, found 10ft below the surface during building work at the Priory, Shepherd's Hill Road.

1843   400 gold coins from the 18th and19thC found in Tufnell Park; thought to have been concealed in 1842.

1896   16 gold coins from the 18th and19thC, thought to have been concealed between 1837 and 1901.

HORNCHURCH, HAVERING

1938   448 silver pennies, the bulk of which were Henry III short-cross pennies, all dated before 1265, found under Hornchurch Road.

HORNSEY, HARINGEY

1897   120 gold coins from the 18th and19thC; thought to have been concealed between 1760 and 1816.

HOUNSLOW

1861   376 silver coins from the 15thC, made up of English, Irish and foreign coins; believed to have been concealed *c*. 1495–1500.

ISLEWORTH, HOUNSLOW

1859–60   A large quantity of George III silver shillings found in a box during alterations at Sion House, having been concealed in 1763.

1886   28 silver Anglo-Saxon pennies from the 10thC found in a field, having been scattered during ploughing. They are believed to be part of a much larger hoard, yet to be discovered. It is thought this hoard may be connected with the unsuccessful attack on London by Danes under Sweyn and Norwegians under Olaf Trygvesson. They sailed up the Thames and besieged London before being bought off by Aethelred.

ISLINGTON

[date?]   78 gold coins from the 19th and 20thC, thought to have been concealed between 1901 and 1936.

KENTISH TOWN, CAMDEN

1981   99 gold coins from the 19th and 20thC found in a tin box beneath floorboards at 37 Falkland Road, NW5. They were found by policeman James Long at his son's house and were Australian gold sovereigns from the reign of Victoria and one Edward VII sovereign, dated 1853–1903. They are thought to have been deposited in 1903 or later and were declared treasure trove before being returned to the finder.

ROYAL BOROUGH OF KINGSTON UPON THAMES

c. **1530**   Roman gold, silver and copper coins, and silver plate from the 4th and 5thC AD.

1848   More than 10 6thC gold tremisses found in the bed of the River Thames.

1974   8 forged pewter half-crowns of Charles I found during building work; thought to have been deposited after 1645.

1976   1 silver coin and several false coins and blanks from the reign of George III, found during excavations of a cesspit.

LAMBETH

1842 Some thousands of gold coins found on the Thames foreshore. Initially two men found a Tudor gold coin and didn't search any more. Soon the news spread and people began arriving at the site with shovels and discovered a vast quantity.

LEWISHAM

1837 420 gold coins from the 16th and 17thC found in Southend Lane; thought to have been concealed in 1645, although it may have been after the failed Kentish Royalist uprising in 1648.

1896 A large quantity of 19th and 20thC gold coins, thought to have been concealed between 1837 and 1901.

LEYTONSTONE, WALTHAM FOREST

In Daniel Defoe's *Tour of Britain* (1720) he wrote 'That the great road lay this way; and that it was one of those famous highways made by the Romans, there is undoubted proof, by the several marks of Roman work, and by Roman coins, and other antiquities found there.'

MUSWELL HILL, HARINGEY

1928 654 Roman silver coins from the 1st to the 3rdC AD found in a pot by a boy digging 4–5ft below the surface in the garden of 104 Cranley Gardens. Along with the coins, which all except one were *denarii*, was a silver spoon, a broken bronze ring, and pottery fragments.

NEW BARNET, BARNET

1946 21 silver coins from the 16thC, thought to have been concealed in 1587.

ORPINGTON, BROMLEY

1934 376 Roman *denarii* from the 1st to the 3rdC AD found in a pot by a labourer 18in below the surface while digging a trench on the O'Sullivan estate, in Forest Way.

PECKHAM, SOUTHWARK

1830 19thC gold coins found in the kitchen wall of a house. Some time later £1,000 in banknotes was found in a piece of furniture in the same house.

RICHMOND UPON THAMES

1972 9 gold sovereigns and 2 half-sovereigns dated 1878–1906 found in a cork-sealed glass bottle in the ground in Richmond Park.

SOUTHWARK

1755 Roman silver coins and a large silver ingot from the 4th and 5thC AD found during the digging of foundations for a meeting house in Redcross Street.

1761 Some gold and Elizabeth I silver coins found during the demolition of the Bear Tavern, at the Southwark end of London Bridge. They were thought to have been concealed c. 1558–1603.

1786 Coins in a vessel found while digging a well for a steam engine in Park Street, near the spot where the Globe Theatre formerly stood.

1864 554 Roman copper coins dating from the 3rdC AD found in a pot, together with two skeletons, while digging a trench on the corner of Grove Street.

1977 A silver bowl of 1634–5 found under Southwark Bridge by Anthony Pilson, who took it home. It wasn't until he began to clean it that he saw the silver hallmark and so reported it to the police. It had the inscription 'Johannes Downing', who was probably its original owner. It was worth well over £1,000.

[date?] 4 pewter spoons from the 13th to the 14thC excavated from the Thames foreshore.

SPITALFIELDS MARKET, TOWER HAMLETS

1999 A gold finger-ring, inscribed and decorated with a human skull, dating from 1674, found during the excavation of a cesspit.

Museum of London

1999 An inscribed 15thC gold finger-ring found during excavations of a medieval road surface.

Museum of London

SPITALFIELDS, TOWER HAMLETS

2001 8 gold coins (angels of Henry VIII), thought to have been deposited c.1520–30, found by the Museum of London Archaeological Service.

Museum of London

STANMORE, HARROW

1781 Roman gold and silver coins, a gold bracelet and 2 gold rings dating from the 4th and 5thC AD found by labourers while cleaning a ditch, about a mile from the Roman posting station of Sulloniacae on Watling Street. Many coins were dispersed by the finders, along with a silver plate, but 40 gold coins were recovered. Many of the silver coins crumbled when handled.

1836 A large quantity of foreign gold coins, possibly from the 18th and 19thC; thought to have been concealed in 1816.

STOKE NEWINGTON, HACKNEY

1896 47 gold coins from the 18th and 19thC; thought to have been concealed between 1816 and 1820.

SURREY COMMERCIAL DOCKS, SOUTHWARK

1867 1,900 Roman copper coins from the 4th and 5thC AD found in a vase 5ft below the surface during the excavation of the foundations of a warehouse.

RIVER THAMES

1984–5 A 15thC necklace found in the mud by Alan Stewart (M/D). It was valued at £20,000 (worth close to twice that amount today) and he received a reward.

Museum of London

1986 An Anglo-Saxon gold coin in beautiful condition and dated AD 600–70, found at the water's edge on the south bank by James Mathieson. It was valued at over £3,000.

[date?] An Anglo-Saxon long-knife, known as a 'scramaseax', with copper bronze and silver wire inlay of the 'futhorc' or runic alphabet.

[date?] 6 16th–17thC pewter spoons excavated from the Thames foreshore.

[date?] An early 17thC pewter feeding bottle found on the Thames foreshore. It is one of the earliest feeding bottles found.

[date?] A Roman bronze helmet from the 1stC AD was found in the river, having probably been lost between AD 43 and 60. This helmet, known as a coolus, was used by both cavalry and infantry, and has the names of its four successive owners on the neck-guard.

British Museum

WANDSWORTH

1944 1,395 banknotes, 84 gold sovereigns, 33 half-sovereigns, a box of jewellery, and several gold watches from the 19th and 20thC found under the floorboards of a house in West Hill by a young electrician working in the house.

WAPPING, TOWER HAMLETS

1895–1910? Coins discovered on the Thames foreshore. Hundreds of people descended on the area, digging up gardens, pavements, roads, and even the railway, before the police put a stop to it.

WATERLOO BRIDGE AREA, SOUTHWARK

[date?] A 1stC bronze helmet, probably belonging to a chieftain, dating from about 50 BC.

WATERLOO BRIDGE, LONDON

1938 3 gold, 6 silver and 4 copper coins dating from the 18th and19thC found in the foundation stone of the bridge; thought to have been concealed in 1811.

WILLESDEN, BRENT

1840 16thC silver coins; found on Wormwood Scrubs, thought to have been concealed between 1544 and 1561.

Central London

ALDERSGATE STREET , LONDON EC1

>1909 Roman *denarii* from the 1st to the 3rdC AD found in a vase.

ALDGATE, CITY OF LONDON

1926 Gold coins and more than 3 silver coins, probably from the 16th or 17thC; thought to have been concealed between 1685 and 1697.

BERMONDSEY, LONDON SE1

1945 361 Roman copper coins from the 4th and 5thC AD found in a pot while preparing a housing site in Chilton Street.

Museum of London

BILLINGSGATE, LONDON EC3

1975 200 Roman copper coins from the 4th and 5thC AD found during excavations of the bath-house.

[date?]   A late 13thC pewter mirror case. This highly decorated case had originally contained a small convex mirror backed with lead.

Museum of London

BLOOMSBURY, LONDON WC1

1924   About 700 Roman copper coins from the 4thC AD found in the remains of a lead box 7ft below the surface by workmen building a new hotel in Tavistock Square. Some were given away by the finders, but 667 coins were retained.

BROAD STREET, LONDON EC2

1758   An unknown quantity of coins in two vessels, of 'considerable value', found by bricklayers digging at the rear of a house in Broad Street.

BUCKLERSBURY, CITY OF LONDON

1872   King Alfred silver pennies, dating from the 9thC.

BULL WHARF, CITY OF LONDON

[date?]   A 14thC pewter pyx lid. A pyx is a small vessel in which the sacrament can be kept for future use.

CHEAPSIDE, CITY OF LONDON

1838   11thC pewter jewellery, including partly finished beads, brooches and rings, found opposite St Mary-le-Bow church.

1842   Roman coins and a bronze figure of an archer from the 3rdC AD found by a bricklayer beside a newly discovered Roman wall in Queen Street, a short distance from Watling Street. The bronze figure is at the Museum of London.

Museum of London

1912   A 16thC hoard was found over 15ft below the surface during the digging of foundations for a new building. It was thought to be the whole stock of a city jeweller's shop, and consisted of about 150 pieces of jewellery, including crucifixes, pins, watches and old gemstones. Thought to have been buried *c.* 1640, during the Civil War.

CITY OF LONDON

1958   More than 74 Roman silver coins from the 1stC BC to the 2ndC AD found on a building site near Budge Row. A workman discovered them 16ft down on the site of Temple House. The coins were shared among his companions, who were mostly, like himself, of Polish origin. 74 coins were later recovered.

COVENT GARDEN, LONDON WC2

2000   An Early Saxon brooch dating from the 7thC was found in a grave during excavations near the Royal Opera House. With it were three glass beads and some rings of silver wire. The brooch had a face embellished with gold strip, with five domed garnets in bosses, and a mosaic of tiny garnet slabs elsewhere. The theory is that it belonged to a lady of noble or royal birth.

Museum of London

EAST LONDON

1804   An immense quantity of 1st to 3rdC AD Roman coins was found by workmen enlarging a pleasure ground. Contemporary reports say they were 'of different metals, and in good preservation'.

FENCHURCH STREET, LONDON EC3

1922   12 Roman *denarii* from the 1st and 2ndC AD found 18in below the surface while relaying a drain by No.146 Fenchurch Street.

FETTER LANE, CITY OF LONDON

[date?]   An 8th–9thC Anglo-Saxon parcel gilt-silver sword pommel, adorned with writhing snakes and leaves.

British Museum

HONEY LANE, CITY OF LONDON

1837   Nearly 20 silver pennies from the 11thC found at Honey Lane Market.

KING WILLIAM STREET, OR ST SWITHIN'S LANE, CITY OF LONDON

1845   Roman coins found during the digging of foundations for a house. They were plated Roman *denarii*: some Consular, some Augustus, Marc Antony, Tiberius, and a very few Claudius. They were probably brought to England by the Roman troops during Claudius's reign. According to contemporary reports they 'are of iron, coated with a thick plate of silver. They are much oxidised and, in consequence, when found were in masses, but it is evident that they had been placed in tiers in a box or some other enclosure.' It was later discovered that they were not iron but copper.

KING'S REACH, CITY OF LONDON

[date?]   A 10thC sword, found in the Thames close to the Temple.

LIME STREET , CITY OF LONDON

1881–2   251 Roman *denarii* and *antoniniani* from the 3rdC.

1882   About 600 Roman silver and copper coins from the 2nd and 3rdC AD, found in an urn 18ft below the surface during excavations; about 320 of these were *denarii*.

LINCOLN'S INN FIELDS, CITY OF LONDON

c. 1750   Several hundred Roman copper coins from the 3rdC AD, found in an urn in the foundations of an old house.

1893   9thC AD coins, thought to have been concealed *c.* AD 842, found while laying conduits for electrical cables in the Middle Temple.

LOMBARD STREET, CITY OF LONDON

1785–6   About 300 Roman copper coins from the 3rd and 4thC AD found about 7ft below the surface, close to a chalk wall, opposite the end of Nicholas Lane.

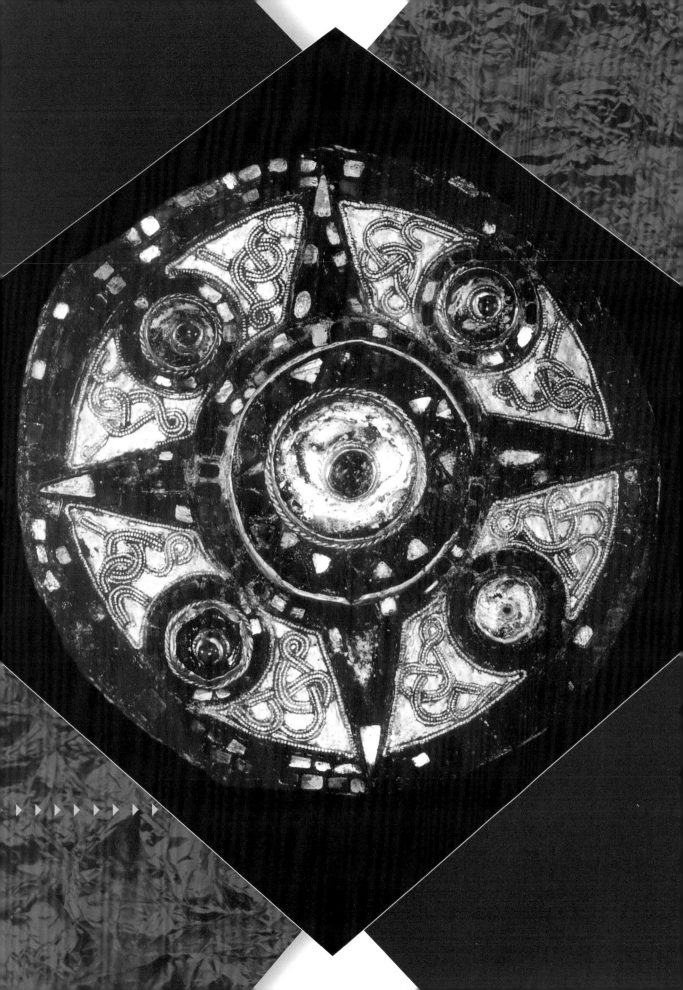

LONDON BRIDGE, SE1

1758   16thC gold and silver coins found in 3 pots in a house on old London Bridge when it was being demolished. They were thought to have been deposited in 1558–1603.

1850   12thC silver pennies.

1853   Roman coins found in an urn when the old London Bridge was pulled down.

LONDON BRIDGE (APPROACH), SE1

>1921   17 Roman bronze coins from the 1stC AD found 15ft down on the site of Lloyds Bank. The coins were asses of Claudius (15) and Agrippa (2) and were bound together. They were buried along with some fragments of Samianware pottery.

Museum of London

1975   448 tokens dated *c.* 1870–1939 found in the Thames mudflats. These were checks of the Royal Arsenal Co-operative Society Limited, probably dumped by the issuers.

1981   More than 447 lead tokens from the 15th to the 16thC found in the Thames mudflats at the city end of the bridge. They are thought to have been concealed in the late 15th to early 16thC.

British Museum

[date?]   Viking battleaxes and spears retrieved along with tongs and an anchor from the Thames at London Bridge. They date from *c.* 840–1020 and were possibly left after a battle, or may have been thrown into the river as an offering to the gods.

Museum of London

LOVAT LANE, CITY OF LONDON

1775   Over 300 coins and a gold filigree brooch dating from the 11thC found in two earthenware pots, one inside the other, at St Mary-at-Hill Church. The coins were silver pennies of Edward, Harold and William I, and the brooch was set with a sapphire and pearls.

NORTON FOLGATE, LONDON E1

[date?]   A Pewter paten, thought to date from *c.* 1600.

OLD FORD, EAST LONDON

>1846   About 500 Roman silver and copper coins from the 3rd and 4thC AD, found over a period of years by a man digging in his garden.

1866   Roman *antoniniani* from the 3rdC AD found in a small vase 3ft deep during the digging of foundations for a house, between the two Roman roads entering London at Aldgate.

PLANTATION PLACE, LONDON EC3

2000   43 Roman *aurei* from AD 65/6 to 174, including two word coins of Nero, found during the development work for an office

block and shops. They were originally in a bag, probably of leather, and concealed in a floor safe next to a wall within a large family home. They were declared treasure trove and donated to the Museum of London by the owners of the site, the British Land Company.

Museum of London

QUEEN VICTORIA STREET, LONDON EC4

1872   183 silver pennies of Edward the Confessor, thought to have been concealed *c.* 1070.

1872   More than 7,000 11thC silver pennies and foreign coins found near Walbrook. This hoard had coins from the reigns of Harold, Edward, and earlier kings. They may have been concealed as William I advanced on London.

QUEENHITHE, LONDON EC4

1980   More than 500 silver coins of Edward IV, all lightweight forgeries, found on the north foreshore of the Thames; thought to have been concealed *c.* 1490.

1982   15thC crucifix found among stones on the foreshore by the Three Cranes Wharf site at the Vintry between Queenhithe and Southwark Bridge. It is Gothic in design, resembling a tree with fresh budding branches.

[date?]   15thC pewter candlestick excavated from Thames foreshore, dated *c.* 1400.

Museum of London

[date?]   Late 15thC pewter pilgrim badge found on the Thames foreshore.

ST MARTIN'S LANE, CITY OF LONDON

1747   16th and 17thC gold and silver coins found in a Delft shoe, next to Douglas's Coffee House in St Martin's Lane, having probably been buried *c.* 1600–62.

ST MARTIN'S LE GRAND, CITY OF LONDON

1800s   35 silver pennies dating from the early 11thC; thought to have been concealed *c.* 1016, at the end of Ethelred the Unready's reign, when London was under virtual siege by the Vikings.

ST PANCRAS, LONDON NW1

1770   A large quantity of 16th and 17thC silver coins, thought to have been concealed between 1625 and 1649.

1950s   Late Roman silver coins found in the window box of a house. We can only assume that the earth was dug up and used to fill the box.

1963   62 gold coins from the 18th and 19thC, thought to have been concealed *c.* 1875.

ST THOMAS'S HOSPITAL, BOROUGH, CITY OF LONDON

1863   12thC silver pennies.

SWAN LANE, CITY OF LONDON

1981   7 highly decorated tin-lead tokens from the 13thC found during excavations.

THREADNEEDLE STREET, CITY OF LONDON

>1924   10thC silver coins, thought to have been deposited *c.* AD 950.

1978   4 gold and 1,739 silver coins of 15th–17thC found at the Bank of England. They were in 4 bags and a wooden box and had been deposited at the bank on 9 July 1725. There were coins from the reigns of Edward VI, Henry VIII, Philip and Mary, Elizabeth I, James I and Charles I and II. They were declared treasure trove.

WATLING STREET, CITY OF LONDON

1980   More than 12 Roman bronze coins from the 1stC AD found in a leather purse, during building works at Watling Court in Watling Street. The vast majority were probably shared among the workers and those that were recovered were all asses of Nero. Of these, 11 were minted at Lugdunum and 1 at Rome in AD 65 or 66. The fact that there were none of the more common Flavian bronzes from Lugdunum indicates that they were deposited *c.* AD 70.

CITY OF WESTMINSTER

1863   An unknown quantity of gold nobles was said to have been disposed of to a refiner who paid the finders £212 10*s* 0*d*. (This would equate to nearly £12,000 today.)

1871   54 gold coins from the reign of Henry VIII (1509–44), thought to have been concealed in 1544 or earlier.

Items from Bill's collection, including coins from the Roman period and 16th and 17thC belt mounts.

Ancient history is everywhere in the West of England, and where there is no tangible evidence of our ancestors, the gaps are filled by myth and legend.

There have been some wonderful Civil War finds in this area, often associated with rich Royalists burying their wealth to avoid its being found by Cromwell's New Model Army. In 1693 near the Isle of Athelney, Somerset, 30 years after the end of the Civil War, arguably the greatest single find in this country was made: the Anglo-Saxon 'Alfred Jewel' from the 9[th]C AD was found at Newton Park. King Alfred probably owned it as it bears the Anglo-Saxon inscription 'Aelfred Mec Heht Gewyrcan' – 'Alfred Had Me Made'. Evidence of the earlier occupation of the area could not be better demonstrated than the discovery of 55,000 Roman coins at Mildenhall in Wiltshire in 1978. In the same year a Viking bracelet was found on the beach at Paignton near Torbay by a lady on holiday from Lincolnshire. A year earlier her mother had found a hoard of Roman coins in Lincolnshire.

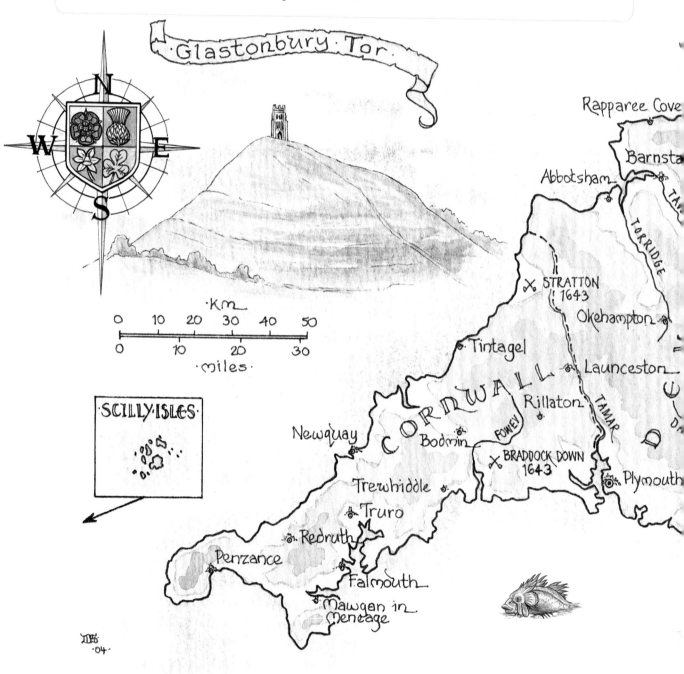

·Glastonbury·Tor·

N
W · E
S

·Km·
0   10   20   30   40   50
0   10   20   30
·miles·

SCILLY ISLES

Rapparee Cove
Barnsta
Abbotsham
TORRIDGE
TAM
STRATTON 1643
Okehampton
Tintagel
Launceston
CORNWALL
Rillaton
TAMAR
Newquay
Bodmin
FOWEY
D
BRADDOCK DOWN 1643
Plymouth
Trewhiddle
Truro
Redruth
Penzance
Falmouth
Mawgan in Meneage

·04·

The WEST

GLOUCESTERSHIRE

TEWKESBURY 1471
Cheltenham
Gloucester
Birdlip
Bourton-on-the Water
Lydney
SEVERN
Cirencester
Thornbury
Bristol
Swindon
LANSDOWN 1643
Mildenhall
Marlborough
AVON
Bromham
Stanchester
Weston-super-mare
Bath
Blagan Hill
Wilcot
ROUNDWAY DOWN 1643
Radford
Devizes
Savernake Forest
Minehead
WILTSHIRE
SOMERSET
Wells
Warminster
Shapwick
Stonehenge
Amesbury
Bridgwater
Glastonbury
SEDGEMOOR 1685
WYLYE
Roughmoor
LANGPORT 1645
Salisbury
Taunton
PARRETT
Ilchester
Bowerchalke
East Worlington
Isle of Athelney
Shaftesbury
EXE
Ham Hill
Yeovil
Fontmell Magna
STOUR
Membury
Pulham
Blandford
DORSET
AVON
Exeter
Dorchester
Poole
Lyme Regis
Bournemouth
TEIGN
Weymouth
Torquay
Paignton
Dartmouth

Stonehenge

ABBOTSHAM, DEVON

2001 495 gold and silver coins of Edward VI, Mary, Elizabeth I, James I, Charles I, Commonwealth, and two of Philip IV of Spain found by T. Prouse and Tony Elphick (M/D), thought to have been deposited *c.* 1650–60; they were later declared treasure trove and valued at £30,000.

ALDBOURNE, WILTSHIRE

1980–1 4,780 Roman copper *antoniniani* coins from the 3rdC AD found by E.R.A. Sewell, while field-walking on Ewins Hill. After his initial find he and the landowner returned and recovered the entire hoard.

Wiltshire Heritage Museum

ALDBOURNE AREA, WILTSHIRE

1867 280 silver coins from the 16th and 17thC found at Crowood; thought to have been concealed between 1625 and 1649.

ALLER, DEVON

1982 4 Elizabeth I sixpences, 4 Elizabeth I threepences, 1 Charles I shilling, and 1 Charles I sixpence found by a metal detectorist in scrubland. It is presumed that they were buried during the Civil War.

ALLINGTON, WILTSHIRE

1972 106 silver coins from the 16th and 17thC found by B. Ham (M/D); thought to have been concealed in 1644.

ALTON, WILTSHIRE

2001 A late 6th or early 7thC Anglo-Saxon silver-gilt pyramidal strap-mount, set with a garnet: finder John Philpotts (M/D).

Wiltshire Heritage Museum

AMESBURY, WILTSHIRE

1767 67 silver coins, consisting of silver groats, half-groats and pence of Henry V and Edward III, most of which were perfect, discovered in a bank, under tree roots, at Lake, near Amesbury, on the former site of a chapel belonging to the priory of Bradenstoke. They were thought to have been concealed after 1415.

1843 4thC AD Roman silver and copper coins, and 3 silver rings with intaglios, found by labourers digging trenches on Long's Farm.

1990 8 Roman gold coins and 1 silver piece from the 4thC found in a small pot at Butterfield Down by a metal detectorist. The 8 coins cover 4 emperors, including 2 of Arcadius (AD 383–408) and 4 of Honorius (AD 393–423). Finds from the site, which has revealed an extensive 15-acre Romano-British settlement, have included over 1,000 coins. The 8 gold coins were later declared treasure trove.

British Museum

AMPNEY ST MARY, GLOUCESTERSHIRE

1931 346 silver coins from the 16th and 17thC, thought to have been concealed in 1646.

AMPNEY ST PETER, NEAR CIRENCESTER, GLOUCESTERSHIRE

1935 115 silver coins from the 16th and 17thC, probably concealed in 1643. It may be the same hoard as the one found in Ampney St Mary.

ASKERSWELL, DORSET

1958 Some silver coins dated 1625 or earlier, thought to have been concealed between 1603 and 1625.

AVEBURY TRUSLOE, WILTSHIRE

2001 Mid-17thC inscribed gold posy ring: finder Peter Cawley (M/D).

Wiltshire Heritage Museum

AVETON GIFFORD, DEVON

1891 More than 200 gold coins, thought to have been concealed between 1697 and 1714.

AXBRIDGE, SOMERSET

>1878 3rdC AD Roman *denarii* and *antoniniani* found in 3 pots by a man digging for ore on Sandford Hill. The workman was given 1 pot and Mr Rich (his boss?) kept the other 2.

> **D IS FOR DENARIUS**
>
> Before the British currency was decimalised in 1971, our pennies, or pence, were denoted by the letter 'd', an abbreviation for *denarius*.

AXMINSTER AREA, DEVON

1724 Gold found on the site of Hawkesdown Hill fort. It was supposedly found by a sailor named Courd, who used his new-found wealth to build a pier on the River Axe. In the 1980s Roman lead sling shot and an *aureus* were found near the fort, which is said to be haunted by a warrior and a fire-breathing dog!

1837 Large quantity of Roman coins from the 1st and 2ndC AD found in a field by workmen hedge-laying on the plantations in Dalwood Down.

BANWELL AREA, NORTH SOMERSET

1967 30 Roman *antoniniani* from AD 286 unearthed on a pathway on Wint Hill beside the site of Romano-British building.

BATH, BATH AND NORTH-EAST SOMERSET

On the River Avon the famous spa and ancient Roman city have the only natural hot springs in Great Britain. In the Dark Ages it was one of King Alfred's defensive centres against the Viking and the Saxon abbey became a cathedral in the 11thC. With the demise of the city's ecclesiastical status at the Reformation, Bath became a fashionable resort, giving rise to the Georgian Bath that is so admired today. The Bath that Jane Austen knew and wrote about was already past its zenith.

'The first view of Bath in fine weather does not answer my expectations; I think I see more distinctly in the rain. The sun was got behind everything, and the appearance of the place from the top of Kingsdown was all vapour, shadow, smoke, and confusion.'

Jane Austen

1755   42 silver coins from the 10thC found in a wooden box under the head of a skeleton, during building work; thought to have been buried *c.* AD 950–5.

1806   Almost 100 Roman coins (some silver) of the 1st and 2ndC AD found by labourers on the south-west side of Trinity Court, near the Turnpike Road, or main street of Walcot (the Fosse Way).

1826   3rd and 4thC AD Roman copper coins, many in an excellent state of preservation, found in a metal pot 10ft below the surface by workmen excavating the ground for the foundations of the New Bridge, at the bottom of Bathwick Street.

1831   16th and 17thC silver coins, thought to have been concealed between 1625 and 1649, found at Leigh House.

>1840   More than 250 Roman bronze coins from 4thC AD, *siliquae* of Constantius II to Eugenius, thought to have been deposited in AD 395. 35 of these are held at the British Museum.

British Museum

1979   27 Roman coins and a priceless Roman bronze brooch found at the bottom of the Roman reservoir, under the Roman baths, during work to remove pollution from the spa water. The brooch was intricately engraved with fish and bird motifs.

1979   1,807 3rdC Roman coins found by a metal detectorist to the north-west of Bath. The coins were all *antoniniani*, but for 1 *denarius* and 1 *quinarius*.

1979   11 copper coins originating from the Netherlands found on the banks of the River Avon. They were perhaps connected with troops or other followers of William of Orange (William III) and possibly deposited after 1660.

1980   1,807 Roman billon coins from the 3rdC AD found in a lead container near Bath by a metal detectorist. The coins were from 16 reigns and were thought to have been deposited in AD 296.

1982   61 gold Iron Age staters found in a hollowed-out flint by Garf Hebden (M/D). They were Iron Age gold 'Corio' staters of the Dobunni tribe, which ruled the West Country about 2,000 years ago. The British Museum said: 'These coins represent a major find, as only 34 of these coins were known, and one of these coins would have bought the services of a fighting man for one season.' Later declared treasure trove.

[date?]   Roman finds from a sacred spring (Aquae Sulis), comprising a mask, a number of paterae, bronze and pewter jugs, a pewter candlestick, a bronze penannular brooch, gemstones, and a large number of worn coins.

BATHFORD, BATH AND NORTH-EAST SOMERSET

1691 Some Roman coins and 2 portable altars found in an urn.

BATSFORD, GLOUCESTERSHIRE

2000 A gold penannular ring of 1150–750 BC: finder Michael Chapman (M/D).

Corinium Museum

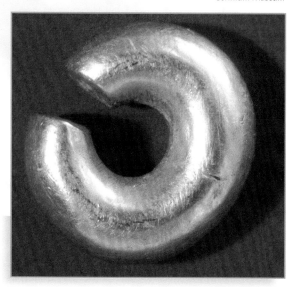

BEAMINSTER AREA, DORSET

1998 15thC gold finger-ring, engraved with the figures of saints, found by M. Henderson (M/D); valued at £4,500.

Dorset County Museum

BEER, DEVON

In 1588 a Spanish galleon was wrecked nearby, and gold and silver coins have been found in the vicinity.

BERKELEY, GLOUCESTERSHIRE

1997 A 16thC silver-gilt dress pin: finder L.F. Hobbs (M/D); valued at £650.

Museum in the Park, Stroud

BERWICK BASSET, WILTSHIRE

1999 Late 15th or early 16thC highly decorated silver-gilt finger-ring: finder George Horton; returned to the finder.

BIRDLIP, GLOUCESTERSHIRE

Late 1800s Iron Age grave goods, including a bronze Celtic mirror from the 1stC BC. There have been fewer than 40 Iron Age mirrors discovered and this is one of the best. Found in a grave, it is a matter of debate as to what exactly people used these mirrors for. It is obvious that you could see your reflection but it is probable that they were indicative

of status above all else. A local antiquarian, John Bellows, heard that two men had discovered some graves while road mending, and it is thanks to him that the treasures were saved. In one of the graves was the skeleton of a woman together with a large amber necklace, 2 bronze bowls, a silver-gilt brooch, a pair of tweezers, an expanding bracelet, 5 bronze rings and the mirror. The burial is assumed to have been at around the time of the Roman invasion.

City Museum and Art Gallery, Gloucester

BISHOPSTROW, WILTSHIRE

1792 Several thousand Roman copper coins from the 4th and 5thC AD found in an urn while digging a ditch on an area to the south-west of the village called the Bury. The find was said to include 'several pieces of iron armour, much Roman ware, and two large urns, one of which contained several coins, said at the time to be "a peck in measure" '.

1798 Vast number of 4th and 5thC AD Roman copper coins, 'nearly sufficient to fill a Winchester bushel', found in 3 urns.

BISLEY AREA, GLOUCESTERSHIRE

1844–5 1,223 Roman copper *antoniniani*, perfectly preserved from the 3rdC AD, found in a pot 6in below the surface in a field called Church Piece, near Lillyhorn, adjoining the highway from Oakridge Common to Bisley.

BLAGAN HILL, WILTSHIRE

1990 1 Roman gold coin, 1,700 silver, over 5,000 bronze, 8 Roman bowls and jewellery from the 4thC AD found in a field. During the summer Philip Gage, a local policeman, found 2 Roman *siliquae* on a field. In the autumn, after harvesting, Alan Aldridge checked the field and found 8 earthenware bowls (all scattered), 2 bead necklaces with silver clasps, a silver bracelet, a copper bracelet, 3 silver rings, a silver ring bezel/brooch with stone, 1 gold coin, 1,700 silver coins, and over 5,000 bronze coins. Known as the Blagan Hill Hoard, it was thought to have originally been in a strong box belonging to a Roman official and was concealed *c.* AD 360–400. It was found on top of a Bronze Age midden.

BLEADON, NORTH SOMERSET

>1968 Silver coins, both English and foreign, thought to have been deposited after 1438.

2003 30 Roman coins of AD 260–74 found by Keith Usher (M/D) on farmland; later declared treasure trove.

BLUNSDON ST ANDREW, WILTSHIRE

1904 About 100 silver trade tokens from the 19thC found at Cold Harbour Inn. They were silver threepenny tokens of the Cold Harbour Friendly Society, thought to have been deposited after 1849.

BOURNEMOUTH

1901 376 silver coins from the 12thC found in a pot. Many of these coins were Henry I silver pennies, thought to have been deposited *c.* 1130

BOURNEMOUTH AREA

[date?]   20 silver pennies of Henry I, thought to have been deposited c. 1135.

BOURTON-ON-THE-WATER, GLOUCESTERSHIRE

c. **1882**   About 1,500 Roman copper coins from the 4thC AD found in a pot on Lower Slaughter Farm. Ryknield Street (in Lower Slaughter Parish, near Bourton-on-the-Water) is a prehistoric track surfaced by the Romans, and intersects the Fosse Way. Roman coins were once so plentiful that they used to be taken to the market at Stow-on-the-Wold and sold by the peck (5lb).

1970   More than 3,297 Roman copper coins from the 4thC AD found in bags about 18in below the surface: finder C. Renfrew (M/D). He first found 2 *antoniniani* and 2,705 copper folles, and a further 590 coins were found in the immediate vicinity where they had been scattered by ploughing. They dated from c. AD 318, and had been concealed beneath flat stones in a field adjoining the Fosse Way, a quarter of a mile south of the village. Coins had regularly been found on the site, causing local people to call it 'Money Ground'.

1999   32 Roman coins from between the 1stC BC and 4thC AD: finder W. Jackman (M/D). They comprised 2 silver and 29 bronze coins and were valued at £100.

2000   Early to middle Bronze Age annular sheet-gold bead found on an archaeological dig.

Corinium Museum

BOVEY TRACEY, DEVON

1998   Highly decorated 16thC silver dress-hook: finder D.W. Hewing; valued at £200.

BOWERCHALKE, WILTSHIRE

1997   19 Roman silver coins and 2 highly ornate Roman gold rings from the late 4thC AD found by Andrew Mitchell and Julian Adams (M/D). On the larger ring, the bezel depicts two clasped right hands, a symbol of allegiance or marriage. They were declared treasure trove.

2003   7 Roman silver coins from AD 356: finders Andrew Mitchell and Julian Adams (M/D). The coins are from the Emperors Julian (AD 356–63), Valens (AD 364–78), Theodosius (AD 379–83), Magnus Maximus (AD 383–8) and Eugenius (AD 389–94), and were declared treasure trove.

BOYTON, WILTSHIRE

1935   4,147 silver coins from the 14thC found by a workman in an earthenware jug. They were silver pennies of Edward III (1327–77), mainly English and Scottish, a few of which were counterfeit. They were thought to have been concealed in 1324.

BREAGE, CORNWALL

1779   About 1,600 Roman coins from the 3rdC AD found with an urn under a large stone (4ft long x 2ft wide x 1ft thick) by Nicholas Pearce, while narrowing a bank forming the boundary of his field, in the Barton of Godolphin, on land belonging to the Duke of Leeds. This site is about half a mile from the Roman fort at Bosense. The coins were dispersed by the finders.

BRENT KNOLL, SOMERSET

>1789   1st to 3rdC AD Roman coins.

BRIDPORT, DORSET

1943   24 gold coins from the 20thC or earlier, thought to have been concealed in 1914.

BRIDZOR FARM, WARDOUR, WILTSHIRE

c. **1786**   16th and 17thC gold coins, about 110 silver coins, and a gold ring found in a stone trough, in a barn, at Bridzor Farm. The coins were mostly of Elizabeth I, Charles I and II, and William III, and were thought to have been deposited after 1695. The farm is close to Wardour Castle, which was built in the late 14thC for John, the 5th Lord Lovel. It was attacked and badly damaged in 1643, during the Civil War, and was even more badly damaged when it was retaken by its owners, the Arundell family, who blew a large part of it down. It was 'maintained' as a ruin when the new castle was built in 1776.

BRIXTON DEVERILL, WILTSHIRE

>1936   Roman silver coins found in an earthen jar.

BRISTOL, CITY OF

>1818   Roman silver and brass coins in a pot found by a man repairing a hedge. He took them to Bristol and sold them.

1820   19thC or earlier gold coins found in the Southville area of the city; thought to have been concealed between 1760 and 1816.

1800s   19thC or earlier silver coins found during demolition work. All the coins were dispersed except 1, which is in the Bristol City Museum.

Bristol City Museum

1869   More than 1,000 Roman coins found on the 'Somerset side of Bristol' in a vase.

1875   Massive quantity of 3rd and 4thC AD Roman bronze coins found in a large pot, thought to have been deposited *c.* AD 336. They were found by labourers laying water pipes at Lower Easton, near the Blackbirds' Gate, between Stapleton and Bristol. 'The coins were so numerous that the finders shared the coins by the double handful, and "bore their prizes away in 3 bowler hats filled to the brim".'

1881   16th and 17thC silver and billon coins found in the Southville area of the city. They were thought to have been concealed between 1625 and 1649.

1920–3 and **1935**   16 Roman coins from the 1stC AD found in the Sea Mills area of the city. This seems to have been a single hoard or part of a single hoard, patination is identical and distinctive. In some cases impressions of lettering from one coin appear in the patina of another.

1923   5,449 silver coins from the 16th and 17thC, thought to have been concealed in 1691, found in the Welshback area.

1932   52 gold coins from the 18th and 19thC found in the Southville area of the city; thought to have been concealed between 1820 and 1837.

1936   Large quantity of silver coins found in the Southville area of the city, thought to have been concealed between 1837 and 1901.

1937   1,478 Roman *denarii* and 2 copper coins from the 1st and 3rdC AD found in Rochester Road, St Anne's, Bristol, in a pit that was being dug for a garage.

Bristol City Museum

1945–6   4thC AD Roman copper coins found in a pot by a bulldozer driver at Ashton Vale during building work. Many were dispersed by the finder; 25 were later recovered.

1969   7 billon coins from the 17thC found during demolition work. They included a James I or Charles I farthing.

Bristol City Museum

BRISTOL AREA

1839   About 250 Roman *siliquae* (4thC AD) found on the line of the Great Western Railway between Bath and Bristol.

1867   2,044 Roman silver coins from the 4th and 5thC AD found in the North Mendip region. The hoard comprised 31 miliarenses, 2,003 *siliquae*, and 10 half-*siliquae*.

BROADWOODWIDGER, WEST DEVON

1972   326 silver coins of Philip and Mary, Elizabeth I, James I and II, Charles I and II, and Scottish coins of Charles I found in the shattered remains of a Bellarmine jug (a round-bellied salt-glazed stoneware jug). Following the coroner's inquest, 2 coins were retained by the British Museum.

BROMHAM, WILTSHIRE

1981   416 Roman silver coins from the 4thC found in a beaker on a farm by brothers Paul and Clyde King, while they were trying out new farm machinery. The vessel was among clay pot fragments, about half a mile east of West Park villa, a large late Roman building and was thought to have been buried *c.* AD 337–83. The hoard comprised 20 miliarenses and 395 *siliquae* of Constantius II, Julian, Jovian, Valentinian, Valens and Gratian, and was later declared treasure trove.

1999   15thC silver strap-end, decorated with flowers: finder Lloyd Earley (M/D).

BROOMFIELD, SOMERSET

On some land called Money Field, finds have been made, including bars of gold, pieces of armour and a gold ring or seal with turquoise.

BUCKFASTLEIGH, DEVON

1932   36 silver coins from the 16th and 17thC. The latest coin, an Exeter half-crown, was dated 1644, and the hoard was thought to have been concealed then or soon after.

BUDOCK WATER, CORNWALL

1865   1,022 Roman copper coins from the 3rd and 4thC AD found while ploughing at a depth of between 12 and 18in in a field on a hillside at Pennance Farm near the shore, about a mile south of Falmouth.

BURNHAM-ON-SEA, SOMERSET

1983   2 gold Bronze Age bracelets from 900 BC were found; declared treasure trove.

British Museum

CAMBORNE, CORNWALL

c. **1906**   Some hundreds of Roman copper coins from the 4thC AD found in an urn while clearing away an ancient mound in Rosewarne Park.

1931   13 Roman *denarii* from the 2nd and 3rdC AD found in a fitted wall recess, during excavations of a Roman villa at Magor Farm.

CAMERTON, BATH AND NORTH-EAST SOMERSET

c. **1814–17**   26 Roman silver coins from the 4th and 5thC AD found during the unmethodical excavations of three Roman villas. Over the next few years more coins were found from the 3rdC AD including 334 by a workman, underneath 2 large stones. Besides coins, 4lb of lead ore, a good deal of Samian and other pottery, a thumb vase, and an iron lamp stand were discovered.

CASTLE COMBE, WILTSHIRE

1826   About 300 Roman copper coins, and a small engraved stone slab, from the 4th and 5thC AD, found by labourers planting trees opposite the site of a Roman villa in North Wraxall, which was discovered in 1950.

CATSGORE, SOMERSET

1971 and **1972**   13 Roman billon coins from the 4thC AD were found during excavations in 1971 and another 27 billon coins the following year.

Somerset County Museum

CHAPMANSLADE, WILTSHIRE

1993   5,362 4thC Roman bronze coins found in a pot by Steve Martie and Brent Pullen, in a field about half a mile from a Roman villa on land belonging to farmer Colin Forward. The pot was about 3ft below the surface. Wiltshire Heritage Museum dated the find AD 320–37.

CHARD, SOMERSET

1831   500 Roman gold coins from the 1stC AD found in an urn. 'The gardener of Henry Host Henley Esq., of Leigh House dug up the urn containing a number of gold coins of the emperor Claudius.'

1836   Roman copper coins from the 4thC AD found in a heap 1½ft below the surface by labourers digging for chalk in a field called Court Pitts at Chard Farm, about a quarter of a mile from Chard church.

CHARLTON, SOMERSET

1880   Roman silver coins from the 1st to 3rdC AD found in a vase.

CHARLTON MARSHALL, DORSET

2003   Medieval finger-ring engraved with flowers and a merchant's mark discovered in a field by John Hinchcliffe; it was declared treasure trove.

CHEDDAR, SOMERSET

1846   99 Roman copper coins (all *antoniniani*) from the 3rdC AD found during ploughing.

[date?]   376 Roman copper coins from the 3rd and 4thC AD found during the excavation of Gough's Old Cave, on the steep slope known as Slitters, adjacent to the cave.

CHELTENHAM, GLOUCESTERSHIRE

1818   250–300 Roman coins in a jar found by labourers near New Bath Turnpike.

CHELTENHAM AREA, GLOUCESTERSHIRE

1924   5 silver pennies from the kingdoms of Mercia and Wessex from the 9thC AD found at Leckhampton Hill; thought to have been deposited *c*. AD 875.

1980–1   More than 381 Roman billon coins from the 3rdC AD, spread across the reigns of eight emperors; thought to have been deposited in AD 274.

CHELVEY, NORTH SOMERSET

1808   About 274 Roman silver coins in a stone bottle found by workmen some 4ft below the surface while digging the foundations for a new schoolroom. One of the workmen unearthed a large pot or urn containing a hard blackish substance, apparently ashes and human bones. Another labourer struck the stone bottle containing the coins of Julius Caesar. At the time it was reported that the coins were to be presented to the British Museum but nothing has been recorded there.

CHESIL BEACH, DORSET

1748?   Large quantity of 14thC gold coins found on the seashore. There have been numerous shipwrecks along this stretch of coast, resulting in gold bars and silver coins, as well as many ingots, being found.

CHICKERELL, DORSET

1999   2 gold neck-rings of 1150–800 BC found by 2 metal detectorists, R. Acton and R. Howse. These Late Bronze Age plain necklaces were valued at £110,000.

Dorset County Museum

CHILTON FOLIAT, WILTSHIRE

1966   61 silver coins from the 16th and 17thC, thought to have been concealed in 1680.

CHILTON POLDEN, SOMERSET

A Romano-British settlement was located to the east of the village, and to the north numerous Roman coin moulds and salt-making mounds have been found. At around the time of the finds, the antiquarian William Stradling built Chilton Priory and he was responsible for much of what was found in the area.

Early 1800s   About 48 Roman silver coins from the 4th and 5thC AD found in a pot by workmen in a field. They apparently broke the pot by throwing stones at it.

1838   4th and 5thC AD Roman silver and copper coins found in small leather purses, which turned to dust on being touched, in mounds at Turbary. 62 of these *siliquae* were later sold at Seaby's.

CHIPPENHAM, WILTSHIRE

1762   17thC or earlier gold and silver coins found, including some of James I.

CHRISTOW, DEVON

>1891   1stC BC and 1stC AD Roman gold and silver coins.

CHUDLEIGH, SOUTH DEVON

1986   7 James I hammered gold coins found by 2 members of the Torbay Metal Detectors' Club on farmland. Each coin was in superb condition, dated 1604–18.

CHURCHILL, DEVON

1952   8 gold coins from the 18th and possibly 19thC, thought to have been concealed in 1804.

CHUTE FOREST, WILTSHIRE

1927   5 gold staters of 75–55 BC found inside a hollow flintstone in the north-east part of the forest. This particular type of coin became known as a 'Chute' stater.

CINDERFORD AREA, GLOUCESTERSHIRE

1974   Bronze Age palstave of 1350–1200 BC found by G. Phelps while working in clay beds at Hawkwell Brickworks.

CIRENCESTER, GLOUCESTERSHIRE

The Romans called it Corinium Dobunnorum, which derived from the name of the local tribe, the Cornovii. It was the Roman's most important town after London, with a population that may have approached 10,000; in AD 150 the Greek writer Ptolemy mentions Korinion in his *Geography*, written about AD 150. After the Romans left, the town went into decline and by the time of the Domesday Book (1086) it was a small farming settlement with a population of 350. In 1117 Henry I founded Cirencester Abbey, which survived until the Reformation. In 1643, during the Civil War, the Royalists seized the town and held it for two years until the war was coming to an end. From then on the town settled into the existence of a typical English market town.

1900   31 4thC AD Roman silver coins were released after cleaning from a clump of coins fused together; thought to have been deposited *c.* AD 380.

>1929   924 Roman copper coins from the 4th and 5thC AD.
Corinium Museum

1960   480 4thC AD Roman copper coins found on St Mary's Abbey estate during excavations in the silt of a diverted river.

1975   11 silver coins from the 1stC AD found during excavations. These were Republic *denarii* from the reigns of Vitellius, Vespasian, Titus and Domitian, thought to have been deposited *c.* AD 93.
Corinium Museum

1975   22 Roman silver coins from 1stC AD found during excavations at St Michael's Field, in King Street. They were Republic *denarii* from the reigns of Vitellius, Vespasian and Domitian, thought to have been deposited *c.* AD 94.

1995   Decorated silver belt buckle from the 5thC AD: finder E. Wooton (M/D); valued at £1,250.

CLAPTON-IN-GORDANO, NORTH SOMERSET

1922–4   About 3,500 Roman copper coins from the 3rdC AD found about 1ft below the surface during ploughing. It was thought the coins had been originally buried in a wooden box; they were found with broken pottery, animal bones, 2 bronze brooches, and spindle whorles. The bulk of the hoard remained with the finder.

COCKINGTON, TORBAY

1900s   6 silver 17thC coins found on farmland. 4 Charles I half-crowns, 1 Charles I Scottish 30s piece, and 1 Charles II crown. They were found by a metal detectorist scattered over a small area, and were all very worn and clipped.

1982   2 late 16th or early 17thC gold finger-rings found in a pasture field near the Elizabethan Cockington Court by Brian A. Read (M/D) in the same field at different times. One was inset with 9 rubies or spinels.

COLATON RALEIGH COMMON, DEVON

1986   3 Late Bronze Age gold bracelets found by Nigel Hague while walking along a footpath churned up by horses' hooves. He saw something glinting, dug the items out of the ground with a penknife and took them to the Royal Albert Memorial Museum in Exeter, which sent them on to the British Museum for identification. The British Museum named it the 'Colaton Raleigh Hoard', valuing it at £5,000 (the equivalent to about £9,000 today). The find was later declared treasure trove.

COLEFORD, GLOUCESTERSHIRE

1839   Large hoard of Roman coins from the 3rdC AD found at Crab Tree Hill. The coins were all *antoniniani* except for 1 *denarius*.

1847 More than 5,000 Roman bronze coins from the 3rdC AD found in 5 pots by workmen digging the foundations of a house in the winter of this year. The coins, apart from several hundred, were disposed of by the finders.

1848–9 About 3,000 Roman copper coins from the 3rdC AD, in 3 pots found by workmen raising blocks of gritstone in an oak copse called Perry Grove, a mile from Coleford.

1850 Several thousand Roman bronze coins from the 3rdC AD found in a pot near the 1847 hoard.

COLERNE, WILTSHIRE

1941 About 200 Roman silver coins from the 4th and 5thC AD found in a jar about 1ft below the surface by John Matthews while digging a trench for footings of an RAF hut. The site was 1 mile from a fairly extensive Roman villa.

COMPTON, CITY OF PLYMOUTH

1888 300–1,000 Roman brass coins from the 3rdC AD in a pot found by a labourer near the surface, at the foot of a hedge, during preparations for building work on Vinstone estate. They were in fair condition, and were disposed of by the finder.

CONDURROW, CORNWALL

1735 Large quantity of Roman copper coins from the 4thC AD found at Helford Haven. At the time they were referred to as '24 gallons of Roman Brass Money'.

CONGRESBURY AREA, NORTH SOMERSET

1828 138 gold and silver 15thC coins, consisting of Henry V and VI gold nobles and silver groats, and an Edward IV gold royal. The coins were dated 1413–83, and were buried c. 1470, at the time of the Wars of the Roses.

COOMBE BISSETT, WILTSHIRE

2001 A highly decorated 16thC silver-gilt dress-hook: finder Richard Cranham (M/D).

Wiltshire Heritage Museum

CORFE COMMON, DORSET

1980 1 gold stater and 35 silver Gallo-Belgic silver staters and quarter-staters, and 75 Roman coins from c. 70 BC found by Peter Hobby (M/D) at a depth of approx. 2ft. The coins were in extremely fine condition and were thought to be worth over £8,000 (over £21,000 today). The hoard was later declared treasure trove.

CORSLEY HEATH, WILTSHIRE

2001 Medieval silver brooch from about 1300: finder H. Green (M/D).

Salisbury and South Wiltshire Museum

CORTON DENHAM, SOMERSET

1722–3 3rdC AD Roman copper coins in a small urn found by labourers digging in a field. At the time it was described as 'about 2 quarts of coins'.

COTSWOLDS, GLOUCESTERSHIRE

1909 168 silver coins from the 16th and 17thC, thought to have been concealed in 1645.

CREDITON, DEVON

1896 1,884 silver coins from the 16th and 17thC, thought to have been concealed in 1683.

CREWKERNE, SOMERSET

1872 About 150 Roman copper coins from the 4thC AD found by labourers digging for sand on a hillside on Combe Farm, a few hundred yards from Lady Down, on the road from Clapton to Wayford. They were in a good state of preservation.

[date?] 6 Roman billon coins from the 4thC AD covering three reigns, thought to have been deposited c. AD 335.

CRICKLADE AREA, WILTSHIRE

1864–5 About 70 Roman coins from the 1st and 2ndC AD found in the bed of the River Churn, near its junction with a cut called the New Brook, in the parish of Latton. The finds included iron implements, a fine bronze bowed fibula brooch, part of a twisted bronze armlet, and an iron spearhead. The site is close to Ermin Way.

CROYDE, NORTH DEVON

1997 32 modern sixpences of 1942–66 found together in the sand on the beach: finder Frederick Bason (M/D).

DAWLISH, DEVON

1978 3,000-year-old Bronze Age axe found at Secmanton Farm.

DEVIZES, WILTSHIRE

1828 Nearly 100 silver coins of Mary, Elizabeth I, James I and Charles I found in Angel Street; it was deemed to be a Civil War hoard.

1983 Gold ring found on the surface of a ploughed field: finder Richard Green. Devizes Museum did an initial identification before passing it to the British Museum, who dated it as late 14th or 15thC. It was declared not treasure trove and returned to the finder, who sold it to the Wiltshire Heritage Museum, Devizes for £400.

Wiltshire Heritage Museum

1983 Gold sovereigns and half-sovereigns of 1821–59 found in the roof of a house; they were declared treasure trove and said to be worth £8,000 (the equivalent of about £16,000 today).

DEVIZES AREA, WILTSHIRE

1699 Several hundred Roman copper coins from the 4thC AD found in a pot 2ft below the surface during digging on land belonging to Sir John Eyles, the Lord Mayor of London, in 1688.

DEVON

1981 Late Bronze Age spearhead in excellent condition, dated 1000–600 BC found at a depth of approx 8in by Tony Jackson (M/D) at the entrance of a small cove.

DILTON MARSH, WILTSHIRE

1973 2,500 Roman copper coins of the 4thC AD found in 2 pots in the grounds of Chalcot House.

DORCHESTER, DORSET

The Roman town of Durnovaria was established in the late 1stC AD; it was supplied with water by a famous 7-mile-long aqueduct. In literature the town is 'Casterbridge' in Thomas Hardy's novels.

1898 54 Roman silver coins, 2 silver spoons, and several fragments from the 4th and 5thC AD found in the ground on the Somerleigh Court estate.

Dorset County Museum

1936 22,121 2nd and 3rdC Roman coins found on a building site at the back of 48 South Street. The builders initially uncovered the foundations of a Roman villa and a week later one of them, E.M. McIntyre, drove his pick into a wooden keg and was amazed to see a stream of bronze coins fall from it. From then on Col. C.D. Drew, the Curator of the Dorset County Museum, took charge of the excavations and the full extent of the hoard was soon revealed. Besides the keg, which was made of yew with bronze fittings, there was a bronze bowl and a large bronze jug, the handle of which was inlaid with silver in the design of a bunch of grapes. Altogether there were just over 22,000 *antoniniani* and a dozen or so *denarii* dated AD 198–268. Some of the early coins were of fair-quality silver, but the great majority were of silver-washed bronze.

1969 More than 650 Roman copper coins from the 4th and 5thC AD found scatered in the ground among the destruction rubble during excavation at Somerleigh Court.

1986 21 1stC BC silver coins found in a field beside a road, close to Maiden Castle: finder Keith Bickmore (M/D). The hoard comprised 19 silver staters, 1 cut stater, and 1 quarter-stater. They were sent to the British Museum, which dated them at 30 BC. They were declared treasure trove and the finder was paid a reward of £1,000.

British Museum

1986–7 About 7,500 Roman copper coins from the late 3rdC AD were found of which 1,836 were retrieved, the remainder being sold overseas.

1988 42 silver and 8 bronze 1stC BC coins found in a field beside a road close to Maiden Castle by Keith Bickmore (M/D). The hoard comprised 30 silver staters, 12 quarter-staters, and 8 bronze staters from 30 BC and was worth £2,000.

2000 Roman gold finger-ring from the 1st or 2ndC AD found during an archaeological excavation by Peter Ireland (M/D). The ring had a gem setting but the gem was lost.

[date?] Gold ring depicting interlaced snakes with wire decoration, dated as *c*. 800.

Ashmolean Museum

DORCHESTER AREA, DORSET

1840 300–400 Roman copper coins from the 1st to the 4thC AD found by men cleaning out and lowering the bed of a river in a meadow to the east of the town. Besides the coins there were fragments of thin brass, pieces of brass instruments, a fibula, brass rings, rings of twisted wire, the front of a heart-shaped clasp inlaid with enamel, remnants of Samian pottery, and iron fragments.

1986 7 silver coins and 2 silver ingots found in the ground in a small village close to Dorchester. The 6 silver staters of the Durutriges tribe, 1 silver quarter-stater, and 2 silver ingots of the same period were found at depths of 3–4in in a field after stubble-burning by John House (M/D). They were declared not treasure trove.

1997 2 silver-gilt dress-hooks from the 16thC: finder J. Adams; valued at £525.

Dorset County Museum

DORSET

1986 Bronze dagger from 1500 BC found by Keith Bickmore (M/D) in an old burial mound in a field.

1986 7 silver coins of Burgred, King of Mercia (AD 852–78): finder Clive Gibbs (M/D); declared treasure trove and valued at £960.

1987–8 82 silver coins of Elizabeth I, James I, and Charles I and II found by Rex Burton (M/D) in a lane beside a field; later declared treasure trove.

1990–1 17 gold Chute-type staters dated 85–55 BC found by Julian Adams and another metal detectorist in a field on a farm. Later in the same field they found another 26. Both hoards were declared treasure trove.

2000–1 A copper-alloy zoomorphic mount from the 11thC: finder R. Reeves.

[date?] 34 gold coins from 85 BC found by Jim McGovern and his son Mike (M/D) in a downland field. They turned out to be Celtic staters and quarter-staters of the Cheriton type and were unique. The finders received a modest reward.

British Museum

DUNKERTON, BATH AND NORTH-EAST SOMERSET

1958 164 19thC silver coins found; thought to have been concealed in 1886.

EAST COULSTON, WILTSHIRE

1830 More than 345 4thC AD Roman copper coins, in a pot found in ground at Baynton.

EAST HARPTREE, BATH AND NORTH-EAST SOMERSET

1887 Almost 1,496 Roman silver coins from the 4thC AD, in a metal vessel found 6in below the surface by William Currell while digging for water, a mile south-west of the village, to the west of the Frances Plantation. With the coins were 5 cast silver ingots cut into strips, and a silver ring with an intaglio.

EAST HOLME, DORSET

1988 151 Roman copper coins from the 3rd and 4thC AD found by S.J. Dereham (M/D) in a field south-west of the village, together with some pot shards. They were thought to have been deposited *c.* AD 308.

EAST LOOE, CORNWALL

1837 Immense quantity of gold coins found in a cupboard of the elegant house, built in 1652, of Thomas Bond, the town clerk and local historian. The hoard was discovered after his death and was so large that it had to be removed in a farmer's wagon.

EAST PARLEY, DORSET

1868 80 gold coins from the 18th and 19thC, thought to have been concealed between 1760 and 1816.

EAST STOKE, DORSET

2001 Plain gold 18thC, or possibly later, finger-ring found by T.E. Allen (M/D), who returned it to the landowner.

EAST WORLINGTON, DEVON

1895 5,188 silver coins from the 16th and 17thC found on farmland, having been concealed in 1646. It seems likely that this vast hoard was hidden to avoid it being found by Fairfax's army during the Civil War. Fairfax captured Exeter in early 1646, having laid siege to the town. Afterwards his attentions were turned elsewhere and he marched towards Barnstaple, where his route took him close to the village.

EASTERTON, WILTSHIRE

>1866 4thC AD Roman copper coins were found in a pot, together with a bronze bow brooch. Many coins were dispersed, but some were later retrieved.

EASTINGTON, GLOUCESTERSHIRE

>1865 Roman coins found in an urn by a labourer digging his garden. This was a few hundred yards from the ancient camp known as Ranbury Rings.

ELTON, SOMERSET

1780 200 silver pennies of Henry II found in the churchyard by the verger of St Michael and All Angels who received a £10 reward (worth £850 today).

EMBOROUGH, SOMERSET

1930 18 silver coins from the 16th and 17thC, thought to have been concealed in 1645.

EXETER, DEVON

The Second Augustan Legion of the Roman army established a fort at Exeter *c.* AD 50. (In fact there were two separate forts in the area covered by modern-day Exeter.) They called it Isca Dumnoniorum – the Riverside Settlement of the Dumnonii, after the local Celtic tribe. Around 150 years later the Romans built the city walls. Like many Roman towns Exeter went into decline after they departed. Viking attacks took place in the 9thC, and the city was occupied by the Danes for a short while. Early in the 12thC the Normans began building the cathedral, and the twin Norman towers can still be seen.

>1630 1st and 2ndC AD Roman gold and silver coins found in a pot, near the castle. Others were found nearby, together with a ring with a stone representing Cleopatra and the asp.

1715–16 2nd and 3rdC Roman silver and brass coins found in a pot near St Martin's church. At the time it was said to be 'about half a bushel of Roman coins, most silver'.

1774 Roman coins dated 27 BC–AD 14 found in an earthen vessel in St Catherine's Lane when some houses were rebuilt; one of Augustus Caesar was in a fine state of preservation.

1820 30 silver coins from the 16th and 17thC found at Old King John Tavern; thought to have been concealed between 1625 and 1649.

1874 33 Roman billon coins from the 4thC AD, thought to have been concealed *c.* AD 340.

>1891 40 Roman silver coins from the 1stC AD found in Taphouse Road.

1937 16 gold and 24 silver coins from the 18thC found at 1 Hampton Place. These were George III guineas and William III half-crowns and shillings, thought to have been deposited after 1798.

1973 11 billon coins, thought to have been deposited *c*. AD 75, discovered in a sealed deposit during the excavation of some timber buildings in the area outside the city's south gate, placing it outside the limits of the legionary fortress. This looks like being the second fortress.

EXETER AREA, DEVON

1986 7 gold coins from the 17thC found by Val and Ken MacRae M/D) on an old track on a farm. These James I gold unites were sent to the British Museum and were later declared treasure trove. Unites replaced the sovereign in 1804 and were so called to mark the unification of England and Scotland; they were, like the sovereigns valued at one pound.

EXMOUTH AREA, DEVON

1997–8 15thC gold ring: finder James Autton (M/D). It was 3in below the surface in a field and was later declared treasure trove.

FAILAND RIDGE, NORTH SOMERSET

1997 16thC silver-gilt dress pin: finder M. Vowles (M/D); valued at £80.
North Somerset Museum

FAIRFORD, GLOUCESTERSHIRE

[date?] 6thC gilded bronze saucer brooches.
Ashmolean Museum

FARMBOROUGH, BATH AND NORTH-EAST SOMERSET

1953 3 gold and over 500 silver coins from the 16th and 17thC, thought to have been concealed in 1638.

FIFIELD BAVANT, WILTSHIRE

1999 Silver-gilt thimble from the mid-17thC: finder Chris Plummer; valued at £300.

1999 Late 13th or early 14thC inscribed silver finger-ring: finder Chris Plummer; valued at £350.
Salisbury and South Wiltshire Museum

FILTON, SOUTH GLOUCESTERSHIRE

1880 Large quantity of Roman copper coins from the 4thC AD found by a man throwing a stone at a pot in the bank of a brook near Filton. The pot broke and out poured an avalanche of coins. He gathered up the coins from the bank, leaving most of those that had fallen into the water.

FILWOOD, CITY OF BRISTOL

1869 1st to 3rdC AD Roman copper coins found by a labourer when he disturbed a pot while levelling the bank for a water-course. Sometime later a boy found about 500 coins in the bank and later still many people collected a large quantity of coins from the field.

FONTHILL GIFFORD, WILTSHIRE

1861 9 silver coins from the 15th and 16thC found when an old bank was pulled down at West End Lodge. The coins were silver pennies and groats of Edward IV, Richard II and Henry VII, thought to have been deposited *c*. 1505–10.

FONTMELL MAGNA, DORSET

1819 Large quantity of silver coins from the 16th and 17thC found in a pot 1ft deep on the edge of Lynchet in a potato field. They included coins of Edward VI, Elizabeth I, James I, and Charles I, thought to have been deposited before 1649.

2004 Piece of ornamental gold from 3000 BC found in a field by Clive Gibbs (M/D). It is only the second such find in the UK, presumed to have come from Ireland or France. Claire Pinder, senior archaeologist at Dorset County Council, said: 'One side of the strip is decorated with thin lines, the other side is quite plain. It's meant to be decorative, maybe it would have been set into something like a wooden object or wrapped around clothing. It could also have been part of an earring or twisted into someone's hair, we just don't know. It probably belonged to someone wealthy or of high status. It looks flimsy but is very heavy because of its high gold content.' It was declared treasure trove.

FOREST OF DEAN, GLOUCESTERSHIRE

1852 More than 1,168 Roman coins from the 3rdC AD found in a jar near Park End, on the Coleford Road. All of the coins were *antoniniani* except for 1 *denarius*, and were in a solid mass.

FOXCOTE, GLOUCESTERSHIRE

1863 300–400 Roman copper coins from the 3rd and 4thC AD found by workmen with a group of antiquaries opening one of the large Foxcote tumuli. The coins were found scattered, together with a female skeleton. At the time the hoard was referred to as 'about a hundredweight' and 'many thousands of the very small coins thinking them as of no value'. Many hundreds of coins were later picked up from the brook by the villagers.

FRAMPTON, DORSET

1998 511 Roman base-silver radiates from the 3rdC AD found in a pot: finders A. Brown, C. Plummer and S. Jones (M/D). Thought to have been deposited *c*. AD 280; returned to the finders.

FRITTISCOMBE, DEVON

1999 2 gold penannular rings of 1150–750 BC found by G.P. Fisher (M/D), valued at £900.
Plymouth City Museum and Art Gallery

FROME AREA, SOMERSET

1865 About 452 Roman copper coins from the 4thC AD found by a workman 1ft below the surface in the Mendip Hills.

FROXFIELD, WILTSHIRE

1725 Roman bronze cup known as 'The Rudge Cup' found in Rudge Coppice. Made of bronze and decorated with enamel, it appears to be a souvenir of Hadrian's Wall. Around its rim are the names of some of the forts on the Wall: Mais (Bowness), Aballava (Burgh-by-Sands), Vxelod[Vn]Vm (Stanwix), Camboglan[ni]S (Castlesteads) and Banna (Birdoswald).

GARE AREA, CORNWALL

1967   47 gold *denarii* and *antoniniani*, 1,029 copper coins (sestertii) and 8 Assis from AD 270 found by workmen while harrowing a field near Sett Bridge.

Royal Cornwall Museum

GLOUCESTER, GLOUCESTERSHIRE

1952   140 silver coins from 16th and 17thC, thought to have been concealed in 1653.

1960   About 15,544 Roman copper *antoniniani* from the 3rdC AD found in a large pot by workman Patrick O'Shea during city centre building work in the corner of Northgate and Eastgate. They were later declared treasure trove.

1966   181 Roman copper coins from the 4th and 5thC AD found scattered among roofing tiles and charcoal during excavations. They had probably been hidden in the roof, and fell when the building was burnt.

1971   652 Roman copper coins from 4th and 5thC AD found in a trench during work on the telephone exchange extension at 13/17 Berkeley Street.

1972   21 silver coins of 1560–1644, buried during the Civil War.

City Museum and Art Gallery, Gloucester

1980   Romano-British silver torc brachiale with very nice finials found by Philip Hartley in the garden of a house near the site of a Roman villa. It was in 4 pieces.

1983   A Norman backgammon board and counters dating from the 11thC found during an archaeological dig at Gloucester Castle. Ian Stewart was working in a trench that contained an early medieval midden when he unearthed some decorated gaming pieces. Eventually the board was discovered, along with a large number of counters carved from red deer antlers. The counters depict astronomical themes, figures eating and drinking, serpents, birds and even a stylised elephant. The board measures 60cm by 48cm and is decorated with dragons, serpents and a boar hunt. What made this find so important is the fact that previously it was thought that backgammon had not been played before the 14thC. When displayed recently in Germany the board was insured for £8 million.

GLOUCESTERSHIRE

1972   21 silver coins of Elizabeth I, James I, and Charles I, thought to have been deposited after 1642.

City Museum and Art Gallery, Gloucester

1990   A 6in long Bronze Age palstave found on farmland: finder D.C. Allen (M/D).

GOATHURST, SOMERSET

2001   A highly decorated silver buckle from the late 16th and 17thC: finder B.R. Wilson (M/D).

Somerset County Museums

GREAT BEDWYN, WILTSHIRE

2001   Late Saxon coin brooch, made from a modified silver penny coin of Edward the Confessor (1042–66): finder Andrew Day (M/D).

British Museum

GREAT CHEVERELL, WILTSHIRE

1695   3rdC AD Roman copper coins found in a field called Sand; the find was referred to as 'about a gallon of copper coins'.

GREAT WISHFORD AREA, WILTSHIRE

1906   300 Roman silver coins and 6 silver rings from the 4th and 5thC AD found in a pot by Samuel William Doughty while digging for stones in old earthworks, around the north side of Groveley Wood. The silver coins were almost all *siliquae* with a few miliarenses. There were an additional 1,000 Roman bronze coins from the 4thC AD, in a pot, in a very bad state of preservation.

GRITTLETON, WILTSHIRE

1903   About 50 silver pennies of Edward I and II, thought to have been buried *c.* 1320.

GWITHIAN, CORNWALL

2001   A highly decorated silver finger-ring from the 16th and 17thC: finder A. Bolton (M/D).

HAM HILL, SOMERSET

There was a very large hill fort here, a stronghold of the Durotriges, with double-banked enclosures dating from the Bronze Age. Among the finds dating to this time are iron currency bars and chariot parts. A large number of Roman military pieces have been found at the site, probably dating to the immediate postwar invasion period. It is probably one of the 20 places destroyed by Vespasian when he was a legionary legate in Claudius's invading army. Much of the site has been substantially altered by quarrying.

c. **1802–14**   491 Roman copper-alloy coins from the 3rdC AD found in a pot by labourers digging for limestone in the eastern extreme of the Roman camp.

1816   3rdC AD Roman silver and bronze coins found in a vase during ploughing to the south of the hill.

>1853   4th and 5thC AD Roman copper coins found in a pot.

1882   About 1,066 Roman copper-alloy sestertii from 1stC BC to the 3rdC AD, in three pots, found during digging in an orchard at Batemore Barn. 773 of these coins are held at the Somerset County Museum in Taunton.

Somerset County Museum

>1901   166 Roman copper *antoniniani* from the 3rdC AD.

HAMBROOK, SOUTH GLOUCESTERSHIRE

1998   28 Roman base-silver coins from the 3rdC AD found by D. Upton (M/D). They were thought to have been deposited *c.* AD 274 and were valued at £100.

Bristol City Museum

HANHAM ABBOTS, CITY OF BRISTOL

1951   4thC AD Roman copper coins found by workmen clearing a bank of a hedgerow for the construction of Westfield Close Road. At the time they were described as 'half a bucketful' and 'a couple of shovels full'. Fewer than 200 coins were later retrieved.

HARESFIELD, GLOUCESTERSHIRE

1832   2,000–3,000 Roman copper coins from AD 328 to 340 found in a pot in a field.

HARNHAM, WILTSHIRE

1871   Almost 4,000 Roman coins from the 3rdC AD found by a labourer, when a cow trod through the earth and broke an urn buried in a meadow, near the bank of a small rivulet at Harnham. The coins were all *antoniniani* apart from 4 *denarii*.

HARNHILL, GLOUCESTERSHIRE

2002   Roman gold ring found by David Ebbage (M/D) on land occupied and managed by the Royal Agricultural College at Harnhill, near Cirencester. The site was once a Roman building complex, and previous finds there have included roof tiles, remnants of mosaic, and evidence of under-floor heating. The ring was bent but intact. The finder said: 'I think it was lost when it was fairly new as it showed little sign of wear.' It has been named the Harnhill ring and was declared treasure trove.

HAYLE, CORNWALL

1825   3rdC AD Roman copper coins found in a copper vessel about 3½ft below the surface, by workmen building a causeway.

HEDDINGTON, WILTSHIRE

1653   4thC AD Roman silver, bronze and copper coins found in a pot while digging deeper than the plough to sow carrots in Weeke Field, by Sandy Lane in Heddington. It turned out to be the site of a Roman villa.

HENGISTBURY HEAD, BOURNEMOUTH

1911   3,000 Iron Age, and more than 100 Roman, gold, silver and bronze coins, many of them British and Gaulish from the 1stC BC to the 2ndC AD found during excavations. While the coins had probably been deposited in bundles within basketwork, they had been scattered by the activities of rabbits over the intervening years. The find included a few gold and some silver Iron-Age coins, and some *denarii*. This site was occupied from the Stone Age to the departure of the Romans from Britain in the early 5thC AD.

1977   Gold bullet stater, minted in Gaul in 75 BC.

HENSTRIDGE, SOMERSET

1936   4 gold coins of Henry VII (1500–9), thought to have been concealed in 1544 or earlier.

HIGHER MELCOMBE AREA, DORSET

Both the following finds were reported as Melcombe Horsey, but this medieval village is no longer in existence.

1999   38 Roman *siliquae* and 1 bronze coin from the 4thC AD found in a pot: finders A. Mitchell, J. Adams, J. Hutchins and F. Hutchins (M/D). They were thought to have been deposited about AD 402 and were returned to the finders. A further 45 silver coins were found in 2002 by the same people.

2003   6 Roman coins: finder Julian Adams (M/D); declared treasure trove.

HOLDENHURST, DORSET

1905   677 coins from the 1stC BC to the 1stC AD found in a pot. The hoard had 93 silver and 513 ancient British coins, and 18 silver and 53 copper-alloy Roman coins; they are now held in various museums and universities.

HOLWAY, SOMERSET

1821   430 Roman silver coins from the 4th and 5thC AD in a Samian pottery urn found during the ploughing of Ten Acres field on the estate of Downing Blake Esq. The coins, comprising 43 miliarenses, 2 argentei, 384 *siliquae*, and 2 half-*siliquae*, were mostly in perfect preservation and were found along with two skeletons.

ILCHESTER, SOMERSET

Standing at the junction of the Fosse Way and another Roman road, this town was established by the Romans in the late 2nd and early 3rdC. There are reports of Roman coins being found in 1947, but nothing of significance or note.

1840   16th and 17thC coins (weighing over 40lb) found in a canvas bag in an old cottage. A local innkeeper bought the derelict cottage and workmen were demolishing it. The large canvas bag, hidden in the recess above a window, burst under its weight and the workmen were deluged with coins. Several hundred coins were rescued, but the bulk of the hoard was lost to the workmen and townsfolk. The hoard, which was mainly silver pieces of Elizabeth I, Charles and James II, was thought to have been hidden during the Monmouth Rebellion, the original owner dying at the Battle of Sedgemoor in 1685.

1999   Folded fragment of gold of 1150–750 BC: finder G. Sinfield.

ILCHESTER AREA, SOMERSET

1977 Unique Norman silver penny from 1130 found on a mud bank
beside a layby on the A37. Bob Taylor from Bristol was on his way back
from a family holiday in Weymouth when he stopped to answer the call of
nature. He spotted the coin on a mud bank, as it was amazingly clean and
free from dirt. He took it home and showed it to local experts, who said it
was probably a forgery. He sent it to Peter Seaby who told him it was
worth £600 (the equivalent of £2,300 today). According to Seaby, 'It is the
first Henry I penny of this type to be found from the Bristol mint, and is
therefore unique.' Back then a penny would buy a chicken or 20 eggs, and
4 pennies would be the rent of a cottage for a year.

ISLAND OF ATHELNEY AREA, SOMERSET

1693 The Anglo-Saxon 'Alfred Jewel' from the 9thC AD found at Newton
Park, a few yards from the junction of the rivers Parrot and Thone, and is
arguably the greatest single find ever made in this country. It was probably
owned by King Alfred (871–99) as it bears the Anglo-Saxon inscription
'Aelfred Mec Heht Gewyrcan', which translates as 'Alfred Had Me Made'. The
battledore-shaped aestal, or reading pointer, has exquisite gold filigree work
along with gold and cloisonné enamel that form the setting of the stone. It
was found near the Island of Athelney, where Alfred took refuge from the
Danes in AD 878. (It is no longer an island, but in Alfred's time it was.) It seems
likely that the monks from the monastery at Athelney hid the 'jewel' 500 years
after Alfred's time to avoid it being lost when the monastery was plundered
during Henry VIII's time. Newton Park belonged to Sir Thomas Wroth and on
his death the Alfred Jewel passed to his maternal uncle, Colonel Nathaniel
Palmer, who bequeathed it to Oxford University in the belief that Alfred was
its founder. In 1997 the jewel was the object of a failed robbery attempt.

Ashmolean Museum

There is every indication that these reading pointers were made in
sets in Anglo-Saxon and early medieval times, as Salisbury Cathedral
had a dozen of them in the 13thC, while Canterbury Cathedral had a
similar number.

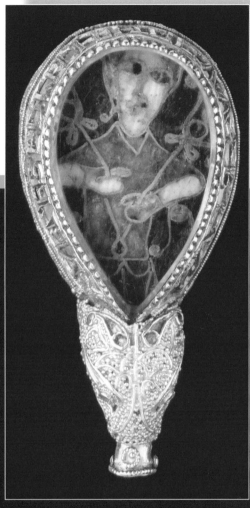

KEMPSFORD, GLOUCESTERSHIRE

1978 31 Roman silver coins from the 1stC AD found in the bank of the River Thames on various occasions by metal detectorists. It seems unlikely that they all comprise the same hoard.

KILTON, SOMERSET

c. **1700** A great quantity of 2nd and 3rdC Roman coins found near the village.

KILVE, SOMERSET

c. **1700** 3rdC Roman copper coins found in the hamlet of Putsham.

KINGSCOTE, GLOUCESTERSHIRE

1980 38 Roman billon coins from the 3rdC, thought to have been deposited in AD 285. The villa was originally discovered in 1691 and coins were found then and subsequently.

KINGSKERSWELL, DEVON

1982 10 coins from the 16th and 17thC found beside a footpath. The coins, 8 Elizabethan and 2 of Charles I, were valued at £100 and were thought to have been lost in about 1650.

KINGSKERSWELL AREA, DEVON

1838–9 2,000 Roman copper coins from the 3rdC AD found on the high land to the south-west of Kerswell Down church.

KINGSTON DEVERILL, WILTSHIRE

1998 A highly decorated Anglo-Saxon silver-gilt pinhead from the 9thC AD: finder D. Smith (M/D).

KINGSTON SEYMOUR, NORTH SOMERSET

1884 About 800 Roman bronze coins from the 3rdC AD found by Mr Smyth-Pigott during excavation of the Roman villa at Wemberham, Yatton, about 2 miles from the house at Kingston Seymour.

LACOCK, WILTSHIRE

1990 93 Roman *antoniniani* in a poor state of preservation from the 3rdC AD found by Chris Bultitude (M/D) on land at Halfway House Farm, Lacock. The site is very close to the Roman road leading from Cunetio to Bath.

LAKE, WILTSHIRE

c. **1770** 18 silver Elizabeth I shillings from the 16thC found under the roots of a large tree, probably concealed after 1558.

LANGTON MATRAVERS, DORSET

c. **1842** 4th and 5thC AD Roman copper coins found in a pot during the digging of foundations for the new dining room at Leeson House.

LATTON, WILTSHIRE

1860 or **1882** 50–60 12thC English silver pennies of Stephen found in Latton churchyard.

LAVERSTOCK, WILTSHIRE

[date?] A 9thC gold ring decorated with niello, belonging to Aethelwulf, King of Wessex.

British Museum

LAWRENCE WESTON, CITY OF BRISTOL

1982 6 gold and 228 silver coins from the 14thC found under a large boulder during the digging of a trench near a substation by David Platt and Bob Peacock, on land belonging to the city of Bristol. The gold coins were 5 half-nobles and a quarter-noble of Edward III; the silver coins were 36 groats, 16 half-groats, 138 pennies, 29 halfpennies, and a Scottish half-groat, penny and halfpenny. The entire hoard was valued in the region of £6,000 (worth double that today), and later declared treasure trove.

1986 598 silver Roman coins from the 1stC BC to 2ndC AD found in the front garden of a house under a sandstone slab and later declared treasure trove.

British Museum

LERRYN, CORNWALL

1980s Hoard of 103 Roman coins from the 3rdC found in the mud and gravel, between the bridge and car park: finder S.M. Pelling (Crawley).

Royal Cornwall Museum

2001 1,092 Roman coins, in a pot, from AD 249 to 274 found by Jonathan Clemes and Trevor Bird (M/D) on National Trust land at Ethy Creek near Lerryn. All but 68 of the bronze coins were found inside an earthenware storage jar. The men first of all came across 1 coin 2in below the surface on a track by the river. Next they found 3 more coins a few feet away before discovering the pot containing the bulk of the coins. Next morning they took them to the Royal Cornwall Museum at Truro. They were thought to be worth several thousand pounds and were later declared treasure trove. Half the money went to the finders and the rest to the museum.

LIDDINGTON, SWINDON

1999 Gold ingot of 1150–750 BC: finder J. Noble; valued at £1,500.

LILLESDON, SOMERSET

1748 About 150 Roman silver coins, in mint condition, from the 4th and 5thC AD found in an urn during ploughing where a hedge had once stood.

Somerset County Museum

LISKEARD, CORNWALL

Possibly 1907 More than 87 gold coins from the 17th and 18thC, thought to have been concealed in 1725.

LITTLE LONDON AREA, SOMERSET

>1863   1st and 2ndC AD Roman coins found in a pot on the Fosse Way, which runs to the north of the Iron Age hill fort Maesbury Castle.

LITTLE SOMERFORD, WILTSHIRE

1888   About 30 or 40 Roman coins from the 1stC AD found by workmen digging a well. The find was not reported and the coins were distributed locally.

LODERS, DORSET

1840   500 silver coins of Henry VIII, thought to have been concealed in 1544 or earlier.

LONG ASHTON, NORTH SOMERSET

1815   About 300 Roman copper coins from the 4thC AD found in broken urns by workmen during the demolition of a tumulus, within 50yd of a small round enclosure called 'Old Fort' on the hill above Ashton Water. Many of the coins were dispersed by the finders.

1817   About 1,000 Roman *denarii* from the 1stC BC to the 3rdC AD found 6in below the surface by workmen while digging on Leigh Down in Ashton Parish. They were dispersed by the finders.

LONGBRIDGE DEVERILL, WILTSHIRE

1999   Early Bronze Age gold disc of 2200–1600 BC: finder Brian Read (M/D). The disc of thin gold sheet was crumpled and valued at £50.

Wiltshire Heritage Museum

LOSTWITHIEL, CORNWALL

1983   103 Roman silver *antoniniani* from the 3rdC AD found on a riverbank.

Royal Cornwall Museum

LOWER LANGFORD, NORTH SOMERSET

1998   Middle Bronze Age gold penannular ring of 1300–1100 BC: finder Ted Chaffey (M/D). It was discovered to be two rings fused together.

LOWER SLAUGHTER, GLOUCESTERSHIRE

1958   134 Roman copper coins from the 3rdC AD found in the remains of a wooden box under rough stone paving during grave-digging on the site of an earlier find. The coins were all *antoniniani* except for 1 sestertius.

LOXBEARE, DEVON

1980   17 silver pennies of King John, Henry II and Richard I found 18in deep in the garden of Highgate Cottage by the owner, R.M. Vickery, and his 2 sons while building a wall. They were thought to have been concealed *c.* 1216 and were valued at around £700.

Royal Albert Memorial Museum

LUDGVAN, CORNWALL

1793   1,000–1,500 Roman copper-alloy coins from the 3rdC AD found in an urn 2 or 3ft below the surface by labourers digging a trench about 100yd from the sea, about half a mile north-west of St Michael's Mount.

LYDBROOK, GLOUCESTERSHIRE

1848   Large quantity of Roman coins from the 3rdC AD found by workmen searching for sandstone. Hundreds were sold off at 10d to 2s a dozen.

LYDEARD ST LAWRENCE, SOMERSET

1666   3rdC AD Roman coins, 'weighing 80lb', found in a large pitcher that was dug up by labourers in a ploughed field.

LYDNEY, GLOUCESTERSHIRE

1805   700 Roman coins found by the Hon. C. Bathurst when the Roman site, including villas and a temple, was first investigated.

1929   1,646 Roman copper coins from the 4thC AD found in the floor while excavations of the Roman temple were taking place. Together with the coins were coin fragments and pieces of corroded bronze.

1939   1,296 Roman copper coins from the 4thC AD.

LYDNEY AREA, GLOUCESTERSHIRE

1854   More than 155 Roman *denarii* from the 1st and 2ndC AD found in two vases by men opening coal-workings (or an ancient iron mine). Many were disposed of at the time.

LYME REGIS, DORSET

1786   Large quantities of 16th and 17thC gold and silver coins, thought to have been concealed 1660–85. Coins dating back to before medieval times have been found on the local beaches after storms.

MALPAS, CORNWALL

1749   About 3,000 Roman copper coins from the 3rdC AD found by a boy digging in a field near the highway. They were said to weigh 20lb and it was thought that the hoard had originally been buried in an oak box.

MANATON, DEVON

1897 2 Elizabeth I, 3 James I, and 6 Charles I silver coins, presumed to have been buried during the Civil War.

MANSTON, DORSET

2001 7 Roman *denarii* from the 1st and 2ndC AD found by G.W. Wyatt and D.P. Waxman (M/D). They were thought to have been deposited about AD 152 and were deemed not to be treasure trove.

MANTON AREA, WILTSHIRE

1883 About 40 Roman silver and copper coins from the 4th and 5thC AD found while digging on Manton Downs. 26 *siliquae* were preserved.

1883 A quantity of Roman pewter items found by workmen levelling the ground near the house at Alec Taylor's racing stables. The find included 12 dishes, the largest of which was 2ft in diameter; others had designs and ornamental borders. There were two skeletons nearby.

MARLBOROUGH, WILTSHIRE

1818 or **1819** About 300 Roman copper coins from the 4thC AD found in a vessel while ploughing a field in the vicinity of Marlborough Forest. Most of the coins, in a good state of preservation, were dispersed by the finders, although 21 were retrieved.

1901 More than 2 gold and 300–400 silver coins, and spoons from the 16th and 17thC, found with the skeleton of a horseman 'in spurs with whip in hand' (were these 'spurs' the spoons?) They were thought to have been deposited after 1625.

1911 12th and 13thC silver coins found during drainage work at Crabbes Close. The find, thought to be silver pennies of Henry II and III (1154–1272), was not declared to the authorities.

MARLBOROUGH AREA, WILTSHIRE

1999 3rdC AD Roman gold ring found by M. Thomas (M/D). The ring contains a nicolo engraved with a figure of Fortuna, is complete and in very good condition; it was returned to the finder.

MAWGAN IN MENEAGE, CORNWALL

1817 or **1822** About 1,600 Roman silver and copper coins from the 1st and 3rdC AD, found in an urn during ploughing, about a mile from Telowarren. The ploughman turned up a flat stone and disclosed a cavity containing the urn and the coins, which were in a generally good state of preservation. The finder sold them at a penny a piece. Some sources give the find spot as Trevassack, in the parish of Mawgan.

MEARE HEATH, SOMERSET

1972 385 silver coins, 869 imitations and 150 blanks for 3rdC AD Roman coins found by Roy Harvey while digging for peat. The coins were all *antoniniani* of very debased silver, and cover the period AD 253–74.

MEMBURY, DEVON: ROMAN CAMP

1814 Large quantity of Roman copper coins from the 3rdC AD found in a pot in a heap of stones at Hill Common. Many were dispersed by locals.

1823 20–30 Roman copper and brass coins from the 1st and 2ndC AD found in an urn by a labourer while taking away an irregular heap of stones.

>1833 A very large quantity of Roman coins, found in a lane leading from the village of Wambrook to Bewley Down, about 2 miles from the Roman camp.

1988 256 Roman *denarii* from *c.* 149 BC to the reign of Tiberius (AD 14–37) found in a field by Douglas Wilson (M/D). They were approximately half a mile north-west of the Iron Age hill-fort at Membury and approximately 2 miles south of the Roman road, scattered over an area of about 20 by 10yd to a depth of 13in. 8 fragments of local Savemake ware were found in the central area but it is unclear whether they are associated with the hoard. The coins were valued at more than £3,000 and declared treasure trove.

MERE, WILTSHIRE

1856 About 270 Roman *denarii* from the 1st and 2ndC AD found in a pot by workmen draining land for a new cemetery to the south of Mere.

MIDDLE CHINNOCK AREA, SOMERSET

1805 About 4,000 Roman copper coins from the 3rdC AD found in 2 small pots together with human bones. They were discovered by a poor woman getting limestones in a newly ploughed field called Barrow field, adjoining the turnpike road from Yeovil to Crewkerne. In the 2 days following the discovery she sold or gave away all of the coins.

MILBORNE PORT, SOMERSET

[date?] A bronze palstave.

MILDENHALL, WILTSHIRE

>1888 23 16thC silver coins found on the site of a Roman town. These were coins of Elizabeth I from three-farthings to a shilling and were thought to have been deposited after 1578.

1978 About 54,951 3rdC Roman silver-washed and silver coins from AD 193 and AD 274 found in a large earthenware urn in Black field: finders Peter Humphreys and John Booth. Peter Humphreys said: 'It was an amazing thing to find so many coins. We put some in a box and it took 4 people to lift it.' The coins, deposited after AD 274, were mostly *antoniniani*, but included 620 *denarii*, and today would be worth well over a £1 million. The hoard has been named the Cuntio Treasure and it is the largest number of Roman coins so far found in one location in Britain. The Mildenhall site was the Roman crossroads town of Cunetio, which later became an important military base, said to be one of the most formidable fortresses in Britain with large fortified walls being introduced in AD 367. The coins were taken to the British Museum where they were cleaned and assessed, before being declared treasure trove. The finders received a reward.

MILVERTON, SOMERSET

>1847 45 Roman *siliquae* from the 4thC AD found in an urn.

MINCHINHAMPTON, GLOUCESTERSHIRE

1904 1st to the 3rdC AD Roman silver coins found at Amberley, near Minchinhampton.

MONKTON FARLEIGH, WILTSHIRE

1980 3,466 Roman copper coins from the 3rdC AD found in a pot by a man digging in his garden. The coins were all copper except for 1 *denarius*, and date from AD 253 to 285/6.

MORCHARD BISHOP, DEVON

c. 1813 1stC AD Roman silver coins found by labourers repairing a hedge in Bishop's Morchard (it's known both ways round!).

MUCKLEFORD, DORSET

1935 115 gold coins from the 16th and 17thC, thought to have been concealed in 1636.

NAILSEA, NORTH SOMERSET

>1789 Large quantity of Roman copper coins from the 3rd and 4thC AD found in 3 urns not far from Cadbury Camp, at a place called Nailsea wall, which divides Ken moor and Nailsea moor.

NETHERHAMPTON AREA, WILTSHIRE

>1988 Large hoard of Iron Age artefacts of 240–200 BC found in a field. Known as the 'Salisbury Hoard', it had been plundered by detectorists some time before 1988. In 1993 a team from the British Museum excavated the site, when additional artefacts were discovered.

NETTLETON, WILTSHIRE

1938 61 Roman coins and 26 fragments from the 3rdC AD found during excavations by W.C. Priestley.

NEWENT, GLOUCESTERSHIRE

1969 44 18thC gold coins, thought to have been concealed in 1798. Bronze Age weapons and Roman coins have also been found.

NEWTON ABBOT, DEVON

1880 72 17thC silver coins found at Barton Old Hall. The oldest was of 1644–5 and it is presumed they were buried during the Civil War.

NEWTON ST LOE AREA, BATH AND NORTH-EAST SOMERSET

1983 255 Roman 4thC AD *siliquae* found by a detectorist in a hedgerow in Newton Park.

NORTH CERNEY, GLOUCESTERSHIRE

1998 Silver finger-ring, probably Roman, with 8 decorated facets. It was returned to the finder.

NORTH CURRY, SOMERSET

[date?] Saxon coin found in the churchyard some years ago.

Somerset County Museum

NORTH PETHERTON, SOMERSET

1897 A large quantity of 19th and 20thC gold coins, thought to have been concealed between 1837 and 1901.

NUNNEY, SOMERSET

1860 More than 10 gold Celtic coins, 236 Roman silver coins, 4 Roman copper coins, and a Roman bronze fibula brooch found in a small urn, in Eleven Acres field, West Down Farm. 'It was on the 15th of October last that two men, ploughing in a field known as the Eleven Acres, and forming a portion of West Down Farm in the parish of Nunney, broke open a small urn, and thus brought to light the hoard of coins I am now about to describe . . . The urn was so shattered by the first finders, and the fragments so dispersed, that only a few small pieces could be recovered, and nothing can now be learned as to its form, except that it was circular, with the sides sloping outwards, and having an exterior diameter of about four and half inches at its base. A small bow-shaped fibula in bronze was found upon the spot, but it is uncertain whether it formed part of the contents of the urn or no.' Sometime

afterwards Sir John Evans succeeded in examining about 250 of the coins and found that the 10 gold coins and 232 silver coins were of the Dobunni, 4 Roman *denarii* coins.

NYNEHEAD, SOMERSET

1922? 35 16thC silver coins, thought to have been concealed in 1549.

OKEHAMPTON, DEVON

1897 About 200 Roman copper coins from the 4thC AD found by a workman under a rock on Park Hill, above the railway station, within a stone's throw of the old Roman road. The coins were dated AD 320–30.

OKEHAMPTON AREA, DEVON

Early 1800s This middle to later Iron Age fort (500 BC–AD 50) is one of at least 12 hill-forts that survive on Dartmoor. In the 19thC it was reported that a hoard of 200 Roman coins was found in the area of East Hill fort. A small-scale examination in 1840 revealed nothing more.

OLD SARUM AREA, WILTSHIRE

1865 Large quantity of Roman coins found in 3 pots between Old Sarum and Winterbourne Earls.

OLDCROFT, GLOUCESTERSHIRE

1971–2 2 Roman silver and 3,333 billon coins, a pin, a small loop, 4 small silver bars, and fragments of a linen purse from the 4thC found on land belonging to the Bathurst family, immediately west of Dean Road. The hoard was discovered by P. Croal, near his home, and over half the coins were found to be 4thC forgeries. The hoard was thought to have been concealed *c.* AD 345–9. The silver objects are held at the British Museum.

British Museum

OTTERY ST MARY, DEVON

1998 11 silver pennies of Edward I, II and III found by W. Weller and T. Cobley (M/D), thought to have been deposited *c.* 1344–51; returned to the finders.

OVER, GLOUCESTERSHIRE

1999 14 Roman base-*siliquae* from the 3rd and 4thC AD: finder S. Mason (M/D); returned to the finder.

OVER COMPTON, DORSET

1997 A 16thC silver-gilt dress pin and mount found by R. Lovett and valued at £850.

Dorset County Museum

PAIGNTON, TORBAY

1978 A three-strand gold Viking bracelet from the 10th or 11thC was found on Goodrington beach by Kay Creasey, from Lincoln, who was on honeymoon. She and her husband Stephen were walking along the seashore looking for shells, when she spotted what she thought was a piece of twisted wire, which she ignored twice before eventually picking it up. She said: 'I saw it was a bracelet but thought it was something a

[date?] 36 Roman coins from the 1stC AD, including coins of Claudius and Nero, found in the roots of an old oak tree.

PAINSWICK, GLOUCESTERSHIRE

1914 34 gold and 8 silver coins from the 16th and 17thC found in a field at Blakeways Farm. Farmer Cuthbert Webb was walking across one of his fields when he found a gold coin in the deep impression of a cow's hoof in the soft earth. He searched for others, and eventually found a dozen, mostly gold, but also a few silver ones. He reported his finds to the curator of the Gloucester City Museum. On a further search 30 more coins were found. Some of the gold coins had been clipped. With no trace of any container, it was concluded that they had probably been in a bag that had rotted away. They were thought to have been concealed in 1641.

City Museum and Art Gallery, Gloucester

PAMPHILL, DORSET

1736 20 small Roman silver coins from the 2nd and 3rdC AD found in an urn by a workman digging in a field. The coins and fragments of the urn were claimed by John Bankes, lord of the manor of Kingston Lacy, as treasure trove.

PAUL, CORNWALL

Site of the oldest coin hoard ever found in Britain. It dated from 150 BC and contained only coins from northern Italy. The coins, which were imitation Massilia *drachms*, probably belonged to a merchant trader who came here to process tin.

PAULTON, BATH AND NORTH-EAST SOMERSET

1956 77 Roman silver coins from the 4th and 5thC AD.

kiddy had made at school and painted. A few days later I went home and showed it to my father who is interested in history.' He advised her to take it to the police. Following analysis by the British Museum it was found to be 99 per cent gold. It was auctioned at Sotheby's, and acquired by the British Museum for £6,150. Kay Creasey's mother, Dorothy Harrison, had previously discovered a large hoard of Roman coins in 1977 in Lincolnshire.

PAWLETT, SOMERSET

[date?]   A bronze palstave found on Pawlett Hill; there are also reports of Roman finds from the area.

PILTON AREA, SOMERSET

1691   4thC AD Roman coins found in a pot at Elm Farm.

PITNEY, SOMERSET

1853   Anglo-Scandinavian bronze and gilded openwork disc brooch of AD 1050–1100, depicting the body of an interlaced animal with its neck being bitten by a snake, found in the churchyard. The animal struggling with snakes was a symbol of Christianity's fight against heathenism.

British Museum

CITY OF PLYMOUTH

1776   240 gold coins of James I found by 'a poor man with a wife and several children' who needed firewood, and who cut up an old chest which was in the house. He found it had a false bottom and underneath were the coins.

POLDEN HILLS, NEAR BRIDGWATER, SOMERSET

1991   5 silver groats of Elizabeth I and Mary found on a farm: finder Rose Attridge (M/D). They were found in a straight line over a distance of about 30ft, so they may have fallen from a torn purse; they were declared not treasure trove.

POOLE

1833   Several hundred Roman *antoniniani* in the finest state of preservation from the 3rdC AD found in an urn by labourers digging a meadow about half a mile from the town. 366 coins were recovered.

1930   984 Roman copper *antoniniani* found in a pot during work to lay a water main in the Sterte area in the east of Poole.

1936   34 Roman *antoniniani* from the 3rdC AD found in a pot in an allotment at the east end of Week's Quay, near Poole Harbour. It was later suggested that these coins were possibly part of the Dorchester hoard found in the same year.

1986   1,663 Roman nummi, together with about 90 coin fragments, from the 4thC AD found in 2 pots 9in apart in a field near Upton: finders George Fletcher and Ken Emery (M/D).

PORTESHAM, DORSET

1994   Iron Age mirror and grave goods found just below the surface by Mr Smith (M/D). The highly decorated mirror is cast bronze; other items in the hoard were an iron razor, an ear scope, 2 broken tweezers, a dragonesque fibula brooch, and part of a ceramic bowl. The mirror was later purchased by Dorset County Museum for £75,000.

Dorset County Museum

1998   A 16th or early 17thC gold finger-ring, with a missing stone: finder John Rule; returned to the finder.

2001   A decorated silver-gilt brooch from the first half of the 14thC: finder C. Walmsley (M/D).

Dorset County Museum

PORTISHEAD, NORTH SOMERSET

[date?]   Roman coins from the 2ndC onwards found in the grounds of Gordano School.

POTTERNE, WILTSHIRE

1874   A large quantity of English and foreign 18thC gold coins, concealed in a box beneath the floorboards of Church House; thought to have been deposited sometime after 1716.

1982   Late Bronze Age gold pennanular bracelet found by grave-digger William Sims on land belonging to Potterne Parish Council. The British Museum identified it and valued it at £500–£5,000; later declared not treasure trove.

POTTINGTON, DEVON

1998   A 16thC gold seal ring inscribed with a family crest: finder P. Allaway (M/D).

POUGHILL, DEVON

1836   40 Roman silver coins from the 1st and 2ndC AD found in a field at the Barton; 28 are in the Ashmolean Museum.

Ashmolean Museum

PRESTON, DORSET

1812   300 silver coins from the 3rdC AD found in an urn in a field on Jordan Hill. Nearby are the remains of a Roman temple.

1816   Several hundred Roman copper coins from the 4th and 5thC AD found in an urn during ploughing half a mile from Rimbury. Many coins were disposed of by the finder.

1979   Giant double-handed 14thC sword found among rocks at Preston beach by Graham Farmer, aged 11, from Paignton. The sword was over 5ft long, and so heavy that Graham had to drag it up the beach before the sea came in. It was similar to swords carried by the crusaders, and probably once belonged to a medieval knight.

PROBUS, CORNWALL

1966–7   47 Roman silver and 1,009 bronze coins from the 1st and 3rdC AD found in a field at Gare Farm by farm labourer William Chapman. The silver coins were later declared treasure trove.

PULHAM, DORSET

1983   100 gold coins of 1354–1460 found in a pot in a field on Grange Farm by the farmer Simon Drake. Climbing down from his tractor to inspect his ploughing, he noticed a small yellow disc. On examination it turned out to be a gold coin. Over the next few weeks Simon and his wife, using a borrowed metal detector, covered the area and found 99 more over an area of 20 sq. yd. This hoard comprised 96 nobles, 2 half-nobles, and 2 quarter-nobles, from the reigns of Edward III, Henry IV, Henry V and Henry VI, minted between 1354 and 1460. 1 is a Henry IV 'heavy coinage' noble, minted before the devaluation of 1412. This extremely rare coin was worth approx. £6,000. The hoard was deemed to be treasure trove but returned to the finder as the British Museum did not wish to acquire them. They were sold at Christie's for £63,000 (the equivalent of around £118,000 today). The farm had belonged to Bindon Abbey and a medieval road had run close to the find site.

PUNCKNOWLE, DORSET

1791 About 1,200 Roman coins found in a vessel while ploughing a field known as Walls.

c. **1850** 3rdC AD Roman copper coins found in a jar while ploughing a field near the Knoll, which lies to the south of the village. Many coins were scattered and were taken by people in the neighbourhood; 107 *antoniniani* were retrieved.

PYLLE, SOMERSET

1836 3rdC AD Roman copper coins, referred to as 'a peck of coins', found in a large vessel during ploughing at Cockmill, near Pylle.

RADFORD, BATH AND NORTH-EAST SOMERSET

1827 A hoard of 26 vessels that are partly silver-gilt, from 1581 to 1601, found in a potato barn and subsequently named 'The Armada Service'. Originally made for Sir Christopher Harris (1553–1625), of Radford, Devon, according to British Museum records, the dishes were so named not for any direct involvement in the Armada but because there was a tradition of making high-quality items with silver captured from the Spanish Armada. It was thought to have been concealed *c.* 1645–8 to avoid loss during the Civil War.

British Museum

RAMSBURY, WILTSHIRE

c. **1730** 1stC AD Roman coins found in a pot beneath a tessellated pavement; they were said to be of the Emperor Vespasian.

[date?] 17 gold and 44 17thC silver coins found in pot by workmen digging drains. They exposed the earthenware pot which contained a Charles I gold crown, 16 Charles II crowns, and 44 half-crowns.

RAPPAREE COVE, NEAR ILFRACOMBE, DEVON

1978 10 gold coins were found with metal detectors. The area has several wrecks, and there have been numerous reports of gold coins being found over the last two centuries. In 1796 the treasure ship *London* sank off the cliff. In 1997, bones of Africans captured in the Caribbean were dug up along with some iron fetters. They were probably being taken to Bristol to be sold as slaves, just a decade before the British Parliament abolished the slave trade. The ship contained 5 treasure chests of which only 4 were ever found.

REDRUTH, CORNWALL

1745 Roman copper coins, referred to as 'about a quart', found at the foot of Carn Brae.

1749 A sack-full of gold coins found on Carn Brae, a hill of huge granite blocks and deep caves, which overshadows the town of Redruth. Nearby is prehistoric Carn Brea Castle.

1749 4thC AD Roman copper coins, referred to as 'one pint of copper Roman coins', found in a pot, 3ft below the surface: finder Mr Bevan. They were found with the brass head of an animal, possibly a ram.

1889 88 copper tokens/jettons from the 16th and 17thC, thought to have been concealed in 1666.

RILLATON, CORNWALL

1818   Gold cup and bronze dagger of *c.* 1900–1600 BC found during the excavation of a barrow at Rillaton Manor. Archaeologists unearthed the 3¼in-high 'Rillaton Cup' and dagger with a skeleton. The cap is very similar to the one found recently at Ringlemere and was probably made in Britain. For hundreds of years the local moor was said to be haunted by the ghost of a Druid priest, who would emerge from a nearby barrow and offer passers-by a golden cup which contained a magic potion. When the traveller drank from the cup it was impossible to drain the cup dry. During one of these supposed encounters the traveller was said to have thrown the remaining liquid in the spectre's face, and soon afterwards he and his horse both died in an accident. It is not known whether sightings of the Druid stopped after the Rillaton Cup was excavated.

ROUGHMOOR, SOMERSET

2000–1   Roman cornelian intaglio ring in a 16ct gold setting found by P. Saxon in a lover's glade in woods at Roughmoor. This Renaissance gold finger-ring, engraved with 4 oxen and fashioned in the Augustine period (1stC BC to early 1stC AD), has become known as the 'Roughmoor Ring'. It was later declared treasure trove.

Somerset County Museum

ROUNDWAY, WILTSHIRE

1714   A large quantity of Roman silver coins and bronze statues in a large urn found buried under the ruins of a Roman building, between flat stones and covered with Roman brick. The find included several brass statues of heathen deities.

1999   16th or 17thC gold posy ring, inscribed with lettering: finder Lloyd Alexander Earley (M/D); returned to the finder. The ring was engraved with an imperial bust and carries the Greek word NIKE, meaning Victory. It is possible that this may be linked to the campaign by the commander known as the 'Valentinian General' (the Emperor Valentinian I, AD 363–75).

1999   A silver brooch from the late 13th or early 14thC: finder M.P. O'Donovan (M/D).

Wiltshire Heritage Museum

ROUNDWAY DOWNS, WILTSHIRE

[date?] Late 7thC gold jewellery, including a triangular pendant, found during the excavation of a barrow grave.

Wiltshire Heritage Museum

ST JUST, CORNWALL

c. **1737** Almost 100 bronze Roman coins from the 1st and 2ndC AD found by workmen removing a bank in a field.

ST JUST IN ROSELAND, CORNWALL

1942–5 Large quantity of Roman copper coins from the 4thC AD found by American soldiers digging gun emplacements at Turnaware Point, on the River Fal. The coins, which were in excellent condition, were dispersed by the finders.

ST MICHAEL CAERHAYS, CORNWALL

1869 About 2,500 Roman copper *antoniniani* from the 3rdC AD found in a tin vessel, 3ft below the surface by two labourers digging a drain on moorland below a spot known as Beech Tree Wood.

SALISBURY, WILTSHIRE

1777–8 200 silver coins of James I and Charles I found in a catskin bag, under the floorboards of a house; thought to have been deposited after 1650.

1869 About 250 Roman copper coins from the 3rdC AD found in the wall of the cellar of the Old George Inn during restoration work. Apparently Samuel Pepys stayed at the inn some time during 1668, but for just one night. He left because of the outrageous expense. 'Came about ten at night to a little Inn, where we were fain to go into a room where a peddler was in bed and made him rise, and here wife and I lay. Good beds and the master of the house sober, understanding man, and I had good discourse with him about the county's matters as wool and corn and other things.'

SALISBURY PLAIN, WILTSHIRE

c. **1865** More than 1,850 Roman copper coins from the 4thC AD found in 2 jars 2ft below the surface by labourers.

SALISBURY AREA, WILTSHIRE

1986 55 rare Greek coins.

2000 3 gold and 1,193 silver Roman coins from the 4th and 5thC AD found in the remains of a pot on farmland by Dave Philpotts and his son John (M/D). Dave had swapped his fishing rod for a metal detector before finding the hoard, which comprised 3 gold solidi, 3 miliarenses and 1,190 *siliquae*; estimated to be worth £50,000.

SALTFORD, BATH AND NORTH-EAST SOMERSET

1983 255 Roman silver coins of AD 100–200 found under a hedgerow between Saltford and Newton St Loe by James Sewell (M/D); the coins were in mint condition.

SANCREED, CORNWALL

1829 About 200 Roman copper coins from the 3rdC AD found by a man digging and clearing round a large stone, in a field in the parish of Sancreed, near Land's End.

SAPPERTON, GLOUCESTERSHIRE

1759 About 3,000 2nd and 3rdC AD Roman copper coins, including 37 of silver, found in 3 pots by a man driving over Sheepscomb field, near Cirencester, when one of his back wheels sank deeply into the ground, breaking a large stone urn. The urn contained a large quantity of copper coins and as he was digging out his wheel he found the other 2 urns.

1844 70 Roman coins from the 3rdC AD found with a skeleton by labourers digging for the railroad at the north of the Sapperton Tunnel.

SAVERNAKE FOREST, WILTSHIRE

1857 Iron Age and Roman gold and silver coins found in a pot not far from Cunetium, at the top of the Salisbury Hill. Some men digging clay for a brickfield came upon the pot, which contained a considerable number of coins, almost all British. It is said 1 Roman coin of Tiberius was among them, which has been taken as a clue to their date. The coins were dispersed but they included some small silver coins of Epaticcus.

>1881   Roman silver coins found in brick kilns in the forest. 'Many were silver coins of Julius Caesar found at the forest brick kilns', according to Canon J.E. Jackson in the *Wiltshire Archaeological Magazine* of 1881. It is just possible that these coins came from the 1857 Savernake hoard.

c. **1890**   About 531 Roman copper coins from the 4thC AD found in a pot on Grantham Hill.

SEEND, WILTSHIRE

1969   5 gold and 33 silver coins, probably 17th or 18thC, thought to have been concealed in 1719.

SEMLEY AREA, WILTSHIRE

1985   86 Celtic silver coins found in a pot in woodland by Michael A'Court (M/D), together with a broken earthenware pot. They were sent to the British Museum for an expert appraisal.

SENNEN, NEAR LAND'S END, CORNWALL

1807   300 small copper Roman coins from the 3rdC AD found between 2 flat stones under a large projecting rock, in a field.

SEVINGTON, WILTSHIRE

1834   About 70 silver coins and other silver items from the 9thC found. This hoard was made up of Anglo-Saxon silver pennies, a silver spoon and fork, a silver circular brooch, and fragments of silver, thought to have been buried *c.* AD 840–50.

SHAFTESBURY, DORSET

1940   More than 20 11thC silver pennies, thought to have been buried in 1003, when the Vikings were harrying West Wessex. King Cnut died here in 1035.

SHAPWICK, SOMERSET

1936   (First hoard) About 120 Roman *siliquae* and pewter articles from the 4th and 5thC AD 2ft below the surface by James Crane while cutting peat on Shapwick Moor. The pewter items included a plate, a saucer and cup with one handle.

1937   (Second hoard) 125 Roman *siliquae* from the 4thC AD found in a beaker and pewter jug by Percy Spiller Mullins while cutting peat on Shapwick Moor.

1938   (Third hoard) Over 1,100 Roman copper coins from the 4thC AD found in a pewter vessel by Percy Spiller Mullins in the peat-beds of Shapwick Moor.

1999   9,238 Roman coins, mostly *denarii*, from the 1stC BC to the 3rdC AD: finders Kevin Elliott and his cousin Martin Elliott (M/D). They had to use milking buckets to carry the hoard. There were 3 smaller hoards from the 1stC BC to the 4thC AD found during subsequent archaeological examination in November 1998 and May 1999. The coins were thought to have been deposited in a leather or textile sack, and range from Mark Antony (31–30 BC) to Severus Alexander (AD 222–35), with the latest coin dating to AD 224. Among the haul are 2 exceptionally rare coins of Didius Severus Julianus (AD 193) who was murdered a month after he became emperor. The 9,238 coins made up the largest hoard of *denarii* ever to have been found in Britain: they were valued at £265,000 and declared treasure trove. Not only was there the wonderful find of coins through the work of the detectorists, but the site proved to be a grand villa complex, in an area where there was not thought to be anything but small farmsteads.

Somerset County Museum

SHEPTON MALLET, SOMERSET

1826 23 silver coins from the 16th and 17thC, thought to have been concealed between 1625 and 1649.

1826 Large hoard of coins found by workmen hidden in the rafters of an old house of a wealthy tailor who had died that year.

SHEPTON MALLET AREA, SOMERSET

1987 More than 1,800 bronze and copper Roman coins found on farmland by Michael Ashford (M/D) 13in below the surface.

SHIPHAM, SOMERSET

1986 About 860 4thC AD Roman copper coins found in a flagon by L. Hayes using a mechanical excavator to dig trenches for drains, while extending Kulu Lodge, Horseleaze Lane.

SIDBURY, DEVON

2000 Late 15th or early 16thC silver-gilt finger-ring found by C.D. Roberts while gardening.

SIXPENNY HANDLEY, DORSET

1877 More than 400 Roman *denarii* from the 1st and 2ndC AD found just over a foot below the surface in a pot during the digging of an allotment near the Turnpike Road. The site is about 1½ miles north of the Roman road from Old Sarum to Dorchester.

> **HUNDREDS**
>
> The name Sixpenny Handley has no connection with money; it relates to the 2 medieval hundreds of Saxpena and Hanlege meaning, 'Saxon hilltop' and 'high clearing'. A hundred was an area of land sufficient to support 100 families. It was made up of 100 hides, an area of between 60 and 120 acres.

SNOWSHILL, GLOUCESTERSHIRE

[date?] A Bronze Age dagger and pin, along with a Stone Age axe-hammer.

British Museum

SOMERSET

1925 13 billon coins from the 17thC. These rose farthings, which were manufactured privately by the Duchess of Richmond (1624–34) were found on the body of a soldier who was thought to have died between 1625 and 1649.

1953? 480 silver coins from the 16th and 17thC, thought to have been concealed in 1645.

1973 191 Roman billon coins, thought to have been deposited in AD 291. They were *antoniniani* from Gallienus to Maximian.

SOUTH PETHERTON, SOMERSET

c. **1720** Some Roman coins, 'to the quantity of 6 pecks', found in a pot in a field near Petherton Bridge.

1889 32 silver coins from the 16th and 17thC, thought to have been concealed between 1625 and 1649.

SPARKFORD, SOMERSET

1973 350–400 Roman copper *antoniniani* from the 3rdC AD.

SPETISBURY, DORSET

c. **1790** 3 silver coins from the 10thC found in Spetisbury Rings hill-fort during ploughing; thought to have been deposited *c.* AD 982. In 1857, during the construction of the railway, a mass grave of 120 skeletons, thought to be the victims of the Roman invasion, was uncovered.

1999 Gold penannular ring of 1100–800 BC.

STANCHESTER, WILTSHIRE

2000 1,196 Roman coins found in a plain pottery jar by schoolboy John Philpotts in a field at Wilcot; the latest coin was dated AD 406, making it the latest coin struck to be found in Wiltshire. The find comprised 3 gold solidi, 33 silver miliarenses, 1,159 *siliquae*, and a bronze nummus. Known as the 'Stanchester Hoard', it was bought by the local museum for £50,000 after it was declared treasure trove. The find site was close to a Roman villa.

Wiltshire Heritage Museum

STAVERTON, DEVON

1998 37 silver coins from the 13th and 14thC: finders P.H.J. Wills and R. Hill. They were 35 silver pennies of Edward I and II, and 2 others, thought to have been deposited around the late 1340s. They were returned to the finders.

STOGURSEY, SOMERSET

1999 1,097 Roman base-silver coins from the 3rdC AD were found in a pot by T. Phillips and K. Usler (M/D), thought to have been deposited *c.* AD 276. Three coins were valued at £100 and are held at the British Museum; the remainder were returned to the finders.

1999 Bronze Age gold 'basket ornament' of 2500–2000 BC: finders T. Phillips and D. Hines (M/D). This small parcel of tightly folded very thin sheet gold was found close to a plough-scattered hoard of Roman coins (above) and was valued at £200.

British Museum

STOKE TRISTER, SOMERSET

1999 15thC silver finger-ring, inscribed with lettering: finder Derek Bradfield (M/D).

Somerset County Museums

STRATTON ON THE FOSSE, SOMERSET

1987 538 Roman copper coins from the 3rd and 4thC AD found in a pot about 18in below the surface by Frances Pugsley and David Massey (M/D) in a field to the north of Downside Abbey. The site is about 450yd to the west of the Fosse Way.

STREET OR WINSHAM, SOMERSET

1684 Roman coins in an urn found between the two villages.

SWANAGE, DORSET

1987–8 Gold coin from the 1stC BC: finder Barry Dillon. It is one of Britain's rarest coins, as only 2 others have ever been found in the UK. Later declared not treasure trove, it was returned to the finder, who was offered £4,000 for it, which he turned down.

SWINDON

1890 17thC pewter baluster found at Kingshill House.

SWINDON AREA

2000 161 Roman *denarii* from the 1st and 2ndC AD found on farmland, near the roman road of Ermin Street: finder Peter Hyams (M/D); later declared treasure trove.

TADWELL, BATH AND NORTH-EAST SOMERSET

1999 13th or 14thC highly decorated silver-gilt annular brooch fragments: finder David Horsbrugh (M/D).

TARRANT HINTON, DORSET

>1866 4thC AD Roman copper coins found in an urn during excavations of a barrow, together with a skeleton.

TARRANT RUSHTON, DORSET

1998 17thC silver bodkin: finder J. Adams; valued at £700.

Dorset County Museum

TARRANT VALLEY, DORSET

1999 A late 13thC silver seal matrix, decorated and inscribed with lettering: finder Rex Burton (M/D).

2001–2002 16 Iron Age gold coins, probably from the late 1stC BC found by 8 separate detectorists (M/D).

Dorset County Museum

TAUNTON, SOMERSET

1980 275 silver coins from the 16th and 17thC found in a pot by excavator driver Graham Sulley, who was digging a trench on a building site at 32 East Street, when his machine knocked the bottom off an old earthenware pot. The hoard consisted of a crown, 6 half-crowns and 268 shillings of Edward VI, Philip and Mary, Elizabeth I, James I and Charles I, and dated 1551–1644. They were thought to have been buried in 1643–4 by someone fleeing the town while it was under siege during the Civil War. Graham Sulley received £3,335 for the find (worth over £8,000 today), which was declared treasure trove, and bought by Somerset County Museum.

Somerset County Museum

TAUNTON AREA, SOMERSET

1999 Almost 1,000 Roman bronze coins (some were washed silver) found in a pot 9–12in below the surface by Keith Usher and another metal detectorist. They later unearthed a lead cremation urn 2ft below the surface in a nearby field.

2000? 16thC gold ring found in a field by Paul Saxton. It held an engraved Roman carnelian from the 1stC BC to the 1stC AD.

TAYNTON, GLOUCESTERSHIRE

1999 50 Roman base-silver coins from the 4thC AD: finders D. Sherratt and D. Hutton (M/D). They were thought to have been deposited *c.* AD 317 and were returned to the finders.

2000 98 base-silver Roman coins and a silver finger-ring from the 4thC AD found by D. Sherratt and D. Hutton (M/D). The items were returned to the finders.

TEIGNMOUTH, DEVON

1978 Two 19thC £1 notes found by Jimmy Wright, who was knocking out part of a wall in the basement of the Royal Hotel when he revealed some old fireplace bricks. Carefully tucked away behind them were the notes, both perfectly preserved. They were issued from the Andover Old Bank, and dated September and October 1822.

TEMPLE CLOUD, BATH AND NORTH-EAST SOMERSET

1953 Over 500 gold and silver coins unearthed during road works.

THORNBURY, SOUTH GLOUCESTERSHIRE

2004 15,000–20,000 Roman coins from the 4thC unearthed when Ken Allen dug a hole for his new fishpond in his back garden, 20yd from his house. According to Bristol Museum, the find was the biggest to come out of the area in 30 years. Kurt Adams, the Gloucestershire and Avon Finds Liaison Officer, said: 'The coins identified so far can be attributed to Constantine the Great (AD 307–37). So far they seem to consist of three different types which show soldiers in between two standards, twins suckling from a she-wolf and Victory on the prow of a boat. The mint marks – a letter or symbol used to indicate the mint which produced the coin – suggest Trier, Germany and Constantinople (Istanbul), Turkey as possible places of origin. Some are in such good condition they may never have been in circulation.'

TICKENHAM, NORTH SOMERSET

1789 Roman coins found in a pot in the ramparts of Cadbury Camp; disposed of by the finders.

TIDENHAM, GLOUCESTERSHIRE

1999 1 gold and 117 silver coins from the 16th and 17thC: finder M.T. Meakin (M/D). The gold and silver coins of Elizabeth I, James I and Charles I were thought to have been deposited *c.* 1642–3, and were valued at £4,000.

Chepstow Museum

TIDWORTH AREA, WILTSHIRE

1985   Hoard of stolen 18thC silver items found in a plastic bag in an open manhole by 15-year-old Kevin Johnston and his friend, while playing in a wood near their home. The treasure had been stolen 2 years before from the strong room of the officers' mess at Moolton Barracks in Tidworth. It was the prized possession of the 1st Battalion, the Queen's Own Highlanders, and was valued at £128,000. The collection included 16 silver statuettes, a large centrepiece, plates, cups, ashtrays and goblets. The boys each received a cheque for £3,000 from the insurance company.

TINTAGEL, CORNWALL

1939   17 silver coins of Henry VIII found at Tintagel Castle; thought to have been concealed in 1544 or earlier.

TISBURY, WILTSHIRE

1643   A large quantity of 16th and 17thC gold coins found at Wardour Castle; thought to have been concealed in 1643.

TIVERTON AREA, DEVON

1845   Several hundred Roman *denarii* from the 2nd and 3rdC AD found in a jar about 2ft below the surface in an orchard at Little Gornhay Farm, near Tiverton. They were plated and of billon; most were dispersed, but a few were preserved.

TORQUAY AREA, TORBAY

17thC   The Torre Abbey Jewel from *c.* 1540 found by a member of the Ridgeway family in the grounds of Torre Abbey. In 1856 it was sold to the Victoria and Albert Museum for £21, the equivalent of about £1,030 today.

Victoria and Albert Museum

TOTNES, DEVON

1930s   176 silver coins of various reigns from Edward VI to James I found by R. McBride and T. Treacey, while laying storm-water sewers in the High Street. They were thought to have been deposited *c.* 1644–5 and it was reportedly one-third of the hoard originally found by building workers in the High Street. They were delivered to Totnes Museum on 9 July 1999.

Totnes Museum

TREWHIDDLE, NEAR ST AUSTELL, CORNWALL

1774 or **1777**   114 silver coins and silver items from the 9thC found under a pile of loose stones beside a stream in abandoned mine workings. The Trewhiddle Hoard, as it was called, consisted of 114 Anglo-Saxon silver coins buried in a silver chalice, a unique silver whip of plaited silver wires with a large glass bead as a handle (a scourge for religious services), drinking horn mounts, strap-ends and slides, and other silver items. It was probably hidden by a priest *c.* AD 871–5, a time when Viking raids were at their height.

British Museum

TYWARDREATH, CORNWALL

>1769   4thC AD Roman copper coins of which only 53 were recovered.

UPAVON, WILTSHIRE

1980   111 Roman bronze coins probably from the 3rd and 4thC AD found by Peter Stephens on Upavon Hill on the edge of Salisbury Plain, just north of the extensive 'Celtic' field system. Presumed to be of Iron Age and Romano-British date, they were later declared not treasure trove.

Wiltshire Heritage Museum

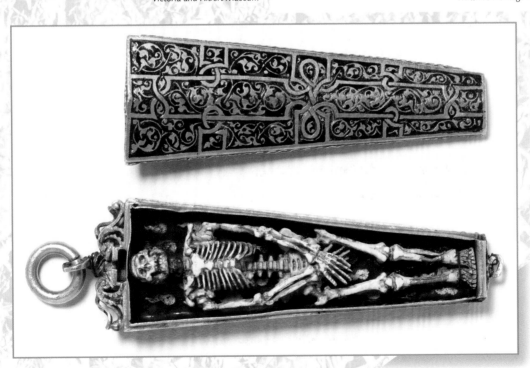

UPHILL, NORTH SOMERSET

1846 129 Roman silver and copper coins from the 3rd and 4thC AD found when a labourer, raising some stones near a lime kiln, discovered a large cavern in which the coins were deposited, in a fine state of preservation. Later scores more coins were found by locals.

UPHILL AREA, NORTH SOMERSET

1983 2 Bronze Age gold bracelets from 900 BC found by Keith Crabtree, a university lecturer, when he was visiting Brean Down with a party of geography and archaeology students. According to the British Museum, the bracelets were 'almost priceless'. They were declared treasure trove.

British Museum

UPLYME, DEVON

>1833 Very large quantity of Roman coins found by a man removing a heap of stones in a field called Holcombe Bottom. He apparently took them to Exeter and sold them.

UPTON, DORSET

1986 1,647 Roman bronze coins, with a trace of silver, of AD 310–18, found by Ken Emery (M/D) 17in below the surface in the remains of two clay pots. They were taken to the Russell Cotes Museum in Bournemouth, before being sent to the British Museum, who identified them as being from the reign of Constantine I.

UPWEY, DORSET

1950 279 silver coins from the 16th and 17thC, thought to have been concealed in 1662.

WANBOROUGH, SWINDON

1689 1600–2000 Roman coins from the 1st and 2ndC AD found in an earthenware vessel.

c. **1888** 22 Roman *aurei*, probably from the 2ndC AD.

2001 A 13thC highly decorated silver-gilt brooch: finder D. Alesbury (M/D).

Swindon Museum and Art Gallery

WAREHAM, DORSET

1992 and ongoing 1,500 Roman coins and several hundred pieces of jewellery discovered by Lilian Ladle over a 10-year period beginning in 1992. The finds were on the floor of Bestwall quarry on the outskirts of this Saxon town. The site has revealed a Bronze Age field system as well as the remains of a Roman pottery that was producing pots on an industrial scale. (www.bestwall.co.uk)

WARMINSTER, WILTSHIRE

1764 About 150 Roman copper coins and a small brass image from the 4thC AD found in an urn by a labourer digging stone on Warminster Common.

1780 Roman *denarii* from the 1st to 3rdC AD found in a pot by workmen when the land on Warminster Common was enclosed.

1972 32 16thC silver coins, made up of silver pennies, half-groats and groats of Henry VII, thought to have been concealed *c.* 1505–10.

WARMINSTER AREA, WILTSHIRE

1990 Gold torc from 1000 BC: finders Dennis Chaddock and Reg Day (M/D). It was later declared treasure trove and acquired by Salisbury Museum for £75,000 (the equivalent of over £100,000 today).

> **1999** Anglo-Saxon jewel from the 9thC, set with a 5th or 6thC rock crystal, found by David Rylett in a field at Cley Hill Farm. The jewel was an aestel, and originally named 'The Wessex Jewel'. It belongs to the same family as the Alfred Jewel, the Minster Lovell Jewel, and the Bowleaze Jewel. The jewel has now been renamed the 'Warminster Jewel' and was originally estimated to be worth more than £50,000. Having been declared not treasure trove it was returned to the finder. Subsequently Christie's in London estimated the value to be £200,000–£300,000 at auction. It eventually sold for £102,000.

WATCHET, SOMERSET

A mint is known to have existed here making coins for the southern English King Harthacnut (1040–2) in the 11thC. A coin bearing its mint mark is in Somerset County Museum.

WATERMOOR AREA, GLOUCESTERSHIRE

1975 22 Roman coins from 209 BC to AD 93 found by tennis coach Godfrey Evans in St Michaels field. They were valued at over £3,000 (around £15,000 today) and declared treasure trove.

WEDMORE, SOMERSET

1853 200 Anglo-Saxon silver pennies from the 11thC, some of them from the Somerset mints, found in an earthen vessel by Tucker Coles when the path near the north-eastern boundary of the churchyard was being widened. Many of the Danish landowners in the area lost their estates when the Saxon monarchy was restored in 1042, and it seems likely that one of them hid the hoard of coins. In the churchyard there is a stone marking the spot where the coins were found. Most of the coins were bought for the British Museum.

British Museum

1891 57 silver coins from the 16th and 17thC, thought to have been concealed between 1625 and 1649.

WELSH BICKNOR, GLOUCESTERSHIRE

c. **1817** Large quantity of Roman copper coins from the 4th and 5thC AD found on Copped-Wood Hill about a mile west of Courtfield between it and Welsh Bicknor.

1980 3 gold and 151 silver coins of Edward VI, Mary, Elizabeth I, James I, and Charles I found with fragments of a lead vessel near Parkwood Cottage while ploughing an area from which a large stone had recently been removed. They were thought to have been concealed in 1643 or later.

1845 99 gold coins from the 17thC or earlier found in a cavity of an old beam at the Old George Inn.

WESTBURY AREA, WILTSHIRE

1877 32 gold coins from the 14thC, mainly Edward III gold nobles, found at Bremeridge Farm; believed to have been concealed *c.* 1390–1400. Most of these coins are held by the Phipps family at Chalcot.

WESTLECOT, SWINDON

1874 Some silver coins of Edward I, II and III, thought to have been deposited during the 14thC.

WESTON-SUB-EDGE, GLOUCESTERSHIRE

1981 2 gold and 307 silver coins of Edward VI, Philip and Mary, Elizabeth I, James I, and Charles I found in a sealed lead pipe, under the floor of the village hall. They were thought to have been deposited in 1642 or later.

Corinium Museum

WESTWARD HO BEACH, DEVON

1980–1 Piece of gold plate, probably from the 9thC and thought to be Norse, was found by Pat Barrow (M/D). It has a pattern on both sides and the Norse connection relates to the activities of Hubba the Dane in the 9thC. Roman coins and artefacts have also been found in the area.

WEYMOUTH, DORSET

Bronze weapons, Roman remains and several Roman coins found along the shore since 1972.

1928 About 4,450 Roman copper coins and fragments from the 4th and 5thC AD found by workmen on the Weymouth Bay estate. The coins were fused together in one piece.

1990 An Anglo-Saxon gold aestel (a manuscript pointer) from the 9thC AD found on the beach at Bowleaze Cove. Named 'The Bowleaze Jewel', it has a central fitting of cobalt blue glass and it is in the same family as the Alfred Jewel. It was found below the cliffs at low tide: finder Bernard Yarosz (M/D). Having been studied by the British museum, it was declared not treasure trove. The museum subsequently bought it for £42,000 (the equivalent of £55,000 today).

British Museum

1998–9 2 Late Bronze Age gold torcs of *c.* 1000–800 BC found by a metal detectorist in a field on the outskirts of the town. They were later declared treasure trove.

WHITCHURCH, DEVON

1818 22 Roman *denarii* from the 2nd and 3rdC AD found by workmen removing a heap of stones in a field called Shellacres on Higher Wild Farm, a quarter of a mile from the Ikeneld Way, near Greenway Head.

WEST BAGBOROUGH, SOMERSET

2001 669 Roman silver coins and silver fragments from the 1st to the 4thC AD found in a ploughed field at the foot of the Quantocks by James Hawkesworth (M/D). The hoard comprised 2 *denarii*, 8 *miliarenses*, 659 *siliquae*, and 64 cut fragments of hacksilver (56 coins were forgeries). Thought to have been buried *c.* AD 365, this hoard would have been around a year's pay from a Roman legionary soldier; it was later declared treasure trove and valued at £40,650.

Somerset County Museum

WEST LAVINGTON, WILTSHIRE

1998 Roman silver pin fragment: finder B. King; returned to the finder.

WHITCHURCH, SOMERSET

1891–3 Small quantity of Roman bronze coins from the 2nd and 3rdC AD found by workmen in a ditch, together with some coin-casting moulds.

1961–2 Small quantity of Roman bronze coins from the 2nd and 3rdC AD found by farmer E.W. George while cleaning a ditch at Lyons Court Farm. He informed local archaeologists and about 300 coin moulds were found during a later excavation.

WICK, SOUTH GLOUCESTERSHIRE

1998 2 highly decorated Anglo-Saxon silver strap-ends from the 9thC AD: finder David Woodhouse (M/D).

WIGBOROUGH, SOMERSET

1830 3 Late Bronze Age palstaves.

Royal Albert Memorial Museum

WILCOT, WILTSHIRE

[date? Hoard of Roman gold and silver coins found by John Philpots (M/D), for which he was later rewarded with £50,000.

WILLERSEY, GLOUCESTERSHIRE

1968 1 silver ring and 56 silver coins from the 4thC AD found at a burial site containing 2 skeletons. The coins were thought to have been deposited in AD 363. They were found by two workmen digging holes for a barn extension at Hill Farm.

WILLITON, SOMERSET

1999 2 16thC silver-gilt dress-hooks: finder J. Slade (M/D); valued at £1,500.

Somerset County Museum

WILTON AREA, WILTSHIRE

1998 Gold ingot from between 1150 and 750 BC: finder J. Eden (M/D); returned to the finder.

WILTSHIRE

1986 53 gold Gallo-Belgic staters found by policeman and metal detectorist Peter Cracknell (M/D) in a field. He had decided to try his luck in the field having been told by a friend of his uncle's amazing find in the 1930s. Back then the 13-year-old boy had been one of a group of beaters for a shooting party, and he had picked up a stone and bowled it along the ground only to see it shatter on a larger stone and break open to reveal 65 gold coins. By the time Peter Cracknell came to the site, the farmer warned him that many had searched it before him without success.

1988 203 Roman *denarii* of 147 BC–AD 37 were found in a field: finder Doug Wilson (M/D).

Ashmolean Museum

1993–4 88 12thC silver pennies from King Stephen were found by a metal detectorist in a field. They were only found because the detectorist had kept his machine switched on as he walked back to his car. Among the coins was an unrecorded baron's issue, as well as a rare West Country mint, and while probably worth in the region of several thousand pounds, the historical significance outweighs the monetary value. The coins were declared treasure trove.

WINCANTON, SOMERSET

>1724 3rdC AD Roman bronze coins, described as 'half a peck', found in an urn a little above Sutton towards Beacon Ash.

WINCHCOMBE, GLOUCESTERSHIRE

2001 A 13thC decorated silver-gilt brooch: finder Gilbert Stirling Lee (M/D).

WINFORD, NORTH SOMERSET

1800s 11 silver pennies of Edward I, II and III from the 14thC found in a churchyard; believed to have been buried after 1369. 4 coins are held in the Bristol City Museum.

WINTERBOURNE EARLS, WILTSHIRE

1865 Roman copper coins from the 3rd and 4thC AD found while ploughing between Winterbourne Earls and Old Sarum. The coins were in an urn and a further search revealed 2 more urns and coins and some indication of a Roman villa. The coins were in an excellent state of preservation and looked as if they had never been in circulation.

WINTERBOURNE MONKTON, WILTSHIRE

1988 14 Iron Age silver coins (10 silver staters and 4 quarter-staters of the Durotriges) from the 1stC BC: finder C. Walmsley (M/D); returned to the finder.

WINTERBOURNE STOKE, WILTSHIRE

1797   301 silver coins from the 16th and 17thC, thought to have been concealed between 1625 and 1649.

WINTERBOURNE WHITCHURCH, DORSET

1999   An Anglo-Saxon silver finger-ring with decorated oval bezel from the 9thC AD: finder R. Tory (M/D).

WINTERSLOW, WILTSHIRE

1804   11th and 12thC silver coins found in a chalk pit, having probably been concealed c. 1154. The precise number of coins is unknown as only 18 coins were officially handed over. They were all silver pennies and cut halfpennies, including Henry of Anjou, William of Gloucester, and 2 baronial issues.

1910   50 silver coins of Mary and Philip, Edward VI, Elizabeth I, Charles I, and James I found in an earthenware jar in the garden of the village constable, who was having building work done.

WIVELISCOMBE, SOMERSET

1719   1,600 Roman copper folles from the 3rd and 4thC AD.

1946   1,087 Roman coins from the 3rd and 4thC AD found in a pot.
Somerset County Museum

WOODBURY, DEVON

2000   A 13thC gold finger-ring, set with an emerald: finder Nigel Tucker (M/D).
Royal Albert Memorial Museum

WOOKEY HOLE, SOMERSET

1975   15 Roman silver *antoniniani* from the 3rdC found in the remains of what may have been a purse. They were found by potholers exploring this famous limestone cave, and came from the reigns of Gallienus to Tetricus.

WOOLASTON, GLOUCESTERSHIRE

1862   Several hundred 4thC AD Roman copper coins found by a labourer excavating a ditch at the foot of Bowlash Hill. The find site was equidistant from the Roman works at 'The Chesters' and the 'Oldbury Field'.

1885   About 250 4thC AD Roman copper coins found in the ground under a stone near Woolaston, close to the road between Gloucester and Caerwent.

WORLE, NORTH SOMERSET

1852   241 Roman copper coins from the 4th and 5thC AD found during the excavation of the Iron Age settlement of Worle Camp. Along with the coins were a large quantity of pottery fragments, a great many glass beads, and fragments of bronze ornaments.

WRAXALL, NORTH SOMERSET

1950   Some Roman coins found when the Roman villa was discovered.

WRINGTON, NORTH SOMERSET

1984   1,283 Roman copper coins and fragments from the 4thC AD: finder D. Cook (M/D).

YATTON, NORTH SOMERSET

>1851   4th and 5thC AD Roman copper coins found in a large urn 18in below the surface together with two skeletons in the Roman cemetery at the foot of the encampment known as Cadbury Hill. Contemporary reports spoke of 'a large urn holding nearly 2 gallons'. Most coins were sold locally by the finders.

YEOVIL, SOMERSET

1916   About 1,000 Roman copper coins from the 4thC AD found 3ft below the surface in a field, by a workman digging a trench to lay a water-main, 144ft south of the pavement at Seaton Road.

1951   227 gold coins, possibly 19th and 20thC, thought to have been concealed in 1913.

[date?]   A gold Bronze Age ornament made from composite gold strip and measuring about 3in.
Somerset County Museum

YEOVIL AREA, SOMERSET

1989   About 22,500 Roman bronze coins from the 4thC AD found in a large pot by Mike Pittard (M/D). They were 18in below the surface and mostly of Constantine (AD 307–37).

ZENNOR, CORNWALL

1702   About 80 Roman silver coins from the 4th and 5thC AD found in an urn in a field, under a large rock called the Giant's Rock in the parish of Towednack, between St Ives and Land's End. The coins were well preserved.

Isles of Scilly

SAMSON

1957   27 gold, silver, or copper coins from the 18th and 19thC, thought to have been concealed between 1820 and 1837.

TRESCO

1744   About 500 silver coins, including Charles I half-crowns, thought to have been deposited c. 1651.

1946   9 silver coins, copper forgeries of Edward VI profile shillings, thought to have been concealed between 1544 and 1561.

This landlocked region often throws up finds that originated outside the area, perhaps lost by those travelling through. There is no better example than a Roman bowl found near Ashbourne in Derbyshire which originally belonged to a Roman legionnaire who had been based on the western end of Hadrian's Wall. It seems likely that it was a retirement gift but quite how it came to be left at what may have been a religious site is unclear. A hoard of up to 20,000 silver pennies found at Tutbury on the River Dove may well have been the pay chest of the Earl of Lancaster's army who sided with the Scots in their war with Edward II in 1322. In 1981 a man renovating a 15thC village hall found a piece of sealed lead pipe which to his amazement contained over 300 gold and silver coins: a Royalist soldier fleeing from the Battle of Evesham in 1645 had probably buried them.

What links these three particular finds, and many others from this region and across the whole of Britain and Ireland, is that their discovery is only the start of the detective story. Serious work is required to piece together the circumstance of why objects appear in a particular location and for many detectorists, this is half the fun.

THE WEST·MIDLANDS

Kenilworth Castle

STAFFORDSHIRE

Stoke-on-Trent

Newcastle-under-Lyme

Oswestry

Tutbury

Stafford

Burton-upon-Trent

1403
Shrewsbury

Penkridge

Lichfield

SHROPSHIRE

Wroxeter

Pattingham

Tamworth

Much Wenlock

Wolverhampton

Bridgnorth

Birmingham

Nuneaton

SEVERN

Solihull

Coventry

Ludlow

Kidderminster

Rugby

WORCESTERSHIRE

Kenilworth

MORTIMER'S CROSS
1461

Warwick

Leamington

Leominster

Alcester

WARWICKSHIRE

Stoke Prior

TEME

Worcester
1651

Stratford-upon-Avon

LUGG

Bidford-on-Avon

Cleve Prior

Hereford

Evesham
1265

EDGEHILL
1642

WYE

AVON

HEREFORDSHIRE

Ross-on-Wye

Shakespeare's Birthplace~Stratford-upon-Avon

Km
0   10   20   30   40

0   10   20

Miles

ALCESTER, WARWICKSHIRE

At the crossing of the Roman Icknield Way and the Salt Way from Droitwich, many artefacts have been found, including coins, pottery, glass and leatherwork.

c. **1638** 16 perfectly preserved gold and about 800 silver Roman coins from the 1st to the 5thC AD found 9in below the surface by labourers, while digging a cellar for a house next to the churchyard.

1890 A Saxon Tau cross.

British Museum

1925 A 1stC Roman vase.

1964 146 Roman coins (95 *antoniniani* and 51 *sestertii*), dating from the reign of Trajan (AD 98–117) to the 3rdC AD, found by 2 workmen digging a trench at Oversley Mill caravan park.

Warwickshire Museum

1979 4 gold sovereigns from King George IV, dated 1821–2, found in the grounds of Ragley Hall: finders Anthony Perry and Michael Pearson. They were valued at £1,400 (the equivalent of over £4,000 today).

ALREWAS AREA, STAFFORDSHIRE

1994 3 unfinished Iron Age gold torcs of 150 BC–AD 43 found just under the topsoil in a field: finder Emma Gray (M/D). At first they were taken to be a mass of brass wire, and it is thought that their maker was responsible for hiding them. They were declared treasure trove and bought by the Potteries Museum and Art Gallery for £8,000.

ALTON, STAFFORDSHIRE

1725 3 Roman gold coins from the 1stC AD found while ploughing near Wooton Lodge, about 900yd below Alton Castle.

ARELEY COMMON, STOURPORT ON SEVERN, WORCESTERSHIRE

>1979 A quantity of coins dated 1920–51 found in a biscuit tin in a garden; they were valued at £563.

ASHBOURNE AREA, DERBYSHIRE

2003 Roman bronze bowl or patera from the 2ndC AD found about 12in deep by Kevin Blackburn, Julian Lee, Flo Worsley and Ken Gameson on the Staffordshire moorlands. Decorated with Celtic-style motifs in blue, red, turquoise and yellow, it features an engraved inscription, AELI DRACONIS, which can be translated as 'by the hand – or property – of Aelius Draco'. There are also the names of 4 forts at the western end of Hadrian's Wall: Bowness, Drumburgh, Stanwix and Castlemeads. It has also been suggested that the inscription may imply that the Romans called the wall the Aelian Frontier. Kevin's view is that it was a retirement present to a soldier who had done his time on the wall. It is very similar, although slightly smaller, to the Rudge Cup found in Wiltshire, and is estimated to be worth £100,000. Since finding the cup the team have found 16 Roman fibula brooches at the same site, all in excellent condition. There is a theory that the place where the water disappeared underground was used as a votive offering site.

British Museum

ASHTON-UNDER-HILL AREA, WORCESTERSHIRE

1979 3 Saxon brooches found in a gravel path.

ASTLEY CASTLE, WARWICKSHIRE

1764 A James I silver penny, a Charles I rose farthing and a French silver coin dating from the 17thC found in the gardens of the castle. They were probably deposited during the Civil War, *c.* 1640. The castle was built *c.* 1266, but was demolished in the 16thC. In 1554 it was held by Henry, Duke of Staffordshire, who was executed with his daughter, Lady Jane Grey, who reigned as queen for nine days.

ATHERSTONE, WARWICKSHIRE

1957 184 silver coins from the 16th and 17thC found in an upper floor of a house, having probably been concealed in 1645.

1964 146 gold, 246 silver and some copper coins from the 19th and 20thC, thought to have been concealed in 1928.

BAGINTON, WARWICKSHIRE

1970 23 Roman *denarii* and 14 copper-alloy coins from the 1stC BC to the 2ndC AD found in a ditch during excavations at the Lunt, a Roman fort used for horse training.

BEDWORTH, WARWICKSHIRE

1938 19thC gold and silver coins, thought to have been concealed between 1837 and 1901.

BEESTON TOR, NEAR WETTON, STAFFORDSHIRE

1924 49 silver Anglo-Saxon silver pennies, 3 rings and a silver Saxon disc brooch, thought to have been buried in AD 871, found in St Bertram's Cave. The brooch is on display at the British Museum.

British Museum

BIDFORD-ON-AVON, WARWICKSHIRE

Warwickshire Archaeology Research Team began the excavation of an Anglo-Saxon cemetery in the town in 1990, uncovering a number of graves, some containing jewellery as well as weapons.

1999   9thC AD Anglo-Saxon highly decorated polyhedral socketed gold terminal: finder Robert Laight (M/D). The precise use of this object is unclear but it may have been hung from a rich garment and could have been ecclesiastical in nature.

2001   Gold-covered penannular ring of 1150–750 BC: finder Robert Laight (M/D).

Warwickshire Museum

2001   Anglo-Saxon triangular gold and garnet pendant dating from the 7thC: finder Robert Laight (M/D).

Warwickshire Museum

BIRMINGHAM

1816   1stC AD Roman coins, many in excellent condition, found by a man digging his garden near the 'Jews Burying Ground', which disappeared in 1845 with the building of the railway and New Street Station.

1890   1stC AD Roman coins found by a workman excavating a sewer at the junction of Dudley Street and Smallbrook Street.

1899   6 gold and 12 silver coins of George III found in the foundations of Christ Church. They were in a foundation deposit, buried 22 July 1805.

Birmingham Museum and Art Gallery

1923   18th and 19thC gold and silver coins , thought to have been concealed in 1899.

[date]   14thC pewter cruet found at Weoley Castle, originally a fortified manor house built in *c.* 1260.

BREDICOT, WORCESTERSHIRE

1839   3rdC AD Roman copper coins found in a pot about 2ft below the surface under a very large and ancient elm tree, close to Bredicot Court. The workmen who found them were building the Birmingham and Gloucester railway line and they shared most of the coins among themselves, but 62 coins and the urn were saved.

BREDON, WORCESTERSHIRE

1969   57 gold and 2 silver coins dating from the 18thC, thought to have been concealed in 1794.

BRIDGENORTH, SHROPSHIRE

1908   144 silver coins, dating from the 16th and 17thC. The town sided with Charles I in the Civil War and endured a month-long siege in 1646, which is when the hoard may well have been hidden.

BROWNHILLS, WALSALL

1955   4 gold and 9 silver coins, possibly from the 19th and 20thC; thought to have been concealed in 1915.

BURTON-UPON-TRENT AREA, STAFFORDSHIRE

1984   26 silver coins dating from Mary and Elizabeth I (1553–97) found on farmland: finder Rod Johnson (M/D). The hoard comprised 8 groats of Mary, 1 shilling, 3 sixpences, 1 threepence, 1 half-groat and 12 groats of Elizabeth I and ranged from depths of 3–11in, scattered over a large area. The finder handed them in at the local police station.

CALLINGWOOD, STAFFORDSHIRE

1788 or **1793**   32 Roman gold coins, from the reigns of 5 emperors from the 1stC AD, found on the north side of Needwood Forest, about a mile west from the Ryknield Way.

CANWELL HALL NEAR TAMWORTH, STAFFORDSHIRE

1991   46 silver short-cross pennies, 8 cut halves and 3 broken coins of Henry II, Richard I and John (1154–1216) found by Mel Hill and his son Andrew (M/D) beside a dried-up pond in a field. They were later declared treasure trove. Close by was the site of Canwell Priory founded *c.* 1120.

CASTLE BROMWICH, SOLIHULL

1909   181 Roman *denarii* and 18 base *denarii* dating from the 1st and 2ndC AD found in a pot about 3ft below the surface during ploughing at Shard End Farm.

1979–80   1 gold and 25 silver coins from the 16thC found scattered, about 6in below the surface on land earmarked for housing: finder Tony Patterson. The hoard was declared treasure trove, and sent to the British Museum.

CHADDESLEY CORBETT, WORCESTERSHIRE

1999   419 Roman base-silver coins from the 3rd and 4thC AD: finder Mr Harriman (M/D). Thought to have been deposited *c.* AD 317, they were valued at £1,800.

CHILD'S ERCALL, SHROPSHIRE

1980   2,897 Roman copper *antoniniani* from the 3rdC AD found in a pot 18in below the surface by an earth-moving machine stripping topsoil at Hatton Farm during irrigation work.

CLAVERDON AREA, WARWICKSHIRE

1972   2 silver and 5 billon coins of Elizabeth I, James I and Charles II found on Yarningdale Common; they were probably concealed *c.* 1680 or a little later.

CLEEVE PRIOR, WORCESTERSHIRE

1811   500–600 Roman gold and about 2,500–3,000 silver coins dating from the 4th and 5thC AD found in two large pots about 18in below the surface by a man getting stone from the quarry. The first pot, said to hold about 2 quarts, contained the gold coins, which were in mint condition and 'about 6lb in weight'. The second pot, which would hold a gallon, had about 3,000 silver coins, which were more worn. The finder was offered £700 (the equivalent of £27,000 today) for the coins, but thinking they were worth nearer £1,000 disposed of them in various lots himself. Today a find like this would be worth perhaps £500,000–£1 million.

CLENT, WORCESTERSHIRE

Clent relates to the Old English word for cleavage: the hills around the village give the impression that it nestles in their 'cleavage'. There is a legend of a battle between the Saxons and Romans in the area.

c. **1790**   Roman gold and silver coins found in a large jar while making a new pool on Clent Heath.

>1852   Roman gold and silver coins found in separate jars by labourers.

CLEOBURY MORTIMER, SHROPSHIRE

2000   A Roman gilded silver dolphin brooch dating from the 1stC AD: finder Mark Anthony Nash.

British Museum

COLESHILL, WARWICKSHIRE

1931   3,237 Roman copper coins from the 4thC AD, thought to have been deposited *c.* AD 354–5, found in a jar by workmen in Ennersdale Close on a new housing estate. The coins were found about 500yd south of a Roman temple site to the east of Grimstock Hill.

CORLEY, WARWICKSHIREHIRE

1999   14 silver pennies and groats from the 15th and 16thC: finder R. Chester (M/D); thought to have been deposited *c.* 1540–50.

COUNDON, COVENTRY

1998   Late 15th or early 16thC gold rectangular pendant, which was engraved with the head of Christ: finder R. Chester (M/D); valued at £4,000.

Herbert Art Gallery and Museum, Coventry

COVENTRY

1784? 16th and 17thC silver coins, thought to have been concealed between 1561 and 1634.

1847 100–200 English, Irish and Scottish silver pennies, dated 1280–1300.

1931 23 gold guineas, 17 half-guineas, and 5 smaller coins of George III found in the garden of 245 Broad Lane. Hens scratching about found the coins, thought to have been concealed *c.* 1804.

1937 About 500 silver coins and 2 silver brooches from the 13thC found under the floor of the old laundry at the Coventry and Warwick Hospital. A workman digging about 6ft below floor-level unearthed the slightly tarnished silver coins, which were otherwise in a good state of preservation. Careful sifting revealed the coins and the brooches, which were thought to have been buried in 1298. The works foreman took 6 coins and the 2 brooches to a local archaeologist, who forwarded them to the British Museum before handing the rest of the coins to the police. The 2 brooches are now displayed in the British Museum, and 106 coins can be seen in Coventry's Herbert Art Gallery and Museum.
British Museum and Herbert Art Gallery and Museum, Coventry

1967 225 silver coins from the 14thC found in pot during the digging of foundations; thought to have been buried *c.* AD 1365.
Herbert Museum and Art Gallery, Coventry

CURBOROUGH, STAFFORDSHIRE

1997 13thC gold finger-ring, set with a ruby: finder A.J. Southwell (M/D); valued at £1,800.
Potteries Museum and Art Gallery

DONNINGTON, SHROPSHIRE

1938 522 16th–17thC silver coins, thought to have been concealed in 1641. The village is about a mile from the site of a Roman fort.

DROITWICH, WORCESTERSHIRE

1973 14 Roman silver *antoniniani* of Carausius and Allectus found during archaeological excavations of a Roman villa at Bays Meadow site.

DUNCHURCH, WARWICKSHIRE

1961 89 billon halfpennies from various reigns during the 17th and 18thC; they included a large number of forgeries and were thought to have been concealed in 1751.
Birmingham Museum and Art Gallery

EATON CONSTANTINE, SHROPSHIRE

2000 Roman gold amulet case found by Niall Menice (M/D). This simple cylindrical tube had 3 loops and probably dated from the 1st or 2ndC AD. There was a large Roman fortress established here *c.* AD 47.
Shrewsbury Museum and Art Gallery

ELLESMERE AREA, SHROPSHIRE

1950 362 Roman coins dating from the 3rdC found in a pot in field at Hordley Grange.

ERDINGTON, BIRMINGHAM

1957 32 silver coins, probably from the 16th–17thC; thought to have been concealed in 1644.

EVESHAM, WORCESTERSHIRE

1979 20 17th–18thC lead tokens found below floorboards in an upper room of the Almonry Museum. With them was a brass button and buckle, and a piece of lead waste; they were thought to have been deposited *c.* 1650–1750.

1984 Edward II solid silver sixpence minted in 1277, 2 years after the Battle of Evesham, found by former mayor Frank Hampton, while picking runner beans on his allotment in town.

1998 2 silver groats and 1 silver coin of Edward IV, thought to have been deposited about 1480: finder S. Jackson (M/D); valued at *c.* £250.

EVESHAM AREA, WORCESTERSHIRE

1981 2 gold and over 300 silver coins, dated 1566–1642, found under the floor of the 15thC village hall by builder Howard Middlicott during extensive alterations. He discarded a piece of sealed lead pipe about 2ft below the floor level. The next day, thinking it might have some scrap value, he opened the end of the pipe and the coins, all of which were in excellent condition, fell to the ground. They were thought to have been hidden by fleeing Royalist soldiers during the Civil War, possibly after the storming of Evesham in 1645.

1996 9 saucer brooches, a shield-boss, a spearhead, a cruciform brooch and a girdle hanger, found at the site of an Anglo-Saxon cemetery dating from AD 550. The site, in a field on the side of a hill, was found by Mark Wilkinson (M/D) before the search was taken over by an archaeological excavation.

FAIRFIELD, WORCESTERSHIRE

1833 More than 100 Roman coins from the 2nd and 3rdC AD found 6in below the surface in a jar by workmen digging on Leigh Down in Ashton parish. The coins were dispersed by the finders.

FAULD, STAFFORDSHIRE

2000 Early 11thC Anglo-Saxon silver brooch: finder Peter Bell.
The design of the brooch (which, although damaged, had clearly been originally a very fine piece) was influenced by German designs, which caused a good deal of interest as to how it came to be in this area.

FILLONGLEY, WARWICKSHIRE

1997 2 silver brooches and a silver finger-ring from *c.* 1220–30: finders Roy English and Robert Foster (M/D); valued at £1,500.
Warwickshire Museum

1997 127 short-cross pennies and fragments, mostly from the reigns of John and Henry III, along with a silver ring brooch, dating from 1199 to 1220, found on farmland: finders Roy English and Robert Foster (M/D). The hoard was later declared treasure trove.

FISHERWICK, STAFFORDSHIRE

2001 Highly decorated late 16th or early 17thC gold signet ring: finder Mark Stephen (M/D).

Birmingham Museum and Art Gallery

FOLESHILL, COVENTRY

1792–3 More than 1,800 Roman copper coins found by 2 men digging a drainage ditch on a farm on 17 December 1792. They uncovered a sealed pot containing coins of the Emperors Constantine, Constans, Constantius and Magentus. On 12 January 1793 a second broken pot was found containing around 1,000 Roman silver and copper coins. Further searching revealed a number of other coins and fragments of a third pot of a similar age to the 2 already found.

FORSBROOK, STAFFORDSHIRE

[date?] Early 7thC Anglo-Saxon pendant containing a Roman gold coin (AD 375–9) and cloisinné garnet setting.

FRODESLEY, SHROPSHIRE

1999 2 highly decorated Anglo-Saxon strap-end fragments from the 9thC AD: finders J.S. Martin and R. Thompson (M/D).

GLASCOTE, STAFFORDSHIRE

1943 Iron Age gold torc from 50 BC containing 15oz of gold found in a boatyard by the canal in the Glascote area of Tamworth. The torc, made of twisted strands of gold alloy, was declared treasure trove and the local museum was offered it but turned it down. Following the discovery of the Ipswich torcs in 1968 Birmingham Museum had a change of mind and launched an appeal for £7,500 (the equivalent of £80,000 today) to buy the torc. Local legend has linked the torc to Queen Boudicca, who fought her last battle along Watling Street, which runs close to the town. In actual fact the craftsman who made it had rejected the torc, owing to a fault in the connecting terminals. He cast it aside where it was found 2,000 years later.

Birmingham Museum and Art Gallery

GOLDENHILL, STOKE ON TRENT

1832 36 gold coins and possibly 24 silver coins, from the 16th and 17thC; thought to have been concealed in 1648.

GLEWSTONE, HEREFORDSHIRE

1980 87 silver coins of Edward VI, Philip and Mary, Elizabeth I, James I and Charles I found by a metal detectorist in the bank of a drainage ditch close to Sunray Park Cottage. They were thought to have been concealed in 1641 or later.

GREAT BARR, SANDWELL

1956 45 gold, silver or copper forgeries of William Booth, thought to have been concealed 1760–1812. Booth lived at Squire Gough's Farm at Perry Barr, now known as Booth's Farm. A tunnel supposedly ran from the farm to a pub, the Hare and Hounds, at West Bromwich, where he was said to do business. He was arrested for murder while he was attempting to burn the evidence of his forging business. Tried at Staffordshire assizes in 1812, he was sentenced to hang. The executioner failed to hang him properly, whereupon he had to be revived and hanged again two hours later.

GREAT PACKINGTON, WARWICKSHIRE

1999 10 Roman *denarii* from the 1stC AD: finder M. Longfield (M/D); thought to have been deposited about AD 50 and were valued at £300.

HAMSTALL RIDWARE, STAFFORDSHIRE

1810 Silver chalice found by a ploughman while working alongside the old churchyard.

1998 Late 13th or early 14thC silver seal matrix, highly decorated with insignia: finder M.J.B. Hicks (M/D); valued at £3,000.

Potteries Museum and Art Gallery

HEREFORD, HEREFORDSHIRE

1933 18th and 19thC silver coins, thought to have been concealed in 1819.

HEREFORD AREA, HEREFORDSHIRE

1980 87 silver coins of Edward IV to Charles I found in a gully beside a footpath: finder Ruth Churchill (M/D). The silver half-crowns, shillings and sixpences lay scattered over a 12 sq. ft area 9–12in deep. The coins were thought to have been buried *c.* 1646, during the Civil War, when Goodrich Castle was under a long siege. The hoard was declared treasure trove.

HOLBERROW GREEN, WORCESTERSHIRE

2001 Late 10th or early 11thC highly decorated gold brooch fragment: finder B.R. Melly (M/D).

British Museum

HONINGTON, WARWICKSHIRE

1741 About 121 silver coins of Elizabeth I, James I and Charles I found in a pot, during the rebuilding of Honington Hall. They were thought to have been concealed in 1645–9.

HORDLEY, SHROPSHIRE

1950 362 Roman copper coins from the 3rdC AD found with a pot, scattered across a field near Hordley Grange. The coins were all *antoniniani* apart from 7 *denarii*.

Shrewsbury Museum and Art Gallery

HUDDINGTON, WORCESTERSHIRE

1903 1 silver and 31 copper mostly Scottish coins found together with a skeleton, thought to have been buried in 1637.

HURLEY, WARWICKSHIRE

1999 A gold foil disc pendant, decorated with geometric designs and dating from the 7thC AD: finder J. Stanfield (M/D).

INGESTRE, STAFFORDSHIRE

1798 16th and 17thC silver coins, thought to have been concealed 1660–85.

KEMPSEY, WORCESTERSHIRE

1954 Gold coin inscribed with the head of Emperor Nero found at the Roman cemetery by schoolboys from King's School during a summer term archaeological dig. Other coins of an undisclosed number and nature were found in the area of the Roman fort.

KINGSLEY, STAFFORDSHIRE

1941 48 silver coins from the 16thC, thought to have been concealed in 1573, found at Little Broad Oak.

KNOWLE, SOLIHULL

1778 A large quantity of Roman bronze coins from the 3rdC AD found during ploughing. The coins were in a solid mass in a pot and weighed 15lb. The site was 1½ miles north of the remains of a Roman station called Arborough Banks.

LEEK AREA, STAFFORDSHIRE

***c.* 1770** 3rdC AD Roman coins found where cattle had broken up the ground on a farm at Frier-Moor, about 2 miles south of Leek. They were fused together and taken out of the ground in lumps as big as fists, and were said to be 'more than would fill the largest whisket [straw basket]'.

LEEK WOOTTON, WARWICKSHIRE

1971 17 gold coins – 9 sovereigns and 8 half-sovereigns – of George IV, dated 1825–59; thought to have been buried after 1859. They were estimated to be worth £1,000 (the equivalent of almost £9,000 today).

LICHFIELD, STAFFORDSHIRE

1788 16th and 17thC silver coins found at Bore Street; thought to have been concealed 1625–49.

LICHFIELD AREA, STAFFORDSHIRE

1998 18 Roman *denarii* from the 1st and 2ndC AD found by a metal detectorist. Valued at £250, they were thought to have been deposited about AD 180.

Potteries Museum and Art Gallery

1998 13 silver groats of Edward IV and Henry VII, and 5 foreign coins: finders A. Harper and I. Malvgani; thought to have been deposited *c.* 1500, they were valued at £500.

Potteries Museum and Art Gallery

LIGHTHORNE AREA, WARWICKSHIRE

1972 93 silver coins of Edward VI, Elizabeth I, James I and Charles I, dated 1551–1646, thought to have been deposited after 1646.

Warwickshire Museum

LITTLE MALVERN, WORCESTERSHIRE

1847 200–300 well-preserved Roman coins from the 3rd and 4thC AD found in an urn by a party of visitors rambling over the hills on the western side of the road leading to Ledbury, opposite the premises called Little Malvern Grove, and within half a mile of the foot of a hill called Herefordshire Beacon (a 32-acre Iron Age fort). One of the party stuck his stick into the turf, where it dislodged some earth and exposed the urn.

LLANGARREN, HEREFORDSHIRE

1912 2,810 Roman copper coins, in good or excellent condition, dating from the 4thC AD, found in a pot 18in below the surface during ploughing at Hill Farm.

LONGFORD, SHROPSHIRE

1898 700–1,000 Roman *antoniniani* from the 3rdC AD found by a boy ploughing a field opposite the 'Fabric' Cottages. He disposed of most of the coins at Market Drayton.

LONGTON, STOKE-ON-TRENT

1960 1,739 identifiable Roman coins and a further 722 irregular pieces and fragments from the 3rdC, many of which were corroded, found by J.T. Allen while he was digging his garden at 698 Lightwood Road, Longton. They were discovered in a pot that also contained a pair of silver bracelets and a fragment of a silver clasp. The silver bracelets were later declared treasure trove.

Potteries Museum and Art Gallery

LOW HILL, WOLVERHAMPTON

1999 88 silver coins of Henry VIII and Charles I found by R. McBride and T. Treacey, while digging a trench to lay storm drains. They were thought to have been deposited *c.* 1644.

LOWER BRAILLES, WARWICKSHIRE

1999   9 silver coins of Elizabeth I, James I and Charles I: finder A.D. Gardner (M/D). They were thought to have been deposited *c.* 1640 and were valued at £180.

Warwickshire Museum

LUDLOW AREA, SHROPSHIRE

1784–5?   17thC gold and silver coins found in a pot by a farmer during ploughing; thought to have been concealed *c.* 1648. There is a sad twist to the tale: the farmer was so excited with his newfound wealth that he drank too much and 48 hours later he was dead.

MADELEY, STAFFORDSHIRE

1817   3rd and 4thC AD Roman coins found in 2 urns during ploughing on Little Madeley Parks Farm.

MADELEY WOOD, NEAR IRONBRIDGE SHROPSHIRE

1839   A large quantity of gold coins from the 16th and 17thC, thought to have been concealed 1603–25.

MANCETTER, WARWICKSHIRE

1960   16 Roman coins from the 1stC AD found just outside the main gates of Mancetter Manor. Other finds of pottery and Samianware in the area have provided the likely date for the hoard being deposited: AD 50–70. (The site was a large Roman fortress called Mandvessedvm.) The coins were at a depth of about 18in along with fragments of a red jug.

MARKET DRAYTON, SHROPSHIRE

1980   About 3,000 Roman coins from the 3rdC AD found by Don Ford, while working with a bulldozer in the field of farmer Jim Hollins. The hoard was concealed in a clay pot, 18in deep.

MARTLEY, WORCESTERSHIRE

2003   Silver brooch from the 13th or early 14thC: finder David Cole (M/D). This small brooch was interesting in that it was not a sign of particularly high status and probably belonged to a merchant or farmer's wife.

MAYFIELD, STAFFORDSHIRE

***c.* 1676**   Roman coins found during the digging up of a tumulus in Church-town field in Dale Close, Upper Mayfield.

MEON HILL, WARWICKSHIRE

1824   394 currency bars found in the earthwork on the summit of Meon Hill, which dates from the Iron Age, though Neolithic artefacts have also been found. There is a story of a labourer ploughing the field on the top of the hill and unearthing a stash of gold coins. Instead of handing them to his employer he kept them and grew so prosperous that he was able to marry his daughter to one of Warwickshire's most noble families.

MERIDEN, SOLIHULL

1783   200 gold guinea pieces of Charles II, in immaculate condition and dated 1660–85, found by 3 labourers digging a drainage pit. They kept the find a secret to begin with and divided the coins between themselves.

MILVERTON, WARWICKSHIRE

1885   About 200 Roman copper coins from the 3rdC AD found by a man working in a gravel pit. He broke the jar to get at the coins and many seem to have been collected by people who heard of his discovery.

MUCH WENLOCK, SHROPSHIRE

1977   2,591 Roman billon coins from the 3rdC AD found at Westwood Farm, half a mile from a Roman burial ground. Initially a tractor driver, David Merrick, discovered some coins while ploughing at David Craig's farm. There followed a thorough search, with the aid of three local archaeologists, which revealed the whole hoard. The coins were bronze and some bore the heads of Emperors Caligula and Claudius and were probably originally buried in a wooden box. Thought to have been deposited in AD 284, they were declared treasure trove, and placed in the hands of the British Museum for valuation.

NASEBY AREA

1990s?   44 silver coins from the 17thC were found close to a ditch about 1½ miles from the site of the Battle of Naseby: finder J.Ellis (M/D). There is conjecture that it may have been hidden prior to the battle (1645) but it seems somewhat close to the battle site. In any event, whoever buried the money failed to return to retrieve it.

NEWCASTLE-UNDER-LYME, STAFFORDSHIRE

1946   Many gold coins and banknotes found by a man who took up the floorboards in the bedroom of his house and found a stocking filled with coins and notes worth £500.

NUNEATON, WARWICKSHIRE

1889   About 400 silver pennies, dated 1470–90, probably concealed during the Wars of the Roses. They were dispersed by the finders, 20 coins being located in 1933.

1920   29 Roman *denarii* from the 1st and 3rdC AD found in a pot at the Griff granite quarry. They were assumed to be part of a hoard.

NUNEATON AREA, WARWICKSHIRE

1977   223 silver coins found on Woody Farm, Galley Common. In 1974 farmer Maurice Pointon found 2 or 3 coins and then Fred James found 5 more. Fred James bought a metal detector, and, assisted by Maurice Pointon, located the hoard. An old cottage had stood on the spot, which Maurice Pointon had demolished before ploughing the area and it was probably the plough that caught the top of the dark brown glazed jar and spilled some of the coins. The hoard comprised 31 shillings and 53 sixpences of Elizabeth I; 18 shillings and 5 sixpences of James I; and 32 half-crowns, 72 shillings and 12 sixpences of Charles I. This is a fairly typical Civil War hoard of the 1640 period and was thought to have been deposited after 1645.

OFFCHURCH, WARWICKSHIRE

2002   Roman silver finger-ring fragment from the 3rd or 4thC AD: finder Stephen A. Wright (M/D); returned to the finder.

OSCOTT, BIRMINGHAM

>1977   33 silver coins of Elizabeth I, James I and Charles I found in the Roman Catholic College of St Mary, a centre for the historical heritage of Catholicism in England, founded in 1794. It is thought the coins were deposited c. 1641–3 or later.

Birmingham Museum and Art Gallery

OSWESTRY, SHROPSHIRE

1904   4 gold and 401 silver coins from the 16th and 17thC found in a field; thought to have been concealed in 1641.

1999   10thC silver penannular bracelet: finder J.H. Moore (M/D); returned to the finder.

OULTON, STAFFORDSHIRE

1795   11thC silver coins, thought to have been deposited c. AD 1070. The 25 known coins are of Edward the Confessor and William I.

OVERLEY HILL, TELFORD AND WREKIN

1990   1 *aureus* and 13 *denarii* from the 1stC AD found by John Nicholls and another metal detectorist while searching an area being prepared for a new road passing over the A5, which was formerly Watling Street. The site was just a few miles from the old Roman city of Wroxeter. The coins were declared treasure trove.

2004   77 Silver coins dating between 1280 and 1430: finder Kevin Blackburn and Julian Lee (M/D). The hoard comprised hammered silver pennies, half-groats and groats.

PATTINGHAM, STAFFORDSHIRE

Pattingham is close to Penkridge, previously the Roman town of Pennocrucium, an important junction where roads from the south and west meet Watling Street.

1700   Roman gold torc found at Copley Farm, by a farm worker, who was preparing to plough a field at Fantley Hill and had moved a large stone. Beneath it was the gold torc, which he assumed was brass, selling it to a Wolverhampton metal merchant named Orm for a few pence. He in turn sold it to a London goldsmith for a handsome price, whereupon it was melted down. When the lord of the manor (a member of the Astley family) found out what his farmhand had done, he ordered him to be arrested. Protesting his innocence (claiming he thought it was brass) did him no good, until Orm made a torc of brass and presented it as the object that had been found.

1760   Loaf-shaped gold ingot found in the field adjoining Fantley Hill at Copley Farm.

1920?   2 16th–17thC silver coins, thought to have been concealed in 1643.

PENKRIDGE, STAFFORDSHIRE

1750   A large quantity of gold coins, possibly dating from the 17thC found at Pillaton Hall. Its owner, Sir Edward Littleton, was a Parliamentarian during the opening years of the Civil War but later decided to change sides. In 1643, while still a Parliamentarian, he was entrusted with a pay chest containing a large amount of money, which he stole and then hid at Pillaton Hall, planning to hand it over to the king. His plot was discovered and Sir Edward had to flee for his life leaving the hidden hoard behind. At the end of the war Sir Edward was imprisoned and died before Charles II was restored to the crown. Sir Edward's nephew inherited Littleton Hall in 1750 and discovered the money behind some oak panelling. It is said that a second hoard came to light within the next decade.

PERSHORE, WORCESTERSHIR

c. **1750**   A 10thC bronze censer cover with the inscription '*Godric me wvorht*' (Godric made me): finder Revd Thomas Beale. The censer would have been used for burning incense in a church and this one takes the form of a tower with a square openwork arcaded base. On each of the four faces is a gable, one of which has the inscription. It was bought in 1960 for £2,730 (the equivalent of £38,000 today).

British Museum

PILLERTON PRIORS, STAFFORDSHIRE

1750   Chalice and paten, and many gold coins dating from the 16thC found in a chimney of an old hall that was being demolished by Sir Edward Littleton in 1750. They were sold at Christie's in 1960. A mosaic floor disturbed by ploughing, but still beautiful, found in the site in 1998 – the remains of a Roman villa.

POLESWORTH, WARWICKSHIRE

1762   4thC AD Roman copper coins found in a large pot by labourers digging a trench.

1849   Large hoard of Roman coins from the 1st and 2ndC AD found during ploughing at Hall End on land belonging to the Earl of Beauchamp.

ROSS-ON-WYE, HEREFORDSHIRE

1980   3 gold and 151 silver coins from the 16th and 17thC found by Stephen Kirby (aged 16) while ploughing a field. The hoard included a Queen Mary gold angel and 2 gold coins of James I. The silver coins were mostly of Elizabeth I, James I and Charles I.

ROWLEY REGIS, SANDWELL

1794   About 1,200 Roman silver coins found in an earthen vessel. They were dispersed by the finder, but about 300 were retrieved.

SANDFIELDS, STAFFORDSHIRE

1999   15 Roman *denarii* from the 1st and 2ndC AD: finder C.M. Pearson (M/D). Thought to have been deposited about AD 175, they were returned to the finder.

SEVERN STOKE, WORCESTERSHIRE

1992–6 17 Anglo-Saxon silver pennies, of various 9thC rulers: finder C.L. Thompson (M/D); thought to have been deposited c. AD 874.

1999 Anglo-Saxon silver penny of Burgred, King of Mercia (852–74): finder C.L. Thompson.

SHREWSBURY, SHROPSHIRE

1999 14thC inscribed silver finger-ring found by Trevor Robin Mason near the 16thC moated manor house of Albright Hussey; it was valued at £800. Albright Hussey was on the site of the Battle of Shrewsbury, fought in 1603 between Henry IV's army and the rebels led by Henry Percy (Hotspur). It was the first time that English longbowmen had faced each other on a battlefield.

Shrewsbury Museums Service

1999 13thC gold finger-ring set with a ruby: finder Mark Walton (M/D).

SHREWSBURY AREA, SHROPSHIRE

1982 21 gold guineas and half-guineas, dated 1666–1701, found between a stream and a footpath by Desmond Hogg (M/D) on land belonging to Sam Gumbley. The coins were thought to be worth at least £6,000.

SOLIHULL

1930 7 gold coins, possibly from the 18th and 19thC, thought to have been concealed in 1821.

1997–8 14 silver coins of various reigns from the 13th to 17thC: finder J. Jones (M/D); returned to the finder.

STAFFORD, STAFFORDSHIRE (1929)

1929 2 silver and 13 billon coins, including many forgeries, from the reigns of William III, and George II and III, found in Mill Street. They were thought to have been concealed after 1775, and possibly as late as 1800.

STAPELEY HILL, SHROPSHIRE

1974 16 silver coins of Victoria, Edward VII and George V, dated 1887–1921.

STAUNTON-UPON-ARROW, HEREFORDSHIRE

1953 Bronze Age gold bracelet from c. 1000 BC found in Mill Street.

STOKE-ON-TRENT

1982 3,000-year-old bronze axe, in very good condition, found by a man digging the garden of his new house.

STOKE PRIOR, HEREFORDSHIRE

1891 A chalice hallmarked 1578, a large and ornate vessel in 3 separate parts dated 1594, a small bell-shaped vessel (1596), a paten (a dish for the consecrated communion wafers) dated 1639, and three small cups from the reign of Charles I found in a small coppice. A farmer's son, Vincent Godfrey, and a farm labourer went hunting rabbits in the wood about 250yd from the road from Leominster to Stoke Prior, near an old cottage named the Slough. Near to a large elm tree they put their rabbit down the hole but it failed to surface so they began to dig it out. They soon came upon the first piece of treasure, followed by the other 5 objects. They reported their discovery to the police and the Treasure of Stoke Prior, as it has become known, is now in the Victoria and Albert Museum

Victoria and Albert Museum

STONELEIGH, WARWICKSHIRE

[date?] 14thC pewter sepulchral chalice found during excavations for a croquet lawn at Stoneleigh Abbey.

STOURPORT-ON-SEVERN, WORCESTERSHIRE

1973 4,073 silver and 46 other coins from the reigns of Victoria, Edward VII, and George V and VI, and dated 1889–1951, found wrapped in newspaper.

STRATFORD-UPON-AVON, WARWICKSHIRE

1786 4thC AD Roman gold and silver coins found in an urn during ploughing 2½ miles from Stratford at Monk's Close, adjoining the London Road.

1830 Over 1,000 short-cross silver pennies, a silver seal inscribed 'Christ the head of all things' in Latin and a gold ring set with emeralds dating from the 12thC. A man walking with his horse and cart at Cross-on-the-Hill ('a crossroads about half a mile south of Stratford-on-Avon, where the track to Stratford Mill left Cross-on-the-Hill', according to contemporary reports) found what he thought to be sixpences in the mud on his cartwheels. He found the remainder of the hoard where his cart had disturbed it.

STRETTON SUGWAS, HEREFORDSHIRE

>1964 Some Roman coins, of which 170 were recovered.

TAMWORTH, STAFFORDSHIRE

1863 900 silver coins reported to have been found at Cumberford, now an area in the town. King Offa established a mint at Tamworth during the time he had a palace in the area c. 780. The mint remained operational until the 12thC and coins originating from here often come up for sale through dealers. In 2004 a hammered silver penny of Edward the Confessor was being offered online for £900, which gives some idea as to the possible value of the find.

TAMWORTH AREA, STAFFORDSHIRE

1877   300 silver pennies unearthed in a leaden box during excavations for a new school. The box was believed to have been deposited in 1090 and 30 of the coins originated from the Tamworth mint.

2001   2 Roman *aurei* and 92 *denarii* from the 1stC AD found by members of the Tamworth Search Society. They were thought to have been deposited about AD 90 and the silver coins were returned to the finders. The gold coins are held at the Potteries Museum, Stoke-on-Trent.

Potteries Museum and Art Gallery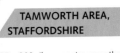

TELFORD, TELFORD AND WREKIN

1982   368 silver coins of Charles I, thought to have been buried *c.* 1648–9. They were found by 3 workmen building a new motorway in Telford, which had previously been part of a garden. The hoard was declared treasure trove.

TUTBURY, STAFFORDSHIRE

1831   About 20,000 silver pennies from the 13th and 14thC found in the bank of the River Dove. The owner of the corn and cotton mill, John Webb, had decided to deepen the river to improve the fall of water from the wheel. On 1 June some of the workmen found a few blackened and corroded coins and soon they came across more with recognisable designs so they told John Webb of their discovery. Over the next week more and more coins came to light until on 8 June the main hoard was discovered, buried under 4ft of gravel in the riverbed on the Derbyshire side of the river. Contemporary reports talk of workmen lifting 150 in a shovelful. The workmen began selling coins at 6 or 7s a hundred and as better coins came to light they were selling some for as much as £1 each. The site was on land belonging to the crown and so commissioners were appointed to supervise the excavations on behalf of the Duchy of Lancaster. By 1 July the search was finally abandoned. No record was kept of the number of coins that were discovered. Contemporary reports talk of as many as 200,000 while others say 100,000. Today the figure of 20,000 is readily accepted as a better assessment – which is still a staggering number. In the end 1,500 were submitted to the British Museum, along with a chased gold ring found in the same place. Among the find were coins of Henry III, Edward I and Edward III, Scottish coins of Alexander III and Robert Bruce, and kings of Bohemia and Poland. One theory as to how the coins got into the river is that they belonged to the Earl of Lancaster, who sided with the Scots against his cousin King Edward II in the early 1300s. Lancaster was beaten at the Battle of Burton Bridge in 1322 and it may have been his paymaster who lost them while trying to cross the flooded river after the Earl and his men had taken refuge in Tutbury Castle. Or they may have been buried in a field near the river and over time the river changed its course. Either way, it would seem likely that whoever buried or lost them was killed in battle or in some other way since he did not return to search for the huge hoard.

2000   11thC gold brooch found 3in below the surface: finder Peter Bell (M/D). It was part of a crucifix and one of only 4 pieces of medieval German jewellery so far found in Britain; it was declared treasure trove.

UPPER ARLEY, WORCESTERSHIRE

c. 1798   In a *History of Staffordshire* published in 1798 it said: 'Hawkbatch is certainly a very antique site, and the roads from thence through the woods tend towards Wall town, evidently a Roman station, from several gold coins dug up near it; one of Tiberius, very fresh, in the possession of Mr. James Pardoe of Bewdley.'

UPPER BRAILES, WARWICKSHIRE

1999   Fragment of gold ingot that could date from anywhere between 800 BC and the 5thC AD: finder A. Gardner (M/D).

2001   An iconographic 15thC gold finger-ring depicting saints, found 3in below the surface: finder A. Gardner (M/D); later declared treasure trove.

Warwickshire Museum

UPTON UPON SEVERN, WORCESTERSHIRE

>1883   'Roman coins and relics have been found in the field tradition has marked out as "The Camp"', according to the book *Hanley Castle* by William Symonds. It was chosen as the site of a camp to protect the river crossing by the Romans.

WALFORD, HEREFORDSHIRE

1895   More than 17,550 Roman copper coins, nearly all from the Constantine period (AD 290–360) found in 3 large jars just below the surface by workmen getting stones to mend a road, at Bishop's Wood. More coins were found the next day by schoolchildren, but were subsequently lost.

WALSALL

1888   1 gold and 25 silver coins, possibly of the 18th–19thC and thought to have been concealed in 1819.

WARWICK, WARWICKSHIRE

1998   Elaborately engraved and decorated 15thC gold finger-ring found during archaeology monitoring; returned to the finder.

2001   Highly decorated gold brooch from *c.* 1300: finder C. Kibblewhite (M/D).

2001   Enamelled and decorated late 10thC gold finger-ring: finder J. Cahill (M/D).

WARWICK AREA, WARWICKSHIRE

1700s   200 gold guineas of Charles II.

WARWICKSHIRE

1994   10 gold staters and 1 fragment from the Corieltauvi tribe, from 45 BC to AD 15: finder Dave Morris (M/D); declared not treasure trove and returned to the finder.

WATER ORTON, WARWICKSHIRE

1979   1 gold and 25 silver coins of Henry VII, Mary, Philip and Mary, Elizabeth I, James I and Charles I, with a few Scottish coins, thought to have been concealed in 1640 or later.

WEDNESBURY, SANDWELL

1817   A small number of well-preserved Roman coins from the 1st and 2ndC AD.

WELLINGTON, TELFORD AND WREKIN

1903   60 silver forged half-crowns, thought to have been concealed between 1816 and 1820.

WHITCHURCH, SHROPSHIRE

1945   4 gold and 39 silver coins from the 16th and 17thC, thought to have been concealed in 1640.

WINSHILL, STAFFORDSHIRE

1960   Some silver coins discovered by a DIY enthusiast removing floorboards in his house. They were valued at £400.

WISHAW, WARWICKSHIRE

1988   156 Roman coins from the 3rdC AD found by Bob Hall 15–18in below the surface in a field to the east of Wishaw Hill Farm.

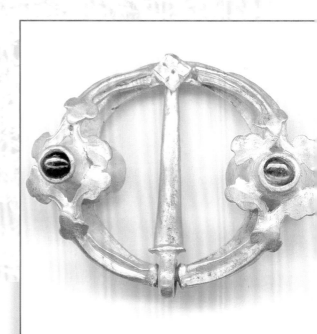

WOLVERHAMPTON

1979 A cache of stolen jewellery, valued at £80, found under a bush: finder schoolboy Robert Allcott. He handed his find to police and his honesty earned him a £10 reward from the Staffordshire Crown Court.

1981 13thC church altar stand made of cast bronze found on farmland: finder Keith Fellows (M/D).

WORCESTER, WORCESTERSHIRE

1698 Some Roman coins (contemporary reports spoke of 'a peck') found in a pot beside a Roman hearth, within 100yd of the city walls.

1850 or **1853** 210 silver pennies and 7 silver finger-rings found in the Lark Hill area of the city; believed to have been buried c. 1180.

>1963 10 Roman coins from the 1stC AD found during a redevelopment excavation in Worcester before February 1963. 9 are copies of Claudian prototypes and the other is a commemorative As of M. Agrippa.

◄ WORCESTERSHIRE

1990s Roman buckle plate found by a metal detectorist.

SOUTH WORCESTERSHIRE

1993 Almost 1,000 Iron Age coins from the 1stC AD found in a leather bag in a field. 7 of the coins were gold staters; most of the others were debased silver of the Celtic Dubunni tribe and were thought to have been concealed c. AD 45. The estimated market value of the entire hoard was £70,000–£100,000.

WROXALL, WARWICKSHIRE

1999 5 silver coins of Philip and Mary to Charles I found while walking in a field: finder G.J. Jones. Thought to have been deposited c. mid-17thC, they were returned to the finder.

WROXETER, SHROPSHIRE

This was the administrative and commercial centre of the Celtic tribe known as the Cornovii and became Viroconium in Roman times. A stone slab found some years ago carried the words 'Civitas Cornoviorum' or 'The Civitas of the Cornovii'. There are a number of Roman military sites close to the village: 3 miles to the south-east there was a large fortress at Eaton Constantine; about half a mile to the south is a small auxiliary fort; and just north of the present village a legionary fortress was established in AD 58. Viroconium was built on the site of the legionary fortress after the army left to move north to Chester in c. AD 80, and became the fourth largest town in Roman Britain.

c. **1798** Roman silver and copper coins found in two urns.

>1872 402 Roman *denarii* from the 1st to the 3rdC AD found in a vessel under a bush in a lane. Apparently the finder, Betty Fox, dreamed about the coins in a crock buried by an alder bush beside a lane running from Wroxeter to the Horse Shoe inn at Uckington. When she woke up she went to the spot and found the coins, which she subsequently sold for £28 (the equivalent of £1,300 today).

1914 23 silver and copper-alloy Roman coins from the 1stC BC to the 2ndC AD found during excavation of the Roman town.

[date?] 22 silver and copper-alloy Roman coins and a dragonesque brooch from the 1stC BC to the 2ndC AD found during excavation of the Roman town.

1966 47 Roman billon coins and 26 fragments from the 4thC AD found during excavations of a spoil heap. They were thought to have been concealed c. AD 378.

British Museum

WYRE, WORCESTERSHIRE

1978 219 silver coins from the 15thC found 1ft below the surface during the making of a new lawn at Wyre House.

YARDLEY, BIRMINGHAM

1935 4thC AD Roman copper coins found during building works in Bilton Grange Road. Many coins were dispersed, but 62 were retrieved.

YOXALL, STAFFORDSHIRE

1997 10 silver coins of James II and William III: finder F. Simpson (M/D); thought to have been deposited c. 1697, they were valued at £80.

Potteries Museum and Art Gallery

The laws governing metal detecting in the Republic of Ireland make for an obvious difference with the way the hobby is carried out in Britain. But there is another – the Romans never invaded the island and so typical finds are quite different too. However, there has been, and continues to be, no shortage of remarkable discoveries.

Many of the finds in Ireland, like Scotland, reflect the artistry of Celtic craftsmen. An 8thC brooch found at Bettystown, County Meath, in 1850 and known as the 'Tara Brooch' is among the finest Celtic jewellery ever discovered. Both Queen Victoria and Prince Albert bought copies of it and in so doing helped to fuel the Celtic revival. Another found in Dublin prior to 1700 and known as the Kilmainham Brooch is thought to have been inspired by the opening page of St Luke's Gospel in the *Book of Kells*. (This magnificent example of illumination is on display at Trinity College in Dublin – it is without doubt one of the wonders of the world.) Ireland is also rich in Bronze Age discoveries and the quality of some of the island's gold torcs is simply stunning.

Other finds can be linked to Ireland's troubled history, for example the terrible hardships inflicted by Oliver Cromwell's army in the 17thC, gun money dating from the Battle of the Boyne in 1690 and the 18thC fight for Irish independence.

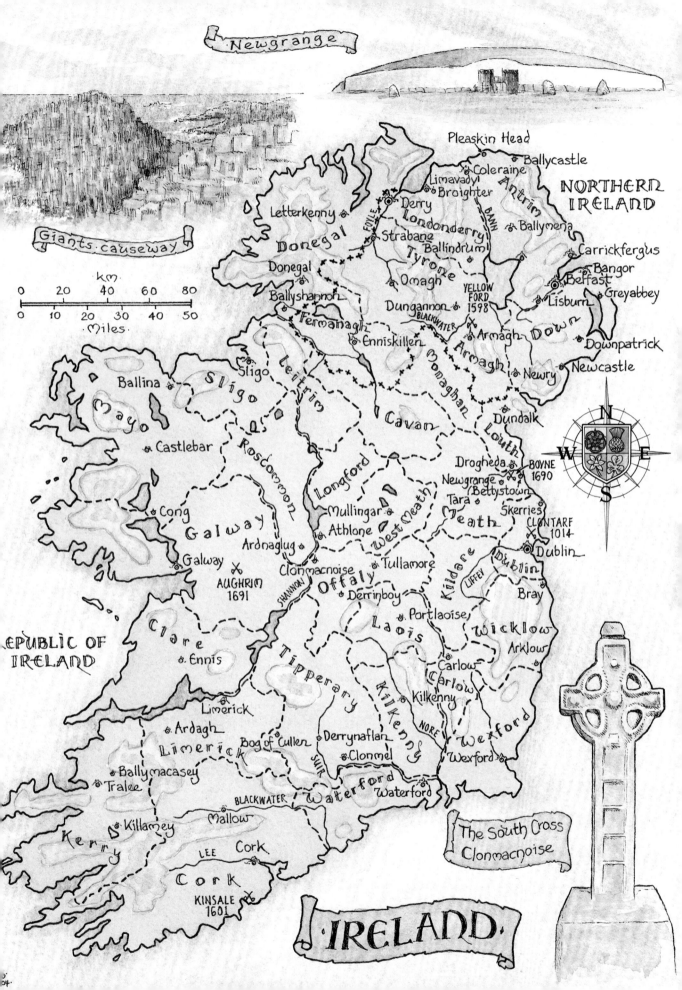

·Newgrange·

Giants·causeway·

km.
0   20   40   60   80
0   10   20   30   40   50
·Miles·

Pleaskin Head

Ballycastle

Coleraine

Limavady   Broighter

Derry   Antrim

NORTHERN
IRELAND

Letterkenny

Donegal

Londonderry

Ballymena

Strabane

Ballindrum

Carrickfergus

Donegal

Tyrone

Bangor

Ballyshannon

Omagh

Dungannon   YELLOW
FORD
1598

Belfast

Greyabbey

BLACKWATER

Lisburn

Fermanagh

Armagh

Down

Enniskillen

Armagh

Downpatrick

Sligo   Leitrim

Monaghan

Newry   Newcastle

Ballina   Sligo

Cavan

Dundalk

Mayo

Roscommon

Louth

Castlebar

Longford

Drogheda   BOYNE
1690

Cong

Newgrange

Bettystown

Galway

Mullingar

Tara   Meath   Skerries

Ardnaglug

Athlone   West Meath

CLONTARF
1014

Galway   AUGHRIM
1691

Clonmacnoise   Tullamore

Dublin   Dublin

SHANNON   Offaly

Derrinboy

Kildare   LIFFEY   Bray

REPUBLIC OF
IRELAND

Clare

Laois

Portlaoise

Wicklow

Ennis

Tipperary

Arklow

Limerick

Kilkenny   Carlow
Carlow

Ardagh

Bog of Culler   Derrynaflan

Kilkenny

NORE   Wexford

Limerick

SUIR   Clonmel

Ballymacasey

Wexford

Tralee

BLACKWATER   Waterford

Waterford

Killarney   Mallow

Kerry   LEE   Cork

The South Cross
Clonmacnoise

Cork

KINSALE
1601

·IRELAND·

Irish Treasure Laws

In 1930 the Irish Government passed the National Monuments Act, which included legislation that covered the excavation, export, as well as the conservation of archaeological objects. The act required that people needed a licence to carry out archaeological work and all finds had to be reported to the national museum. After the proliferation of metal detectors in the 1970s Ireland seemed to have a greater problem in controlling the activities of amateur archaeologists and in 1987 a law was passed making it illegal to search for archaeological objects with a metal detector. This explains why there are so few metal detector finds recorded in the Republic of Ireland.

ABBEYLAND, CASTLEDERMOT, KILDARE

1912   226 silver coins dating from the 16th and 17thC, thought to have been deposited in 1643.

ABBEYLAND, CO. MEATH

1921   474 silver coins dating from the 16th and 17thC, thought to have been deposited in 1645.

ABBEYSHRULE, CO. MEATH

1906   Bronze Age implements found, including the Clonbrin Shield.
National Museum of Ireland

ABBEYSIDE, DUNGANNON, CO. TYRONE

1852   11 gold coins found, dating from the 17th and 18thC.

ADARE, CO. LIMERICK

1834   24 coins found, dating from the Viking era.

AHOGHILL, ANTRIM, BALLYMENA

1849   16thC silver coins, thought to have been deposited c. 1559.

AIRD TOWNLAND AREA, CO. ANTRIM

>1893   6 silver testoons of Mary of Scotland, dated 1556–61, believed to have been deposited c. 1563.

ARBOE AND KILLYCOLPY, CO. TYRONE

Early 1800s   Hoard of gold ear ornaments were found of 800–700 BC.
National Museum of Ireland

ARDAGH, CO. LIMERICK

1868   Anglo-Saxon silver chalice, a smaller bronze chalice and four ornate brooches, dating from c. 800 AD, found by two men digging in a potato field at Reerasta Rath fort. It is thought that the men may have believed that the potatoes would be safe from the blight that had afflicted the crop during the Great Famine. The Ardagh Chalice, which stands 6in high and is made of gold, silver and bronze, is one of Ireland's foremost treasures, as well as one of the finest examples of Anglo-Saxon metalwork ever to have been found. The chalice may have been stolen from Clonmacnois in 1125 by a Viking and buried at the fort. A Mrs Quin rented the land from the Sisters of Mercy and sold the hoard to the Bishop of Limerick for £50; he in turn sold the chalice to the Royal Irish Academy for £500 (the equivalent of around £25,000 today). In *The Treasures of Thomond* by Bishop Newman he reported that in the Earl of Dunraven's papers it was stated that Mrs Quin had found a chalice about 50yd from the fort some time around 1848 but it was lost. 'One day her children took it out of the house to play with and she never saw it again.'

National Museum of Ireland

ARDCRONY, CO. TIPPERARY

1842   Gold collar of 800–700 BC found in a bog.

National Museum of Ireland

ARDGLASS, CO. DOWN

1971   Four silver coins dating from the 16thC, thought to have been deposited *c.* 1540.

ARDNAGLUG, CO. ROSCOMMON

1861   2 gold torcs made from twisted gold and dating from the 3rdC BC found in a bog. Known as the Knock Ribbon Torc it was found by a man who claimed that he found it and a buffer torc in a cavern in Clonmacnoise, Co. Offaly. It was not until 1992 that archaeologists proved that it was found in the bog at Ardnaglug. They assumed that the finder's motives in saying it was found elsewhere was to enable him to continue searching the real site for additional items.

National Museum of Ireland

ARDSTRAW, NEWTOWNSTEWART, CO. TYRONE

1860   150 16thC silver coins, thought to have been concealed in 1593.

ARMAGH, CO. ARMAGH

1831   3 coins dating from the Viking era.

c. **1911**   16th and 17thC silver coins.

1970   8 copper coins of Charles II and James II, dated 1678–86, found during excavation of the Franciscan friary church. They were thought to have been concealed in 1686.

1976   92 silver coins of Henry VIII, Edward VI and Philip and Mary found during archaeological excavations at the Bank of Ireland site in Scotch Street. They were thought to have been deposited after 1555–8.

1976 135 silver coins of Henry VIII, Philip and Mary, and Elizabeth I found behind loose bricks in the remains of a medieval wall in Castle Street. They were thought to have been deposited after 1558–60.

1998 35 silver pennies of Edward I and III (England), and David II and Robert II (Scotland), thought to have been deposited before 1390: finder J.P. Nugent (M/D); valued at £ 1,800.

Ulster Museum

ARMAGH AREA, CO. ARMAGH

1850 16thC copper coins, thought to have been concealed in 1601–2.

1850 16th and 17thC gold coins.

ATHENRY, CO. GALWAY

1964 10 18thC gold coins, thought to have been deposited in 1779, found in the area of Prospect House.

BALBRIGGAN, CO. DUBLIN

1969 Large quantity of gold coins dating from the 19th and 20thC, thought to have been deposited *c.* 1914, found in Drogheda Street.

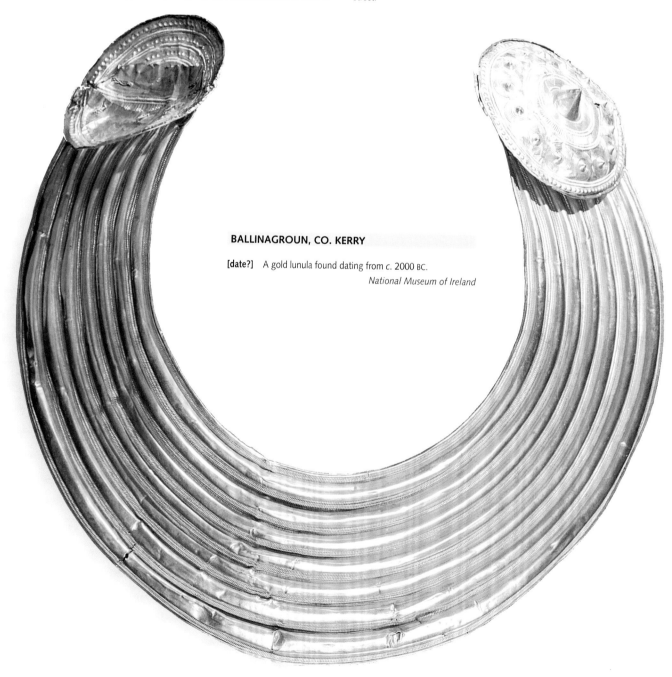

BALLINAGROUN, CO. KERRY

[date?] A gold lunula found dating from *c.* 2000 BC.
National Museum of Ireland

LUNULA

These crescent-shaped beaten gold necklaces are among the most beautiful pieces of craftsmanship to have survived from the Bronze Age. Named for their moon-like shape they were thought to have been used to fasten garments at the neck. Over 80 have been found in Ireland, more than half of which are on display in the National Museum. Others have been found in Europe in places accessible to Ireland and it may be that these are native to Ireland, having found their way to continental Europe by means of trade, or as booty from raids.

BALLINDERRY, CO. WESTMEATH

1928–32 Decorated Viking iron sword dating from the 9th or 10thC found during excavations on a crannog site by the Harvard Archaeological Mission to Ireland. The sword is of Frankish manufacture and is inscribed with the name Ulfberth, its maker. Other finds at the site have included combs, a knife and a pair of linen glass-smoothers.

National Museum of Ireland

BALLINDRUM TOWNLAND, MONEYMORE, CO. LONDONDERRY

1973 39 silver coins dating from the 16thC found in Springhill Forest by two forestry workers at a depth of roughly 15in, during the clearing of roots for a road being built through the forest. The coins were in small piles, and over the years had fused together. They dated from a 1553 English groat of Mary, to an 1594 English sixpence of Elizabeth I and were thought to have been deposited shortly after 1594. They were declared treasure trove and the two finders were awarded the full market value of the coins.

BALLINE, CO. LIMERICK

1940? Hoard of Roman silver objects comprising 4 ingots and hacksilver tableware dating from the late 4thC AD found in gravel pit. The hacksilver is similar to that found at Traprain Law in Scotland.

National Museum of Ireland

BALLINEANIG, CO. KERRY

1964 5 silver groats of Henry VIII found stuck together in a sod of turf; thought to have been concealed after 1544.

BALLINESKER, CO. WEXFORD

1990 Hoard of gold ornaments dating from 900 to 700 BC found in topsoil that had originated in Ballinesker. The first2 gold items were found in a garden at Maudlin town in Co. Wexford. Archaeologists from the National Museum searched the site from where the topsoil came, as well as 8 other locations to which soil had been taken. In all, 2 dress fasteners, a bracelet, 3 ear spools and part of a fourth spool were found at three separate sites.

National Museum of Ireland

BALLINLOUGH, CO. MEATH

c. **1950** 13 16thC silver coins, thought to have been deposited *c.* 1550.

BALLINREA, CO. CORK

1956? Gold ring brooch dating from the 13th or 14thC.

National Museum of Ireland

BALLINREES, CO. LONDONDERRY

1854 1,500–2,000 Roman silver coins and 341oz of silver items dating from the 4th and 5thC AD found by a labourer. The hoard included more than 20 silver lumps or ingots, 6 ornamental pieces for horses and several battleaxes.

BALLINTOGHER, CO. SLIGO

1854 100 gold coins dating from the 18thC.

BALLOO TOWNLAND, CO. ANTRIM

1973 11 silver coins, mainly silver pennies, groats and half-groats of Edward IV and Henry VII, dating from the 16thC found in ditch sludge, during archaeological excavations at Massereene Friary. They were thought to have been deposited *c.* 1501–5.

Ulster Museum

1974   12 Elizabeth I copper pennies of 1601 found during archaeological excavations at Massereene Friary.

BALLYBUNION, CO. KERRY

1839   16th and 17thC silver coins, thought to have been deposited in 1605.

BALLYCASTLE, CO. ANTRIM

1890   70 coins dating from the Viking era found in or around an urn, in an area known as the Trench (which was a Viking burial ground). It comprised English and Irish coins, including a penny of King Edgar of England (957–75), a penny of King Ivarus of Dublin (c. 872), 2 pennies of King Canute of England (1014–39), and 13 pennies of Sithric III, King of Dublin (982–1029).

BALLYCONAGAN, RATHLIN ISLAND, CO. ANTRIM

1931   101 17thC silver coins, thought to have been deposited in 1640.

BALLYCULTER UPPER, CO. DOWN

1979   Bronze Age gold dress fastener found in a potato field on farmland.

BALLYCULTRA, CULTRA, CO. DOWN

1822   More than 3 16thC silver coins, thought to have been deposited in 1580.

BALLYCURRIN, SHRULE, CO. MAYO

1862   16th and 17thC silver coins.

BALLYDEHOB, CO. CORK

1978–9   87 gold sovereigns (possibly 19th or 20thC) found behind a brick, in the fireplace of a cottage by Joseph O'Sullivan, who was carrying out alterations. He kept the coins but they were eventually returned to the cottage owner, William Martin, after a court case in Dublin.

BALLYHARNEY, CO. WESTMEATH

1965?   Bronze sword dating from 900 to 700 BC found during dredging operations on the left bank of the River Inny.

National Museum of Ireland

BALLYHAUNIS, CO. MAYO

1903   Small quantity of 16th–17thC silver coins.

BALLYHOLME, BANGOR, CO. DOWN

1922   17 15th–16thC silver coins, thought to have been deposited c. 1529.

BALLYMACASEY. CO. KERRY

1871   Gold and silver processional cross dating from 1479 found in pieces in a ploughed field. It was made by Irish craftsman William Cornell, and is one of the few that can definitely be so attributed; it

represents workmanship of the highest quality. It was found 2 miles from the Franciscan friary of Lislaughtin, which was destroyed in 1580.

National Museum of Ireland

BALLYMACMORIARTY, DOAGH ISLAND, CO. DONEGAL

c. 1945   5 16thC silver coins, thought to have been deposited in 1573.

BALLYMAHON, CO. MEATH

1840   16thC silver coins, thought to have been deposited c. 1554.

1861?   Bronze bracelet dating from the 2ndC AD found during drainage work at the junction of the Deel and Boyne rivers.

National Museum of Ireland

BALLYMENA, CO. ANTRIM

1846   50 silver coins dating from the 16th and 17thC.

BALLYMONEY, CO. ANTRIM

1853   About 3,600 17thC silver coins, thought to have been deposited c. 1661.

2001   Hoard of 17thC silver coins, including some foreign issues, found sealed in the remains of a leather pouch by workmen during a dig outside the town. They were thought to have been buried c. 1680.

BALLYMOTE, CO. SLIGO

1941   2 silver and 5 copper coins dating from the 17thC, thought to have been deposited in 1694.

BALLYNAGLOGH, CO. ANTRIM

1930?   Late 8th or early 9thC AD silver-gilt and amber penannular brooch found in a bog.

National Museum of Ireland

BALLYNAHINCH, CO. DOWN

c. 1818   19 16thC silver coins, thought to have been deposited c. 1548.

BALLYRASHANE, CO. LONDONDERRY

1835   8 16thC silver coins, thought to have been deposited c. 1559, found beneath some old buildings.

BALLYSAKEERY, CO. MAYO

1950   41 16thC silver coins, thought to have been deposited in 1590.

BALLYSHANNON, CO. DONEGAL

In 1423 the O'Donnells, chieftains of Donegal, built a castle which was the scene of a siege and disastrous defeat of the crown forces by Red Hugh O'Donnell in 1597.

c. 1916   Bronze sword hilt dating from the 1stC BC dredged up from the sea bed by a trawler.

National Museum of Ireland

c. **1965**   15 silver coins dating from the 16th and 17thC, thought to have been deposited in 1603.

BALLYSPELLAN, CO. KILKENNY

1983?   Silver bossed, highly decorated, penannular brooch dating from *c.* AD 900 to 1000.

National Museum of Ireland

BALLYVARLEY, CO. DOWN

1931   20 17thC silver coins, thought to have been deposited in 1677.

BALLYVESEY, CO. ANTRIM

1816   350 17thC silver coins, thought to have been deposited in 1669.

BALTINGLASS, CO. WICKLOW

1882   84 coins dating from the Viking era.

BARNESMORE GAP, CO. DONEGAL

1956?   More than 10 16thC silver coins, thought to have been deposited in 1591.

BELFAST

1861   8 17thC copper coins found in the High Street, thought to have been deposited in 1650.

1960   5 silver coins dating from the 16th and 17thC found at Cave Hill, thought to have been deposited in 1636.

1963   8 silver coins from the 18th and 19thC found at the castle, thought to have been deposited in 1828.

1969   Large quantity of 19thC gold coins found in Christopher Street, thought to have been deposited *c.* 1893.

1993   Solid gold Bronze Age dress fastener found at Cave Hill by James and Alfreda Carson (M/D). It weighed 3oz and was declared treasure trove; the finders received a reward of £18,000.

BELFAST AREA

1840   About 50 16thC silver coins, thought to have been deposited *c.* 1534.

1845   150 silver coins dating from the 16th and 17thC.

1846   50 silver coins dating from the 16th and 17thC.

1848   Small quantity of 16thC silver coins.

1850   1,200 silver coins dating from the 16th and 17thC.

1850   About 5 17thC gold coins.

BELVEDERE, CO. WESTMEATH

1875   2 silver coins dating from the 17thC.

BELVILLE, CO. CAVAN

1852   5 gold bands dating from 2300 to 2100 BC found in the bed of a tributary of the River Erne.

National Museum of Ireland

BETTYSTOWN, CO. MEATH

1850   Early 8thC AD cast and gilt-silver brooch with gold filigree found in a box on the seashore near the Hill of Tara by a peasant woman; it was thought that a cliff fall had deposited the box on the beach. Known as the 'Tara Brooch' it was made around AD 700 and is among the finest Celtic brooches ever found. Unusually it has an intricate design on both the back and the front. The Hill of Tara was traditionally the seat of the kings of Ireland. When the 1851 Crystal Palace Exposition took place, reproductions of the Tara Brooch were offered for sale. Both Queen Victoria and Prince Albert, who had recently bought the Balmoral estate in Scotland, bought copies of the brooch and in so doing helped to fuel the Celtic revival.

National Museum of Ireland

BLESSINGTON, CO. WICKLOW

[date?]   Early Bronze Age gold lunula necklace.

BOG OF ALLEN, CO. KILDARE ▶ ▶ ▶ ▶ ▶ ▶ ▶ ▶ ▶ ▶

[date?]   Gold foil-covered bullae (bulla) dating from 800 to 700 BC.

National Museum of Ireland

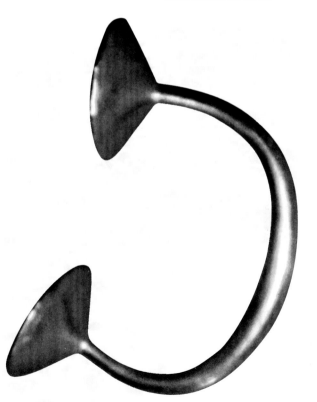

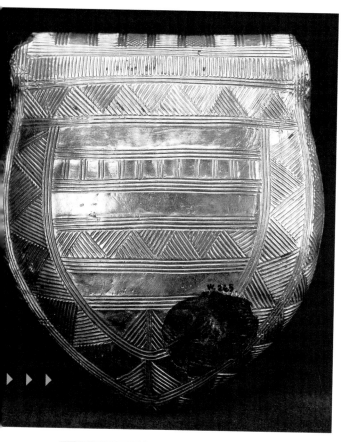

BOG OF CULLEN, CO. TIPPERARY

1800s Over a long period of years peat-cutters found over 40 gold objects, but only one piece has survived. In a letter from the Revd Mr Armstrong, some time around 1750, he tells of a large wooden image found in the bog: 'little pins or pegs were stuck in different parts of it; and . . . the little gold plates found there (4 inches by 3 each), one of which I saw, were suspended by these pegs in different parts of that image.' Subsequently the wooden image became a gatepost and was lost.

BOMACKATALL LOWER, DRUMQUIN, CO. TYRONE

c. **1950** 11 17thC silver coins.

BOOTERSTOWN, CO. DUBLIN

1866 About 610 silver coins dating from the 17thC, thought to have been deposited *c.* 1649.

BORRISNOE, CO. TIPPERARY

1836 Gold torc, known as the Borrisnoe Collar, of 800–700 BC, found under a bog.

National Museum of Ireland

BOYLE, CO. SLIGO

1941 1 silver and 15 copper coins dating from the 17thC.

BRAY, CO. WICKLOW

1834 Several 2ndC AD Roman coins, together with several human skeletons, found by workmen levelling a bank of sand near the sea.

1981 5 silver pennies of Edward I (1272–1307) found near a cliff-top edge, south of Bray Head by Christopher Kearney.

1981–2 11 silver shillings and sixpences of Elizabeth I (1558–1603) found in a landslide from the cliffs by Christopher Kearney (M/D).

1985 26 silver coins dated 1558–1603 found on the cliff top at Bray Head: finder John O'Toole (M/D). These hammered coins comprised 11 shillings, 11 sixpences, a threepence, 2 groats, and a fourpence.

1986 3 gold coins of George III dating from 1797 found by Ann O'Higgins while turning over the soil in a flower bed in her back garden.

BRAY AREA, CO. WICKLOW

1986 321 Elizabethan sixpences and 79 shillings, dated 1560–1601, found by John O'Toole (M/D) on a building site. A tentative value of £8,000 was put on the hoard, which equates to about £14,500 today.

BETWEEN BRAY AND GREYSTONES, CO. WICKLOW

1986 162 silver coins from the 16thC comprising 2 Spanish reals, 2 Queen Mary groats, 1 Phillip and Mary shilling, 45 Elizabeth I shillings, 98 Elizabeth I sixpences, and 8 shillings, 2 sixpences, and 4 Irish shillings of James I were found by Christopher Kearney (M/D) on the cliff tops. The coins were at a depth of about 18in and in a pile measuring about 3in across.

BRIGHT, INISHOWEN, CO. DONEGAL

1848 1,680 16thC silver coins, thought to have been deposited *c.* 1559.

BROIGHTER, CO. LONDONDERRY

1896 Hoard of gold objects dating from the 1stC BC found by a farmer while ploughing, near the shore of Lough Foyle. The hoard comprised a model boat with fittings, a bowl, 2 neck chains, 2 twisted bar torcs, and a large decorated buffer torc. The hoard was found in a floodplain and is believed to have been used as a votive offering to a Celtic sea god. There were persistent rumours that part of the Broighter Hoard had been found in an umbrella and had perhaps been deposited by robbers, but recent analysis has proved their authenticity. There have also been conflicting opinions about where the items were made but scholars now agree that they were all produced in Ireland.

National Museum of Ireland

BULLOCK, DALKEY, CO. DUBLIN

1838 3 silver coins of Eadgar (*c.* 970); two years later 65 more silver coins of Eadgar came to light.

BURT, CO. DONEGAL

[date?] 11 Anglo-Saxon silver pennies of King Eadgar dated 957–65 found beneath a stone during the construction of the Letterkenny railway.

BUSHMILLS AREA, CO. ANTRIM

1827   About 300 Roman silver coins dating from the 1st and 2ndC AD found at Flower Hill by Alexander McKinlay, who concealed them and disposed of all but two of them over a protracted period.

CAHERCIVEEN, CO. KERRY

1868   55 silver groats and half-groats of Edward III, Henry VI, Edward IV, Richard III and Henry VII found, thought to have been deposited c. 1495.

CALEDON, CO. TYRONE

1851   Small quantity of silver coins dating from the 15th and 16thC found, thought to have been deposited c. 1529.

1900   16thC silver coins, thought to have been deposited in 1594.

CALEDON AREA, CO. TYRONE

1751   More than 100 16thC coins found in a bag, thought to have been deposited after 1596.

CALLAN AREA, CO. KILKENNY

[date?]   Silver cross pendant dating from c. 1500 found in an old church near Callan.

National Museum of Ireland

CAMOLIN, CO. WEXFORD

1913   77 17thC silver coins found, possibly deposited in 1644.

CO. CARLOW

1918   55 17thC gold coins.

CARNEARNY TOWNLAND, CO. ANTRIM

1974   14 silver shillings and sixpences dating from 1558 to 1619 found during drainage operations on farmland. There were 2 Irish shillings, 4 English shillings, and 1 English sixpence of James I, and 3 English shillings and 4 English sixpences of Elizabeth I. They were found over an area of roughly 1 sq. yd and no container of any type was evident. 1 sixpence dated 1604 was in practically mint condition, which was amazing considering they were deposited sometime shortly after 1607.

CARNTALL HILL, CARNMONEY, CO. ANTRIM

1835   17thC silver coins.

CARRICKABWEEHAN TOWNLAND, CO. FERMANAGH

1975   4 silver groats of Henry VIII found in a well.

CARRICKATLIEVE, CO. DONEGAL

1962   11 17thC silver coins, thought to have been deposited c. 1645.

CARRICKFERGUS, CO. ANTRIM

1855   About 360 silver groats and shillings of Elizabeth, Mary and Philip, weighing about 3lb, were found in North Street, thought to have been hidden c. 1559.

1895   4 silver coins of Henry VIII, Elizabeth, Mary and Philip found in North Street, thought to have been hidden c. 1559.

1903   15 silver coins dating from the 16thC that included coins of Mary and Philip, and an Irish sixpence of Edward IV, found in North Street; they were thought to have been hidden c. 1559.

1903   Over 150 14thC silver coins found by workmen clearing a site in Trooper's Lane. The hoard included coins of Edward III (1327–77), silver halfpennies, pennies, and groats, pennies minted in Scotland for Robert the Bruce, and a silver denier from Poitiers for Edward the Black Prince, son of Edward III. There were also some Irish coins from Dublin.

1909   12 silver coins dating from the 18thC found in St Nicholas churchyard.

1910   50–60 Anglo-Irish silver coins of Elizabeth, Mary and Philip found in Governor's Place, North Street; they were thought to have been hidden c. 1559.

1975   4 Nuremberg jettons dating from the late 16thC found during the laying out of a park in Market Place.

Carrickfergus Museum

JETTONS

These coin-like counters were used in the calculation of accounts and had no monetary value. They were mostly made of brass or copper but some silver ones appeared in the 17thC. English jettons first appeared in the reign of Edward I but by the mid-16thC the most frequently used came from Nuremberg. Jettons were often used as counters for various games from the 15thC onwards.

CARRIGTWOHILL, CO. CORK

1955   58 silver coins dating from the 16th and 17thC, thought to have been deposited in 1639, found near Barryscourt Castle. The castle was taken by Lord Inchiquin on 7 May 1645 by quarter. This may have been when the coins were hidden.

CARROWEN, CO. DONEGAL

1863   11 coins dating from the Viking era.

CASHEL, CO. TIPPERARY

1998   9thC zoomorphic penannular brooch found in a pocket of gravel at an excavation at the sewage works.

CASHELTOWN, CO. ANTRIM

1937   181 16thC silver coins, thought to have been deposited in 1592.

CASTLE ARCHDALE, CO. FERMANAGH

[date?]   5 Ptolemaic bronzes and 4 billon tetra*drachm*s from Roman Egypt found in a leather bag, thought to have been concealed between 1850 and 1950.

CASTLE BERNARD, CO. OFFALY

1851   8 17thC silver coins.

CASTLE ENIGAN, CO. DOWN

1814   About 200 14thC coins found inside a cow's horn. The coins were of Robert Bruce, his grandfather David, and Edward I.

CASTLEBROOK AREA, CO. DUBLIN

1978   22 16thC iron spearheads.

CASTLEDERG, CO. TYRONE

1933?   Bronze cauldron of 700–600 BC found in a bog. This is a superb example of the technical brilliance of the metalworkers of this period. Made from sheet bronze, it has a decorative rivet pattern and may have originated in the eastern Mediterranean; it is one of around 30 to have been found in Ireland.

National Museum of Ireland

CASTLEDERG AREA, CO. TYRONE

1888   6 17thC silver coins, thought to have been deposited in 1696.

CASTLEFINN, GORTNAGRACE, CO. DONEGAL

1962   Small quantity of 17thC copper coins, thought to have been deposited in 1685.

CASTLEGAL, CO. SLIGO

1876   Small quantity of 17thC silver coins, thought to have been deposited *c*. 1649.

CASTLEKELLY AREA, CO. ROSCOMMON

1819   Gold dress fastener with very large hollow circular terminals and a short handle, dating from 900 to 700 BC, found about 20ft below the surface, in gravel under a bog.

National Museum of Ireland

CASTLEREAGH, CO. DOWN

1844   150 17thC silver coins .

CASTLETOWN KILPATRICK, CO. MEATH

1848   2 decorated silver pins from the late 4th or early 5thC AD.

National Museum of Ireland

CASTLETOWN MOUNT, CO. LOUTH

1984   12th or 13thC gold finger-ring, decorated with a diamond-shaped bezel. The Normans arrived in Ireland in 1169 and in 1185 a Norman noble, Bertrum De Verdon, erected a manor house at Castletown Mount.

National Museum of Ireland

CASTLETOWNROCHE, CO. CORK

1847   Large quantity of 17thC silver coins.

CO. CAVAN

1853   Late 8th or early 9thC AD cast and silver-gilt annular brooch with gold filigree, known as the Queen's Brooch. A replica of this brooch was given to Queen Victoria during her visit to the Great Exhibition in Dublin in 1853.

National Museum of Ireland

CELBRIDGE, CO. KILDARE

>1920   Silver-gilt thistle brooch dating from the late 9th or early 10thC.

National Museum of Ireland

CLANDALKIN, CO. DUBLIN

1830   Large quantity of Viking-era coins.

CLARE CASTLE, LISSANE, CO. CLARE

1958   1 gold and 14 silver coins dating from the 17thC , thought to have been deposited in 1633.

CLAREMONT, CO. DUBLIN

1838   9 coins dating from the Viking era.

CLOGHEEN, CO. TIPPERARY

1847   40 silver coins dating from the 15th and 16thC found, thought to have been deposited *c*. 1536.

CLONARD, CO. MEATH

1839   17thC silver and copper coins found, thought to have been deposited *c*. 1690.

CLONASLEE, CO. LAOIS

1948   2 gold and 1 silver coin dating from the 18thC, thought to have been deposited in 1720.

CLONBULLOGE, CO. OFFALY

1968   60 16thC silver coins, thought to have been deposited in 1596, found in Cloncreen bog.

CLONCA, CO. DONEGAL

1849   Large quantity of silver coins dating from the 15th and 16thC, thought to have been deposited *c*. 1529.

CLONES AREA, CO. MONAGHAN

1820   Gold dress fastener dating from 900 to 700 BC.

National Museum of Ireland

CLONMEL AREA, CO. TIPPERARY

1981 12 Viking silver and 2 pewter pieces dating from the 9th or 10thC found on farmland.

CLOONCAM, DRUMOD, CO. LEITRIM

1951 15 16thC silver coins, thought to have been deposited c. 1529.

CLOONFAD, CO. ROSCOMMON

1887 40 17thC silver coins.

CLOONSHARRAGH, CLOGHANE, CO. KERRY

1847 35 silver coins dating from the 15th and 16thC, thought to have been deposited c. 1529.

CLOUGHJORDAN AREA, CO. TIPPERARY

1885 31 silver coins dating from the late 15thC.

COLERAINE, CO. LONDONDERRY

1843 16thC silver coins.

1854 1,506 Roman coins, silver tableware, and ingots dating from the 4th and 5thC AD found in a pot by men digging a ditch. Unusually, among the coins were some of Constantine III (AD 408–11). The entire hoard stretched from Constantius II (AD 337–61) to Honorius (AD 395–423). It is thought that the coins and the silver were taken back to Ireland by compatriots of King Niall, who plundered both mainland Britain and France.

2001 13th or 14thC highly decorated gold brooch found by archaeologist Ann Marie Denvir during excavations on the site of the Baptist church; the brooch was declared treasure trove.

Ulster Museum

COLERAINE AREA, CO. LONDONDERRY

1841 137 16thC silver coins, thought to have been deposited c. 1559.

COLLIGAN, DUNGARVAN, CO. WATERFORD

1841 More than 100 16thC silver coins, thought to have been deposited in 1580.

COLMANSTOWN, CO. GALWAY

1942 321 17thC silver coins, thought to have been deposited around 1645.

COMBER, CO. DOWN

1847 30 silver coins dating from the 16th and 17thC.

CONG, CO. MAYO

[date?] An early 12thC large processional cross, decorated with gold filigree, a large rock crystal, niello and blue and white glass bosses, was found. Known as the Cross of Cong it stands 30in high and is one of Ireland's foremost treasures. In the middle of the cross is a large polished crystal, under which was a relic sent from Rome to King Turloch O'Conor, in 1123, according to the *Annals of Innisfallen*: 'A bit of the true cross came into Ireland and was enshrined at Roscommon by Turloch O'Conor.' How it ended up at Cong Abbey is unclear, as is what happened to it from around the mid-1300s to 1839, when it was bought and presented to the Royal Irish Academy. Local stories have it residing beneath the altar in an iron box.

National Museum of Ireland

COOLNACRAN TOWNLAND, CO. ARMAGH

2001 3 silver groats and 2 half-groats dating from the 14thC found by Tom Crawford (M/D); they were thought to have been deposited c. 1380–90.

Ulster Museum

CORBETSTOWN, CO. WESTMEATH

c. **1870** 28 silver halfpennies, pennies, half-groats and groats of Edward I, II and III, and David II of Scotland, thought to have been concealed c. 1365.

CORK CITY AREA, CO. CORK

1837 Large quantity of 16thC silver coins, thought to have been deposited c. 1559.

CORNAMAGH, ATHLONE, CO. WESTMEATH

1835 Large quantity of 17thC silver coins, thought to have been deposited in 1679.

COROFIN, CO. GALWAY

1953 65 silver coins dating from the 16th and 17thC, thought to have been deposited in 1639.

COURTOWN, CO. KILKENNY

1862   Copper coins dating from the late 17thC found in a leather purse. Some of the coins were 'Gun Money', half-crowns of James II. When James II fled to France in 1688 he decided to return early in 1689 to claim the throne from William III. James landed at Kinsale in Co. Cork to rally a Catholic army from local Irish supporters along with the Frenchmen who came with him. Because there was a lack of precious metal James had to strike brass coins in Dublin and Limerick and these 'tokens' were known as Gun Money. After James was defeated at the Battle of the Boyne the Gun Money was devalued by William, making the £22,500 (the equivalent of £2.7 million today) that had been struck worth just £600 (£73,000 today).

CREGGS AREA, CO. GALWAY

1895   22 silver coins dating from the 16thC, thought to have been deposited in 1590, found in Cloncanny bog.

CRUMLIN, CO. ANTRIM

1911   95 17thC silver coins.

1937   11 18thC gold coins, thought to have been deposited in 1791.

CUILLEENOOLAGH, CO. ROSCOMMON

1943   55 silver coins, shillings and sixpences of Philip and Mary, and Elizabeth I, found during the digging of a stubble field, thought to have been concealed in 1602.

CURRYGRAN LAKE, CO. LONGFORD

1896   Silver coins of Elizabeth I and Philip and Mary, thought to have been deposited after 1596.

CUSHENDALL, CO. ANTRIM

1849   2 coins from the Viking era.

DALKEY, CO. DUBLIN

1840   80 coins from the Viking era.

DELGANY, CO. WICKLOW

1874   115 coins from the Viking era.

DERAMFIELD, BELTURBET, CO. CAVAN

c. **1943**   14 silver coins dating from the 16th and 17thC, thought to have been deposited in 1643.

DERRINBOY, CO. OFFALY

1959   Hoard of Bronze Age gold ornaments of 1200–1000 BC found 12ft deep during turf-cutting. It included five objects surrounded by copper wire. There were two gold armlets that demonstrated outstanding craftsmanship, made of heavy gold sheets, 2 gold tress rings, and a neck-ring. It is thought the objects were related to a funeral of an important individual.

National Museum of Ireland

DERRY CITY, CO. LONDONDERRY

1825   12 17thC silver coins, thought to have been deposited in 1678, found in the Prehen area.

1843   15th and 16thC silver coins, thought to have been deposited *c.* 1529.

DERRYAD, LISNASKEA, CO. FERMANAGH

1976   58 silver coins of Victoria and George V, dated 1845–1916, found in 2 tins, in an internal wall of a farmhouse.

DERRYGORRY WOOD, CO. MONAGHAN

1956   23 17thC silver coins , thought to have been deposited *c.* 1645.

DERRYKEIGHAN, CO. ANTRIM

1843   280 coins from the Viking era.

DERRYLIN, KNOCKNINNY, CO. FERMANAGH

1938   Large quantity of 18thC gold coins.

DERRYMORE, CO. WESTMEATH

1872   11 coins from the Viking era.

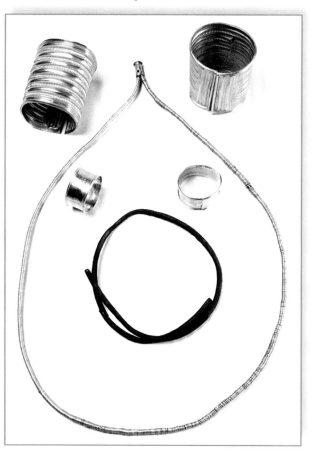

DERRYNAFLAN, CO. TIPPERARY

1980 The hoard comprised a silver chalice, a silver paten with stand, and a copper-alloy strainer/ladle, all covered by a plain copper-alloy basin and dating from the late 8th to the 9thC, found on the site of a monastery by Michael Webb and his son Michael, using metal detectors on land where they had not received permission to search. A court case followed, at which the Webbs argued that they should receive £25,000, as the landowners had done, when all they received was £10,000; they won their case.

National Museum of Ireland

DOOEY, LETTERMACAWARD, CO. DONEGAL

1957 50 17thC silver coins.

DOON CASTLE, CO. OFFALY

Late 1850s 17thC copper coins, including some James II gun money, found near the entrance of an underground passage.

DOOYORK, CO. MAYO

2001–2 2 gold torcs of 300 BC–AD 200 found by P.J. Deane while walking on Geesala beach. A team from the National Museum visited

DERRYVILLE, PORTARLINGTON, CO. OFFLAY

1946–8 105 gold and 5 silver coins dating from the 17thC, thought to have been deposited in 1651.

DERVOCK, CO. ANTRIM

1877 More than 77 16thC silver coins, thought to have been deposited in 1594.

DONERAILE, CO. CORK

1853 About 450 silver coins dating from the 16th and 17thC, thought to have been deposited in 1610.

the site and found another torc, 7 amber beads, and 2 bronze bracelets, along with some fragments.

National Museum of Ireland

DOWNPATRICK, CO. DOWN

1808 About 2,500 17thC silver coins.

1809 Large quantity of silver coins dating from the 15th and 16thC, thought to have been deposited c. 1529.

DOWNPATRICK AREA, CO. DOWN

1820 12 16thC silver coins, thought to have been deposited c. 1559.

c. **1900**   13 16thC silver coins, thought to have been deposited in 1593.

DOWRIS, CO. OFFALY

c. **1825**   200 bronze objects dating from 800 to 600 BC found by two men who were trenching potatoes on the shore of Lough Coura. Some 190 of the pieces have been saved; there are 111 in the National Museum of Ireland and 79 in the British Museum. The hoard included 44 spearheads, 43 axes, 24 trumpets, 44 crotal bells, 5 swords, tools, a bronze bucket made from sheet bronze riveted together and 2 other buckets. The objects were removed and collected by the Earl of Rosse and T.D. Cooke, who in 1848 reported the find to the Royal Irish Academy.

National Museum of Ireland

DREMINSTOWN, CO. MEATH

1970   1 silver and 47 billon coins dating from the 19thC, thought to have been deposited after 1870.

DROMARA, CO. DOWN

1940   A considerable quantity of silver coins dated 1880–1930 found in the chimney piece of a cottage, near Stewart's Corner.

DROMKEEN WEST, CAUSEWAY, CO. KERRY

1961   35 gun money coins, thought to have been deposited after May 1690.

DROMORE, CO. DOWN

1844   About 200 17thC silver coins.

DRUMENAGH, MAGHERAFELT, CO. LONDONDERRY

1955   132 17thC silver coins, thought to have been deposited in 1641.

DUBLIN

>late 1700s   Late 8th or possibly early 9thC AD penannular brooch made of cast and gilt silver, with gold filigree and red enamel. It has become known as the Kilmainham Brooch and it has been suggested that the terminals are similar to the opening page of St Luke's Gospel in the Book of Kells. It is thought to have been found in a Viking burial in the Kilmainham area of the city.

National Museum of Ireland

1771   About 3,000 coins dating from the late 17thC found in an iron chest in the foundations of a wall at St Mary's Abbey, thought to have been concealed in the late 17thC.

1832   4 silver coins, thought to have been deposited *c.* 1546.

1923   100 17thC silver coins found in Harristown.

1968   413 gold coins dating from the 19th and early 20thC found in the Ballsbridge area, thought to have been deposited in 1909.

>1979   Hoard of Anglo-Irish coins, mostly halfpennies but including 5 farthing coins, found in a pint-sized meal container in the Loughlinstown area.

[date?]   13th or 14thC gold ring brooch found in Marlborough Street.

National Museum of Ireland

1986   400 Elizabethan silver coins found by a metal detectorist.

DUNBOYNE, CO. MEATH

c. **1942**   17thC copper coins, thought to have been deposited in 1690.

DUNBRODY, CO. WEXFORD

1836   1,400–1,600 11thC silver coins, thought to have been deposited *c.* 1050.

DUNDALK AREA, CO. LOUTH

1980–1   8 silver Anglo-Saxon coins of King Athelred (978–1016) found when a JCB operator, preparing a building site for a new factory, noticed the outline of an underground passage. An archaeological team were called in, and during the four-day excavation the coins were found.

DUNDONALD, CO. DOWN

1928   32 17thC silver coins, thought to have been deposited in 1676, found in the Churchquarter area.

DUNDRUM, CO. DUBLIN

c. **1885**   200 17thC copper coins, thought to have been deposited *c.* 1690.

1895   650 17thC copper coins, thought to have been deposited *c.* 1690.

DUNMORE CAVE, CO. KILKENNY

1973   9 silver coins, thought to have been concealed *c.* AD 929.

1999   Hoard of silver and bronze artefacts dating from the late 10thC AD, including 7 silver cones (buttons), Anglo-Saxon silver pennies and bracelets, hacksilver, bent bars, and bronzes.

National Museum of Ireland

DURROW, CO. OFFALY

>1850   11 silver coins dating from the 10thC, thought to have been deposited *c.* 940.

National Museum of Ireland

ELLISTOWN, RATHANGAN, CO. KILDARE

1945   30 silver coins from 16th and 17thC, possibly deposited in 1607.

ENNIS, CO. CLARE

1855?   16thC silver coins.

ENNISKILLEN AREA, CO. FERMANAGH

1975   4 16thC coins found by a schoolboy in a pond used by cattle as a watering hole. Local people used to throw coins into this pond for good luck, and the boy's mother, being superstitious, made him throw them back in. They were never recovered, but according to the description given by the boy, it is supposed that the coins were of King Henry VIII.

ESKRAGH, CO. TYRONE

1894   Small quantity of 18thC copper coins.

FENNOR, CO. MEATH

1869   2 coins dating from the Viking era.

FERBANE, CO. OFFLAY

2000   6thC crozier, stuck vertically in the mud, was discovered by Ellen O'Carroll of the Archaeological Development Services. Broken into several pieces, it was about 4ft in length, probably carved from a single bow of cherry wood. It is probably the earliest example and was dated by dendrochronology to AD 596. It was found next to a raised oak pathway above the surface of the bog that connected Killiaghintober to Leamanaghan Island, where St Manchan's church had stood.

FERMOY, CO. CORK

1839   180 16thC silver coins, thought to have been deposited in 1594.

FETHARD, CO. TIPPERARY

1825–37   17thC gold and silver coins. In 1650, Oliver Cromwell arrived in Fethard on his way to take Kilkenny. He wrote to the Speaker of the House of Commons in London about the town 'as having a very good wall with round and square bulwarks, after the old manner of fortification'. He stationed his troops 'in an old abbey in the suburbs', while he agreed the town's surrender.

FINGLAS, CO. DUBLIN

2004   A 10thC brooch was discovered along with the remains of a woman while building work was being carried out near the ruins of St Canice's Church. Archaeologists also discovered the closing ditch of the Finglas monastery, wells and defensive ramparts. It is believed that Finglas acted as a kind of 'buffer zone' between Viking Dublin and the surrounding Gaelic kingdoms. It is thought that the town traded with the Vikings, making it an important area for potential finds; although reports suggest an unsympathetic local council towards archaeology.

FORE, MOORETOWN, CO. WESTMEATH

1988   A 2ndC BC bronze bowl found at the burial site containing the cremated remains of an adult male within an inland promontory fort.

National Museum of Ireland

FOUNTAINSTOWN, CO. CORK

1835   17thC copper coins, thought to have been deposited in 1646.

FOURKNOCKS, CO. MEATH

1950   29 coins of the Viking age.

CO. GALWAY

[date?]   An elaborate Irish-Viking silver penannular brooch dating from the late 9th or early 10thC.

British Museum

GALWAY CITY, CO. GALWAY

1904   8 17thC silver coins, thought to have been deposited *c.* 1645.

GALWAY AREA, CO. GALWAY

1980   2 canoes, about 2,000 years old, found in the bed of the River Corrib. Inside the canoes were forks, a reaping hook, a sword, and a musket dating from the Iron Age to early medieval times.

GARVAGH, CO. LONDONDERRY

1958   36 gold coins dating from the 19th and early 20thC, thought to have been deposited in 1911.

GEASHILL, CO. OFFALY

1862   5 coins from the Viking era.

GILFORD, CO. DOWN

1779   13thC silver pennies found in a clay pot in earthworks.

GLANMIRE, CO. CORK

1847   16thC silver coins.

GLASLOUGH, CO. MONAGHAN

1860   23 16thC silver coins, thought to have been deposited in 1590.

GLENARM, CO. ANTRIM

c. **1950**   Small quantity of 16thC silver coins.

GLENAVY, CO. ANTRIM

1954   32 18thC gold coins, thought to have been deposited in 1794.

GLENDALOUGH, CO. WICKLOW

1821   50 coins from the Viking era.

GLENGEEN, CO. TYRONE

>1945   10 English silver shillings and sixpences dated 1561–1638 found in a cloth bag during peat-cutting. There were 4 shillings and 4 sixpences of Elizabeth I, 1 sixpence of James I, and 1 shilling of Charles I; most of the coins were worn and were thought to have been deposited after 1638.

GLENINSHEEN, CO. CLARE

1932   Gold collar, or gorget, dating from 800 to 700 BC, found in a cleft in the rock on the Burren (an area of 300 sq kms or 115 sq miles that looks like a lunar landscape). The Gleninsheen Collar is 12¼in long: finder Paddy Nolan, a farmer.

National Museum of Ireland

GLENNAMADDY, CO. GALWAY

1957   17thC silver coins.

GORTALOWRY, COOKSTOWN, CO. TYRONE

1959   11 16th and 17thC silver coins, thought to have been deposited in 1639.

GORTEENREAGH, CO. CLARE

1948   Hoard of gold objects of 800–700 BC found by a man clearing stones from a field. The hoard comprised a collar (which was in pieces), 2 lock-rings, 2 bracelets and an ear ornament.

National Museum of Ireland

GOWRAN, CO. KILKENNY

1855   500 17thC silver coins found in Castle Ellis Road.

GREYABBEY, CO. DOWN

The Cistercian abbey was founded in 1193 by Affreca, daughter of Godred, the King of the Isle of Man. She married John de Courcy, the Somerset knight who conquered Ulster. It was the first complete Gothic-style building in Ireland, with almost every window, arch and door pointed, not rounded, a style introduced by the monks, who came from Holm Cultram in Cumbria.

1795   16 16thC silver coins, thought to have been deposited *c.* 1559.

c. **1812**   6 16thC silver coins, thought to have been deposited *c.* 1548.

1858   4 silver coins dating from the 16thC, thought to have been deposited in 1584.

1966   8 copper coins dating from the 18th and 19thC, thought to have been deposited in 1826.

GRIFFINSTOWN, CO. WESTMEATH

c. **1837**   17thC silver coins, thought to have been deposited *c.* 1649.

HARE ISLAND, LOUGH REE, CO. WESTMEATH

1802   10 gold arm-rings dating from the late 10th to the early 11thC. They weighed about 11lb and were melted down soon after discovery.

HAUGHEY'S FORT, CO. ARMAGH

[date?]   Pieces of scrap gold dating from *c.* 1260 to 910 BC found in the fill of a number of pits during archaeological excavation.

HILLSBOROUGH, CO. DOWN

1743   Large quantity of 17thC silver coins.

ISLANDMAGEE, CO. ANTRIM

1920–30   4 or 5 silver coins of William and Mary, dated 1689–94, found during the construction of Gobbins Road.

KANTURK, CO. CORK

1971   9 silver and 9 copper coins from the 19thC, thought to have been deposited in 1881, found in Greenfield Road.

KESHCARRIGAN, CO. LEITRIM

1852?   Early 1stC BC bronze bowl found in a stretch of water between Lough Scur and Lough Marrive

National Museum of Ireland

KILBRIDE, CO. MAYO

>1988   2 bronze socketed axes, a gold bracelet and a gold dress fastener of 800–700 BC found by workmen removing rocks from the land of John Dyra on Drumlin hill. The Dyra Hoard, as it is known, was buried under a large rock over 3ft tall.

National Museum of Ireland

KILCLIEF, CO. DOWN

1999   5 silver pennies of Edward I, and a halfpenny of John as Lord (Ireland) were found by Gerald McQuoid (M/D) near the 15thC Kilclief Castle; thought to have been deposited *c.* 1320–50.

KILDARE, CO. KILDARE

1840   6 coins dating from the Viking era.

1923   34 coins dating from the Viking era.

KILGORMAN, CO. WEXFORD

1865   459 silver coins from the 15th and 16thC, thought to have been deposited *c.* 1529.

KILKENNY, CO. KILKENNY

1792   Large quantity of coins dating from the Viking era.

1819   17thC silver coins.

KILKENNY AREA, CO. KILKENNY

1852   6 17thC silver coins.

KILLALA AREA, CO. MAYO

c. **1965**   10 George III Bank of Ireland silver coins, dated 1805–13, found in a ruined cottage.

KILLAMERY, CO. KILKENNY

1980s?   Early 9thC AD pseudo-penannular silver, gold and glass brooch. This brooch has become known as the Killamery Brooch and is the earliest pseudo-penannular brooch to be found; they became popular in the 9thC. With its animal designs on the back of the brooch and the elongated pin, it is very different from earlier examples and shows the influence of the Vikings, who brought silver to Ireland and created trade routes.

National Museum of Ireland

KILLARNEY AREA, CO. KERRY

Late 1700s Gold lunula of *c.* 2000 BC.

National Museum of Ireland

KILLEAGH, CO. CORK

1839   16thC coins.

KILLENAULE AREA, CO. TIPPERARY

Hoard of Viking silver found at Rathmoley Fort, which is a complete double-ring fort.

National Museum of Ireland

KILLISKEY, CO. WICKLOW

c. **1837**   17thC silver coins.

KILLYLEA, CO. ARMAGH

1852   400 17thC silver coins.

KILLYMOON, CO. TYRONE

1816   Gold dress fastener of 900–700 BC found in a carved alder wood box in a bog.

National Museum of Ireland

KILLYMORGAN, CO. TYRONE

c. **1900**   7 16thC silver coins, thought to have been deposited in 1593.

KILLYON MANOR, NAVAN, CO. MEATH

1876   88 coins from the Viking era found at Killyon Manor.

KILMARONEY, CO. LAOIS

1786   Large quantity of Viking-era coins.

KILMORE, CO. CAVAN

c. **1863**   Bronze seal matrix of Bishop Hugh O'Reilly found in the parish.

KILMOYLEY NORTH, CO. KELLY

1940   3 gold bracelets and dress fastener dating from 900 to 700 BC found in an oak box in a bog; the box didn't survive.

National Museum of Ireland

KILROOT, CO. ANTRIM

c. **1845**   4 silver coins of the 16th and 17thC, thought to have been deposited in 1609.

KILSKEERY EAST, CO. TYRONE

1862   3 17thC silver coins, thought to have been deposited in 1676.

KILWAUGHTER, CO. ANTRIM

1894   3 silver and 6 copper coins of the 17thC, thought to have been deposited in 1687.

1934   Small quantity of 16th and 17thC silver coins, thought to have been deposited in 1632.

KINCASLOUGH, CO. DONEGAL

c. **1943**   34 17thC silver coins, thought to have been deposited in 1638.

KIRKHILL, CO. ANTRIM

2001   22 silver coins of the 16th and 17thC found while digging a pit for a cattle-grid: finder Michael Miller and George Henry.

Ulster Museum

KNOCKNABOUL, CO. LIMERICK

1943   More than 117 16thC silver coins, thought to have been deposited in 1585.

KNOWTH, CO. MEATH

1969   2 coins from the Viking era.

LACKEN, CO. KILKENNY

1868   About 50 silver groats and pennies from the late 14thC.

LAGHY, CO. DONEGAL

c. **1907**   More than 24 17thC silver coins, thought to have been deposited *c.* 1641.

LAMBAY ISLAND, CO. DUBLIN

Mid-1800s   Gold band of AD 50–100, possibly a head-dress, found with an iron sword in an ancient burial site during harbour works.

National Museum of Ireland

LATTOON, CO. CAVAN

1919 2 dress fasteners, 2 bracelets and a disc, all made of gold and dating from 900 to 700 BC found deep in a bog.

National Museum of Ireland

LAURENCETOWN, CO. DOWN

1876 400 17thC silver coins.

LEGGAGH, CO. MEATH

c. **1843** 10 silver coins and some ingots of silver dating from AD 925 or earlier.

National Museum of Ireland

LIMAVADY AREA, CO. LONDONDERRY

1896 A collection of gold objects dating from the 1stC BC, made up of a buffer collar, a small boat with oars, a bowl, 2 bracelets and 2 neck-laces, found by two ploughmen, Tom Nicholl and James Morrow. They were working for a local farmer when the plough hit something hard; it was only when they took them back to the farmhouse and washed them that they realised what they really were. The farmer sold the hoard to a Mr Day for £200 (£13,000 in today's money), who realised that one of the boat's seats was missing and initiated a search, but to no avail. Later one of the ploughmen found the seat and sold it to a jeweller in Limavady. Later still Mr Day sold the objects to the British Museum for £600 (the equivalent of almost £40,000 today). In 1903 the Royal Irish Academy claimed the hoard was treasure trove and in June a four-day court case took place at which the British Museum argued it was a votive offering and therefore the owners had no inten-tion of recovering the items, meaning they were not treasure trove. The crown argued the opposite case, and the judge agreed, ordering the British Museum to hand them over to King Edward VII. In his summing-up the judge said, 'The court had been occupied for some considerable time in listening to fanciful suggestions more suited to the poem of a Celtic bard than to the prose of a legal reporter.' The King decided that the hoard should be returned to Ireland. In 2000 the National Museum of Ireland decided that the Broighter Hoard most aptly represented the best in Irish history and culture; it is hard to disagree.

LIMERICK, CO. LIMERICK

1833 108 coins from the Viking era.

1848 30 gold coins dating from the 18th and 19thC found in the Castleconnell area.

1853 500 17thC silver coins found at the New Shambles.

1921 22 16thC silver coins, thought to have been deposited *c.* 1573, found at St John's Hospital.

1979 More than 80 12thC silver coins, thought to have been deposited *c.* 1195.

LIMERICK AREA, CO. LIMERICK

1874? 2 early 10thC silver kite brooches found during the construction of the Limerick to Tipperary railway line.

National Museum of Ireland

LISBURN, CO. ANTRIM

1810 1 silver and 2 copper coins from the 17thC, thought to have been deposited in 1697, found in Magheragall Road.

LISBURN AREA, CO. ANTRIM

1915 Coins found on the banks of the Stoneyford river near Knockcairn Bridge by a man out rabbiting.

Ulster Museum

LOUGH ACKRICK, CO. ROSCOMMON

1967 16thC gold, silver and copper coins, thought to have been deposited in 1561, found near a crannog.

LOUGH BELTRA, CO. MAYO

[date?] Bronze Age bronze sword recovered from the lake bed. It measured over 16in and was in good condition.

LOUGH ESKE, CO. DONEGAL

c. **1926** Small quantity of 17thC silver coins.

LOUGH GUR, CO. LIMERICK

There are a large number of prehistoric remains around the lough, including standing stones, stone circles, wedge-tombs, hut foundations, and crannogs.

1872? Bronze shield dating from *c.* 700 BC found in a bog between Ballinamoona and Herbertstown.

National Museum of Ireland

(possibly 1939) 2 pieces of scrap gold dating from 1400 to 1300 BC found during archaeological excavation.

LOUGH ISLAND, REAVY, CO. DOWN

c. **1965** Small quantity of 17thC silver coins.

LOUGH LENE, CO. WESTMEATH

1843 28 coins dating from the Viking era.

LOUGHAN, COUNTY LONDONDERRY

1878? 9thC AD penannular gold, silver and glass brooch found at an ancient ford on the River Bann.

National Museum of Ireland

LOUGHBRICKLAND, CO. DOWN

1950? 17thC silver coins .

LOUGHMOE, CO. TIPPERARY

1842 Late 8th–early 9thC AD brooch composed of silver with gold filigree and amber studs. It is known as the Tipperary Brooch.

National Museum of Ireland

1851 1 silver and 11 copper coins dating from the 17thC.

CO. LOUTH

1984   A 12thC gold ring found by 11-year-old schoolboy James Wykes. The ring was complete with a gemstone and the carved figure of an animal.

National Museum of Ireland

LURGAN, CO. ARMAGH

1968   164 silver coins dating from the 19th and 20thC, thought to have been deposited in 1918, found in Lake Street.

MACOSQUIN, CO. LONDONDERRY

1910   432 coins found by a farmer carrying out reclamation work at Dunderg Fort. They were contained in a bag, which disintegrated on touch.

MACROOM, CO. CORK

1840   17 coins from the Viking era.

1850   Large quantity of 18thC gold coins .

MAGHERA, CO. LONDONDERRY

1862   48 17thC copper coins.

MAGHERAFELT, CO. LONDONDERRY

1975   8 George III copper halfpennies found during renovations of old house in Rainey Street. They were thought to have been deposited *c.* 1830.

Ulster Museum

MAGHERRALOGAN, CO. DOWN

1835   2 foreign coins and coin fragments, a silver arm-ring and ring fragments dating from the 9th and 10thC. The hoard was thought to have been buried in the late 9th or early 10thC The coins were *dirhem*, and had been minted in Baghdad in about AD 775. One coin had a hole in it, suggesting it had been used as a pendant or charm. The arm-ring was formed from a broad silver band, decorated by stamping its outer surface with various shapes.

MANGERTON, CO. KERRY, IRELAND

[date?]   An early Bronze Age gold lunula, of about 2000–1500 BC.

British Museum

MARL VALLEY, CO. WESTMEATH

1841   130 coins dating from the Viking era.

MEELICK, CO. GALWAY

1954   21 silver coins dating from the 17thC, thought to have been deposited in 1630.

MOIG SOUTH, ASKEATON, CO. LIMERICK

1954   86 silver coins that were dated 1534 or earlier.

MONAGHAN TOWN, CO. MONAGHAN

c. **1965**   2 gold coins dating from the 18thC, thought to have been deposited *c.* 1790.

MONASTERADEN, CO. SLIGO

1849   Matching pair of gold foil-covered lead split-ring ornaments of 800–700 BC found in a ceramic vessel on the shore of Lough Gara.

National Museum of Ireland

MONASTERBOICE, CO. LOUTH

1746   3 coins dating from the Viking era.

MOOGHAUN, CO. CLARE ▶ ▶ ▶ ▶ ▶ ▶ ▶ ▶ ▶   ▶ ▶ ▶

1854   Over 200 Bronze Age gold bracelets, of 800–700 BC, each one with a unique design and decoration and each crafted from a solid ingot. Found at the site of a hill-fort during the building of the railway, close to the lake shore; it is thought that they may have been buried as an offering. Whatever the reason, it confirmed the importance of the site. Unfortunately most of the objects were sold off or melted down, and only 34 items survive.

National Museum of Ireland

▶ ▶ ▶ ▶ ▶ ▶ ▶ ▶ ▶ ▶ ▶ ▶

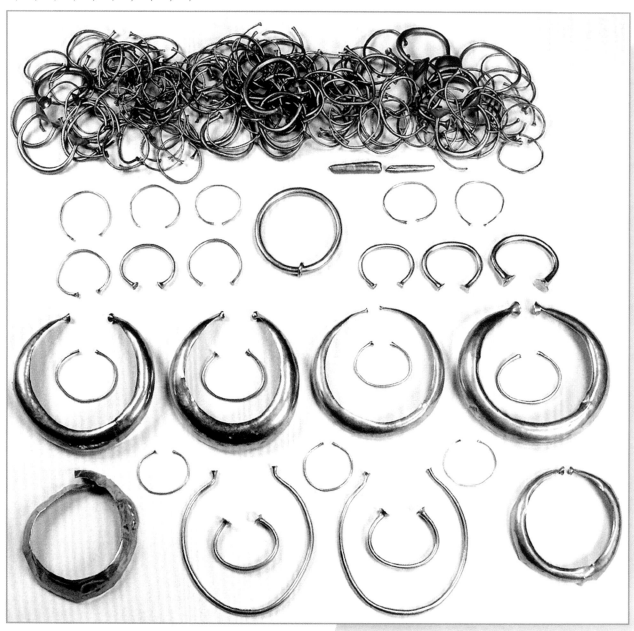

MOUNT STEWART, CO. DOWN

1820   16[th]C silver coins, thought to have been deposited *c.* 1559.

MOUNTNUGENT AREA, CO. CAVAN

c. **1876**   An iron javelin head found near Crover Castle on the shores of Lough Sheelin.

MOYLOUGH, CO. SLIGO

1945?   8[th]C AD belt shrine found in a bog. It is highly decorated with silver foils.

National Museum of Ireland

MOYNALTY, CO. MEATH

1984   Elaborately decorated bronze door handle in 3 parts was found in the bank of the River Borora.

MUCKAMORE PRIORY, CO. ANTRIM

1973   22 silver coins, thought to have been concealed around 1315 or earlier, found during archaeological excavations at the site of an Augustinian priory. It was founded after 1183, possibly on the site of a 6thC monastery; it was thought that the buildings were erected some time after 1185 because a John de Courcy farthing was found under the west cloister arcade wall.

Ulster Museum

MULLAGHBAWN, CO. KILDARE

1871   11 coins dating from the Viking era.

MULLINAHONE, CO. TIPPERARY

1856   Large quantity of 17thC copper coins, thought to have been deposited *c.* 1690.

MULLINGAR, CO. WESTMEATH

1856   17 coins dating from the Viking era.

MULLINGAR AREA, CO. WESTMEATH

1994   2 gold ear spools of 800–700 BC.

National Museum of Ireland

MUNGRET, CO. LIMERICK

c. **1840**   9 silver coins and 7 ingots, thought to have been deposited around AD 950, found during the opening of a quarry in a field near the old churches of Mungret.

NENAGH, CO. TIPPERARY

1936 47 17thC copper coins, thought to have been deposited in 1690.

NEWCASTLE, BALLYMAHON, CO. LONGFORD

1863   17 17thC silver coins, thought to have been deposited in 1679.

NEWGRANGE, CO. MEATH

>1977   2 bronze disc brooches, with gilded fronts, dating from the 4thC AD, found near three standing stones at the entrance to the Passage Tomb.

National Museum of Ireland

>1977   2 silver spiral rings dating from the 2ndC AD found near three standing stones at the entrance to the Passage Tomb.

National Museum of Ireland

>1977   2 gold coin pendants dating from the 4thC AD found near three standing stones at the entrance to the Passage Tomb. The coins were dated AD 320–37.

National Museum of Ireland

NEWPORT, GORTNAHELTIA, CO. MAYO

1945   9 17thC silver coins found, thought to have been deposited in 1666.

NEWPORT AREA, CO. MAYO

>1915   Bronze Age hoard found comprising 2 socketed axe heads, a spearhead, part of a sword, 4 pins and fragments of a plain ring dating from 1700 to 1500 BC.

NEWRY (SHIP) CANAL, CO. DOWN

1849   9 17thC gold coins.

NEWRY AREA, CO. DOWN

1815   16thC silver coins.

1875? Large and highly decorated 2ndC AD bronze armlet.

National Museum of Ireland

NEWTOWNARDS, CO. DOWN

1977   1 penny and 13 groats of Edward I and III, and David II of Scotland were found during the digging of a trench on a building site in the High Street; they were thought to have been deposited *c.* 1360.

NEWTOWNARDS AREA, CO. DOWN

1820   18th and 19thC gold coins.

OLDCASTLE, CO. MEATH

1899   12 coins dating from the Viking era.

OMAGH AREA, CO. TYRONE

1809   200 silver coins, thought to have been concealed *c.* 1500.

PLEASKIN HEAD AREA, CO. ANTRIM

1831   About 500 Roman *denarii* from Vespasian (AD 69–79) to Commodus (AD 180–92) found in a field on the Faugh Mountain, near Pleaskin, one of the headlands of the Giant's Causeway. A farmer was shovelling potatoes, when his shovel struck a flagstone,

underneath which was a heap of silver Roman coins, originally in a leather bag. Apparently the finder sold 190 of them to an English gentleman for a pound note (about £50 today). It has been suggested that the same farmer found two other hoards which he concealed.

PORTAFERRY, CO. DOWN

1882   9 17thC copper coins, thought to have been deposited in 1692.

RAHAN, CO. OFFALY

1820 and **1828**   2 large quantities of Viking-era coins.

RAHANS LOUGH, MAGHERACLOONE, CO. MONAGHAN

1863   5 16thC silver coins, thought to have been deposited c. 1553. There was another find of fused coins in 1976 but there is no dating evidence available.

RAPPA CASTLE, CO. MAYO

>1856   2 gold discs dating from 2200 to 2000 BC.
National Museum of Ireland

RATHBARRY, CO. CORK

1799   10thC silver coins found in a leather bag at the entrance to a souterrain at Castlefreke during land-levelling work; they were thought to have been concealed c. AD 950.

RATHCONRATH, CO. WESTMEATH

1911   700 17thC silver coins.

RATHCORMACK, CO. CORK

1837   17thC copper coins, thought to have been deposited in 1690.

RATHEDEN, CO. CARLOW

[date?]   Late 10th–early 11thC AD gold arm-ring.
National Museum of Ireland

RATHKEALE, CO. LIMERICK

c. **1839**   17thC copper coins, thought to have been deposited c. 1690.

RATHLIN ISLAND, CO. ANTRIM

1916   7 coins of the Viking era [?].

1977?   9thC silver penannular found in a Viking cemetery.
National Museum of Ireland

RATHNURE, CO. WEXFORD

1966   10 18thC gold coins found, thought to have been deposited in 1798.

THE IRISH REBELLION OF 1798
In 1791 the United Society of Irishmen in Belfast and Dublin demanded a number of democratic reforms that included Catholic emancipation. Over the next two years the British Government granted some reforms but with the coming of the war between France and England in 1793 they effectively stopped. The French gave their backing to the Irish reformists and in 1796 the United Irishmen almost stole a victory when a large force of French troops anchored off Bantry Bay; only bad weather prevented the force from landing. From then on Ireland divided into pro-British loyalists and those seeking independence. By 1798 a campaign against the United Irishmen by the British Army was having results and those Irish leaders who had avoided capture organised a full-scale uprising in May. French aid was slow to arrive, and the planned Dublin uprising failed to go according to plan. There were major risings in Wexford and in the north of the country, but these were defeated. By the end of the year the rebellion was over.

RICHHILL, CO. ARMAGH

1851   60 17thC silver coins, thought to have been deposited in 1662.

ROSCOMMON, CO. ROSCOMMON

1968   24 16thC silver coins, thought to have been deposited in 1582, found on the outskirts of the town.

ROSCREA, CO. TIPPERARY ▷ ▷ ▷ ▷ ▷ ▷ ▷ ▷ ▷ ▷

1983?   9thC silver annular brooch.
National Museum of Ireland

ROSSCARBERY, CO. CORK

1925   16thC silver coins.

ROSSINVER, CO. LEITRIM

1947 10 16thC silver coins, thought to have been deposited *c.* 1541.

ROSSLEA, CO. FERMANAGH

c. **1965** 3 gold and 3 silver coins dating from the 19thC, thought to have been deposited in 1897.

ROSSMORE PARK, CO. MONAGHAN

1928 Gold lunula of *c.* 2000 BC.

National Museum of Ireland

ROSSNOWLAGH, CO. DONEGAL

1965 3 16thC silver coins, thought to have been deposited *c.* 1541.

ROSTREVOR, CO. DOWN

c. **1835–40** About 2,000 15th and 16thC silver coins. All that remains from the hoard are 24 silver groats of Edward IV and Henry VII.

Ulster Museum

SCARBO HILL, CO. DOWN

1854 100 coins from the Viking era.

SCARTAGLEN, MULLIN, CO. KERRY

1964 108 17thC copper coins, thought to have been deposited in 1691.

SCARVA AREA, CO. DOWN

1978 A brass cauldron, many silver coins, spearheads and other objects dating from the 13th to the 14thC found during work to clear out the moat of Lisnagade Fort.

RIVER SHANNON, CO. ATHLONE

1978 More than 80 silver Prince John farthings, halfpennies and pennies dating from about AD 1180 found in the riverbank by Frank Keane and Billy Conlon over successive days.

1981 Bronze Age shield of 800 BC found by novice scuba diver, Louis Fleming, making his first dive. He found the shield in 12ft of water, in remarkably good condition despite having been in the river for 3,000 years.

SHANNONGROVE, CO. LIMERICK

1973 Bronze Age gold gorget or collar.

SHEEPHOUSE, CO. MEATH

1899? Hoard of altar furnishings of *c.* 1500, comprising a processional cross, a bell, and a candlestick, found in a quarry on land owned by the nearby Cistercian Monastery of Mellifont.

National Museum of Ireland

SKERRIES, FINGAL, CO. DUBLIN

1963 12 gold coins of the 17th and 18thC, thought to have been deposited in 1714, found near Baldongan Castle. The Knights Templar in the 13thC built the castle and in 1642 it fell to Cromwell's Parliamentary forces, who, having besieged the castle, destroyed it with artillery fire, and killed the garrison of 200.

SLEATY, CO. LAOIS

c. **1800** About 400 gold and many silver coins, including gold guineas and Spanish dollars, dating from the 18thC, found in a cow's horn in the thatch of a house.

SLIGO, CO. SLIGO

1948 46 16thC silver coins, thought to have been deposited *c.* 1532, found at Sligo Abbey.

1954 14 silver coins of the 15th and 16thC found during restorations of a wall at Sligo Abbey. The silver groats and half-groats of Henry VII and VIII, and Edward IV were thought to have been deposited *c.* 1520.

SMARMORE, CO. LOUTH

1929 72 Anglo-Saxon silver pennies dating from the 10thC, and thought to have been buried about AD 965–70, found under a rock, in a field during ploughing.

STEWARTSTOWN, CO. TYRONE

1956 2 silver and 23 copper coins dating from the 17thC, thought to have been deposited in 1696, found at Castle Farm.

TAGHMON, CO. WESTMEATH

1901 3 late 12thC silver bowls. One is held at the British Museum, and the other two at the National Museum of Ireland.

British Museum and National Museum of Ireland

TANDRAGEE, CO. ARMAGH

c. **1900** 18th and 19thC gold coins.

TARA, CO. MEATH

Tara was a site of both mystical and mythical importance, the centre of the Celtic High Kings of Ireland until the 11thC. The spread of Christianity brought about the decline of Tara, but in 1843 Daniel 'the Liberator' O'Connell chose it for one of his rallies in search of Catholic emancipation; over a million people attended.

1810 2 gold torcs of 1200–1000 BC found at the Rath of the Synods, Hill of Tara.

National Museum of Ireland

c. **1800s** Late 8th or early 9thC silver brooch, with additional gilding, filigree work and amber, found by Thomas Bateman, a pioneering Derbyshire archaeologist. It is thought that the empty recesses at the back of the brooch were for lead, to make it heavier than it really was.

British Museum

TEDAVNET, CO. MONAGHAN

1872? 2 gold discs of 2200–2000 BC found in the roots of an old tree.

National Museum of Ireland

TEMPLEMICHAEL, CO. LONGFORD

1928 218 17thC silver coins.

TEMPLETOUHY, CO. TIPPERARY

1944 5 17thC silver coins, thought to have been deposited in 1645.

TERMON MAGRATH, CO. DONEGAL

1860 60 17thC silver coins found, possibly deposited in 1639.

THREE ROCK MOUNTAIN, CO. DUBLIN

1849 197 16thC silver coins found, thought to have been deposited *c.* 1557.

TOORADOO, CO. LIMERICK

1927? Hoard of gold and other ornaments of 800–700 BC found in a bog called Cnoc na bPoll. There were 4 bronze rings, 4 gold foil-covered lead split-ring ornaments, and a lignite bead and an amber necklace.

National Museum of Ireland

TORYHILL, CO. LIMERICK

>1920 A gold collar of 800–700 BC found in two pieces.

National Museum of Ireland

TRILLICK, CO. TYRONE

1884 A gold lunula dating from *c.* 2000 BC found under a rock.

National Museum of Ireland

TRIM, COUNTY MEATH

c. **1942** 5 17thC copper coins, thought to have been deposited in 1683.

TULLAMORE, CO. OFFALY

1922 140 16thC silver coins found, possibly deposited in 1589.

TULLYHOMMON, CO. FERMANAGH

1861 2 gold and 22 silver coins dating from the 17thC.

TULLYLOUGH, CO. LONGFORD

[date?] A 16thC iron sword.

National Museum of Ireland

TULLYMORE, BENBURB, CO. TYRONE

1800s 19thC gold and silver coins found by an Ulster Defence Regiment patrol.

ULLARD, LACKEN, CO. KILKENNY

c. **1862** 62 17thC copper coins found, possiblydeposited *c.* 1682.

UPPER CULMORE, CO. LONDONDERRY

[date?] Large quantity of 13thC silver coins found on farmland, thought to have been deposited in 1290.

WEST CORK, CO. CORK

[date?] 1 silver and 126 copper James II crowns, half-crowns and shillings, thought to have been deposited in 1690 or later, found in a cave.

WESTPORT, CO. MAYO

1880 24 16thC silver coins found, possibly deposited *c.* 1532.

WEXFORD, CO. WEXFORD

c. **1920** 278 17thC silver coins, possibly deposited in 1645.

WHITTY'S HILL, WELLINGTON BRIDGE, CO. WEXFORD

1954 199 gold and 144 silver coins dating from the 18th and 19thC, thought to have been deposited in 1807.

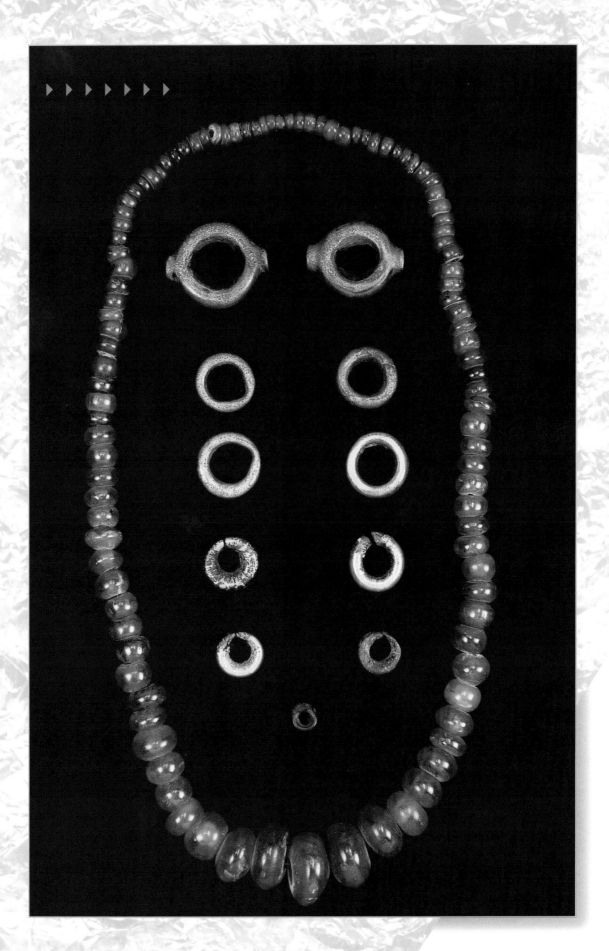

Some people assume that having built Hadrian's Wall, the Romans never ventured further north – they did. Amazing discoveries have been made, for example, at the Roman settlement at Newstead in the Scottish Borders and work on understanding this important site continues.

The cross-border fighting that provides finds in the north of England also supplies similar discoveries north of the border. Heading north and west from the central belt brings forth widely diverse discoveries. Scotland's islands in particular have yielded some wonderful finds.

The Isle of Lewis chessmen, the Viking hoard from Skaill on Orkney, finds on Iona linked to the Christian settlement and a hoard of Pictish objects found in Shetland reveal the country's riches.

Perhaps Scotland's greatest ever treasure find was made at Traprain Law in East Lothian in 1919. The 53lb of Roman silver, including jugs, dishes and plates, may have been stolen from the south of England or could have been payment by the Romans for mercenary aid.

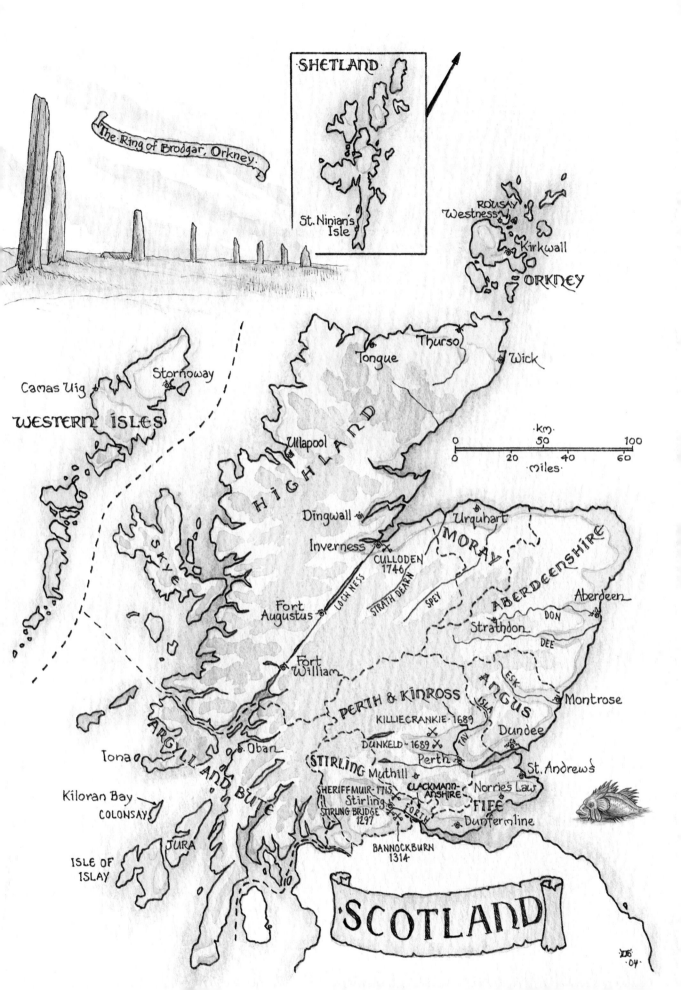

The Ring of Brodgar, Orkney.

SHETLAND

St. Ninian's Isle

ROUSAY
Westness
Kirkwall
ORKNEY

Camas Uig
Stornoway
WESTERN ISLES

Tongue
Thurso
Wick

HIGHLAND

Ullapool

Dingwall

SKYE

Inverness
CULLODEN
1746

Urquhart

MORAY

STRATH DEARN

SPEY

Aberdeen

DON

Strathdon

DEE

Fort
Augustus

LOCH NESS

ABERDEENSHIRE

Fort
William

ESK

ANGUS

ISLA

Montrose

PERTH & KINROSS

KILLIECRANKIE·1689

Dundee

ARGYLL AND BUTE

Iona

Oban

DUNKELD·1689

TAV

Perth

STIRLING

Muthill

St. Andrews

Kiloran Bay
COLONSAY

SHERIFFMUIR·1715
Stirling
STIRLING BRIDGE
1297

CLACKMANN-
ANSHIRE

Norrie's Law

FIFE

FORTH

JURA

Dunfermline

BANNOCKBURN
1314

ISLE OF
ISLAY

SCOTLAND

·km·
0   50   100
0   20   40   60
·miles·

DB
·04·

Scottish Treasure

All ancient objects newly discovered in Scotland, whether of precious metal or not, belong to the crown because the heirs of the previous owner can never be known. Under Scots common law the maxim *quod nullius est fit domini regis* (that which belongs to nobody becomes our Lord the King's [or Queen's]) prevails. The law is the same whether such objects were hidden or just lost, in natural ground or in buildings, but the archaeological value will vary. They are often called treasure trove, although strictly that term is confined to gold and silver just as in other parts of the United Kingdom where the crown's claims are limited to those metals. The crown does not always exercise its claim, but all objects found should be reported so that a decision can be made.

It is important to report anything that could be claimed – coins of gold and silver, and hoards of coins or other items, whether in pots or loose. Such finds should be reported direct to the Treasure Trove Secretariat at the National Museums of Scotland (address at the end of this section), or to a local museum or council archaeologist. As skeletons or other human remains are covered by different laws, graves should always be reported to the police, who will contact museum staff if necessary. Expert staff can assess needs in terms of conservation, archaeological investigation, etc. A receipt will be issued by the police for all objects handed in.

The police or museum will report the discovery to the Procurators Fiscal and the Queen's and Lord Treasurer's Remembrancer (the Q&LTR) who act on the crown's behalf. As the intention is always to record or preserve such things for the public good, the Q&LTR consults an advisory panel about which museums should be entrusted with the finds. The panel also advises on the importance and value of the find. All the articles will have to be examined fully and this may take some time.

The panel consists of an independent chairman and three members appointed by the Scottish Ministers, together with ex-officio representation of The National Museums of Scotland and the Scottish Museums Council. Allocation of treasure trove objects is a response to expressions of interest by relevant museums.

Rewards for items selected for retention by the state are paid to the finders by the Q&LTR at the receiving museum's expense and are based on the market value of the find. Valuations for reward purposes may be affected by the promptness with which a find is reported and the care taken by the finder in not destroying important evidence by untrained cleaning or by unskilled digging on the site or by breaking up a number of objects, which may have considerably more value as a group than as individual items. In all cases a major concern is the care of the find, which may need conservation treatment, and so early reporting is essential.

After examination articles not required for museum collections are returned to the finder.

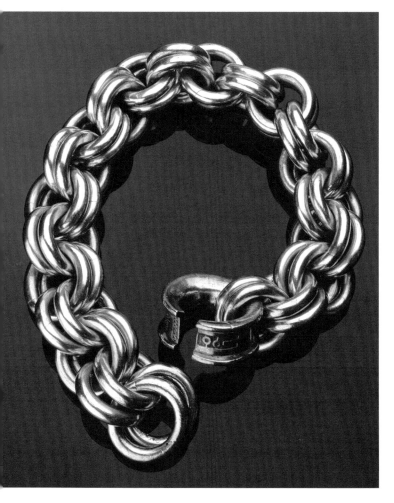

A decorated silver chain dating from *c.* AD 500–600, found at Whitecleugh, South Lanarkshire.

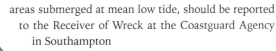

areas submerged at mean low tide, should be reported to the Receiver of Wreck at the Coastguard Agency in Southampton

Further advice may be obtained from the Archaeology Department, The National Museums of Scotland, Chambers Street, Edinburgh EH1 lJF (tel: 0131 225 7534), or www.treasuretrove.org.uk

A bronze ceremonial shield dating from 1150–750 BC found at Yetholm in the Scottish Borders in 1837.

Conditions contained in public works contracts or contracts of employment take second place to the rights of the crown. When archaeological excavators have made prior arrangements with the landowner about the permanent preservation of finds, this will be taken into account if any of the finds are, in exceptional cases, claimed on behalf of the crown.

Treasure hunters are reminded that unauthorised disturbance of sites may lead to prosecution under the Ancient Monuments Acts. It is an offence to use a metal detector on the site of a scheduled monument or any monument under the ownership or guardianship of the Secretary of State or of a local authority, or in an area of archaeological importance, by virtue of the 1979 Ancient Monuments and Archaeological Areas Act. The removal of any object from such a protected place, or the disturbance of the ground, is also an offence.

Inland underwater finds are treated legally as those on land. Maritime finds, from the sea and from coastal

ABERDEEN

1802   Large hoard of 14thC coins found by workmen digging in Union Street.

1807   Large quantity of 14thC English and Scottish silver pennies found near the church of St Nicholas, in St Nicholas Street, believed to have been concealed after 1320.

1827   A few gold coins of Edward III and a 'hoard' of silver pennies of Edward I and II, concealed after 1344, found in the Footdee area during some excavations to build some cottages.

1841   Small quantity of copper coins from the 16thC, thought to have been concealed between 1542 and 1567, found at 'Norman Dykes', which lies to the south-west of Old Aberdeen.

1847   More than 100 Scottish billon coins from the 16thC found near Marischal College, thought to have been concealed in 1558.

1858   Billon coins possibly from the 15th and 16thC, thought to have been concealed in 1584.

1886   9,755 silver coins (although some reports talk of over 12,000) found when a workman put his pickaxe through a three-legged bronze cooking pot during building excavations, at Upperkirkgate. The majority of the coins were Edward I and II silver pennies. The remainder were of Scottish, Irish and continental origin. Some of the last were French, and there were also 7 coins of the blind King John of Bohemia. It is thought that they were buried after 1330. The British Museum kept 60 coins, and 400 went to the National Museum of Scotland, while the remainder, with the bronze pot, are in the Aberdeen Museum.

British Museum, Museum of Scotland
and Aberdeen Art Gallery and Museum

1893   4thC AD copper coins of the Emperor Constantine the Great and his son, Constantius II, found at Windmill Brae.

c. **1906**   Copper coins probably from the 17thC, thought to have been concealed between 1625 and 1660.

1937   183 coins (mainly Edward III groats), buried in 1466, found in a small red clay jug near Bridge of Don.

1979   2 silver pennies of Edward I found on a demolition site in Drums Lane.

1983–4   Several hundred silver pennies from the late 13th and early 14thC found in a ceramic jug during the digging of a drain in the construction of the St Nicholas Street shopping centre. The following year another 7,000 medieval coins were found.

ABERDOUR, FIFE

1978   277 English, Irish and Scottish silver coins from the 14thC, thought to have been concealed *c.* 1380 in a rock crevice: finder R.M. Black; he received a settlement close to £4,000 (equating to £14,000 today).

1981   Robert II silver groat, and 16 long-cross pennies of Edward II and III, as well as some continental issues: finder R.M. Black. They were buried more deeply and scattered over a wider area than the hoard he found three years earlier.

ABERLADY, EAST LOTHIAN

1972   13 Scottish billon coins of James IV, James V, and Mary, and a French coin of Francis I, thought to have been deposited *c.* 1546.

ABERNETHY, PERTH AND KINROSS

1866   8 silver and 510 copper coins from the 15th and 16thC, thought to have been concealed in 1560.

ALFORD, ABERDEENSHIRE

1795?   17thC silver coins, thought to have been concealed between 1625 and 1660.

AMULREE AREA, PERTH AND KINROSS

1845   A quantity of 13th–14thC silver coins, described as Edwardian sterlings, found in a field near the head of Loch Freuchie.

ANNAT, ARGYLL AND BUTE

1872   102 17thC silver coins, thought to have been concealed *c.* 1675.

ANWOTH, DUMFRIES AND GALLOWAY

1784?   16th and 17thC silver coins, thought to have been concealed between 1567 and 1625.

ARDCHATTAN, BY OBAN, ARGYLL AND BUTE

1829   A quantity of silver coins from the 13th and 14thC found in Baile Mhaodain burial ground. Thought to have been deposited between 1280 and 1360, they were probably coins of Edward minted in London, Canterbury and perhaps Exeter. There was a priory at Ardchattan, founded by the monks of the Valliscaulian order in the 13thC.

ARDNAVE POINT, ISLE OF ISLAY, ARGYLL AND BUTE

1968   81 silver coins of Edward VI, Elizabeth I, James I, Charles I, and including coins from the Spanish Netherlands, Belgium, Austria, and other foreign territories from the 16th and 17thC. They were thought to have been concealed *c.* 1639. They are held at the Museum of Scotland.

The National Museums of Scotland

ARKLETON AREA, DUMFRIES AND GALLOWAY

1883   176 English, Irish, Scottish and foreign coins from the 14thC, believed to have been concealed in 1340.

ASCOG, ISLE OF BUTE, ARGYLL AND BUTE

1813   Several thousand coins, described at the time as an 'immense quantity of ancient silver coin', found by workmen building a road at Ascog Bank, Millbank. Most were dispersed among the workers but some were recovered and included some Irish pennies, as well as some late 13th and early 14thC Scottish and continental coins.

ATHELSTANEFORD, EAST LOTHIAN

1882 14thC silver engraved ring brooch found during the digging of a fresh grave in the Kirkyard.

The National Museums of Scotland

AUCHENTAGGART, DUMFRIES AND GALLOWAY

1850 Gold collar or breastplate from 2000 BC and associated with the Druids discovered at McCall Farm.

AUCHMITHIE, ANGUS

c. **1794** 33 silver coins, thought to have been concealed *c.* 1689–1707.

AYR, SOUTH AYRSHIRE

1793 About 20 either silver or billon coins, thought to have been concealed in 1562.

1804 About 42 silver coins from 1685 or earlier, thought to have been concealed between 1649 and 1685.

c. **1873** A very considerable number of coins from the 13th and 14thC found in a small greyware cooking pot. Many of the coins were dispersed before being reported, but 227 coins and the pot were recovered. These were English, Irish and Scottish silver pennies of Edward I and II, and Alexander III, thought to have been buried *c.* 1320.

The National Museums of Scotland

1874 135 English and Scottish groats and half-groats from 1490 found during renovations to the Wheatsheaf Inn.

1892 2 silver engraved brooches from the 13thC, along with 155 coins of Alexander III, John Balliol, Edward I and Edward II, found in an earthenware pot at the old fort in Ayr, thought to have been deposited *c.* 1280–1300.

The National Museums of Scotland

1914 7 silver and 685 copper coins from the 16thC, thought to have been concealed in 1567.

AYR AREA, SOUTH AYRSHIRE

1973 Testoons and half-testoons of Mary and Francis and Mary from 1555 to 1561 found in a pot 3 miles from Ayr.

AYRSHIRE

1782 Large quantity of silver coins, said to weigh several pounds, dated 1466–80, found in a field after a lady dreamed of treasure being buried there. Several ounces were sold for 5s 8d each, the equivalent of around £23 today.

BALGREGGAN, DUMFRIES AND GALLOWAY

1913 125 Roman copper coins from the 4thC AD found in a jug by three council workmen while stripping the soil from the top of a rock at Balgreggan Quarry.

BALLINGHARD, COLONSAY, ARGYLL AND BUTE

1859 9 silver coins from the 17th and 18thC, thought to have been deposited *c.* 1689–1707.

BANFF, ABERDEENSHIRE

>1836 A quantity of silver coins that included 11 Edwardian pennies and an Alexander III sterling, thought to have been deposited *c.* 1300, found on the site of a house at the bottom of the Castlehill.

1952 3 17thC silver coins, thought to have been concealed in 1631.

BANKHEAD, ABERDEEN

1862 32 17thC silver coins, thought to have been concealed in 1640.

BARABHAS, ISLE OF LEWIS, WESTERN ISLES

1960 12 18thC copper coins found, thought to have been concealed in 1793.

BARR, SOUTH AYRSHIRE

1955 578 Scottish billon placks and pennies from the reigns of three consecutive Scottish kings, James III (1460–88), James IV (1488–1513) and James V (1513–42) found in a field on a hillside at Baligmorie Farm by a young farmhand while ploughing. Having been working the area for several days he finally noticed a spherical object which turned out to be a medieval earthenware bank, known in Scotland as a 'pirlie-pig'. Looking similar to an onion it had a slot for coins in its side. Although it had been broken by the ploughing it seems that all the coins stayed close together and they were all collected. They were thought to have been concealed between 1513 and 1542.

BARROCK, HIGHLAND

1921 19 17thC copper coins found on a skeleton at Quintfall Hill, thought to have been deposited *c.* 1694.

BEINN NAN GUDAIREAN, COLONSAY

[date?] Late Bronze Age sword.

BEITH, NORTH AYRSHIRE

1958 13 silver and 6 copper coins from the 16thC found at Mossend Farm, thought to have been concealed in 1574.

BERSCAR, DUMFRIES AND GALLOWAY

1900 1,382 silver pennies, dated 1322, found in an earthenware pot, covered in a cloth, surprisingly intact. The coins were thought to have been concealed *c.* 1335.

BIRDSTON, EAST DUNBARTONSHIRE

1790 17thC silver coins, thought to have been concealed 1625–60.

BIRNIE, NEAR ELGIN, MORAY

2000   300 Roman *denarii* from Nero (AD 54–68) to Septimius Severus (AD 193–211) found in a pot in what had been a post hole during the excavation of an Iron Age settlement by archaeologists from the National Museums of Scotland. This hoard poses the question whether the Romans were paying off local tribes even this far north. The excavations were only initiated after several random Roman coins had been found at the site by detectorists.

2002   A second Roman coin hoard found in a pot at the same site as the first, and just 10 yards away. Both hoards are thought to have been buried as offerings to the gods. An Iron Age enamelled finger-ring was also found at the site.

BLACKBURN MILL, SCOTTISH BORDERS

[date?]   Large hoard of 1stC AD metalwork, including a phallic-handled sickle; it was probably part of a votive offering.

The National Museums of Scotland

BONGATE, SCOTTISH BORDERS

1827   More than 90 Anglo-Saxon silver pennies and ornaments. The coins were from the reign of Ecgberht, King of Wessex (AD 802–39) and were said to be worth £700 each. An ancient cross once stood there and today there is a large stone, covered with indistinct characters. The coins were found in a field close by and could be related to Ecgberht's campaign to subdue Northumbria.

BONNINGTON, EDINBURGH

1853   16thC copper coins, thought to have been concealed between 1567 and 1625.

BORERAY, NORTH UIST, WESTERN ISLES

1836   Small quantity of gold coins and 400 silver coins from the 16thC, thought to have been concealed in 1592.

BOTHWELL, LANARKSHIRE

1983   £1,940 in old (20thC) £5 and £10 banknotes discovered in two tins by two men digging in the garden of a house.

BOTRIPHNIE, NEAR DRUMMUIR, MORAY

1864   129 silver and 3 copper coins from the 17th and 18thC thought to have been deposited c. 1689–1707.

BRAEMORE, HIGHLAND

1850–1900   More than 6 silver pennies, including 2 silver pennies of Edward I, and Scottish coins of Alexander III and others from the 14thC, thought to have been deposited in the early 1300s.

BRAESIDE, INVERCLYDE

1955   More than 11 silver testoons and more than 39 copper bawbees, struck between 1543 and 1559 during the reign of Queen Mary, found by three labourers digging a sewer. They dug up an ancient cow's horn,

which contained the coins. They were thought to have been concealed in 1573.

> **TESTOON**
>
> Testoons were the precursor of the English shilling and were first struck in Scotland during Mary's reign (1542–67). The first ones appeared in 1553 and were in actual fact the first milled coins (struck in presses driven by a mill) ever produced in Britain.

BRANXHOLM AREA, SCOTTISH BORDERS

1860   Silver pennies of David II and Robert II as well as jewels, including a silver engraved brooch, from the 14thC, thought to have been deposited c. 1370. Branxholme Castle was the seat of the Scotts of Buccleuch, the family of the writer Sir Walter Scott; they had acquired the lands in 1420.

The National Museums of Scotland

BRECHIN, ANGUS

1785   A large quantity of silver was found, mainly English pennies of Edward I and II and silver spoons, thought to have been buried c. 1280–1307.

1891   Coins of Edward I and II, 4 silver ring brooches, and a ring brooch fragment from the 13th and 14thC were found, thought to have been deposited 1280–1320.

The National Museums of Scotland

BRIGLANDS, RUMBLING BRIDGE AREA, PERTH AND KINROSS

1938 and **1957**   179 Roman *denarii* from the 1st and 2ndC AD found when opening up a rabbit hole, two-thirds of the way up the steep east bank of the River Devon, by Lord Clyde. In 1938 9 *denarii* had been found on Lord Clyde's estate.

BRIMMOND HILL, CITY OF ABERDEEN

1942   4 silver and 73 copper coins from the 17thC, thought to have been concealed in 1632.

BROUGHTY FERRY, CITY OF DUNDEE

1881   15thC gold engraved iconographic ring found during the demolition of a cottage.

BROWNLEE, SOUTH LANARKSHIRE

1770   Coins of David II and Robert II of Scotland, with some of Edward III, concealed after 1340, possibly at the time of the Black Death.

BUCKIE, MORAY

1805   17thC silver coins, thought to have been concealed between 1625 and 1660.

BURNSWARK, DUMFRIES AND GALLOWAY

1950s?   An enamelled bronze horse bit and lead sling bolts from the second half of the 1stC AD found during excavations. Two Roman camps and a hill-fort are nearby and it is known to have been used by the Roman army for training exercises. By 1985, 133 lead sling shot had been recovered from the site as well as arrowheads and ballista bolts.

BURRAY, ORKNEY ISLANDS

1889   3 Anglo-Saxon coins, a silver rod, an intertwined necklet, an armlet, 30 silver rings and 108 pieces of silver cut from rings. The 3 coins determined the date of concealment as 1016.

The National Museums of Scotland

BUTE, ARGYLL AND BUTE

1873   27 English and Scottish silver pennies and some gold and silver ornaments from the 12thC, thought to have been concealed *c.* 1140; there were coins of Stephen, David I of Scotland (1124–53), and his sons Henry, Earl of Northumberland, and Malcolm IV of Scotland.

The National Museums of Scotland

[date?]   7 gold finger-rings and 3 gold ingots were found, believed to be of Viking origin.

CADDER, EAST DUNBARTONSHIRE

1815   141 lions (gold crowns) of James I and II found on land belonging to James Stirling of Kier, believed to have been hidden after 1438.

CAKEMUIR AREA, MIDLOTHIAN

1865   22 gold, silver, or bronze coins, possibly from the 17th and 18thC, possibly concealed between 1727 and 1760. They may possibly have been buried on Fala Moor. The nearby castle was built in the mid-16thC.

CALDALE, ORKNEY ISLANDS

1774   300 coins of King Cnut (1016–35) and several silver fibulae brooches in the form of crescents of different sizes from the 11thC found 2ft below the surface, hidden in a horn, by a man digging peat. The hoard was hidden *c.* AD 1030–5.

British Museum

CAM A' BHARRAICH, COLONSAY

[date?]   Oval Berdal brooches (cast with a cloth, wax or clay mould) found here and are among the earliest examples of Viking material found in Scotland.

CAMAS UIG, ISLE OF LEWIS, WESTERN ISLES ▶ ▶ ▶

1831   78 ivory chess pieces and 14 pieces for draughts made from walrus ivory and whale tooth and carved *c.* 1135–50 were found by a crofter from Uig on the shores of Loch Resort. Working near some sand dunes he saw that some stonework had been exposed by the recent storms. He found the chessmen about a foot below the surface in a kind of box. Some had crowns, others mitres, some were on horseback and all were dressed in medieval costume. One theory is that a Scandinavian trader was shipwrecked near the spot and hid the pierces, intending to return, but never doing so. All but 11 pieces, in the National Museum of Scotland, are in the British Museum, the cause of great consternation north of the border.

Museum of Scotland and British Museum

CAMBS, CLACKMANNAN

1797   A large quantity of silver coins, including some of Elizabeth I and Charles II as well as German coins, was found by workmen while levelling the floor of an old house. The men took many of the coins; they were thought to have been deposited *c.* 1649–85.

CAMPBELTOWN, ARGYLL AND BUTE

>1979   Silver coins, mostly Victorian silver crowns, half-crowns and florins, the majority of which were in mint condition, found in an old biscuit tin on the beach. The latest coin was dated 1913 and the hoard was valued at around £400.

CANONBIE, DUMFRIES AND GALLOWAY

1811   Medieval coins found in a purse in some marshy ground where the Rowan Burn joins the River Liddle.

1863   Mid- to late 13thC gold, sapphire and emerald ring, a gold ruby ring, 2 silver ring brooches, 15 jet beads, silver ring brooch fragments, 70 silver pennies and 3 halfpennies of Edward I and II, a penny of Alexander III, and 2 pennies of John Balliol found during ploughing at Woodhead Farm.

The National Museums of Scotland

CARLINGWARK, DUMFRIES AND GALLOWAY

1860?   Over 100 Iron Age tools and weapons, including a bronze dagger, recovered from Carlingwark Loch. It was a votive offering, found in a huge cauldron.

CARLUKE, SOUTH LANARKSHIRE

>1782   About 52 17thC silver coins, thought to have been concealed between 1625 and 1660.

1793   Silver coins, including some Scottish of Alexander III, from the 13th and 14thC found in a field called Friar's Croft. They were thought to have been deposited 1280–1360.

1872   20 German thaler from the 17thC, deposited *c.* 1679.

CARMUNNOCK, CITY OF GLASGOW

c. **1839**   17thC silver coins, thought to have been deposited *c.* 1649–85.

CARNOCK, FIFE

1774   18thC copper coins .

CARNWATH, SOUTH LANARKSHIRE

1928   Small quantity of copper coins from the 16thC, thought to have been concealed between 1513 and 1542.

CARSPHAIRN AREA, DUMFRIES AND GALLOWAY

1913   2,225 14thC silver coins, mainly English silver pennies with a few Scottish and foreign coins, found in a broken earthenware jug in a marshy hollow on Goat Craig Hill at Craigengillan Farm. The hoard was thought to have been concealed in 1330.

CARSTAIRS, LANARKSHIRE

1838 36 silver Edwardian sterlings from the 13th and 14thC found on the side of a reclaimed moss (a bog). They were thought to have been deposited 1280–1360.

CASTLE NEWE, ABERDEENSHIRE

[date?] Enamelled and decorated bronze armlet from the 1st and 2ndC AD.

CATHCART, CITY OF GLASGOW

1840? 17thC continental silver coins found at Newlands Farm, thought to have been concealed between 1625 and 1660.

CAULDHAME, KEITH, MORAY

1881 Between 80 and 100 13thC short-cross silver pennies, thought to have been deposited in 1205 or later.

CAVERS, SCOTTISH BORDERS

c. **1796** Large quantity of 18thC gold coins.

CLOSEBURN, DUMFRIES AND GALLOWAY

1844 More than 10,000 14thC English and Scottish silver pennies and groats found in a tripod cooking pot. This is probably the largest hoard of coins ever found in Scotland but large numbers were dispersed by the finders. Two years later several more coins of the same period were also discovered, and probably formed part of the original hoard.

COLDINGHAM, SCOTTISH BORDERS

1853 693 12thC English and Scottish silver pennies, believed to have been buried in the 12thC when England and Scotland were at war. There was a church founded here in 1098 that became a priory in 1150.

COLDINGHAM AREA, SCOTTISH BORDERS

1915 28 18thC silver coins found at Moorhouse, on Coldingham Moor. They were thought to have been concealed between 1727 and 1760, but were almost certainly deposited c. 1800.

COLLIN, DUMFRIES AND GALLOWAY

1963 10 gold, 134 silver and more than 374 copper coins, thought to have been concealed in 1553.

CORRIMONY, HIGHLAND

1870 570 14thC silver pennies found packed neatly on edge in a copper pot in a churchyard at the head of Glen Urquhart.

COULNAKYLE, HIGHLAND

1870 Silver pennies of Edward I and II, thought to have been concealed in the early 14thC, many of which were disposed of by the finders. 23 coins were recovered, 1 of which was from Berwick mint.

COVESEA, MORAY

1929–30 230 Roman copper coins from the 4thC AD found during the excavation of the Sculptor's Cave, together with Samianware, potsherds, bracelets, netting needles, and bronze toilet instruments.

COWIE, FETTERESSO AREA, ABERDEENSHIRE

1843 Roman *denarii* from the 1st to the 3rdC AD found in an urn by a man digging on the forest or common of Cowie. The find spot is about 1½ miles from the ancient encampment of Raedyke.

COYLTON, SOUTH AYRSHIRE

1841? 16th and 17thC silver coins found at Bargannoch Farm, thought to have been concealed between 1625 and 1660.

CRAIGHOUSE, JURA, ARGYLL AND BUTE

1793 16th and 17thC silver coins found at Sanniag Farm, thought to have been concealed between 1625 and 1660.

CRAIGIE AREA, SOUTH AYRSHIRE

1893 79 Scottish silver coins and 1 Irish silver coin from the 14thC, believed to have been hidden *1380–90*.

The National Museums of Scotland

CHAPELHALL, NORTH LANARKSHIRE

1921 23 17thC silver coins, thought to have been deposited c. 1677.

CLAYMORE, GALSTON, AYR

1782 22 silver coins from the 16th and 17thC, thought to have been concealed in 1622.

CLEUCHHEAD, MINTO AREA, SCOTTISH BORDERS

1897 138 silver coins from the 14thC. They were all foreign silver coins, thought to belong to a foreign trader who buried them for safe keeping c. 1310, at the time of Edward II's march into Scotland. At the same time Robert the Bruce's agents were blackmailing people in Roxburgh and it may be that the money was hidden to avoid paying.

CRATHES CASTLE AREA, ABERDEENSHIRE

1863 21 silver pennies of Edward I and II found at Bush Farm to the north of the castle, thought to have been deposited 1320–40.

CRAWFORDJOHN, SOUTH LANARKSHIRE

>1836 A quantity of silver coins from the 13th and 14thC, including Irish coins of Dublin and Waterford, thought to have been deposited 1280–1360.

CREGGANS, ARGYLL AND BUTE

1876 1 silver and 218 copper coins from the 15th and 16thC, thought to have been concealed between 1500 and 1513.

CRIEFF AREA, PERTH AND KINROSS

1787 Some coins dated 1390–1406.

CROMARTY, HIGHLAND

1916 42 silver and 1 copper coin from the 16th and 17thC, thought to have been concealed in 1635.

CROOKSTON AREA, CITY OF GLASGOW

1797 Large quantity of coins, mainly of Henry IV, V and VI, believed to have been concealed c. 1460–65, during the Wars of the Roses.

CROOKSTON, SCOTTISH BORDERS

1859 A 14thC silver ring brooch.

CROSSCRYNE, BIGGAR AREA, SCOTTISH BORDERS

>1868 Very large number of 14thC silver coins found in this area. Details are few as the finders disposed of the coins without notifying the authorities. Later 21 were recovered and these were mainly of Edward I and II, and Alexander III of Scotland, which dated the hoard to c. 1320.

CROY, HIGHLAND

1875 2 coins and 12 pieces of jewellery from the mid-9thC.

The National Museums of Scotland

CULDUTHEL, HIGHLAND

[date?] Bronze Age wrist-guard with four gold studs found in a cist burial.

CUMMERTREES, DUMFRIES AND GALLOWAY

1833 13thC silver coins were found in a moss (a bog), thought to have been concealed 1280–1360.

DAILLY AREA, SOUTH AYRSHIRE

1818 Coins of Edward I and II, and 2 counterfeit sterlings of the Count of Flanders and Porcieu, found in a circular brass pyx at Dalquharran Castle. They were believed to have been concealed in 1320.

DALRYMPLE, EAST AYRSHIRE

[date?] A few silver coins found from the reigns of James I of Scotland and Edward I and Edward III of England.

DERVAIG AREA, ISLE OF MULL, ARGYLL AND BUTE

c. 1833 Mid-15thC silver octagonal and highly decorated ring brooch found at Kengharair Farm.

DINGWALL AREA, HIGHLAND

1979 Hoard of 9 Bronze Age gold objects from c. 700 BC found by 79-year-old Donald MacDonald while he was ploughing. He thought they were just some dull metal trinkets and kept them in the house, barely giving them another thought. Ten years later his wife was prompted to contact the National Museum of Scotland after watching a TV archaeological programme. The museum identified the pieces as a gold armlet and dress fastener. This sparked a full-scale dig on the site which yielded 7 more items, giving in total 5 bracelets, a gold armlet, 3 dress fasteners, and other Late Bronze Age items. Mr MacDonald received a cheque for £40,700, the equivalent of around £123,000 today.

The National Museums of Scotland

DINWOODIE MAINS, DUMFRIES AND GALLOWAY

1780 17th and 18thC silver coins.

DORNOCK AREA, DUMFRIES AND GALLOWAY

1871 90 silver pennies of Edward I, II and III, believed to have been deposited after 1330; they were all returned to the finder.

DOUNE, STIRLING

c. 1830 Late 14th or early 15thC gold ring brooch found by a boy while fishing in the Water of Ardoch, near Doune Castle.

The National Museums of Scotland

DRUMNADROCHIT, HIGHLAND

1931   34 silver coins from the 14thC found near Temple Pier on the supposed site of St Ninian's chapel; they were thought to have been deposited *c.* 1390.

DRUMOAK, ABERDEENSHIRE

1812   Small quantity of 16thC silver coins found at Dalmaik Farm, thought to have been concealed between 1542 and 1567.

DUMBARTON, WEST DUNBARTONSHIRE

1896   Large quantity of silver coins of Edward I, II and III, and Scottish coins of Alexander III and David II from the 14thC found during the construction of a railway station. They were thought to have been concealed *c.* 1351–71.

1975   Silver pennies of Edward I and II (1272–1327) found during excavations at Castle Rock.

DUMFRIES, DUMFRIES AND GALLOWAY

1615   18 gold coins from the 15th and 16thC, possibly concealed between 1500 and 1513.

1849   Large quantity of silver coins, mainly silver pennies, from the early 14thC. The majority were sold to a silversmith in Carlisle for their bullion value.

1870?   1 gold and 5 silver coins from the 16thC, thought to have been concealed between 1542 and 1567.

1878   213 silver pennies of Alexander II, Edward I, and Robert de Bethune and jewellery, deposited in 1310. The hoard comprised a silver brooch, 2 silver brooch fragments, a silver pendant cross, a length of chain and a silver hook bow.

The National Museums of Scotland

DUNBAR, EAST LOTHIAN

1773   290 silver coins from the 16th and 17thC, thought to have been concealed between 1625 and 1660.

DUNBLANE, STIRLING

1869   180 gold coins from the 15th and 16thC, thought to have been concealed between 1513 and 1542.

DUNFERMLINE, FIFE

1896   Around 300 silver pennies of Edward I and II and 2 foreign sterlings from the 14thC found buried in a large bronze jug. They were believed to have been deposited after 1345, possibly in 1348 when the Black Death hit Scotland. The jug is in the British Museum.

British Museum

1902   4 silver and 3 copper coins of George III, dated 1787–1815, found in a bottle, in a cavity in the foundation stone of the Old High School; they were deposited in 1815.

Pittencrieff House Museum

DUNKELD, PERTH AND KINROSS

>1925   Late 14th or early 15thC gold ruby ring found buried near Dunkeld Cathedral. It was presented to the museum by HM Office of Works in 1925.

DUNROSSNESS, SHETLAND

1830   11thC Anglo-Saxon coins, a number of which were presented to the Society of Antiquaries in 1831.

DUNS, SCOTTISH BORDERS

1811   2,361 English and Scottish silver pennies from early 14thC, buried in a pewter jug and wooden cup, in the meadow in front of Duns Castle.

1859   22 17thC silver coins, thought to have been concealed in 1645. However, they may have been buried in 1639 during what has been called the First Bishop's War, when Charles I's men were humiliated by Covenanters under Alexander Leslie. Leslie's vastly inferior force lined up on the heights of Duns Law and duped the king into thinking there were many more men behind him; it worked and the king negotiated.

DUNSCORE, DUMFRIES AND GALLOWAY

1945   16thC copper coins, thought to have been concealed 1542–67.

DUNTULM, ISLE OF SKYE, HIGHLAND

1975   13 silver English, Scottish and foreign coins of various 17thC reigns found in a metal container that had disintegrated. They were returned to the finder.

EARLSTON, SCOTTISH BORDERS

1787   200 gold, silver or copper coins from the 15th and 16thC, thought to have been concealed 1542–67.

EASSIE, ANGUS

>1795   13th and 14thC silver coins, several of which were Edward I, found on a large circular mound about a mile from the old church of Eassie.

EASTER ROSS, HIGHLAND

1979   A gold and silver hoard containing 5 bracelets, 3 cloak or dress fasteners, and a circular strip from *c.* 700 BC found by a farmer while ploughing. The jewellery was probably made in Ireland and was declared treasure trove.

EASTER WOODEN, SCOTTISH BORDERS

1793?   15th and 16thC silver coins, thought to have been concealed between 1542 and 1567.

EDDLESTON, SCOTTISH BORDERS

1794   Large quantities of gold and silver coins from the 15th and 16thC found at Kingside Farm, thought to have been concealed 1513–42.

c. **2000**   14thC silver brooch found by Louise Forsyth in a paddock where she kept her horse. When she found it she believed it was a part of a horse's harness. 3 silver plates have survived out of the 5 that would have been soldered to the hoop, which was originally gilded. It is believed that the brooch came from the Borders or Northumberland and it resembles similar ones found with 14thC coin hoards in Langhope and Canonbie.

EDINBURGH

>1741   1st and 2nd AD Roman silver coins found in urn during the demolition of an old Roman arch.

1778   Hoard of bronze items was dredged from the bottom of Duddingston Loch. It included broken weapons, with 32 sword fragments and 14 spearheads. There were also the traces of a cauldron handle making this a votive offering. Some of the items were given to King George III, others to the writer Sir Walter Scott, but the majority passed into the hands of the Society of Antiquaries of Scotland, becoming their first acquisition in 1781.

The National Museums of Scotland

1786   14 copper coins from the 16thC thought to have been concealed in 1583.

>1787   Vast quantity of silver coins from the 13th and 14thC found by workmen digging house foundations in Niddry's Wynd. They were thought to have been deposited 1280–1360.

1821   16th and 17thC silver and copper coins, thought to have been concealed between 1567 and 1625, found in the Canongate.

1830   15th and 16thC gold coins and more than 300 silver coins, possibly concealed between 1513 and 1542, found in Clifton Terrace.

1831   More than 12 silver and a large quantity of copper coins from the 16th and 17thC found at Arthur's Seat, thought to have been concealed in 1831.

1872   1 silver and 3 copper coins from the 17thC, thought to have been concealed in 1671, found near Leith Harbour.

>1917   Gold diamond ring from *c.* 1300 found in shrubbery in the gardens of the palace of Holyroodhouse.

1979–80   250 £1 notes found by an antique dealer in a wooden blanket chest. As he was moving it, the box tumbled down the stairs and smashed open to reveal the pristine 20-year-old £1 banknotes.

1980   7 Bronze Age axe heads of 800–700 BC found in an old quarry by William Wilson. They were deemed to be treasure trove and the finder was awarded £1,200.

1992   A trumpet brooch and a hairpin found in earth that had been moved by a bulldozer during the building of a car park in Cramond. Nearby a stone lioness was found sticking out of the mud bottom of the River Almond by a boatman. It was thought to have been a part of the gate at the entrance to a Roman fort.

EDZELL, ANGUS

1852?   28 16thC copper coins found, possibly concealed in 1588.

ELGIN, MORAY

1759   16thC gold coins found, thought to have been concealed between 1567 and 1625.

1838   2 foreign thalers from the 17thC, possibly deposited *c.* 1663.

FALKIRK

1933   More than 1,923 Roman *denarii*, 1 *drachm*, and 1 bronze coin dated 83 BC–AD 235 found in a pot by a workman cutting away the face of a hill during levelling operations for the Town Council in Bell's Meadow. The coins were fused together in what remained of some cloth; the coins that fell loose were kept by the man. It is thought that the coins may have belonged to a trader who dealt with the Romans or it could have been a payment from the Romans to a local tribe to 'buy' their allegiance. Ironically, the hoard site is now the location for a Tesco store. Parts of the Antonine Wall, built *c.* AD 142, can still be seen in the Falkirk area. Unlike Hadrian's Wall this one was made with earth that was banked up on a stone foundation. It originally stood 12ft high, with a 40ft wide and 12ft deep V-shaped ditch on the north side; a network of forts at around 2-mile intervals were placed along the line of the wall.

The National Museums of Scotland

FAULDHOUSE, WEST LOTHIAN

1913   37 silver coins, mainly of Edward I and II, found in a field on the boundary between the parishes of Fauldhouse and Eastfield Moss, believed to have been buried in 1320. After a treasure trove inquest they were returned to the finder, except one coin which was retained by the National Museum.

The National Museums of Scotland

FETLAR, SHETLAND ISLANDS

1737   Large amounts of silver coins found on the beach several months after the *Wendela*, a Danish frigate bound for India, broke up on the reef beneath Heilinabretta headland.

FIFE

1979   287 silver coins, possibly from the 14th and 15thC, found at the foot of an embankment.

FISHERTON AREA, SOUTH AYRSHIRE

1830   A coin, about the size of a crown-piece, of Albert and Elizabeth of Bruges and Brabant from *c.* 1630 was turned up during ploughing close to Dunduff Castle.

FITFUL HEAD, SHETLAND ISLANDS

1830   10th and 11thC Anglo-Saxon pennies.

FORGANDENNY AREA, PERTH AND KINROSS

1876   Silver coins, mainly groats and half-groats thought to have been deposited *c.* 1440, found in an earthenware pot. Most of the coins were dispersed by the finders, although the pot and 37 coins were later recovered.

The National Museums of Scotland

FORT AUGUSTUS, HIGHLAND

1767   About 300 Roman bronze coins, probably *antoniniani* and folles, possibly from the 3rd and 4thC AD, found in an urn by labourers digging a trench for the repair of the fortifications.

FYVIE, ABERDEENSHIRE

1898   Quantity of 13thC silver coins, listed as continental sterlings, found in an abandoned quarry. They were thought to have been deposited *c.* 1300.

GALSTON, EAST AYRSHIRE

1922   231 silver coins, the majority of which were continental sterlings, but including seven silver pennies of Edward I, dated *c.* 1300, found in a small unglazed earthware jug.

GEORGEMAS HILL, HIGHLAND

1876   8 silver and 139 copper coins from the 17thC, thought to have been deposited *c.* 1676.

GLAMIS, ANGUS

>1707   A great quantity of Roman silver coins from the 1stC AD found in an urn. According to a report in 1726: 'On digging up a small Tumulus, called the Green Cairn, near the Castle of Glames, in Strathmore, an Urn was lately discovered, with great quantities of Roman Medals of Silver, many of which are still in the Possession of the Earl of Strathmore. I procured one of them myself from a Countryman; it was a Silver Coin of Galba, and is now in Baron Clark's Collection.'

GLASGOW

1787   About 9 17thC silver coins, thought to have been concealed between 1625 and 1660.

1795   More than 800 gold coins from the 15th and 16thC, thought to have been concealed between 1542 and 1567.

1902   18 gold coins from the 16thC, thought to have been concealed in 1556.

1980   2 gold sovereigns and 2 half-sovereigns from the 19th and 20thC found inside a purse, in a gramophone by 12-year-old Gary McPherson and his father. The boy had bought an old gramophone at a jumble sale and finding it did not work asked his father to fix it. Inside they found the purse fouling the mechanism. The coins were sold for £190.

GLEN ETIVE, HIGHLAND

1830   A quantity of silver coins from the 13th and 14thC found by a shepherd, close to a large upright stone near the river at Inbhirfhaolain Farm.

GLEN GARRY, HIGHLANDS

Early 1800s   Many old solid gold bracelets found beneath a rock in a newly drained field that was being prepared for ploughing. The rock had been blasted revealing the 'antique patterned' bracelets.

GLEN QUAICH, PERTH AND KINROSS

1876   349 17th–18thC copper coins, thought to have been deposited *c.* 1689–1707.

GLENELG, HIGHLAND

1958   25 silver coins from the 16th and 17thC, thought to have been concealed in 1620.

GOLSPIE, HIGHLAND

1853   Flat bronze axe.

[date?]   Decorated pin of AD 600–700.

GRANGEMOUTH, FALKIRK

1899   1,094 silver coins from the 16th and 17thC, thought to have been concealed between 1625 and 1660.

GREENOCK, INVERCLYDE

1927   5 silver coins from the 19thC found in the foundation stone of the Memorial to Highland Mary; concealed in 1842.

GRETNA, DUMFRIES AND GALLOWAY

>1791   25 14thC silver coins found in a small wooden box in moss, near the Hirst. Contemporary reports spoke of '25 Edwardian sterlings and 4 somewhat smaller coins'. These were possibly halfpence and it is believed they had been deposited 1280–1360.

GULBERWICK, SHETLAND ISLANDS

[date?]   12thC silver ornaments and several precious items found close to the cliffs.

HADDINGTON, EAST LOTHIAN

1830   52 16thC silver coins, thought to have been concealed between 1542 and 1567.

HAWICK, SCOTTISH BORDERS

1876 3 gold, 24 silver and 533 copper coins from the 15th and 16thC, thought to have been concealed in 1555.

c. 1935 Carved sandstone figure found in the garden at Appletreehall. It is thought it may have some religious significance.

c. 1965 Roman coin, possibly of Marcus Aurelius (AD 161–80) found in a garden in Maclagan Drive.

HIGH BLANTYRE, SOUTH LANARKHIRE

1797 About 12 silver coins from the 16th and 17thC found at Blantyre Well; thought to have been concealed between 1567 and 1625.

HISLOP, SCOTTISH BORDERS

1845 14thC silver coins, 1 of which was a silver penny of Alexander III, found in moss ground, believed to have been deposited 1280–1360.

HUME, SCOTTISH BORDERS

>1940 Silver-gilt iconographic ring from the 15thC found at Hume Castle.

The National Museums of Scotland

HUNTERSTON, EAST AYRSHIRE

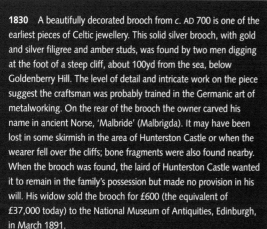

1830 A beautifully decorated brooch from *c.* AD 700 is one of the earliest pieces of Celtic jewellery. This solid silver brooch, with gold and silver filigree and amber studs, was found by two men digging at the foot of a steep cliff, about 100yd from the sea, below Goldenberry Hill. The level of detail and intricate work on the piece suggest the craftsman was probably trained in the Germanic art of metalworking. On the rear of the brooch the owner carved his name in ancient Norse, 'Malbride' (Malbrigda). It may have been lost in some skirmish in the area of Hunterston Castle or when the wearer fell over the cliffs; bone fragments were also found nearby. When the brooch was found, the laird of Hunterston Castle wanted it to remain in the family's possession but made no provision in his will. His widow sold the brooch for £600 (the equivalent of £37,000 today) to the National Museum of Antiquities, Edinburgh, in March 1891.

The National Museums of Scotland

INCHKENNETH, INNER HEBRIDES, ARGYLL AND BUTE

1831 24 Anglo-Saxon and Danish silver coins and jewellery from the 11thC.

British Museum and The National Museums of Scotland

INGLESTONE, DUMFRIES AND GALLOWAY

1815–20 Over 1,000 14thC silver coins found in a horn, believed to have been deposited 1280–1360.

INNERLEITHEN, SCOTTISH BORDERS

1980 Bronze Age axe head from *c.* 1000 BC found in woodland on a hill: finder Mary Wilson; declared treasure trove.

INNERWICK, EAST LOTHIAN

1979 250 silver and 2 billon coins were found, thought to have been deposited *c.* 1480; they comprised English coins of Edward III, Henry V and VI, and Edward IV, Irish coins of Edward IV, and Scottish coins of David II, Robert II and III, and James I, II and III.

INVERARAY AREA, ARGYLE AND BUTE

1981 Silver crowns, shillings, and copper coins of Elizabeth I, and Charles I and II found buried near a boulder close to an old track in the hills: finder R.M. Black (M/D).

INVERGORDON, HIGHLAND

1852 60 silver coins, mostly Spanish, with a few English coins, from the 16th and 17thC, thought to have been concealed in 1638.

INVERLOCHY, HIGHLAND

1982 9 bronze 'Flat Axe' heads and 4 fragments of 2000–1800 BC.

IONA, ARGYLL AND BUTE

1922 Decorated gold fillet and 4 decorated silver spoons of the late 12th to the early 13thC found during routine maintenance work underneath a stone in the nunnery.

1950 338 Anglo-Saxon silver pennies of 924–1016 found by workmen digging a ditch to lay a drain, near Abbot's House, on the north side of the cathedral. Two feet below the surface they came upon a layer of stones and beneath them they discovered a mass of silver coins, with some fragments of gold and silver ornaments.

1963 Late 12thC gold finger-ring and decorated gold fillet found by workmen removing loose earth from the corner of St Ronan's church.

IRVINE, NORTH AYRSHIRE

1923 351 silver coins from the 16th and 17thC, thought to have been concealed between 1625 and 1660.

ISBISTER, ORKNEY ISLANDS

1832 150 silver coins from the 16th and 17thC found at Cottascarth, thought to have been concealed between 1625 and 1660.

ISLAY, ARGYLL AND BUTE

1850 10thC coins and silver ingots found at Macrie Farm, near Kildalton. Later 90 Anglo-Saxon, Danish and oriental silver coins and 4 ingots were recovered. They were deposited in AD 960–70.

1852 5 10thC Anglo-Saxon silver pennies found in the parish of Knowe; they were deposited in AD 960–70.

1901 74 silver coins from the 16thC found at Ballynaughton Cist; they were thought to have been concealed in 1558.

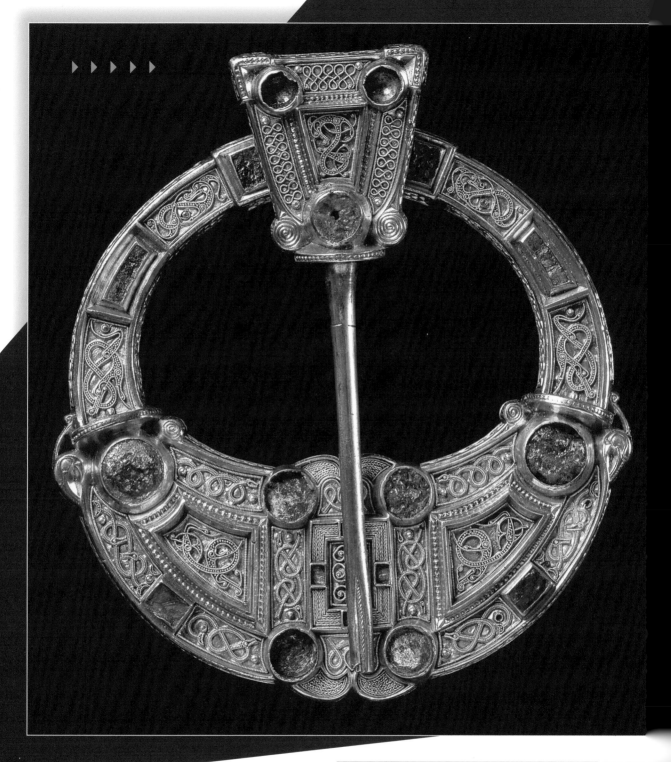

▶ ▶ ▶ ▶ ▶

ISLE OF MAY, FIFE

1842   2 silver and 35 copper coins discovered in a tin box, in the stomach of a shark caught by a fisherman close to the Isle of May, which lies in the outermost reaches of the Firth of Forth. The coins were thought to have been placed in the box sometime *c.* 1811 but there are no thoughts as to when the shark actually swallowed the box.

JARLSHOF, SHETLAND

[date?]   Decorated pin of AD 700–900 .

JED WATER, SCOTTISH BORDERS

>2000   At a book launch in 2000, local historian Walter Elliot was contacted by a man who said he had a friend, now dead, who used to regularly fish the Jed Water. One day while he was fishing he found a gold coin. It turned out to be gold stater of the

mention of a small quantity of silver coins found at Kerse of Kinnel Farm from the same period; these were thought to have been buried between 1567 and 1625, also found in 1827.

JURA, ARGYLL AND BUTE

1981 A 10thC Viking gold armlet weighing about 4½oz, and made from gold rods twisted together was found on the seabed, in the Sound of Jura, by Martin Brown, a petty officer in the Royal Navy, while skin-diving. It was valued at £8,500 and the finder received £7,500 as a salvage award.

KAMES, ARGYLL AND BUTE

1966 More than 6 16thC copper coins, thought to have been concealed between 1542 and 1567.

KEIR MILL, DUMFRIES AND GALLOWAY

1866 141 English silver pennies from *c.* 1300.

KELLS, DUMFRIES AND GALLOWAY

1828 9 16thC silver coins, thought to have been concealed between 1567 and 1625.

KELSO, SCOTTISH BORDERS

1789 A small number of 16thC gold coins , thought to have been concealed between 1567 and 1625.

1910 Large quantity of jewellery found in a chest, in a mound of garden refuse at Sunlaws House. It was believed to have been dumped there when the building was cleared after being burnt down in 1885.

KELSO AREA, SCOTTISH BORDERS

1992 10 gold and 1,270 silver English and foreign coins, the oldest coin of 1546 and the latest of 1638, found in a pot on farmland at Wooden: finder William Swanson (M/D). At 18in below the surface, the find included coins of Edward VI, Elizabeth I, James VI, Mary, and Charles I, as well as foreign pieces from Poland, Spain, Germany, Austria and the Holy Roman Empire. They were thought to have been buried *c.* 1639–42, which may be a little early. They were not buried by the monks at Kelso as some have suggested, because the abbey had long gone. It was more likely *c.* 1644 when the ruins of Kelso Abbey were used by General Leslie's Covenanter army. The coins have been valued at £500,000.

KENMORE, PERTH AND KINROSS

1755 12 to 14 silver Roman coins from the 2ndC AD found in a vase 3in below the surface by workmen making a road across the hill from Taymouth to Glenquaich.

1915 3 copper coins, possibly from the 18th and 19thC, found at Inschedney Well, thought to have been concealed in 1806.

Eastern Emperor Flavius Julius Valens (AD 364–78), who was based in Syria.

JEDBURGH, SCOTTISH BORDERS

Large numbers of coins along with some old medals found at Stewartfield, Bongate, near the abbey, as well as at other places in the town. These include coins of Cnut, Edred, Edwy, Ethelred, Edward I., Edward III and later monarchs.

1822 14 16thC silver coins found at Castlehill, thought to have been concealed in 1556.

1833 More than 3 16thC silver coins, thought to have been concealed between 1513 and 1542.

1834 More than 300 16thC silver coins found at Swinnie near Jedburgh, thought to have been concealed between 1542 and 1567.

JEDBURGH AREA, SCOTTISH BORDERS

1897 538 silver coins, including 138 continental sterlings, from the 13th and 14thC found at Hill End field, Cleuchhead Farm; they were thought to have been deposited *c.* 1296–1302.

JOHN O'GROATS AREA, HIGHLAND

1969 More than 82 silver coins, mainly silver pennies of Henry III, Edward I and II, and Alexander III, believed to have been buried in *c.* 1320, found at Duncansby Head.

The National Museums of Scotland

JOHNSTONEBRIDGE, DUMFRIES AND GALLOWAY

1827 1 gold and a large quantity of silver coins from the 17th and 18thC, thought to have been deposited *c.* 1689–1707. There is also a

KILBRANDON, ARGYLL AND BUTE

1955   45 silver shillings, sixpences and merk pieces of Elizabeth I, and James VI of Scotland and I of England found by a young boy camping on a knoll a few hundred yards from Ardmaddy Castle. He found a single coin and upon clearing away the soil found the remainder of the hoard, thought to have been concealed in 1605.

KILDRUMMY CASTLE, ABERDEENSHIRE ▶ ▶ ▶ ▶

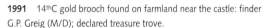

1991   14thC gold brooch found on farmland near the castle: finder G.P. Greig (M/D); declared treasure trove.

Aberdeen Art Gallery and Museum

KILKERRAN AREA, ARGYLL AND BUTE

1892   66 silver coins from *c.* 1490.

KILLICHONATE, SPEAN BRIDGE, HIGHLAND

1830   37 14thC silver coins found at the farm of Killichonate. Only 1 coin was viewed by experts, a Robert III groat of 1390.

KILMARNOCK, EAST AYRSHIRE

1785   About 168 silver coins from the 16th and 17thC, thought to have been concealed between 1625 and 1660.

1788   16th and 17thC silver coins, mostly shillings and sixpences of Elizabeth and James I of England, with some half-crowns and sixpences of Charles I, thought to have been concealed 1625–60.

1863   113 German thalers, from the 17thC, and 14 British 16th and 17thC coins found in Fore Street, thought to have been concealed *c.* 1649–85. Some coins were dispersed prior to what remained being examined.

1920   20 silver coins from the 16th and 17thC, thought to have been concealed *c.* 1671, found during building work in the Strand.

KILORAN BAY, COLONSAY

1882   3 mid-9thC Northumbrian stycas (coins) and an iron sword, a spearhead, an axe head, a shield-boss, fragments of an iron pot, 4 bronze studs and a balance with 7 decorated weights were found along with the crouched burial of a man which, from the evidence, took place after AD 850. There were 4 stones with crosses carved upon them, which indicates that this may have been a Christian burial as it looked out towards Iona.

The National Museums of Scotland

KINCARDINE AREA, ABERDEENSHIRE

1806   19 gold coins from the 16th and 17thC found at the Mearns, thought to have been concealed in 1604.

KINDROCHIT CASTLE, BRAEMAR, ABERDEENSHIRE

1925   Late 15thC silver ring brooch found in the pit prison of Kindrochit Castle by a party of Boy Scouts on a supervised excavation.

The National Museums of Scotland

KINGHORN, FIFE

1864   More than 1,000 silver pennies found near the railway and close to the old mansion house of Abden, 50yd north of the church. It included coins of Alexander II, III and David II and their condition suggested that the hoard was buried early in the reign of David II, *c.* 1340.

KINGHORNIE, ABERDEENSHIRE

1893   Over 1,000 English, Scottish and foreign silver coins from the 14thC were found in a light brown stoneware cooking pot at Inverbervie Farm. Nine years later more coins were found during ploughing.

KINNELL, ANGUS

1790   Quantity of silver pennies from the 13th and 14thC found in an earthenware pot in a bank above River Lunan, between Hatton and Hatton Mill.

KINROSS, PERTH AND KINROSS

1829   15thC gold seal matrix found by men digging the foundations for a new house.

KIRKCOWAN, DUMFRIES AND GALLOWAY

1815–20   Over 1,000 silver coins from the 13th and 14thC found at Glassnock Farm, believed to have been deposited 1280–1360.

KIRKCUDBRIGHT, DUMFRIES AND GALLOWAY

In 1843 the minister of the town wrote a history of the area and said, 'quantities of silver coin have been found, within the last twenty years, on the farm of Lochfergus'. In the same history he said, 'Small coins called "Charles' placks" have been often found in and near the town of Kirkcudbright.' These may have been forgeries of placks first struck in the reign of James III (1460–88). Counterfeits have occasionally been found elsewhere in Scotland.

1912   2 silver and 108 billon coins from the 16thC, thought to have been concealed in 1558.

1912   Quantity of 13thC silver coins.

1967?   16th and 17thC silver coins, thought to have been concealed *c*. 1625.

KIRKCUDBRIGHT AREA, DUMFRIES AND GALLOWAY

1850, or earlier   84 silver coins , thought to have been deposited *c*. 1296–1302. The hoard included a long cross of Henry III and 77 continental sterlings.

KIRKINTILLOCH, EAST DUNBARTONSHIRE

1797   About 16 silver coins from the 17thC, thought to have been concealed between 1625 and 1660.

1893   24 Roman *denarii*, and an iron spearhead, from the 1st and 2ndC AD, found by a labourer digging sand to be used in the Lion Foundry.

1902   2 Roman *denarii* and 11 tin coins from the 1st and 2ndC AD found during excavations of the well at the Bar Hill fort on the Antonine Wall. The coins lay among the detritus; 1 coin was lost but the rest are held by Hunterian Museum.

Hunterian Museum, Glasgow University

KIRKMABRECK, DUMFRIES AND GALLOWAY

1871   More than 10 silver and more than 40 copper coins found at Holecroft Farm, thought to have been concealed in 1560.

KIRKMICHAEL MAINS, DUMFRIES AND GALLOWAY

1821   Quantity of 14thC silver coins found between Nether Garrel and Courance. They were believed to have been deposited 1280–1360.

KIRKMICHAEL AREA, PERTH AND KINROSS

1867   5 silver pennies from the 14thC found by workmen; they were concealed in 1320.

KIRKPATRICK DURHAM, DUMFRIES AND GALLOWAY

1967?   16th and 17thC silver coins, thought to have been concealed between 1567 and 1625.

KIRKTOWN OF ALVAH AREA, ABERDEENSHIRE

1866   13 copper coins from the 17th and 18thC found at Mountblairy, thought to have been concealed *c*. 1689–1707.

KIRKTOWN OF DESKFORD, MORAY

>1726   More than 27 Roman coins from the 2ndC AD found during digging.

1816   Ornate bronze musical instrument shaped in the form of a boar's head from the Celtic Iron Age, and from *c*. 1stC AD discovered by ditch diggers. It is assumed it was taken apart and cast into a loch as a votive offering.

KIRKWALL, ORKNEY ISLANDS

>1880   In a contemporary book it was reported that 'A small Roman silver coin about the size of a silver sixpenny piece but much thicker and bearing date 140 was said to have been found a few years ago hereabouts in the Graveyard attached to the Cathedral of St. Magnus. The coin had the name of Sabina the wife of the Emperor Hadrian on it.'

KIRKWALL AREA, ORKNEY ISLANDS

1774   300 coins of Cnut, with many fibulae and fragments of silver, found in two horns at Caldale House. Many of the coins were dispersed but the fibulae and some coins along with the horn were saved.

KYLEAKIN, ISLE OF SKYE, HIGHLAND

1951   13 silver and 59 copper coins of the 16th–17thC found at Caisteal Maol; they were thought to have been concealed in 1601.

LANARK AREA, SOUTH LANARKSHIRE

1847   About 700 Roman coins, mostly *denarii*, apart from a few gold and bronze coins from the 1st and 2ndC AD, found 1½ miles east from Lanark during the building of the Caledonian Railway, in the lower part of a cairn of stones.

LANGHOLM, SCOTTISH BORDERS

[date?]   6 or 7 Roman *aurei* from Nero, Vespasian, Otho, and Domitian found by workmen on a farm. The Roman fort at Broomholm was close by. It was in use *c*. AD 80 during the reign of Agricola. Other periods of use followed, the last being *c*. AD 120 in the reign of Hadrian.

LANGHOPE, SCOTTISH BORDERS

1880 or 1882   Over 4,000 English and Scottish sterlings of Edward I, II and III; Henry III, Alexander III, John Balliol and Robert I, together with continental copies, 2 silver ring brooches and a silver pin, found in a bronze three-legged cooking pot. It was found 'about a mile and a quarter up the Langhope Burn, in a small gulley which branches off to the left. Opposite are 2 vertical ridges of bare rock which may have been the mark by which the depositor hoped to identify the place of burial.' They were thought to have been concealed in the 14thC, possibly in 1356, during the 'Burnt Candlemas'. This was Edward III's campaign of burning and looting through the south of Scotland as he marched from Roxburgh to Haddington after Edward Balliol renounced his claim to the Scottish throne in January. This theory is supported by the fact that many of the English pennies were minted shortly before 1356.

The National Museums of Scotland

SSWADE AREA, MIDLOTHIAN

6 41 Roman *denarii* from the 1stC AD found during excavations of Roman marching camp at Elginhaugh.

UDER AREA, SCOTTISH BORDERS

21 Silver-gilt fede-ring from the late 15thC found near Earnscleugh ter, which runs into the Leader Water near Thirlestone Castle. A fede-is so called because of the 2 hands that are clasped in troth (faith).

URENCEKIRK, ABERDEENSHIRE

8 40 silver coins from the 16th and 17thC found at Northhill Farm, ught to have been concealed in 1623.

LAXDALE, SHETLAND ISLANDS

1962 5 17thC silver coins, thought to have been concealed *c.* 1649–85.

LESMAHAGOW, SOUTH LANARKSHIRE

1815 Quantity of silver coins from the 13th and 14thC found underneath a large stone, thought to have been deposited 1280–1360.

LEUCHARS, FIFE

1808 Almost 100 Roman *denarii*, in near perfect state, from the 1st to the 3rdC AD, found in a jar during ploughing on Craigie Hill. Among the emperors represented in the hoard were Severus, Antoninus and Faustina.

LINDORES, FIFE

1814 9thC Anglo-Saxon coins, including some of Ecgbeorht, found inside a triangular-shaped stone near the abbey church. Other coins possibly found in the area include some of David II and Robert II.

LINLITHGOW, WEST LOTHIAN

1789 Large quantities of gold and silver coins from the 16th and 17thC, thought to have been concealed between 1567 and 1625.

1910 2 silver and 192 16thC copper coins, concealed in 1559.

1963? 10 silver and 368 copper coins from the 16thC, thought to have been concealed between 1513 and 1542.

LOCH BROOM, HIGHLAND

1968 15 silver pennies and 9 cut halfpennies from the late 12th to early 13thC found during excavations at the Dun Lagaidh hill-fort; they were thought to have been concealed after 1242.

Hunterian Museum

LOCH DOCHART CASTLE, STIRLING

1906? 87 copper coins from the 17thC, thought to have been concealed in 1639. The two-storey tower house was built *c.* 1590.

LOCH DOON, EAST AYRSHIRE

1966 1,887 silver pennies, the majority English of Edward I and II, as well as 45 Scottish from Alexander III to Robert I and some continental coins, found in the remains of a pottery jug on the east shore of the loch just below Muckle Eriff Hill. They are thought to be associated with Edward II's campaign in 1332–5.

The National Museums of Scotland

LOCH MIGDALE, HIGHLAND

1900 Hoard of Bronze Age jewellery, including a bronze axe head, bronze hair ornaments, bronze bangles and anklets, and carved jet and shale buttons, found in a rock crevice above Loch Migdale. Apparently not all the pieces made it out of the Highlands. It is now believed that smaller pieces may have been kept by children playing in the area.

LOCH SWEEN, ARGYLL AND BUTE

1880 16th and 17thC silver coins found on the Island of Danna, thought to have been concealed in 1643.

LOCHGELLY, FIFE

1971 1 gold and 159 silver English, Scottish and French coins from the 17th and 18thC found while digging the foundations for an extension to the Old Ship Inn. They were probably deposited after 1762, as the latest dated coin was a gold Portuguese escudos.

The National Museums of Scotland

LOCHMABEN, DUMFRIES AND GALLOWAY

Lochmaben Castle was originally earthworks but a wooden tower was added c. 1290. The castle was seized by Edward I c. 1297, and attacked in 1306 by Robert the Bruce, whose childhood home it had been, and returned to the Scots after Bannockburn in 1314, only to be attacked again by the English in 1333. The castle got its first stonework while Edward I had the castle and it was the more impressive castle that the Earl Douglas retook for the Scots in 1384. Mary, Queen of Scots, and her husband Darnley attended a banquet at the castle in 1565. A few years later in 1588 it was besieged by James VI and taken. From then on the castle was abandoned and fell into the ruin it is today.

>1823 13th and 14thC silver coins found at Whitehills Moss, thought to have been deposited *c.* 1280–1360.

1845? 15th and 16thC silver coins, originally thought to have been concealed between 1542 and 1567, but given the castle siege of 1588, that may be a more likely date.

LOCHMABEN AREA, DUMFRIES AND GALLOWAY

1904 476 silver pennies from the 13th and 14thC found in a conical broken red-ware pot; the coins were dated from before 1325 and their concealment may have coincided with the English attack on the castle in 1333.

LONGFORGAN, PERTH AND KINROSS

1775 1 silver coin and small quantity of copper coins from the 17thC, thought to have been concealed between 1625 and 1660.

>1797 Over 700 silver Edwardian sterlings and 4 coins of Alexander III were found near a barrow called Market Knowe.

LUCE SANDS, DUMFRIES AND GALLOWAY

1935? 14 silver coins from the 16th and 17thC ,possibly concealed in 1614.

LUMPHANAN, ABERDEENSHIRE

>1750 14thC silver coins found in a pot on the edge of churchyard, thought to have been deposited *c.* 1390.

***c.* 1793** 2,000 silver coins from the 18thC, thought to have been concealed between 1697 and 1714.

MARNOCH AREA, ABERDEENSHIRE

1863 2 silver and 2,000 copper coins from the 17thC found close to a house called the Knowhead of Crombie; they were thought to have been concealed *c.* 1649–85.

MAYBOLE AREA, SOUTH AYRSHIRE

1919 197 copper coins from the 15th and 16thC found near Crossraguel Abbey; thought to have been concealed between 1500 and 1513.

1990s Medieval silver cross found near Crossraguel Abbey.

MEGRAY, NEAR STONEHAVEN, ABERDEENSHIRE

1852 141 Roman *denarii* from the 1st and 3rdC AD found in an urn by labourers digging a trench on the site of Megray Market.

MELROSE AREA, SCOTTISH BORDERS

1900–10 About 50 14thC silver coins, thought to have been concealed *c.* 1360; it is another hoard that may well be related to the Burnt Candlemas.

MIDCALDER, WEST LOTHIAN

1843? Small quantity of 17thC gold, silver, or copper coins, thought to have been deposited *c.* 1660.

MIDDLEBIE, DUMFRIES AND GALLOWAY

1851 3 silver ring brooches from the 14thC found at Middlebie church and given to the museum by the Revd A.E. Macdonald Dawson in 1851.

The National Museums of Scotland

MILLHEUGH, SOUTH LANARKSHIRE

1820 Quantities of 17thC gold and silver coins found, thought to have been deposited *c.* 1660.

MONIFIETH AREA, ANGUS

1854 More than 700 silver pennies from the 14thC found on land belonging to Lord Panmure. The finders disposed of most of the coins; however, 200 of the hoard that dated from 1320 were successfully recovered.

MONTCOFFER, ABERDEENSHIRE

1915 215 silver and 172 copper coins from the 18thC, thought to have been concealed in 1796.

MONTRAVE, FIFE

1877 9,615 silver English, Scottish and foreign coins from the 13th and 14thC found in a bronze tripod cooking pot during drainage work at a field called Well Park; they were estimated to have been buried in 1356.

The National Museums of Scotland

MONTROSE, ANGUS

1836 20 copper coins from the 16thC, thought to have been concealed between 1542 and 1567.

1859 19 silver coins and a spoon from the 13thC, thought to have been deposited *c.* 1296.

1973 77 silver coins, mainly silver pennies of Edward I and II, and Alexander III and Robert I of Scotland, found in a leather bag on a building site in Castle Street. They were thought to have been deposited after 1332–40.

MORAY FIRTH, MORAY

1847 4thC AD gold crossbow brooch.

British Museum

MOULIN, PERTH AND KINROSS

>1835 More than 20 silver coins, Edwardian pennies and sterlings of Alexander III, from the 13th to the 14thC found at Stronchane Farm.

MUSSELBURGH, EAST LOTHIAN

1951 318 17thC silver coins found in the area of Fisherrow Harbour; they were thought to have been deposited *c.* 1646.

MUTHILL, PERTH AND KINROSS

***c.* 1672** Roman silver coins and a large ring of gold from the 1st and 2ndC AD were found by men digging deep foundations for a new kiln for corn in the area of Drummond Castle (featured in the film *Rob Roy*). The coins, described as 'more than a bushel of them', ended up being sold to goldsmiths in Perth.

1837 2 bronze armlets from *c.* AD 50–150 found on Pitkelloney Farm, about 2 miles from Drummond Castle. They were probably cast flat, then hammered flat before being inlaid with yellow and red glass.

British Museum

NAIRN, HIGHLAND

1460 Roman silver coins found in a marble vessel on the common where Brehan Castle was built in the 17thC; it has since been demolished.

NETHERFIELD AREA, DUMFRIES AND GALLOWAY

1860 194 silver pennies of Edward I and II from the 13th and 14thC. Reports have suggested they were concealed *c.* 1300–7, but this seems too early. They may well be related to the finds around Lochmaben Castle which is just a few miles to the east.

NEW CUMNOCK, EAST AYRSHIRE

***c.* 1828** About 100 Edward I silver pennies and Scottish sterlings of Alexander III found in a small earthenware jar/pot by a farm worker digging with a spade at Whitehill Farm. They were believed to have been deposited *c.* 1280–1360.

1882 41 gold and 142 silver coins from the 15thC found in a pot near Whitehill Farm; they were believed to have been hidden *c.* 1480.

NEWCASTLETON, SCOTTISH BORDERS

1937 14 English long-cross silver pennies from about 1260, around the time of the Baron's Revolt.

NEWMILNS, EAST AYRSHIRE

1783 16th and 17thC copper coins, thought to have been concealed between 1567 and 1625.

NEWSTEAD, SCOTTISH BORDERS

1863 1 silver and 97 copper coins from the 16thC, thought to have been concealed in 1560.

Scale armour and a wine jug featuring the head of Bacchus were just two of the numerous finds from the Newstead site.

NIGG, HIGHLAND

1793? 16thC silver coins, thought to have been concealed in 1559.

NORANSIDE, ANGUS

1962 1 silver and 93 copper coins from the 16thC, thought to have been concealed in 1587.

NORRIE'S LAW, NEAR CUPAR, FIFE

***c.* 1817** Many large silver items were found by a 'tinker' on the Norrie's Law estate in a mound. He did not declare the finds and sold items to a silversmith in nearby Cupar. These included a suit of silver armour and some coins. The owner of the estate, General Durham, had the mound excavated and found many more items, including 3 hand-pins, a pair of large penannular rings, 2 leaf-shaped brooches, a large silver roundel, a bowl, finger-rings and many pieces of bracelets and some silver mounts. It was at first thought that the tumulus dated to the 7thC but the finds indicate that it was probably earlier, around the 5thC AD. Local legend says that it contained the body of the Danish warrior Norroway, buried in a suit of silver armour.

The National Museums of Scotland

OLD MONKLAND, NORTH LANARKSHIRE

1877 8 silver and 88 copper coins from the 17thC, thought to have been deposited *c.* 1672.

PARTICK, CITY OF GLASGOW

1766 About 30 silver coins from the 17thC, thought to have been deposited *c.* 1660.

PARTON, DUMFRIES AND GALLOWAY

1911 2,026 mostly silver pennies and foreign coins, thought to have been buried in 1320, were found in a wooden bowl during ploughing at Blackhills Farm, about 700yd from Corsock Tower. Since that time, and prior to 1975, the farmer has found 7 English and 3 Scottish silver pennies, thought to have been concealed *c.* 1323. These latter coins were returned to the finder and may well have been part of the original hoard.

PEELHILL, SOUTH LANARKSHIRE

[date?] 28 Bronze Age spearheads and fragments of a sword found during ploughing on a farm at Peelhill. It is unclear if they were an offering to the gods or belonged to a metal worker and were buried for some reason prior to being reworked.

PENICUIK, MIDLOTHIAN

1898 273 silver coins, mainly silver pennies of Edward I and II, the earliest of the latter king from 1320, found in a small yellowware jug on farmland near the parish boundary with Falhills.

PERTH, PERTH AND KINROSS

1803 Silver and copper coins from the 15th and possibly 16thC found in the Castle Gable; they were thought to have been concealed between 1500 and 1513.

c. 1812 Large hoard of silver coins said to be 'almost 6lbs weight' found at the site of the Parliament House. Most of the coins were fused together but those that were able to be identified included 1 of Alexander I (1107), 1 of John Baliol (1293), a groat of James I, a penny of Edward II, a Danish silver coin, and another foreign coin. The hoard was probably deposited between 1318 and 1360.

1836 Small quantity of 16thC silver coins, thought to have been concealed between 1542 and 1567.

1896 25 French, Spanish and Portuguese gold coins found in an earthenware pirlie pig during the building of the new Post Office; they were thought to have been concealed between 1513 and 1542.

1920 18 gold, 611 silver and 499 copper coins of AD 1249–1513 found during the building of a new cinema at the corner of King Edward Street. 1,001 coins, including 8 gold coins, were returned to the finders.

The National Museums of Scotland

[date?] 2 Roman coins, one of Licinius I and a billon coin of Nero, found while digging a trench; both coins were minted in Alexandria.

PETERCULTER, ABERDEEN

1841 Small quantity of Scottish billon coins from *c.* 1560.

1852 22 silver and 2 copper coins of foreign origin, thought to have been deposited *c.* 1660.

PHILIPHAUGH, SCOTTISH BORDERS

1845 9 silver coins from the 17thC. They were thought to have been deposited *c.* 1660, but it seems more likely to have been 1645 when the Battle of Philiphaugh took place between Leslie's Covenanter army and the Royalists under General Montrose.

PIEROWALL, WESTRAY, ORKNEY ISLANDS

1800s Viking brooches and a Celtic bronze brooch along with other 9thC items found during the excavation of a Viking cemetery.

PITCULLO, FIFE

1781 19 Roman silver coins from Nero, Domitian, Trajan, Hadrian, Antoninus Pius, Marcus Aurelius, Commodus, and the Empress Faustina found during ploughing.

PITREAVIE, FIFE

c. 1850 17thC silver coins found by men digging a trench in a field.

PITTENWEEM, FIFE

1981 Coins, clay pipes and foreign pottery from 17thC found in a garden.

1998 2 silver pennies from Edward I: finder R. Nee (M/D).

PLAN FARM, ISLE OF BUTE

1863 4 decorated gold fillets (strips), 2 rings, and coins of David I and Stephen from *c.* 1200 found at Plan Farm.

PLUSCARDEN PRIORY, MORAY

1827 4 copper coins from the 16thC found at the priory, which fell into disuse after the Reformation. The coins were thought to have been concealed in 1558.

PORTMAHOMACK, HIGHLAND

1998 8thC coin from Frisia (Holland) found during excavations on the site of a Pictish monastery. It became the most northerly pre-Viking coin ever found; a coin at Dunbar in the south of Scotland, over 130 miles away, had previously been the most northerly coin. Other items, including pins and combs, showed that the monastery was in use from the 6th to the 11thC.

PORTMOAK, PERTH AND KINROSS

1851 600–700 Roman *denarii*, a sword and a silver piece of the 1st–2ndC AD found by a boy working in a cornfield which had once been a bog on the banks of Loch Leven. They were found just 4in below the surface with the iron sword and the silver piece, which is thought to be from the crest of a helmet.

PORTOBELLO, EDINBURGH

1852 About 600 silver coins found on the links, thought to have been deposited 1280–1360.

1980 Large quantity of 19thC jewellery found on the beach at Portobello by Harry Wordon (M/D). It included a fragile necklace, a hallmarked gold ring, gold locket, necklaces, bracelets, and brooches, which he took to a local police station. A month later he found a smaller quantity of miscellaneous jewellery about 15yd from the first hoard.

PORTREE, ISLE OF SKYE, HIGHLAND

1891 110 Anglo-Saxon, Danish, and oriental silver coins and 23 silver ingots and ornaments from the 10thC. This Viking hoard dated from about AD 950.

PORTSONACHAN, ARGYLL AND BUTE

1871 6 silver German thalers from the 17thC found at Barbreck Farm, thought to have been deposited *c.* 1645.

PRESTONPANS, EAST LOTHIAN

1869 1 gold, 2 silver and more than 101 copper coins from the 16thC found at Bankton House. It has been proposed that they were concealed in 1559, but in 1547 the Battle of Pinkie took place a few miles from Bankton. Without precise knowledge of the coins it is impossible to say if this was the date.

RAFFORD, MORAY

c. 1864 64 silver and 557 copper coins from the 17thC, thought to have been deposited *c.* 1649–85.

RANNOCH, PERTH AND KINROSS

1875   155 silver coins, thought to have been deposited *c.* 1643.

RATHO, CITY OF EDINBURGH

[date?]   2 Bronze Age axes found at Hillwood (formerly North Platt Hill) at what may well have been a hill-fort.

REDGORTON, PERTH AND KINROSS

1834   About 1,500 silver pennies of Henry III and Edward I, and sterlings of John Balliol, found under a large stone near Thistle Bridge; 23 coins included 1 from Berwick mint. Possibly concealed as late as *c.* 1300.

ROSEMARKIE, HIGHLAND

1788   17thC silver coins, thought to have been deposited *c.* 1660.

ROTHESAY AREA, ARGYLL AND BUTE

1813   Many hundreds of silver coins, including Edward I and II silver pennies and Scottish coins of Robert I and John Baliol, from the 14thC found during the construction of the coast road at Ascog Quarry. They were thought to have been concealed between 1335 and 1381.

ROXBURGH, SCOTLAND

c. 1878–1890s   About 1,000 silver coins from the reigns of Edward I and II and Alexander III of Scotland found in a pot, about 100yd from Cocklaw Castle. Given the reigns from which the coins came, they were probably concealed sometime after 1330. Whether it was as late as 1403 when Cocklaw was besieged by Henry 'Hotspur' Percy is pure conjecture. However, given the few that were recovered, just 37, it may be that the ones that were dispersed were of later origin.

Hawick Museum

RUTHERGLEN, CITY OF GLASGOW

>1793   Large quantity of silver coins, rings and trinkets found in a pot during ploughing, thought to have been deposited *c.* 1320.

ST ANDREWS, FIFE

1792   8 gold and about 150 silver coins, including some of Robert I and James I, found in a broken pot in North Castle Street.

1794   3 18thC French coins.

1845   47 19thC copper coins found in the old College buildings.

1983   Silver shilling of James VI from 1605 found in a molehill near a footpath at Kinkell Braes.

[date?]   6 19thC copper coins found in South Street.

ST MUNGO'S, DUMFRIES AND GALLOWAY

1834?   40 silver coins, thought to have been concealed between 1567 and 1625.

ST NINIAN'S ISLE, SHETLAND ISLANDS

1958   Hoard of Pictish silver objects from the 7th and 8thC found in a larchwood box under a slab, beneath the chancel of the church that had been in use during the Iron Age. A schoolboy, who had joined a dig, found the items, which included some that were magnificently decorated with animals and other designs. There was a silver hanging bowl, 7 other silver bowls, 2 sword chapes, 3 pepper pot shapes, a sword pommel, a spoon, a silver pronged instrument, and 12 silver brooches.

The National Museums of Scotland

SANDAY, ORKNEY ISLANDS

1991   23ft long Viking burial boat found containing a sword, a quiver of arrows, 22 gaming pieces, brooches, a sickle and a carved whalebone plaque as well as the bodies of men, women and children.

SHOTTS, NORTH LANARKSHIRE

1842   Several hundred Roman *denarii* from the 1st and 2ndC AD found while removing sods on the line of the Roman road.

SILVERBURN, ABERDEENSHIRE

>1726   A great quantity of Roman silver coins from the 1st and 3rdC AD.

SKAILL, ISLE OF ORKNEY

1858   10thC Viking hoard was found by a boy named David Linklater who was digging at Muckle Brae, near the Sandwick parish church, when he came across a few pieces of silver lying in the earth. He was soon joined by others working nearby and they unearthed over 100 items. The hoard was made up of 15lb of silver and included 12 silver Anglo-Saxon, Danish and oriental coins, 9 silver brooches, 8 silver wire armlets, 1 small decorated silver armlet, 7 silver bars and ingots, 15 silver rings, and many pieces of decorated silver. Many of the pieces in the hoard show signs of being owned, or used by a number of people, giving rise to the theory that this was a Viking 'pirate's' hoard. It was thought to have been hidden *c.* AD 950–70 and while it may have been hidden by such a man it may also have been an offering to the gods as part of a burial ritual. One factor against such a theory is that the hoard was buried in a stone kist, which could indicate that someone was expecting to return for what was an exceptionally valuable amount of goods. The hoard was declared crown property and was sent to The National Museums in Edinburgh.

SKIRLING, SCOTTISH BORDERS

c. 1814   Roman coins of Hadrian and Antoninus from the 1st and 2ndC AD found near Greatlaws.

SORN, EAST AYRHIRE

1837   500 coins, thought to have been concealed between 1567 and 1625.

SPROUSTON AREA, SCOTTISH BORDERS

1911   890 English, Irish, Scottish, and foreign silver pennies and 2 silver brooches found at Mellendean Farm. There were coins from Edward I, as well as 103 continental coins; they were thought to have been buried *c.* 1296–*c.* 1302.

STENNESS, ORKNEY ISLANDS

1879   4 Viking gold rings.

[date?] 9 Viking silver rings found at Ring o'Brodgar, the finest known truly circular late Neolithic or early Bronze Age stone ring. The Viking rings were buried there centuries later.

STEVENSTON SANDS, AYRSHIRE

[date?] Arabic coin minted in Tashkent and Samarkand *c.* 921–2.

STIRLING

1863 50 silver coins from the 16th and 17thC, thought to have been concealed between 1625 and 1660, found at Kippendavie.

STITCHILL, SCOTTISH BORDERS

1747 Hinged collar and pin and two armlets from the late 1stC AD found 7ft below the surface by 2 workmen digging a well. It is thought that the collar originated in the West Midlands. One of the armlets was complete, the other broken in two, half of which had disappeared. It is possible that they may have been inlaid with enamel or glass.

STORNOWAY, ISLE OF LEWIS, WESTERN ISLES

1954 120 English, Scottish, Irish and continental silver coins from the reigns of Elizabeth I, James IV of Scotland and I of England, Charles I and Charles II found at Stornoway Castle by a 15-year-old schoolboy. He accidentally unearthed the hoard with his foot while playing on the bank of a burn that runs through the castle grounds. They were thought to have been concealed in 1669.

1876 24 silver and two copper coins from 1572 or earlier found in the Steinish area.

STORR ROCK, ISLE OF SKYE, HIGHLAND

1876 Arabic coin from *c.* 935–40 found with other coins.

STRATHAVEN AREA, SOUTH LANARKSHIRE

1803 About 400 Roman *denarii* from the 1st and 2ndC AD discovered in an oblong square glass bottle by a boy cleaning out a drain at Torfoot Farm, about 7 miles south-west of Strathaven.

STRATHBLANE, STIRLING

1793 Small quantity of gold coins and a large quantity of silver coins, thought to have been deposited *c.* 1660.

STRATHDON AREA, ABERDEENSHIRE

1694 Hoard of silver, including coins of Charles I, discovered on the north side of Tom a'Bhuraich.

1822 Several hundred silver coins and 2 finger-rings found by workmen building a stone dyke on the 1,600ft contour line on the north-west slope of Tom a'Bhuraich. There were coins from the reigns of William the Lion (1174–1214) and Henry III (1216–72). The hoard was thought to have been hidden *c.* 1240.

STRATHMIGLO, FIFE

[date?] 6 bronze vessels, a large number of military weapons and 2 Roman coins, 1 of which belonged Domitian (AD 81–96).

STROMNESS, ORKNEY ISLANDS

1955 134 (some reports say 124) copper Scottish turners (Scots *2d* pieces), all from Charles I, found in a cloth bag, inside a chimney by the farmer demolishing a wall at the Old Croft at Pow.

SULLOM, SHETLAND ISLANDS

1951 2 silver and 1 copper coin from the 17thC found with a skeleton; they were thought to have been deposited *c.* 1690.

TANTALLON CASTLE, EAST LOTHIAN

1852 15thC old engraved iconographic ring; Captain Henry James gave it to the museum in 1854.

The National Museums of Scotland

TARBAT, HIGHLAND

1820 17thC copper coins found at Balone Castle, thought to have been deposited *c.* 1660.

TARVES, ABERDEENSHIRE

1811 Large quantity of gold and silver coins of James VI, from 1569, found at Mains of Cairnbrogie; they were thought to have been concealed in 1601.

THORNHILL, DUMFRIES AND GALLOWAY

1866 10 silver coins of Edward I found in a horn, thought to have been deposited between 1280 and 1360.

1964 Coin of Constantius II from AD 324–61 found in soil that had been scraped away by a rabbit on the site of what is thought to be a Roman signal station.

THREAVE, DUMFRIES AND GALLOWAY

1920s 15thC decorated silver locket found in a trench during excavations.

TOROSAY, ARGYLL AND BUTE

1840 3 silver coins from the 17thC found in a purse; they were thought to have been deposited *c.* 1649–85.

TRANENT, EAST LOTHIAN

1828 Small quantity of gold, silver, or copper coins, thought to have been concealed between 1542 and 1567.

1967 7 17thC copper coins found, thought to have been deposited *c.* 1697.

1980 150 silver coins of Edward I, II and III, and Scottish coins of David II and Robert II, and a few continental coins . They were thought to have been concealed in the late 14thC. They were found in the area of Blindwells, the site of an open-cast mine, to be redeveloped for housing.

TRAPRAIN LAW, EAST LOTHIAN

1919   160 pieces of bowls and drinking vessels weighing over 53lb from the 4th and 5thC AD found during an archaeological dig. Besides the silver pieces there were 4 silver coins (1 of Valens and 3 of Arcadius and Honorius) found in the hoard, which indicates dates from c. AD 410–25, although it could be later. While there are some Christian pieces the majority are tableware including 8 large jugs, 5 goblets, 50 bowls, 22 round dishes, 6 square dishes, 6 spoons, and various pieces including a small ladle with a dolphin handle and 2 panther-shaped handles. There are also items from a lady's dressing table. Most of the items were crushed flat or broken in some way as though packed for storage. Various theories have been put forward as to its history, including Saxon raids on the continent; some of the pieces can be traced to Hungary. More recently it has been suggested it could have been 'stolen' from the south of England. It could also have been payment from the Romans for Saxon mercenary aid.
The National Museums of Scotland

TURNBERRY AREA, SOUTH AYRSHIRE

1909   16thC gold finger-ring set with a diamond and with some enamelling.
The National Museums of Scotland

1978   Nearly 100 coins from the reigns of Edward I, II and III, and Alexander III found in a field.
Dick Institute

UDDINGSTON, SOUTH LANARKSHIRE

1835   Engraved Roman gem showing a winged kneeling spirit.

1848   Roman bronze coins, many dating to Tetricus (AD 271–3) found during the building of the railway at Clydesdale Junction.

URQUHART , MORAY

1857   Hoard of middle to late Bronze Age torcs that were all gold barring 1 in bronze was found at the Law Farm, Wallfield, during ploughing. The spot was about 40yd from the base of the Law itself and had at one time apparently been marked with a cairn. The number of torcs has never been definitively established but it was around 33. 10 are in the Museum of Scotland, 7 in the British Museum, and the rest in various other museums. Some, however, have been lost. In 1929 the farmer found another gold torc while planting turnips.
The National Museums of Scotland and British Museum

2002   Enamelled brooch and a bead from a beaded torc, both from the Iron Age at Binn Hill: finder F. Hunter (M/D); declared treasure trove.
Elgin Museum

WEISDALE VOE, SHETLAND ISLANDS

1914   Early 14thC gold engraved ring found during road works.
The National Museums of Scotland

WEST KILBRIDE, NORTH AYRSHIRE

1870   216 silver coins from Mary Tudor to Charles I found during ploughing at Chapelton Farm, thought to have been deposited c. 1645.

1876   360 coins from Edward VI to Charles II as well as German, Austrian and other foreign coins, originally in a canvas bag, found during ploughing on the hill face in front of Chapelton Cottages.

WEST LINTON, SCOTTISH BORDERS

1808   Silver coins of Mary and James V, thought to have been concealed c. 1625. A reward of £5 5s (worth over £200 today) was paid to the finder.

WESTNESS, ROUSAY, ORKNEY ISLANDS

1963   2 early to mid-9thC tortoise brooches, a Celtic brooch from c. AD 750 and a bronze mount found by a farmer while digging a hole to bury a cow. It turned out to be the site of a Viking cemetery and further bodies were discovered along with 40 beads, fragments of a bronze bowl and some iron implements.

1971   Early 10thC shield-boss found during an archaeological dig at the site of the 1963 find. The grave, of a very large man, also contained 23 objects, which appeared to belong to some sort of game.

1980   Weapons, jewellery and tools found during the excavation of a boat grave containing a male skeleton dating from the 9thC.

WESTRUTHER, SCOTTISH BORDERS

>1834   Large quantity of silver coins from the 17thC discovered in a cave at the ruins of the chapel in Wedderlie. They were thought to have been hidden during covenanting times c. 1660.

WHITECLEUGH, SOUTH LANARKSHIRE

[date?] Decorated silver chain from *c.* AD 500–600.
National Museum of Antiquities in Edinburgh

WHITHORN, DUMFRIES AND GALLOWAY

1957 Early 13thC gold ring and silver-gilt chalice and paten found in the grave of a bishop at the cathedral church. There was also a gold and amethyst ring, 2 bronze buckles, a fragment of gold braid, and the remains of a wooden crosier.
The National Museums of Scotland

[date?] 14thC silver ring found in a grave at Whithorn priory.
The National Museums of Scotland

WHITTON, SCOTTISH BORDERS

1819 190 copper coins, thought to have been deposited *c.* 1649–85.

WICK, HIGHLAND

1969 73 English silver coins of Elizabeth I, James I, Charles I, Scottish coins of James IV, and many 17thC foreign coins found at Hillhead during the building of a new school, thought to have been concealed in 1684.
The National Museums of Scotland

1881 15thC gold and silver coins were unearthed by workmen during the building of Temperance Hall Park; the men shared them out among

themselves. Later a bronze three-legged pot was found close by and later still 30 gold and 2 silver coins were recovered. Of the gold coins there were 16 Scottish, 8 English and 6 French. The earliest dated from Robert III of Scotland (1390–1406) and the latest were Edward IV of England and Louis XI of France (both 1461–83). The 2 silver coins were Scottish (James II 1437–60). It is thought that they were buried *c.* 1490–1500.

WOODEND, ISLE OF SKYE, HIGHLAND

1884 53 silver coins from the 16th and 17thC were found, thought to have been concealed in 1605.

YETHOLM, SCOTTISH BORDERS

[date?] 500 Roman coins found in a brass bottle. This may be a hoard found by a child in 1836 while playing in a field at Hayhope.

1837 and **1869** 2 bronze ceremonial shields from AD 1150–750 found by men draining a boggy field. A third one was found at the latter date in the same field. The shields have become famous in that others of a similar kind are always referred to as Yetholm-type shields.

2003 A Bronze Age circular mirror from *c.* 1000 BC found by Alf Slingsby and Roger Elliot (M/D) about half a mile from Yetholm. The mirror was about 14in in diameter and in many pieces. The find site was believed to have been the bottom of a small loch during the Bronze Age and was close to the shield finds of the previous century.

Wales, like Scotland, has yielded a rich and diverse range of treasures. The late Bronze Age hoard of mostly horse harness fittings found near Abergale, Conwy, and the fabulous gold cape found at Mold in Flintshire attest to the sophisticated culture that was present in Wales before the coming of the Romans. Numerous finds throughout the country – especially those at Caerleon, the City of the Legion, in Newport and at Caerwent in Monmouthshire – show how seriously the Romans took the conquest of Wales. Caerleon in Welsh means 'the fortress of the legion'; it has fuelled the legend of King Arthur holding court on the site.

Rome's retreat from Wales allowed the country to return to its pre-conquest status. Less has been found in Wales from this period than in many other parts of Britain. While this is no proof of a lack of activity it perhaps does show that there is ample opportunity for the detectorist to discover fragments of history that will help fill in the detail of this period. However, Viking treasure, Civil War hoards and numerous finds from the Middle Ages have made Wales a vital part of Britain's treasure trove past.

WALES

ISLE OF ANGLESEY

Holyhead

Llanbedrgoch
ANGLESEY 60
Beaumaris

Little Ormes Head

Llanrhos

Rhyl
Abergele
Conwy
Colwyn Bay

FLINTSHIRE

Bangor

Mold

Rossett

Wrexham

Caernarfon

CONWY

CLWYD

DENBIGHSHIRE

GWYNEDD

DEE

Porthmadog

Harlech

Barmouth

VYRNWY 1402

SEVERN

CAER CARADOC 51

Welshpool

BUTTINGTON 893

AFON DYFI

MONTGOMERY 1644

Aberystwyth
HYDDGEN 1401

SEVERN

POWYS

Rhyader

PILLETH 1402

Harlech Castle

CEREDIGION

Llangeitho

Lampeter

Llanwrtyd Wells

OREWIN BRIDGE 1282

Builth Wells

Cardigan

TEIFI

Fishguard

1797
Pentre-Ifan

Tregwynt
St. Davids

PEMBROKESHIRE

CARMARTHENSHIRE

TAF

Llandovery

Brecon

WYE

Carmarthen

TOWY

USK

Abergavenny

Monmouth

Haverfordwest

MERTHYR TYDFIL

Llandeilo

MONMOUTHSHIRE

Milford Haven

Llanelli

Merthyr Tydfil

BLAENAU GWENT

Pembroke

Tenby

SWANSEA
PORT TALBOT

Neath

RHONDDA CYNON TAFF

Pontypool

Usk

Caerleon

Chepstow

Swansea

CAERPHILLY

Caerphilly

Port Talbot

BRIDGEND

Caerwent

Magor

Newport

Coed-y-Wanallt

ST. FAGANS 1648

Cardiff

Monknash

THE VALE OF GLAMORGAN

Pentre Ifan Burial Chamber

km
0 10 20 30 40 50

miles
0 10 20 30

268

ABBEY CWMHIR, POWYS

[date] 13 silver coins from the 12thC, including coins of Henry II and Richard I, thought to have been concealed after 1176.

ABERAVON, NEATH, PORT TALBOT

1999 Highly decorated 14thC silver seal matrix: finder A. Malin (M/D); valued at £6,000.

National Museums and
Galleries of Wales

ABERGAVENNY, MONMOUTHSHIRE

1848 Roman gold and silver coins found in vases by workmen at the nursery a few miles north of the town. The finders sold the coins for profit.

2003–4 Roman leopard cup from the 1stC AD found on farmland: finder Gar Mapps.

ABERGELE, DENBIGHSHIRE

1842 400–800 Roman *denarii* in excellent condition from the 1st and 3rdC AD found by men digging a ditch in a field at Bron-y-Berlan Farm. Many of the coins were disposed of by the finders but 350 were retained and examined.

ABERGELE AREA, CONWY

>1868 Late Bronze Age hoard of over 100 items, mostly made up of horse harness fittings, found below the western defences of Dinorben hill-fort, which in itself is one of the earliest known examples from Britain to have survived. The hoard includes a rattle pendant, one of only 2 to be discovered, which was fixed to the horse bit. When these items were first discovered, it was suggested they might be from a warrior burial.

ABERGWYNGREGYN, GYWNEDD

1700s Gold image 5in high found by a local man near a cairn, known today as Carnedd-y-Ddelw (the Cairn of the image). He took it home but was dogged by so much bad luck that he eventually threw it away.

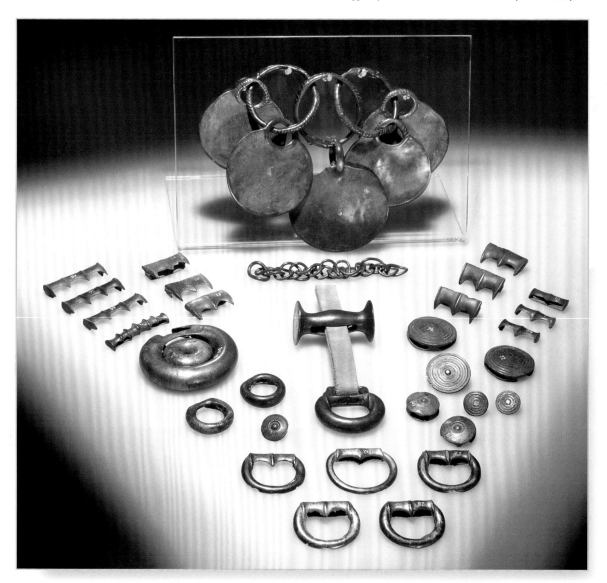

ABERKENFIG, BRIDGEND

>1879 About 550 Roman copper coins from the 3rdC AD found by workmen at the bottom of an 8ft crevice in rocks.

ABERNANT, CARMARTHENSHIRE

1823 60 silver coins from the 16th and 17thC, thought to have been concealed between 1625 and 1649.

ABERYSTWYTH, CARDIGANSHIRE

1841 Many hundreds of Roman copper coins from the 3rdC AD found in 2 bronze vessels near Nantoes, a Georgian mansion where a cup supposed to be the Holy Grail (known as the Nantoes Cup) was housed until 1950, when the last member of the Powells, who built the house, moved out.

1880–1 About 7,000 Roman copper *antoniniani* dated AD 260–85 found in a pot by a man ploughing a field south-west of Rhiw Arthen-Isaf farmhouse, near Goginan, about 4½ miles east of the town. The site is very close to the Roman road, which crosses the Rheidol at Pwlleynawon by Blaengenfford.

ACTON-PARK, WREXHAM

[date?] 7 Bronze Age palstaves found at Acton Park. They have since given their name to the innovative style of axes from this area of North Wales.

National Museum and Galleries of Wales

AMLWCH, ISLE OF ANGLESEY

1937 428 Roman copper coins and two silver rings from the 3rdC AD found underneath a stone during the widening of the road between Amlwch and Bull Bay.

ANGLE, PEMBROKESHIRE

1999 A late 13th–early 14thC gold finger-ring with a missing stone: finder J.R. Tree (M/D); valued at £550.

BANGOR, GWYNDD

1894 13 coins, a silver ingot, and a decorated fragment of a silver bracelet from the 10thC, believed to have been buried *c.* AD 930. The hoard is almost certainly a Viking pirate's plunder as it included Danish and oriental money, including at least 2 coins minted in Samarkand, along with the Anglo-Saxon coins.

BANGOR AREA, GWYNEDD

1978 37 Roman coins from the late 2ndC to the early 3rdC found on the beach.

BARMOUTH, GWYNEDD

1923 17th and 18thC copper coins, thought to have been concealed *c.* 1775.

BASSALEG, NEWPORT

1986 904 Roman silver *antoniniani*, except for 1 *denarius*, from the 3rdC AD found in the remains of pot by V. Thomas and K. Evans (M/D) at Craig-y-Saeson Farm, on the western outskirts of Newport; later declared treasure trove.

BEDDGELERT, GWYNEDD, WALES

1853 24 English silver long-cross pennies of Henry III dated 1248–60 found when a grave was opened in the churchyard. They were probably concealed at the time of the Barons' Revolt in 1264.

BIGLIS, VALE OF GLAMORGAN

1979 52 Roman silver coins from the 3rdC AD found during excavations of a Romano-British site. They were thought to be a scattered hoard of *antoniniani*.

BISHOPTON VALLEY, GOWER PENINSULA, SWANSEA

1939 Two Bronze Age pennanular brooches from AD 100 found on the site of a hill-fort.

Swansea Museum

BLAENAU, GWENT

1977 23 copper coins of George II, George IV and Victoria.

1986   900 silver and bronze Roman coins, including 90 *denarii*, dated AD 200–70, found by Viv Thomas and Ken Evans (M/D).

Museum of Wales

BODFARI, DENBIGHSHIRE

1927   16th and 17thC silver coins, thought to have been concealed between 1625 and 1649.

BORTH AREA, CARDIGANSHIRE

1930   31 gold nobles from the 15thC found loose in the ground. They were in very good condition and were thought to have been buried in 1425. In 1979 they were estimated to be worth £15,000, which equates to about £47,000 today.

BOVERTON, VALE OF GLAMORGAN

1798   38 Roman *denarii* from the 1st and 2ndC AD found by men removing soil on a farm.

BRECON, POWYS

1924–5   9 Roman *denarii* from the 1st and 2ndC AD found among the debris during excavation of the Roman fort at Brecon.

BREIDDIN HILL, NEAR WELSHPOOL, POWYS

>1865   1 Roman billon, 3 copper and more than 8 other coins, thought to have been deposited *c.* AD 306–37.

BRONYSKAWEN, NEAR LLANBOIDY, CARMARTHENSHIRE

1692   200–300 Roman silver coins from the 1stC BC to the 1stC AD found in 2 round leaden boxes (pewter canisters) just below the surface by 2 shepherd boys at the entrance of Bronyskawen, a Roman camp.

BRYN GWYDION, GLYNLLIFON, GYNEDD

1875   46 Roman *denarii* from the 1st and 2ndC AD found in a farmyard at Bryn Gwydion, sticking out of the ground.

BRYNDEDWYDD, NEAR LLANGWM, CONWAY

1863   About 2,000 Roman copper coins from the 4thC AD found in a vessel about a foot below the surface while draining a field called Gwann Yr Alt about half a mile from the Goat Inn, near Maesmore, Corwen, on the right side of the lane leading from the inn to the village of Bettws Gwerfyl Goch.

BUTTINGTON, POWYS

1955   11 silver coins, thought to have been concealed in 1579.

CAERLEON, NEWPORT

In Nennius's Historia Brittonum, *written in AD 830, there is reference to one of King Arthur's battles at 'The City of the Legion'. This may be Caerleon, which in Welsh means 'The Fortress of the Legion'. In Geoffrey of Monmouth's* Historia Regum Britanniae *(1133) (History of the Kings of Britain) he described how Arthur held court at Caerleon.*

Monmouth is 20 miles away so he may have made the link. Such is the complexity of the legend that we will never know for sure.

1926   5 billon farthing tokens of 1652–62.

National Museum of Wales

1926   10 Roman coins, of which 7 were *denarii*, from the 1stC BC to the 2ndC AD, found underneath the floor of the Roman legionary fortress.

1927–9   295 Roman *denarii* and brass coins from the 1st and 2ndC AD found in a barrack building at the fortress.

Roman Legionary Museum, Caerleon

1986   51 Roman *antoniniani* from the 3rdC AD found during excavations of the civil settlement on the Cambria House site.

CAERLEON AREA, NEWPORT

c. **1850**   1,700 Roman copper coins from the 3rd and 4thC AD found by an old woman in the side of an old quarry at Hendrew Farm.

CAERNARVON, GWYNEDD

>1789   Some coins found in a brass pot near the gallows on the river bank not far from the Roman fort.

1966–7   4 Roman sestertii from the 3rdC found in a bronze box.

CAERWENT, MONMOUTHSHIRE

The remains of the Roman city cover some 44 acres; it was originally surrounded by a 16ft-high wall, some of which can still be seen today. Known as Venta Silurum, it became the tribal capital of the Silures, and was on the route to the legionary fortress of Caerleon. The remains of a house, shops, a temple and the Forum Basilica can be seen today. Much of Caerwent, which was renamed when it was taken back by the Celts after the Romans left, is built from robbed out stone from the Roman city. Kelly's Directory of Monmouthshire of 1901 reads, 'Roman coins are found in great numbers'.

1850   116 Roman *denarii* from the 2nd and 3rdC AD found by a labourer.

1860   1,000–1,200 Roman copper coins from the 3rdC AD found in a pot in a quarry called Wentwood Mill. 1,051 coins (all *antoniniani*) are held at the Caerleon Legionary Museum.

Roman Legionary Museum, Caerleon

c. **1902**   7,000–8,000 Roman copper coins from the 4th and 5thC AD found in the ground during excavation of the site of a Roman house.

c. **1904**   About 250 Roman copper coins from the 4th and 5thC AD found 2ft below the surface during excavation of the site of a Roman house.

1908   About 200 Roman copper coins from the 4th and 5thC AD found in a vase during excavation of the site of a Roman house.

1909   About 1,000 Roman copper coins from the 4th and 5thC AD found in ground during excavation of the site of a Roman house.

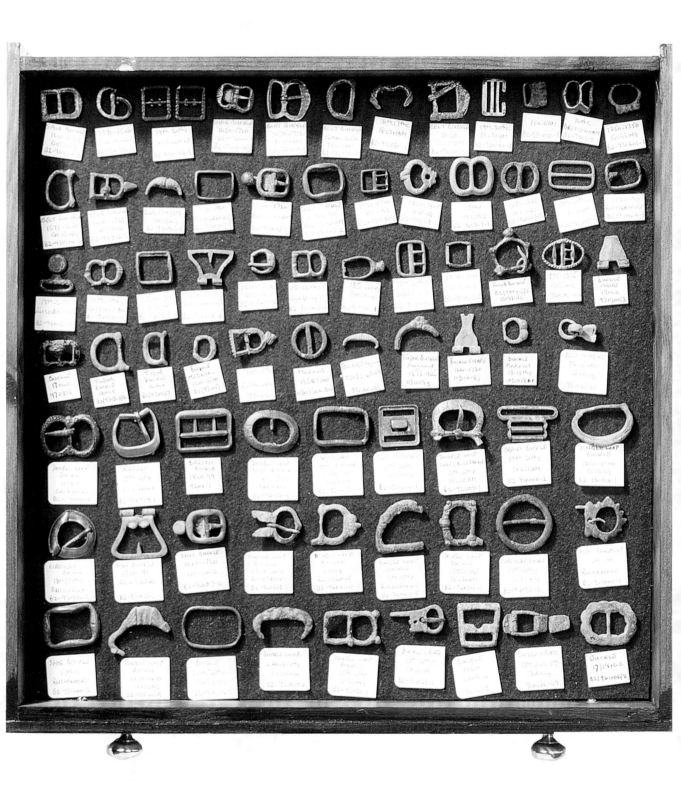

Bill annotates his finds and stores them in a set of drawers for ease of reference. These buckles have all been found close to Bill's home in Suffolk.

1909   About 430 Roman copper coins from the 4th and 5thC AD found in the ground during excavation of the site of a Roman house.

1909   About 1,450 Roman copper coins from the 4th and 5thC AD found in the ground during excavation of the site of a Roman house.

1917   Small hoard of early Saxon silver coins found by a farmer while digging.

1925   Small hoard of Henry VIII silver groats found in a field.

1947   151 Roman copper coins from the 4th and 5thC AD were found scattered in the ground during excavation of the Pound Lane site of a Roman house and shop.

1973   About 25 Roman *antoniniani*, including 8 counterfeit coins from the late 3rdC, found during the excavation of a Roman building, outside the eastern gate of the Roman town.

CALDICOT, MONMOUTHSHIRE

1998   2 12thC silver finger-rings and a 13thC silver decorated annular brooch: finder B. Stephenson (M/D); valued at £840.

National Museum and Art Gallery of Wales

CALDY ISLAND, PEMBROKESHIRE

>1693   Roman coins and a glass vessel found in an urn.

CAMROSE, PEMBROKE

1956   45 gold coins, possibly from the 19thC, thought to have been concealed in 1882.

CAPEL ISAF, NEAR MANORDEILO, CAMARTHENSHIRE

1975   4 gold bracelets and part of a gold torc from the Bronze Age found beneath a large glacial boulder during pipe-laying operations.

CARDIFF

1890   3rdC AD Roman coins found near Holybush Road.

1904   46 gold and more than 33 silver coins from the 17th and 18thC, thought to have been concealed between 1697 and 1714.

1978   Large hoard of Bronze Age axe heads found by Peter Halewood (M/D) in a field near his home.

National Museum of Wales in Cardiff

1981   110 Roman coins dated AD 251–74 found by Derek Stowe (M/D) on three separate occasions. They were mostly made of base metal and were declared not treasure trove.

CARDIFF AREA

1999   8 Bronze Age axes and 1 fragment from 1150 to 750 BC found about 15in below the surface of a field by A. Learner.

CARMARTHEN AREA, CARMARTHENSHIRE

1750   3,000 Roman coins from the 3rdC AD found at Cynwyl Caio, 4 miles from Carmarthen.

CARREGHOFA, LLANYMYNECH, POWYS

>1878   Roman gold, silver and bronze coins found in an urn by a man in a stone quarry. The coins were sold to the visitors for a fraction of their value.

CASTELLIOR, TY CROES, ISLE OF ANGLESEY

1871   Some English leather token currency from 1280, used to pay workmen building Beaumaris Castle. These were well-formed circles of leather with pieces of silver neatly inserted and riveted in their centres, without any impression of character.

CASTLETON, NEWPORT

1999   4 silver shillings, 1 sixpence, and 1 half-groat of Elizabeth I (1558–1603), thought to have been deposited *c.* 1600: finder D. Groves (M/D); valued at £125.

Newport Museum and Art Gallery

CEFN, NEAR LLANWRTHWL, POWYS

1958   4 gold Bronze Age torcs found near a derelict farmhouse beneath a pile of small slabs with a large upright slab surmounting the mound.

National Museums and Galleries of Wales

CILYMAENLLWYD, CARMARTHENSHIRE

>1586 Large quantity of 2nd and 3rdC AD Roman silver coins found in pot by 'county people', as a contemporary report put it.

COED-Y-WENALLT CARDIFF

1980 86 silver coins and 16 fragments from the 12thC found in the bank of a trench in woodland on the west side of Caerphilly Mountain just 3in below the surface by brothers Stephen and Cyril Shepherd (M/D). The 102 silver pennies and cut halves were of Stephen and the Empress Matilda (Maud), who were cousins and at war over the succession to the English throne. One coin was a baronial issue in the name of Henri de Neubourg, a previously unknown coin and the first from the Swansea mint. The discovery of the hoard, mainly from the Cardiff mint, and thought to have been deposited c. 1141, trebled the number of known examples of Matilda's coinage. The coins were declared treasure trove and valued at £103,040 (over £270,000 today). The National Museum of Wales bought 34 coins for £43,670, and the British Museum bought 16 for £8,000. Other museums bought single pieces. The rest were auctioned at Spink's.

COWBRIDGE, VALE OF GLAMORGAN

1747 2nd and 3rdC AD Roman coins found near the castle.

COYGAN, CARMARTHENSHIRE

1965 315 Roman copper coins from the 3rdC AD found during an excavation of the prehistoric Romano-British and Dark Ages settlement at Coygan Camp.

CWMHEYOPE, NEAR KNUCKLAS POWYS

1955 3 Bronze Age gold neck-rings were ploughed up on a sloping piece of ground that was being ploughed for the first time in living memory. They were very close to the surface.

CYMYRAN, ISLE OF ANGLESEY

1998–2001 10 Roman silver and copper-alloy coins from the 3rd and 4thC found by A. Tommis (M/D), thought to have been deposited after AD 367.

CYNWYL ELFED, CARMARTHENSHIRE

c. 1870   2ndC AD Roman coins, *aurei* of Hadrian, found in a burial mound.

DINAS DINILE FORT, LLANDWROG, GWYNEDD

>1803 3rdC AD Roman coins found by a shoemaker inside the Dinas Dinile fort. He is reported to have sold the coins, become rich, bought houses, and turned himself into a gentleman.

DOLAUCOTHI, NEAR LLANDOVERY, CARMARTHENSHIRE

1960s? Roman gold necklace and necklace clasp from the 1st or 2ndC AD found close to the gold mines that were worked by the Romans and which may have started as early as the Bronze Age. The mine was under military control before going into private ownership and gold mined here was sent to the Roman mints. The gold was mined by slaves who hammered away at the rock to get to the veins of gold. Last worked in 1938, the site is owned by the National Trust, and they have been working with a team of French archeologists who are responsible for investigating the much older history of this site.

British Museum

DOLYDD, GWYNEDD

>1845 More than 16 billon coins from the late 3rdC were beneath the foundations of a house called Llwynygwalch.

National Museum of Wales

DRWSDANGOED AREA, CAERNARVONSHIRE

>1850 18 Anglo-Saxon silver pennies of King Cnut.

DYSERTH, DENBIGHSHIRE

1860 About 60 Roman coins from the 2nd and 3rdC AD found at the base of a hill called Graig Bach, during the construction of the railway line.

ERWHEN FARM, NEAR PUMSAINT, CARMARTHENSHIRE

1965 684 Roman copper and bronze coins from the 3rdC AD found by Forestry Commission workers using a bulldozer to improve a track 200yd north-north-east of Erwhen Farmhouse, a little over 2 miles from Dolaucothi, the site of the Roman gold mine. The coins were declared treasure trove and the 2 workmen were awarded £89 each (about £1,000 today).

Carmarthenshire County Museum, and the National Museum and Gallery Wales

ERYRYS, DENBIGHSHIRE

1982 2 Bronze Age bracelets, a jewellery clip, a tiny gold ingot, and a bronze axe head from *c.* 1000 BC found in a crevice in the rock face by Colin Keely. The find was one of the most significant of its kind and was worth *c.* £3,000 (£6,500 today).

National Museum of Wales in Cardiff

FELINRHYD, GWYNEDD

c. 1850   3,000–5,000 Roman copper coins, mainly copper folles of AD 335–40 found by labourers moving stones on Tyddyn Isaf Penrhyndeudraeth Farm, opposite the ford of Felinrhyd. Contemporary reports described them as 'about 2 quarts'.

FISHGUARD, PEMBROKESHIRE

c. 1780   3rdC AD Roman bronze coins found in an urn near a large stone during ploughing.

NEAR FISHGUARD, PEMBROKESHIRE

>1816 3rdC AD Roman silver and copper coins, thought to have originally been buried in a wooden box, found on Esgarn Moor.

GLASCOED, MONMOUTHSHIRE

1979 11 worn silver coins of Philip and Mary, Elizabeth I, James I and Charles I, dated 1555–1646, found in woodland: finder G.Whitney; later declared treasure trove.

GLYNTAWE, POWYS

1972 6 Roman billon coins from the 4thC AD found in a crevice in the Ogof yr Esgyrn cave, thought to have been deposited c. AD 337. Ogof Yr Esgyrn means 'bone cave'; and is so called because 42 human skeletons have been discovered in its chamber. Many of the bones date back to the Bronze Age over 3,000 years ago.

GOWERTON, SWANSEA

1938 About 30 Roman coins from the 1st and 2ndC AD found during the building of Gowerton County School for Girls in Dunvant Road.

GRAIG LLWYD, CONWY

c. **1871** About 60 Roman coins, mostly *denarii*, from the 1st and 2ndC AD found by 2 men removing soil. A number of coins were thrown away before they were recognised.

GREAT ORME, CONWY

1981 4 silver coins from the 10thC found in a molehill by a Leeds University student taking part in a field-course. 3 coins were fused together. The find was declared treasure trove.

National Museum of Wales, Cardiff

GUILSFIELD, POWYS

1935 288 Roman copper coins, probably from the 4thC AD found in a wooden box by H.K. Jones while ploughing on his farm at Caebardd, Broniarth.

1981 4,716 Roman copper coins from AD 316 to 328 found in 2 vessels just below the surface by F. Jones while ploughing the same field that yielded the 1935 find.

HARLECH CASTLE, GWYNEDD

c. **1695** 3rdC AD Roman copper coins found in an urn. The finder left the country shortly after selling the coins for 30 guineas (the equivalent of over £3,000 today).

HAVERFORDWEST, PEMBROKESHIRE

1864 3 gold coins from the 18thC, thought to have been concealed between 1727 and 1760.

NEAR HAVERFORDWEST, PEMBROKESHIRE

1984 A Bronze Age axe head and Celtic terret ring found by Tenby hotelier Kenneth Lunn.

County Museum, Haverfordwest

HOLYHEAD, ISLE OF ANGLESEY

1710 4thC AD Roman copper coins, many in mint condition.

1837 A great quantity of Roman copper coins from the 4th and 5thC AD found in a vessel near Treaddur, near the Coetan Arthur cromlech. They were taken to the British Museum, then posted back to the finder, but were stolen in transit.

ILSTON, SWANSEA

1823 More than 200 silver Roman coins from the 1st and 2ndC AD found about a foot below the surface among loose stones and rubbish from a limestone quarry and close to a kiln at Pengwern Farm, adjoining Leithryd.

1933 91 Roman copper *antoniniani* from the 3rdC AD found with a skeleton in a quarry.

KINSLEY WOOD, NEAR KNIGHTON, POWYS

>1852 A large quantity of 15thC coins, containing a considerable number of gold coins, 2 of which have been identified as Henry VI angels.

LITTLE ORME'S HEAD, CONWY

c. **1873** 6,000–7,000 Roman copper coins (all folles apart from a few *antoniniani*) from the 3rd and 4thC AD found in a large jar by a farmer on his land while altering the level of the road. Found in some old masonry, the coins were in a corroded mass, and were separated and carefully cleaned. The farmer's nephew later sold them.

1907 500 Roman coins and gold ornaments.

LLANARMON DYFFRYN CEIRIOG, DENBIGHSHIRE

1918 551 Roman *denarii* from the 1st and 3rdC AD found about 3ft below the surface in a drain cut in dry ploughed land. Some were sold or given away, but 504 were recovered.

British Museum

LLANBEDR DYFFRYN CLWYD, DENBIGHSHIRE

1816 About 1,500 Roman copper coins from the 4thC AD found lying on the inner side of the main ramparts of Moel Fenlli, an Iron Age hill-fort that was occupied during the Romano-British period.

1999 A late medieval–early post-medieval silver fede ring with clasped hands: finder P. Richardson (M/D).

LLANBEDRGOCH, ISLE OF ANGLESEY ▶ ▶ ▶ ▶ ▶ ▶ ▶

A Viking settlement was discovered on the eastern side of Anglesey in 1994 after a number of metal detector finds had been brought to the Museum of Wales for identification. In the field where some Viking weights had been found, an enclosure ditch was discovered and through radio carbon dating it was found to have been in use from the 1st to the 11thC.

>1994 An Anglo-Saxon penny of Cynethryth, struck between 787 and 792, a Wulfred of Canterbury penny struck c. 810, 9thC Carolingian deniers of Louis the Pious and Charles the Bald, and 3 lead weights of Viking type were all taken to the Museum of Wales for identification.

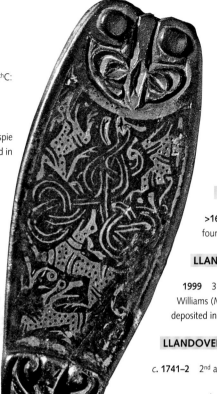

1997 A silver finger-ring from the 10thC: finder A. Gillespie.

1997–8 3 Carolingian silver coins of 814–77: finders P. Corbett and A. Gillespie (M/D); thought to have been deposited in the 9thC.

1998 A 10thC silver hammered rod: finder A. Gillespie.

1999 3 silver sheet fragments from the 10thC: finder A. Gillespie and P. Corbett.

2000 A 9thC Anglo-Saxon silver strap-end: finder P. Corbett (M/D).
National Museums and Galleries of Wales

2000 5 fragments of 10thC hacksilver found during excavations.
National Museums and Galleries of Wales

LLANBETHERY, NEAR BARRY, VALE OF GLAMORGAN

1957 814 Roman copper coins of AD 313–46 found in a vessel by Leonard Borlase while ploughing on a farm, along with traces of a Roman building.

LLANDDEWI FELFFRE, PEMBROKESHIRE

>1693 Roman silver and bronze coins of 1stC BC–1stC AD found in 1 pot, or possibly 2 pots, on a farm.

LLANDDONA, ISLE OF ANGLESEY

1999 311 silver pennies of Edward I and II found by G. Williams (M/D) on a beach. Thought to have originally been deposited in a cloth bag c. 1320–40, many were poorly preserved.

LLANDOVERY, CARMARTHENSHIRE

c. **1741–2** 2nd and 3rdC AD Roman silver and copper coins.

c. **1755** More than 12 Roman silver coins (Gordian III to Gallienus Antoniniani) from the 3rdC AD.

LLANDRILLO YN RHOS, CONWY

c. **1902** 3rd and 4thC AD Roman copper coins found in a vessel during digging for gravel.

278

LLANDUDNO, CONWY

1907 About 700 Roman copper coins from the 3rdC AD found 2½ft below the surface by workmen during the construction of the New Mostyn Broadway in the town. They were probably deposited in a wooden or metal box, as corroded fragments were found.

LLANDYBIE AREA, CARMARTHENSHIRE

c. **1736** Great quantities of Roman copper coins from the 4th and 5thC AD found in a quarry near Landevane Bath.

LLANDYFEISANT, CARMARTHENSHIRE

c. **1800** Well-preserved 1stC AD Roman *denarii* found in an earthen vessel in the kitchen garden of Dynevor Castle.

LLANEDEYRN, CARDIFF

The Cambrian Archaeological Trust undertook excavations at the site of these Roman domestic pottery kilns in 1978.

1892 About 800 Roman billon coins from the 3rdC AD found in a pot on the breast of a hill, on the line of an old watercourse, during ploughing.

National Museum of Wales in Cardiff

1975 1,094 billon *antoniniani* from the 3rdC, thought to have been deposited *c.* AD 275, found in a pot on the site of a pottery kiln. Daniel Lynch was clearing a site for a new housing estate near Hollybush Road when he came across 2 cracked jars containing *antoniniani* from 18 different 3rdC AD rulers.

National Museum of Wales in Cardiff

1992 110 Roman *antoniniani* of AD 251–74 found by D.B. Stowe on a housing estate, on the north-eastern outskirts of Cardiff.

National Museum of Wales in Cardiff

LLANELEN, MONMOUTHSHIRE

1961 A gold Roman *aureus* of Claudius I, struck at Rome AD 51–2, found by Edward Jones while cultivating a field on Ty Aur Farm. It was a very fortunate find as just the tip of the coin was protruding from the ground. The Museum of Wales confirmed that it was an almost mint *aureus* (probably lost or buried within a year or so of being minted). Ysgubor Aur, the name of the farm and adjoining barn, incorporates the Welsh word for metallic gold. This may indicate that a hoard had been found in the past but a careful search of the site using a Territorial Army mine detector revealed nothing (this was in the days well before metal detectors). The slope of the fields surrounding the place where the coin was found could have meant that it had been washed downhill by natural forces over the centuries.

LLANELIDAN, DENBIGHSHIRE

1866 200–300 Roman copper coins from the 4thC AD, together with a gold ring with a stone setting, found in a vessel by an old woman on Bodlowydd Ucha Farm. The finders disposed of many of the coins and sold the ring for £1 (equates to about £50 today). In 1987 two more coins were found at the same site by a detectorist.

LLANELLTUD, NEAR DOLGELLAU, GWYNEDD

1890 13thC silver-gilt chalice and paten found in a crack in rocks on a hillside by two gold prospectors who later sold them for 50s. They were probably associated with the nearby Cymmer Abbey. The crown claimed them as treasure trove, but found they had been sold at Christie's for £710. The buyer sold them to a Baron Schroder for £3,000 (around £190,000 in today's monetary values) who agreed that they would be handed back to the crown on his death. They are now in the National Museum of Wales.

National Museum of Wales in Cardiff

LLANELLY, MONMOUTHSHIRE

1897 19thC gold coins, thought to have been concealed sometime after 1837.

LLANELWEDD. POWYS

1984 672 silver coins from the late 17thC found in a bank, in a cleft between two rocks, by Andrew Nelson (aged 9), his two sisters, and cousin, on the farm belonging to his grandparents Mr and Mrs Ken Gethin. They were mainly silver shillings spanning the reigns of Elizabeth I to Charles II and were later declared treasure trove.

National Museum of Wales in Cardiff

LLANENDDWYN, GWYNEDD

c. **1848** A large hoard of Roman silver and bronze coins and 5 bronze vessels (the coins were in one of the vessels) from between the 1stC BC and the 1stC AD found at a place known as Vortigern's Isle, Ynys Gwrtheyrn, between Harlech and Barmouth.

LLANFACHRETH, GWYNEDD

[date?] Bucket made of sheet bronze from 700 BC found in a peat bog near Arthog. It was probably a votive offering and originated from the Danube Valley; it is the only item of its type ever found in Britain.

LLANFAETHLU, ISLE OF ANGLESEY

c. **1870s** 32 silver and 7 bronze Roman coins from the 1stC AD found during the digging of the foundations of Western Heights, in a field called Parc Stryd.

LLANFAIR CAEREINION, POWYS

1740 Large quantity of 4thC AD Roman copper coins found in an urn while digging in a field near the River Banwy.

LLANFAIR AREA, GWYNEDD

[date?] 10thC Anglo-Saxon silver coins, including 1 gold coin, unearthed along with skeletons near Plas Gwyn, a country house not far from the village.

LLANFAIRFECHAN, CONWY

>1955   30 Roman billon coins from the 3rdC AD, thought to have been concealed *c.* AD 293.

LLANFIHANGEL DIN SYLWY, ISLE OF ANGLESEY

1831   A great number of Roman silver and copper coins, along with several rings, keys, buckles and clasps of copper.

1900   61 Roman copper coins from the 3rdC AD found by a dog scratching at a rabbit hole.

LLANGEINWEN, ISLE OF ANGLESEY

1856   3rdC AD Roman copper coins found by men digging the foundations for a new wall. Along with the coins were animal bones, fragments of Samianware pottery, and glass beads.

LLANGEITHO AREA, CEREDIGION

c. **1792**   700 guineas found in the garden and house of Miss Lloyd, a wealthy spinster, who lived in the 'Big House' and was murdered in 1792 by John Benjamin, who was later caught and hanged. He swore he only found a handful of coins, and during the weeks following his hanging the old lady's relatives found a total of 700 guineas in several small parcels hidden or buried in various parts of the house and garden, but they all felt this was far less than the lady had possessed.

LLANGYNLLO, CEREDIGION

1804   80–90 gold nobles of Edward III and Henry IV, believed to have been hidden after 1400, found in a black crock on the bank of a little stream on farmland. They sold in London for 100 guineas, little more than their face value (a little over £5,000 in today's money).

1814   16th and 17thC silver coins, thought to have been concealed between 1625 and 1649.

LLANHAMLACH, POWYS

1999   12 Roman *denarii* and 3 copper-alloy coins from the 1stC AD found by M. Preece (M/D). Thought to have been deposited *c.* AD 50–60, they were valued at £180. Two years later the same man found a Roman *denarius* and 11 copper-alloy coins from the 1stC AD, thought to have been deposited around the same time as first find.

LLANIDAN, NEAR BRYNSIENCYN, ISLE OF ANGLESEY

1844   Roman coins, probably brass, from the 2nd or 3rdC AD, found in a vessel in a hedge running across an enclosure.

LLANRHOS, CONWY

1979   202 silver coins and 29 fragments of 1017–35 found on a footpath by John Jones (M/D) on land belonging to Mostyn Estates. Initially he found 16 King Cnut silver pennies minted in Chester and later he returned with Derek Blaymar and found more coins. They informed the Gwynned Archaeological Trust and a team uncovered the rest of the hoard, which was valued at £17,284 (equates to £54,000 today). The hoard was declared treasure trove. He only located the first find because he wanted to go to the lavatory and went into the bushes. He left his detector switched on and got a signal!

National Museum of Wales in Cardiff

LLANSAMLET, SWANSEA

1835   About 500 Roman copper coins from the 3rdC AD found in a pot after a tremendous thunderstorm. The rain washed away some soil and the coins were found by a small girl who thought they were buttons. She took some home and when it was realised they were coins, many people went to the spot and collected many others; only 260 coins were retained.

LLANTRITHYD, VALE OF GLAMORGAN

2001   Silver flat annular hawk ring made *c.* 1650: finder Scott Delafontaine (M/D). It was engraved 'John Awbrey Esqr' and would have identified a hawk as belonging to John Awbrey. It was found close to the remains of Llantrithyd Place, whose owner, Sir John Aubrey, fought for Charles I in the 1646 Royalist rising in Glamorgan.

National Museums and Galleries of Wales

LLANTWIT MAJOR AREA, VALE OF GLAMORGAN

1990s   Medieval copper-alloy rotary key.

LLANWRTHWL, POWYS

1958 Bronze Age gold earring found near a spring east of Talwyn Farm; it had apparently been washed out of the spring.

LLANYMYNECH, POWYS

1965 33 Roman *denarii* from the 1st and 2ndC AD found by a party of schoolboys in a lamp concealed in a pile of rubble in the shaft of old mine-workings on Llanymynech Hill. They were later declared treasure trove.

National Museum of Wales in Cardiff, and Oswestry Museum

LYN CERRIG BACH, ISLE OF ANGLESEY

1942 Roman coins found by men working on the construction of RAF Valley. The coins spanned 2 centuries of Roman occupation and were religious offerings, having been thrown into a shallow well near the site of a wayside temple.

MAGOR, GWENT

c. **1998** 3,778 Roman coins, including 700 coins from the time of the usurper Allectus, who reigned in Britain AD 293–6, found in a field by Colin Roberts, a member of the Gwent Metal Detecting Club.
Mr Roberts, aged 46, of Newport, Gwent, dreamed of digging up coins in a field he had previously searched. He said, 'When I had the same dream a few nights later I took a few hours off work the next day and went to the field. Normally I would start by the gate and work my way across, but this time I went straight to the middle. I took just two paces and my metal detector bleeped.' The coins were declared treasure trove.

MANORBIER AREA, PEMBROKESHIRE

2001 18thC gold inscribed posy ring: finder Gary Whatling (M/D); returned to the finder.

MARFORD, WREXHAM

1887 433 Roman copper coins from the 4thC AD found in the garden of the Elms.

MARGAM SANDS, NORTH PORT TALBOT

1972–5 1 gold and 12 silver coins and other objects from the 16thC found on the beach. The hoard included a Portuguese gold piece of John III, and silver coins of Spanish and Portuguese origin, along with other artefacts, all from before 1557. They are believed to have come from an unidentified and unrecorded Armada wreck lying somewhere close by.

MATHERN, MONMOUTHSHIRE

1998 A late 16thC silver-gilt dress pin: finder B. Stephenson (M/D); valued at £850.

National Museums and Galleries of Wales

THE MENAI BRIDGE AREA, ISLE OF ANGLESEY

1978 8 Roman *denarii* and 29 silver *antoniniani* from the 2nd and 3rdC AD found by K.P. Wynne and Haydon Williams (M/D) in earth that had fallen from a crevice in a steep rock, beside a path leading from the beach, in wooded ground known as Coed Cyrnol. They were later declared treasure trove.

Gwynedd Museum and Art Gallery

MILFORD HAVEN, PEMBROKESHIRE

>1901 A quantity of silver coins from the 12thC found but not declared and then sold off secretly. Some fell into the hands of numismatists, who identified them as Henry I silver pennies from 1129.

MOEL FAMAU AREA, FLINTSHIRE

1953 13 Roman coins, including 11 *denarii*, from the 1st and 2ndC AD found during excavations of a Bronze Age cairn on Cefn-Goleu.

MOEL FENLLI, DENBIGHSHIRE

1816 38 Roman billon coins from the 4thC AD, thought to have been concealed *c.* AD 348.

Grosvenor Museum, Chester

MOLD, FLINTSHIRE

1833 A Bronze Age gold cape from *c.* 1900–1600 BC found by workmen quarrying for road stone. In 1825 an elderly man and his wife claimed to have seen a ghostly warrior wearing golden armour while they were walking home from market but local people were sceptical. Then, some years later, the workmen uncovered a skeleton with a gold breastplate/cape. The field in which the cape was found is known as Bryn-yr-Ellyllon (Goblin or Fairies' Hill). The naming of the field probably relates to the fact that there was a burial mound in the centre and it was in a stone-lined grave that the workmen found this most fantastic of finds – one that has no equal anywhere in Britain. The cape was acquired by the British Museum in 1836 and initially they thought it was an elaborate horse harness. As more pieces of the cape were acquired by the museum (it had initially been split up between the workmen who discovered it), it became clear that the cape was beaten from a single piece of gold, which would have been worn over the shoulders of a man or woman. It had probably been worn on ceremonial occasions and would have been used like the 'coat of gold' seen in the apparition of 1825.

British Museum

1903 72 gold coins from the 18th and 19thC, thought to have been concealed in 1885.

MONKNASH, VALE OF GLAMORGAN

2000 103 Roman silver coins found in a pot about 17in below the surface by Steven McGrory on farmland. The coins cover 11 emperors, from Nero (AD 54–68) to Antoninus Pius (AD 138–61) and 3 of their relations. They include Vespasian, Trajan and Hadrian, as well as the short-lived Emperors Galba, Otho and Vitellius from AD 69. There are coins of Vespasian's sons (Titus, 79–81, and Domitian, 81–96) and Nerva (AD 96–8). There are also coins of 3 empresses: Sabina, the wife of Hadrian; Faustina, wife of Antoninus Pius, struck after her death in 141; and an extremely rare issue of Marciana, Trajan's sister, who died in 114. The find was declared treasure trove.

MONKTON, PEMBROKESHIRE

2000 A 15thC gold finger-ring, engraved with representations of saints: finder B. Williams (M/D).

National Museum and Galleries of Wales

MONMOUTH, MONMOUTHSHIRE

1728 Almost 2,000 Roman copper coins, all perfectly preserved, from the 3rd and 4thC AD, found in a vessel in the town.

1868 15 silver coins of Philip and Mary, Elizabeth I, James I, and Charles I, dated from the Civil War, thought to have been concealed some time after 1644.

MOUNTAIN ASH AREA, RHONDDA

1947 3 Richard II gold nobles of 1367–1400. Following a coroner's inquest 1 of the nobles was retained by the National Museum of Wales, and the other 2 were returned to the finder.

National Museum and Galleries of Wales

NEWPORT AREA, NEWPORT

1917 Small quantity of early Saxon silver pennies found in a field (*see* next entry).

1925? Small quantity of silver Henry VIII groats from the 16thC found in a field.

1978? Rare George II gold guinea found near a reservoir.
1985 7 gold sovereigns and 12 half-sovereigns from the 19thC found on farmland: finders Tom Smith and Terry Ackerman (M/D); valued at £2,000–3,000, they were handed to the police.

1989 Bronze Age hoard of 3 socketed axes, a spearhead (in 2 pieces), the tip of a sword blade, and 3 other fragments found in a field: finder Richard Jones (M/D).

NEWTON NORTH, PEMBROKESHIRE

1999 28 Roman base-silver coins from the 3rdC AD: finder K. Lunn (M/D). Thought to have been deposited *c.* AD 292, they were returned to the finder.

OLDCASTLE AREA, MONMOUTHSHIRE

1754–64   Roman coins possibly from the 1st and 2ndC AD found in a jug.

PEMBROKE AREA, PEMBROKESHIRE

1982   3 pewter dishes from the 17thC found in a fishpond near a vicarage: finder Arthur Duncan (M/D). They were lying on top of each other at a depth of about 10–12in. One dish was stamped 1624 and bears a maker's mark; they were thought to have been hidden during the Civil War.

PEN Y CORDDYN MAWR, CONWY

1985   4 Roman copper coins, 129 billon coins (including 12 imitations) and a bronze ring from the 3rdC AD found on gently sloping ground close to the hill-fort finder J.J. Kinsella. They were thought to have been originally buried in a leather purse, which had perished. There were coins from the reigns of 16 emperors and the latest coin was dated AD 320.

PEN Y GAER, POWYS

1998   Inscribed silver posy ring of 1600–50: finder B. Elliott (M/D); valued at £425.

PENARD, SWANSEA

1966   More than 2,583 Roman copper coins, all *antoniniani* except for 1 *denarius*, from the 3rdC AD, found in a badly damaged bronze bowl during excavations for a septic tank on a new housing development.

PENARTH FAWR, GWYNEDD

1860   Anglo-Saxon silver coins of King Cnut, dated 1016–35.

PENBOYR, CARMARTHENSHIRE

>1804   Roman silver coins found in a pot near the churchyard.

PENBRYN, CAREDIGION

>1845   Roman gold, silver and bronze coins, from the 1stC BC to the 1stC AD found in a pot containing ashes; they were below an inscribed erect stone.

PENCAEMAWR, NEAR USK, MONMOUTHSHIRE

2000   A 15thC gold finger-ring, engraved with the Virgin Mary and child: finder K. Evans. The image itself was very worn, indicating that it may frequently have been touched.

National Museums and Galleries of Wales

PENCARREG AREA, CARMARTHENSHIRE

1846   36 silver coins from the late 13th to the early 14thC.

PENDOYLAN, VALE OF GLAMORGAN

1640–50   27 silver coins of Edward VI, Elizabeth I and Charles I found in the thatch of a cottage.

PENNAL, GWYNEDD (CEFN CAER)

>1693   Roman silver coins, a gold chain and a brass pan found at the Roman fort. In a letter from Revd Maurice Jones, rector of Dolgelly, to Edward Lhuyd on 21 August 1693, he describes it so: 'As for Cefn Caer in all probability it was first built by the Romans by reason that the coyns of severall of the Cesars have been found there, as the coyns of Julius, Tyberius Augustus with many others (as Mr. Owen Wynne, the late owner of the land, assuredly informs me) . . . Besides the coyne there was found there a little gold chayne, and by digging further for treasure there was found a huge brass pann, which was bestowed upon Hugh Owen of Caer Berilan Esq., who made use of it for his brewing vessel!.'

PENRICE, SWANSEA

1830   Small quantity of silver pennies of King Ethelred.

PENTREGWYDDEL, LLYSFAEN, CONWY

1856   Roman silver coins, probably *antoniniani*, from the 3rd and 4thC AD, found by a farmer while looking for lost sheep.

PENYCAE

1979   105 coins spanning 90 years, from the mid-16thC to the Civil War. The last coin is dated 1644–5, but most dated to the reign of Charles I and were found in a culvert pipe on farmland by Bruce Davidson (aged 16), son of the farmer, who noticed some coins: 'At first I thought they were 50p pieces.' Valued at £4,450 they were declared treasure trove.

PETERSTON-SUPER-ELY AREA, VALE OF GLAMORGAN

1978   Bronze Age axe heads from 700 BC found in a field.

PONTYPRIDD, RHONDDA

1884   300 silver coins from the 16th and possibly 17thC, thought to have been concealed in 1605.

PONTYPRIDD AREA, RHONDDA

1988   35 hammered silver coins from the 16th and 17thC found on farmland: finder Tony Maz (M/D); valued at less than £1,000, they were declared treasure trove.

PORT EYNON, SWANSEA

1999   A penannular hair-ring of gold, electrum and copper from 1100 to 750 BC: finder R. Sanders (M/D); valued at £750.

National Museums and Galleries of Wales

PRESCELLY HILLS, PEMBROKESHIRE

1837   Roman coins found in an urn. A contemporary magazine reported: 'Another correspondent of Sylvanus Urban speaks of the discovery of an urn full of coins on Precilly mountain in Carmaithenshire, over which the Roman road to St David's passes. One of these coins is the very common *denarius* of the Julian family with the elephant. Reverse – the pontifical instruments.'

PRESTATYN, DENBIGHSHIRE

1868   1 gold and about 20 Roman silver coins from the 4th and 5thC AD found by men building the railway from Prestatyn Station to the foot of Cwm Mountain; they quickly disposed of the coins.

1934   519 silver coins from the 16th and 17thC, thought to have been concealed in 1643.

PRESTEIGNE, POWYS

c. **1940**   24 Roman silver coins from the 1st and 2ndC AD found by two gardeners converting a tennis court into a vegetable patch on the south side of Corton House, about half a mile south-east of Presteigne. They were in a metal container, which crumbled to pieces when touched. In 1951 7 more Roman silver coins from the 1st and 2ndC AD were dug up in the vegetable patch.

Radnorshire Museum

PYLE, BRIDGEND

1957   10 Roman coins from the 3rdC, thought to have been deposited *c.* AD 280.

National Museums and Galleries of Wales

RAGLAN, MONMOUTHSHIRE

1998   Large, highly decorated, 15thC gold signet ring: finder R. Treadgold (M/D). Known as the Raglan Ring it was too big to be worn over a finger and was probably worn over a glove. It was valued at £30,000.

National Museums and Galleries of Wales

RHAYADER, POWYS

1886   Roman ring, bracelet and necklet from the 2nd or 3rdC AD found a few miles north-west of the fort at Castell Collen, Llandrindod Wells. A young man was rolling stones down a hill 'to scare the foxes', and when he tried to dislodge a piece of rock the jewellery fell out of a crevice. He took one of his finds to the High Sheriff, who sent it to London where it was melted down and was discovered to be 22.5ct gold. The remaining pieces were then handed over to the sheriff, who sent them to the British Museum. There is speculation that the hoard may have belonged to the wife of Vortigern, the legendary 5thC Romano-British king who was on the run through Wales.

ROGIET, MONMOUTHSHIRE

1998   3,778 Roman base-silver coins, 7 *denarii* and 3,771 radiates, from the 3rdC AD: finder C. Roberts (M/D). Thought to have been deposited *c.* AD 295, they were valued at £40,000.

National Museums and Galleries of Wales

ROSSETT, WREXHAM

2002   Bronze Age hoard including a faceted axe, a knife (in 2 pieces), and 4 gold bracelet fragments, found inside the axe, dating from *c.*1000 to 800 BC, found by P. Williams and Mike Sheen (M/D) during a metal-detecting rally.

Wrexham County Borough Museum

2004   14 gold, bronze and ancient pottery artefacts of 1300–1100 BC: finders Peter Skelly, William May and Joseph Perry. They were members of the South Lancashire and Cheshire Metal Detectors Club. They first found a Bronze Age axe head about 8in below the surface which was soon followed by a gold torc. The final haul was a twisted gold wire bracelet, a spiralled gold wire pendant, the torc, a pendant, a collection of beads, rings and a bracelet. The bracelet was 25yd from the other finds and was probably disturbed by ploughing.

National Museums and Galleries of Wales

RUABON, WREXHAM

1979   105 silver coins of Edward VI, Mary I, Philip and Mary, Elizabeth I, James I, and Charles I, thought to have been concealed in 1644–5 at Penybryn Hall.

RUMNEY, CARDIFF

1980   64 silver coins, mostly silver pennies of Edward I and a few Scottish silver pennies, found during archaeological excavation at Caer Castell (Rumney Castle). They were thought to have been deposited *c*. 1290.

RUTHIN AREA, DENBIGHSHIRE

1776   600 silver pennies of Edward II (1307–27) found by a man cutting down an old hedge.

ST DONATS, VALE OF GLAMORGAN

>1760   In a description of the castle published in this year it said: 'Several ancient coins have been dug up here among which are some of "Aemilianus" and "Marius", which are very scarce.' Aemilianus reigned in AD 253 and Marius in AD 269.

ST NICHOLAS, VALE OF GLAMORGAN

2000   An inscribed late 17thC or early 18thC gold finger-ring: finder Gwyn Rees (M/D).

2001   A decorated 13th or 14thC silver brooch: finder Gwyn Rees (M/D).

2002   Bronze Age hoard of 10 socketed axes, a socketed knife, 9 sword fragments, 2 spearheads, a sword scabbard mount, and a penannular bronze bracelet fragment, found by a metal detectorist.

National Museums and Galleries of Wales

SALEM, CEREDIGION

1998   48 Roman base-silver radiates from the 3rdC AD found by Patrick McKeown, T. Driver and J.L. Davies. This chance find came during pipe trench excavation by Dwr Cymru (Welsh Water). The scattered coins, valued at £50, were recovered (M/D) and were thought to have been deposited *c*. AD 290.

Ceredigion Museum

STOW HILL, GWENT

1830   Large quantity of 13th and 14thC silver coins found by poachers digging out a rabbit warren to retrieve their ferret. Just 3 coins were recovered by the authorities, these being silver pennies of 1280–1300.

SULLY, VALE OF GLAMORGAN

1899 More than 300 Roman gold, silver and copper coins and gold rings from the 3rdC AD found in a metal vessel by a labourer digging foundations for a building on Sully Moor. He later sold his 'treasure' to a Cardiff antiquarian for 18 guineas. Many other items were hidden and later dispersed by the other workmen. The recovered items included 4 gold rings, 7 *aurei*, 96 *denarii* and 219 *antoniniani*.

SWANSEA, WALES

1840 157 silver pennies, mainly of Edward I and II.

1980 3,500-year-old spearhead found in a garden near Neath Abbey.

TENBY, PEMBROKESHIRE

1998 Late 16th or early 17thC gold finger-ring, set with stones of enamel or glass: finder G. Griffiths (M/D); valued at £150.

Tenby Museum

TIERS CROSS, PEMBROKESHIRE

c. **early 1990s** 3 gold Bronze Age torcs from the 12th and 11thC BC: finders Simon and Andrew Bevans (M/D). These are probably 1 torc and 2 armlets, and were later declared treasure trove. They were acquired for over £105,000.

National Museums and Galleries of Wales

TONGWYNLAIS, CARDIFF

1984 3 early Bronze Age halberds of 2250–1750 BC found on Forestry Commission land.

TREFEGLWYS, POWYS

c. **1835** More than 200 Roman *denarii* from the 1st and 2ndC AD found in a pot by farm workers near an old farmhouse at Cilhaul. A few days later a horse pawed up the gravel and laid bare an earthen vase containing more coins. Many were carried off, but nearly 200 were saved.

TREGARE, MONMOUTHSHIRE

1962 9 gold coins of Henry VIII, thought to have been concealed in 1544 or earlier.

TREGWYNT, PEMBROKESHIRE

1996 33 gold and 467 silver coins and a gold posy ring found during the making of a tennis court at Tregwynt Mansion by Roy Lewis (M/D), while checking spoil heaps. This was the last hoard of gold and silver coins from Wales to be declared treasure trove under the old common law, which has been superseded by the Treasure Act. The Tregwynt Hoard was probably buried during the Civil War and after applications for ownership of the hoard from descendants of the 17thC owners of Tregwynt were unsuccessful,

it was claimed by the National Museum of Wales. The coins ranged in date across the reigns of Henry VIII, Philip and Mary, Elizabeth I, James I, and Charles I, and included a number of Civil War 'emergency coinages' minted for the king while on campaign, with the latest dated 1647–9. There is another legend of buried treasure associated with Tregwynt, but this one is concerned with the Napoleonic invasion of South Wales in 1797. The story goes that a ball was taking place at Tregwynt and as the concerned and frightened guests heard of the threatened invasion they buried their valuables in the garden.

National Museums and Galleries of Wales

TREHAFOD, RHONDDA

1943 28 silver coins from the 16th and 17thC , thought to have been concealed between 1625 and 1649.

USK, MONMOUTHSHIRE

The Roman legionary fort known as Burrium was probably constructed c. AD 54.

1967 6 Roman *denarii* from the 1stC AD found while excavating the Roman fort. The latest coin was of Claudius, minted AD 51–4. It is thought that the hoard had been disturbed after deposition.

1969 4 bronze coins of AD 85–90 found while excavating the Roman fort.

1971 35 bronze folles of AD 310–35 found in a pot during excavations of the Roman fortress.

1971 Large quantity of Roman copper coins from the 4thC AD found in 3 pots. 35 coins were retrieved from a field; the rest had been ploughed off.

1971 6 Roman bronze coins and 6 copies of AD 348–50 found in a well during excavations of the Roman fortress (No.4). They were thought to have been deposited *c.* AD 350.

1973 7 bronze coins, 5 *dupondii* (Antonia type) and 2 asses (Minerva type), all counterfeit and well worn, found during excavations of the Roman fort. They were probably buried *c.* AD 64.

USKMOUTH, NEWPORT

1953 Coins found by workman pumping water from the river for the Uskmouth Power Station. Among the coins sucked up was an extremely rare silver tetra*drachm* of the Syrian King Demerius III (162–150 BC).

WALES

[date?] Middle Bronze Age gold torc made from a twisted bar and wound into 3½ coils, thought to date about 1200–900 BC.

WHITESANDS BAY, PEMBROKESHIRE

c. **1996** Small gold nugget, possibly dating from the late Bronze Age, found by a metal detectorist.

WILLINGTON, FLINTSHIRE

1840 16th and 17thC silver coins, thought to have been concealed between 1603 and 1625.

WREXHAM AREA

2004 Middle Bronze Age gold hoard found near Burton: finders Pat Skelly, Billy May and Joe Perry (M/D). It comprised a torc, bracelet, neck pendant, rings and beads. There were also two palstaves and a chisel in a small pot. It was later declared treasure trove.

YNYSFOR, GWYNEDD

1900 10 silver coins from the 16thC, thought to have been concealed in 1592.

YSTRADGWYN, GWYNEDD

1963 18 pieces of Bronze Age ware including shield-bosses found high on the slopes of Cader Idris. They were thought to be 2,000 years old.

The National Council for Metal Detecting

1. Do not trespass. Obtain permission before venturing on to any land.

2. Respect the Country Code. Do not leave gates open, and do not damage crops or frighten animals.

3. Wherever the site, do not leave a mess or an unsafe surface for those who may follow. It is perfectly simple to extract a coin or other small object buried a few inches below the ground without digging a great hole. Use a suitable digging implement to cut a neat flap (do not remove the plug of earth entirely from the ground), extract the object, reinstate the grass, sand or soil carefully, and even you will have difficulty in locating the find spot again.

4. If you discover any live ammunition or any lethal object such as an unexploded bomb or mine, do not disturb it. Mark the site carefully and report the find to the local police and landowner.

5. Help keep Britain tidy. Safely dispose of refuse you come across.

6. Report all unusual historical finds to the landowner, and acquaint yourself with current NCMD policy relating to the Voluntary Reporting of Portable Antiquities.

7. Remember it is illegal for anyone to use a metal detector on a protected area (e.g. scheduled archaeological site, SSSI, or Ministry of Defence property) without permission from the appropriate authority.

8. Acquaint yourself with the definitions of Treasure contained in the Treasure Act 1996 and its associated Code of Practice, making sure you understand your responsibilities.

9. Remember that when you are out with your metal detector you are an ambassador for our hobby. Do nothing that might give it a bad name.

10. Never miss an opportunity to explain your hobby to anyone who asks about it.

For more information on the Council contact:

General Secretary
51 Hilltop Gardens
Denaby
Doncaster
DN12 4SA
Phone: 01709 868521

E-mail: trevor.austin@ncmd.co.uk or visit the website at www.ncmd.co.uk

Museums

This is by no means a complete list of museums in Great Britain and Ireland with artefacts featured in this book. Neither does the information provided here detail every museum with items of interest to the detectorist or armchair treasure hunter; to attempt such would require another book entirely. However, we have tried to indicate which museums have especially interesting finds among their collections, which may perhaps encourage you to visit your local museum: our museums contain some of our finest treasures and are in themselves one of our greatest national assets.

Opening times are generally available on museum websites. For a listing of Britain's 3,500 museums, galleries, and heritage sites visit www.24hourmuseum.org.uk/

Aberdeen Art Gallery and Museum
Schoolhill
Aberdeen · AB10 1FQ
01224 523673
www.aagm.co.uk/code/emuseum.asp

Andover Museum
6 Church Close
Andover
Hampshire · SP10 1DP
01264 366283

Ashmolean Museum
Beaumont St
Oxford
Oxfordshire · OX1 2PH
01865 278015
http://www.ashmol.ox.ac.uk/

Ashwell Village Museum
Swan Street
Ashwell
Baldock
Hertfordshire · SG7 5NY
01462 742956

Bassetlaw Museum
Amcott House
40 Grove Street
Retford
Nottinghamshire · DN22 6JU
01777 713749

Roman Baths Museum
Pump Room
Stall Street
Bath · BA1 1LZ
01225 477774
www.romanbaths.co.uk

Bedford Museum
Castle Lane
Bedford · MK40 3XD
01234 353323
www.bedfordmuseum.org/

Bideford Museum
Kingsley Road
Bideford · EX39 2QQ
01237 471455

Birmingham Museum
Chamberlain Square
Birmingham · B3 3DH
0121 303 2834
www.bmag.org.uk/

Blackburn Museum
Museum St
Blackburn
Lancashire · BB1 7AJ
01254 667130

Bowes Museum
Newgate
Barnard Castle
Durham · DL12 8NP
01833 690606
www.bowesmuseum.org.uk/

Braintree District Museum Town Hall Centre Gallery
Market Place
Braintree
Essex · CM7 3YG
01376 325266

Brewhouse Yard Museum
Castle Boulevard
Nottingham · NG7 1FB
0115 915 3600

Bristol City Museum
Queen's Road
Bristol · BS8 1RL
0117 922 3571

British Museum
Russell Street
LondonvWC1B 3DG
020 7323 8000 (switchboard)
020 7323 8299 (information desk)
http://www.thebritishmuseum.ac.uk/

Bromley Museum
The Priory
Church Hill
Orpington · BR6 0HH
01689 873826

Buckinghamshire County Museum
Church Street
Aylesbury
Buckinghamshire · HP20 2QP
01296 337889
www.buckscc.gov.uk/museum/

Buxton Museum
Terrace Road
Buxton
Derbyshire · SK17 6DU
01298 24658

Calverton Village Museum
Main Street
Calverton
Nottinghamshire · NG14 6FQ
0115 965 2836

Cambridge University Museum of Archaeology and Anthropology
Downing Street
Cambridge · CB2 3DZ
01223 333 516
http://museum.archanth.cam.ac.uk/

Carisbrooke Castle Museum
Newport
Isle of Wight · PO30 1XY
01983 523112

Carmarthenshire County Museum
Abergwili
Carmarthen
West Wales · SA31 2JG
01267 - 231691

Carrickfergus Museum
Antrim Street
Carrickfergus · BT38 7DG
Tel: 028 9335 8000

Ceredigion Museum
Terrace Road
Aberystwyth
Dyfed · SY23 2AQ
01970 633088

Chelmsford and Essex Museum
Oaklands Park
Moulsham Street
Chelmsford
Essex · CM2 9AQ
01245 615100

Chepstow Museum
Gwy House
Bridge Street
Chepstow · NP16 5EZ
01291 625981

Chesters Museum
Chesters Roman Fort
Chollerford
Humshaugh
Hexham · NE46 4EP
01434 681 379

Chichester Museum
29 Little London
Chichester
West Sussex · PO19 1PB
01243 784683

City and County Museum, Lincoln
12 Friars Lane
Lincoln
Lincolnshire · LN2 5AL
01522 530401
http://www.lincolnshire.gov.uk/ccm/

City Museum, Winchester
The Square
Winchester
Hampshire
01962 848269

City Museum and Art Gallery, Gloucester
Brunswick Road
Gloucester · GL1 1HP
01452 396131

Cliffe Castle Museum
Spring Gardens Lane
Keighley
West Yorkshire · BD20 6LH
01535 618230

Clifton Park Museum
Clifton Lane
Rotherham
Rotherham · S65 2AA
South Yorkshire
01709 823635

Colchester Castle Museum
Castle Park
Colchester
Essex · CO1 1TJ
01206 282939

Corinium Museum
Park Street
Cirencester
Gloucestershire · GL7 2BX
01285 655611

Dales Countryside Museum
Station Yard
Hawes
North Yorkshire · DL8 3NT
01969 667450

Dartford Borough Museum
Market Street
Dartford
Kent · DA1 1EU
01322 343555

Dick Institute
Dean Castle Country Park
Dean Road
Kilmarnock
Ayrshire · KA3 1XB
01563 522 702

Doncaster Museum
Chequer Road
Doncaster
South Yorkshire · DN1 2AE
01302 734293
www.doncaster.gov.uk/Leisure_in_Doncaster/Museums_and_history/Museums_and_History.asp

Dorman Museum
Linthorpe Road
Middlesbrough · TS5 5DL
01642 813781
www.dormanmuseum.co.uk/

Dorset County Museum
High West Street
Dorchester
Dorset · DT1 1XA
01305 262735

Dunwich Museum
St James' Street
Dunwich
Suffolk · IP17 3EA
01728 648 796

Durham Heritage Centre and Museum
St Mary-le-Bow
North Bailey
Durham · DH1 3ET
0191 384 5589

Fitzwilliam Museum
Trumpington Street
Cambridge
Cambridgeshire · CB2 1RB
01223 33290
http://www.fitzmuseum.cam.ac.uk/

Grosvenor Museum
27 Grosvenor Street
Chester
Cheshire · CH1 2DD
01244 402008

Guildford Museum
Castle Arch
Guildford
Surrey · GU1 3SX
01483 444750

Guildhall Museum, Rochester
High Street
Rochester
Kent · ME1 1PY
01634 848717

Gwynedd Museum & Art Gallery
Ffordd Gwynedd,
Bangor,
Gwynedd · LL57 1DT
01248 353368

Harris Museum
Market Square
Preston
Lancashire · PR1 2PP
01772 258248

Haverfordwest Town Museum
Castle House
Haverfordwest
Pembrokeshire · SA61 2EF
01437 763087

Hawick Museum
Wilton Lodge Park
Hawick
Scottish Borders · TD9 7JL
01450 373457

Herbert Art Gallery and Museum
Jordan Well
Coventry · CV1 5QP
024 7683 2386
www.coventrymuseum.org.uk/

Hertford Museum
18 Bull Plain
Hertford
Hertfordshire · SG14 1DT
01992 582686
www.hertfordmuseum.org/

Hitchin Museum
Paynes Park
Hitchin
Hertfordshire · SG5 1EQ
01462 434476

Hull and East Riding Museum
36 High Street,
Hull · HU1 1PS
01482 300300.
http://www.hullcc.gov.uk/museums/index.php

Hunterian Museum
University of Glasgow
Glasgow · G12 8QQ
0141 330 4221
www.hunterian.gla.ac.uk/

Ipswich Museum
High Street
Ipswich
Suffolk · IP1 3QH
01473 433550

Kingston Museum
Wheatfield Way
Kingston upon Thames · KT1 2PS
020 8546 5386

Lancaster City Museum
Market Square
Lancaster
Lancashire · LA1 1HT
01524 64637

Letchworth Museum
Broadway
Letchworth
Hertfordshire · SG6 3PF
01462 685647

Littlehampton Museum
Manor House
Church Street
Littlehampton
West Sussex · BN17 5EP
01903 715149

Liverpool Museum
William Brown Street
Liverpool
Merseyside · L3 8EN
0151 478 4399
www.liverpoolmuseums.org.uk/livmus/index.aspx

Maidstone Museum
St. Faiths Street
Maidstone
Kent · ME14 1LH
01622 754497

Malton Museum
Old Town Hall
Market Place
Malton
North Yorkshire · YO17 7LP
01653 695136

Manx Museum
Kingswood Grove
Douglas
Isle of Man · IM1 3LY
01624 648000
www.gov.im/mnh/heritage/museums/manxmuseum.xml

Mildenhall Museum
6 King Street
Mildenhall
Bury St Edmonds
Suffolk · IP28 7ES
01638 716970
http://www.mildenhallmuseum.co.uk/

Moyse's Hall Museum
Cornhill
Bury St Edmonds
Suffolk · IP33 1DX
01284 706183

Museum in the Park, Stroud
Stratford Park
Stratford Road
Stroud
Gloucestershire · GL5 4AF
01453 763394

Museum of Antiquities, Newcastle
University of Newcastle
Newcastle · NE1 7RU
0191 222 7846

Museum of London
London Wall
London · EC2Y 5HN
0870 444 3852
www.museumoflondon.org.uk/

Museum of Scotland
Chambers Street
Edinburgh · EH1 1JF
Tel: 0131 247 4422
www.nms.ac.uk/home/index.asp?m=4&s=1&ss=6

National Museum and Gallery of Wales
Cathays Park
Cardiff · CF10 3NP
029 2039 7951
http://www.nmgw.ac.uk/nmgc/

National Museum Of Ireland
Kildare Street
Dublin 2
Ireland
(00353) 01 6777444
http://www.museum.ie/

Newarke House Museum
The Newarke,
Leicester · LE2 7BY
0116 225 4980

Newport Museum and Art Gallery
John Frost Square
Newport
South Wales · NP20 1PA
01633 840064
http://www.newport.gov.uk

New Walk Museum
53 New Walk
Leicester
Leicestershire · LE1 7EA
0116 225 4900

Northampton Museum
Guildhall Road
Northampton
Northamptonshire · NN1 1DP
01604 838111
www.northampton.gov.uk/museums/

North Lincolnshire Museum
Oswald Road
Scunthorpe
Lincolnshire · DN15 7BD
01724 853433

North Somerset Museum
Burlington Street
Weston-super-Mare
Somerset · BS23 1PR
01934 621028

Norwich Castle Museum
Shirehall
Market Avenue
Norwich
Norfolk · NR1 3JQ
01603 493625
http://www.museums.norfolk.gov.uk/

Nottingham Castle Museum
off Friar Lane
Nottingham
Nottinghamshire · NG1 6EL
0115 9153700

Pittencrieff House Museum
Pittencrieff Park
Dunfermline · KY12 8QU
01383 722 935

Plymouth City Museum and Art Gallery
Drake Circus
Plymouth
Devon · PL4 8AJ
01752 30477
www.plymouthmuseum.gov.uk/

Portsmouth Museum
Museum Road
Old Portsmouth
Portsmouth
Hampshire · PO1 2LJ
023 9282 7261
www.portsmouthmuseums.co.uk/

Potteries Museum and Art Gallery
Bethesda Street
Hanley
Stoke-on-Trent
Staffordshire · ST1 3DW
01782 232323

Radnorshire Museum
Temple Street
Llandrindod Wells
Powys · LD1 5DL
01597 824513

Reading Museum
Town Hall
Blagrave Street
Reading
Berkshire · RG1 1QH
0118 939 9800
www.readingmuseum.org.uk/

Roman Legionary Museum, Caerleon
High Street
Caerleon
Gwent · NP18 1AE
01633 423 134
http://www.nmgw.ac.uk/rlm/

Rotunda Museum
Vernon Road
Scarborough · YO11 2NN
North Yorkshire
01723 374839

Royal Albert Memorial Museum
Queen Street
Exeter
Devon · EX4 3RX
01392 665858

Royal Cornwall Museum
River Street
Truro
Cambridgeshire · TR1 2SJ
01872 272205
www.royalcornwallmuseum.org.uk/

Royal Pump Room Museum
Crown Place
Harrogate
North Yorkshire · HG1 2RY
01423 556188
www.harrogate.gov.uk/museums/

Rutland County Museum
Catmose Street
Oakham
Rutland · LE15 6HW
01572 75844

Saffron Walden Museum
Museum Street
Saffron Walden
Essex · CB10 1JL
01799 51033

Salford Museum
Peel Park
The Crescent
Salford
Lancashire · M5 4WU
0161 736 2649

Salisbury and South Wiltshire Museum
The King's House
65 The Close
Salisbury · SP1 2EN
01722 332151
www.salisburymuseum.org.uk/

Sewerby Hall and Gardens
Church Lane
Sewerby
Bridlington
East Riding of Yorkshire · YO15 1EA
01262 677874

Shrewsbury Museum and Art Gallery
Rowley's House
Barker Street
Shrewsbury
Shropshire · SY1 1QH
01743 361196
www.shrewsburymuseums.com/

Somerset County Museum
Taunton Castle
Castle Green
Taunton
Somerset · TA1 4AA
01823 320 201

Southend Museum
Victoria Avenue
Southend-on-Sea
Essex · SSO 8AD
01702 434449

Stevenage Museum
St Georges Way
Stevenage
Hertfordshire · SG1 1XX
01438 218881
www.stevenage.gov.uk/museum/index.htm

Swansea Museum
Victoria Road,
The Maritime Quarter,
Swansea · SA1 1SN
01792 653763
http://www.swansea.gov.uk

Swindon Museum and Art Gallery
Bath Road
Old Town
Swindon
Wiltshire · SN1 4BA
01793 466556

Tenby Museum and Art Gallery
Castle Hill
Tenby · SA70 7BP
01834 842809
http://www.tenbymuseum.free-online.co.uk/

Tolson Museum
Ravensknowle
Wakefield Rd
Huddersfield · HD5 8DJ
01484 223830

Tullie House Museum
Castle Street
Carlisle · CA3 8TP
01228 534781
www.tulliehouse.co.uk/index2.htm

Ulster Museum
Ulster Museum
Botanic Gardens
Belfast
Antrim · BT9 5AB
Northern Ireland
028 9038 3000

Verulamium Museum
St Michaels
St Albans
Hertfordshire · AL3 4SW
01727 751810
www.stalbansmuseums.org.uk/

Victoria and Albert Museum
Cromwell Road
South Kensington
London · SW7 2RL
020 7942 2000
www.vam.ac.uk/

Wardown Park Museum
Wardown Park
Luton
Bedfordshire · LU2 7HA
01582 546722

Warwickshire Museum
Market Hall
Market Place
Warwick · CV34 4SA
01926 412 500

Watford Museum
194 High Street
Watford
Hertfordshire · WD1 2HG
01923 232297
www.watfordmuseum.org.uk/

West Berkshire Museum
The Wharf
Newbury
Berkshire · RG14 5AS
01635 30511

Wiltshire Heritage Museum
41 Long Street
Devizes
Wiltshire · SN10 1NS
01380 727369
www.wiltshireheritage.org.uk/

Wisbech and Fenland Museum
Museum Square
Wisbech
Cambridgeshire · PE13 1ES
01945 583817

Wrexham County Borough Museum
County Buildings
Regent Street
Wrexham · LL11 1RB
01978 317 970

Yorkshire Museum
Museum Gardens
York · YO1 7FR
01904 687687
www.yorkshiremuseum.org.uk/

Bedfordshire & Hertfordshire
01727 751826
j.watters@stalbans.gov.uk

Berkshire & Oxfordshire
01635 30511 / 07795 092524
ksutton@westberks.gov.uk

Buckinghamshire
01296 624519
rtyrrell@buckscc.gov.uk

Cambridgeshire
01223 717573 / 07990 803551
chris.montague@cambridgeshire.gov.uk

Cheshire, Greater Manchester & Merseyside
0151 478 4259
nick.herepath@liverpoolmuseums.org.uk

Cornwall
01872 272205
anna.tyacke@royalcornwallmuseum.org.uk

Derbyshire & Nottinghamshire
01332 716665
rachel.atherton@derby.gov.uk

Devon
01392 665983
nicola.powell@exeter.gov.uk

Essex
01206 282931/2
caroline.mcdonald@colchester.gov.uk

Gloucestershire & Avon
0117 9223571 / 01452 425705
kurt_adams@bristol-city.gov.uk

Hampshire
01962 848269
jmccrohan@winchester.gov.uk

Hereford & Shropshire
01584 813641
Peter.Reavill@shropshire-cc.gov.uk

Isle of Wight
01983 823810 / 07970 009508
frank.basford@IOW.gov.uk

Kent
01622 221544
andrew.richardson@kent.gov.uk

Lancashire & Cumbria
01772 264061
vacant@mus.lancscc.gov.uk

Leicestershire
0116 2658325
wscott@leics.gov.uk

Portable Antiquities Scheme

The Portable Antiquities Scheme is a voluntary scheme for recording archaeological objects found by members of the public. Every year many thousands of objects are discovered, many of these by metal detector users, but also by people out walking, gardening or going about their daily work. Such discoveries offer an important source for understanding our past.

The scheme encourages finders to record these discoveries with their local Finds Liaison Officer or museum. Finds Liaison Officers welcome enquiries in their region and are also happy to record any archaeological objects that you might discover. A full list of the such officers can be found on the Portable Antiquities website (www.finds.org.uk).

The Portable Antiquities Scheme is the largest community archaeological project in the country. In 2003–4 some 2,376 finders volunteered 47,099 objects for recording, spanning 500,000 years of our history. While the majority of these finds were made using a metal-detector, over one third of the objects were discovered by other means, such as field-walking, often by chance. The long-term aim of the scheme is to change public attitudes to recording archaeological discoveries, so that it becomes normal practice for finders to report them for the benefit of all.

The best way of keeping up to date with what has been found, both in the past, and more recently, is to check out the Portable Antiquities finds database at www.findsdatabase.org.uk. Here you can access over 119,000 objects and 41,000 images, from prehistoric flints to post-medieval buckles. This resource can be helpful in identifying your finds, in comparing them with existing finds, and can act as a guide to the type of things most commonly found in your region.

Portable Antiquities Scheme
The British Museum
London WC1B 3DG
Tel: 0207 323 8611/8618
Email: info@finds.org.ukAcknowledgements

Witch bottle and contents (*c*.1820–80) – Often filled with cloth, human hair, nail-clippings or urine, glass witch bottles protected the victim of witchcraft by throwing the evil spell back onto the witch. This was common practice in the 17th and 18thC, but this example, found during building work, shows that witches were still being warded off in Lincolnshire in the Victorian era.

Aureus of Nero (AD 65–68) – An exceptionally rare find. An aureus was equivalent to a month's wages for a legionary soldier of the period, and may have been buried deliberately rather than being an accidental loss. This is only the second early gold coin to be reported under the scheme, and the first ever to be found in Cornwall.

Medieval silver gilt brooch (13thC) – An elaborately decorated silver gilt brooch of a knight and a lion, which some experts believe may represent figures from the Arthurian romance *The Knight of the Lion* described in tales by Chrétien de Troyes in the late 12thC. The brooch was discovered by a metal detectorist in Northamptonshire.

Lincolnshire
01522 553112 / 07717 303680
adam.daubney@lincolnshire.gov.uk

London
020 7814 5733 / 07766 303057
fsimpson@museumoflondon.org.uk

Norfolk
01603 493647 / 01362 869289/290
adrian.marsden@norfolk.gov.uk /
erica.darch@norfolk.gov.uk

North East
0191 222 5076
p.j.walton@ncl.ac.uk

North Lincolnshire
01724 843533
lisa.staves@northlincs.gov.uk

Northamptonshire
01604 237249
tbrindle@northamptonshire.gov.uk

Somerset & Dorset
01305 224921 / 01823 320200
c.h.trevarthen@dorsetcc.gov.uk

Staffordshire & West Midlands
0121 303 4636 / 07766 925351
Caroline_a_Johnson@birmingham.gov.uk

Suffolk
01284 352447/449
faye.minter@et.suffolkcc.gov.uk /
steven.plunkett@et.suffolkcc.gov.uk

Surrey
01737 247296
david.williams@surreycc.gov.uk

Sussex
01273 405731 / 07958 919226
flo@sussexpast.co.uk

Warwickshire & Worcestershire
01905 361827
abolton@cityofworcester.gov.uk

Wiltshire
01380 727369
katiehinds@btinternet.com

Yorkshire (South & West)
01924 305359
amarshall@wyjs.org.uk

Yorkshire (North & East)
01904 687666/668
simon.holmes@ymt.org.uk /
david.evans@ymt.org.uk

Wales
02920 573226
mark.lodwick@nmgw.ac.uka

Treasure on the Web

Apart from the wealth of knowledge and information available on the larger museum websites, and of course the Portable Antiquities Scheme site, there are many other very useful internet resources. Many are maintained by professional bodies and organisations, but there are also some well-designed amateur sites. As always with the net, be prepared to use your discretion and do not accept everything as fact. However, this should not imply that amateur sites are either unhelpful or not worth visiting; they contain much that is invaluable, particularly on a local basis.

As with the list of museums, this is just to whet your appetite for the vastness of cyber space: just go to Google, 'metal detecting' and see what happens – at the last count 693,000 sites!

Magazines and Journals

Antiquity: www.antiquity.ac.uk
BBC History: www.bbchistorymagazine.com
Current Archaeology: www.archaeology.co.uk
History Ireland: www.historyireland.com
History Scotland: www.historyscotland.com

History Today: www.historytoday.com
The Searcher: www.thesearcher.co.uk
Treasure Hunting:
   www.greenlightpublishing.co.uk/treasure

Professional Websites

SCRAN is an award-winning learning image website with access to quality images, sounds, movies and learning resources. There are over 300,000 images from museums, galleries and archives:
   www.scran.ac.uk

BRITISH HISTORY ONLINE
The digital library of text and information about people, places and businesses from the medieval and early modern period, built by the Institute of Historical Research and the History of Parliament Trust:
www.british-history.ac.uk

ARCHAEOLOGY DATA SERVICE (ADS)
The ADS supports research, learning and teaching with high quality and dependable digital resources. It does this by preserving digital data in the long term, and by promoting and disseminating a broad range of data in archaeology:
   http://ads.ahds.ac.uk/

COUNCIL FOR BRITISH ARCHAEOLOGY
The CBA is the principal UK-wide non-governmental organisation that promotes knowledge, appreciation and care of the historic environment for the benefit of present and future generations. Their web site has a huge amount of very useful information:
   www.britarch.ac.uk/

THE ORDNANCE SURVEY
This site was used to check locations and spellings and is an exceptional useful resource:
   www.ordnancesurvey.co.uk

THE NATIONAL ARCHIVES
Explore over 1,000 years of history from Domesday to the present day:
   www.nationalarchives.gov.uk/

Other Useful Websites

THE MODERN ANTIQUARIAN
Based on Julian Cope's guidebook of the same name this site is a massive resource for news, information, images, folklore & web links on the ancient sites across the UK & Ireland:
   www.themodernantiquarian.com/home/

ROMAN BRITAIN
This one has over 1,500 pages, with a wealth of information:
   www.roman-britain.org
The other is almost as big:
   www.romans-in-britain.org.uk/

ARCHAEOLOGY NEWS

A daily update of archaeological stories from around the world, this is a fascinating site:

www.archaeologica.org/NewsPage.htm

THE INTERNET MEDIEVAL SOURCEBOOK

This fascinating portal has no end of links including one to an online translation of the Anglo Saxon Chronicles and Bede's *Ecclesiastical History of England* – just to name two!

www.fordham.edu/halsall/sbook1n.html

Coin-Related Websites

THE BRITISH CELTIC COIN INDEX

Access to over 28,000 records and images of British Celtic coins:

www.writer2001.com/cciwriter2001/index.htm

THE ROYAL NUMISMATIC SOCIETY

www.rns.dircon.co.uk/

THE BRITISH NUMISMATIC SOCIETY

www-cm.fitzmuseum.cam.ac.uk/coins/britnumsoc/

IRELAND

A database of all the excavations carried out in Ireland – north and south – from 1970 to 2000. It contains almost 6000 reports and can be browsed or searched:

www.excavations.ie

A portal to many other Irish archaeologically oriented websites.

www.xs4all.nl/~tbreen/links.html

SCOTLAND

A fantastic portal to many other history-related sites in and about Scotland:

www.rampantscotland.com/

Another portal to a huge amount of archaeological data about Scotland:

www.gla.ac.uk/archaeology/scotland/

The official website for Treasure Trove in Scotland. This site provides information on all aspects of how finds of archaeological and historical significance in Scotland are recorded and protected:

www.treasuretrove.org.uk/

ENGLISH REGIONAL SITES

The Cumberland and Westmoreland Archaeological and Antiquarian Society:

www.cwaas.org.uk/index.html

East Anglian Archaeology:

www.eaareports.demon.co.uk/

Northern Archaeology:

www.n-a-g.freeserve.co.uk/

Staffordshire Metal Detectors Limited:

www.staffsmetaldetectors.co.uk/index.htm

DETECTOR MANUFACTURERS

There are a large number of retailers for detectors but these are the principal manufacturers:

www.cscope.co.uk
www.fieldmastermetaldetectors.co.uk
www.fisherlab.com
www.garrett.com
www.minelab.com
www.saxons.uk.com
www.tesoro.com
www.metaldetectors.co.uk (Viking)
www.troycustomdetectors.com
www.whites.co.uk
www.xpmetaldetectors.com

Bibliography

During the writing of this book numerous books and publications were consulted to both collate information and to give historical context to the finds.

Abdy, Richard Anthony, *Romano-British Coin Hoards* (Shire Publications, 2002)

Bahn, Paul, ed., *The Penguin Archaeology Guide* (Penguin, 2001)

British Museum Guide (British Museum, 1976)

Brown, I.D., and Michael Dolley, *Coin Hoards of Great Britain and Ireland, 1500–1967* (Royal Numismatic Society, 1971)

Burke, John, *Roman England* (Artus, 1983)

Campbell, James, ed., *The Anglo-Saxons* (Phaidon, 1982)

Care Evans, Angela, *The Sutton Hoo Ship Burial* (British Museum, 1986)

Casey, John, and Richard Reece, ed., *Coins and the Archaeologist* (Seaby, 1988)

Coin Hoards, Volumes I–VI (The Royal Numismatic Society, 1975, 1976, 1977, 1978, 1979, 1981 and 1983)

Cottrell, Leonard, *Seeing Roman Britain* (Evans, 1956)

Cribb, Joe, Barrie Cook and Ian Carradice, *The Coin Atlas* (Macdonald Illustrated, 1990)

Crummy, Philip, *City of Victory: The Story of Colchester, Britain's First Roman Town* (Colchester Archaeological Trust, 2001)

Cunliffe, Barry, ed., *The Oxford Illustrated Prehistory of Europe* (Oxford University Press, 1994)

de la Bedoyere, Guy, *The Finds of Roman Britain* (B.T. Batsford, 1989)

Falkus, Malcolm, and John Gillingham, eds, *Historical Atlas of Britain* (Crescent Books, 1987)

Faulkner, Neil, *Hidden Treasure: Digging Up Britain's Past* (BBC Books, 2003)

Fletcher, Edward, *Buried British Treasure Hoards* (Greenlight Publishing, 1996)

Friar, Stephen, *The Local History Companion* (Sutton, 2001)

Glenn, Virginia, *Romanesque and Gothic Decorative Metalwork and Ivory Carvings in the Museum of Scotland* (National Museums of Scotland, 2003)

Hadrian's Wall Path (Harvey Map Services, 2003)

Historical Map & Guide to Ancient Britain (Ordnance Survey, 1996)

Historical Map & Guide to Roman Britain (Ordnance Survey, 2001)

Hobbs, Richard, *Treasure: Finding Our Past* (British Museum, 2003)

Hornblower, Simon, and Antony Spawforth, eds, *The Oxford Companion to Classical Civilization* (Oxford University Press, 1998)

Hornsby, Peter R.G., Rosemary Weinstein and Ronald F. Homer, *Pewter: A Celebration of the Craft 1200–1700* (Museum Of London, 1989)

Illustrated Road Book of England & Wales, The (The Automobile Association, 1965)

Jessup, Ronald, *Curiosities of British Archaeology* (Butterworths, 1961)

Keay, John and Julia, *Encyclopaedia of Scotland* (Collins, 2000)

Kinealy, Christine, *A New History of Ireland* (Sutton, 2004)

Lee, Christopher, *This Sceptred Isle, 55BC–1901* (BBC Books, 1997)

McQuarrie, Alan, *Medieval Scotland* (Sutton, 2004)

Magnusson, Magnus, *Scotland: The Story of a Nation* (Harper Collins, 2000)

Moffat, Alistair, *The Borders* (Deerpark Press, 2002)

Museum of Scotland (brochure) (National Museums of Scotland, 1998)

Oakeshott, Ewart, *Records of the Medieval Sword* (The Boydell Press, 1991)

Past All Around Us, The (Reader's Digest Association, 1979)

Portable Antiquities Annual Report 2000–2001, 2001/02– 2002/03 and 2003–2005 (Department of Culture, Media & Sport)

Potter, T.W., *Roman Britain* (British Museum, 1983)

——, and Catherine Johns, *Roman Britain* (British Museum, 1992)

Robertson, Anne S., *An Inventory of Romano-British Coin Hoards* (Royal Numismatic Society Special Publication, 2000)

Seymour, William, *Battles in Britain 1066–1746* (Sidgwick & Jackson, 1975)

Teeple, John B., *Timelines of World History* (DK Publishing, 2002)

Thomas, Nicholas, *A Guide to Prehistoric England* (Batsford, 1960)

Wakeman, William, *Handbook of Irish Antiquities* (Hodges, Figgis & Co, 1891)

Wallace, Patrick F., and Raghnall O Floinn, eds, *Treasures Of The National Museum Of Ireland* (Gill & Macmillan, 2002)

Williams, Geoffrey, *Stronghold Britain* (Sutton, 2003)

Wilson, Sir David M., ed., *The Collections of the British Museum* (British Museum, 1989)

Wood, Michael, *In Search of the Dark Ages* (BBC Books, 1981)

——, *Domesday: In Search of Rural England* (BBC Books, 1996)

Greenlight Publishing, the company behind the monthly magazine *Treasure Hunting*, produces a number of excellent specialist books of interest to detectorists including:

Evan-Hart, Julian, and Dave Stuckey, *Beginner's Guide to Metal Detecting*

Bailey, Gordon, *Buttons & Fasteners 500BC–AD1840*

——, *Detector Finds*, vols 1–3, 5

——, *Finds Identified (Detector Finds 4)*

Blair, Dennis, *British Buttons,19th–20th Century*

Buck, Ivan, *Medieval English Groats*

Fletcher, Ted, *Reading Beaches*

——, *Reading Land*

——, *Reading Tidal Rivers*

——, *Tokens & Tallies 1850–1950*

——, *Tokens & Tallies Through the Ages*

——, *Treasure Hoards*Laing, Lloyd, *Pottery in Britain 4000BC to AD1900*

Marsden, Adrian, *Roman Coins Found in Britain*

Mills, Nigel, *Medieval Artefacts*

——, *Saxon & Viking Artefacts*

Murawski, Paul, *Benet's Artefacts*, 2nd Edition

Read, Brian, *Metal Artefacts of Antiquity*

The other essential monthly magazine for British metal detectorists is *The Searcher*. Both *Treasure Hunting* and *The Searcher* were extensively consulted during the writing of this book.

Acknowledgements

I have been helped by numerous people over the years in pursuit of my passion for metal detecting. In particular my old friend Terry Taylor has accompanied me on many days in the fields around my home in Suffolk. Terry has found lots of interesting things that have added to my understanding of the local area.

I would particularly like to thank Edward and Joanna Martin, who have helped me in so many ways over many years, as has Faye Minter in Edward's office. During the writing of this book Richard and I have been helped by numerous people who all receive our grateful thanks. Edward Besly, Maggie Bone, Kevin Blackburn, Hannah Bolton, Gary Brown, Ian Cartwright, Carol and Rob Carr, Andy Chopping, Julie Cochrane, Stephanie Fawcett, Trish Gant, Jackie Gill, Sally Gillespie, Alan Golbourn, Heather Graham, Nick Holmes Alan Hughes, Ron Humphrey, Jim McBeth, Josephine McGlade, Julie Mearns, Kirstin Munro, Helen Osmani, Ian Stewart, Charlotte Stokes, Anne Taylor, Chris Vezey, Elizabeth Walker and Diana Welsh. One person deserving of special thanks is Derek Stone for his beautiful maps.

Michael Lewis and Roger Bland at the Portable Antiquities Scheme have been very supportive and helped in a number of different ways. Chris Bain at the *Searcher* and Greg Payne at *Treasure Hunting* have done likewise. Gina De Maria in my office, Michael and Julie Haugh at Gedding and my lawyer James Wyllie have as always been very helpful. Our picture researcher Maria Gibbs has yet again proved that there is more to the art of finding good pictures then we'll ever learn! She has helped to realise my vision of what the book has become.

Richard and I have met many people at Sutton Publishing who have been tireless in the support from the outset. Nazia Ahmed-White, Sarah Bryce, Jane Entrican, Helen Holness, Bow Watkinson and Chris Jones have worked especially hard. Glad Stockdale's design for this challenging book is wonderful. Elizabeth Stone's cool and calm approach has helped to guide the book to fruition. Finally a big thank you to Jim Crawley for introducing us to Sutton Publishing and to him, Christopher Feeney and Jeremy Yates-Round for having the vision to see what this book could become.

As usual Suzanne and Christine have been there in support, working behind the scenes to allow us the freedom to do what we love doing best!

Bill Wyman in Suffolk
Richard Havers in The Scottish Borders
February 2005

Picture Credits

©Aberdeen Art Gallery and Museum 255; © Amgueddfeydd ac Orielau Cenedlaethol Cymru/National Museums and Galleries of Wales 105, 268, 269, 270–1, 274 below, 277 below, 279, 282, 284, 286; © AOC Archaeology 161; ©Ashmolean Museum, University of Oxford xvi, 73, 85, 179; reproduced courtesy of Bath Archaeological Trust 167; photograph courtesy of Kevin Blackburn 201; © copyright The Trustees of The British Museum xii centre, xiii above, xix above left, xxii above 4 below right, 6, 7 below, 9 above right, 10, 14, 15, 16 below, 16 above right, 16 above left, 16 centre right, 19 below right, 22 above, 22 below, 29, 31, 32 below, 32 above, 33, 34, 36, 38, 46 above, 46 below, 49, 51, 54, 59, 64, 65, 66 below, 66 above, 67, 69, 72 below, 76, 84, 87, 94, 101 below left, 113, 119 above, 119 below, 129, 131 left, 131 above right, 135 above, 135 below, 144, 146, 152, 153, 155, 159, 181, 183, 184, 187, 188 above, 200, 204, 231, 246 below, 281, 283; © copyright The Trustees of The British Museum/Braintree District Museum, Essex 4 below left; © copyright The Trustees of The British Museum/ Royal Museum and Art Gallery, Canterbury 140; © copyright The Trustees of The British Museum/Cheshire Museum Service 120; © copyright The Trustees of The British Museum/Chichester Museum 126 above; © copyright The Trustees of The British Museum/Corinium Museum, Cirencester 168; © copyright The Trustees of The British Museum/Colchester Castle Museum 8; © copyright The Trustees of The British Museum/Herbert Art Gallery and Museum, Coventry 202; © copyright The Trustees of The British Museum/St Edmundsbury Borough Council (Moyse's Hall Museum). Purchased with the assistance of the National Art Collections Fund, the National Lottery Fund and a local benefactor 5; © copyright The Trustees of The British Museum/Hampshire County Museum 143; © copyright The Trustees of the British Museum/courtesy of Harrogate Museums and Arts/Harrogate Borough Council xxiii; © copyright The Trustees of The British Museum/Lancashire County Museums 110 above; © copyright The Trustees of The British Museum/City and County Museum, Lincoln 53; © copyright The Trustees of The British Museum/courtesy of owner 13; © copyright The Trustees of The British Museum/Museum of Reading 72 above; © copyright The Trustees of The British Museum/Somerset County Museum 188 below; © copyright The Trustees of The British Museum/courtesy of Suffolk County Council 19 left; © copyright The Trustees of The British Museum/Somerset County Museum 190; © copyright The Trustees of The British Museum/Yorkshire Museum 277 above; © Christie's Images Ltd 1999 195; reproduced with permission from Colchester Museums xi below, 20; courtesy of Dorset County Museum 171; © Trish Gant Photographer v right, vii right; © Trish Gant Photographer/courtesy of Bill Wyman Collection, v left, vi all, vii left, viii all, xii below, xvii below, xviii above, xx, xxi below, xxii below, xxii centre, xxv, 163, 221, 273; © Gloucester City Museum & Art Gallery xi above; © Institute of Archaeology Oxford, photograph R.L. Wilkins 139 above; Dave King © Dorling Kindersley, courtesy of the University Museum of Archaeology and Anthropology, Cambridge 9 above left; Andy Chopping/ MoLAS 26 above, 26 below; photograph courtesy of Jeremy de Montfalcon xxiv above; The Museum of Antiquities of the University and Society of Antiquaries of Newcastle upon Tyne 91, 100; © National Museum of Ireland xi centre, 214 below, 215 above, 216, 217, 220, 224, 225, 226, 232, 233, 234, 235, 237; © The Trustees of The National Museums of Scotland 240, 241, 246 above, 248, 249, 253, 254, 257 all, 260 above, 260 centre, 264--5; © Norfolk Museums and Archaeology Service 25 above left; Nottingham City Museums and Galleries 44 above left; image provided courtesy of the Portable Antiquities Scheme xii below, xiii centre, xxvi, 2 above, 7 above, 18, 23, 24, 25 below right, 28, 57, 71 above, 109, 111, 128, 131 below right, 139 left, 175, 211, 279 below; image provided courtesy of the Portable Antiquities Scheme/Hull and East Riding Museum 83; image provided courtesy of the Portable Antiquities Scheme/Ipswich Borough Council Museums and Galleries xix above right; image provided courtesy of the Portable Antiquities Scheme/Yorkshire Museum 101 right; image provided courtesy of the Portable Antiquities Scheme/© Somerset County Council 166; © Sheffield Galleries and Museums Trust 44 below; ©Ian Stewart 177; © Suffolk County Council/courtesy of Suffolk County Council Archaeological Service 39; image provided courtesy of *The Searcher*; xxi above, 71 below, 97, 121, 126 below, 133, 137 right, 150, 196, 219; photograph courtesy of *Treasure Hunting* magazine x below left, 52 above, 99, 169; photograph © Ulster Museum 2005. Reproduced with the kind permission of The Trustees of The Museums and Galleries of Northern Ireland 223; V&A Images/Victoria and Albert Museum 193, 209; photograph courtesy of Watford Museum Collection 78; by permission of Warwickshire Museum 210; © Wessex Archaeology Ltd 148; © Wiltshire Heritage Museum, Devizes xv, 189; York Museums Trust (Yorkshire Museum) 96, 115

Every effort has been made to trace copyright holders. Sutton Publishing apologises for any unintentional omissions and would be pleased, if any such case should arise, to add an appropriate acknowledgement in future editions.